Leibniz, Gottfried 1646–1716
Leucippus ca. 490–430 B.C.
Locke, John 1632–1704
Lucretius ca 96–55 B.C.
Marx, Karl 1818–1883
Mill, John Stuart 1806–1873
Montaigne, Michel de 1533–1592
Newton, Sir Isaac 1642–1727
Nietzsche, Friedrich 1844–1900
Paley, William 1743–1805
Pascal, Blaise 1623–1662
Peirce, Charles S. 1839–1914
Plato ca. 428–ca. 348 B.C.
Protagoras ca. 490–421 B.C.
Pyrrho ca. 361–ca. 270 B.C.
Pythagoras active ca 525–500 B.C.
Quine, W. V. O. 1908–
Radhakrishnan, Sarvepalli 1888–1975
Rawls, John 1921–
Rorty, Richard 1931–
Rousseau, J. J. 1712–1778
Russell, Bertrand 1872–1970
Ryle, Gilbert 1900–1976
Sartre, Jean-Paul 1905–1980
Schopenhauer, Arthur 1788–1860
Searle, John 1932–
Sextus Empiricus ca. 200
Skinner, B. F. 1904–1990
Socrates ca. 470–399 B.C.
Spinoza, Baruch 1632–1677
Thales 624–546 B.C.
Tolstoy, Lev 1828–1910
Trebilcot, Joyce 1933–
Warnock, Geoffrey 1923–
Whitehead, Alfred North 1861–1947
Wittgenstein, Ludwig 1889–1951
Zeno b. ca. 489 B.C.

Elements of Philosophy
An Introduction

Elements of Philosophy

An Introduction

THIRD EDITION

Samuel Enoch Stumpf
Vanderbilt University

McGraw-Hill, Inc.
New York St. Louis San Francisco Auckland Bogotá
Caracas Lisbon London Madrid Mexico City Milan
Montreal New Delhi San Juan Singapore
Sydney Tokyo Toronto

Elements of Philosophy: An Introduction

Copyright © 1993, 1986, 1979 by McGraw-Hill, Inc. All rights reserved. Printed in the United States of America. Except as permitted under the United States Copyright Act of 1976, no part of this publication may be reproduced or distributed in any form or by any means, or stored in a data base or retrieval system, without the prior written permission of the publisher.

7890   DOC DOC   909876

ISBN 0-07-062468-2

This book is printed on acid-free paper.

This book was set in Palatino by The Clarinda Company.
The editors were Cynthia Ward and Eleanor Castellano;
the production supervisor was Kathryn Porzio.
The cover was designed by Wanda Siedlecka.
R. R. Donnelley & Sons Company was printer and binder.

Cover credit: Plato and Socrates; from a treatise on astronomy (St. Albans, mid 13th century). Ms. ASMM. 304 foc 31 v; The Bodleian Library, Oxford, England.

Library of Congress Cataloging-in-Publication Data
Stumpf, Samuel Enoch, (date).
    Elements of philosophy: an introduction / Samuel Enoch Stumpf. —
    3rd ed.
        p.   cm.
    Includes bibliographical references and index.
    ISBN 0-07-062468-2
    1. Philosophy—Introductions.   I. Title.
BD21.S825   1993
100—dc20   92-43670

ABOUT THE AUTHOR

Samuel Enoch Stumpf holds the Ph.D. from the University of Chicago. He was a Ford Fellow at Harvard University and a Rockefeller Fellow at Oxford University. For fifteen years he was chairman of the philosophy department at Vanderbilt University; he then served a term as president of Cornell College of Iowa, and subsequently returned to Vanderbilt as professor of the philosophy of law in the School of Law and as research professor of medical philosophy in the School of Medicine. He participates in various national organizations and lectures widely in the fields of philosophy, medical ethics, and jurisprudence.

To
the next generation of philosophers
NICHOLAS, ANNA, LAWRENCE, and GILLIAN
who wonder why they can catch a ball, but can't catch the dark

CONTENTS

PREFACE

This book is intended for the student just beginning the study of philosophy. The third edition of *Elements of Philosophy* presents philosophers' thinking on these important questions: "What Should I Do and Why Should I Do It?," "Why Should I Obey?," What Can I Know?," What Can I Believe?," What Is There?," "What Am I?," "Is My Will Free?," and "What Is the Meaning of Life?".

Elements of Philosophy examines the ways philosophers throughout history have addressed the questions of today's readers, and presents selections from their thinking and writing on those questions. In selecting the philosophers to be studied, I have sought a balance of representatives from the major historical periods of philosophy in order to achieve a sense of the ongoing "dialogue" as the emphasis and insights in philosophy change. In this third edition, additional emphasis has been placed on our contemporary period with the inclusion of philosophers such as Annette Baier, Simone de Beauvoir, Carol Gilligan, John Hospers, Richard Rorty, John Searle, B. F. Skinner, Joyce Trebilcot, and Geoffrey Warnock. In addition, a selection from Radhakrishnan's *Karma* gives readers an idea of how the past has an effect on the present according to ancient Indian philosophy.

The organization of the book is straightforward and simple, and the length relatively brief, as befits an introductory text. Each of the eight problem areas is self-contained so that instructors can elect to present topics in any sequence they prefer. An introduction to each problem focuses on elements of the particular subject under discussion; brief biographical sketches of the philosophers discussed locate them in time and place; an analysis of the philosophers' ideas makes them more accessible; selections from the philosophers' original works provide a sample of their modes of thought and style of writing; and, new to this edition are "Questions for Review and Discussion" at each chapter's end. An expanded Glossary of Key Terms and list of suggested additional readings is included.

As always, I am grateful to my wife, Jean, for her constant and incomparable assistance along the way.

Samuel Enoch Stumpf

Female Thinker (© *Succession H. Matisse 1992/ARS, New York. Matisse, Henri "La Serpen-
tine." Issy-les-Moulineauz (autumn 1909). Bronze, 22 ¼ x 11 x 7 ½", including base. Collection.
The Museum of Modern Art. New York. Gift of Abby Aldrich Rockefeller.*)

What Is Philosophy?

Philosophy is for everyone. In fact, we all engage in philosophy every day. Even when we do not know how to define philosophy, we will make such statements as "My philosophy about eating is . . ." or "Let me tell you my philosophy about taxes."

Philosophy begins with our ordinary everyday experiences. We not only *do* things, we *think* about them. Such a simple experience as eating is capable of leading to some major philosophical questions. How much should we eat? Animals do not ask this question. We ask it because it makes a difference in our daily life. The amount we eat can affect the pleasure we get out of life, especially if we eat too much. But eating is in itself a pleasure. We begin to philosophize when we try to decide which pleasures are most important to us, for example, looking slim and trim on the one hand or enjoying bountiful meals on the other. We even ask whether pleasure is the proper standard for making our decisions in life. Before long, we no longer talk about eating but about the more general question that the experience of eating makes us think about, namely, What values are most important to us? How, in short, do we achieve the good life?

Similarly, the person who says "Let me tell you my philosophy about taxes" starts to think about this matter because of the experience of paying taxes. Paying taxes is not always pleasant. We want to know more about this part of our experience. Who should pay and how much? Once again, the discussion soon becomes philosophical. From being only about the inconvenience of paying taxes, the discussion moves to such questions as "What is the purpose of the tax?" or "What is a fair tax?" Before long, this line of thought leads to the philosophical question "What is justice?"

From these examples of eating and paying taxes we learn at least one thing about philosophy—that it is a quest for knowledge. That, after all, is what the Greek roots of the word "philosophy" mean, namely, *philo* (love) and *sophia* (knowledge or wisdom)—hence the love of knowledge. To say that philosophy is the love of knowledge still leaves the question "What kind of knowledge does philosophy involve?"

There was a time when philosophy included almost every kind of knowledge of which human beings were capable. There was no sharp distinction between science and philosophy. Indeed, the term "natural philosophy" was until relatively recently used to describe various sciences, especially physics. Among early philosophers, then, we find thinkers concerned with explaining the structure of nature, including the realm of physical things, the world, and the whole universe. In time, this subject matter was separated from philosophy and became the various sciences, such as physics, astronomy, and astrophysics. Similarly, the philosophical concern regarding human nature in its various aspects represented an attempt to understand the functioning of the body and mind, the elements of health and disease, the causes of pain and pleasure, and the requirements for orderly and peaceful communities and societies. Here too over the years new disciplines arose, as biology, medicine, psychology, sociology, political science, and economics became independent sciences. To some extent, therefore, it appears that the scope of knowledge which philosophy pursues has been reduced to the extent that the special sciences have achieved a certain independence from philosophy.

It is usually said that philosophy deals with those problems which have not as yet been solved by science. To put the matter another way, as soon as science has solved certain problems, there is no further need for the philosopher. This may be true to the extent that the various sciences generate facts and solutions through their unique methods of investigation. But in virtually every area of science there remains the need to understand, interpret, and above all evaluate the body of facts. Facts do not assess themselves. Nor does the body of facts clearly reveal what should or should not be done. That the mind can be altered by drugs, that behavior can be controlled, that genetic engineering or eugenics can modify the course of human reproduction—in all these cases the question remains whether from the simple fact that we can do all these things it follows that we should. There is, then, another kind of knowledge which the philosopher pursues, a knowledge that assimilates and understands these facts and seeks to put them into a larger and more general context, which includes humanity's quest for a rational and fulfilling destiny. But this activity of the philosopher does not necessarily provide a new set of facts, nor does it provide precise answers to all the questions raised by these facts. We are concerned not so much with specific issues as with fundamental principles or modes of thinking which enable us to deal most effectively with the problem areas of philosophy.

Why do we engage in philosophy? What is there about human beings that leads us to engage in reflective thought, thinking about questions which do not appear to produce practical results? It could be argued that in the long run philosophical thought does produce widespread practical consequences. In the political realm, for example, the writings of John Locke significantly influenced the development of American democracy, while the theories of Karl Marx brought into being a radically new form of government. It could also be said that what separates us from the animal world and from uncivilized human beings is just this intellectual endeavor, which could be justified as valuable even if only for its own sake. But there is a deeper reason for engaging in philosophy, and that is that we simply cannot turn away from certain questions which constantly confront us. Our human constitution or our human condition predisposes us to want to know. It was Ludwig Wittgenstein (1889–1951) of Cambridge University who compared our situation to that of a fly in a bottle. The fly is trying to get out of the bottle but does not know how. The function and aim of philosophy is to show the fly how to get out of the bottle. For us this means that, like the fly, we feel trapped and have difficulty finding our way out. In our case, this fly bottle represents certain levels of ignorance or problems and questions that are difficult to solve and we look to philosophy for help in finding our way out.

Again, to emphasize the many functions of philosophy, Wittgenstein said that philosophy is like a toolbox. We use words and ideas for different purposes, just as we use different tools to do different jobs. Pounding nails calls for a hammer, screws require a screwdriver, and to cut wood we need a saw. All these jobs are different, but in each case they are done with a tool taken from the toolbox.

Philosophy is in a similar way called on to do many jobs. These jobs reflect the richness of our daily experience. For example, there is the job of helping us to decide how to behave. We want to know how to distinguish right and wrong, good and bad, morality and immorality, and between what we ought to do and ought not to do. In our private moments we wonder how we can achieve the happiest and best life for ourselves. This is the job for *ethics*. Because we cannot avoid constant contact with other persons or groups, the quality of our life is affected by the behavior of others and we realize the need for public rules or laws in order to provide a peaceful and cooperative community based on an appropriate form of government. Working out the principles and design for laws and government is the job of *political philosophy*. As we extend our thinking beyond ourselves and beyond our communities, we wonder how we fit into the larger setting of the universe and beyond. To deal with questions of our destiny is the job of *religion*. We all have the experience of discovering new insights which affect our ways of thinking. Sometimes we are sure of what we know, while at other times we are not so sure. To help us understand how our minds work in our quest to know is a special job for philosophy. The tool for this job is the *theory of knowledge* (epistemology). We all have the common experience of seeing things appear and disappear, come into being and pass out of being, trees growing, dying, and disintegrating, indeed everything constantly changing. All this fluctuation in things raises the question of whether there is anything that is permanent. What, in short, are things made of, and what does it mean for anything to *be?* This is the special concern of *metaphysics*. These "jobs" and such additional questions as "What am I?" "Is my will free?" and "What is the meaning of life?" will serve as our introduction to the fundamental elements of philosophy.

It is time now to sample some typical philosophical activity. The leading philosophers rarely ever formulated specific definitions of philosophy, and it would not be fruitful for us to do so either. We discover what philosophy is not from definitions but rather from the way these philosophers *do* philosophy. A good example of doing philosophy is found in one of Plato's early dialogues, the *Euthyphro*.

The *Euthyphro* is a classic example of the method used by Socrates to pursue clarity of thought. For both Socrates and Plato, philosophy meant a personal pursuit of truth and goodness. The *Euthyphro* exemplifies this relentless analysis of ideas not only to promote logical consistency but also to urge that the way one thinks can affect the quality of one's life. Intellectual and moral integrity, he held, go together. That is why Socrates makes the point (in the *Apology*) that not only is the unexamined idea not worth having but also "the unexamined life is not worth living."

Euthyphro is a confident young man whom Socrates encounters on the steps of the courthouse. Euthyphro asks why Socrates is there and learns that Socrates has been charged with the offense of "impiety." When Socrates discovers that Euthyphro is there because he is suing someone for the same offense, Socrates starts the dialogue with powerful irony. To paraphrase, Socrates asks: "How can I be so lucky as to find someone who is bringing such a lawsuit since you, Euthyphro, can be of considerable help to me, because I do not think I know what impiety is. And, by the way, whom are you suing?" When Euthyphro says "my father," Socrates replies, "Then you must really know what impiety is. Tell me, what is impiety?"

The rest of the dialogue is a perfect example of the "Socratic method." It is a form of cross-examination, a *dia*logue, a series of searching questions and answers, an intellectual process whose aim is to arrive at clear definitions. In this process, ideas must pass through various people's minds reflecting different perspectives before an idea becomes clear. But since Euthyphro has never had a clear idea of what impiety is in the first place, the cross-examination by Socrates is quite unsettling for Euthyphro, who says, "But Socrates, I really don't know how to explain to you what is in my mind. Whatever statement we put forward always somehow moves around in a circle, and will not stay where we put it."

As Socrates presses the question "What is piety?", Euthyphro fails to define the one characteristic of a person's behavior which, when present, makes an action pious. Euthyphro gives various *examples* instead of a *definition* of piety. To say that "piety is what is pleasing or dear to the gods and impiety is what is not pleasing to them" is not helpful because one still has to ask what it is that makes it pleasing to them. Morever, in the literature about the gods, the stories say that the gods disagree among themselves about various matters. A given behavior could therefore please some gods and displease others. Also, is it simply because the gods approve of an act that it is pious; or, do the gods approve of it because it conforms to piety? As we turn now to Plato's *Euthyphro*, we will find that Socrates will not allow Euthyphro to get away with sloppy thinking.

Reading ————————————————————————————————

Euthyphro, A Model of the Socratic Method
Plato

INTERLOCUTORS: Socrates and Euthyphro
SCENE: The Porch of the King Archon

EUTHYPHRO: Why have you left the Lyceum, Socrates? and what are you doing in the Porch of the King Archon? Surely you cannot be concerned in a suit before the King, like myself?

SOCRATES: Not in a suit, Euthyphro: impeachment is the word which the Athenians use.

EUTH.: What! I suppose that some one has been prosecuting you, for I cannot believe that you are the prosecutor of another.

SOC.: Certainly not.

EUTH.: Then some one else has been prosecuting you?

SOC.: Yes.

EUTH.: And who is he?

SOC.: A young man who is little known, Euthyphro: and I hardly know him: his name is Meletus, and he is of the deme of Pitthis. Perhaps you may remember his appearance: he has a beak, and long straight hair, and a beard which is ill grown.

EUTH.: No, I do not remember him, Socrates. But what is the charge which he brings against you?

SOC.: What is the charge? Well, a very serious charge, which shows a good deal of character in the young man, and for which he is certainly not to be despised. He says he knows how the youth are corrupted and who are their corruptors. I fancy that he must be a wise man, and seeing that I am the reverse of a wise man, he has found me out, and is going to accuse me of corrupting his young friends. And of this our mother the state is to be the judge. Of all our political men he is the only one who seems to me to begin in the right way, with the cultivation of virtue in youth; like a good husbandman, he makes the young shoots his first care, and clears away us who are the destroyers of them. This is only the first step; he will afterwards attend to the elder branches; and if he goes on as he has begun, he will be a very great public benefactor.

EUTH.: I hope that he may; but I rather fear, Socrates, that the opposite will turn out to be the truth. My opinion is that in attacking you he is simply aiming a blow at the foundation of the state. But in what way does he say that you corrupt the young?

SOC.: He brings a wonderful accusation against me, which at first hearing excites surprise: he says that I am a poet or maker of gods, and that I invent new gods and deny the existence of old ones; this is the ground of his indictment.

EUTH.: I understand, Socrates; he means to attack you about the familiar sign which occasionally, as you say, comes to you. He thinks that you are a neologian, and he is going to have you up before the court for this. He knows that such a charge is readily received by the world, as I myself know too well; for when I speak in the assembly about divine things, and foretell the future to them, they laugh at me and think me a madman. Yet every word that I say is true. But they are jealous of us all; and we must be brave and go at them.

SOC.: Their laughter, friend Euthyphro, is not a matter of much consequence. For a man may be thought wise; but the Athenians, I suspect, do not much trouble themselves about him until he begins to impart his wisdom to others; and then for some reason or other, perhaps, as you say, from jealousy, they are angry.

EUTH.: I am never likely to try their temper in this way.

SOC.: I dare say not, for you are reserved in your behaviour, and seldom impart your wisdom. But I have a benevolent habit of pouring out myself to everybody, and would even pay for a listener, and I am afraid that the Athenians may think me too talkative. Now if, as I was saying, they would only laugh at me, as you say that they laugh at you, the time might pass gaily enough in the court; but perhaps they may be in earnest, and then what the end will be you soothsayers only can predict.

EUTH.: I dare say that the affair will end in nothing, Socrates, and that you will win your cause; and I think that I shall win my own.

SOC.: And what is your suit, Euthyphro? are you the pursuer or the defendant?

EUTH.: I am the pursuer.

SOC.: Of whom?

EUTH.: You will think me mad when I tell you.

SOC.: Why, has the fugitive wings?

EUTH.: Nay, he is not very volatile at his time of life.

SOC.: Who is he?

EUTH.: My father.

SOC.: Your father! my good man?

EUTH.: Yes.

SOC.: And of what is he accused?

EUTH.: Of murder, Socrates.

SOC.: By the powers, Euthyphro! how little does the common herd know of the nature of right and truth. A man must be an extraordinary man, and have made great strides in wisdom, before he could have seen his way to bring such an action.

EUTH.: Indeed, Socrates, he must.

SOC.: I suppose that the man whom your father murdered was one of your relatives—clearly he was; for if he had been a stranger you would never have thought of prosecuting him.

EUTH.: I am amused, Socrates, at your making a distinction between one who is a relation and one who is not a relation; for surely the pollution is the same in either case, if you knowingly associate with the murderer when you ought to clear yourself and him by proceeding against him. The real question is whether the murdered man has been justly slain. If justly, then your duty is to let the matter alone; but if unjustly, then even if the murderer lives under the same roof with you and eats at the same table, proceed against him. Now the man who is dead was a poor dependant of mine who worked for us as a field labourer on our farm in Naxos, and one day in a fit of drunken passion he got into a quarrel with one of our domestic servants and slew him. My father bound him hand and foot and threw him into a ditch, and then sent to Athens to ask of a diviner what he should do with him. Meanwhile he never attended to him and took no care about him, for he regarded him as a murderer; and thought that no great harm would be done even if he did die. Now this was just what happened. For such was the effect of cold and hunger and chains upon him, that before the messenger returned from the diviner, he was dead. And my father and family are angry with me for taking the part of the murderer and prosecuting my father. They say that he did not kill him, and that if he did, the dead man was but a murderer, and I ought not to take any notice, for that a son is impious who prosecutes a father. Which shows, Socrates, how little they know what the gods think about piety and impiety.

Soc.: Good heavens, Euthyphro! and is your knowledge of religion and of things pious and impious so very exact, that, supposing the circumstances to be as you state them, you are not afraid lest you too may be doing an impious thing in bringing an action against your father?

Euth.: The best of Euthyphro, and that which distinguishes him, Socrates, from other men, is his exact knowledge of all such matters. What should I be good for without it?

Soc.: Rare friend! I think that I cannot do better than be your disciple. Then before the trial with Meletus comes on I shall challenge him, and say that I have always had a great interest in religious questions, and now, as he charges me with rash imaginations and innovations in religion, I have become your disciple. You, Meletus, as I shall say to him, acknowledge Euthyphro to be a great theologian, and sound in his opinions; and if you approve of him you ought to approve of me, and not have me into court; but if you disapprove, you should begin by indicting him who is my teacher, and who will be the ruin, not of the young, but of the old; that is to say, of myself whom he instructs, and of his old father whom he admonishes and chastises. And if Meletus refuses to listen to me, but will go on, and will not shift the indictment from me to you, I cannot do better than repeat this challenge in the court.

Euth.: Yes, indeed, Socrates; and if he attempts to indict me I am mistaken if I do not find a flaw in him; the court shall have a great deal more to say to him than to me.

Soc.: And I, my dear friend, knowing this, am desirous of becoming your disciple. For I observe that no one appears to notice you—not even this Meletus; but his sharp eyes have found me out at once, and he has indicted me for impiety. And therefore, I adjure you to tell me the nature of piety and impiety, which you said that you knew so well, and of murder, and of other offences against the gods. What are they? Is not piety in every action always the same? and impiety, again—is it not always the opposite of piety, and also the same with itself, having, as impiety, one notion which includes whatever is impious?

EUTH.: To be sure, Socrates.

SOC.: And what is piety, and what is impiety?

EUTH.: Piety is doing as I am doing; that is to say, prosecuting any one who is guilty of murder, sacrilege, or of any similar crime—whether he be your father or mother, or whoever he may be—that makes no difference; and not to prosecute them is impiety. And please to consider, Socrates, what a notable proof I will give you of the truth of my words, a proof which I have already given to others:—of the principle, I mean, that the impious, whoever he may be, ought not to go unpunished. For do not men regard Zeus as the best and most righteous of the gods?—and yet they admit that he bound his father (Cronos) because he wickedly devoured his sons, and that he too had punished his own father (Uranus) for a similar reason, in a nameless manner. And yet when I proceed against my father, they are angry with me. So inconsistent are they in their way of talking when the gods are concerned, and when I am concerned.

SOC.: May not this be the reason, Euthyphro, why I am charged with impiety—that I cannot away with these stories about the gods? and therefore I suppose that people think me wrong. But, as you who are well informed about them approve of them, I cannot do better than assent to your superior wisdom. What else can I say, confessing as I do, that I know nothing about them? Tell me, for the love of Zeus, whether you really believe that they are true.

EUTH.: Yes, Socrates; and things more wonderful still, of which the world is in ignorance.

SOC.: And do you really believe that the gods fought with one another, and had dire quarrels, battles, and the like, as the poets say, and as you may see represented in the works of great artists? The temples are full of them; and notably the robe of Athene, which is carried up to the Acropolis at the great Panathenaea, is embroidered with them. Are all these tales of the gods true, Euthyphro?

EUTH.: Yes, Socrates; and, as I was saying, I can tell you, if you would like to hear them, many other things about the gods which would quite amaze you.

SOC.: I dare say; and you shall tell me them at some other time when I have leisure. But just at present I would rather hear from you a more precise answer, which you have not as yet given, my friend, to the question, What is 'piety'? When asked, you only replied, Doing as you do, charging your father with murder.

EUTH.: And what I said was true, Socrates.

Soc.: No doubt, Euthyphro; but you would admit that there are many other pious acts?

Euth.: There are.

Soc.: Remember that I did not ask you to give me two or three examples of piety, but to explain the general idea which makes all pious things to be pious. Do you not recollect that there was one idea which made the impious impious, and the pious pious?

Euth.: I remember.

Soc.: Tell me what is the nature of this idea, and then I shall have a standard to which I may look, and by which I may measure actions, whether yours or those of any one else, and then I shall be able to say that such and such an action is pious, such another impious.

Euth.: I will tell you, if you like.

Soc.: I should very much like.

Euth: Piety, then, is that which is dear to the gods, and impiety is that which is not dear to them.

Soc.: Very good, Euthyphro; you have now given me the sort of answer which I wanted. But whether what you say is true or not I cannot as yet tell, although I make no doubt that you will prove the truth of your words.

Euth.: Of course.

Soc.: Come, then, and let us examine what we are saying. That thing or person which is dear to the gods is pious, and that thing or person which is hateful to the gods is impious, these two being the extreme opposites of one another. Was not that said?

Euth.: It was.

Soc.: And well said?

Euth.: Yes, Socrates, I thought so; it was certainly said.

Soc.: And further, Euthyphro, the gods were admitted to have enmities and hatreds and differences?

Euth.: Yes, that was also said.

Soc.: And what sort of difference creates enmity and anger? Suppose for example that you and I, my good friend, differ about a number; do differences of this sort make us enemies and set us at variance with one another? Do we not go at once to arithmetic, and put an end to them by a sum?

Euth.: True.

Soc.: Or suppose that we differ about magnitudes, do we not quickly end the differences by measuring?

Euth.: Very true.

Soc.: And we end a controversy about heavy and light by resorting to a weighing machine?

Euth.: To be sure.

Soc.: But what differences are there which cannot be thus decided, and which therefore make us angry and set us at enmity with one another? I dare say the answer does not occur to you at the moment, and therefore I will suggest that these enmities arise when the matters of difference are the just and unjust, good and evil, honourable and dishonourable. Are not these the points about which men differ, and about which when we are unable satisfactorily to decide our differences, you and I and all of us quarrel, when we do quarrel?

EUTH.: Yes, Socrates, the nature of the differences about which we quarrel is such as you describe.

SOC.: And the quarrels of the gods, noble Euthyphro, when they occur, are of a like nature?

EUTH.: Certainly they are.

SOC.: They have differences of opinion, as you say, about good and evil, just and unjust, honourable and dishonourable: there would have been no quarrels among them, if there had been no such differences—would there now?

EUTH.: You are quite right.

SOC.: Does not every man love that which he deems noble and just and good, and hate the opposite of them?

EUTH.: Very true.

SOC.: But, as you say, people regard the same things, some as just and others as unjust,—about these they dispute; and so there arise wars and fightings among them.

EUTH.: Very true.

SOC.: Then the same things are hated by the gods and loved by the gods, and are both hateful and dear to them?

EUTH.: True.

SOC.: And upon this view the same things, Euthyphro, will be pious and also impious?

EUTH.: So I should suppose.

SOC.: Then, my friend, I remark with surprise that you have not answered the question which I asked. For I certainly did not ask you to tell me what action is both pious and impious: but now it would seem that what is loved by the gods is also hated by them. And therefore, Euthyphro, in thus chastising your father you may very likely be doing what is agreeable to Zeus but disagreeable to Cronos or Uranus, and what is acceptable to Hephaestus but unacceptable to Herè, and there may be other gods who have similar differences of opinion.

EUTH.: But I believe, Socrates, that all the gods would be agreed as to the propriety of punishing a murderer: there would be no difference of opinion about that.

SOC.: Well, but speaking of men, Euthyphro, did you ever hear any one arguing that a murderer or any sort of evil-doer ought to be let off?

EUTH.: I should rather say that these are the questions which they are always arguing, especially in courts of law: they commit all sorts of crimes, and there is nothing which they will not do or say in their own defence.

SOC.: But do they admit their guilt, Euthyphro, and yet say that they ought not to be punished?

EUTH.: No; they do not.

SOC.: Then there are some things which they do not venture to say and do: for they do not venture to argue that the guilty are to be unpunished, but they deny their guilt, do they not?

EUTH.: Yes.

SOC.: Then they do not argue that the evil-doer should not be punished, but they argue about the fact of who the evil-doer is, and what he did and when?

EUTH.: True.

SOC.: And the gods are in the same case, if as you assert they quarrel about just and unjust, and some of them say while others deny that injustice is done among them. For surely neither God nor man will ever venture to say that the doer of injustice is not to be punished?

EUTH.: That is true, Socrates, in the main.

SOC.: But they join issue about the particulars—gods and men alike; and, if they dispute at all, they dispute about some act which is called in question, and which by some is affirmed to be just, by others to be unjust. Is not that true?

EUTH.: Quite true.

SOC.: Well then, my dear friend Euthyphro, do tell me, for my better instruction and information, what proof have you that in the opinion of all the gods a servant who is guilty of murder, and is put in chains by the master of the dead man, and dies because he is put in chains before he who bound him can learn from the interpreters of the gods what he ought to do with him, dies unjustly; and that on behalf of such an one a son ought to proceed against his father and accuse him of murder. How would you show that all the gods absolutely agree in approving of his act? Prove to me that they do, and I will applaud your wisdom as long as I live.

EUTH.: It will be a difficult task; but I could make the matter very clear indeed to you.

SOC.: I understand; you mean to say that I am not so quick of apprehension as the judges: for to them you will be sure to prove that the act is unjust, and hateful to the gods.

EUTH.: Yes indeed, Socrates; at least if they will listen to me.

SOC.: But they will be sure to listen if they find that you are a good speaker. There was a notion that came into my mind while you were speaking; I said to myself: 'Well, and what if Euthyphro does prove to me that all the gods regarded the death of the serf as unjust, how do I know anything more of the nature of piety and impiety? for granting that this action may be hateful to the gods, still piety and impiety are not adequately defined by these distinctions, for that which is hateful to the gods has been shown to be also pleasing and dear to them.' And therefore, Euthyphro, I do not ask you to prove this; I will suppose, if you like, that all the gods condemn and abominate such an action. But I will amend the definition so far as to say that what all the gods hate is impious, and what they love pious or holy; and what some of them love and others hate is both or neither. Shall this be our definition of piety and impiety?

EUTH.: Why not, Socrates?

Soc.: Why not! certainly, as far as I am concerned, Euthyphro, there is no reason why not. But whether this admission will greatly assist you in the task
of instructing me as you promised, is a matter for you to consider.

Euth.: Yes, I should say that what all the gods love is pious and holy, and the
opposite which they all hate, impious.

Soc.: Ought we to enquire into the truth of this, Euthyphro, or simply to
accept the mere statement on our own authority and that of others? What
do you say?

Euth.: We should enquire; and I believe that the statement will stand the test
of enquiry.

Soc.: We shall know better, my good friend, in a little while. The point which
I should first wish to understand is whether the pious or holy is beloved by
the gods because it is holy, or holy because it is beloved of the gods.

Euth.: I do not understand your meaning, Socrates.

Soc.: I will endeavour to explain: we speak of carrying and we speak of being
carried, of leading and being led, seeing and being seen. You know that in
all such cases there is a difference, and you know also in what the difference lies?

Euth.: I think that I understand.

Soc.: And is not that which is beloved distinct from that which loves?

Euth.: Certainly.

Soc.: Well; and now tell me, is that which is carried in this state of carrying
because it is carried, or for some other reason?

Euth.: No; that is the reason.

Soc.: And the same is true of what is led and of what is seen?

Euth.: True.

Soc.: And a thing is not seen because it is visible, but conversely, visible
because it is seen; nor is a thing led because it is in the state of being led, or
carried because it is in the state of being carried, but the converse of this.
And now I think, Euthyphro, that my meaning will be intelligible; and my
meaning is, that any state of action or passion implies previous action or
passion. It does not become because it is becoming, but it is in a state of
becoming because it becomes; neither does it suffer because it is in a state of
suffering, but it is in a state of suffering because it suffers. Do you not
agree?

Euth.: Yes.

Soc.: Is not that which is loved in some state either of becoming or suffering?

Euth.: Yes.

Soc.: And the same holds as in the previous instances; the state of being loved
follows the act of being loved, and not the act the state.

Euth.: Certainly.

Soc.: And what do you say of piety, Euthyphro: is not piety, according to
your definition, loved by all the gods?

Euth.: Yes.

Soc.: Because it is pious or holy, or for some other reason?

Euth.: No, that is the reason.

Soc.: It is loved because it is holy, not holy because it is loved?

EUTH.: Yes.

SOC.: And that which is dear to the gods is loved by them, and is in a state to be loved of them because it is loved of them?

EUTH.: Certainly.

SOC.: Then that which is dear to the gods, Euthyphro, is not holy, nor is that which is holy loved of God, as you affirm; but they are two different things.

EUTH.: How do you mean, Socrates?

SOC.: I mean to say that the holy has been acknowledged by us to be loved of God because it is holy, not to be holy because it is loved.

EUTH.: Yes.

SOC.: But that which is dear to the gods is dear to them because it is loved by them, not loved by them because it is dear to them.

EUTH.: True.

SOC.: But, friend Euthyphro, if that which is holy is the same with that which is dear to God, and is loved because it is holy, then that which is dear to God would have been loved as being dear to God; but if that which is dear to God is dear to him because loved by him, then that which is holy would have been holy because loved by him. But now you see that the reverse is the case, and that they are quite different from one another. For one (θεοφιλὲ·) is of a kind to be loved because it is loved, and the other ('ὁσιον) is loved because it is of a kind to be loved. Thus you appear to me, Euthyphro, when I ask you what is the essence of holiness, to offer an attribute only, and not the essence—the attribute of being loved by all the gods. But you still refuse to explain to me the nature of holiness. And therefore, if you please, I will ask you not to hide your treasure, but to tell me once more what holiness or piety really is, whether dear to the gods or not (for that is a matter about which we will not quarrel); and what is impiety?

EUTH.: I really do not know, Socrates, how to express what I mean. For somehow or other our arguments, on whatever ground we rest them, seem to turn round and walk away from us.

SOC.: Your words, Euthyphro, are like the handiwork of my ancestor Daedalus; and if I were the sayer or propounder of them, you might say that my arguments walk away and will not remain fixed where they are placed because I am a descendant of his. But now, since these notions are your own, you must find some other gibe, for they certainly, as you yourself allow, show an inclination to be on the move.

EUTH.: Nay, Socrates, I shall still say that you are the Daedalus who sets arguments in motion; not I, certainly, but you make them move or go round, for they would never have stirred, as far as I am concerned.

SOC.: Then I must be a greater than Daedalus: for whereas he only made his own inventions to move, I move those of other people as well. And the beauty of it is, that I would rather not. For I would give the wisdom of Daedalus, and the wealth of Tantalus, to be able to detain them and keep them fixed. But enough of this. As I perceive that you are lazy, I will myself endeavor to show you how you might instruct me in the nature of piety; and I hope that you will not grudge your labour. Tell me, then,—Is not that which is pious necessarily just?

EUTH.: Yes.

SOC.: And is, then, all which is just pious? or, is that which is pious all just, but that which is just, only in part and not all, pious?

EUTH.: I do not understand you, Socrates.

SOC.: And yet I know that you are as much wiser than I am, as you are younger. But, as I was saying, revered friend, the abundance of your wisdom makes you lazy. Please to exert yourself, for there is no real difficulty in understanding me. What I mean I may explain by an illustration of what I do not mean. The poet (Stasinus) sings—

> Of Zeus, the author and creator of all these things,
> You will not tell: for where there is fear there is also reverence.

Now I disagree with this poet. Shall I tell you in what respect?

EUTH.: By all means.

SOC.: I should not say that where there is fear there is also reverence; for I am sure that many persons fear poverty and disease, and the like evils, but I do not perceive that they reverence the objects of their fear.

EUTH.: Very true.

SOC: But where reverence is, there is fear; for he who has a feeling of reverence and shame about the commission of any action, fears and is afraid of an ill reputation.

Euth.: No doubt.

SOC.: Then we are wrong in saying that where there is fear there is also reverence; and we should say, where there is reverence there is also fear. But there is not always reverence where there is fear; for fear is a more extended notion, and reverence is a part of fear, just as the odd is a part of number, and number is a more extended notion than the odd. I suppose that you follow me now?

EUTH.: Quite well.

SOC.: That was the sort of question which I meant to raise when I asked whether the just is always the pious, or the pious always the just; and whether there may not be justice where there is not piety; for justice is the more extended notion of which piety is only a part. Do you dissent?

EUTH.: No, I think that you are quite right.

SOC.: Then, if piety is a part of justice, I suppose that we should enquire what part? If you had pursued the enquiry in the previous cases; for instance, if you had asked me what is an even number, and what part of number the even is, I should have had no difficulty in replying, a number which represents a figure having two equal sides. Do you not agree?

EUTH.: Yes, I quite agree.

SOC.: In like manner, I want you to tell me what part of justice is piety or holiness, that I may be able to tell Meletus not to do me injustice, or indict me for impiety, as I am now adequately instructed by you in the nature of piety or holiness, and their opposites.

EUTH.: Piety or holiness, Socrates, appears to me to be that part of justice which attends to the gods, as there is the other part of justice which attends to men.

Soc.: That is good, Euthyphro; yet still there is a little point about which I should like to have further information, What is the meaning of "attention"? For attention can hardly be used in the same sense when applied to the gods as when applied to other things. For instance, horses are said to require attention, and not every person is able to attend to them, but only a person skilled in horsemanship. Is it not so?

Euth.: Certainly.

Soc.: I should suppose that the art of horsemanship is the art of attending to horses?

Euth.: Yes.

Soc.: Nor is every one qualified to attend to dogs, but only the huntsman?

Euth.: True.

Soc.: And I should also conceive that the art of the huntsman is the art of attending to dogs?

Euth.: Yes.

Soc.: As the art of the oxherd is the art of attending to oxen?

Euth.: Very true.

Soc.: In like manner holiness or piety is the art of attending to the gods?—that would be your meaning, Euthyphro?

Euth.: Yes.

Soc.: And is not attention always designed for the good or benefit of that to which the attention is given? As in the case of horses, you may observe that when attended to by the horseman's art they are benefited and improved, are they not?

Euth.: True.

Soc.: As the dogs are benefited by the huntsman's art, and the oxen by the art of the oxherd, and all other things are tended or attended for their good and not for their hurt?

Euth.: Certainly, not for their hurt.

Soc.: But for their good?

Euth.: Of course.

Soc.: And does piety or holiness, which has been defined to be the art of attending to the gods, benefit or improve them? Would you say that when you do a holy act you make any of the gods better?

Euth.: No, no; that was certainly not what I meant.

Soc.: And I, Euthyphro, never supposed that you did. I asked you the question about the nature of the attention, because I thought that you did not.

Euth.: You do me justice, Socrates; that is not the sort of attention which I mean.

Soc.: Good: but I must still ask what is this attention to the gods which is called piety?

Euth.: It is such, Socrates, as servants show to their masters.

Soc.: I understand—a sort of ministration to the gods.

Euth.: Exactly.

Soc.: Medicine is also a sort of ministration or service, having in view the attainment of some object—would you not say of health?

Euth.: I should.

Soc.: Again, there is an art which ministers to the ship-builder with a view to the attainment of some result?

Euth.: Yes, Socrates, with a view to the building of a ship.

Soc.: As there is an art which ministers to the housebuilder with a view to the building of a house?

Euth.: Yes.

Soc.: And now tell me, my good friend, about the art which ministers to the gods: what work does that help to accomplish? For you must surely know if, as you say, you are of all men living the one who is best instructed in religion.

Euth.: And I speak the truth, Socrates.

Soc.: Tell me then, oh tell me—what is that fair work which the gods do by the help of our ministrations?

Euth.: Many and fair, Socrates, are the works which they do.

Soc.: Why, my friend, and so are those of a general. But the chief of them is easily told. Would you not say that victory in war is the chief of them?

Euth.: Certainly.

Soc.: Many and fair, too, are the works of the husbandman, if I am not mistaken; but his chief work is the production of food from the earth?

Euth.: Exactly.

Soc.: And of the many and fair things done by the gods, which is the chief or principal one?

Euth.: I have told you already, Socrates, that to learn all these things accurately will be very tiresome. Let me simply say that piety or holiness is learning how to please the gods in word and deed, by prayers and sacrifices. Such piety is the salvation of families and states, just as the impious, which is unpleasing to the gods, is their ruin and destruction.

Soc.: I think that you could have answered in much fewer words the chief question which I asked, Euthyphro, if you had chosen. But I see plainly that you are not disposed to instruct me—clearly not: else why, when we reached the point, did you turn aside? Had you only answered me I should have truly learned of you by this time the nature of piety. Now, as the asker of a question is necessarily dependent on the answerer, whither he leads I must follow; and can only ask again, what is the pious, and what is piety? Do you mean that they are a sort of science of praying and sacrificing?

Euth.: Yes, I do.

Soc.: And sacrificing is giving to the gods, and prayer is asking of the gods?

Euth.: Yes, Socrates.

Soc.: Upon this view, then, piety is a science of asking and giving?

Euth.: You understand me capitally, Socrates.

Soc.: Yes, my friend; the reason is that I am a votary of your science, and give my mind to it, and therefore nothing which you say will be thrown away upon me. Please then to tell me, what is the nature of this service to the gods? Do you mean that we prefer requests and give gifts to them?

Euth.: Yes, I do.

Soc.: Is not the right way of asking to ask of them what we want?

EUTH.: Certainly.

SOC.: And the right way of giving is to give to them in return what they want of us. There would be no meaning in an art which gives to any one that which he does not want.

EUTH.: Very true, Socrates.

SOC.: Then piety, Euthyphro, is an art which gods and men have of doing business with one another?

EUTH.: That is an expression which you may use, if you like.

SOC.: But I have no particular liking for anything but the truth. I wish, however, that you would tell me what benefit accrues to the gods from our gifts. There is no doubt about what they give to us; for there is no good thing which they do not give; but how we can give any good thing to them in return is far from being equally clear. If they give everything and we give nothing, that must be an affair of business in which we have very greatly the advantage of them.

EUTH.: And do you imagine, Socrates, that any benefit accrues to the gods from our gifts?

SOC.: But if not, Euthyphro, what is the meaning of gifts which are conferred by us upon the gods?

EUTH.: What else, but tributes of honour; and, as I was just now saying, what pleases them?

SOC.: Piety, then, is pleasing to the gods, but not beneficial or dear to them?

EUTH.: I should say that nothing could be dearer.

SOC.: Then once more the assertion is repeated that piety is dear to the gods?

EUTH.: Certainly.

SOC.: And when you say this, can you wonder at your words not standing firm, but walking away? Will you accuse me of being the Daedalus who makes them walk away, not perceiving that there is another and far greater artist than Daedalus who makes them go round in a circle, and he is yourself; for the argument, as you will perceive, comes round to the same point. Were we not saying that the holy or pious was not the same with that which is loved of the gods? Have you forgotten?

EUTH.: I quite remember.

SOC.: And are you not saying that what is loved of the gods is holy; and is not this the same as what is dear to them—do you see?

EUTH.: True.

SOC.: Then either we were wrong in our former assertion; or, if we were right then, we are wrong now.

EUTH.: One of the two must be true.

SOC.: Then we must begin again and ask, What is piety? That is an enquiry which I shall never be weary of pursuing as far as in me lies; and I entreat you not to scorn me, but to apply your mind to the utmost, and tell me the truth. For, if any man knows, you are he; and therefore I must detain you, like Proteus, until you tell. If you had not certainly known the nature of piety and impiety, I am confident that you would never, on behalf of a serf, have charged your aged father with murder. You would not have run such a risk of doing wrong in the sight of the gods, and you would have had too much respect for the opinions of men. I am sure, therefore, that you know the nature of piety and impiety. Speak out then, my dear Euthyphro, and do not hide your knowledge.

EUTH.: Another time, Socrates; for I am in a hurry, and must go now.

SOC.: Alas! my companion, and will you leave me in despair? I was hoping that you would instruct me in the nature of piety and impiety; and then I might have cleared myself of Meletus and his indictment. I would have told him that I had been enlightened by Euthyphro, and had given up rash innovations and speculations, in which I indulged only through ignorance, and that now I am about to lead a better life.

From Plato, "Euthyphro," in *The Dialogues of Plato,* trans. Benjamin Jowett, Oxford University Press, Oxford, 1920.

In some respects, the material in this book will represent a conversation between various philosophers concerning various subjects from various points of view as expressed at various times all the way from antiquity to the very present. For this reason, the history of philosophy can be seen as a dialogue. Whereas a dialogue as presented by Plato is a neatly crafted conversation, the dialogue or, more accurately, the many dialogues in this book will not be as neat because each party to the "conversation" speaks in pages instead of sentences. This means that you, the reader, will have to participate in creating the character of a dialogue for everything you read. Actually, at this stage in the study of philosophy this should not be too complicated because you are called upon to do a relatively simple task, namely, to ask yourself what differentiates the ideas of the philosopher you are reading from those of the philosopher or philosophers who came earlier. What, for example, is the difference between Aristotle and John Stuart Mill when they try to describe what it means to be "good" or when they try to provide a foundation for Ethics? You should also participate in the conversation by giving your own views on the subject being discussed, but you should be prepared to give reasons for your views.

Control and balance, the classical formula for ethics. *Dancer,* Degas *(Hilaire Germain Edgar Degas, 1834–1917. "Arabesque over the Right Leg." Bronze. Height 11 3/8". The Metropolitan Museum of Art, Bequest of Mrs. H.O. Havemeyer Collection.)*

PART ONE

Ethics

What Should I Do?
And Why Should I Do It?

Imagine that you are forced by circumstances to borrow money. You know that you will not be able to repay it. Nevertheless, you know that no one will lend you money unless you promise to repay it at a definite time. You are about to make such a promise to repay but you ask yourself whether you should try to get yourself out of a difficulty in this way. To make such a false promise will no doubt solve your immediate problem, but you ask yourself, Is it right?

Kant
Fundamental Principles of the Metaphysics of Ethics (1785)

Why can't we just do what we want to do? What difference does it make to anyone how we behave? Why does the question of ethics arise in the first place? These questions bother us especially because we resent any limitation on our behavior. We also have the suspicion that nobody knows what is right or good. After all, we see very nice people behaving in opposite ways and each one thinks he is right. Why should we think that one way of behaving is better than another, that telling the truth is better than trying to get ourselves out of trouble by telling a falsehood? And who has the authority to tell us what to do?

We study ethics in order to find answers to the questions "What should I do?" and "Why should I do it?" But before we try to answer these questions, we need to consider what ethics is all about. If we examine the person who is considering making a false promise, we will find in that example some elements which help us to understand what ethics is about.

THE ELEMENTS OF ETHICS

Facing Alternatives

Ethics begins with our being aware that we face alternative possibilities in our behavior. We can either tell the truth or tell a falsehood. These two

21

possibilities are presented to us as options. We are capable of doing either one. We can control our action. A stone does not face this kind of alternative because it cannot distinguish between different courses of action. A stone can behave only in the way an outside force makes it behave. Unlike a stone, a person can start an action by himself. The difference, then, is that a stone is not aware of options, is not conscious of possibilities, whereas human beings are conscious that they face genuine alternatives.

Sometimes we do not want to admit that our behavior is under our control. After all, there are some things about us which are fixed even before we have anything to say about them. The color of our eyes, the general shape of our body, and even the sound of our voice may be the result of our family inheritance. In this respect, we could resemble a stone in that within a certain range we do not face any alternatives. But while a stone faces no alternatives at all, we as human beings do. What is more, we *know* that we face alternative ways of behaving.

Deliberating

When a person wonders whether to tell the truth or tell a falsehood in order to get out of trouble, he is engaged in the process of weighing the pros and cons of each alternative action. In short, he is "deliberating." Deliberation always has to do with future actions that are within our power. We do not deliberate about the past. Nor do we deliberate about those actions about which we have no choice. Deliberation means that we are considering what we should do. Sartre speaks of the young woman who deliberates over whether to remove her hand or leave it resting in her companion's. She also deliberates about whether she wants to be involved in the actions that leaving her hand there would make possible. Deliberation means asking the question "Should I do it?" or "What ought I to do?" To a certain extent, we know in general what we want to achieve through our actions—we want to achieve a sense of well-being, of happiness. What we deliberate over is how we shall achieve that end, or as Aristotle says, it is "the mark of a man of practical wisdom to be able to deliberate well about what is good and expedient . . . about what sort of things conduce to the good life in general." Certainly, deliberation has to do with action, and that is why Aristotle calls deliberation "practical wisdom." That is what we mean when we say a person made a conscious, deliberate choice.

Choosing

Our ability to make choices is what makes ethics possible. If we were machines, the question of ethics would never arise. The keys on the typewriter do not wake up in the morning, look out the window at the bright sunshine, and decide not to make words indoors on such a nice day. The keys have no choice. Although no one would describe a human being in such a thoroughly mechanical way, there are those who say that human behavior resembles the way machines work, that to think we are free to make choices is an illusion.

But again, if we did not have the power of choice, it would not be possible to evaluate our behavior or to praise or blame anyone, since we would always be doing what we are programmed to do. Could we ever say about an action that it is "wrong" if the person doing it "had no choice"? Moreover, could we ever praise someone for doing "the right thing" if that person did not choose to do it? Aristotle said "there are three objects of choice . . . the noble, the advantageous, and the pleasant." We also have the power to choose to avoid their opposites, namely, "the base, the injurious, and the painful." Virtue, then, says Aristotle, "is a state of character concerned with choice. . . ." Affirming our power of choice, Immanuel Kant said, "because I must, I can."

Being Responsible

In ethics, being responsible for our behavior means that we understand what we are doing, that we are aware of a moral rule which tells us to behave in a certain way, and that we have chosen to obey or disobey that moral rule. If we deliberate over whether to tell the truth and then choose instead to make a false promise, we are responsible for that action because it is the product of our choice. Being responsible means also that it is appropriate that we should be blamed for our actions. But being responsible is not limited to "bad" behavior only. We can also be responsible for "good" actions. In this case, being responsible means that it is appropriate that we should be praised for our behavior. It would not be appropriate, nor would it make any sense, to blame or punish or to praise anyone for those actions for which he is not responsible, that is, for actions which are not the result of his choice. There are many other ways to use the word "responsible," but our concern is with its ethical meaning. In ethics, being responsible focuses on our capacity to deliberate and to choose and therefore on our capacity to originate our actions. It is because these actions are *our* actions that we are said to be responsible for them.

Being Aware of Others

As in most ethical situations, making a true or false promise involves other people. Almost every time we ask "What should I do?" we are aware that other people are involved in our behavior. Why should someone ask himself before making a false promise, "Is it right?" It may be that he is afraid of being found out. He may, however, wonder whether it is fair to the other person. How we relate ourselves to others or how our behavior affects others makes up most of the subject matter of ethics. Being aware of others is more than wondering how our actions will affect them; we are also concerned about how the behavior of others will affect us. There is no satisfactory way for us to avoid the presence of other people. The most we can do is try to arrange the rules of behavior, of ethics, in order to reduce the amount of friction and conflict and thereby achieve the greatest amount of harmony. Whether our actions are right and good will depend to a great extent on the effect they will have on others. Actions such as telling a falsehood, stealing, injuring, and killing are considered wrong most of the time because they result in varying degrees of harm to someone. They also produce reactions from the victims, who in effect say, "If it is right for you to do that to me, then I will not hesitate to do the same thing to you."

Being Concerned with Oneself

When we ask such questions as "Is it right?" or "Why should I do it?" we are concerned not only about how our behavior will affect other people, but also about how it will affect ourselves. For one thing, we want to know whether our behavior will make us liable for punishment. We are also concerned about what people will think about us. Sometimes we decide that it is more important to behave in a certain way than to worry about other people's opinions. We also want to know whether our behavior will make us happy or unhappy. In a broader sense, we are concerned with what kind of a person we want to be or at least how our behavior will affect our character. This personal element in ethics focuses our attention on our individual selves and how we view the purpose of our lives. Our ideas about ethics will reflect our ideas about ourselves.

DEFINING "GOOD"

The purpose of moral rules is to guide human behavior toward actions which may be considered good. In most cases, these moral rules grow out of a particular insight into human nature. Theories of ethics will vary, since they reflect different views of human capacities and human possibilities. In some cases, however, a description of human nature and the cultural setting in which human beings find themselves can produce theories of ethics in which moral rules have a very restricted scope and relevance. This is true in such theories as, for example, "psychological egoism" and "cultural relativism."

Suppose that we say that the only motive at work in human behavior is our own self-interest or what is usually called self-love or psychological egoism. From this assumption, it would be possible to fashion a basis for ethics, but it would be the ethics of egoism, from which no moral rules of altruism or concern for others could be drawn. For the psychological egoist, everything turns on the love of self. This is not so much a theory as a description of what human beings in fact do. For example, Helvetius says that "self-love makes us totally what we are. . . . Why are we so coveteous of honors and dignity? Because we love ourselves. . . . The love of power, and the means of preventing it, is therefore, necessarily connected in man with the love of himself. . . . Power is the only object of man's pursuit."

Similarly, the ethical relativist calls good whatever a given culture considers good. Accordingly, William Graham Sumner says in his *Folkways*, "Morals can never be intuitive. They are historical. . . . The notion of right is in the folkways. . . . whatever is, is right." This could mean that what is good and right in our culture could be thought of as bad in another. It may be true, as shown by anthropology and sociology, that different cultures define good and bad in different ways. But moral philosophy goes beyond anthropology by asking whether there are standards of behavior or conceptions of good applicable to all human beings regardless of their unique cultural history.

There is another complication which involves the notion that the word "good" cannot be defined, a view expressed by G. E. Moore in his *Principia Ethica*. Defining good, says Moore, is as difficult as defining the color yellow. What makes it difficult if not impossible is that yellow is a basic and unique quality unlike anything else. But even though we cannot define it, we can confidently use the term "yellow" without difficulty by identifying any object that possesses this quality. One reason it is difficult to define the color yellow is that in the process we shift from what we are trying to define to something else. To say, for example, that the color yellow is present when certain light vibrations strike the normal eye may be an accurate scientific description of the mechanics of perceiving a color. But the word "yellow" is the name of a property we *see* and not the information which results from scientific measurement. In a similar way, when we try to define the word "good," we tend to identify it with something else, as when we say that good can be defined as pleasure. But the problem of defining good in terms of pleasure is that it leaves the question we started with unanswered, namely, "Why is it that we say of pleasure that it is good?" In short, what do we mean by "good"?

Moore said that there are two fallacies involved in this exercise. First, there is the fallacy of thinking that the word could be defined at all. He says,

> If I am asked "what is good?" my answer is that good is good and that is the end of the matter. Or if I am asked "How is good to be defined?" my answer is that it cannot be defined, and that is all I have to say about it.

The other fallacy is what Moore calls the "naturalistic fallacy," which consists of trying to define a nonnatural object *(good)* in terms of a natural object *(pleasure* or *self-realization).* What is unsatisfactory or fallacious here is that this definition is not conclusive because it is still significant to ask why pleasure or self-realization are good. To define good, for example, as pleasure begs the question, because this definition assumes what it is trying to prove, namely, not only that pleasure is good, but that good is pleasure.

Moore's conclusion is therefore that although the concept of good (in general) cannot be defined, it is nevertheless possible to identify good things and indeed to define *the* good. *The* good, according to Moore, is that which is valuable for its own sake, that is, what is intrinsically good, which he defines as follows: "By far the most valuable things which we know or can imagine, are certain states of consciousness, which may be roughly described as the pleasures of human intercourse and the enjoyment of beautiful objects." He continues, "No one . . . has ever doubted that personal affection and appreciation of what is beautiful in Art or nature are good in themselves; nor, if we consider strictly what things are worth having *purely for their own sake,* does it appear probable that anyone will think that anything else has nearly so great a value as the things which are included under these two heads." Therefore, just because he found no adequate way of defining good, Moore did not give up the attempt to provide a basis for the moral life.

However difficult it may be to define the word "good," and whatever fallacies may be involved in the attempt, the theories of ethics described in the following chapters represent some of the most influential attempts by philosophers to understand what is meant by morally good behavior. These philosophers are not so concerned with listing good actions as they are with providing reasons why an action can be called good.

SOME APPROACHES TO ETHICAL THEORIES

Aristotle emphasized that since everything in nature has a purpose, then man too must have a purpose, and therefore, ethics should consist of guiding our behavior in accordance with our purpose. Just as a hammer, or anything else, is called "good" because it does well what it is supposed to do, so also a person is good if his or her behavior is in accordance with what human nature was designed for.

Approaching "purpose" from a different perspective, an early group of philosophers called *"Stoics"* said that few events in our lives can be controlled by us. The script of the drama of life is already written. The only thing in our power is to choose how we will react to what we must do.

When philosophers added religious thought to their theories, as *Saint Augustine* did, it meant that ethics would cover a wider range than just the natural world. It is our nature, says Augustine, to love, that is, to fasten our affections on various objects or subjects, things or persons. We are good when we love the proper things properly. Thus things and other persons cannot be loved properly even though they possess value if they are loved as though they possess more value than God.

One of the most impressive philosophers, *Immanuel Kant,* singles out our faculties of will and reason as the key to ethics. Our conduct is right if it is consistent with human reason; that is, if on *principle* we would be willing for everyone to behave the way we do.

Jeremy Bentham and *John Stuart Mill* place more emphasis on our feelings, especially the feelings of pleasure and pain, as the guide for ethics. Whatever gives us the greatest pleasure and the least amount of pain is the standard for morally good behavior.

Seeking a way to account for our deepest yearnings to express our energy and power, *Friedrich Nietzsche* developed his famous and novel statements about the will to power. The highest morality, he said, is to express all our vital energies, saying "yes" to life and its urgings, expressing our will, using reason primarily to direct, not to deny, our powerful life forces.

Moral philosophers use the word "man" to refer generically to all human beings, both male and female. But this does raise a significant question: To the extent that there are natural differences as well as similarities between men and women, what significance do the differences between male and female have on the process of formulating a theory of ethics? Prof. *Carol Gilligan* presents an illuminating analysis of the question of whether there is a distinctive feminine voice that is relevant to the formulation of moral philosophy. Similarly, Prof. *Annette Baier* addresses the question "What do women want in a moral theory?"

1

Fulfilling Human Purpose

Aristotle

Aristotle (382–322 B.C.) was born in Stagira, a small town northeast of Athens. His father was physician to the King of Macedonia. As a boy, Aristotle was introduced to Greek medicine by his father, and this stimulated his lifelong interest in science. At age fifteen he was sent to Athens, where for the next twenty years he studied with Plato at Plato's Athenean Academy. Here he was known as "the mind of the school." Later Aristotle traveled widely, married a king's adopted daughter, and became the tutor of the future Alexander the Great for three years. In 355 B.C. he opened his own school, called the Lyceum, a rival of Plato's Academy. For twelve or thirteen years Aristotle remained as head of the Lyceum, where he lectured, taught classes, but most important of all, formulated his ideas about the classification of the sciences, invented logic, and wrote books in every major area of philosophy and science. The forty-seven books of his that remain cover the whole range of universal knowledge.

Aristotle's theory of ethics centers on his belief that man (a term which refers to both men and women), as everything else in nature, has a special "end" to achieve or a function or purpose to fulfill. For this reason, his theory is called "teleological" (from the Greek word *telos,* meaning end or purpose). He begins his book *Ethics* by saying that "every art and every inquiry, and similarly every action and pursuit, is thought to aim at some good. . . ." If this is so, the question for ethics is "What is the *good* at which human behavior aims?"

For Aristotle, the principle of good and right was embedded within each man; moreover, this principle could be discovered by studying the essential nature of man and could be attained through his actual behavior in daily life. Aristotle warns his reader, however, not to expect more precision in a discussion of ethics than "the subject matter will admit." Still, just because this subject is susceptible of "variation and error" does not mean, said Aristotle, that ideas of right and wrong "exist conventionally only [that is, by local agreement], and not in the nature of things." With this in mind, Aristotle set out to discover the basis of morality in the structure of human nature.

Aristotle. *(Scala/Art Resource)*

TYPES OF "ENDS"

Aristotle sets the framework for his ethical theory with a preliminary illustration. Having said that all action aims toward an end, he now wants to distinguish between two major kinds of ends, which can be called "instrumental" ends (acts that are done as *means* for other ends) and "intrinsic" ends (acts that are done *for their own sake*). These two types of ends are illustrated, for example, in "every action connected with war."

When we consider step by step what is involved in the total activity of a war, we find, says Aristotle, that there is a series of special kinds of acts. These acts have their own ends, but when they are completed, they are only means by which still other ends are to be achieved. There is, for one thing, the art of the bridle maker. But the bridle is a means for the horseman to guide his horse in battle. Also, a carpenter builds a barrack, and when it is completed, he has fulfilled his function as a carpenter. The barracks also fulfill their function when they provide safe shelter for soldiers. But the ends here achieved by the carpenter and the building are not ends in themselves but are merely instrumental in housing soldiers until they move on to their next stage of action. Similarly, the builder of ships fulfills his function when the ship is successfully launched, but again this end is in turn a means for transporting the soldiers to the field of battle. The doctor fulfills his function to the extent that he keeps the soldiers in good health. But the "end" of health in this case becomes a "means" for effective fighting. The officer aims at victory in battle, but victory is the means to peace. Peace itself, though sometimes taken mistakenly as the final end of war, is the means for creating the conditions under which men, *as men*, could fulfill their function as men. When we discover what men aim at, not as carpenters, doctors, or generals, but as *men*, we will then arrive at action *for its own sake*, and for which all other activity is only a means, and this, says Aristotle, "must be the Good of Man."

How shall the word "good" be understood? As Plato before him, Aristotle tied the word "good" to the special function of a thing. A hammer is good if it does what hammers are expected to do. A carpenter is good if he fulfills his function as a builder. This would be true for all the crafts and professions. But here Aristotle distinguishes between a man's craft or profession and his activity as a man. To be a good doctor, for example, did not for Aristotle mean the same thing as being a good man. One could be a good doctor without being a good man, and vice versa. There are two different functions here, the function of doctoring and the function of acting as a man. To discover the good at which a man should aim, Aristotle said we must discover the distinctive function of human nature. The good man, according to Aristotle, is the man who is fulfilling his function as a man.

THE FUNCTION OF MAN

Aristotle asks, "Are we then to suppose that while carpenter and cobbler have certain works and courses of action, Man as Man has none, but is left by Nature without a work?" Or if "the eye, hand, foot and in general each of the parts evidently has a function, may one lay it down that man similarly has a function apart from all these?" Surely man too has a distinctive mode of activity, but what is it? Here Aristotle analyzes man's nature in order to discover his unique activity, saying, first of all, that man's end "is not mere life," because that plainly is shared with him even by vegetables, and, says Aristotle, "we want what is peculiar to him." Next there is the life of sensation, "but this again manifestly is common to horses, oxen and every animal." There remains then "an active life of the element that has a rational principle. . . . if the function of man is an activity of soul which follows or implies a rational principle . . . then the human good turns out to be activity of soul in accordance with virtue. . . ."

Since man's function as a man means the proper functioning of his soul, Aristotle sought to describe the nature of the soul. The soul is the form of the body. That is, the soul is what provides the body with its unique life and operation and makes it the kind of body which is human. As such, the soul refers to the total person. Accordingly, Aristotle said that the soul has two parts, the irrational and the rational. The irrational part, in turn, is composed of two subparts, the vegetative and the desiring or "appetitive" parts. For the most part, these are "something contrary to the rational principle, resisting and opposing it." The conflict between the rational and irrational elements in man (that is, the conflict between reason and our desires) is what raises the problems and subject matter of morality.

Morality involves action, for nothing is called good unless it is functioning. Thus Aristotle says that "as at the Olympic games it is not the finest and strongest men who are crowned, but they who enter the lists, for out of these the prize-men are selected; so too in life, of the honorable and good, it is they who act who rightly win the prizes." The particular kind of action implied here, if we have in mind Aristotle's analysis of the soul, is rational control and guidance of the irrational parts of the soul. Moreover, the good man is not the one who does a good deed here and there, now and then, but whose whole life is good, "for as it is not one swallow or one fine day that makes a spring, so it is not one day or a short time that makes a man blessed and happy."

HAPPINESS AS THE END

Human action should aim at its proper end. Everywhere men aim at pleasure, wealth, and honor. But none of these ends, although they have value, can occupy the place of the chief good for which man should aim. To be an ultimate end, an act must be *self-sufficient* and *final*, "that which is always desirable in itself and never for the sake of something else," and it must be *attainable* by man. Aristotle seems certain that all men will agree that *happiness* is the end that alone meets all the requirements for the ultimate end of human action. Indeed, we choose pleasure, wealth, and honor only because we think that "through their instrumentality we shall be happy." Happiness, it turns out, is another word or name for good, for like good, happiness is the fulfillment of our distinctive function, or as Aristotle says, "Happiness . . . is a working of the soul in the way of excellence or virtue. . . ."

How does the soul work to attain happiness? The general rule of morality is "to act in accordance with Right Reason." What this means is that the rational part of the soul should control the irrational part. That the irrational part of the soul requires guidance is obvious when we consider what it consists of and what its mechanism is. Referring now only to the appetites or the appetitive part of the soul, we discover first that it is affected or influenced by things outside of the self, such as objects and persons. Also, there are two basic ways in which the appetitive part of the soul reacts to these external factors, these ways being *love* and *hate* or through the *concupiscent* and *irascible* "passions." The concupiscent passion leads one to desire things and persons, whereas the irascible passion leads one to avoid or destroy them. It becomes quickly apparent that these passions or capacities for love and hate, attraction or repulsion, creation or destruction, taken by themselves, could easily "go wild." In themselves they do not contain any principle of measure or selection. What should a person desire? How much? Under what circumstances? How should he relate himself to things, wealth, honor, and other persons?

We do not automatically act the right way in these matters; as Aristotle says, "none of the moral virtues arises in us by nature; for nothing that exists by nature can form a habit contrary to its nature." Morality has to do with developing habits, the habits of right thinking, right choice, and right behavior.

VIRTUE AS THE "GOLDEN MEAN"

Since the passions are capable of producing a wide range of action, all the way from too little to too much, a person must discover the proper meaning of excess and defect and thereby discover the appropriate *mean*, the middle ground. Virtue is concerned with our various feelings and actions, for it is in them that there can be *excess* and *defect* (too much and too little). For example, it is possible, says Aristotle, to feel the emotion of fear, confidence, lust, anger, compassion, pleasure, and pain too much or too little and in either case wrongly. To feel these when we ought to, on appropriate occasions, toward whom, and as we should, is the mean; that is the best state for man to be in, and this is *virtue*. Vice, again, is either extreme, excess or defect, and virtue is the mean. It is through the rational power of the soul that the passions are controlled and action is guided.

The virtue of *courage*, for example, is the mean between two vices, namely, fear (defect) and foolhardiness (excess). Virtue, then, is a state of being, "a state apt to exercise deliberate choice, being in the relative mean, determined by reason, and as the man of practical wisdom would determine."

The mean is not the same for every person, nor is there a mean for every act. Each mean is relative to each person inasmuch as the circumstances will vary. In the case of eating, the mean will obviously be different for an adult athlete and a little girl. But for each person, there is nevertheless a proportionate or relative mean. For example, the excess (too much) in eating is called "gluttony," and the defect (too little) is called "fasting." For both the athlete and the little girl there is the right amount of eating, and this is the "mean"; but these amounts would be different because of their physical differences. For both, the mean between these extremes is the virtue of *temperance*. Similarly, when one gives money, *liberality*, as the mean between prodigality and stinginess, is not an absolute figure but is relative to one's assets. Moreover, for some acts there is no mean at all; their very nature already implies badness, such as spite, envy, adultery, theft, and murder. These are bad in themselves and not in their excesses or deficiencies. One is always wrong in doing them.

DELIBERATION AND CHOICE

There are in the rational soul two kinds of reasoning. The first is theoretical, giving us knowledge of fixed principles or philosophical wisdom. The other is practical, giving us a rational guide to our action under the particular circumstances in which we find ourselves, and this is practical wisdom. What is important about the role of reason is that without this rational element, man would not have any moral capacity.

Again, Aristotle stressed that although man has a natural capacity for *right* behavior, he does not act rightly *by nature.* A man's life consists of an indeterminate number of possibilities. Goodness is in man *potentially,* but unlike the acorn out of which the oak will grow with almost mechanical certitude, man must move from what is potential in him to its actuality by knowing what he must do, deliberating about it, and then choosing in fact to do it. Unlike Plato and Socrates, who thought that to know the good was sufficient to do the good, Aristotle saw that there must be deliberate choice in addition to knowledge. Thus Aristotle said that "the origin of moral action . . . is choice, and [the origin] of choice is desire and reasoning with a view to an end." There cannot be *choice* without reason: "intellect itself . . . moves nothing, but only the intellect which aims at an end and is practical."

Morality and moral choice imply human responsibility. If some ways of behaving are right and others wrong, it is necessary to discover why a person acts in a wrong instead of a right way. If we are to praise or blame—praise virtue and blame vice—a person must be truly capable of making a choice. Aristotle assumed that an act for which a person could be held responsible must be a voluntary act. A genuine choice is a voluntary action. But not all our actions are voluntary. Thus Aristotle said that "praise and blame arise upon such acts as are voluntary, while for the involuntary allowance is made, and sometimes compassion is excited." The distinction, as he saw it, between voluntary and involuntary acts was in general this: *Involuntary* acts are those for which a person is not responsible because they are (1) done out of ignorance of particular circumstances, (2) done as a result of external compulsion, or (3) done to avoid a greater evil. *Voluntary* acts are those for which a person is responsible because none of these three extenuating circumstances obtain.

THE VIRTUES

In a general way we have already defined virtue as the fulfillment of man's distinctive function and as the mean between extremes. Another way to describe Aristotle's concept of virtue is to consider each virtue as the product of rational control of the passions. In this way we can combine all aspects of human behavior. Human nature consists for Aristotle not simply of rationality but of the full range covered by the vegetative, sensitive or appetitive, and the rational souls. Virtue does not imply the negation or rejection of any of these natural capacities. The moral man employs all his capacities, *physical* and *mental.* Corresponding to these two broad divisions in man there are two functions of reason, the intellectual and the moral, and each has its own virtues. There are accordingly *intellectual virtues* and *moral virtues.*

The intellectual virtues are philosophical wisdom and understanding, and they owe their birth and growth to teaching and learning. Moral virtue comes about as a result of habit, whence comes the name "ethics" *(ethike),* "formed by a slight variation from the word *ethos* (habit)." All the moral virtues have to be learned and practiced, and they become virtues only through action, for "we become just by doing just acts, temperate by doing temperate acts, brave by doing brave acts." The "cardinal" moral virtues are courage, temperance, justice, and wisdom. In addition to these, Aristotle considered also the virtues of magnificence, liberality, friendship, and self-respect. And although he acknowledged the central role of reason as a guide to practical and moral action, he nevertheless concluded that philosophical wisdom is superior to practical wisdom, that *contemplation* is most likely to lead to happiness.

CONTEMPLATION

Aristotle concludes that if happiness is the product of our acting according to our distinctive nature, it is reasonable to assume that it is acting according to our highest nature; "that this activity is contemplative we have already said." This activity is the best, says Aristotle, "since not only is reason the best thing in us, but the objects of reason are the best of knowable objects." Moreover, contemplation "is most continuous, since we can contemplate truth more continuously than we can *do* anything." Finally, "we think happiness has pleasure mingled with it, but the activity of philosophical wisdom is admittedly the pleasantest of virtuous activities."

Reading _____

Basing Ethics on Human Nature
Aristotle

Every art and every inquiry, and similarly every action and pursuit, is thought to aim at some good; and for this reason the good has rightly been declared to be that at which all things aim. Now, as there are many actions, arts and sciences, their ends also are many; the end of the medical art is health, that of shipbuilding a vessel, that of strategy victory, that of economics wealth.

If, then, there is some end of the things we do, which we desire for its own sake (everything being desired for the sake of this), and if we do not choose everything for the sake of something else (for at that rate the process would go on to infinity, so that our desire would be empty and vain), clearly this must be the good and the chief good. Will not the knowledge of it, then, have a great influence on life? Shall we not, like archers who have a mark to aim at, be more likely to hit upon what is right? If so, we must try, in outline at least, to determine what it is. . . .

Our discussion will be adequate if it has as much clearness as the subject-matter admits of, for precision is not to be sought for alike in all discussions, any more than in all the products of the crafts. . . .

Let us resume our inquiry and state, in view of the fact that all knowledge and every pursuit aims at some good, . . . what is the highest of all goods achievable by action? Verbally there is very general agreement; for both the general run of men and people of superior refinement say that it is happiness, and identify living well and doing well with being happy; but with regard to what happiness is they differ, and the many do not give the same account as the wise. For the former think it is some plain and obvious thing, like pleasure, wealth, or honour; they differ, however, from one another—and often even the same man identifies it with different things, with health when he is ill, with wealth when he is poor; but, conscious of their igno– rance, they admire those who proclaim some great ideal that is above their comprehension. Now some thought that apart from these many goods there is another which is self-subsistent and causes the goodness of all these as well. . . .

Let us again return to the good we are seeking, and ask what it can be. It seems different in different actions and arts; it is different in medicine, in strategy, and in the other arts likewise. What then is the good of each? Surely that for whose sake everything else is done. In medicine this is health, in strategy victory, in architecture a house, in any other sphere something else, and in every action and pursuit the end; for it is for the sake of this that all men do whatever else they do. Therefore, if there is an end for all that we do, this will be the good achievable by action, and if there are more than one, these will be the goods achievable by action.

So the argument has by a different course reached the same point; but we must try to state this even more clearly. Since there are evidently more than one end, and we choose some of these (e.g., wealth, flutes, and, in general, instruments) for the sake of something else, clearly not all ends are final ends; but the chief good is evidently something final. Therefore, if there is only one final end, this will be what we are seeking, and if there are more than one, the most final of these will be what we are seeking. Now we call that which is in itself worthy of pursuit more final than that which is worthy of pursuit for the sake of something else, and that which is never desirable for the sake of something else more final than the things that are desirable both in themselves and for the sake of that other thing, and therefore we call final without qualification that which is always desirable in itself and never for the sake of something else.

Now such a thing happiness, above all else, is held to be; for this we choose always for itself and never for the sake of something else, but honour, pleasure, reason, and every virtue we choose indeed for themselves (for if nothing resulted from them we should still choose each of them), but we choose them also for the sake of happiness, judging that by means of them we shall be happy. Happiness, on the other hand, no one chooses for the sake of these, nor, in general, for anything other than itself. . . .

Presumably, however, to say that happiness is the chief good seems a platitude, and a clearer account of what it is is still desired. This might perhaps be given, if we could first ascertain the function of man. For just as for a flute-player, a sculptor, or any artist, and, in general, for all things that have a function or activity, the good and the "well" is thought to reside in the function, so would it seem to be for man, if he has a function. Have the carpenter, then, and the tanner certain functions or activities, and has man none? Is he born without a function? Or as eye, hand, foot, and in general each of the parts evidently has a function, may one lay it down that man similarly has a function apart from all these? What then can this be? Life seems to be common even to plants, but we are seeking what is peculiar to man. Let us exclude, therefore, the life of nutrition and growth. Next there would be a life of perception, but *it* also seems to be common even to the horse, the ox, and every animal. There remains, then, an active life of the element that has a rational principle. . . . Now if the function of man is an activity of soul which follows or implies a rational principle, and if we say "a so-and-so" and "a good so-and-so" have a function which is the same in kind, e.g., a lyre-player and a good lyre-player, and so without qualification in all cases, eminence in respect of goodness being added to the name of the function (for the function of a lyre-player is to play the lyre, and that of a good lyre-player is to do so well): if this is the case, (and we state the function of man to be a certain kind of life, and this to be an activity or actions of the soul implying a rational principle, and the function of a good man to be the good and noble performance of these, and if any action is well performed when it is performed in accordance with the appropriate excellence: if this is the case,) human good turns out to be activity of soul in accordance with virtue, and if there are more than one virtue, in accordance with the best and most complete.

But we must add "in a complete life." For one swallow does not make a summer, nor does one day; and so too one day, or a short time, does not make a man blessed and happy. . . .

Since happiness is an activity of soul in accordance with perfect virtue, we must consider the nature of virtue; for perhaps we shall thus see better the nature of happiness. . . . But clearly the virtue we must study is human virtue; for the good we were seeking was human good and the happiness human happiness. By human virtue we mean not that of the body but that of the soul; and happiness also we call an activity of soul. . . .

Some things are said about it [the soul], adequately enough, even in the discussions outside our school, and we must use these; e.g., that one element in the soul is irrational and one has a rational principle. . . .

Of the irrational element one division seems to be widely distributed, and vegetative in its nature, I mean that which causes nutrition and growth; for it is this kind of power of the soul that one must assign to all nurslings and embryos, and this same power to full-grown creatures; this is more reasonable than to assign some different power to them. Now the excellence of this seems to be common to all species and not specifically human; for this part or faculty seems to function most in sleep, while goodness and badness are least manifest in sleep (whence comes the saying that the happy are no better off than the wretched for half their lives; and this happens naturally enough, since sleep is an inactivity of the soul in that respect in which it is called good or bad), unless perhaps to a small extent some of the movements actually penetrate to the soul, and in this respect the dreams of good men are better than those of ordinary people. Enough of this subject, however; let us leave the nutritive faculty alone, since it has by its nature no share in human excellence.

There seems to be also another irrational element in the soul—one which in a sense, however, shares in a rational principle. For we praise the rational principle of the continent man and of the incontinent, and the part of their soul that has such a principle, since it urges them aright and towards the best objects; but there is found in them also another element naturally opposed to the rational principle, which fights against and resists that principle. For exactly as paralysed limbs when we intend to move them to the right turn on the contrary to the left, so is it with the soul; the impulses of incontinent people move in contrary directions. But while in the body we see that which moves astray, in the soul we do not. No doubt, however, we must none the less suppose that in the soul too there is something contrary to the rational principle, resisting and opposing it. In what sense it is distinct from the other elements does not concern us. Now even this seems to have a share in a rational principle, as we said; at any rate in the continent man it obeys the rational principle—and presumably in the temperate and brave man it is still more obedient; for in him it speaks, on all matters, with the same voice as the rational principle. . . .

Virtue, then, being of two kinds, intellectual and moral, intellectual virtue in the main owes both its birth and its growth to teaching (for which reason it requires experience and time), while moral virtue comes about as a result of habit; for nothing that exists by nature can form a habit contrary to its nature. For instance the stone which by nature moves downwards cannot be habituated to move upwards, not even if one tries to train it by throwing it up ten thousand times; nor can fire be habituated to move downwards, nor can anything else that by nature behaves in one way be trained to behave in another. Neither by nature, then, nor contrary to nature do the virtues arise in us; rather we are adapted by nature to receive them, and are made perfect by habit.

If happiness is activity in accordance with virtue, it is reasonable that it should be in accordance with the highest virtue; and this will be that of the best thing in us. Whether it be reason or something else that is this element which is thought to be our natural ruler and guide and to take thought of things noble and divine, whether it be itself also divine or only the most divine element in us, the activity of this in accordance with its proper virtue will be perfect happiness. That this activity is contemplative we have already said.

Now this would seem to be in agreement both with what we said before and with the truth. For, firstly, this activity is the best (since not only is reason the best thing in us, but the objects of reason are the best of knowable objects); and, secondly, it is the most continuous, since we can contemplate truth more continuously than we can *do* anything. And we think happiness has pleasure mingled with it, but the activity of philosophic wisdom is admittedly the pleasantest of virtuous activities; at all events the pursuit of it is thought to offer pleasures marvellous for their purity and their enduringness, and it is to be expected that those who know will pass their time more pleasantly than those who inquire. And the self-sufficiency that is spoken of must belong to the contemplative activity. For while a philosopher, as well as a just man or one possessing any other virtue, needs the necessaries of life, when they are sufficiently equipped with things of that sort the just man needs people towards whom and with whom he shall act justly, and the temperate man, the brave man, and each of the others is in the same case, but the philosopher, even when by himself, can contemplate truth, and the better the wiser he is; he can perhaps do so better if he has fellow-workers, but still he is the most self-sufficient. And this activity alone would seem to be loved for its own sake; for nothing arises from it apart from the contemplating, while from practical activities we gain more or less apart from the action. And happiness is thought to depend on leisure; for we are busy that we may have leisure, and make war that we may live in peace. . . .

But such a life would be too high for man; for it is not in so far as he is man that he will live so, but in so far as something divine is present in him; and by so much as this is superior to our composite nature is its activity superior to that which is the exercise of the other kind of virtue. If reason is divine, then, in comparison with man, the life according to it is divine in comparison with human life. But we must not follow those who advise us, being men, to think of human beings, and, being mortal, of mortal things, but must, so far as we can, make ourselves immortal, and strain every nerve to live in accordance with the best thing in us; for even if it be small in bulk, much more does it in power and worth surpass everything. This would seem, too, to be each man himself, since it is the authoritative and better part of him. It would be strange, then, if he were to choose not the life of his self but that of something else. And what we said before will apply now; that which is proper to each thing is by nature best and most pleasant for each thing; for man, therefore, the life according to reason is best and pleasantest, since reason more than anything else *is* man. This life therefore is also the happiest.

From Aristotle, *Nichomachean Ethics*, vol. V, *The Student's Oxford Aristotle*, trans. W. D. Ross, by permission of the Oxford University Press, New York, 1946.

QUESTIONS FOR REVIEW AND DISCUSSION

1. Why can you say that it is possible for someone to be a good doctor but a bad person and vice versa?
2. If the "good" is defined as the Golden Mean, how would you apply the standard of temperance to two individuals who are unlike physically in size, weight, and age?
3. What is the difference between *instrumental* ends and *intrinsic* ends?
4. Everything has a function, the eye to see, the ear to hear, the feet to walk, etc. What is a human being's function *as a person?*
5. What did Aristotle mean when he said that "one swallow does not make a summer" when describing a good person?

2

What Can We Control?

The Stoics

The Stoics were members of a school founded in Athens by Zeno (334–262 B.C.). They held their meetings on the *stoa* (the Greek word for porch, hence the term "stoic"). Their ideas spread to Rome, where such famous people as Cicero, Seneca, and the Emperor Marcus Aurelius became followers. One of the outstanding Roman Stoics was Epictetus (A.D. 60–117). He overcame major hurdles in his life: He was lame either by birth or through accident, and early in life he was not a free man. He tried to develop an intensely practical guide for how life is to be carried out with satisfaction.

Epictetus based his moral philosophy on this simple teaching: There are "two rules we must ever bear in mind—that apart from the will there is nothing either good or bad, and that we must not try to anticipate or direct events, but merely accept them with intelligence." We must do this, says Epictetus, because "the Gods put in our hands the one blessing that is best of all and master of all, that and nothing else, the power to deal rightly with our impressions, but everything else they did not put in our hands. . . ."

As human beings, we should think of ourselves as actors in a drama. It would be a mistake to think of this drama as being limited to our family, community, or even country. The drama Epictetus has in mind involves the whole universe, and people everywhere are members of the cast. As actors, we do not choose our role. The author and director of the drama is God or universal reason, who determines what each person will be and how and where each person will be situated in the course of his or her life. If everything is "set" for each person, if the "script" of our lives is already written, what, if anything, can we do about it? Do we have any choice at all?

There is something we can do, says Epictetus. We can recognize and accept what our part or role in this drama is and then perform that part well. Some people have "bit" parts, while others are cast into leading roles. "If it be [God's] will that you should act a poor man, see that you act it well; or a cripple or a ruler, or a private citizen. For this is your business," says Epictetus, "to act well the given part."

Stoa of Attalos. *(Agora Excavations, American School of Classical Studies at Athens)*

The actor develops a great indifference to those things over which he has no control, for example, the shape and form of the scenery or who the other players will be. He especially has no control over the story or its plot. But there is one thing that the actor can control, and that is his attitude and emotions. He can sulk because he has only a bit part, or he can be consumed with jealousy because someone else was chosen to be the hero, or he can be terribly insulted because the makeup artist put a particularly ugly nose on his face. But neither sulking, nor jealousy, nor feeling insulted can in any way alter the fact that he has a bit part, is not a hero, and must wear an ugly nose. The only thing these feelings and attitudes can do is rob him of his happiness. Therefore, the wise person will choose to control his feelings.

Epictetus. *(New York Public Library Picture Collection)*

Reading —————————————————————————————————

Controlling Our Feelings and Attitudes
Epictetus

1

Of all existing things some are in our power, and others are not in our power.
In our power are thought, impulse, will to get and will to avoid, and, in a
word, everything which is our own doing. Things not in our power include
the body, property, reputation, office, and, in a word, everything which is not
our own doing. Things in our power are by nature free, unhindered,
untrammelled; things not in our power are weak, servile, subject to hindrance,

dependent on others. Remember then that if you imagine that what is naturally slavish is free, and what is naturally another's is your own, you will be hampered, you will mourn, you will be put to confusion, you will blame gods and men; but if you think that only your own belongs to you, and that what is another's is indeed another's, no one will ever put compulsion or hindrance on you, you will blame none, you will accuse none, you will do nothing against your will, no one will harm you, you will have no enemy, for no harm can touch you. . . .

Make it your study then to confront every harsh impression with the words, "You are but an impression, and not at all what you seem to be." Then test it by those rules that you possess; and first by this—the chief test of all—"Is it concerned with what is in our power or with what is not in our power?" And if it is concerned with what is not in our power, be ready with the answer that it is nothing to you.

2

Remember that the will to get promises attainment of what you will, and the will to avoid promises escape from what you avoid; and he who fails to get what he wills is unfortunate, and he who does not escape what he wills to avoid is miserable. If then you try to avoid only what is unnatural in the region within your control, you will escape from all that you avoid; but if you try to avoid disease or death or poverty you will be miserable.

Therefore let your will to avoid have no concern with what is not in man's power; direct it only to things in man's power that are contrary to nature. But for the moment you must utterly remove the will to get; for if you will to get something not in man's power you are bound to be unfortunate; while none of the things in man's power that you could honourably will to get is yet within your reach. Impulse to act and not to act, these are your concern; yet exercise them gently and without strain, and provisionally. . . .

5

What disturbs men's minds is not events but their judgements on events. For instance, death is nothing dreadful, or else Socrates would have thought it so. No, the only dreadful thing about it is men's judgement that it is dreadful. And so when we are hindered, or disturbed, or distressed, let us never lay the blame on others, but on ourselves, that is, on our own judgements. To accuse others for one's own misfortunes is a sign of want of education; to accuse oneself shows that one's education has begun; to accuse neither oneself nor others shows that one's education is complete. . . .

8

Ask not that events should happen as you will, but let your will be that events should happen as they do, and you shall have peace.

9

Sickness is a hindrance to the body, but not to the will, unless the will consent. Lameness is a hindrance to the leg, but not to the will. Say this to yourself at each event that happens, for you shall find that though it hinders something else it will not hinder you. . . .

12

If you wish to make progress, abandon reasonings of this sort: "If I neglect my affairs I shall have nothing to live on"; "If I do not punish my son, he will be wicked." For it is better to die of hunger, so that you be free from pain and free from fear, than to live in plenty and be troubled in mind. It is better for your son to be wicked than for you to be miserable. Wherefore begin with little things. Is your drop of oil spilt? Is your sup of wine stolen? Say to yourself, "This is the price paid for freedom from passion, this is the price of a quiet mind." Nothing can be had without a price. When you call your slave-boy, reflect that he may not be able to hear you, and if he hears you, he may not be able to do anything you want. But he is not so well off that it rests with him to give you peace of mind.

13

If you wish to make progress, you must be content in external matters to seem a fool and a simpleton; do not wish men to think you know anything, and if any should think you to be somebody, distrust yourself. For know that it is not easy to keep your will in accord with nature and at the same time keep outward things; if you attend to one you must needs neglect the other. . . .

15

Remember that you must behave in life as you would at a banquet. A dish is handed round and comes to you; put out your hand and take it politely. It passes you; do not stop it. It has not reached you; do not be impatient to get it, but wait till your turn comes. Bear yourself thus towards children, wife, office, wealth, and one day you will be worthy to banquet with the gods. . . .

16

When you see a man shedding tears in sorrow for a child abroad or dead, or for loss of property, beware that you are not carried away by the impression that it is outward ills that make him miserable. Keep this thought by you: "What distresses him is not the event, for that does not distress another, but his judgement on the event." Therefore do not hesitate to sympathize with him so far as words go, and if it so chance, even to groan with him; but take heed that you do not also groan in your inner being.

17

Remember that you are an actor in a play, and the Playwright chooses the manner of it: if he wants it short, it is short; if long, it is long. If he wants you to act a poor man you must act the part with all your powers; and so if your part be a cripple or a magistrate or a plain man. For your business is to act the character that is given you and act it well; the choice of the cast is Another's. . . .

20

Remember that foul words or blows in themselves are no outrage, but your judgement that they are so. So when any one makes you angry, know that it is your own thought that has angered you. Wherefore make it your first endeavour not to let your impressions carry you away. For if once you gain time and delay, you will find it easier to control yourself. . . .

22

If you set your desire on philosophy you must at once prepare to meet with ridicule and the jeers of many who will say, "Here he is again, turned philosopher. Where has he got these proud looks?" Nay, put on no proud looks, but hold fast to what seems best to you, in confidence that God has set you at this post. And remember that if you abide where you are, those who first laugh at you will one day admire you, and that if you give way to them, you will get doubly laughed at.

23

If it ever happen to you to be diverted to things outside, so that you desire to please another, know that you have lost your life's plan. Be content then always to be a philosopher; if you wish to be regarded as one too, show yourself that you are one and you will be able to achieve it. . . .

33

Lay down for yourself from the first a definite stamp and style of conduct, which you will maintain when you are alone and also in the society of men. Be silent for the most part, or, if you speak, say only what is necessary and in a few words. Talk, but rarely, if occasion calls you, but do not talk of ordinary things—of gladiators, or horse-races, or athletes, or of meats or drinks—these are topics that arise everywhere—but above all do not talk about men in blame or compliment or comparison. If you can, turn the conversation of your company by your talk to some fitting subject; but if you should chance to be isolated among strangers, be silent. Do not laugh much, nor at many things, nor without restraint. . . .

Refuse the entertainments of strangers and the vulgar. But if occasion arise to accept them, then strain every nerve to avoid lapsing into the state of the vulgar. For know that, if your comrade have a stain on him, he that associates with him must needs share the stain, even though he be clean in himself.

For your body take just so much as your bare need requires, such as food, drink, clothing, house, servants, but cut down all that tends to luxury and outward show.

Avoid impurity to the utmost of your power before marriage, and if you indulge your passion, let it be done lawfully. But do not be offensive or censorious to those who indulge it, and do not be always bringing up your own chastity. If some one tells you that so and so speaks ill of you, do not defend yourself against what he says, but answer, "He did not know my other faults, or he would not have mentioned these alone. . . ."

34

When you imagine some pleasure, beware that it does not carry you away, like other imaginations. Wait a while, and give yourself pause. Next remember two things: how long you will enjoy the pleasure, and also how long you will afterwards repent and revile yourself. And set on the other side the joy and self-satisfaction you will feel if you refrain. And if the moment seems come to realize it, take heed that you be not overcome by the winning sweetness and attraction of it; set in the other scale the thought how much better is the consciousness of having vanquished it. . . .

44

It is illogical to reason thus, "I am richer than you, therefore I am superior to you," "I am more eloquent than you, therefore I am superior to you." It is more logical to reason, "I am richer than you, therefore my property is superior to yours," "I am more eloquent than you, therefore my speech is superior to yours." You are something more than property or speech. . . .

46

On no occasion call yourself a philosopher, nor talk at large of your principles among the multitude, but act on your principles. For instance, at a banquet do not say how one ought to eat, but eat as you ought. Remember that Socrates had so completely got rid of the thought of display that when men came and wanted an introduction to philosophers he took them to be introduced; so patient of neglect was he. And if a discussion arise among the multitude on some principle, keep silent for the most part; for you are in great danger of blurting out some undigested thought. And when some one says to you, "You know nothing," and you do not let it provoke you, then know that you are really on the right road. For sheep do not bring grass to their shepherds and show them how much they have eaten, but they digest their fodder and then produce it in the form of wool and milk. Do the same yourself; instead of displaying your principles to the multitude, show them the results of the principles you have digested.

From "The Manual of Epictetus," in *The Stoic and Epicurean Philosophers,* ed. Whitney J. Oates, Random House, New York, 1940.

QUESTIONS FOR REVIEW AND DISCUSSION

1. What point does Epictetus want to make when he says that we are all actors in a drama?
2. Epictetus says that some things are in our control and some are not. Give an example and indicate how this fact plays a significant role in shaping Epictetus's philosophy.
3. Epictetus says that "what disturbs men's minds is not events but their judgements on events." How should a person judge events?

3

The Modes of Love

Augustine

Saint Augustine was born in northern Africa in A.D. 354. His father was a pagan, but his mother, Monica, was a devout Christian. During his student days in the bawdy port town of Carthage, while he vigorously pursued his studies, he abandoned his religious faith and took a mistress. He could never overcome his intense concern about his personal morality and destiny. He read widely in philosophy and moved to Milan to study rhetoric. While there, he was influenced by Ambrose, the Bishop of Milan. He finally discovered a version of Platonic thought which helped overcome his intellectual difficulties with Christianity. Eventually he became the author of an astonishing number of books whose influence can be felt even today. His life was emotionally tempestuous, and his deepest concerns focused on the problem of moral evil. With his massive learning, he brought together philosophy and theology to form a unique way of looking at morality. He concluded his career in North Africa, where he was Bishop of Hippo, dying in the posture of prayer at the age of seventy-five.

As a student, Augustine found Christianity unsatisfactory, especially because he could not understand why there should be so much moral evil among people if there is a good God. How can one explain the existence of evil in human experience? The Christians had said that God is the Creator of all things and that God is good. How, then, is it possible for evil to arise out of a world that a perfectly good God had created? Because Augustine could find no satisfactory answer in the Christianity he learned as a youth, he turned to a group called Manichaeans who were sympathetic to much of Christianity but who, boasting of their intellectual superiority, rejected the idea of the Old Testament that there is only one God who is both the Creator and Redeemer of man. Instead, the Manichaeans taught the doctrine of "dualism," according to which there were two basic principles or powers in the universe, the principle of light or goodness on the one hand and the principle of darkness or evil on the other. These two principles or powers were said to be equally eternal and were seen as eternally in conflict with each other. This conflict was reflected in human life as the conflict between the soul, composed of light, and the body, composed of darkness. This seemed to make sense to Augustine. He could

Augustine. *(Scala/Art Resource)*

now blame his sensual desires on the external power of darkness. But this did not solve his personal problem. The presence of fierce passion was just as bothersome even when he shifted the blame for it to something outside himself. He gave up his interest in the Manichees, became a skeptic for awhile, and was attracted to the notion that everything is material in nature, that there are no nonmaterial substances, such as, for example, the soul. Augustine eventually found the best solution to his intellectual problems, especially the problem of evil, in some new forms of Plato's philosophy. He now understood that evil is not a positive thing but rather the absence of good, just as darkness is the absence of light. Through Platonic thought Augustine was able to make Christianity intellectually reasonable.

In describing man's moral situation, Augustine put together his insights about human nature, the nature of God, and the idea of creation. Man's condition, says Augustine, is that he is made in such a way that he always seeks happiness. Although the ancient Greeks had also considered happiness the goal of life, Augustine went farther because to the natural ends or purposes of man he added the supernatural element. He expressed this key idea in both religious and philosophical language. In his *Confessions* he wrote, "Oh God Thou hast created us for Thyself so that our hearts are restless until they find their rest in Thee." In more philosophical language he makes this same point by saying that human nature is so made that "it cannot itself be the good by which it is made happy." There is, in short, no purely "natural" man. The reason there is no purely natural man, says Augustine, is that nature did not produce man. God did. Consequently, man always bears the marks of his creation, which means, among other things, that there are some permanent relations, actual and possible, between man and God. It is not by accident that man *seeks* happiness. That he seeks it is a consequence of his incompleteness, his finitude. That he can find happiness only in God is also no accident, since he was made by God to find happiness only in God. Augustine elaborates this aspect of man's nature through his doctrine of love.

THE ROLE OF LOVE

Man inevitably loves. To love is to go beyond oneself and to fasten one's affection on an object of love. What makes it inevitable that man will love is, again, his incompleteness. There is a wide range of objects that man can choose to love, reflecting the variety of ways in which man is incomplete. A person can love (1) physical objects, (2) other persons, or even (3) himself. From these he can derive satisfaction for some of his desires and passions. Augustine stressed that all things in the world are good because all things come from God, who is goodness itself. Consequently, all things are legitimate objects of love. Everything that man loves will provide him with some measure of satisfaction and happiness. Nothing is evil in itself; evil is not a positive thing but the absence of something. Man's moral problem consists not so much in loving or even in the objects he loves. What causes man's moral problem is the *manner* in which he attaches himself to his objects of love and his *expectations* regarding the outcome of his love. Everyone expects to achieve happiness and fulfillment from love, yet men are miserable, unhappy, restless. Why? Augustine lays the blame on man's "disordered" love.

Evil and Disordered Love

Each object of love is different, and for this reason the consequences of loving them will be different. Similarly, the human needs which prompt the act of love are also different. Augustine thought that there is some sort of correlation between various human needs and the objects that can satisfy them. Love is the act that harmonizes these needs and their objects. What constitutes the chief fact about man is that the range of his needs includes not only (1) objects, (2) other persons, and (3) himself, but also, and most of all, (4) God. There is no way to unmake this fact about man. Augustine formulates this point in virtually quantitative terms. Each object of love can give only so much satisfaction and no more. Each of man's needs likewise has a measurable quantity. Clearly, satisfaction and happiness require that an object of love contain a sufficient amount of whatever it takes to fulfill or satisfy the particular need. Thus we love food and we consume a quantity commensurate with our hunger. But our needs are not all physical in that primary sense. We love objects of art, too, for the aesthetic satisfaction they give. At a higher level we have the need for love between persons. Indeed, this level of affection provides quantitatively and qualitatively more in the way of pleasure and happiness than mere physical things, such as the various forms of property, can.

From this it becomes clear that certain human needs cannot be met by an interchange of objects; the deep human need for human companionship cannot be met any other way than by a relationship with another person. Things cannot be a substitute for a person, because things do not contain within themselves the unique ingredients of a human personality. Therefore, although each thing is a legitimate object of love, one must not expect more from it than its unique nature can provide. The basic need for human affection cannot be satisfied by things. But this is particularly the case with man's spiritual need. Man was made, said Augustine, to love God. God is infinite. In some way, then, man's nature was made so that only God, the infinite, can give him ultimate satisfaction or happiness. "When," says Augustine, "the will which is the intermediate good, cleaves to the immutable good . . . man finds therein the blessed life," for "to live well is nothing else but to love God. . . ." To love God is, then, the indispensable requirement for happiness, because only God, who is infinite, can satisfy that peculiar need in man that is precisely the need for the infinite.

If objects are not interchangeable, if things cannot substitute for a person, neither can any finite thing or person substitute for God. Yet all men confidently expect that they can achieve true happiness by loving objects, other persons, and themselves. While these are all legitimate objects of love, man's love of them is disordered when these are loved for the sake of ultimate happiness. "Disordered love" consists in expecting more from an object of love than it is capable of providing. Disordered love produces all forms of pathology in human behavior. Normal self-love becomes pride, and pride is the cardinal sin that affects all aspects of man's conduct. The essence of pride is the assumption of self-sufficiency. Yet the permanent fact about man is precisely that he is not self-sufficient, neither physically, nor emotionally, nor spiritually.

Man's pride, which turns him away from God, leads him to many forms of overindulgence, since he tries to satisfy an infinite need with finite entities. He therefore loves things more than he should in relation to what they can do for him. His love for another person can become virtually destructive of the other person, since he tries again to derive from that relationship more than it can possibly give. Appetite flourishes, passion multiplies, and there is a desperate attempt to achieve peace by satisfying all desires. The soul becomes seriously disfigured and is now implicated in envy, greed, jealousy, trickery, panic, and a pervading restlessness. It does not take long for disordered love to produce a disordered person, and disordered persons produce a disordered community. No attempt to reconstruct an orderly or peaceful community or household is possible without reconstructing each human being. The rigorous and persistent fact is that personal reconstruction, salvation, is possible only by reordering love, by loving the proper things properly. Indeed, Augustine argued that we can love a person properly only if we love God first, for then we will not expect to derive from human love what can be derived only from our love of God. Similarly, we can love ourselves properly only as we subordinate ourselves to God, for there is no other way to overcome the destructive consequences of pride than by eliminating pride itself.

FREE WILL AS THE CAUSE OF EVIL

Augustine did not agree with Plato that the cause of evil is simply ignorance. To be sure, there can be some circumstances under which a person does not know the ultimate good, is not aware of God. Still, Augustine says that "even the ungodly" have the capacity to "blame and rightly praise many things in the conduct of men." The overriding fact is that in daily conduct men understand praise and blame only because they already understand that they have an obligation to do what is praiseworthy and to abstain from what is blameworthy. Under these circumstances, man's predicament is not that he is ignorant but that he stands in the presence of alternatives. He must choose to turn toward God or away from God. He is, in short, free. Whichever way man chooses, he does so with the hope of finding happiness. He is capable of directing his affections exclusively toward finite things, persons, or himself and away from God. Augustine says that "this turning away and this turning to are not forced but voluntary acts." Evil, or sin, is a product of the will. It is not, as Plato said, ignorance, nor, as the Manichaeans said, the work of the principle of darkness permeating the body. In spite of the fact of original sin, all men still possess the freedom of their will. This freedom (liberum) of the will is not, however, the same as spiritual freedom (libertas), for true spiritual liberty is no longer possible in its fullness in this life. Man now uses his free will to choose wrongly, but even when man chooses rightly, he does not, says Augustine, possess the spiritual power to do the good he has chosen. He must have the help of God's grace.

Reading _____

Love of God the Highest Good

St. Augustine

How then, according to reason, ought man to live? We all certainly desire to live happily, and there is no human being but assents to this statement almost before it is made. But the title happy cannot, in my opinion, belong either to him who has now what he loves, whatever it may be, or to him who has what he loves if it is hurtful, or to him who does not love what he has, although it is good in perfection. For one who seeks what he cannot obtain suffers torture, and one who has got what is not desirable is cheated, and one who does not seek for what is worth seeking for is diseased. Now in all these cases the mind cannot be but unhappy, and happiness and unhappiness cannot reside at the same time in one man: so in none of these cases can the man be happy. I find, then, a fourth case, where the happy life exists—when that which is man's chief good is both loved and possessed. For what do we call enjoyment but having at hand the objects of love? And no one can be happy who does not enjoy what is man's chief good, nor is there any one who enjoys this who is not happy. We must then have at hand our chief good, if we think of living happily.

We must now inquire what is man's chief good, which of course cannot be anything inferior to man himself. For whoever follows after what is inferior to himself, becomes himself inferior. But every man is bound to follow what is best. Wherefore man's chief good is not inferior to man. Is it then something similar to man himself? It must be so, if there is nothing above man which he is capable of enjoying. But if we find something which is both superior to man, and can be possessed by the man who loves it, who can doubt that in seeking for happiness man should endeavor to reach that which is more excellent than the being who makes the endeavor. For if happiness consists in the enjoyment of a good than which there is nothing better, which we call the chief good, how can a man be properly called happy who has not yet attained to his chief good? or how can that be the chief good beyond which something better remains for us to arrive at? Such, then, being the chief good, it must be something which cannot be lost against the will. For no one can feel confident regarding a good which he knows can be taken from him, although he wishes to keep and cherish it. But if a man feels no confidence regarding the good which he enjoys, how can he be happy while in such fear of losing it?

Let us then see what is better than man. This must necessarily be hard to find, unless we first ask and examine what man is. I am not now called upon to give a definition of man. The question here seems to me to be—since almost all agree, or at least, which is enough, those I have now to do with are of the same opinion with me, that we are made up of soul and body—What is man? Is he both of these? or is he the body only, or the soul only?

Now if we ask what is the chief good of the body, reason obliges us to admit that it is that by means of which the body comes to be in its best state. But of all the things which invigorate the body, there is nothing better or greater than the soul. The chief good of the body, then, is not bodily pleasure, not absence of pain, not strength, not beauty, not swiftness, or whatever else is usually reckoned among the goods of the body, but simply the soul. For all the things mentioned the soul supplies to the body by its presence, and, what is above them all, life. Hence I conclude that the soul is the chief good of man, whether we give the name of man to soul and body together, or to the soul alone.

If, again, the body is man, it must be admitted that the end is the chief good of man. But clearly, when we treat of morals—when we inquire what manner of life must be held in order to obtain happiness—it is not the body to which the precepts are addressed, it is not bodily discipline which we discuss. In short, the observance of good *customs* belongs to that part of us which inquires and learns, which are the prerogatives of the soul. . . . So the question seems to me to be not, whether soul and body is man, or the soul only, or the body only, but what gives perfection to the soul. . . .

EVERYTHING IN NATURE IS GOOD; EVIL IS A PRODUCT OF THE WILL

All natures, then, inasmuch as they are, and have therefore a rank and species of their own, and a kind of internal harmony, are certainly good. And when they are in the places assigned to them by the order of their nature. . . . they preserve such being as they have received.

Let no one, therefore, look for an efficient cause of the evil will; for it is not efficient, but deficient, as the will itself is not an effecting of something, but a defect. For defection from that which supremely is, to that which has less of being—this is to begin to have an evil will.

This I do know, that the nature of God can never, nowhere, nowise be defective. . . . I know likewise, that the will could not become evil, were it unwilling to become so; and therefore its failings are justly punished, being not necessary, but voluntary. For its defections are not to evil things, but are themselves evil; that is to say, are not towards things that are naturally and in themselves evil, but the defection of the will is evil, because it is contrary to the order of nature, and an abandonment of that which has supreme being for that which has less. For avarice is not a fault inherent in gold, but in the man who inordinately loves gold, to the detriment of justice, which ought to be held in incomparably higher regard than gold. Neither is luxury the fault of lovely and charming objects, but of the heart that inordinately loves sensual pleasures, to the neglect of temperance, which attaches us to objects more lovely in their spirituality, and more delectable by their incorruptibility. Nor yet is boasting the fault of human praise, but of the soul that is inordinately fond of the applause of men, and that makes light of the voice of conscience. Pride, too, is not the fault of him who delegates power, nor of power itself, but of the soul that is inordinately enamored of its own power, and despises the more just dominion of a higher authority. Consequently he who inordinately loves the good which any nature possesses, even though he obtains it, himself becomes evil in the good, and wretched because deprived of a greater good. . . .

And therefore there is a nature in which evil does not or even cannot exist; but there cannot be a nature in which there is no good. Hence not even the nature of the devil himself is evil, in so far as it is nature, but it was made evil by being perverted. . . .

THE LOVE OF GOD

. . . Following after God is the desire of happiness; to reach God is happiness itself. We follow after God by loving Him; we reach Him, not by becoming entirely what He is, but in nearness to Him, and in wonderful and immaterial contact with Him, and in being inwardly illuminated and occupied by His truth and holiness. He is light itself; we get enlightenment from Him. The greatest commandment, therefore, which leads to happy life, and the first, is this: "Thou shalt love the Lord thy God with all thy heart, and soul, and mind." For to those who love the Lord all things issue in good, and if, as no one doubts, the chief or perfect good is not only to be loved, but to be loved so that nothing shall be loved better, as is expressed in the words, "With all thy soul, with all thy heart, and with all thy mind," who, I ask, will not at once conclude, when these things are all settled and most surely believed, that our chief good which we must hasten to arrive at in preference to all other things is nothing else than God? And then, if nothing can separate us from His love, must not this be surer as well as better than any other good?

The farther the mind departs from God, not in space, but in affection and lust after things below Him, the more it is filled with folly and wretchedness. So by love it returns to God—a love which places it not along with God, but under Him. And the more ardor and eagerness there is in this, the happier and more elevated will the mind be, and with God as sole governor it will be in perfect liberty. Hence it must know that it is a creature. It must believe what is the truth—that its Creator remains ever possessed of the inviolable and immutable nature of truth and wisdom, and must confess, even in view of the errors from which it desires deliverance, that it is liable to folly and falsehood. But then again, it must take care that it be not separated by the love of the other creature, that is, of this visible world, from the love of God Himself, which sanctifies it in order to lasting happiness. No other creature, then—for we are ourselves a creature—separates us from the love of God which is in Christ Jesus our Lord.

THE CONVERSION OF THE GREEK VIRTUES

As to virtue leading us to a happy life, I hold virtue to be nothing else than perfect love of God. For the fourfold division of virtue I regard as taken from four forms of love. For these four virtues (would that all felt their influence in their minds as they have their names in their mouths!), I should have no hesitation in defining them: that *temperance* is love giving itself entirely to that which is loved; *fortitude* is love readily bearing all things for the sake of the loved object; *justice* is love serving only the loved object, and therefore ruling rightly; *prudence* is love distinguishing with sagacity between what hinders it and what helps it. The object of this love is not anything, but only God, the chief good, the highest wisdom, the perfect harmony. So we may express the definition thus: that temperance is love keeping itself entire and incorrupt for God; fortitude is love bearing everything readily for the sake of God; justice is love serving God only, and therefore ruling well all else, as subject to man; prudence is love making a right distinction between what helps it towards God and what might hinder it. [Italics mine.]

From Augustine, "City of God," *The Writings against the Manichaeans and against the Donatists (a Select Library of the Nicene and post-Nicene Fathers)*, First Series, ed. Philip Schaff, vol. IV, The Christian Literature Publishing Co., New York, 1886–1890.

QUESTIONS FOR REVIEW AND DISCUSSION

1. Why do human beings love, and what is the range of their objects of love?
2. Why are human beings unhappy, according to Augustine, and is "unhappy" the right word to describe the human condition?
3. What does Augustine mean by "disordered love"? Isn't every object of love a "good" one?
4. If God is goodness itself and creates everything as good, why then is there evil in the world, according to Augustine?

4

A Sense of Duty

Kant

Immanuel Kant lived all his eighty years (1724–1804) in the small town of Konigsburg in East Prussia. At the university he studied classics, physics, and philosophy. The strongest influences shaping his early thinking were Sir Isaac Newton's physics, the tradition of philosophy which emphasized the power of human reason, and the pietistic religious nurture in his family. A bachelor all his life, he worked with incredible discipline—the story is told that neighbors could set their watches when he stepped out of the house each day at half past four to walk up and down the street eight times. His books revolutionized philosophy. Philosophers who came after might disagree with what he wrote, but no one could ever ignore him.

"Two things fill the mind with ever new and increasing admiration and awe," says Kant, "the starry heavens above and the moral law within." To him the starry heavens were a reminder that the world, as pictured by Sir Isaac Newton, is a system of physical bodies in motion, where every event has a specific cause. At the same time, all men experience the sense of moral duty which implies that human beings, unlike physical objects, possess freedom of choice in their behavior. Because human beings have this freedom of choice, we can ask ourselves "What shall I do?" But this was not the question of greatest importance for Kant. That question merely asks "Which of the various alternative ways of behaving do I want to choose?—as if I were asking myself which street I should take on my way home today." The key question in ethics according to Kant is this: "Given the fact that I face alternatives, which choice *ought* I to make?" That is, "What *must* I do?"

The task of moral philosophy, said Kant, is to discover how we can arrive at principles of behavior that apply to all persons. To include all persons is a way of testing whether my own personal behavior is right, just as we test if a scientific theory works for every scientist. That is, if I am not willing for others to act according to my rule of behavior, there could be something wrong with my ethical idea. He was sure that we cannot find these principles simply by studying the actual behavior of people. Such a study

Immanuel Kant. *(Culver Pictures)*

would give us interesting anthropological information about how people *do* behave. What impressed Kant was that we do make moral judgments when we say, for example, that we ought to tell the truth. How do we know that we should tell the truth? Kant's answer is that our knowledge of moral principles resembles our knowledge of scientific principles in an important way. For Kant, the moral judgment that "we ought to tell the truth" is on principle the same kind of mental activity as the scientific judgment that "every change must have a cause." How do we know that every change must have a cause? We have not observed every change. Our mind, our rational power, enables us to think of every change even though we see or experience only one or a few changes. This represents our capacity for theoretical thinking. We know that two and two equals four no matter two of what. This knowledge does not come from simply looking at two apples or two dollars. Similarly, the conclusion that we must tell the truth does not come from observing Mary and John. Our reason *brings* to the objects or events in our experience certain ways of thinking about them, as though we were looking at them through intellectual glasses or lenses. Our knowledge begins with our experience but is not limited to it.

Both in science and in moral philosophy we use concepts that go beyond any particular facts we experience at any one time. In both science and morality, experience is the occasion for triggering the mind to think in broader, universal terms. When we experience a given example of change, our minds bring to this event the idea of causality, which makes it possible to explain the relation of cause and effect not only in this case but in all cases of change. Similarly, in our human relations, our practical reason is able to determine how we should behave, not only at this moment, but at all times. Our practical reason can make judgments about "ought" just as our theoretical reason can make judgments about "cause." In both cases, our reason is dealing with a *principle* which applies to all cases. Just as there are laws of physics, so there are "laws" of moral behavior. Ethics, then, is for Kant the study of principles that apply to all rational beings and that lead to behavior that we call "good."

GOOD DEFINED AS THE GOOD WILL

According to Kant, "Nothing can possibly be conceived in the world, or even out of it, which can be called good, without qualification, except a good will." He would admit, of course, that other things can be considered good, such as, for example, the control of the passions, "and yet," he says, "one can hardly call this unreservedly good . . . for without the principles of a good will this may become evil indeed. The cold-bloodedness of a villain not only makes him far more dangerous, but also makes him seem more despicable to us than he would have seemed without it." Kant's chief point is that the essence of the morally good act is the principle that a person acts on when he behaves. "The good will is good not because of what it accomplishes, not because of its usefulness in the attainment of some set purpose, but alone because of the willing, that is to say, it is good of itself."

GOOD WILL AND THE MOTIVE OF DUTY

The will is good in the moral sense when it acts out of the proper motive. Kant distinguishes between three motives behind our actions, namely, (1) inclination, (2) self-interest, and (3) duty. It makes a difference in judging the morality of our behavior whether we act out of inclination (which means that we will do a particular act if we happen to feel like doing it at that moment), self-interest (where we calculate the benefit to us in a given action), or out of duty (because we believe it is the right thing to do). The reason Kant makes the startling statement that "the good will is good not because of what it accomplishes" is that he wants to emphasize the dominant role of the will in ethics. It is not enough for the effects or the consequences of our behavior to *agree with* the moral law; the truly moral act is done *for the sake of* the moral law, "for all these effects—even the promotion of the happiness of others— could have also been brought about by other causes, so that there would have been no need of the will of a rational being. . . ." Instead of acting out of inclination or self-interest, we must act out of a sense of duty "so that nothing remains which can determine the will except objectively the (moral) *law* and subjectively *pure respect* for this practical law."

MOTIVES AND TYPES OF IMPERATIVES

Our sense of duty implies that we are under some kind of obligation, a moral law. As rational beings, says Kant, we are aware of this obligation when it comes to us in the form of an *imperative*. Not all imperatives or commands are connected with morality. To be a moral imperative, the command must be directed to all men, to all rational beings. There are three types of imperatives: (1) *Technical imperatives*—these are rules of skill, and they command us to do certain things *if* we want to achieve certain ends. Thus *if* we want to build a bridge, we *must* use materials of a certain strength. But we do not absolutely have to build a bridge. We can either build a tunnel or use surface craft to get to the other side. (2) *Prudential imperatives*—which say, for example, that *if* I want to be popular with certain people, I *must* do and say certain things. But again, it is not absolutely necessary that I should achieve this popularity. (3) *Moral imperatives*—these moral commands are directed to us as rational human beings, requiring of us in each case "an action necessary of itself without reference to another end, that is, as objectively necessary." So the moral imperative requires that we tell the truth not to achieve this or that purpose but because, as we will see later, our rationality, our being human, requires it.

HYPOTHETICAL AND CATEGORICAL IMPERATIVES

We have just seen that the technical and prudential imperatives are connected with the condition "if"; if I want to build a bridge—if I want to be popular. For this reason, these two imperatives are *hypothetical*, that is, they command our behavior only if we want to achieve bridges or popularity or other ends. By contrast, the moral imperative contains nothing hypothetical—moral commands always require necessarily that we should behave in certain ways. For this reason, the moral imperative is categorical, meaning that there are no "ifs" about what we must do.

Having discussed motives and types of imperatives and having indicated which are hypothetical and which are categorical, we can arrange and relate these ideas in the following way:

Motives	Imperatives	
1. Inclination	1. Technical	A. Hypothetical: "if"
2. Self-interest	2. Prudential	
3. Duty	3. Moral	B. Categorical: no "ifs"

THE CATEGORICAL IMPERATIVE

We have emphasized the difference between the behavior of physical objects and the behavior of rational human beings. Kant has a striking way of stating this difference: "Everything in nature works according to laws. Rational beings alone have the faculty of acting according to the conception of laws. . . ." And what is our *conception* of the moral law? The moral law does not give us a list of dos and don'ts. Instead, Kant defined the categorical imperative in terms of basic principles. His point is that once we understand these principles, we will be prepared to know what we ought to do in any given set of circumstances.

The categorical imperative can be formulated in three ways as follows:

1. "Act only on that maxim [principle] whereby you can at the same time will that this maxim should become a universal law."
2. "So act as to treat humanity, whether in your own person or in that of any other, in every case as an end withal, never as a means only."
3. "Always so act that the will could regard itself at the same time as making universal law through its own maxim."

Again, it is clear that the categorical imperative does not give us specific rules of conduct, for it appears to be simply an abstract formula. Still this was what Kant thought moral philosophy should provide us in order to guide our moral behavior, for once we understand the fundamental principle of the moral law, we can then apply it to specific cases. To illustrate how the categorical imperative enables us to discover our moral duties, Kant gives the following example.

> [A man] finds himself forced by necessity to borrow money. He knows that he will not be able to repay it, but sees also that nothing will be lent to him unless he promises stoutly to repay it in a definite time. He desires to make this promise, but he has still so much conscience as to ask himself: Is it not unlawful and inconsistent with duty to get out of a difficulty in this way? Suppose, however, that he resolves to do so, then the maxim of his action would be expressed thus: When I think myself in want of money, I will borrow money and promise to repay it, although I know that I never can do so. Now this principle of self-love or of one's own advantage may perhaps be consistent with my whole future welfare; but the question now is, Is it right? I change then the suggestion of self-

love into a universal law, and state the question thus: How would it be if my maxim were a universal law? Then I see at once that it could never hold as a universal law of nature, but would necessarily contradict itself. For supposing it to be a universal law that everyone when he thinks himself in a difficulty should be able to promise whatever he pleases, with the purpose of not keeping his promise, the promise itself would become impossible, as well as the end that one might have in view in it, since no one would consider that anything was promised to him but would ridicule all such statements as vain pretenses.

If one were still to ask why he must tell the truth or why he should avoid the contradiction involved in a false promise, Kant answers that there is something about a human being that makes him resist and resent being treated as a *thing* instead of a *person*. What makes us persons is our rationality, and to be a person, or a rational being, is therefore an end in itself. We become a thing when someone uses us as a means for some other end, such as when one tells us a lie. But however necessary such use of us may be at times, we nevertheless consider ourselves as being of absolute intrinsic worth as persons. The individual human being as possessing absolute worth becomes the basis for the supreme principle of morality: "the foundation of this principle is: *rational nature exists as an end in itself.* All men everywhere want to be considered persons instead of things for the same reason that I do, and this affirmation of the absolute worth of the individual leads to a second formulation of the categorical imperative which says: *So act as to treat humanity, whether in thine own person or in that of any other, in every case as an end withal, never as a means only."*

There is a third formulation of the categorical imperative, which is already implied in the first two, but which Kant wants to make explicit by saying that we should "always so act that the *will could regard itself at the same time as making universal law through its own maxim."* Here Kant speaks of the *autonomy** of the will, that each person through his own act of will legislates the moral law. He distinguishes autonomy from *heteronomy,* the deter– mination (of a law or action) by someone or something other than the self. Thus an heteronomous will is influenced or even determined by desires or inclination. An autonomous will, however, is free and independent, and as such is the "supreme principle of morality." Central to the concept of the autonomy of the will is the idea of *freedom,* the crucial regulative idea, which Kant employed to distinguish between the worlds of science and morality, the *phenomenal* and *noumenal* worlds.** Kant says that "the *will* is a kind of causality belonging to living beings in so far as they are rational, and *freedom* would be this property of such causality that it can be efficient, independently of foreign causes determining it; just as *physical* necessity is the property that the causality of all irrational being has of being determined to activity by the

---

*"Autonomy," from the Greek *autos* ("self") and *nomos* ("law"); hence, the self is the lawgiver and is therefore independent of someone else's law.

**In Kant, "phenomenal" refers to the observable, physical world, and "noumenal" to the rational, or mental, world.

influence of foreign causes." And again, " . . . I affirm that we must attribute
to every rational being which has a will that it has also the idea of freedom
and acts entirely under this idea. For in such a being we conceive a reason that
is practical, that is, has causality in reference to its objects." The categorical
imperative, therefore, speaks of the universality of the moral law, affirms the
supreme worth of each rational person, and assigns freedom or autonomy to
the will.

POSTULATE OF FREEDOM

Our experience of the moral law suggested to Kant some further insights
concerning the postulate of, or assumptions about, our freedom of the will.
Kant did not think it possible to prove or demonstrate that the human will is
free. Freedom is an idea that it is necessary to assume because of our
experience of moral obligation; that is, "because I must, I can." Although we
cannot demonstrate that our wills are free, we are intellectually compelled to
assume such freedom, for freedom and morality "are so inseparably united
that one might define practical freedom as independence of the will of
anything but the moral law alone." How can a person be responsible or have a
duty if he is not able or free to fulfill his duty or respond to the moral
command? Freedom must be assumed, and as such, it is a major postulate of
morality.

Reading _____

The Categorical Imperative
Kant

THE CHIEF GOOD IS A GOOD WILL

Nothing can possibly be conceived in the world, or even out of it, which can
be called good without qualification, except a *good will*. Intelligence, wit,
judgment, and other *talents* of the mind, however they may be named, or
courage, resolution, perseverance, as qualities of temperament, are
undoubtedly good and desirable in many respects; but these gifts of nature
may also become extremely bad and mischievous if the will which is to make
use of them, and which, therefore, constitutes what is called *character*, is not
good. It is the same with the *gifts of fortune*. Power, riches, honor, even health,
and the general well-being and contentment with one's condition which is
called *happiness*, inspire pride, and often presumption, if there is not a good

will to correct the influence of these on the mind, and with this also to rectify the whole principle of acting, and adapt it to its end. The sight of a being who is not adorned with a single feature of a pure and good will, enjoying unbroken prosperity, can never give pleasure to an impartial rational spectator. Thus a good will appears to constitute the indispensable condition even of being worthy of happiness.

There are even some qualities which are of service to this good will itself, and may facilitate its action, yet which have no intrinsic unconditional value, but always presuppose a good will, and this qualifies the esteem that we justly have for them, and does not permit us to regard them as absolutely good. Moderation in the affections and passions, self-control, and calm deliberation are not only good in many respects, but even seem to constitute part of the intrinsic worth of the person; but they are far from deserving to be called good without qualification, although they have been so unconditionally praised by the ancients. For without the principles of a good will, they may become extremely bad; and the coolness of a villain not only makes him far more dangerous, but also directly makes him more abominable in our eyes than he would have been without it.

THE GOODNESS OF THE WILL INDEPENDENT OF CONSEQUENCES

A good will is good not because of what it performs or effects, not by its aptness for the attainment of some proposed end, but simply by virtue of the volition—that is, it is good in itself, and considered by itself is to be esteemed much higher than all that can be brought about by it in favor of any inclination, nay, even of the sum-total of all inclination. Even if it should happen that, owing to special disfavor or fortune, or the niggardly provision of a stepmotherly nature, this will should wholly lack power to accomplish its purpose, if with its greatest efforts it should yet achieve nothing, and there should remain only the good will (not, to be sure, a mere wish, but the summoning of all means in our power), then, like a jewel, it would still shine by its own light, as a thing which has its whole value in itself. Its usefulness or fruitlessness can neither add to nor take away anything from this value. . . .

FIRST PROPOSITION: TO HAVE MORAL WORTH, AN ACTION MUST BE DONE FROM DUTY

. . . We can readily distinguish whether the action which agrees with duty is done *from duty* or from a selfish view. It is much harder to make this distinction when the action accords with duty, and the subject has besides a *direct* inclination to it. For example, it is always a matter of duty that a dealer should not overcharge an inexperienced purchaser; and wherever there is much commerce the prudent tradesman does not overcharge, but keeps a fixed price for everyone, so that a child buys of him as well as any other. Men are thus *honestly* served; but this is not enough to make us believe that the tradesman has acted from duty and from principles of honesty; his own advantage required it; it is out of the question in this case to suppose that he might besides have a direct inclination in favor of the buyers, so that, as it were, from love he should give no advantage to one over another. Accordingly the action was done neither from duty nor from direct inclination, but merely with a selfish view.

On the other hand, it is a duty to maintain one's life; and, in addition, everyone has also a direct inclination to do so. But on this account the often anxious care which most men take for it has no intrinsic worth, and their maxim has no moral import. They preserve their life   *as duty requires,* no doubt, but not *because duty requires.* On the other hand, if adversity and hopeless sorrow have completely taken away the relish for life, if the unfortunate one, strong in mind, indignant at his fate rather than desponding or dejected, wishes for death, and yet preserves his life without loving it—not from inclination or fear, but from duty—then his maxim has a moral worth.

EXAMPLE OF THE PHILANTHROPIST

To be beneficent when we can is a duty; and besides this, there are many minds so sympathetically constituted that, without any other motive of vanity or self-interest, they find a pleasure in spreading joy around them, and can take delight in the satisfaction of others so far as it is their own work. But I maintain that in such a case an action of this kind, however proper, however amiable it may be, has nevertheless no true moral worth, but is on a level with other inclinations, for example, the inclination to honor, which, if it is happily directed to that which is in fact of public utility and accordant with duty, and consequently honorable, deserves praise and encouragement, but not esteem. For the maxim lacks the moral import, namely, that such actions be done *from duty,* not from inclination. Put the case that the mind of that philanthropist was clouded by sorrow of his own, extinguishing all sympathy with the lot of others, and that while he still has the power to benefit others in distress, he is not touched by their trouble because he is absorbed with his own; and now suppose that he tears himself out of this dead insensibility and performs the action without any inclination to it, but simply from duty, then first has his action its genuine moral worth. . . .

SECOND PROPOSITION: MORAL WORTH OF AN ACTION DERIVES NOT FROM RESULTS BUT BECAUSE IT WAS BASED ON PRINCIPLE

The second proposition is: That an action done from duty derives its moral worth, *not from the purpose* which is to be attained by it, but from the maxim by which it is determined, and therefore does not depend on the realization of the object of the action, but merely on the principle of volition by which the action has taken place, without regard to any object of desire. The purposes which we may have in view in our actions, or their effects regarded as ends and springs of the will, cannot give to actions any unconditional or moral worth. In what, then, can their worth lie if it is not to consist in the will and in reference to its expected effect? It cannot lie anywhere but in the *principle of the will* without regard to the ends which can be attained by the action. For the will stands between two roads, and as it must be determined by something, it follows that it must be determined by the formal principle of volition when an action is done from duty, in which case every material principle has been withdrawn from it.

THIRD PROPOSITION: DUTY IS THE NECESSITY OF ACTING FROM RESPECT OF THE (MORAL) LAW

The third proposition, which is a consequence of the two preceding, I would express thus: *Duty is the necessity of acting from respect for the law.* I may have *inclination* for an object as the effect of my proposed action, but I cannot have respect for it just for this reason that it is an effect and not an energy of will. Similarly, I cannot have respect for inclination, whether my own or another's; I can at most, if my own, approve it; of another's, sometimes even love it, that is, look on it as favorable to my own interest. It is only what is connected with my will as a principle . . . in other words, simply the law of itself, which can be an object of respect, and hence a command. Now an action done from duty must wholly exclude the influence of inclination, and with it every object of the will, so that nothing remains which can determine the will except objectively the *law,* and subjectively *pure respect* for this practical law, and consequently the maxim that I should follow this law even to the thwarting of all my inclinations.

Thus the moral worth of an action does not lie in the effect expected from it, nor in any principle of action which requires to borrow its motive from this expected effect. For all these effects—agreeableness of one's condition, and even the promotion of the happiness of others—could have been also brought about by other causes, so that for this there would have been no need of the will of a rational being; whereas it is in this alone that the supreme and unconditional good can be found. The pre-eminent good which we call moral can therefore consist in nothing else than *the conception of law* in itself, *which certainly is only possible in a rational being,* in so far as this conception, and not the expected effect, determines the will.

PROMISE—AN EXAMPLE OF MORAL LAW

But what sort of law can that be the conception of which must determine the will, even without paying any regard to the effect expected from it, in order that this will may be called good absolutely and without qualification? As I have deprived the will of every impulse which could arise to it from obedience to any law, there remains nothing but the universal conformity of its actions to law in general, which alone is to serve the will as a principle, that is, I am never to act otherwise than *so that I could also will that my maxim should become a universal law.* Here, now, it is the simple conformity to law in general, without assuming any particular law applicable to certain actions, that serves the will as its principle, and must so serve it if duty is not to be a vain delusion and a chimerical notion. The common reason of men in its practical judgments perfectly coincides with this, and always has in view the principle here suggested. Let the question be, for example: May I when in distress make a promise with the intention not to keep it? I readily distinguish here between the two significations which the question may have: whether it is prudent or whether it is right to make a false promise? The former may undoubtedly often be the case. I see clearly indeed that it is not enough to extricate myself from a present difficulty by means of this subterfuge, but it must be well considered whether there may not hereafter spring from this lie much greater inconvenience than that from which I now free myself, and as, with all my supposed *cunning*, the consequences cannot be so easily foreseen but that credit once lost may be much more injurious to me than any mischief which I seek to avoid at present, it should be considered whether it would not be more *prudent* to act herein according to a universal maxim, and to make it a habit to promise nothing except with the intention of keeping it. But it is soon clear to me that such a maxim will still only be based on the fear of consequences. Now it is a wholly different thing to be truthful from duty, and to be so from apprehension of injurious consequences. In the first case, the very notion of the action already implies a law for me; in the second case, I must first look about elsewhere to see what results may be combined with it which would affect myself. For to deviate from the principle of duty is beyond all doubt wicked; but to be unfaithful to my maxim of prudence may often be very advantageous to me, although to abide by it is certainly safer. The shortest way, however, and an unerring one, to discover the answer to this question whether a lying promise is consistent with duty, is to ask myself, Should I be content that my maxim (to extricate myself from difficulty by a false promise) should hold good as a universal law, for myself as well as for others; and should I be able to say to myself, "Every one may make a deceitful promise when he finds himself in a difficulty from which he cannot otherwise extricate himself"? Then I presently become aware that, while I can will the lie, I can by no means will that lying should be a universal law. For with such a law there would be no promises at all, since it would be in vain to allege my intention in regard to my future actions to those who would not believe this allegation, or if they over-hastily did so, would pay me back in my own coin. Hence my maxim, as soon as it should be made a universal law, would necessarily destroy itself.

IMPERATIVES: HYPOTHETICAL AND CATEGORICAL

Everything in nature works according to laws. Rational beings alone have the faculty of acting according to *the conception* of laws—that is, according to principles, that is, have a *will.*

Now all imperatives command either *hypothetically* or *categorically.* The former represent the practical necessity of a possible action as means to something else that is willed (or at least which one might possibly will). The categorical imperative would be that which represented an action as necessary of itself without reference to another end, that is, as objectively necessary. . . .

If [an] action is good only as a means to *something else,* then the imperative is *hypothetical;* if it is conceived as good *in itself* and conforms to reason, then it is *categorical.* . . .

There is therefore but one categorical imperative, namely, this: *Act only on that maxim whereby you can at the same time will that it should become a universal law.* . . .

SOME EXAMPLES

A [man] finds in himself a talent which with the help of some culture might make him a useful man in many respects. But he finds himself in comfortable circumstances and prefers to indulge in pleasure rather than to take pains in enlarging and improving his happy natural capacities. He asks, however, whether his maxim of neglect of his natural gifts, besides agreeing with his inclination to indulgence, agrees also with what is called duty. He sees then that a system of nature could indeed subsist with such a universal law, although men (like the South Sea islanders) should let their talents rest and resolve to devote their lives merely to idleness, amusement, and propagation of their species—in a word, to enjoyment; but he cannot possibly *will* that this should be a universal law of nature, or be implanted in us as such by a natural instinct. For, as a rational being, he necessarily wills that his faculties be developed, since they serve him, and have been given him, for all sorts of possible purposes.

[Another] who is in prosperity, while he sees that others have to contend with great wretchedness and that he could help them, thinks: What concern is it of mine? Let everyone be as happy as Heaven pleases, or as he can make himself; I will take nothing from him nor even envy him, only I do not wish to contribute anything to his welfare or to his assistance in distress! Now no doubt, if such a mode of thinking were a universal law, the human race might very well subsist, and doubtless even better than in a state in which everyone talks of sympathy and good-will, or even takes care occasionally to put it into practice, but, on the other side, also cheats when he can, betrays the rights of men, or otherwise violates them. But although it is possible that a universal law of nature might exist in accordance with that maxim, it is impossible to *will* that such a principle should have the universal validity of a law of nature.

For a will which resolved this would contradict itself, inasmuch as many cases might occur in which one would have need of the love and sympathy of others, and in which, by such a law of nature, sprung from his own will, he would deprive himself of all hopes of the aid he desires.

THE SUPREME PRACTICAL PRINCIPLE OF ETHICS

Let us suppose that there were something *whose existence* has *in itself* an absolute worth, something which, being *an end in itself*, could be a source of definite laws, then in this and this alone would lie the source of a possible categorical imperative, that is, a practical law.

Now I say: man and generally any rational being *exists* as an end in himself, *not merely as a means* to be arbitrarily used by this or that will, but in all his actions, whether they concern himself or other rational beings, must be always regarded at the same time as an end. All objects of the inclinations have only a conditional worth; for if the inclinations and the wants founded on them did not exist, then their object would be without value. But the inclinations themselves, being sources of want, are so far from having an absolute worth for which they should be desired that, on the contrary, it must be the universal wish of every rational being to be wholly free from them. Thus the worth of any object which is *to be acquired* by our action is always conditional. Beings whose existence depends not on our will but on nature's, have nevertheless, if they are not rational beings, only a relative value as means, and are therefore called *things;* rational beings, on the contrary, are called *persons*, because their very nature points them out as ends in themselves, that is, as something which must not be used merely as means, and so far therefore restricts freedom of action (and is an object of respect). These, therefore, are not merely subjective ends whose existence has a worth *for us* as an effect of our action, but *objective ends*, that is, things whose existence is an end in itself—an end, moreover, for which no other can be substituted, which they should subserve *merely* as means, for otherwise nothing whatever would possess *absolute worth*; but if all worth were conditioned and therefore contingent, then there would be no supreme practical principle of reason whatever.

If then there is a supreme practical principle or, in respect of the human will, a categorical imperative, it must be one which, being drawn from the conception of that which is necessarily an end for everyone because it is *an end in itself*, constitutes an *objective* principle of will, and can therefore serve as a universal practical law. The foundation of this principle is: rational nature exists as an end in itself. Man necessarily conceives his own existence as being so; so far then this is a *subjective* principle of human actions. But every other rational being regards its existence similarly, just on the same rational principle that holds for me; so that it is at the same time an objective principle from which as a supreme practical law all laws of the will must be capable of being deduced. Accordingly the practical imperative will be as follows: *So act as to treat humanity, whether in thine own person or in that of any other, in every case as an end withal, never as a means only.*

From Immanuel Kant, "Fundamental Principles of the Metaphysics of Morals," in *Kant's Critique of Practical Reason and Other Works on the Theory of Ethics*, trans. T. K. Abbott, Longmans, London, 1909.

QUESTIONS FOR REVIEW AND DISCUSSION

1. In your judgment, what is the difference between the definitions of the "good person" according to Aristotle and Kant?
2. What are the various motives behind our behavior, and which one of these, according to Kant, produces moral behavior?
3. Can a person be called "good" simply because his or her actions produce good results or consequences?
4. What is the difference between *hypothetical* imperatives and the *categorical* imperative?
5. According to Kant, why is it that lying cannot be considered morally right?
6. What are the various ways of stating or formulating the categorical imperative?
7. Is it enough for a person's actions to be in harmony with the categorical imperative in order to call that person "good." Why or why not?

5

Pleasure versus Pain

Bentham and Mill

Bentham

Jeremy Bentham was born in London in 1748. A brilliant youngster, he entered Oxford when he was twelve years old. He was not happy at Oxford, because he disapproved of the vice and laziness of his fellow students. Nevertheless, at the age of fifteen he took his B.A. and then entered Lincoln's Inn in London to study law in accordance with his father's wishes. He returned to Oxford to hear the lectures of the University's first professor of jurisprudence, Sir William Blackstone, who was expounding his theory of "natural rights." Bentham rejected Blackstone's theory of natural rights, calling it "rhetorical nonsense, nonsense on stilts." After taking an M.A. degree, he returned once again to London but decided against the practice of law. Instead, he entered on a literary career in which he sought to bring some order out of the deplorable condition both of the law and of the social realities which that law made possible. He became an effective reformer. His first book, *Fragment on Government,* an attack on Blackstone, appeared in 1776, the same year as the Declaration of Independence, which Bentham thought was a confused and absurd jumble of words in which the authors had all along assumed the natural rights of man, which was what they wanted to demonstrate. His most famous book is his *Introduction to the Principles of Morals and Legislation.* He remained a powerful public figure until his death in 1832 at the age of eighty-four.

For more than a hundred years, the moral and political philosophy of Jeremy Bentham and John Stuart Mill influenced the thinking and political action of Englishmen. Rarely has a way of thinking captured the imagination of generations of men so completely as did this philosophy called "utilitarianism." What attracted people to it was its simplicity and its way of confirming what most men already believed, for it set forth the general thesis that pleasure and happiness are what everyone desires. From this simple fact that everyone desires pleasure and happiness, the utilitarians inferred that the whole moral idea of what is "good" can be best understood in terms of the principle of happiness, which they spoke of as "the greatest happiness of the greatest number," and by which they meant that "good" is achieved when the aggregate of pleasure is greater than the aggregate of pain. An act is good, therefore, if it is useful in achieving pleasure and diminishing pain.

Such a swift account of what is good had not only the merit of simplicity but had, according to Bentham and Mill, the additional virtue of scientific accuracy. Whereas earlier theories of ethics, which defined the good as the commands of God or the dictates of reason or the fulfillment of the purposes of human nature or the duty to obey the Categorical Imperative,* raised vexing questions as to just what these commands, dictates, purposes, and imperatives consist of, the principle of utility seemed to measure every act by a standard everyone knows, namely, pleasure. To bypass the moral teachings of theology and the classical theories of Plato and Aristotle as well as the recently formulated ethics of Kant, the utilitarians followed in the philosophical footsteps of their own countrymen, Locke and Hume.

In moral philosophy, Bentham and Mill were not innovators, for the principle of utilitarianism had already been stated in its general form by their predecessors Hobbes and Hume. What makes Bentham and Mill stand out as the most famous of the utilitarians is that they, more than the others, succeeded in connecting the principle of utility with the many problems of their age, thereby providing nineteenth-century England with a philosophical basis not only for moral thought but also for practical reform.

PRINCIPLE OF UTILITY

Bentham begins his *Introduction to the Principle of Morals and Legislation* with the classic sentence: "Nature has placed mankind under the governance of two sovereign masters, *pain* and *pleasure*. It is for them alone to point out what we ought to do, as well as determine what we shall do." To be subject to pleasure and pain is a fact we all recognize, and that we desire pleasure and want to avoid pain is also a fact. But in a few sentences, without indicating just how he does it, Bentham moves from the *fact* that we *do* desire pleasure to the *judgment* that we *ought* to pursue pleasure. He moves from a psychological fact to the moral principle of utility. By the *principle of utility* he means "that principle which approves or disapproves of every action whatsoever, according to the tendency which it appears to have to augment or diminish . . . happiness. . . ." In Bentham's language, to *approve* or *disapprove* is the same as saying about an act that it is *good* or *bad*, or *right* or *wrong*. Between saying that men desire pleasure and saying that they *ought* to or that it is *right* that they should, there is a gap that Bentham does not fill with any careful argument. Still he says that it is only about an action "that is conformable to the principle of utility" that one can always say either that it

*See p. 62 (Kant).

Jeremy Bentham. *(The Bettmann Archive)*

"ought to be done" or that "it is a right action. . . ." Tying "ought" to
"pleasure," says Bentham, is the only way "the words *ought*, and *right* and
wrong, and others of that stamp have a meaning: when, otherwise, they have
none." Bentham was aware that he had not proved that happiness is the basis
of "good" and "right," but this was not an oversight. It is rather the very
nature of the principle of utility, he says, that one cannot demonstrate its

validity: "Is it susceptible to any proof? It should seem not: for that which is used to prove every thing else, cannot itself be proved: a chain of proofs must have their commencement somewhere. To give such proof is as impossible as it is needless."

But if Bentham could not *prove* the validity of the principle of utility, he felt that he could at least demonstrate that so-called higher theories of morality were either reducible to the principle of utility or else were inferior to this principle because they had no clear meaning or could not be consistently followed. For example, Bentham takes the Social Contract theory as an explanation for our obligation to obey the law. Apart from the difficulty of determining whether there ever was such a contract or agreement, Bentham argues that the obligation to obey, even in the Social Contract theory itself, rests on the principle of utility, for it really says that the greatest happiness of the greatest number can be achieved only if we obey the law. This being the case, why develop an involved and scientifically dubious theory when the whole problem can be swiftly solved by saying simply that obedience is better because disobedience does more harm than good? The case is the same when others say that goodness and right in an act are determined by our *moral sense* or *understanding* or *right reason* or the *theological principle* of the will of God. All these, says Bentham, are similar to each other and are reducible to the principle of utility. For example, "The principle of theology refers everything to God's pleasure. But what is God's pleasure? God does not, he confessedly does not now, either speak or write to us. How then are we to know what is his pleasure? By observing what is our own pleasure and pronouncing it to be his." Only pains and pleasures, therefore, give us the real value of actions, and in private and public life we are in the last analysis all concerned with maximizing happiness.

SANCTIONS

Just as pleasure and pain give the real values to acts, so do they also constitute the efficient causes of our behavior. Bentham distinguishes four sources from which pleasure and pain can come and identifies these as causes of our behavior, calling them *sanctions*. A "sanction" is what gives binding force to a rule of conduct or to a law, and these four sanctions are termed the *physical*, the *political*, the *moral*, and the *religious* sanctions. Bentham indicates the special character of each sanction by an example, where "a man's goods, or his person, are consumed by fire." He explains:

> If this happened to him by what is called accident, it was a calamity: if by reason of his own imprudence (for instance, from his neglecting to put his candle out), it may be styled a punishment of the *physical* sanction: if it happened to him by the sentence of the political magistrate, a punishment belonging to the *political* sanction; that is, what is commonly called a punishment: if for want of any assistance which his *neighbor* withheld from him out of some dislike to his moral character, a punishment of the *moral* sanction: if by an immediate act of *God's*

displeasure, manifested on account of some *sin* committed by him . . . a punishment of the *religious* sanction.

In all these areas, then, the sanction, or the efficient cause of behavior, is the threat of pain. In public life, the legislator understands that men feel bound to do certain acts only when such acts have some clear sanction connected with them, and this sanction consists of some form of pain if the mode of conduct prescribed by the legislator is violated by the citizen. The legislator's chief concern is, therefore, to decide what forms of behavior will tend to increase the happiness of society and what sanctions will be most likely to bring about such increased happiness. The word "obligation" was given concrete meaning by Bentham's concept of sanction, for obligation now meant not some undefined duty, but the prospect of pain if one did not obey the moral or legal rule. Unlike Kant, who argued that the morality of an act depends on having the right motive and not on the consequences of the act, the utilitarians took the opposite position, saying that morality depends directly on the consequences. Bentham admits that some motives are more likely than others to lead to more useful conduct, that is, conduct which increases happiness, but it is still pleasure and not the motive that confers the quality of morality on the act. Moreover, Bentham took the position that, especially in the social arena, where the law is at work, the law can punish only those who have actually inflicted pain, whatever their motive may be, although some exceptions were admitted. While it may be true that the legislator cannot always take account of motives, this whole question of motives does loom large in morality. Bentham, however, seemed to regard both the moral and legal obligations as being similar in that in both cases the external consequences of the action were considered more important than the motives behind them.

PLEASURE-PAIN CALCULUS

Each individual and each legislator is concerned with avoiding pain and achieving pleasure. But pleasures and pains differ from each other and therefore have different values. With an attempt at mathematical precision, Bentham speaks of units, or what he calls "lots," of pleasure or pain, suggesting that before we act, we should, and really do, calculate the values of these lots. Their value, taken by themselves, will be greater or less depending, says Bentham, on a pleasure's *intensity, duration, certainty,* and *propinquity* or nearness. When we consider not only the pleasure by itself but what consequences it can lead to, other circumstances must be calculated, such as a pleasure's *fecundity,* or its chances of being followed by more of the same sensations, that is, by more pleasure, and its *purity,* or the chances that pleasure will not be followed by pleasure but by pain. The seventh circumstance is a pleasure's *extent,* that is, the number of persons to whom it extends or who are affected by it.

As this calculus indicates, Bentham was interested chiefly in the quantitative aspects of pleasure, so that all actions are equally good if they produce the same amount of pleasure. Therefore, we "sum up all the values of all the *pleasures* on the one side, and those of all the *pains* on the other. The balance, if it be on the side of pleasure, will give the *good* tendency of the act . . . if on the side of pain, the *bad* tendency. . . ."

Whether we actually do engage in this kind of calculation was a question Bentham anticipated, and he replies that "there are some, perhaps, who . . . may look upon the nicety employed in the adjustment of such rules as so much labor lost: for gross ignorance, they will say, never troubles itself about laws, and passion does not calculate. But the evil of ignorance admits of cure: and . . . when matters of such importance as pain and pleasure are at stake, and these in the highest degree . . . who is there that does not calculate? Men calculate, some with less exactness, indeed, and some with more: but all men calculate."

Reading ───

Of the Principle of Utility
Bentham

I. Nature has placed mankind under the governance of two sovereign masters, *pain* and *pleasure*. It is for them alone to point out what we ought to do, as well as to determine what we shall do. On the one hand the standard of right and wrong, on the other the chain of causes and effects, are fastened to their throne. They govern us in all we do, in all we say, in all we think: every effort we can make to throw off our subjection, will serve but to demonstrate and confirm it. In words a man may pretend to abjure their empire: but in reality he will remain subject to it all the while. The *principle of utility* recognises this subjection, and assumes it for the foundation of that system, the object of which is to rear the fabric of felicity by the hands of reason and of law. Systems which attempt to question it, deal in sounds instead of sense, in caprice instead of reason, in darkness instead of light. By the principle of utility is meant that principle which approves or disapproves of every action whatsoever, according to the tendency which it appears to have to augment or diminish the happiness of the party whose interest is in question: or, what is the same thing in other words, to promote or to oppose that happiness. I say of every action whatsoever; and therefore not only of every action of a private individual, but of every measure of government. . . .

III. By utility is meant that property in any object, whereby it tends to produce benefit, advantage, pleasure, good, or happiness, (all this in the present case comes to the same thing) or (what comes again to the same thing) to prevent the happening of mischief, pain, evil, or unhappiness to the party whose interest is considered: if that party be the community in general, then the happiness of the community: if a particular individual, then the happiness of that individual.

IV. The interest of the community is one of the most general expressions that can occur in the phraseology of morals: no wonder that the meaning of it is often lost. When it has a meaning, it is this. The community is a fictitious *body*, composed of the individual persons who are considered as constituting as it were its *members*. The interest of the community then is, what?—the sum of the interests of the several members who compose it.

V. It is in vain to talk of the interest of the community, without understanding what is the interest of the individual. A thing is said to promote the interest, or to be *for* the interest, of an individual, when it tends to add to the sum total of his pleasures: or, what comes to the same thing, to diminish the sum total of his pains.

VI. An action then may be said to be conformable to the principle of utility, or, for shortness sake, to utility, (meaning with respect to the community at large) when the tendency it has to augment the happiness of the community is greater than any it has to diminish it. . . .

X. Of an action that is conformable to the principle of utility one may always say either that it is one that ought to be done, or at least that it is not one that ought not to be done. One may say also, that it is right it should be done; at least that it is not wrong it should be done: that it is a right action; at least that it is not a wrong action. When thus interpreted, the words *ought*, and *right* and *wrong*, and others of that stamp, have a meaning: when otherwise, they have none.

XI. Has the rectitude of this principle been ever formally contested? It should seem that it had, by those who have not known what they have been meaning. Is it susceptible of any direct proof? It should seem not: for that which is used to prove everything else, cannot itself be proved: a chain of proofs must have their commencement somewhere. To give such proof is as impossible as it is needless. . . .

VALUE OF A LOT OF PLEASURE OR PAIN, HOW TO BE MEASURED

I. Pleasures then, and the avoidance of pains, are the *ends* which the legislator has in view: it behoves him therefore to understand their *value*. Pleasures and pains are the *instruments* he has to work with: it behoves him therefore to understand their force, which is again, in other words, their value.

II. To a person considered *by himself*, the value of a pleasure or pain considered *by itself*, will be greater or less, according to the four following circumstances:

1. Its *intensity*.
2. Its *duration*.

3. Its *certainty* or *uncertainty*.

4. Its *propinquity* or *remoteness*.

III. These are the circumstances which are to be considered in estimating a pleasure or a pain considered each of them by itself. But when the value of any pleasure or pain is considered for the purpose of estimating the tendency of any *act* by which it is produced, there are two other circumstances to be taken into the account; these are,

1. Its *fecundity,* or the chance it has of being followed by sensations of the *same* kind: that is, pleasures, if it be a pleasure: pains, if it be a pain.

2. Its *purity,* or the chance it has of *not* being followed by sensations of the *opposite* kind: that is, pains, if it be a pleasure: pleasures, if it be a pain.

3. These two last, however, are in strictness scarcely to be deemed properties of the pleasure or the pain itself; they are not, therefore, in strictness to be taken into the account of the value of that pleasure or that pain. They are in strictness to be deemed properties only of the act, or other event, by which such pleasure or pain has been produced; and accordingly are only to be taken into the account of the tendency of such act or such event.

IV. To a *number* of persons, with reference to each of whom the value of a pleasure or a pain is considered, it will be greater or less, according to seven circumstances: to wit, the six preceding ones; *viz.*

1. Its *intensity*.

2. Its *duration*.

3. Its *certainty* or *uncertainty*.

4. Its *propinquity* or *remoteness*.

5. Its *fecundity*.

6. Its *purity*.

7. And one other; to wit:

8. Its *extent;* that is, the number of persons to whom it *extends;* or (in other words) who are affected by it.

V. To take an exact account then of the general tendency of any act, by which the interests of a community are affected, proceed as follows. Begin with any one person of those whose interests seem most immediately to be affected by it: and take an account,

1. Of the value of each distinguishable *pleasure* which appears to be produced by it in the *first* instance.

2. Of the value of each *pain* which appears to be produced by it in the *first* instance.

3. Of the value of each pleasure which appears to be produced by it *after* the first. This constitutes the *fecundity* of the first *pleasure* and the *impurity* of the first *pain.*

4. Of the value of each *pain* which appears to be produced by it after the first. This constitutes the *fecundity* of the first *pain,* and the *impurity* of the first pleasure.

5. Sum up all the values of all the *pleasures* on the one side, and those of all the pains on the other. The balance, if it be on the side of pleasure, will give the *good* tendency of the act upon the whole, with respect to the interests of that *individual* person; if on the side of pain, the *bad* tendency of it upon the whole.

6. Take an account of the *number* of persons whose interests appear to be concerned; and repeat the above process with respect to each. *Sum up* the numbers expressive of the degrees of *good* tendency, which the act has, with respect to each individual, in regard to whom the tendency of it is *good* upon the whole: do this again with respect to each individual, in regard to whom the tendency of it is *bad* upon the whole. Take the *balance;* which, if on the side of *pleasure,* will give the general the total number or community of individuals concerned; if on the side of pain, the general *evil-tendency,* with respect to the same community.

VI. It is not to be expected that this process should be strictly pursued previously to every moral judgment, or to every legislative or judicial operation. It may, however, be always kept in view: and as near as the process actually pursued on these occasions approaches to it, so near will such process approach to the character of an exact one.

VII. The same process is alike applicable to pleasure and pain, in whatever shape they appear: and by whatever denomination they are distinguished: to pleasure, whether it be called *good* (which is properly the cause or instrument of pleasure) or *profit* (which is distant pleasure, or the cause or instrument of distant pleasure) or *convenience,* or *advantage, benefit, emolument, happiness,* and so forth: to pain, whether it be called *evil,* (which corresponds to *good*) or *mischief,* or *inconvenience,* or *disadvantage,* or *loss,* or *unhappiness,* and so forth.

VIII. Nor is this a novel and unwarranted, any more than it is a useless theory. In all this there is nothing but what the practice of mankind, wheresoever they have a clear view of their own interest, is perfectly conformable to. An article of property, an estate in land, for instance, is valuable, on what account? On account of the pleasures of all kinds which it enables a man to produce, and what comes to the same thing the pains of all kinds which it enables him to avert. But the value of such an article of property is universally understood to rise or fall according to the length or shortness of the time which a man has in it: the certainty or uncertainty of its coming into possession: and the nearness or remoteness of the time at which, if at all, it is to come into possession. As to the *intensity* of the pleasures which a man may derive from it, this is never thought of, because it depends upon the use which each particular person may come to make of it; which cannot be estimated till the particular pleasures he may come to derive from it, or the particular pains he may come to exclude by means of it, are brought to view. For the same reason, neither does he think of the *fecundity or purity* of those pleasures. . . .

From Jeremy Bentham, *An Introduction to the Principles of Morals and Legislation,* 1789.

Mill

Born in 1806 in London, John Stuart Mill was put through a rigorous "educational experiment" by his father. So intense was his tutoring between the ages of three and fourteen that later he could say, "Through the training bestowed on me by my father, I started, I may fairly say, with an advantage of a quarter of a century over my contemporaries." But the heavy emphasis on memorizing and analytical thinking caused young Mill to fall into "a dull state of nerves." He said later that the overemphasis on analysis, without at the same time developing adequately his emotions and feelings, led to his breakdown. "I was, I said to myself, left stranded at the beginning of my voyage, with a well equipped ship and rudder, but no sail. . . ." He therefore turned to such authors as Coleridge, Carlyle, and Wordsworth, who spoke to his feelings. "The cultivation of the feelings," he said, "became one of the cardinal points in my ethical and philosophical creed." Besides his book on ethics entitled *Utilitarianism*, he published his *System of Logic, Principles of Political Economy,* an *Essay on Liberty,* and other books. He died in 1873 at the age of sixty-seven.

John Stuart Mill said that all ethical philosophies could be reduced, in the last analysis, to the simple principle of *utility*. What is good or bad, right or wrong can be tested by the principle of utility in this way: An action is good if it is useful (has utility) in producing pleasure or happiness. This way of thinking became known as "utilitarianism," which taught that the "good" is achieved when the amount of pleasure is greater than the amount of pain. When people act according to the principle of utility, they will achieve "the greatest happiness for the greatest number."

As we have seen, this principle of utility had been developed earlier by John Stuart Mill's fellow Englishman Jeremy Bentham (1748–1832). Mill had known Bentham well, "owing," he says "to the close intimacy which existed between Mr. Bentham and my father." In his *Autobiography* he describes how influential his father was in making Bentham's ideas of utility well known: "It was my father's opinions which gave the distinguishing character to Benthamic or Utilitarian propagandism . . . [since] my father was the earliest Englishman of any mark, who thoroughly understood and in the main adopted, Bentham's general views of ethics. . . ."

MILL'S VERSION OF UTILITARIANISM

Mill's purpose in writing his famous essay *Utilitarianism* was to defend the principle of utility that he learned from his father and Bentham against their critics. In the course of his defense, however, he made such important changes in this theory that his version of utilitarianism turned out to be different from Bentham's in several ways. His definition of the doctrine of utility was perfectly consistent with what Bentham had taught. Mill writes, "The creed which accepts as the foundation of morals Utility, or the greatest Happiness Principle, holds that actions are right in proportion as they tend to promote

John Stuart Mill. *(The Bettmann Archive)*

happiness, wrong as they tend to produce the reverse of happiness. By happiness is intended pleasure, and the absence of pain; by unhappiness, pain, and the privation of pleasure." But even though he started with the same general ideas as Bentham did, especially relating *happiness* with *pleasure*, Mill soon took a different tack by his novel treatment of the role of pleasure in morality.

QUALITATIVE VERSUS QUANTITATIVE APPROACH

Bentham had said that pleasures differ only in their amount, that is, that different ways of behaving produce different *quantities* of pleasure. He had also said that "pushpin is as good as poetry," by which he meant that the only test for goodness is the amount of pleasure an act can produce. It would have to follow in this calculation that all kinds of behavior that produce the same amount of pleasure would be equally good, whether such behavior be the game of pushpin or the writing or enjoyment of poetry. Bentham was so convinced that the simple quantitative measurement of pleasure is the chief test of the morality of an act that he even suggested that "there ought to be a moral thermometer." Just as a thermometer measures the different degrees of heat or temperature, so also a "moral thermometer" could measure the degrees of happiness or unhappiness. This analogy with a thermometer reveals Bentham's exclusive emphasis on quantity in his treatment of goodness and pleasure. To him, just as it is possible to achieve the same degree of heat whether one burns coal, wood, or oil, so also it is possible to achieve equal quantities of pleasure through pushpin, poetry, or other modes of behavior. Goodness, for Bentham, is not connected with any particular *kinds* of behavior, but only with the amounts of pleasure as measured by his "calculus." Inevitably, the utilitarians were accused of being moral relativists who had rejected all moral absolutes in favor of each person's own opinion about what is good. John Stuart Mill sought to defend utilitarianism against these charges, but in the course of his defense he was drawn into the position of altering Bentham's quantitative approach to pleasure by substituting instead a qualitative approach.

Whereas Bentham had said that "pushpin is as good as poetry," Mill said that he would "rather be Socrates dissatisfied than a pig satisfied." Pleasures, said Mill, differ from each other in kind and quality, not only in quantity. He took his stand with the ancient Epicureans, who had also been attacked for their "degrading" emphasis on pleasure as the end of all behavior. The Epicureans replied that it was their critics who had a degrading conception of human nature, for in their attacks they assumed that men are capable of only those pleasures of which swine are capable. But this assumption is obviously false, said Mill along with the Epicureans, because "human beings have faculties more elevated than the animal appetites, and when once conscious of them, do not regard anything as happiness which does not include their gratification." The pleasures of the intellect, of feelings and imagination, and of the moral sentiments have a higher value than the pleasures of mere sensation.

Although Mill had referred to these higher pleasures originally in order to answer the critics of utilitarianism, his concern over higher pleasures led him to criticize the very foundation of Bentham's doctrine of utility. Mill said that "it would be absurd that . . . the estimation of pleasures should be supposed to depend on quantity alone." For Mill, the mere quantity of pleasure produced by an act was of secondary importance when a choice had to be made between pleasures. If a person, says Mill, is acquainted with two different kinds of pleasures and places one of these far above the other in his preference, "even though knowing it to be attended with a greater amount of discontent, and would not resign it for any quantity of the other pleasure which [man's] nature is capable of, we are justified in ascribing to the preferred enjoyment a superiority in quality, so far outweighing quantity as to render it, in comparison, of small account."

The qualitative aspect of pleasure, Mill thought, was as much an observable fact as was the quantitative element on which Bentham placed his entire emphasis. Mill departed even further from Bentham by grounding the qualitative difference between pleasures in the structure of human nature, thereby focusing on certain human faculties whose full use, instead of pleasure only, were to be the test of true happiness and, therefore, of goodness. For this reason, says Mill, "few human creatures would consent to be changed into any of the lower animals, for a promise of the fullest allowance of a beast's pleasures; no intelligent human being would consent to be a fool, no instructed person would be an ignoramus, no person of feeling and conscience would be selfish and base, even though they should be persuaded that the fool, the dunce, or the rascal is better satisfied with his lot than they are with theirs." Pleasures, according to Mill, have to be graded not for their quantity, but for their quality. But if pleasures must be graded for their quality, pleasure is no longer the standard of morality; if, that is, only the full use of our higher faculties can lead us to true happiness, the standard of goodness in behavior has to do not with pleasure directly, but with the fulfillment of our human faculties.

Bentham had simply assumed that we *ought* to choose those acts which produce for us the greatest quantity of pleasure. He also assumed that we should naturally help other people achieve happiness because in that way we should secure our own, and this was his *greatest happiness principle.* Mill accepted this point but added the quality of *altruism* to this principle, saying that "the happiness which forms the utilitarian standard of what is right in conduct, is not the agent's own happiness, but that of all concerned." Mill modified Bentham's egoistic pleasure seeking by indicating "as between his own happiness and that of others, utilitarianism requires [each of us] to be as strictly impartial as a disinterested and benevolent spectator." Mill thus gives the impression that the true utilitarian interprets the greatest happiness principle to mean not *my* greatest happiness but the greatest happiness of the greatest number. He could say, therefore, that "in the golden rule of Jesus of Nazareth, we read the complete spirit of the ethics of utility. To do as one would be done by, and to love one's neighbor as oneself, constitute the ideal of utilitarian perfection." Mill is here trying to defend utilitarian ethics from the charge of egoism, and to emphasize further the "golden rule" character of utilitarianism, he adds that

> Utility would enjoin, first, that laws and social arrangements should place the happiness, . . . or the interest of every individual, as nearly as possible in harmony with the interest of the whole; and secondly, that education and opinion, which have so vast a power over human character, should so use that power as to establish in the mind of every individual an indissolvable association between his own happiness and the good of the whole . . . so that a direct impulse to promote the general good may be in every individual one of the habitual motives of action. . . .

Reading ———————————————————————————

The Calculus of Pain and Pleasure
Mill

PLEASURE—THE "GREATEST HAPPINESS" PRINCIPLE

The creed which accepts as the foundation of morals "utility" or the "greatest happiness principle" holds that actions are right in proportion as they tend to promote happiness, wrong as they tend to produce the reverse of happiness. By happiness is intended pleasure, and the absence of pain; by unhappiness, pain, and the privation of pleasure. To give a clear view of the moral standard set up by the theory, much more requires to be said; in particular, what things it includes in the ideas of pain and pleasure; and to what extent this is left an open question. But these supplementary explanations do not affect the theory of life on which this theory of morality is grounded—namely, that pleasure and freedom from pain are the only things desirable as ends; and that all desirable things (which are as numerous in the utilitarian as in any other scheme) are desirable either for the pleasure inherent in themselves, or as means to the promotion of pleasure and the prevention of pain.

Now such a theory of life excites in many minds, and among them in some of the most estimable in feeling and purpose, inveterate dislike. To suppose that life has (as they express it) no higher end than pleasure—no better and nobler object of desire and pursuit—they designate as utterly mean and groveling; as a doctrine worthy only of swine, to whom the followers of Epicurus were, at a very early period, contemptuously likened; and modern holders of the doctrine are occasionally made the subject of equally polite comparisons by its German, French, and English assailants.

When thus attacked, the Epicureans have always answered that it is not they, but their accusers, who represent human nature in a degrading light, since the accusation supposes human beings to be capable of no pleasures except those of which swine are capable. If this supposition were true, the charge could not be gainsaid, but would then be no longer an imputation; for if the sources of pleasure were precisely the same to human beings and to swine, the rule of life which is good enough for the one would be good enough for the other. The comparison of the Epicurean life to that of beasts is felt as degrading, precisely because a beast's pleasures do not satisfy a human being's conceptions of happiness. Human beings have faculties more elevated than the animal appetites and, when once made conscious of them, do not regard anything as happiness which does not include their gratification. I do not, indeed, consider the Epicureans to have been by any means faultless in drawing out their scheme of consequences from the utilitarian principle. To do this in any sufficient manner, many Stoic, as well as Christian, elements require to be included. But there is no known Epicurean theory of life which does not assign to the pleasures of the intellect, of the feelings and imagination, and of the moral sentiments, a much higher value of pleasures than to those of mere sensation. It must be admitted, however, that utilitarian writers in general have placed the superiority of mental over bodily pleasures chiefly in the greater permanency, safety, uncostliness, etc., of the former— that is, in their circumstantial advantages rather than in their intrinsic nature. And on all these points utilitarians have fully proved their case; but they might have taken the other and, as it may be called, higher ground with entire consistency. It is quite compatible with the principle of utility to recognize the fact that some kinds of pleasure are more desirable and more valuable than others. It would be absurd that, while, in estimating all other things, quality is considered as well as quantity, the estimation of pleasures should be supposed to depend on quantity alone.

SOME PLEASURES BETTER THAN OTHERS

If I am asked what I mean by difference of quality in pleasures, or what makes one pleasure more valuable than another, merely as a pleasure, except its being greater in amount, there is but one possible answer. Of two pleasures, if there be one to which all or almost all who have experience of both give a decided preference, irrespective of a feeling of moral obligation to prefer it, that is the more desirable pleasure. If one of the two, is, by those who are competently acquainted with both, placed so far above the other that they prefer it, even though knowing it to be attended with a greater amount of discontent, and would not resign it for any quantity of the other pleasure which their nature is capable of, we are justified in ascribing to the preferred enjoyment a superiority in quality so far outweighing quantity as to render it, in comparison, of small account.

Now it is an unquestionable fact that those who are equally acquainted with and equally capable of appreciating and enjoying both, do give a most marked preference to the manner of existence which employs their higher faculties. Few human creatures would consent to be changed into any of the lower animals for a promise of the fullest allowance of a beast's pleasures; no intelligent human being would consent to be a fool, no instructed person would be an ignoramus, no person of feeling and conscience would be selfish and base, even though they should be persuaded that the fool, the dunce, or the rascal is better satisfied with his lot than they are with theirs. They would not resign what they possess more than he for the most complete satisfaction of all the desires which they have in common with him. If they ever fancy they would, it is only in cases of unhappiness so extreme that to escape from it they would exchange their lot for almost any other, however undesirable in their own eyes. A being of higher faculties requires more to make him happy, is capable probably of more acute suffering, and certainly accessible to it at more points, than one of an inferior type; but in spite of these liabilities, he can never really wish to sink into what he feels to be a lower grade of existence.

We may give what explanation we please of this unwillingness; we may attribute it to pride, a name which is given indiscriminately to some of the most and to some of the least estimable feelings of which mankind are capable: we may refer it to the love of liberty and personal independence, an appeal to which was with the Stoics one of the most effective means for the inculcation of it; to the love of power or to the love of excitement, both of which do really enter into and contribute to it; but its most appropriate appellation is a sense of dignity, which all human beings possess in one form or other, and in some, though by no means in exact, proportion to their higher faculties, and which is so essential a part of the happiness of those in whom it is strong that nothing which conflicts with it could be otherwise than momentarily an object of desire to them. Whoever supposes that this preference takes place at a sacrifice of happiness—that the superior being, in anything like equal circumstances, is not happier than the inferior—confounds the two very different ideas of happiness and content. It is indisputable that the being whose capacities of enjoyment are low has the greatest chance of having them fully satisfied; and a highly endowed being will always feel that any happiness which he can look for, as the world is constituted, is imperfect. But he can learn to bear its imperfections, if they are at all bearable; and they will not make him envy the being who is indeed unconscious of the imperfections, but only because he feels not at all the good which those imperfections qualify. It is better to be a human being dissatisfied than a pig satisfied; better to be Socrates dissatisfied than a fool satisfied. And if the fool, or the pig, are of a different opinion, it is because they only know their own side of the question. The other party to the comparison knows both sides.

WHO IS THE BEST JUDGE OF PLEASURES?

It may be objected that many who are capable of the higher pleasures occasionally, under the influence of temptation, postpone them to the lower. But this is quite compatible with a full appreciation of the intrinsic superiority of the higher. Men often, from infirmity of character, make their election of the nearer good, though they know it to be the less valuable; and this no less when the choice is between two bodily pleasures than when it is between bodily and mental. They pursue sensual indulgences to the injury of health, though perfectly aware that health is the greater good. It may be further objected that many who begin with youthful enthusiasm for everything noble, as they advance in years, sink into indolence and selfishness. But I do not believe that those who undergo this very common change voluntarily choose the lower description of pleasures in preference to the higher. I believe that, before they devote themselves exclusively to the one, they have already become incapable of the other. Capacity for the nobler feelings is in most natures a very tender plant, easily killed, not only by hostile influences, but by mere want of sustenance; and in the majority of young persons it speedily dies away if the occupations to which their position in life had devoted them, and the society into which it has thrown them, are not favorable to keeping that higher capacity in exercise. Men lose their high aspirations as they lose their intellectual tastes, because they have not time or opportunity for indulging them; and they addict themselves to inferior pleasures, not because they deliberately prefer them, but because they are either the only ones to which they have access, or the only ones which they are any longer capable of enjoying. It may be questioned whether any one who has remained equally susceptible to both classes of pleasures, ever knowingly and calmly preferred the lower, though many, in all ages, have broken down in an ineffectual attempt to combine both.

From this verdict of the only competent judges, I apprehend there can be no appeal. On a question which is the best worth having of two pleasures, or which of two modes of existence is the most grateful to the feelings, apart from its moral attributes and from its consequences, the judgment of those who are qualified by knowledge of both, or, if they differ, that of the majority of them, must be admitted as final. And there needs be the less hesitation to accept this judgment respecting the quality of pleasures, since there is no other tribunal to be referred to even on the question of quantity. What means are there of determining which is the acutest of two pains, or the intensest of two pleasurable sensations, except the general suffrage of those who are familiar with both? Neither pains nor pleasures are homogeneous, and pain is always heterogeneous with pleasure. What is there to decide whether a particular pleasure is worth purchasing at the cost of a particular pain, except the feelings and judgment declare the pleasures derived from the higher faculties to be preferable *in kind,* apart from the question of intensity, to those of which the animal nature, disjoined from the higher faculties, is susceptible, they are entitled on this subject to the same regard.

QUALITY VERSUS THE QUANTITY OF PLEASURES

According to the greatest happiness principle, the ultimate end, with reference to and for the sake of which all other things are desirable—whether we are considering our own good or that of other people—is an existence exempt as far as possible from pain, and as rich as possible in enjoyments, both in point of quantity and quality; the test of quality and the rule for measuring it against quantity being the preference felt by those who, in their opportunities of experience, to which must be added their habits of self-consciousness and self-observation, are best furnished with the means of comparison. This, being according to the utilitarian opinion, the end of human action, is necessarily also the standard of morality, which may accordingly be defined "the rules and precepts for human conduct," by the observance of which an existence such as has been described might be, to the greatest extent possible, secured to all mankind; and not to them only, but so far as the nature of things admits, to the whole sentient creation.

Against this doctrine, however, arises another class of objectors who say that happiness, in any form, cannot be the rational purpose of human life and action; because, in the first place, it is unattainable; and they contemptuously ask, What right hast thou to be happy?—a question which Mr. Carlyle clinches by the addition, What right, a short time ago, hadst thou even to *be?* Next they say that men can do *without* happiness; that all noble human beings have felt this, and could not have become noble but by learning the lesson of renunciation; which lesson, thoroughly learnt and submitted to, they affirm to be the beginning and necessary condition of all virtue.

PLEASURE AND SELF-SACRIFICE

The utilitarian morality does recognize in human beings the power of sacrificing their own greatest good for the good of others. It only refuses to admit that the sacrifice is itself a good. A sacrifice which does not increase or tend to increase the sum total of happiness, it considers as wasted. The only self-renunciation which it applauds is devotion to the happiness, or to some of the means of happiness, of others, either of mankind collectively or of individuals within the limits imposed by the collective interests of mankind.

I must again repeat what the assailants of utilitarianism seldom have the justice to acknowledge, that the happiness which forms the utilitarian standard of what is right in conduct is not the agent's own happiness but that of all concerned. As between his own happiness and that of others, utilitarianism requires him to be as strictly impartial as a disinterested and benevolent spectator. In the golden rule of Jesus of Nazareth, we read the complete spirit of the ethics of utility. "To do as you would be done by," and "to love your neighbor as yourself," constitute the ideal perfection of utilitarian morality.

IS THERE ENOUGH TIME TO CALCULATE PAINS AND PLEASURES?

Again, defenders of utility often find themselves called upon to reply to such objections as this—that there is not time, previous to action, for calculating and weighing the effects of any line of conduct on the general happiness. This is exactly as if any one were to say that it is impossible to guide our conduct by Christianity because there is not time, on every occasion on which anything has to be done, to read through the Old and New Testaments. The answer to the objection is that there has been ample time, namely, the whole past duration of the human species. During all that time, mankind have been learning by experience the tendencies of actions; on which experience all the prudence, as well as all the morality, of life are dependent. People talk as if the commencement of this course of experience had hitherto been put off, and as if, at the moment when some man feels tempted to meddle with the property or life of another, he had to begin considering for the first time whether murder and theft are injurious to human happiness.

ARE WE BORN WITH THE FEELING OF MORAL DUTY?

It is not necessary, for the present purpose, to decide whether the feeling of duty is innate or implanted. Assuming it to be innate, it is an open question to what objects it naturally attaches itself; for the philosophic supporters of that theory are now agreed that the intuitive perception is of principles of morality and not of the details. If there be anything innate in the matter, I see no reason why the feeling which is innate should not be that of regard to the pleasures and pains of others. If there is any principle of morals which is intuitively obligatory, I should say it must be that. If so, the intuitive ethics would coincide with the utilitarian, and there would be no further quarrel between them. Even as it is, the intuitive moralists, though they believe that there are other intuitive moral obligations, do already believe this to be one; for they unanimously hold that a large *portion* of morality turns upon the consideration due to the interests of our fellow creatures. Therefore, if the belief in the transcendental origin of moral obligation gives any additional efficacy to the internal sanction, it appears to me that the utilitarian principle has already the benefit of it.

On the other hand, if, as is my own belief, the moral feelings are not innate but acquired, they are not for that reason the less natural. It is natural to man to speak, to reason, to build cities, to cultivate the ground, though these are acquired faculties. The moral feelings are not indeed a part of our nature, in the sense of being in any perceptible degree present in all of us; but this, unhappily, is a fact admitted by those who believe the most strenuously in their transcendental origin. Like the other acquired capacities above referred to, the moral faculty, if not a part of our nature, is a natural outgrowth from it; capable, like them, in a certain, small degree, of springing up spontaneously; and susceptible of being brought by cultivation to a high degree of development. Unhappily it is also susceptible, by a sufficient use of the external sanctions and of the force of early impressions, of being cultivated in almost any direction, so that there is hardly anything so absurd or so mischievous that it may not, by means of these influences, be made to act on the human mind with all the authority of conscience. To doubt that the same potency might be given by the same means to the principle of utility, even if it had no foundation in human nature, would be flying in the face of all experience.

From John Stuart Mill, *Utilitarianism,* chap. 2, "What Utilitarianism Is," London, 1863.

QUESTIONS FOR REVIEW AND DISCUSSION

1. What is the "principle of utility"?
2. Bentham said that our behavior is controlled by "sanctions." What are some of these sanctions?
3. What does Bentham mean by his pleasure-pain calculus. How do people "calculate" when they are deciding how to behave?
4. What did Bentham mean when he said that "pushpin is as good as poetry"?
5. By contrast, what did Mill mean when he said that "I would rather be Socrates unsatisfied than a pig satisfied"?
6. If pleasure is the standard of what is right and good, what if someone said, "I get a lot of pleasure from drugs"? How would Bentham and Mill deal with that claim?

6

Turning Values Upside Down
Nietzsche

Friedrich Nietzsche was fifty-five years old when he died in August of 1900. Although he was the son and grandson of Lutheran ministers, he expressed the judgment that "God is dead." He grew up in a German household dominated by females, and yet he advocated the most masculine ethic of the "superman." He urged people to express their fullest human vitality in the name of the "Will to Power." At the same time, he believed that to be truly human requires that we should sublimate and control our passions through reason. He was a brilliant student, was appointed professor at the University of Basel even before he completed his doctor's degree, and produced a steady stream of influential books, including *Beyond Good and Evil* and *A Genealogy of Morals.* As a student, he came under the spell of Wagner's music. "I could not have stood my youth without Wagner's music," he once said. "When one wants to rid oneself of an intolerable pressure, one needs hashish. Well, I needed Wagner." He was also influenced by the atheism of the German philosopher Schopenhauer. As a student of Greek literature, his own thought was significantly shaped by the contrast between Dionysus (the symbol of the dynamic stream of life) and Apollo (the symbol of order and restraint).* For the last eleven years of his life, Nietzsche was hopelessly insane as a result of an infection that affected his brain. He was therefore unable to complete his major work, *Revaluation of Values.*

MASTER MORALITY VERSUS SLAVE MORALITY AND THE WILL TO POWER

Nietzsche rejected the notion that there is a universal and absolute system of morality that everyone must equally obey. People are different, he thought, and to conceive of morality in universal terms is to disregard basic differences among individuals. It is unrealistic to assume that there is only one kind of human nature whose direction can be prescribed by one set of rules. There is, however, one thing that does characterize all human beings, says Nietzsche,

*For the symbolic portrayal in Greek art of these two elements in human behavior, see pp. 100 and 101.

and that is the drive to dominate the environment. This drive, so central to human nature, is the *will to power*. This will to power is more than simply the will to survive. It is, rather, an inner drive to express a vigorous affirmation of all of man's powers. As Nietzsche says, "the strongest and highest Will to Life does not find expression in a miserable struggle for existence, but in a Will to War. A Will to Power, a Will to Overpower!" Whenever someone proposes a universal moral rule, he invariably seeks really to deny the fullest expression of man's elemental vital energies. In this respect, Christianity along with Judaism is the worst offender, for the Judeo-Christian ethic is so contrary to man's basic nature that its antinatural morality debilitates man and produces only "botched and bungled" lives.

How did human beings ever produce such unnatural systems of morality? There is, says Nietzsche, a "twofold early history of good and evil," which shows the development of two primary types of morality, namely, the *master morality* and the *slave morality*. In the master morality, "good" has always meant "noble" in the sense of "with a soul of high calibre" and "evil" meant "vulgar" or "plebeian." The noble type of man regards himself as the creator and determiner of values. He does not look outside of himself for any approval of his acts. He passes judgment on himself. His morality is one of self-glorification. This noble individual acts out of a feeling of power, which seeks to overflow. He may help the unfortunate, but not out of pity, rather from an impulse generated by an abundance of power. He honors power in all its forms and takes pleasure in subjecting himself to rigor and toughness and has reverence for all that is severe and hard.

By contrast, the slave morality originates with the lowest elements of society, the abused, the oppressed, the slaves, and those who are uncertain of themselves. For the slave, "good" is the symbol for all those qualities which serve to alleviate the existence of sufferers, such as "sympathy, the kind helping hand, the warm heart, patience, diligence, humility and friendliness. . . ." This slave morality, says Nietzsche, is essentially the morality of utility, where goodness refers to whatever is beneficial to those who are weak and powerless. Whereas for the slave morality the man who arouses fear is "evil," according to the master morality it is precisely the "good" man who is able to arouse fear.

The challenge to the master morality resulted from a deep-seated *resentment* on the part of the "slaves," a resentment, says Nietzsche, "experienced by creatures who, deprived as they are of the proper outlet of action, are forced to find their compensation in an imaginary revenge." This revenge took the form of translating the virtues of the noble aristocrat into evils. Nietzsche's great protest against the dominant Western morality was that it exalted the mediocre values of the "herd," which "knows nothing of the fine impulses of great accumulations of strength, as something high, or possibly as the standard of all things." Incredibly, the "herd mentality" in time overcame the master morality by succeeding in making all the noble qualities appear to be vices and all the weak qualities appear to be virtues. The positive affirmation of life in the master morality was made to seem "bad" and

Friedrich Nietzsche. *(The Bettmann Archive)*

something for which one should have a sense of "guilt." The fact is, says Nietzsche, that

> men with a still natural nature, barbarians in every terrible sense of the word, men of prey, still in possession of unbroken strength of will and desire for power, threw themselves upon weaker, more moral, more peaceful races. . . . At the commencement, the noble caste was always the barbarian caste: their superiority did not consist first of all in their physical, but in their psychical power—they were *complete* men. . . .

But the power of the master race was broken by the undermining of its psychic strength. Against the natural impulse to exert aggressive strength, the weak races had erected elaborate psychic defenses. New values, new ideals, such as peace and equality, were put forward under the guise of "the fundamental principle of society." This, said Nietzsche, was a not-so-subtle desire on the part of the weak to undermine the power of the strong. The weak have created a negative psychic attitude toward the most natural drives of man. This slave morality is, says Nietzsche, "a Will to the *denial* of life, a principle of dissolution and decay." But a skillful psychological analysis of the herd's resentment and its desire to exact revenge against the strong will show, says Nietzsche, what must be done; namely, one must "resist all sentimental weakness: life is essentially appropriation, injury, conquest of the strange and weak, suppression, severity, obtrusion of peculiar forms . . . and at the least, putting it mildest, exploitation. . . ." Nietzsche wanted particularly to emphasize that "exploitation" is not some depraved act, that it does not belong to an imperfect or primitive society. It belongs, he said, "to the nature of the living being as a primary function." Exploitation is, he said, "a consequence of the intrinsic Will to Power, which is precisely the Will to Life—a *fundamental fact* of all history. . . ." Come now, he said, "let us be so far honest toward ourselves!"

European morality, by denying the primacy of the Will to Power, was basically dishonest, in Nietzsche's view. He assigned primary responsibility for this dishonest morality to Judaism and Christianity. With utter directness he said that "I regard Christianity as the most fatal and seductive lie that has ever existed—as the greatest and most *impious lie*. . . ." He was appalled that Europe should be subjected to the morality of that small group of wretched outcasts who clustered around Jesus. Imagine, he said, "the *morality of paltry people* as the measure of all things. . . ." This he considered "the most repugnant kind of degeneracy that civilization has ever brought into existence." Worse yet was the fact that New Testament ethics is still hanging, under the name of "God," over men's heads. To Nietzsche it was incredible that in the New Testament "the least qualified people . . . have their say in its pages in regard to the greatest problems of existence." With what impudent levity "the most unwieldy problems are spoken of here (life, the world, God, the purpose of life) as if they were not problems at all, but the most simple things which these little bigots know all about!!!"

Christianity contradicts nature when it requires us to love our enemies, for Nature's injunction is to *hate* your enemy. Moreover, the natural origin of morality is denied by requiring that before man can love anything, he must first love God. To inject God into men's affections, said Nietzsche, is to subvert the immediate, natural moral standard of utility. All the vital energies of the strong are diluted by routing men's thinking toward God. Again, this is the revenge that the resentment of the weak has engendered. Among men there is always a surplus of "defective, diseased, degenerating, infirm, and necessarily suffering individuals." These are the "failures," which the Judeo-Christian religions seek to keep alive and preserve.

Nietzsche was willing to admit that the "spiritual men" of Christianity had rendered invaluable services to Europe by offering comfort and courage to the suffering. But at what price was Christian charity achieved? The price, Nietzsche said, was "the deterioration of the European race." It was necessary "to *reverse* all estimates of value—*that* is what they had to do! And to shatter the strong, to spoil great hopes, to cast suspicion on the delight in beauty, to break down everything autonomous, manly, conquering, and imperious." In addition, all instincts that are natural to the full "man" had to be transmuted into "uncertainty, distress of conscience, and self-destruction." Christianity succeeded in inverting "all love of the earthly and of supremacy over the earth into hatred of the earth and earthly things. . . ."

Nietzsche was willing for the weak and the herd to have their own morality, provided that they did not impose it on the higher ranks of men. Why should men of great creative powers be reduced to the common level of mediocrity characteristic of the herd? When Nietzsche spoke of rising "beyond good and evil," he had in mind simply rising above the dominant herd morality of his day. He envisioned a new day, when once again the truly complete man would achieve new levels of creative activity and thereby become a higher type of man. This new man will not reject morality; he will reject only the negative morality of the herd. Again, Nietzsche argued that morality based on the will to power is only an honest version of what the slave morality has carefully disguised. If the "superman" is "cruel," said Nietzsche, one must recognize that, actually, almost everything that we now call "higher culture" is simply a spiritualized intensification of cruelty. "This is my thesis," he said, that "the 'wild beast' has not been slain at all, it lives, it flourishes, it has only been—transfigured." He refers to the Romans' pleasures in the arena, the Christian ecstasy of the cross, the Spaniard's delight at the gory sight of the bullfight, the Parisian workman's homesickness for a bloody revolution, and the Wagnerian who "with unhinged will" *undergoes* a performance of *Tristan and Isolde.* "What all these enjoy and strive with mysterious ardour to drink in," said Nietzsche, "is the philtre of the great Circe 'cruelty.' . . ." Looked at from the vantage point of the master morality, the word "cruelty" refers simply to the basic will to power, which is a natural expression of strength. Men are differentiated into ranks, and it is, he says, "quanta of power, and nothing else, which determine and distinguish ranks." For this reason, such ideals as equality among men are nonsensical. There can be no equality where there are in fact different quanta of power. Equality can only mean the leveling downward of everyone to the mediocrity of the herd. Nietzsche wanted to preserve the natural distinction between the two ranks or types of men, namely, between that "type which represents ascending life and a type which represents decadence, decomposition, weakness." To be sure, a higher culture will always require as its basis a strongly consolidated mediocre herd, but only to make possible the development and emergence of the higher type of man, the "superman" (*Übermensch*). If the superman is to emerge, he must go beyond good and evil as conceived by the lower ranks of men.

REVALUATION OF ALL VALUES

What would Nietzsche want to put in the place of the traditional morality, which he believed was clearly dying? His positive prescriptions are not so clear as his critical analyses. Much of the content of his new values can, however, be inferred from his rejection of the slave morality. If the slave morality originated in resentment and revenge, there must again occur a *revaluation* of all values. By revaluation, Nietzsche did not intend the creation of a new table of moral values. He meant rather to declare war on the presently accepted values, like Socrates, to apply "the knife vivisectionally to the very virtues of the time. . . ." Since traditional morality is a perversion of original natural morality, revaluation must consist of rejecting traditional morality in the name of honesty and accuracy. Revaluation implies, said Nietzsche, that all the "stronger motives are still extant, but that now they appear under false names and false valuations, and have not yet become conscious of themselves." It is not necessary to legislate new values, but only to reverse values once again. Just as "Christianity was a revaluation of all the values of antiquity," so today the dominant morality must be rejected in favor of man's original and deepest nature. Thus Nietzsche's program of revaluation was essentially a critical analysis of modern man's ideals. He showed that what modern man called "good" was not at all virtuous, that his so-called truth was disguised selfishness and weakness and that his religion was a skillful creation of psychological weapons with which moral pygmies domesticated natural giants. Once the disguise is removed from modern morality, he thought, the true values will emerge.

Moral values must in the last analysis be built on the true nature of man and his environment. Unlike Darwin, who laid great stress on external circumstances when describing the evolution of the species, Nietzsche focused on the internal power within man, which is capable of shaping and creating events, "a power which *uses* and *exploits* the environment." Nietzsche's grand hypothesis was that everywhere and in everything the Will to Power is seeking to express itself. "This world," he says, "is the Will to Power—and nothing else." Life itself is a plurality of forces, "a lasting form of processes of assertions of force. . . ." Man's psychological makeup shows that his preoccupation with pleasure and pain reflects a striving after an increase of power. Pain can be the spur for exerting power to overcome an obstacle, whereas pleasure can represent a feeling of increased power.

To move from the present condition of mankind requires, says Nietzsche, that human beings pass through "three metamorphoses," or developments or changes in the human spirit. Nietzsche speaks of "how the spirit becomes a camel; and the camel, a lion; and the lion, finally, a child." Here the camel represents man's spirit as a beast of burden, with the spirit's burden being such things as humility, self-denial, suffering hunger for one's soul, and loving those who despise you. Then the spirit expresses a deep desire to be free and like a lion sets out to conquer the dragon which obstructs the spirit's freedom. What is this dragon? The name of the dragon which the lion seeks to destroy is "Thou shalt." This dragon says to the human spirit, "All value has long been created, and I am all created value. Verily, there shall be no more 'I will.'" But the lion says "No" to all inherited values, affirming the right to create new values. But now the preying lion must become a child, for it is the nature of a child to possess innocence and to forget, to try new beginnings, and in a fresh way to say "Yes"; that is, the spirit now wills its *own* will and creates it own world. In another place, Nietzsche says, "A man's maturity consists in having found again the seriousness one had as a child."

THE SUPERMAN (ÜBERMENSCH)

The will to power has its greatest relevance for Nietzsche's philosophy in his notion of the "superman" *(Übermensch)*—again, the "superior" man, sometimes referred to as the "overman." We have already seen that Nietzsche rejected the concept of equality. He also indicated that morality must suit each rank of man. Even after the revaluation of all values, the "common herd" will not be intellectually capable of reaching the heights of the "free spirits." There can, in short, be no "common good." Great things, says Nietzsche, remain for the great, "everything rare for the rare." The superman will be rare, but he is the next stage in human evolution. History is moving not toward some abstract developed "humanity" but toward the emergence of some exceptional men: "Superman is the goal," says Nietzsche. But the superman will not be the product of an automatic process of evolution. Only when superior individuals have the courage to revalue all values and respond with freedom to their internal will to power can the next stage be reached. "Man is something to be surpassed," and it is the superman who represents the highest level of development and expression of physical, intellectual, and emotional strength. The superman will be the truly free man for whom nothing is forbidden except what obstructs the will to power. He will be the very embodiment of the spontaneous affirmation of life.

Nietzsche did not contemplate that his superman would be a tyrant. To be sure, there would be much of the Dionysian element in him. But his passions would be controlled and his animal nature harmonized with his intellect, giving style to his behavior. Such a superman is not to be confused with a totalitarian bully. Nietzsche had in mind as a model for the superman his hero Goethe, suggesting also as an ideal "the Roman Caesar with Christ's soul." As Nietzsche's thought matured, he realized that his superior man would have to possess a balanced unity of the passionate (Dionysian) and rational (Apollonian) elements. Earlier, when his thought was influenced by Wagner and Schopenhauer, Nietzsche had criticized Socrates for having caused Western man to take a wrong turn in history, the turn toward rationality. Even at the end, Nietzsche believed that knowledge and rationality must be used in the service of life and that life must not be sacrificed for knowledge. Still Socrates was important historically precisely because he saved men from self-destruction, which would have occurred if, says Nietzsche, "this whole incalculable sum of energy [in human striving was] *not* employed in the service of knowledge. . . ." The lust for life, he says, would otherwise have led to wars of annihilation. The Dionysian element by itself could lead to pessimism and destruction. That it was necessary to harness man's vital energies already suggested a basic decadent tendency in man, which could be halted only by the kind of influence Socrates represented. But while the rational, or Apollonian, element could stifle the vital streams of life, Nietzsche did not see how, in the end, life could be lived without its form-giving guidance. Socrates became important for Nietzsche precisely because this ancient philosopher was the first to see the proper relation between thought and life. Socrates recognized, said Nietzsche, that thought serves life, while for previous philosophers, life served thought and knowledge. Here, then, was Nietzsche's ideal, the passionate man who has his passions under control.

APOLLONIAN VERSUS DIONYSIAN

Nietzsche found in Homer's account of Apollo and Dionysus a striking symbolism of the two powerful elements in human nature, the power of passion and the power of reason. Dionysus was for Nietzsche the symbol of the dynamic stream of life, which knows no restraints or barriers and defies all limitations. In the worship of Dionysus, the individual would lapse into intoxication and thereby lose his own identity in the larger ocean of life. In the photo of Dionysus, we see a devotee in the presence of Dionysus who exhibits the stirrings of her deep feelings produced by the drinking of wine and the hearing of appropriate music. Apollo, however, was the symbol of order, restraint, and form, the power to create beauty through art. If the Dionysian mood was best expressed in the feeling of abandonment in some types of music, the Apollonian form-giving force found its highest expression, according to Nietzsche, in Greek sculpture. Thus Dionysus symbolized man's unity with life, where his own individuality is absorbed in the larger reality of the life force, whereas Apollo was the symbol of that power which controls and restrains the dynamic processes of life in order to create a formed work of art or a controlled personal character. Looked at from another point of view, the Dionysian represents the negative and destructive dark powers of the soul, which culminate, when unchecked, as Nietzsche says, in "that disgusting mixture of voluptuousness and cruelty" typical of "the most savage beasts of nature." Again, the Apollonian represents the power to deal with the powerful surge of vital energy, to harness destructive powers and to transmute these into a creative act, just as the charioteer (Apollo), by holding the reins, prevents the powerful horses from running wild (see photo of Apollo).

Greek tragedy, according to Nietzsche, is a great work of art. It represents the conquest of Dionysus by Apollo. But from this account Nietzsche drew the conclusion that man is not faced with a choice between the Dionysian and the Apollonian. To assume that one has such a choice to make is to misunderstand the true nature of the human condition. The fact is that human life inevitably includes the dark and surging forces of passion, and the awareness of these driving forces becomes the occasion for producing a work of art in literature or in the plastic arts through the imposition of form on a resisting material or in one's own character through moderation. Nietzsche

Dionysus, the symbol of the power of dynamic passion. (*Hirmer Fotoarchiv, Munich*)

saw the birth of tragedy or the creation of art as a response of the basically healthy element in man, the Apollonian, to the challenge of the energy and frenzy of the Dionysian.

The Dionysian element in human beings is not necessarily or intrinsically "diseased"—only when it is uncontrolled is it unhealthful. In this view, art could not occur without the stimulus of the Dionysian; at the same time, if the Dionysian were considered either the only element in human nature or the dominant element, one might very well despair and come finally to a negative attitude toward life. But for Nietzsche the supreme achievement of human nature occurred in Greek culture, where the Dionysian and Apollonian elements were brought together. To deny that the Dionysian element had a rightful place in life was to postpone, as Nietzsche saw, to some later date the

Apollo, the symbol of order, restraint, and rational control. *(Courtesy Museum of Fine Arts, Boston)*

inevitable explosion of vital forces which cannot be permanently denied expression. To ask whether life should dominate knowledge or knowledge dominate life is to raise the question of which of these two is the higher and more decisive power. There is no doubt, said Nietzsche, that life is the higher and dominating power, but raw vital power is finally life-defeating. For this reason, Nietzsche looked to the Greek formula, the fusion of the Dionysian and Apollonian elements, by which human life is transformed into an aesthetic phenomenon, a work of art.

Reading ————————————————————————————

Thus Spoke Zarathustra
Nietzsche

ON THE THREE METAMORPHOSES

Of three metamorphoses of the spirit I tell you: how the spirit becomes a camel; and the camel, a lion; and the lion, finally, a child.

There is much that is difficult for the spirit, the strong reverent spirit that would bear much: but the difficult and the most difficult are what its strength demands.

What is difficult? asks the spirit that would bear much, and kneels down like a camel wanting to be well loaded. What is most difficult, O heroes, asks the spirit that would bear much, that I may take it upon myself and exult in my strength? Is it not humbling oneself to wound one's haughtiness? Letting one's folly shine to mock one's wisdom?

Or is it this: parting from our cause when it triumphs? Climbing high mountains to tempt the tempter?

Or is it this: feeding on the acorns and grass of knowledge and, for the sake of the truth, suffering hunger in one's soul?

Or is it this: being sick and sending home the comforters and making friends with the deaf, who never hear what you want?

Or is it this: stepping into filthy waters when they are the waters of truth, and not repulsing cold frogs and hot toads?

Or is it this: loving those who despise us and offering a hand to the ghost that would frighten us?

All these most difficult things the spirit that would bear much takes upon itself: like the camel that, burdened, speeds into the desert, thus the spirit speeds into its desert.

In the loneliest desert, however, the second metamorphosis occurs: here the spirit becomes a lion who would conquer his freedom and be master in his own desert. Here he seeks out his last master: he wants to fight him and his last god; for ultimate victory he wants to fight with the great dragon.

Who is the great dragon whom the spirit will no longer call lord and god? "Thou shalt" is the name of the great dragon. But the spirit of the lion says, "I will." "Thou shalt" lies in his way, sparkling like gold, an animal covered with scales; and on every scale shines a golden "thou shalt."

Values, thousands of years old, shine on these scales; and thus speaks the mightiest of all dragons: "All value of all things shines on me. All value has long been created, and I am all created value. Verily, there shall be no more 'I will.'" Thus speaks the dragon.

My brothers, why is there a need in the spirit for the lion? Why is not the beast of burden, which renounces and is reverent, enough?

To create new values—that even the lion cannot do; but the creation of freedom for oneself for new creation—that is within the power of the lion. The creation of freedom for oneself and a sacred "No" even to duty—for that, my brothers, the lion is needed. To assume the right to new values—that is the most terrifying assumption for a reverent spirit that would bear much. Verily, to him it is preying, and a matter for a beast of prey. He once loved "thou shalt" as most sacred: now he must find illusion and caprice even in the most sacred, that freedom from his love may become his prey: the lion is needed for such prey.

But say, my brothers, what can the child do that even the lion could not do? Why must the preying lion still become a child? The child is innocence and forgetting, a new beginning, a game, a self-propelled wheel, a first movement, a sacred "Yes." For the game of creation, my brothers, a sacred "Yes" is needed: the spirit now wills his own will, and he who had been lost to the world now conquers his own world.

Of three metamorphoses of the spirit I have told you: how the spirit became a camel; and the camel, a lion; and the lion, finally, a child.

Thus spoke Zarathustra.

Reading _____

Beyond Good and Evil

Nietzsche

In a tour through the many finer and coarser moralities which have hitherto prevailed or still prevail on the earth, I found certain traits recurring regularly together and connected with one another, until finally two primary types revealed themselves to me, and a radical distinction was brought to light. There is *master*-morality and *slave*-morality;—I would at once add, however, that in all higher and mixed civilizations, there are also attempts at the reconciliation of the two moralities; but one finds still oftener the confusion and mutual misunderstanding of them, indeed, sometimes their close juxtaposition—even in the same man, within one soul. The distinctions of moral values have either originated in a ruling caste, pleasantly conscious of being different from the ruled—or among the ruled class, the slaves and dependents of all sorts. In the first case, when it is the rulers who determine the conception "good," it is the exalted, proud disposition which is regarded as the distinguishing feature, and that which determines the order of rank. The noble type of man separates from himself the beings in whom the opposite of this exalted, proud disposition displays itself: he despises them. Let it at once be noted that in this first kind of morality the antithesis "good" and "bad" means practically the same as "noble" and "despicable";—the antithesis "good" and "evil" is of a different origin. The cowardly, the timid, the insignificant, and those thinking merely of narrow utility are despised; moreover, also, the distrustful, with their constrained glances, the self-abasing, the dog-like kind of men who let themselves be abused, the mendicant flatterers, and above all the liars:—it is a fundamental belief of all aristocrats that the common people are untruthful. "We truthful ones"—the nobility in ancient Greece called themselves. It is obvious that everywhere the designations of moral value were at first applied to *men,* and were only derivatively and at a later period applied to *actions;* it is a gross mistake, therefore, when historians of morals start with questions like, "Why have sympathetic actions been praised?" The noble type of man regards himself as a determiner of values; he does not require to be approved of; he passes the judgment: "What is injurious to me is injurious in itself." He knows that it is he himself only who confers honour on things; he is a creator of values. He honours whatever he recognises in himself: such morality is self-glorification. In the foreground there is the feeling of plenitude, of power, which seeks to overflow, the happiness of high tension, the consciousness of a wealth which would fain give and bestow:—the noble man also helps the unfortunate, but not—or scarcely—out of pity, but rather from an impulse generated by the superabundance of power. The noble man honours in himself the powerful one, him also who has power over himself, who knows how to speak and how to keep silence, who takes pleasure in subjecting himself to severity and hardness, and has reverence for all that is severe and hard. "Wotan placed a hard heart in my breast," says an old Scandinavian Saga: it is thus rightly expressed from the soul of a proud Viking. Such a type of man is even proud of *not* being made for sympathy; the hero of the Saga therefore adds warningly: "He who has not a hard heart when young, will never have one." The noble and brave who think thus are the furthest removed from the morality which sees precisely in sympathy, or in acting for the good of others, or in *désinteressement*, the characteristic of the moral; faith in oneself, pride in oneself, a radical enmity and irony towards "selflessness," belong as definitely to noble morality, as do a careless scorn and precaution in the presence of sympathy and the "warm heart."—It is the powerful who *know* how to honour, it is their art, their domain for invention. The profound reverence for age and for tradition—all law rests on this double reverence,—the belief and prejudice in favour of ancestors and unfavourable to newcomers, is typical in the morality of the powerful; and if, reversely, men of "modern ideas" believe almost instinctively in "progress" and the "future," and are more and more lacking in respect for old age, the ignoble origin of these "ideas" has complacently betrayed itself thereby. A morality of the ruling class, however, is more especially foreign and irritating to present-day taste in the sternness of its principle that one has duties only to one's equals; that one may act towards beings of a lower rank, towards all that is foreign, just as seems good to one, or "as the heart desires," and in any case "beyond good and evil": it is here that sympathy and similar sentiments can have a place. The ability and obligation to exercise prolonged gratitude and prolonged revenge—both only within the circle of equals,—artfulness in retaliation, *raffinement* of the idea in friendship, a certain necessity to have enemies (as outlets for the emotions of envy, quarrelsomeness, arrogance—in fact, in order to be a good *friend*): all these are typical characteristics of the noble morality, which, as has been pointed out, is not the morality of "modern ideas," and is therefore at present difficult to realise, and also to unearth and disclose.—It is otherwise with the second type of morality, *slave-morality*. Supposing that the abused, the oppressed, the suffering, the unemancipated, the weary, and those uncertain of themselves, should moralise, what will be the common element in their moral estimates? Probably a pessimistic suspicion with regard to the entire situation of man will find expression, perhaps a condemnation of man, together with his situation. The slave has an unfavourable eye for the virtues of the powerful; he has a scepticism and distrust, a *refinement* of distrust of everything "good" that is there honoured—he would fain persuade himself that the very happiness there is not genuine. On the other hand, *those* qualities which serve to alleviate the existence of sufferers are brought into prominence and flooded with light; it is here that sympathy, the kind, helping hand, the warm heart, patience, diligence, humility, and friendliness attain to honour; for there these are the most useful qualities, and almost the only means of supporting the burden of existence. Slave-morality is essentially the morality of utility. Here is the seat of the origin of the famous antithesis "good" and "evil":—power and dangerousness are assumed to reside in the evil, a certain dreadfulness, subtlety, and strength, which do not admit of being despised. According to slave-morality, it is precisely the "good" man who arouses fear and seeks to arouse it, while the bad man is regarded as the despicable being. The contrast attains its maximum when, in accordance with the logical consequences of slave-morality, a shade of depreciation—it may be slight and well-intentioned—at least attaches itself even to the "good" man of this morality; because, according to the servile mode of thought, the good man must in any case be the *safe* man: he is good-natured, easily deceived, perhaps a little stupid, *un bonhomme.* Everywhere that slave-morality gains the ascendency, language shows a tendency to approximate the significations of the words "good" and "stupid."—A last fundamental difference: the desire for *freedom*, the instinct for happiness and the refinements of the feeling of liberty belong as necessarily to slave-morals and morality, as artifice and enthusiasm in reverence and devotion are the regular symptoms of an aristocratic mode of thinking and estimating.—Hence we can understand without further detail why love as a *passion*—it is our European speciality—must absolutely be of noble origin; as is well known, its invention is due to the Provencal poet-cavaliers, those brilliant ingenious men of the "gai saber," to whom Europe owes so much, and almost owes itself.

From Friedrich Nietzsche, *Beyond Good and Evil*, trans. Helen Zimmern, in *The Complete Works of Friedrich Nietzsche*, trans. under Oscar Levy (1909–1911).

Reading _____

The Twilight of Idols
Nietzsche

What then, alone, can our teaching be?—That no one gives man his qualities, neither God, society, his parents, his ancestors, nor himself. . . . No one is responsible for the fact that he exists at all, that he is constituted as he is, and that he happens to be in certain circumstances and in a particular environment. The fatality of his being cannot be divorced from the fatality of all that which has been and will be. This is not the result of an individual attention, of a will, of an aim, there is no attempt at attaining to any "ideal man," or "ideal happiness" or "ideal morality" with him—it is absurd to wish him to be careering towards some sort of purpose. *We* invented the concept "purpose"; in reality purpose is altogether lacking. One is necessary, one is a piece of fate, one belongs to the whole, one is in the whole—there is nothing that could judge, measure, compare, and condemn our existence, for that would mean judging, measuring, comparing and condemning the whole. *But there is nothing outside the whole!* The fact that no one shall any longer be made responsible, that the nature of existence may not be traced to a *causa prima,* that the world is an entity neither as a spirit—*this alone is the great deliverance—* thus alone is the innocence of Becoming restored. . . .

From Friedrich Nietzsche, *The Twilight of Idols,* trans. A. M. Ludovici, in *The Complete Works of Friedrich Nietzsche,* trans. under Oscar Levy (1909–1911).

Reading _____

The Will to Power
Nietzsche

I regard Christianity as the most fatal and seductive lie that has ever yet existed—as the greatest and most *impious* lie: I can discern the last sprouts and branches of its ideal beneath every form of disguise, I decline to enter into any compromise or false position in reference to it—I urge people to declare open war with it.

The morality of paltry people as the measure of all things: this is the most repugnant kind of degeneracy that civilisation has ever yet brought into existence. And this *kind of ideal* is hanging still, under the name of "God," over men's heads!!

However modest one's demands may be concerning intellectual cleanliness, when one touches the New Testament one cannot help experiencing a sort of inexpressible feeling of discomfort; for the unbounded cheek with which the least qualified people will have their say in its pages, in regard to the greatest problems of existence, and claim to sit in judgment on such matters, exceeds all limits. The impudent levity with which the most unwieldy problems are spoken of here (life, the world, God, the purpose of life), as if they were not problems at all, but the most simple things which these little bigots *know all about!!!*

This was the most fatal form of insanity that has ever yet existed on earth:—when these little lying abortions of bigotry begin laying claim to the words "God," "last judgment," "truth," "love," "wisdom," "Holy Spirit," and thereby distinguishing themselves from the rest of the world; when such men begin to transvalue values to suit themselves, as though they were the sense, the salt, the standard, and the measure of all things; then all that one should do is this: build lunatic asylums for their incarceration. To *persecute* them was an egregious act of antique folly: this was taking them too seriously; it was making them serious.

The whole fatality was made possible by the fact that a similar form of megalomania was already *in existence,* the *Jewish* form (once the gulf separating the Jews from the Christian-Jews was bridged, the Christian-Jews *were compelled* to employ those self-preservative measures afresh which were discovered by the Jewish instinct, for their own self-preservation, after having accentuated them); and again through the fact that Greek moral philosophy had done everything that could be done to prepare the way for moral-fanaticism, even among Greeks and Romans, and to render it palat–able. . . . Plato, the great importer of corruption, who was the first who refused to see Nature in morality, and who had already deprived the Greek gods of all their worth by his notion *"good,"* was already tainted with *Jewish bigotry* (in Egypt?). . . .

The *law,* which is the fundamentally realistic formula of certain self-preservative measures of a community, forbids certain actions that have a definite tendency to jeopardise the welfare of that community: it does *not* forbid the attitude of mind which gives rise to these actions—for in the pursuit of other ends the community requires these forbidden actions, namely, when it is a matter of opposing its *enemies.* The moral idealist now steps forward and says: "God sees into men's hearts: the action itself counts for nothing; the reprehensible attitude of mind from which it proceeds must be extirpated. . . ." In normal conditions men laugh at such things; it is only in exceptional cases, when a community lives *quite* beyond the need of waging war in order to maintain itself, that an ear is lent to such things. Any attitude of mind is abandoned, the utility of which cannot be conceived.

This was the case, for example, when Buddha appeared among a people that was both peaceable and afflicted with great intellectual weariness.

This was also the case in regard to the first Christian community (as also the Jewish), the primary condition of which was the absolutely *unpolitical* Jewish society. Christianity could grow only upon the soil of Judaism—that is to say, among a people that had already renounced the political life, and which led a sort of parasitic existence within the Roman sphere of government. Christianity goes a step *farther:* it allows men to "emasculate" themselves even more; the circumstances actually favour their doing so.— *Nature* is *expelled* from morality when it is said, "Love ye your enemies": for *Nature's* injunction, "Ye shall *love* your neighbour and *hate* your enemy," has now become senseless in the law (in instinct); now, even *the love a man feels for his neighbour* must first be based upon something *(a sort of love of God). God* is introduced everywhere, and *utility* is withdrawn; the natural *origin* of morality is denied everywhere: the *veneration of Nature,* which lies in *acknowledging a natural morality,* is *destroyed* to the roots. . . .

Whence comes the *seductive charm* of this emasculate ideal of man? Why are we not *disgusted* by it, just as we are disgusted at the thought of a eunuch? . . . The answer is obvious: it is not the voice of the eunuch that revolts us, despite the cruel mutilation of which it is the result; for, as a matter of fact, it has grown sweeter. . . . And owing to the very fact that the "male organ" has been amputated from virtue, its voice now has a feminine ring, which, formerly, was not to be discerned.

On the other hand, we have only to think of the terrible hardness, dangers, and accidents to which a life of manly virtues leads—the life of a Corsican, even at the present day, or that of a heathen Arab (which resembles the Corsican's life even to the smallest detail: the Arab's songs might have been written by Corsicans)—in order to perceive how the most robust type of man was fascinated and moved by the voluptuous ring of this "goodness" and "purity." . . . A pastoral melody . . . an idyll . . . the "good man": such things have most effect in ages when tragedy is abroad.

The *Astuteness of moral castration.*—How is war waged against the virile passions and valuations? No violent physical means are available; the war must therefore be one of ruses, spells, and lies—in short, a "spiritual war."

First recipe: One appropriates virtue in general, and makes it the main feature of one's ideal; the older ideal is denied and declared to be *the reverse of all ideals.* Slander has to be carried to a fine art for this purpose.

Second recipe: One's own type is set up as a general *standard;* and this is projected into all things, behind all things, and behind the destiny of all things—as God.

Third recipe: The opponents of one's ideal are declared to be the opponents of God; one arrogates to oneself a *right* to great pathos, to power, and a right to curse and to bless.

Fourth recipe: All suffering, all gruesome, terrible, and fatal things are declared to be the results of opposition to *one's* ideal—all suffering is *punishment* even in the case of one's adherents (except it be a trial, etc.).

Fifth recipe: One goes so far as to regard Nature as the reverse of one's ideal, and the lengthy sojourn amid natural conditions is considered a great trial of patience—a sort of martyrdom; one studies contempt, both in one's attitudes and one's looks towards all "natural things."

Sixth recipe: The triumph of anti-naturalism and ideal castration, the triumph of the world of the pure, good, sinless, and blessed, is projected into the future as the consummation, the finale, the great hope, and the "Coming of the Kingdom of God."

I hope that one may still be allowed to laugh at this artificial hoisting up of a small species of man to the position of an absolute standard of all things?

To what extent psychologists have been corrupted by the moral idiosyncrasy!—Not one of the ancient philosophers had the courage to advance the theory of the non-free will (that is to say, the theory that denies morality);—not one had the courage to identify the typical feature of happiness, of every kind of happiness ("pleasure"), with the will to power: for the pleasure of power was considered immoral;—not one had the courage to regard virtue as a *result of immorality* (as a result of a will to power) in the service of a species (or of a race, or of a *polis*); for the will to power was considered immoral. . . .

At the waterfall. In looking at a waterfall we imagine that there is freedom of will and fancy in the countless turnings, twistings, and breakings of the waves; but everything is compulsory, every movement can be mathematically calculated. So it is also with human actions; one would have to be able to calculate every single action beforehand if one were all-knowing; equally so all progress of knowledge, every error, all malice. The one who acts certainly labors under the illusion of voluntariness; if the world's wheel were to stand still for a moment and an all-knowing, calculating reason were there to make use of this pause, it could foretell the future of every creature to the remotest times, and mark out every track upon which that wheel would continue to roll. The delusion of the acting agent about himself, the supposition of a free will, belongs to this mechanism which still remains to be calculated.

Irresponsibility and innocence. The complete irresponsibility of man for his actions and his nature is the bitterest drop which he who understands must swallow if he was accustomed to see the patent of nobility of his humanity in responsibility and duty. All his valuations, distinctions, disinclinations, are thereby deprived of value and become false—his deepest feeling for the sufferer and the hero was based on an error; he may no longer either praise or blame, for it is absurd to praise and blame nature and necessity. In the same way as he loves a fine work of art, but does not praise it, because it can do nothing for itself; in the same way as he regards plants, so must he regard his own actions and those of mankind. He can admire strength, beauty, abundance in themselves; but must find no merit therein— the chemical progress and the strife of the elements, the torments of the sick person who thirsts after recovery, are all equally as little merits as those struggles of the soul and states of distress in which we are torn hither and thither by different impulses until we finally decide for the strongest—as we say (but in reality it is the strongest motive which decides for us). All these motives, however, whatever fine names we may give them, have all grown out of the same root, in which we believe the evil poisons to be situated; between good and evil actions there is no difference of species, but at most of degree. Good actions are sublimated evil ones; evil actions are vulgarized and stupefied good ones. The single longing of the individual for self-gratification (together with the fear of losing it) satisfies itself in all circumstances: man may act as he can, that is as he must, be it in deeds of vanity, revenge, pleasure, usefulness, malice, cunning; be it in deeds of sacrifice, of pity, of knowledge. The degrees of the power of judgment determine whether anyone lets himself be drawn through this longing; to every society, to every individual, a scale of possessions is continually present, according to which he determines his actions and judges those of others. But this standard changes constantly; many actions are called evil and are only stupid, because the degree of intelligence which decided for them was very low. In a certain sense, even, *all* actions are still stupid; for the highest degree of human intelligence which can now be attained will assuredly be yet surpassed, and then, in a retrospect, all our actions and judgments will appear as limited and hasty as the actions and judgments of primitive wild peoples now appear limited and hasty to us. To recognize all this may be deeply painful, but consolation comes after: such pains are the pangs of birth. The butterfly wants to break through its chrysalis: it rends and tears it, and is then blinded and confused by the unaccustomed light, the kingdom of liberty. In such people as are *capable* of such sadness—and how few are!—the first experiment made is to see whether *mankind can change itself* from a *moral* into a *wise* mankind. The sun of a new gospel throws its rays upon the highest point in the soul of each single individual, then the mists gather thicker than ever, and the brightest light and the dreariest shadow lie side by side. Everything is necessity—so says the new knowledge, and this knowledge itself is necessity. Everything is innocence, and knowledge is the road to insight into this innocence. Are pleasure, egoism, vanity *necessary* for the production of the moral phenomena and their highest result, the sense for truth and justice in knowledge; were error and the confusion of the imagination the only means through which mankind could raise itself gradually to this degree of self-enlightenment and self-liberation—who would dare to undervalue these means? Who would dare to be sad if he perceived the goal to which those roads led? Everything in the domain of morality has evolved, is changeable, unstable, everything is dissolved, it is true; but *everything is also streaming toward one goal.* Even if the inherited habit of erroneous valuation, love and hatred, continue to reign in us, yet under the influence of growing knowledge it will become weaker; a new habit, that of comprehension, of not loving, not hating, of overlooking, is gradually implanting itself in us upon the same ground, and in thousands of years will perhaps be powerful enough to give humanity the strength to produce wise, innocent (consciously innocent) men, as it now produces unwise, guilty, conscious men—*that is the necessary preliminary step, not its opposite.*

From Friedrich Nietzsche, *Human, All Too Human,* trans. Helen Zimmern, in *The Complete Works of Friedrich Nietzsche,* trans. under Oscar Levy (1909–1911).

QUESTIONS FOR REVIEW AND DISCUSSION

1. How does Nietzsche distinguish between "master morality" and "slave morality"?
2. In what way did Nietzsche think that the Judeo-Christian ethic is contrary to human nature?

3. What is meant by the "revaluation of all values"?
4. How does Nietzsche use the mythical symbolism of the "Appollonian" and "Dionysian" elements to describe human behavior, and what does he consider the proper relationship between them?
5. Would Kant agree with Nietzsche regarding which kind of behavior is more consistent with human nature?

7

Is There a Characteristically Feminine Voice Defining Morality?

Gilligan and Baier

Carol Gilligan

It is said that women and men develop into adulthood along different paths and that these gender differences produce differences in moral consciousness. Since moral philosophy has been, for the most part, the product of masculine thinking, the question has been raised whether moral philosophy, or an ethical theory, can be completely adequate if it is constructed without explicit recognition of fundamental feminine characteristics, and whether it would be different if such characteristics informed it.

An empirical approach to this question has been undertaken by Prof. Carol Gilligan, who is a developmental psychologist at Harvard University. As her article that follows will show in some detail, women react to moral circumstances and answer ethical questions in ways that frequently differ from the thinking of males. Some evidence of these differences has already been found among children. Referring to the studies by Piaget, Gilligan writes that regarding rules governing children's games, "girls were 'less explicit about agreement [than boys] and less concerned with legal elaboration.' In contrast to boys' interest in the codification of rules, the girls adopted a more pragmatic attitude. . . . As a result, in comparison to boys, girls were found to be 'more tolerant and more easily reconciled to innovations.'"

Among the earlier studies comparing the moral judgments of men versus women, Gilligan cites Freud's comment that "for women the level of what is ethically normal is different from what it is in men. Their superego is never so inexorable, so impersonal, so independent of its emotional origins as we require it to be in men." Similarly, Gilligan refers to a study by Lawrence

Kohlberg, who says that a fully developed capacity for moral judgment is achieved only after a person passes through three significant stages (composed of six substages), progressing from (1) an egocentric view, to (2) a societal view of what is good, and finally to (3) "a universal ethical conception." Only with this gradual expansion of one's perspective can a person develop the capacity for free moral judgment; this involves moving from individual needs, and social conventions, until judgment is anchored in principles of justice that can be universally applied.

Women appear to be caught in a paradox, says Gilligan, "for the very traits that have traditionally defined the 'goodness' of women, their care for and sensitivity to the needs of others, are those that mark them as deficient in moral development." It is "the infusion of feeling into their judgments [that] keeps them from developing a more independent and abstract ethical conception in which concern for others derives from principles of justice rather than from compassion and care."

With these earlier evaluations of women's perspectives as her starting point, Gilligan sets out to record answers from some Radcliffe undergraduate students to her question, "How do we identify the characteristically 'feminine voice'?" In short, how do these women perceive the subject of morality?

Reading ─────────────────────────────────────

In a Different Voice
Carol Gilligan

The men whose theories have largely informed [the] understanding of [human] development have all been plagued by the same problem, the problem of women, whose sexuality remains more diffuse, whose perception of self is so much more tenaciously embedded in relationships with others and whose moral dilemmas hold them in a mode of judgment that is insistently contextual. The solution has been to consider women either as deviant or deficient in their development.

That there is a discrepancy between concepts of womanhood and adulthood is nowhere more clearly evident than in the series of studies on sex-role stereotypes reported by Broverman, Vogel, Broverman, Clarkson, and Rosenkrantz (1972). The repeated finding of these studies is that the qualities deemed necessary for adulthood—the capacity for autonomous thinking, clear decision making, and responsible action—are those associated with masculinity but considered undesirable as attributes of the feminine self. The stereotypes suggest a splitting of love and work that relegates the expressive capacities requisite for the former to women while the instrumental abilities

Carol Gilligan is a professor at Harvard University.

necessary for the latter reside in the masculine domain. Yet, looked at from a different perspective, these stereotypes reflect a conception of adulthood that is itself out of balance, favoring the separateness of the individual self over its connection to others and leaning more toward an autonomous life of work than toward the interdependence of love and care. . . .

The revolutionary contribution of Piaget's work is the experimental confirmation and refinement of Kant's assertion that knowledge is actively constructed rather than passively received. Time, space, self, and other, as well as the categories of developmental theory, all arise out of the active interchange between the individual and the physical and social world in which he lives and of which he strives to make sense. . . .

Kohlberg (1969), in his extension of the early work of Piaget, discovered six stages of moral judgment, which he claimed formed an invariant sequence, each successive stage representing a more adequate construction of the moral problem, which in turn provides the basis for its more just resolution. The stages divide into three levels, each of which denotes a significant expansion of the moral point of view from an egocentric through a societal to a universal ethical conception. With this expansion in perspective comes the capacity to free moral judgment from the individual needs and social conventions with which it had earlier been confused and anchor it instead in principles of justice that are universal in application. These principles provide criteria upon which both individual and societal claims can be impartially assessed. In Kohlberg's view, at the highest stages of development morality is freed from both psychological and historical constraints, and the individual can judge independently of his own particular needs and of the values of those around him.

That the moral sensibility of women differs from that of men was noted by Freud (1925/1961) in the following by now well-quoted statement:

> I cannot evade the notion (though I hesitate to give it expression) that for women the level of what is ethically normal is different from what it is in man. Their superego is never so inexorable, so impersonal, so independent of its emotional origins as we require it to be in men. Character-traits which critics of every epoch have brought up against women—that they show less sense of justice than men, that they are less ready to submit to the great exigencies of life, that they are more often influenced in their judgments by feelings of affection or hostility—all these would be amply accounted for by the modification in the formation of their superego. . . .

While Freud's explanation lies in the deviation of female from male development around the construction and resolution of the Oedipal problem, the same observations about the nature of morality in women emerge from the work of Piaget and Kohlberg. Piaget (1932/1965), in his study of the rules of children's games, observed that, in the games they played, girls were "less explicit about agreement [than boys] and less concerned with legal elaboration." In contrast to the boys' interest in the codification of rules, the girls adopted a more pragmatic attitude, regarding "a rule as good so long as the game repays it." As a result, in comparison to boys, girls were found to be "more tolerant and more easily reconciled to innovations."

Kohlberg (1971) also identifies a strong interpersonal bias in the moral judgments of women, which leads them to be considered as typically at the third of his six-stage developmental sequence. At that stage, the good is identified with "what pleases or helps others and is approved of by them." This mode of judgment is conventional in its conformity to generally held notions of the good but also psychological in its concern with intention and consequence as the basis for judging the morality of action.

That women fall largely into this level of moral judgment is hardly surprising when we read from the Broverman et al. (1972) list that prominent among the twelve attributes considered to be desirable for women are tact, gentleness, awareness of the feelings of others, strong need for security, and easy expression of tender feelings. And yet, herein lies the paradox, for the very traits that have traditionally defined the "goodness" of women, their care for and sensitivity to the needs of others, are those that mark them as deficient in moral development. The infusion of feeling into their judgments keeps them from developing a more independent and abstract ethical conception in which concern for others derives from principles of justice rather than from compassion and care. Kohlberg, however, is less pessimistic than Freud in his assessment, for he sees the development of women as extending beyond the interpersonal level, following the same path toward independent, principled judgment that he discovered in the research on men from which his stages were derived. In Kohlberg's view, women's development will proceed beyond Stage Three when they are challenged to solve moral problems that require them to see beyond the relationships that have in the past generally bound their moral experience.

What then do women say when asked to construct the moral domain; how do we identify the characteristically "feminine" voice? A Radcliffe undergraduate, responding to the question, "If you had to say what morality meant to you, how would you sum it up?," replies:

> When I think of the word morality, I think of obligations. I usually think of it as conflicts between personal desires and social things, social considerations, or personal desires of yourself versus personal desires of another person or people or whatever. Morality is that whole realm of how you decide these conflicts. A moral person is one who would decide, like by placing themselves more often than not as equals, a truly moral person would always consider another person as their equal . . . in a situation of social interaction, something is morally wrong where the individual ends up screwing a lot of people. And it is morally right when everyone comes out better off.

Yet when asked if she can think of someone whom she would consider a genuinely moral person, she replies, "Well, immediately I think of Albert Schweitzer because he has obviously given his life to help others." Obligation and sacrifice override the ideal of equality, setting up a basic contradiction in her thinking.

Another undergraduate responds to the question, "What does it mean to say something is morally right or wrong?," by also speaking first of responsibilities and obligations:

> Just that it has to do with responsibilities and obligations and values, mainly values. . . . In my life situation I relate morality with interpersonal relationships that have to do with respect for the other person and myself. [Why respect other people?] Because they have a consciousness or feelings that can be hurt, an awareness that can be hurt.

The concern about hurting others persists as a major theme in the responses of two other Radcliffe students:

> [Why be moral?] Millions of people have to live together peacefully. I personally don't want to hurt other people. That's a real criterion, a main criterion for me. It underlies my sense of justice. It isn't nice to inflict pain. I empathize with anyone in pain. Not hurting others is important in my own private morals. Years ago, I would have jumped out of a window not to hurt my boyfriend. That was pathological. Even today though, I want approval and love and I don't want enemies. Maybe that's why there is morality—so people can win approval, love and friendship.

> My main moral principle is not hurting other people as long as you aren't going against your own conscience and as long as you remain true to yourself. . . . There are many moral issues such as abortion, the draft, killing, stealing, monogamy, etc. If something is a controversial issue like these, then I always say it is up to the individual. The individual has to decide and then follow his own conscience. There are no moral absolutes. . . . Laws are pragmatic instruments, but they are not absolutes. A viable society can't make exceptions all the time, but I would personally. . . . I'm afraid I'm heading for some big crisis with my boyfriend someday, and someone will get hurt, and he'll get more hurt than I will. I feel an obligation to not hurt him, but also an obligation to not lie. I don't know if it is possible to not lie and not hurt.

The common thread that runs through these statements, the wish not to hurt others and the hope that in morality lies a way of solving conflicts so that no one will get hurt, is striking in that it is independently introduced by each of the four women as the most specific item in their response to a most general question. The moral person is one who helps others; goodness is service, meeting one's obligations and responsibilities to others, if possible, without sacrificing oneself. While the first of the four women ends by denying the conflict she initially introduced, the last woman anticipates a conflict between remaining true to herself and adhering to her principle of not hurting others. The dilemma that would test the limits of this judgment would be one where helping others is seen to be at the price of hurting the self.

The reticence about taking stands on "controversial issues," the willingness to "make exceptions all the time" expressed in the final example above, is echoed repeatedly by other Radcliffe students, as in the following two examples:

I never feel that I can condemn anyone else. I have a very relativistic position. The basic idea that I cling to is the sanctity of human life. I am inhibited about impressing my beliefs on others.

I could never argue that my belief on a moral question is anything that another person should accept. I don't believe in absolutes. . . . If there is an absolute for moral decisions, it is human life. . . .

When women feel excluded from direct participation in society, they see themselves as subject to a consensus or judgment made and enforced by the men on whose protection and support they depend and by whose names they are known. A divorced middle-aged woman, mother of adolescent daughters, resident of a sophisticated university community, tells the story as follows:

As a woman, I feel I never understood that I was a person, that I can make decisions and I have a right to make decisions. I always felt that that belonged to my father or my husband in some way or church which was always represented by a0 male clergyman. They were the three men in my life: father, husband, and clergyman, and they had much more to say about what I should or shouldn't do. They were really authority figures which I accepted. I didn't rebel against that. It only has lately occurred to me that I never even rebelled against it, and my girls are much more conscious of this, not in the militant sense, but just in the recognizing sense. . . . I still let things happen to me rather than make them happen, than to make choices, although I know all about choices. I know the procedures and the steps and all. [Do you have any clues about why this might be true?] Well, I think in one sense, there is less responsibility involved. Because if you make a dumb decision, you have to take the rap. If it happens to you, well, you can complain about it. I think that if you don't grow up feeling that you ever had any choices, you don't either have the sense that you have emotional responsibility. With this sense of choice comes this sense of responsibility.

The essence of the moral decision is the exercise of choice and the willingness to accept responsibility for that choice. To the extent that women perceive themselves as having no choice, they correspondingly excuse themselves from the responsibility that decision entails. Childlike in the vulnerability of their dependence and consequent fear of abandonment, they claim to wish only to please but in return for their goodness they expect to be loved and cared for. This, then, is an "altruism" always at risk, for it presupposes an innocence constantly in danger of being compromised by an awareness of the trade-off that has been made. Asked to describe herself, a Radcliffe senior responds:

I have heard of the onion skin theory. I see myself as an onion, as a block of different layers, the external layers for people that I don't know that well, the agreeable, the social, and as you go inward there are more sides for people I know that I show. I am not sure about the innermost, whether there is a core, or whether I have just picked up everything as I was growing up, these different influences. I think I have a neutral attitude towards myself, but I do think in terms of good and bad. . . . Good—I try to be considerate and thoughtful of other people and I try to be fair in situations and be tolerant. I use the words but I try and work them out practically. . . . Bad things—I am not sure if they are bad, if they are altruistic or I am doing them basically for approval of other people. [Which things are these?] The values I have when I try to act them out. They deal mostly with interpersonal type relations. . . . If I were doing it for approval, it would be a very tenuous thing. If I didn't get the right feedback, there might go all my values.

. . . Women have traditionally deferred to the judgment of men, although often while intimating a sensibility of their own which is at variance with that judgment. Maggie Tulliver, in *The Mill on the Floss* (Eliot, 1860/1965), responds to the accusations that ensue from the discovery of her secretly continued relationship with Phillip Wakeham by acceding to her brother's moral judgment while at the same time asserting a different set of standards by which she attests her own superiority:

> I don't want to defend myself. . . . I know I've been wrong—often continually. But yet, sometimes when I have done wrong, it has been because I have feelings that you would be the better for if you had them. If *you* were in fault ever, if you had done anything very wrong, I should be sorry for the pain it brought you; I should not want punishment to be heaped on you.

The morality of responsibility which women describe stands apart from the morality of rights which underlies Kohlberg's conception of the highest stages of moral judgment. Kohlberg . . . sees the progression toward these stages as resulting from the generalization of the self-centered adolescent rejection of societal morality into a principled conception of individual natural rights. To illustrate this progression, he cites an example . . . of a male college senior whose moral judgment also was scored by Kohlberg as at Stage Five or Six:

> [Morality] is a prescription, it is a thing to follow, and the idea of having a concept of morality is to try to figure out what it is that people can do in order to make life with each other livable, make for a kind of balance, a kind of equilibrium, a harmony in which everybody feels he has a place and an equal share in things, and it's doing that—doing that is kind of contributing to a state of affairs that go beyond the individual in the absence of which, the individual has no chance for self-fulfillment of any kind. Fairness; morality is kind of essential, it seems to me, for creating the kind of environment, interaction between people, that is prerequisite to this fulfillment of most individual goals and so on. If you want other people to not interfere with your pursuit of whatever you are into, you have to play the game.

In contrast, a woman in her late twenties responds to a similar question by defining a morality not of rights but of responsibility:

> [What makes something a moral issue?] Some sense of trying to uncover a right path in which to live, and always in my mind is that the world is full of real and recognizable trouble, and is it heading for some sort of doom and is it right to bring children into this world when we currently have an overpopulation problem, and is it right to spend money on a pair of shoes when I have a pair of

shoes and other people are shoeless. . . . It is part of a self-critical view, part of saying, how am I spending my time and in what sense am I working? I think I have a real drive to, I have a real maternal drive to take care of someone. To take care of my mother, to take care of children, to take care of other people's children, to take care of my own children, to take care of the world. I think that goes back to your other question, and when I am dealing with moral issues, I am sort of saying to myself constantly, are you taking care of all the things that you think are important and in what ways are you wasting yourself and wasting those issues?

. . . From another perspective, however, this judgment represents a different moral conception, disentangled from societal conventions and raised to the principled level. In this conception, moral judgment is oriented toward issues of responsibility. The way in which the responsibility orientation guides moral decision at the postconventional level is described by the following woman in her thirties:

> [Is there a right way to make moral decisions?] The only way I know is to try to be as awake as possible, to try to know the range of what you feel, to try to consider all that's involved, to be as aware as you can be to what's going on, as conscious as you can of where you're walking. [Are there principles that guide you?] The principle would have something to do with responsibility, responsibility and caring about yourself and others. . . . But it's not that on the one hand you choose to be responsible and on the other hand you choose to be irresponsible—both ways you can be responsible. That's why there's not just a principle that once you take hold of you settle—the principle put into practice here is still going to leave you with conflict.

The moral imperative that emerges repeatedly in the women's interviews is an injunction to care, a responsibility to discern and alleviate the "real and recognizable trouble" of this world. For the men Kohlberg studied, the moral imperative appeared rather as an injunction to respect the rights of others and thus to protect from interference the right to life and self-fulfillment. Women's insistence on care is at first self-critical rather than self-protective, while men initially conceive obligation to others negatively in terms of noninterference. Development for both sexes then would seem to entail an integration of rights and responsibilities through the discovery of the complementarity of these disparate views. For the women I have studied, this integration between rights and responsibilities appears to take place through a principled understanding of equity and reciprocity. This understanding tempers the self-destructive potential of a self-critical morality by asserting the equal right of all persons to care.

From Carol Gilligan, "In a Different Voice: Women's Conception of Self and of Morality," *Harvard Educational Review*, 47:4, 481–517; copyright 1977 by the President and Fellows of Harvard College.

Reading _____

What Do Women Want in a Moral Theory?

Annette C. Baier

When I finished reading Carol Gilligan's *In a Different Voice*, I asked myself the obvious question for a philosopher reader, namely what differences one should expect in the moral philosophy done by women, supposing Gilligan's sample of women representative, and supposing her analysis of their moral attitudes and moral development to be correct. Should one expect them to want to produce moral theories, and if so, what sort of moral theories? How will any moral theories they produce differ from those produced by men?

Obviously one does not have to make this an entirely *a priori* and hypothetical question. One can look and see what sort of contributions women have made to moral philosophy. Such a look confirms, I think, Gilligan's findings. What one finds *is* a bit different in tone and approach from the standard sort of moral philosophy as done by men following in the footsteps of the great moral philosophers (all men). Generalizations are extremely rash, but when I think of Philippa Foot's work on the moral virtues, of Elizabeth Anscombe's work on intention and on modern moral philosophy, of Iris Murdoch's philosophical writings, of Ruth Barcan Marcus' work on moral dilemmas, of the work of the radical feminist moral philosophers who are not content with orthodox Marxist lines of thought, of Jenny Teichman's book on illegitimacy, of Susan Wolf's recent articles, of Claudia Card's essay on mercy, Sabina Lovilbond's recent book, Gabriele Taylor's work on pride, love and on integrity, Cora Diamond's and Mary Midgeley's work on our attitude to animals, Sissela Bok's work on lying and on secrecy, Virginia Held's work, the work of Alison Jaggar, Marilyn Frye, and many others, I seem to hear a different voice from the standard moral philosopher's voice. I hear the voice Gilligan heard, made reflective and philosophical. What women want in moral philosophy is what they are providing. And what they are providing seems to me to confirm Gilligan's theses about women. One has to be careful here, of course, for not all important contributions to moral philosophy by women fall easily into the Gilligan stereotype, nor its philosophical extension. Nor has it been only women who recently have been proclaiming discontent with the standard approach in moral philosophy, and trying new approaches. Michael Stocker, Alasdair MacIntyre, Ian Hacking when he assesses the game theoretic approach to morality, all should be given the status of honorary women, if we accept the hypothesis that there are some moral insights which for whatever reason women seem to attain more easily or more reliably than men do. Still, exceptions confirm the rule, so I shall proceed undaunted by these important exceptions to my generalizations.

If Hacking is right, preoccupation with prisoner's and prisoners' dilemma is a big boys' game, and a pretty silly one too. It is, I think, significant

Annette Baier is a professor at the University of Pittsburgh, PA.

that women have not rushed into the field of game-theoretic moral philosophy, and that those who have dared enter that male locker room have said distinctive things there. Edna Ullman Margalit's book *The Emergence of Norms* put prisoners' dilemma in its limited moral place. Supposing that at least part of the explanation for the relatively few women in this field is disinclination rather than disability, one might ask if this disinclination also extends to a disinclination for the construction of moral theories. For although we find out what sort of moral philosophy women want by looking to see what they have provided, if we do that for moral theory, the answer we get seems to be "none." For none of the contributions to moral philosophy by women really count as moral theories, nor are seen as such by their authors.

Is it that reflective women, when they become philosophers, want to do without moral theory, want no part in the construction of such theories? To conclude this at this early stage, when we have only a few generations of women moral philosophers to judge from, would be rash indeed. The term "theory" can be used in wider and narrower ways, and in its widest sense a moral theory is simply an internally consistent fairly comprehensive account of what morality is and when and why it merits our acceptance and support. In that wide sense, a moral theory is something it would take a sceptic, or one who believes that our intellectual vision is necessarily blurred or distorted when we let it try to take in too much, to be an anti-theorist. Even if there were some truth in the latter claim, one might compatibly with it still hope to build up a coherent total account by a mosaic method, assembling a lot of smaller scale works until one had built up a complete account—say taking the virtues or purported virtues one by one until one had a more or less complete account. But would that sort of comprehensiveness in one's moral philosophy entitle one to call the finished work a moral theory? If it does, then many women moral philosophers today can be seen as engaged in moral theory construction. In the weakest sense of "theory," namely coherent near-comprehensive account, then there are plenty incomplete theories to be found in the works of women moral philosophers. And in *that* sense of theory, most of what are recognized as the current moral theories are also incomplete, since they do not purport to be yet really comprehensive. Wrongs to animals and wrongful destruction of our physical environment are put to one side by Rawls, and in most "liberal" theories there are only hand waves concerning our proper attitude to our children, to the ill, to our relatives, friends and lovers.

Is comprehensiveness too much to ask of a moral theory? The paradigm examples of moral theories—those that are called by their authors "moral theories," are distinguished not by the comprehensiveness of their internally coherent account, but by the *sort* of coherence which is aimed at over a fairly broad area. Their method is not the mosaic method, but the broad brushstroke method. Moral theories, as we know them, are, to change the art form, vaults rather than walls—they are not built by assembling painstakingly-made brick after brick. In *this* sense of theory, namely fairly tightly systematic account of a fairly large area of morality, with a key stone supporting all the rest, women moral philosophers have not yet, to my knowledge, produced moral theories, nor claimed that they have.

Leaving to one side the question of what good purpose (other than good clean intellectual fun) is served by such moral theories, and supposing for the sake of argument that women can, if they wish, systematize as well as the next man, and if need be systematize in a mathematical fashion as well as the next mathematically minded moral philosopher, then what key concept, or guiding *motif*, might hold together the structure of a moral theory hypothetically produced by a reflective woman, Gilligan-style, who has taken up moral theorizing as a calling? What would be a suitable central question, principle, or concept, to structure a moral theory which might accommodate those moral insights women tend to have more readily than men, and to answer those moral questions which, it seems, worry women more than men? I hypothesized that the women's theory, expressive mainly of women's insights and concerns, would be an ethics of love, and this hypothesis seems to be Gilligan's too, since she has gone on from *In a Different Voice* to write about the limitations of Freud's understanding of love as women know it. But presumably women theorists will be like enough to men to want their moral theory to be acceptable to all, so acceptable both to reflective women and to reflective men. Like any good theory, it will need not to ignore the partial truth of previous theories. So it must accommodate both the insights men have more easily than women, and those women have more easily than men. It should swallow up its predecessor theories. Women moral theorists, if any, will have this very great advantage over the men whose theories theirs supplant, that they can stand on the shoulders of men moral theorists, as no man has yet been able to stand on the shoulders of any woman moral theorist. There can be advantages, as well as handicaps, in being latecomers. So women theorists will need to connect their ethics of love with what has been the men theorists' preoccupation, namely obligation.

The great and influential moral theorists have in the modern era taken *obligation* as the key and the problematic concept, and have asked what justifies treating a person as morally bound or obliged to do a particular thing. Since to be bound is to be unfree, by making obligation central one at the same time makes central the question of the justification of coercion, of forcing or trying to force someone to act in a particular way. The concept of obligation as justified limitation of freedom does just what one wants a good theoretical concept to do—to divide up the field (as one looks at different ways one's freedom may be limited, freedom in different spheres, different sorts and versions and levels of justification) and at the same time hold the subfields together. . . . But as Aristotelians and Christians, as well as women, know, there is a lot of morality *not* covered by that concept, a lot of very great importance even for the area where there are obligations. . . .

Granted that the men's theories of obligation need supplementation, to have much chance of integrity and coherence, and that the women's hypothetical theories will want to cover obligation as well as love, then what concept brings them together? My tentative answer is—the concept of appropriate trust, oddly neglected in moral theory. This concept also nicely mediates between reason and feeling, those tired old candidates for moral authority, since to trust is neither quite to believe something about the trusted, nor necessarily to feel any emotion towards them—but to have a belief-informed and action-influencing attitude. To make it plausible that the neglected concept of appropriate trust is a good one for the enlightened moral theorist to make central, I need to show, or begin to show, how it could include obligation, indeed shed light on obligations and their justification, as well as include love and the other moral concerns of Gilligan's women, and many of the topics women moral philosophers have chosen to address, mosaic fashion. I would also need to show that it could connect all of these in a way which holds out promise both of synthesis and of comprehensive moral coverage. . . .

. . . Indeed it is fairly obvious that love, the main moral phenomenon women want attended to, involves trust, so I anticipate little quarrel when I claim that, if we had a moral theory spelling out the conditions for appropriate trust and distrust, that would include a morality of love in all its variants— parental love, love of children for their parents, love of family members, love of friends, of lovers in the strict sense, of co-workers, of one's country, and its figureheads, of exemplary heroines and heros, of goddesses and gods.

Love and loyalty demand maximal trust of one sort, and maximal trustworthiness, and in investigating the conditions for maximal trust and maximal risk we must think about the ethics of love. More controversial may be my claim that the ethics of obligation will also be covered. I see it as covered since to recognize a set of obligations is to trust some group of persons to instill them, to demand that they be met, possibly to levy sanctions if they are not, and this is to trust persons with very significant coercive power over others. Less coercive but still significant power is possessed by those shaping our conception of the virtues, and expecting us to display them, approving when we do, disapproving and perhaps shunning us when we do not. Such coercive and manipulative power over others requires justification, and is justified only if we have reason to trust those who have it to use it properly, and to use the discretion which is always given when trust is given in a way which serves the purpose of the whole system of moral control, and not merely self serving or morally improper purposes. Since the question of the justification of coercion becomes, at least in part, the question of the wisdom of trusting the coercers to do their job properly, the morality of obligation, in as far as it reduces to the morality of coercion, is covered by the morality of proper trust. Other forms of trust may also be involved, but trusting enforcers with the use of force is the most problematic form of trust involved.

The coercers and manipulators are, to some extent, all of us, so to ask what our obligations are and what virtues we should exhibit is to ask what it is reasonable to trust us to demand, expect, and contrive to get, from one another. It becomes, in part, a question of what powers we can in reason trust ourselves to exercise properly. But self-trust is a dubious or limit case of trust, so I prefer to postpone the examination of the concept of proper self-trust at least until proper trust of others is more clearly understood. Nor do we distort matters too much if we concentrate on those cases where moral sanctions and moral pressure and moral manipulation is not self applied but applied to others, particularly by older persons to younger persons. Most moral pressuring that has any effects goes on in childhood and early youth. Moral sanctions may continue to be applied, formally and informally, to adults, but unless the criminal courts apply them it is easy enough for adults to ignore them, to brush them aside. It is not difficult to become a sensible knave, and to harden one's heart so that one is insensible to the moral condemnation of one's victims and those who sympathize with them. Only if the pressures applied in the morally formative stage have given one a heart that rebels against the thought of such ruthless independence of what others think will one see any reason *not* to ignore moral condemnation, not to treat it as mere powerless words and breath. Condemning sensible knaves is as much a waste of breath as arguing with them—all we can sensibly do is to try to protect children against their influence, and ourselves against their knavery. Adding to the criminal law will not be the way to do the latter, since such moves will merely challenge sensible knaves to find new knavish exceptions and loopholes, not protect us from sensible knavery. Sensible knaves are precisely those who exploit us without breaking the law. So the whole question of when moral pressure of various sorts, formative, reformative, and punitive, ought to be brought to bear by whom is subsumed under the question of whom to trust when and with what, and for what good reasons.

In concentrating on obligations, rather than virtues, modern moral theorists have chosen to look at the cases where more trust is placed in enforcers of obligations than is placed in ordinary moral agents, the bearers of the obligations. In taking, as contractarians do, contractual obligations as the model of obligations, they concentrate on a case where the very minimal trust is put in the obligated person, and considerable punitive power entrusted to the one to whom the obligation is owed (I assume here that Hume is right in saying that when we promise or contract, we formally subject ourselves to the penalty, in case of failure, of never being trusted as a promisor again). This is an interesting case of the allocation of trust of various sorts, but it surely distorts our moral vision to suppose that *all* obligations, let alone all morally pressured expectations we impose on others, conform to that abnormally coercive model. . . .

Undoubtedly some important part of morality does depend in part on a system of threats and bribes, at least for its survival in difficult conditions when normal goodwill and normally virtuous dispositions may be insufficient to motivate the conduct required for the preservation and justice of the moral network of relationships. But equally undoubtedly life will be nasty, emotionally poor, and worse than brutish (even if longer), if that is all morality is, or even if that coercive structure of morality is regarded as the backbone, rather than as an available crutch, should the main support fail. For the main support has to come from those we entrust with the job of rearing and training persons so that they can be trusted in various ways, some trusted with extraordinary coercive powers, some with public decision-making powers, all trusted as parties to promise, most trusted by some who love them and by one or more willing to become co-parents with them, most trusted by dependent children, dependent elderly relatives, sick friends, and so on. A very complex network of a great variety of sorts of trust structures our moral relationships with our fellows, and if there is a *main* support to this network it is the trust we place in those who respond to the trust of new members of the moral community, namely to children, and prepare them for new forms of trust.

A theory which took as its central question "Who should trust whom with what, and why?" would not have to forego the intellectual fun and games previous theorists have had with the various paradoxes of morality—curbing freedom to increase freedom, curbing self interest the better to satisfy self interest, not aiming at happiness in order to become happier. For it is easy enough to get a paradox of trust, to accompany or, if I am right, to generalize the paradoxes of freedom, self interest and hedonism. To trust is to make oneself or let oneself be more vulnerable than one might have been to harm from others—to give them an opportunity to harm one, in the confidence that they will not take it, because they have no good reason to. Why would one take such a risk? For risk it always is, given the partial opaqueness to us of the reasoning and motivation of those we trust and with whom we cooperate. Our confidence may be, and quite often is, misplaced. That is what we risk when we trust. If the best reason to take such a risk is the expected gain in security which comes from a climate of trust, then in trusting we are always giving up security to get greater security, exposing our throats so that others become accustomed to not biting. A moral theory which made proper trust its central concern could have its own categorical imperative, could replace obedience to self made laws and freely chosen restraint on freedom with security-increasing sacrifice of security, distrust in the promoters of a climate of distrust, and so on. . . .

. . . It is appropriate trustworthiness, appropriate trustingness, appropriate encouragement to trust, which will be virtues, as will be judicious untrustworthiness, selective refusal to trust, discriminating discouragement of trust.

Women are particularly well placed to appreciate these last virtues, since they have sometimes needed them to get into a position to even consider becoming moral theorizers. The long exploitation and domination of women by men depended on men's trust in women and women's trustworthiness to play their allotted role and so to perpetuate their own and their daughters' servitude. However keen women now are to end the lovelessness of modern moral philosophy, they are unlikely to lose sight of the cautious virtue of appropriate distrust, or of the tough virtue of principled betrayal of the exploiters' trust.

Gilligan's girls and women saw morality as a matter of preserving valued ties to others, of preserving the conditions for that care and mutual care without which human life becomes bleak, lonely, and after a while, as the mature men in her study found, not self affirming, however successful in achieving the egoistic goals which had been set. The boys and men saw morality as a matter of finding workable traffic rules for self assertors, so that they not needlessly frustrate one another, and so that they could, should they so choose, cooperate in more positive ways to mutual advantage. Both for the women's sometimes unchosen and valued ties with others, and for the men's mutual respect as sovereigns and subjects of the same minimal moral traffic rules (and for their more voluntary and more selective associations of profiteers) trust is important. Both men and women are concerned with cooperation, and the dimensions of trust-distrust structure the different cooperative relations each emphasizes. . . . A moral theory (or family of theories) that made trust its central problem could do better justice to men's and women's moral intuitions than do the going men's theories. Even if we don't easily agree on the answer to the question of who should trust whom with what, who should accept and who should meet various sorts of trust, and why, these questions might enable us better to morally reason together than we can when the central moral questions are reduced to those of whose favor one must court and whose anger one must dread.

From *Annette C. Baier, "What Do Women Want in a Moral Theory?" Noûs,* vol. 19 (March 1985), 53–63. Copyright 1985 by *Noûs* Publications, Indiana University.

QUESTIONS FOR REVIEW AND DISCUSSION

1. Carol Gilligan refers to a study by Kohlberg concerning the development of moral judgment in which he claims that there are several stages in this development. His point is that only after a person progresses through these stages is it possible to make the best moral judgment of behavior. The stages divide into three levels, each of which denotes a significant expansion of the moral point of view. The progression is from (i) an egocentric, through (ii) a societal, to (iii) a universal ethical conception.
   a. Describe the three stages of this development of moral judgment and give an example of moral judgment typical of each stage.
   b. In general, is there any difference between women and men in their progress through these stages?
   c. From the several interviews recorded with undergraduate women by Gilligan, what stands out as their moral point of view, the right thing to do?
   d. Is there in women "a different voice," and in your judgment should we recognize it in formulating a moral philosophy?
2. Annette Baier says that "women moral philosophers have not yet, to my knowledge, produced moral theories," and she then asks that if they did

want to, "what key concept, or guiding *motif*, might hold together the structure of a moral theory hypothetically produced by a reflective woman?"

To answer this question, Baier compares the key concept of modern moral theory, which is *obligation*, with what could be the key concept of a theory produced by women, namely, the concept of *trust*. How does Baier describe "appropriate trust," and how does this moral insight differ from the concept of obligation as the basis of morality?

Parliament in the 1400s. (*New York Public Library Picture Collection*)

PART TWO

Politics
Why Should I Obey?

The only purpose for which power can be rightfully exercised over any member of a civilized community, against his will, is to prevent harm to others. His own good, either physical or moral, is not a sufficient warrant. He cannot rightfully be compelled to do or forbear because it will be better for him to do so, because it will make him happier, because, in the opinions of others, to do so would be wise or even right. These are good reasons for remonstrating with him, or reasoning with him, or persuading him, or entreating him, but not for compelling him. . . .

John Stuart Mill
On Liberty (1859)

If we did not have any government, would we miss it? If we were completely free, how would we get along? It is difficult to imagine any circumstances where we would not require the power of government to help us achieve many of our human aspirations. Still, the question of what things would be like without government is a useful one to ask, since it is a way of forcing us to explain how government comes into existence and whether government is necessary.

It was in the presence of strong governments that Rousseau wrote that "man is born free: and everywhere he is in chains." He recognized the practical fact that "as long as a people is compelled to obey, and obeys, it does well." At the same time, he said that "as soon as it can shake off the yoke, and shakes it off, it does still better." What Rousseau was driving at was a compromise between his romantic ideal of complete freedom, which he thought was natural to all men, and the fact of governmental control of human behavior, which he considered an artificial creation of selfish men. If, that is, there is going to be government in any case, it should at least be made legitimate by acknowledging the prior rights and values of all citizens.

By contrast, Aristotle thought that the state or government is a perfectly natural institution just as marriage is. When he said that "man is by nature a political animal," he meant that no individual can survive without associating with someone else. This makes the family the basic social unit. But neither is

the family self-sufficient. Families must associate with one another in order
to achieve more than the recurrent daily needs, and this gives rise to the
village. Then, says Aristotle, "when we come to the final and perfect association, formed from a number of villages, we have already reached the *polis*—
an association which may be said to reach the height of full self-sufficiency."

As a political animal, man requires the help of government to perfect his
nature. That is the purpose of government. For this reason, Aristotle believed
that "man, when perfected, is the best of animals, but when separated from
law and justice he is the worst of all." Those who consider government an
artificial and arbitrary creation and those who see it as a natural institution
have contributed quite different points of view to the continuing debate over
the elements of political thought.

THE ELEMENTS OF POLITICS

Freedom

In its simplest definition, "freedom" means the absence of external restraints.
If we were totally free, if we faced no restraints, in short, if there were no
government, it would appear that we could do whatever we wished over a
wide range of possibilities. Physically, we could go wherever we wanted to
go, since nobody would interfere with our bodily movements. Socially, we
would be free to associate with everyone and to join any group. Economically,
we would be free to produce, sell, buy, and use whatever we could acquire,
and we could enter whatever job or profession we chose. Culturally, we
could pursue education at all levels and we could think, believe, say, and
publish whatever we wished. Morally, we could engage in any behavior that
pleased us.

Who has all these freedoms? There was a time when only one person, the
ruler, was free. Later, a small group, the aristocracy, was free. In a democracy
it is assumed that everyone is free. But even in a democracy there are several
restraints to freedom. Some of these restraints are clearly necessary, such as
traffic regulations; others are unavoidable, such as when we lack the ability or
talent to enter a profession; still other restraints are debatable, such as when
the government seeks to enforce a particular mode of moral behavior. There
are other limitations to our freedom which have become the concern of
political society, such as the absence of opportunities because of a disadvantaged childhood or the frustration of a free market caused by an economic
monopoly. If there were no restraints, if there were total freedom as Hobbes
described it in the original state of nature, the result might well be what he
called "the war of all against all." If we had too many restraints, the result
would be tyranny. What political thought and action seek to achieve in society
is an appropriate balance between a wide range of freedom, order, and the
satisfaction of human needs.

Authority

The authority of government can be compared to the authority of an umpire at a baseball game. Both these forms of authority are required for similar reasons. Whenever there is a dispute about a play in the game, each party to the dispute thinks he is right. Not everybody holding opposite views can be right. Nevertheless, a decision has to be made. Only the umpire has the authority to make the official decision. If there were no umpire, there would be no way of resolving the dispute. The argument could become severe and end in violence. Similarly, without some political or legal authority, a multitude of people would become involved in endless arguments about what belongs to whom and who is responsible for injuring someone.

But how do governments acquire their authority to govern the lives of people? Political authority has been accounted for in different ways. Kings once assumed that they governed by divine right. Philosophers developed theories of the Social Contract, saying that sovereigns acquired political authority when individuals handed over some or all of their freedoms in exchange for the benefits of an orderly and secure society. Still others believe that the authority to govern was and even now can be acquired through superior power or the force of conquest. In democratic societies the source of political authority is taken to be the consent of the governed. Most people will agree that in order to have a civil society it is necessary to have a supreme authority. But it makes a difference how civil society will be governed when a people accepts one explanation over another of how the sovereign acquires authority. Some of these differences in sovereign authority become apparent when we consider the nature of law.

Law

We normally think of law as a set of rules telling us how to behave. But the rules which make up the law are different from any other kind of rules. What makes them different, for example, from the rules governing baseball is that if we do not want to play that game, we do not have to pay any attention to its rules. The rules of law, on the other hand, apply to us whether we like them or not. Chief Justice John Marshall once said that "the Judicial Department comes home in its effects to every man's fireside; it passes on his property, his reputation, his life, his all." What used to be a simple set of rules has become an enormous system of rules and regulations.

What makes our obedience to these laws mandatory is that they come from the source of authority. That is why "law" can be defined as a command of the sovereign. Before there was a sovereign, law as we know it did not exist. Everyone, in a sense, was his or her own lawgiver. That was the problem in the state of nature where everyone had complete freedom. With the establishment of a single authority came the beginning of law in the sense of officially announced rules. A rule is not a law unless it comes officially from the sovereign. But is every command of the sovereign a law? Suppose that the sovereign commands a law which is contrary to morality. Is that command still a law? Here is the point where different theories of authority lead to different theories of law. If, for example, authority is achieved simply through power, then it might be argued that might is right. But from the earliest times, philosophers have tried to distinguish between a law, on the one hand, and an arbitrary command, on the other. What makes a command arbitrary, in their judgment, is that it pays no attention to reason or morality. What makes a rule *law* is not only the fact that it is officially created, but that it fits the requirements of reasoned morality. Aquinas went so far as to say that "a tyrannical law, not being according to reason, is not law at all in the strict sense but is a perversion of law."

To say this, however, is to assume that everybody is in agreement over what reason requires. Because of these questions about what really is the nature of law, the concept of law has been expanded to include not only the body of rules but also the process—the judicial process of the courts—by which the rules are interpreted and applied. The judicial process provides the occasion, especially in the American system, for the judges to test a law to see if it is constitutional, that is, to make sure that a law does not violate the various rights set forth in the Constitution. The judicial process represents a continuing effort to clarify and advance the ends and purposes of law. The underlying purpose of law is to achieve justice.

Justice

"Justice" can be defined simply as fairness. This assumes that everybody has an intuitive sense of what constitutes fairness in any particular case. Other definitions are similar. One of the earliest definitions says that "justice is rendering to each his own." This, of course, raises the question of what is each's own, just as the classic definition that "justice means treating equals equally" leaves open the question of who are equals?

One reason for the difficulty of defining justice is that we tend to identify our own self-interest with what is right and just. One way to overcome this is to think of justice as meaning what the law says it is. Hobbes once said that there can be no unjust law. All he meant by that was that justice is defined as any action which complies with the law as it is. But the law itself does not always measure up to a community's sense of justice. Indeed, Justice Cardozo, a member of the United States Supreme Court, wrote that "what we are seeking is not merely the justice that one receives when his rights and duties are determined by the law as it is; what we are seeking is the justice to which the law in its making should conform."

In making its laws, a community always has to balance the pressures from special groups with the common good. But the final test of the justice of a society is to be found in the way individuals are treated—how much freedom, how much opportunity, and how much of a share in the society's resources each has. Justice does not require mathematical equality in all things. Justice does require that everyone should be free, that nobody should be arbitrarily denied opportunities, and that if the distribution of resources is unequal, it should nevertheless be fair.

We began by asking whether government is necessary. To find an answer, we wondered what life would be like under a condition of complete freedom. We discovered that (1) if freedom means the absence of external restraints, then everybody would decide individually what was right, that there would be differences that could not be resolved, and that this would lead to chaos. (2) To avoid anarchy, people, just like contestants in a game, need an umpire, that is, an authority to settle disputes and to make the rules for everyone. (3) Law is a set of rules, but only those rules which the sovereign announces. Are these rules law only because the sovereign made them, or must the sovereign, when making laws, consider the dictates of reason and morality? The broader view that sees law not only as a body of official rules but also as a process, the judicial process, underscores the continuing effort of law to achieve (4) justice. Although justice is very difficult to define with exactness, it includes freedom for everyone, equal opportunities, and a fair distribution of resources. These are some of the elements of political thought that we will find discussed by our selected philosophers.

SOME APPROACHES TO POLITICAL PHILOSOPHY

Both *Plato* and *Aristotle* were aware of the confusion frequently encountered in political discussions. This confusion existed, they thought, because participants in these discussions were simply expressing their opinions. Accordingly, Plato and Aristotle sought to overcome this conflict of opinions by discovering in human nature some objective clue to political and social life. They both made use of the concept of purpose. Plato regarded the state as a large-scale version of the individual. Nature seemed to design the state so that each social class in it represented an extension of the three faculties found in man. Just as each faculty in man has a purpose, so also the corresponding class in society has a special function. For example, the faculty of reason, which governs the individual, finds its counterpart in society in the ruling class. The good or just society exists according to Plato when the social classes are in harmony by fulfilling their special function or purpose.

Aristotle did not visualize the structure of the state in such precise terms. He emphasized chiefly the role of the state as a natural institution whose purpose it is to make men good. Because he approached this subject in a scientific way, he was aware of the different forms a state can take, depending on the number of people and the size of the territory involved. What Plato and Aristotle had in common was their concept of the natural purposefulness of government.

Besides by classes, society is also divided along the two sexes. Does nature prescribe the same or different roles for male and female? Plato spoke of the equality of women, raising a subject on which there is considerable discussion on the contemporary scene, as we see in the articles by *Simone de Beauvoir* and *Joyce Trebilcot*.

Aquinas composed a classic treatise concerning the nature of law. He is known especially as an advocate of natural law. The central feature of his theory is that law is a product of reason. As a theologian and philosopher, he combined these two disciplines in his theory of law. For him, natural law represents those principles of conduct which human reason shares with God's reason. Aquinas argued, therefore, that laws made by governments are morally valid only if they do not violate the principles of natural law.

Hobbes and *Locke* described the condition of human life as it might have been before governments existed. Hobbes takes a pessimistic view of man's nature. He accounts for the authority of government by referring to the Social Contract as the solution to anarchy. Men enter into the Social Contract out of fear, not out of love for one another. By contrast, Locke has an optimistic view of human nature. He argues that human beings have natural rights even before there is a government. People leave the state of nature to set up an independent or impartial authority in order to avoid a glaring unfairness in the state of nature by which a person is both a party and a judge in his own cause.

Bentham and *Mill* were the great exponents of utilitarianism. This was a new philosophy of ethics which had a strong influence on social and political thought. The effect of utilitarianism was to simplify moral and political philosophy by using pleasure and pain as the standard for good and evil, as well as for justice and injustice. Whatever causes pain is evil or unjust; whatever causes or increases pleasure is good and just. Each individual must be his own judge on these matters, and the only justification for the government to compel anyone to obey is to prevent him from doing harm to others. Utilitarianism emphasized individualism and liberty.

Marx thought he had discovered a scientific clue to the dynamic movement of history. What makes history move from one stage to another is the class struggle. This struggle is caused by a contradiction between the way men produce things and earn a living, on the one hand, and the way the fruits of industry and society are distributed, on the other. Only when there is a classless society will the conflicts and alienation be overcome.

Rawls devised a theory of justice based on a novel concept of the Social Contract. Unlike Hobbes, who had a pessimistic view of human nature, Rawls assumes that rational individuals can agree on the basic principles of justice which take into account both the equalities and inequalities among people. He believes, moreover, that if, in the "original position," individuals could step behind a "veil of ignorance," they would in the end agree on "two principles of justice" which would require freedom for all and a distribution of wealth which, although not mathematically equal, would be fair.

8

The Natural Basis for Society

Plato and Aristotle

Plato

Plato (428–348 B.C.) was born in a distinguished family in Athens at a time when culture there was flourishing. Although Plato was aware of the various modes of philosophy circulating in Athens, the most important influence in the formation of his thought was the life and teaching of Socrates (470–399 B.C.). From Socrates he learned that the surest way of going after knowledge is through orderly conversation or dialogue. That is why Plato wrote dialogues, because the dialectic method enabled him to demonstrate how an idea must be constantly subjected to argument and counterargument. Plato wrote about twenty books or dialogues. The first group reflects the influence of Socrates, while the later group shows the development of his new concepts. When he was about forty years old, after writing most of his books, he founded his school, called the Academy of Athens, probably the first university. Aristotle entered this Academy in 367 B.C. at the age of eighteen. The trial and death of Socrates disillusioned Plato about public political life, but he continued to exert great influence through his teaching at the Academy until his death at the age of eighty.

In Plato's thought, political theory is closely connected with moral philosophy. Indeed, Plato considered the state as being "man writ large." But Plato does not simply say that there is an interesting or coincidental connection between the just man and the just society. He argues, rather, that there is a structural and natural as well as logical relation between man and the state.

THE STATE AS MAN WRIT LARGE

Plato's whole argument is that the state grows out of the nature of the individual, so that logically the individual comes prior to the state. The state, said Plato, is a natural institution, natural because it reflects the structure of human nature. The origin of the state is a reflection of man's economic needs, for, says Plato, "a state comes into existence because no individual is self-sufficing; we all have many needs." Our many needs require many skills, and no one possesses all the skills needed to produce food, shelter, and clothing, to say nothing of the various arts. There must, therefore, be a division of labor, for "more things will be produced and the work more easily and better done, when every man is set free from all other occupations to do, at the right time, the one thing for which he is naturally fitted."

Man's needs are not limited to his physical requirements, for his goal is not simply survival but a life higher than an animal's. Still, the healthy state soon becomes affected by a wide range of desires and becomes "swollen up with a whole multitude of callings not ministering to any bare necessity." Now there will be "hunters and fishermen . . . artists in sculpture, painting and music; poets with their attendant train of professional reciters, actors, dancers, producers; and makers of all sorts of household gear, including everything for women's adornment. And we shall want more servants . . . lady's maids, barbers, cooks and confectioners." This desire for more things will soon exhaust the resources of the community and before long, says Plato, "we shall have to cut off a slice of our neighbor's territory . . . and they will want a slice of ours." At this rate, neighbors will inevitably be at war. Wars have their "origin in desires which are the most fruitful source of evils both to individuals and states." With the inevitability of war, it will now be necessary to have "a whole army to go out to battle with an invader, in defence of all this property and of the citizens. . . ." Thus emerge the guardians of the state, who, at first, represent the vigorous and powerful men who will repel the invader and preserve internal order. Now there are two distinct classes of men: those who fill all the crafts—farmers, artisans, and traders—and those who guard the community. From this latter class are then chosen the most highly trained guardians, who will become the rulers of the state and will represent a third and elite class.

THE STATE AND THE INDIVIDUAL

The relation between the individual and the state now becomes plain, for the three classes in the state are an extension of the three parts of the soul. The craftsmen or artisans represent as a class the lowest part of the soul, namely, the appetites. The guardians embody the spirited element of the soul. And the highest class, the rulers, represent the rational element. So far, this analysis seems to have logical rigor, for it does not strain the imagination to see the connection (1) between the individual's appetites and the class of workers who satisfy these appetites, (2) between the spirited element in man and the large-scale version of this dynamic force in the military establishment, and (3) between the rational element and the unique function of leadership in the ruler. But Plato was aware that it would not be simple to convince people to accept this system of classes in the state, particularly if they found themselves in a class that might not be the one they would choose if they had the chance. The assignment of all persons to their respective classes would come only after extensive training, where only those capable of doing so would progress to the higher levels. Although theoretically each person would have the opportunity to reach the highest level, he would in fact stop at the level of his natural aptitudes.

	The Individual			The State	
	Three Parts of the Soul	**The Virtues**	**The Three Classes**		
Justice	1. Rational $\longleftarrow$	1. Wisdom $\longrightarrow$	1. Rulers		**Justice**
	2. Spirited $\longleftarrow$	2. Courage $\longrightarrow$	2. Guardians		
	3. Appetitive $\longleftarrow$	3. Temperance $\longrightarrow$	3. Craftsmen		

The same "virtues" apply to the three parts of a person as well as to the three classes in the state.

To make everyone satisfied with his lot, Plato thought it would be necessary to employ a "convenient fiction . . . a single bold flight of invention." He writes, "I shall try to convince, first the Rulers and the soldiers, and then the whole community, that all that nurture and education which we gave them was only something they seemed to experience as it were in a dream. In reality they were the whole time down inside the earth, being molded . . . and fashioned . . . and at last when they were complete, the earth sent them up from her womb into the light of day."

This "noble lie" would also say that the god who fashioned all men "mixed gold in the composition" of those who were to rule and "put silver in the guardians, and iron and brass in the farmers and craftsmen." This would imply that by nature some would be rulers and others craftsmen and that this would provide the basis for a perfectly stratified society. But whereas later societies in Europe assumed that the children born into such a stratified society would stay at the level at which they were born, Plato recognized that children would not always have the same qualities as their parents. He said, therefore, that among the injunctions laid by heaven on the rulers "there is none that needs to be so carefully watched as the mixture of metals in the souls of children. If a child of their own is born with an alloy of iron or brass, they must, without the smallest pity, assign him the station proper to his nature and thrust him out among the farmers and craftsmen." Similarly, if a child with gold or silver is born to craftsmen, "they will promote him according to his value. . . ." Most important of all, Plato thought that everyone should agree on who is to be the ruler and agree also on the reason why the ruler should be obeyed.

THE PHILOSOPHER-KING

To Plato it seemed natural that competence should be the qualification for authority. The ruler of the state should be the one who has the peculiar abilities to fulfill that function. Disorder in the state is caused by the same circumstances that produce disorder in the individual, namely, the attempt on

the part of the lower elements to usurp the role of the higher faculties. In both
the individual and the state, the uncontrolled drives of the appetites and
spirited action lead to internal anarchy. At both levels, the rational element
must be in control. Who should be the captain of a ship—should it be the most
"popular" man, or the one who knows the art of navigation? Who should rule
the state—should it be someone whose training is in war or commerce? The
ruler, said Plato, should be the one who has been fully educated, one who has
come to understand the difference between the visible world and the
intelligible world, between the realm of opinion and the realm of knowledge,
between appearance and reality. The philosopher-king is one whose
education, in short, has led him up step by step through ever higher degrees
of knowledge until at last he has a knowledge of the Good, that synoptic
vision of the interrelation of all truths to each other.

To reach this point, the philosopher-king will have progressed through
many stages of education. By the time he is eighteen years old, he will have
had training in literature, music, and elementary mathematics. His literature
would be censored, for Plato accused certain poets of outright falsehood and
of impious accounts of the behavior of the gods. Music also would be
prescribed so that seductive music would be replaced by a more wholesome,
martial meter. For the next few years there would be extensive physical and
military training, and at age twenty, a few would be selected to pursue an
advanced course in mathematics. At age thirty, a five-year course in dialectic
and moral philosophy would begin. The next fifteen years would be spent
gathering practical experience through public service. Finally, at age fifty, the
ablest men would reach the highest level of knowledge, the vision of the
Good, and would then be ready for the task of governing the state.

THE VIRTUES IN THE STATE

Whether justice could ever be achieved in a state would depend, Plato
thought, on whether the philosophical element in society could attain
dominance. He wrote that "I was forced to say in praise of the correct
philosophy that it affords a vantage-point from which we can discern in all
cases what is just for communities and for individuals," and he believed that
"the human race will not be free of evils until either the stock of those who
rightly and truly follow philosophy acquire political authority, or the class
who have power in the cities be led by some dispensation of providence to
become real philosophers." But justice is a general virtue. It means that all
parts are fulfilling their special functions and are achieving their respective
virtues. Justice in the state will be attained only when and if the three classes
fulfill their functions.

As the craftsmen embody the element of the appetites, they will also
reflect the virtue of temperance. Temperance is not limited to the craftsmen
but applies to all the classes, for it indicates, when it is achieved, the
willingness of the lower to be ruled by the higher. Still, temperance applies in

Acropolis. *(Royal Ontario Museum, Toronto)*

a special way to the craftsmen insofar as they are the lowest and must be subordinate to the two higher levels.

The guardians, who defend the state, manifest the virtue of courage. To assure the state that these guardians will always fulfill their function, special training and provision are made for them. Unlike the craftsmen, who marry and own property, the guardians will have both property and wives in common. Plato considered these arrangements essential if the guardians were to attain true courage, for courage means knowing what to fear and what not to fear. The only real object of fear for the guardian should be fear of moral evil. He must never fear poverty or privation, and for this reason, his mode of life should be isolated from possessions. Although wives will be held in common, this was by no means to suggest any form of promiscuity. On the contrary, Plato believed that men and women were equal in respect to certain things, saying, for example, that "a man and a woman have the same nature if both have a talent for medicine." This being the case, they should both be assigned to the same task whenever they possess the appropriate talent. For this reason, Plato believed that women could be guardians as well as men.

In order to preserve the unity of the members of the class of guardians, the permanent individual family would be abolished, and the whole class would become a single family. Plato's reasoning here was that the guardians must be free not only from the temptation to acquire property, but free also from the temptation to prefer the advantages of one's family to those of the state. Moreover, he thought it rather foolish to take such pains in breeding racing dogs and horses and at the same time rely on pure chance in producing the guardians and rulers of the state. For this reason, sexual relations would be strictly controlled and would be limited to the special marriage festivals. These festivals would occur at stated times, and the partners, under the illusion that they had been paired by drawing lots, would, instead, be brought together through the careful manipulation of the rulers to ensure the highest eugenic possibilities. Plato does say that "young men who acquit themselves well in war and other duties, should be given, among other rewards and privileges, more liberal opportunities to sleep with a wife," but only for the utilitarian purpose that "with good excuse, as many as possible of the children may be begotten of such fathers." As soon as children are born to the guardians, they will be taken in charge by officers appointed for that purpose and will be reared in a crechè in the care of nurses living in a special part of the city. Under these circumstances, thought Plato, the guardians would be most likely to fulfill their true function of defending the state without being deflected by other concerns and would thereby achieve their appropriate virtue of courage.

Justice in the state is therefore just the same as justice in the individual (see illustration on page 137). It is the product of everyone's staying in his place and doing his special task. Justice is the harmony of the virtues of temperance, courage, and wisdom. Since the state is made up of individuals, it will also be necessary for each of these virtues to be attained by each person. For example, even the craftsman must have the virtue of wisdom, not only to keep his appetites in check, but also to know that he rightly belongs where he is and that he must obey the rules. Similarly, as we have seen, the guardians must have sufficient wisdom to know what to fear and what not to fear so that they can develop genuine courage. Most important of all, the ruler must come as close as possible to a knowledge of the Good,* for the well-being of the state depends on his knowledge and character.

THE DECLINE OF THE IDEAL STATE

If the state is "man writ large," then, said Plato, a state will reflect the kind of people a community has become. What he had in mind was that although the nature of man is fixed, in that all men possess a tripartite soul, the kind of men

---

*To see how Plato describes the knowledge of the Good, see pages 255ff.

people become will depend on the degree of internal harmony they achieve. The state will therefore reflect these variations in human character. For this reason, Plato argued that "constitutions cannot come out of stocks and stones; they must result from the preponderance of certain characters which draw the rest of the community in their wake. So if there are five forms of government, there must be five kinds of mental constitution among individuals." And these five forms of government are *aristocracy, timocracy, plutocracy, democracy,* and *despotism.*

Plato considered the transition from aristocracy to despotism as a step-by-step decline in the quality of the state corresponding to a gradual deterioration of the moral character of the rulers and the citizens. His ideal state was, of course, aristocracy, in which the rational element embodied in the philosopher-king was supreme and where each person's reason controlled his appetites. Plato emphasized that this was only an ideal, although significant, nevertheless, as a target to aim at. He was deeply disenchanted with politics, particularly because of the way Athens had executed Socrates and had failed to produce consistently good leaders. "As I gazed upon the whirlpool of public life," he said, "[I] saw clearly in regard to all States now existing that without exception their system of government is bad." Still, the norm for a state is *aristocracy,* for in that form is found the proper subordination of all classes.

Even if this ideal were achieved, however, there would be a possibility for change, since nothing is permanent, and aristocracy would decline first of all into a *timocracy.* This represents a degeneration, for timocracy represents the love of honor, and insofar as an ambitious member of the ruling class loves his own honor more than the common good, the spirited part of his soul has usurped the role of reason. Although this is only a small break in the structure of the soul, it does begin a process whereby the irrational part assumes a progressively larger role. From love of honor to the desire for wealth is a short step, for it means allowing the appetites to rule.

Even under a timocracy there would be the beginning of a system of private property, and this desire for riches paves the way for a *plutocracy,* where power resides in the hands of men whose main concern is wealth. And, says Plato, "as the rich rise in social esteem, the virtuous sink." What is serious about plutocracy, according to Plato, is that it breaks the unity of the state into two contending classes, the rich and the poor. Moreover, the plutocrat is a consumer of goods, and when he has used up his money, he becomes dangerous because he wants more of what he has become accustomed to. The plutocrat is like the person who seeks constant pleasure. But the very nature of pleasure is that it is momentary and must therefore be repeated. There can never be a time of perfect satisfaction; the seeker of pleasure can never be satisfied any more than a leaky pail can be filled. Still, although the plutocrat is torn between many desires, "his better desires will usually keep the upper hand over the worse," and so the plutocrat, says Plato, "presents a more decent appearance than many."

Democracy is a further degeneration, said Plato, for its principles of equality and freedom reflect the degenerate human characters whose whole range of appetites are all pursued with equal freedom. To be sure, Plato's concept of democracy, and his criticism of it, was based on his firsthand experience with the special form democracy took in the small city-state of Athens. Here democracy was direct in that all citizens had the right to participate in the government. The Athenian Assembly consisted, theoretically at least, of all citizens over eighteen years of age. Thus Plato did not have in mind modern liberal and representative democracy. What he saw in his day was rather a mode of direct popular government that clearly violated his notion that the rulership of a state should be in the hands of those with the special talent and training for it. What produced this spirit of equality was the legitimizing of all the appetites under the plutocracy, where the aim of life was to become as rich as possible, and, said Plato, "this insatiable craving would bring about the transition to democracy," for "a society cannot hold wealth in honour and at the same time establish self-control in its citizens."

Even the dogs in a democracy exhibit equality and independence by refusing to move out of the way in the streets. It is, however, when the rich and poor find themselves in a contest under plutocracy that the turning point is reached, for "when the poor win, the result is a democracy." Then "liberty and free speech are rife everywhere; anyone is allowed to do what he likes." Now "you are not obliged to be in authority . . . or to submit to authority, if you do not like it. . . ." All this political equality and freedom stem from a soul whose order has been shattered. It is a soul whose appetites are now all equal and free and act as a "mob" of passions. The life of liberty and equality declares that "one appetite is as good as another and all must have their equal rights."

But the continuous indulgence of the appetites leads one inevitably to the point where a single master passion will finally enslave the soul. One cannot yield to every craving without finally having to yield to the strongest and most persistent passion. At this point we say that a person is under the tyranny of his master passion. Likewise, in the state, the passion for money and pleasures leads the masses to plunder the rich. Since the rich resist, the masses seek out a strong man who will be their champion. But this man demands and acquires absolute power and makes the people his slaves, and only later do the people realize to what depths of subjugation they have fallen. This is the unjust society, the enlargement of the unjust soul. The natural end of democracy is *despotism*.

Aristotle

In his *Politics,* as in his *Ethics,* Aristotle stresses the element of purpose. The state, as man, is endowed by nature with a distinctive function. Combining these two ideas, Aristotle says that "it is evident that the state is a creation of nature, and that man is by nature a political animal." So closely does he relate man and the state that he concludes, "He who is unable to live in society, or who has no need because he is sufficient for himself, must be either a beast or a god." Not only is man by nature destined to live in a state, but the state, as every other community, "is established with a view to some good," exists for some end. The family exists primarily to preserve life. The state comes into existence in the first instance to preserve life for families and villages, which in the long run are not self-sufficing. But beyond this economic end, the function of the state is to ensure the supreme good of man, namely, his moral and intellectual life.

Unlike Plato, Aristotle did not create a blueprint for an ideal state. Even though Aristotle viewed the state as the agency for enabling men to achieve their ultimate goals as human beings, he nevertheless realized that any practical theory of the state must take note of "what kind of government is adapted to particular states . . . [that] the best is often unattainable . . ." and that the legislator must be acquainted with "which is best relatively to circumstances . . . how a state may be constituted under any given conditions . . . [and] how it may be longest preserved," concluding that "political writers, although they have excellent ideas, are often unpractical." For these reasons, Aristotle had little patience with Plato's most radical ideas. Ridiculing Plato's arrangement for the abolition of the family for the guardian class and providing a public nursery for their children, Aristotle said that "there is no reason why the so-called father should care about the son, or the son about the father, or brothers about one another." The communal ownership of property would likewise destroy certain basic human pleasures as well as engender inefficiency and endless disputes.

TYPES OF STATES

Aristotle was willing to recognize that under appropriate circumstances a community could organize itself into at least three different kinds of government. The basic difference between them is primarily the number of rulers each has. A government can have as its rulers either *one,* a *few,* or *many.* But each of these forms of government can have a true or a perverted form. When a government is functioning rightly, it governs for the common good of all the people. A government is perverted when its rulers govern for their own private gain or interests. The true forms of each type of government, according

For biographical note on Aristotle, see p. 29.

to Aristotle, are *monarchy* (one ruler), *aristocracy* (a few rulers), and *polity* (many rulers). The perverted forms are *tyranny* (one), *oligarchy* (few), and *democracy* (many). His own preference was aristocracy, chiefly because even though ideally an individual of exceptional excellence would be desirable, such persons do not exist with sufficient frequency. In an aristocracy, there is the rule of a group of men whose degree of excellence, achievement, and ownership of property makes them responsible, able, and capable of command.

DIFFERENCES AND INEQUALITIES

Because he relied so heavily on his observation of things, it was inevitable that Aristotle would make some mistakes. Nowhere is this more true than in his estimate of slavery. Observing that slaves invariably were strong and large, he concluded that slavery was a product of nature. "It is clear," said Aristotle, "that some men are by nature free, and others slaves, and that for these slavery is both expedient and right." To be sure, Aristotle took great care to distinguish between those who become slaves by nature, a mode he accepted, and those who became slaves by military conquest, a mode he rejected. He rejected slavery by conquest on the highly defensible grounds that to overpower someone does not mean that one is superior to him in nature. Moreover, the use of force may or may not be justified, in which case enslavement could very well be the product and extension of an unjust act. At the same time, speaking of the "proper treatment of slaves," he proposed that "liberty should be always held out to them as the reward of their services." The fact is that in his own last will and testament Aristotle provided for the emancipation of some of his slaves.

Aristotle also believed in the inequality of citizenship. He held that the basic qualification for citizenship was a person's ability to take his share in ruling and being ruled in turn. A citizen had the right and the obligation to participate in the administration of justice. Since a citizen would therefore have to sit in the assembly and in the law courts, he would have to have both ample time as well as an appropriate temperament and character. For this reason, Aristotle did not believe that laborers should be citizens, as they had neither the time nor the appropriate mental development, nor could they benefit from the experience of sharing in the political process.

GOOD GOVERNMENT AND REVOLUTION

Over and over again Aristotle made the point that the state exists for the sake of man's moral and intellectual fulfillment. "A state," he said, "exists for the sake of a good life, and not for the sake of life only"; also, "the state is the union of families and villages in a perfect and self-sufficing life, by which we mean a happy and honourable life." Finally, he said, "our conclusion . . . is that political society exists for the sake of noble actions, and not mere companionship." Still, whether a state produces the good life depends on how its rulers behave. We have already said that the perverted forms of government are distinguished from the true forms by this, that the good rulers seek to achieve the good of all, whereas the perverted rulers seek their own private gain.

Whatever form a government has, it will rest on some conception of justice and proportionate equality. But these conceptions of justice can bring disagreement and ultimately revolution. Democracy, as Aristotle knew it, arises out of the assumption that those who are equal in any respect are equal in all respects; "because men are equally free, they claim to be absolutely equal." On the other hand, Aristotle said that *oligarchy* is based on the notion that "those who are unequal in one respect are in all respects unequal." Hence "being unequal . . . in property, they suppose themselves to be unequal absolutely." For these reasons, whenever the democrats or oligarchs are in the minority and the philosophy of the incumbent government "does not accord with their preconceived ideas, [they] stir up revolution. . . ."

Aristotle concludes that "the universal and chief cause of this revolutionary feeling [is] the desire of equality, when men think they are equal to others who have more than themselves." He did not overlook other causes, such as "insolence and avarice," as well as fear and contempt. Knowing these causes of revolution, Aristotle said that each form of government could take appropriate precautions against it; for example, a king must avoid despotic acts, an aristocracy should avoid the rule by a few rich men for the benefit of the wealthy class, and a polity should provide more time for its abler members to share in the government. Another precaution is to guard against the beginning of change. Most important of all, Aristotle urged that "there is nothing which should be more jealously maintained than the spirit of obedience to law." In the end, men will always criticize the state unless their conditions of living within it are such that they can achieve happiness in the form of what they consider the good life.

Reading _____

The Natural Basis of Society
Aristotle

Every state is a community of some kind, and every community is established with a view to some good; for mankind always act in order to obtain that which they think good. But, if all communities aim at some good, the state or political community, which is the highest of all, and which embraces all the rest, aims and in a greater degree than any other, at the highest good.

Now there is an erroneous opinion that a statesman, king, householder, and master are the same, and that they differ, not in kind, but only in the number of their subjects. For example, the ruler over a few is called a master; over more, the manager of a household; over a still larger number, a statesman or king, as if there were no difference between a great household and a small state. The distinction which is made between the king and the statesman is as follows: When the government is personal, the ruler is a king; when, according to the principles of the political science, the citizens rule and are ruled in turn, then he is called a statesman.

But all this is a mistake; for governments differ in kind, as will be evident to any one who considers the matter according to the method which has hitherto guided us. As in other departments of science, so in politics, the compound should always be resolved into the simple elements or least parts of the whole. We must therefore look at the elements of which the state is composed, in order that we may see in what they differ from one another, and whether any scientific distinction can be drawn between the different kinds of rule.

He who thus considers things in their first growth and origin, whether a state or anything else, will obtain the clearest view of them. In the first place (1) there must be a union of those who cannot exist without each other; for example, of male and female, that the race may continue; and this is a union which is formed, not of deliberate purpose, but because, in common with other animals and with plants, mankind have a natural desire to leave behind them an image of themselves. And (2) there must be a union of natural ruler and subject, that both may be preserved. For he who can foresee with his mind is by nature intended to be lord and master, and he who can work with his body is a subject, and by nature a slave; hence master and slave have the same interest. Nature, however, has distinguished between the female and the slave. For she is not niggardly, like the smith who fashions the Delphian knife for many uses; she makes each thing for a single use, and every instrument is best made when intended for one and not for many uses. But among barbarians no distinction is made between women and slaves, because there is no natural ruler among them: they are a community of slaves, male and female. Wherefore the poets say,—

It is meet that Hellenes should rule over barbarians;

as if they thought that the barbarian and the slave were by nature one.

Out of these two relationships between man and woman, master and slave, the family first arises, and Hesiod is right when he says,—

First house and wife and an ox for the plough,

for the ox is the poor man's slave. The family is the association by nature for the supply of men's every-day wants, and the members of it are called by Charondas "companions of the cupboard" and by Epimenides the Cretan, "companions of the manger." But when several families are united, and the association aims at something more than the supply of daily needs, then comes into existence the village. And the most natural form of the village appears to be that of a colony from the family, composed of the children and grandchildren, who are said to be "suckled with the same milk." And this is the reason why Hellenic states were originally governed by kings; because the Hellenes were under royal rule before they came together, as the barbarians still are. Every family is ruled by the eldest, and therefore in the colonies of the family the kingly form of government prevailed because they were of the same blood.

When several villages are united in single community, perfect and large enough to be nearly or quite self-sufficing, the state comes into existence, originating in the bare needs of life, and continuing in existence for the sake of a good life. And therefore, if the earlier forms of society are natural, so is the state, for it is the end of them, and the (completed) nature is the end. For what each thing is when fully developed, we call its nature, whether we are speaking of a man, a horse, or a family. Besides, the final cause and end of a thing is the best, and to be self-sufficing is the end and the best.

Hence it is evident that the state is a creation of nature, and that man is by nature a political animal. And he who by nature and not by mere accident is without a state, is either above humanity, or below it; he is the

Tribeless, lawless, hearthless one,

whom Homer denounces—the outcast who is a lover of war; he may be compared to an unprotected piece in the game of draughts.

Now the reason why man is more of a political animal than bees or any other gregarious animals is evident. Nature, as we often say, makes nothing in vain, and man is the only animal she has endowed with the gift of speech. And whereas mere sound is but an indication of pleasure or pain, and is therefore found in other animals (for their nature attains to the perception of pleasure and pain and the intimation of them to one another, and no further), the power of speech is intended to set forth the expedient and inexpedient, and likewise the just and the unjust. And it is a characteristic of man that he alone has any sense of good and evil, of just and unjust, and the association of living beings who have this sense makes a family and a state.

Thus the state is by nature clearly prior to the family and to the individual, since the whole is of necessity prior to the part; for example, if the whole body be destroyed, there will be no foot or hand. . . . The proof that the state is a creation of nature and prior to the individual is that the individual, when isolated, is not self-sufficing; and therefore he is like a part in relation to the whole. But he who is unable to live in society, or who has no need because he is sufficient for himself, must be either a beast or a god: he is no part of a state. A social instinct is implanted in all men by nature, and yet he who first founded the state was the greatest of all benefactors. For man, when perfected, is the best of animals, but, when separated from law and justice, he is the worst of all; since armed injustice is the more dangerous, and he is equipped at birth with the arms of intelligence and with moral qualities which he may use for the worst ends. Wherefore, if he have not virtue, he is the most unholy and the most savage of animals, and the most full of lust and gluttony. But justice is the bond of men in states, and the administration of justice, which is the determination of what is just, is the principle of order in political society. . . .

Of forms of democracy first comes that which is said to be based strictly on equality. In such a democracy the law says that it is just for the poor to have no more advantage than the rich; and that neither should be masters, but both equal. For if liberty and equality, as is thought by some, are chiefly to be found in democracy, they will be best attained when all persons alike share in the government to the utmost. And since the people are the majority, and the opinion of the majority is decisive, such a government must necessarily be a democracy. Here then is one sort of democracy. There is another, in which the magistrates are elected according to a certain property qualification, but a low one; he who has the required amount of property has a share in the government, but he who loses his property loses his rights. Another kind is that in which all the citizens who are under no disqualification share in the government, but still the law is supreme. In another, everybody, if he be only a citizen, is admitted to the government, but the law is supreme as before. A fifth form of democracy, in other respects the same, is that in which, not the law, but the multitude, have the supreme power, and supersede the law by their decrees. This is a state of affairs brought about by the demagogues. For in democracies which are subject to the law the best citizens hold the first place, and there are no demagogues; but where the laws are not supreme, there demagogues spring up. For the people becomes a monarch, and is many in one; and the many have the power in their hands, not as individuals, but collectively. Homer says that "it is not good to have a rule of many," but whether he means by this corporate rule, or the rule of many individuals, is uncertain.

At all events this sort of democracy, which is now a monarch, and no longer under the control of law, seeks to exercise monarchical sway, and grows into a despot; the flatterer is held in honour; this sort of democracy being relatively to other democracies what tyranny is to other forms of monarchy. The spirit of both is the same, and they alike exercise a despotic rule over the better citizens. The decrees of the demos correspond to the edicts of the tyrant; and the demagogue is to the one what the flatterer is to the other. Both have great power;—the flatterer with the tyrant, the demagogue with democracies of the kind which we are describing. The demagogues make the decrees of the people override the laws, by referring all things to the popular assembly. And therefore they grow great, because the people have all things in their hands, and they hold in their hands the votes of the people, who are too ready to listen to them. Further, those who have any complaint to bring against the magistrates say, "let the people be judges"; the people are too happy to accept the invitation; and so the authority of every office is undermined. Such a democracy is fairly open to the objection that it is not a constitution at all; for where the laws have no authority, there is no constitution. The law ought to be supreme over all, and the rulers should judge of particulars, and only this should be considered a constitution. . . .

THE FUNCTION OF A STATE

A state exists for the sake of a good life, and not for the sake of life only: if life only were the object, slaves and brute animals might form a state, but they cannot, for they have no share in happiness or in a life of free choice. Nor does a state exist for the sake of alliance and security from injustice, nor yet for the sake of exchange and mutual intercourse; for then the Tyrrhenians and the Carthaginians, and all who have commercial treaties with one another, would be the citizens of one state. True, they have agreements about imports, and engagements that they will do no wrong to one another, and written articles of alliance. But there are no magistracies common to the contracting parties who will enforce their engagements; different states have each their own magistracies. Nor does one state take care that the citizens of the other are such as they ought to be, nor see that those who come under the terms of the treaty do no wrong or wickedness at all, but only that they do no injus– tice to one another. Whereas those who care for good government take into consideration virtue and vice in states. Whence it may be further inferred that virtue must be the care of a state which is truly so called, and not merely enjoys the name: for without this end the community becomes a mere alliance which differs only in place from alliances of which the members live apart. . . .

It is clear then that a state is not a mere society, having a common place, established for the prevention of mutual crime and for the sake of exchange. These are conditions without which a state cannot exist; but all of them together do not constitute a state, which is a community of families and aggregations of families in well-being, for the sake of a perfect and self-sufficing life. Such a community can only be established among those who live in the same place and intermarry. Hence arise in cities family connexions, brotherhoods, common sacrifices, amusements which draw men together. But these are created by friendship, for the will to live together is friendship. The end of the state is the good life, and these are the means towards it. And the state is the union of families and villages in a perfect and self-sufficing life, by which we mean a happy and honourable life.

From Aristotle, *Politics,* trans. Benjamin Jowett, ed. H. W. C. Davis, Clarendon Press, Oxford, Eng., 1905.

QUESTIONS FOR REVIEW AND DISCUSSION

1. Plato says that the state grows out of (is the logical extension of) the nature and structure of the individual. Describe how and why this is the case.
2. What is Plato's "noble lie," which he would use to convince people to accept their place in society?

3. Did Plato allow for any upward or downward movement, from the lowest class to the highest class and vice versa, in his Republic?
4. How did Plato describe democracy? Did he think it was desirable?
5. Who should be the ruler according to Plato?
6. How does Plato define "justice" as applied to the individual and the state?
7. According to Plato, what causes the state (i.e., society) to decline?
8. Aristotle says that "man is by nature a political animal." What does he mean by that?
9. According to Aristotle, what is the function of the state?
10. "It is clear," says Aristotle, "that some men are by nature free, and others slaves." In what way is it "clear" that some should be slaves and also that by nature some should not be citizens?

9

Political Consequences of Biological Differences

Beauvoir, Plato, and Trebilcot

Beauvoir

The political reality is that there is such a thing as sovereignty, that is, the power to dominate. Beauvoir asks, "Why is it that women do not dispute male sovereignty?" The concept of sovereignty implies at least two major parties, the one that dominates and the one that is dominated. There is always the primary party and then various other individuals or groups, classes or races that are dominated. There are, for example, whites, blacks, Jews, Chinese, and the proletariat. All these parties are what they are because they fit into the category of "the other." What Beauvoir notices about these examples of the other is that they do not include the sexes.

The relations between the sexes do not resemble the relations between any other set of parties that make up the sovereign and the others. Even though "otherness" is considered a fundamental category of human thought, there is something unique about the otherness of women. In a small town, those who do not belong to the village are "strangers"; to natives of a country, those who live in other countries are "foreigners"; Jews are "different" for the anti-Semite; proletarians are the "lower class" for the privileged. In all these cases, the other either is a minority or has become the other by virtue of an historic event such as a revolution. In short, the other is "made" the other by the dominant party. The other could have enjoyed dominance or equality in the past, but some historical event transformed it into the other, as though even now there is the possibility of reversing this process whereby the other becomes once again either equal or dominant.

For woman, says Beauvoir, the cause of her otherness is none of the

For biographical information regarding Simone de Beauvoir, see pp. 562–563.

Simone de Beauvoir. *(Pierre Boulat/Time/Life Pictures)*

above. For one thing, women are not a minority, unlike African Americans or Jews. There are about as many women as there are men on this planet. Moreover, both blacks and Jews were originally independent and in some cases have today regained independence. Not only are women not a minority, but the division between the sexes is not the product of an event in history; instead, this division "is a biological fact." Women are women, says Beauvoir by virtue of their anatomy and physiology, and, she says, "throughout history they have always been subordinated to men." That male and female stand opposed is a "primordial" reality. Women do not constitute a separate group similar to the proletariat or bourgeoisie which as a class can think of themselves as separate from other classes. For, says Beauvoir, male and female "is a fundamental unity with its two halves riveted together, and the cleavage of society along the line of sex is impossible."

   Although woman's status as the other, based on biology, has historically had the political consequence of male domination, Beauvoir is not convinced that such dominance is as necessarily fixed as is the biological fact. For there are also at work many creative forces, for example, the fact that "man seeks in woman the Other as Nature and as his fellow being." There is, says Beauvoir, "a whole world of significance which exists only through woman; she is the substance of men's acts and sentiments, the incarnation of all the values that call out their free activity."

Reading _____

The Second Sex

Simone de Beauvoir

Woman? Very simple, say the fanciers of simple formulas: she is a womb, an ovary; she is a female—this word is sufficient to define her. . . .

. . . Woman is a female to the extent that she feels herself as such. There are biologically essential features that are not a part of her real, experienced situation: thus the structure of the egg is not reflected in it, but on the contrary an organ of no great biological importance, like the clitoris, plays in it a part of the first rank. It is not nature that defines woman; it is she who defines herself by dealing with nature on her own account in her emotional life.

[Again] we must ask: what is a woman? *"Tota mulier in utero,"* says one, "woman is a womb." But in speaking of certain women, connoisseurs declare that they are not women, although they are equipped with a uterus like the rest. All agree in recognizing the fact that females exist in the human species; today as always they make up about one half of humanity. And yet we are told that femininity is in danger; we are exhorted to be women, remain women, become women. It would appear, then, that every female human being is not necessarily a woman; to be so considered she must share in that mysterious and threatened reality known as femininity. Is this attribute something secreted by the ovaries? Or is it a Platonic essence, a product of the philosophic imagination? Is a rustling petticoat enough to bring it down to earth? Although some women try zealously to incarnate this essence, it is hardly patentable. It is frequently described in vague and dazzling terms that seem to have been borrowed from the vocabulary of the seers, and indeed in the times of St. Thomas it was considered an essence as certainly defined as the somniferous virtue of the poppy.

But conceptualism has lost ground. The biological and social sciences no longer admit the existence of unchangeably fixed entities that determine given characteristics, such as those ascribed to woman, the Jew, or the Negro. Science regards any characteristic as a reaction dependent in part upon a *situation.* If today femininity no longer exists, then it never existed. But does the word *woman,* then, have no specific content? This is stoutly affirmed by those who hold to the philosophy of the enlightenment, of rationalism, of nominalism; women, to them, are merely the human beings arbitrarily designated by the word *woman.* Many American women particularly are prepared to think that there is no longer any place for woman as such; if a backward individual still takes herself for a woman, her friends advise her to be psychoanalyzed and thus get rid of this obsession. In regard to a work, *Modern Woman: The Lost Sex*, which in other respects has its irritating features, Dorothy Parker has written: "I cannot be just to books which treat of woman as woman. . . . My idea is that all of us, men as well as women, should be regarded as human beings." But nominalism is a rather inadequate doctrine, and the antifemininists have had no trouble in showing that women simply *are not* men. Surely woman is, like man, a human being; but such a declaration is abstract. The fact is that every concrete human being is always a singular, separate individual. To decline to accept such notions as the eternal feminine, the black soul, the Jewish character, is not to deny that Jews, Negroes, women exist today—this denial does not represent a liberation for those concerned, but rather a flight from reality. Some years ago a well-known woman writer refused to permit her portrait to appear in a series of photographs especially devoted to women writers; she wished to be counted among the men. But in order to gain this privilege she made use of her husband's influence! Women who assert that they are men lay claim none the less to masculine consideration and respect. I recall also a young Trotskyite standing on a platform at a boisterous meeting and getting ready to use her fists, in spite of her evident fragility. She was denying her feminine weakness; but it was for love of a militant male whose equal she wished to be. The attitude of defiance of many American women proves that they are haunted by a sense of their femininity. In truth, to go for a walk with one's eyes open is enough to demonstrate that humanity is divided into two classes of individuals whose clothes, faces, bodies, smiles, gaits, interests, and occupations are manifestly different. Perhaps these differences are superficial, perhaps they are destined to disappear. What is certain is that right now they do most obviously exist.

If her functioning as a female is not enough to define woman, if we decline also to explain her through "the eternal feminine," and if nevertheless we admit, provisionally, that women do exist, then we must face the question: what is a woman?

To state the question is, to me, to suggest, at once, a preliminary answer. The fact that I ask it is in itself significant. A man would never get the notion of writing a book on the peculiar situation of the human male. But if I wish to define myself, I must first of all say: "I am a woman"; on this truth must be based all further discussion. A man never begins by presenting himself as an individual of a certain sex; it goes without saying that he is a man. The terms *masculine* and *feminine* are used symmetrically only as a matter of form, as on legal papers. In actuality the relation of the two sexes is not quite like that of two electrical poles, for man represents both the positive and the neutral, as is indicated by the common use of *man* to designate human beings in general; whereas woman represents only the negative, defined by limiting criteria, without reciprocity. In the midst of an abstract discussion it is vexing to hear a man say: "You think thus and so because you are a woman"; but I know that my only defense is to reply: "I think thus and so because it is true," thereby removing my subjective self from the argument. It would be out of the question to reply: "And you think the contrary because you are a man," for it is understood that the fact of being a man is no peculiarity. A man is in the right in being a man; it is the woman who is in the wrong. It amounts to this: just as for the ancients there was an absolute vertical with reference to which the oblique was defined, so there is an absolute human type, the masculine. Woman has ovaries, a uterus; these peculiarities imprison her in her subjectivity, circumscribe her within the limits of her own nature. It is often said that she thinks with her glands. Man superbly ignores the fact that his anatomy also includes glands, such as the testicles, and that they secrete hormones. He thinks of his body as a direct and normal connection with the world, which he believes he apprehends objectively, whereas he regards the body of woman as a hindrance, a prison, weighed down by everything peculiar to it. "The female is a female by virtue of a certain *lack* of qualities," said Aristotle; "we should regard the female nature as afflicted with a natural defectiveness." And St. Thomas for his part pronounced woman to be an "imperfect man," an "incidental" being. This is symbolized in Genesis where Eve is depicted as made from what Bossuet called "a supernumerary bone" of Adam.

Thus humanity is male and man defines woman not in herself but as relative to him; she is not regarded as an autonomous being. Michelet writes: "Woman, the relative being. . . ." And Benda is most positive in his *Rapport d'Uriel:* "The body of man makes sense in itself quite apart from that of woman, whereas the latter seems wanting in significance by itself. . . . Man can think of himself without woman. She cannot think of herself without man." And she is simply what man decrees; thus she is called "the sex," by which is meant that she appears essentially to the male as a sexual being. For him she is sex—absolute sex, no less. She is defined and differentiated with reference to man and not he with reference to her; she is the incidental, the inessential as opposed to the essential. He is the Subject, he is the Absolute— she is the Other.

The category of the *Other* is as primordial as consciousness itself. In the most primitive societies, in the most ancient mythologies, one finds the expression of a duality—that of the Self and the Other. This duality was not originally attached to the division of the sexes; it was not dependent upon any empirical facts. It is revealed in such works as that of Granet on Chinese thought and those of Dumézil on the East Indies and Rome. The feminine element was at first no more involved in such pairs as Varuna-Mitra, Uranus-Zeus, Sun-Moon, and Day-Night than it was in the contrasts between Good and Evil, lucky and unlucky auspices, right and left, God and Lucifer. Otherness is a fundamental category of human thought.

Thus it is that no group ever sets itself up as the One without at once setting up the Other over against itself. If three travelers chance to occupy the same compartment, that is enough to make vaguely hostile "others" out of all the rest of the passengers on the train. In small-town eyes all per-sons not belonging to the village are "strangers" and suspect; to the native of a country all who inhabit other countries are "foreigners"; Jews are "different" for the anti-Semite, Negroes are "inferior" for American racists, aborigines are "natives" for colonists, proletarians are the "lower class" for the privileged. . . .

. . . Why is it that women do not dispute male sovereignty? No subject will readily volunteer to become the object, the inessential; it is not the Other who, in defining himself as the Other, establishes the One. The Other is posed as such by the One in defining himself as the One. But if the Other is not to regain the status of being the One, he must be submissive enough to accept this alien point of view. Whence comes this submission in the case of woman?

There are, to be sure, other cases in which a certain category has been able to dominate another completely for a time. Very often this privilege depends upon inequality of numbers—the majority imposes its rule upon the minority or persecutes it. But women are not a minority, like the American Negroes or the Jews; there are as many women as men on earth. Again, the two groups concerned have often been originally independent; they may have been formerly unaware of each other's existence, or perhaps they recognized each other's autonomy. But a historical event has resulted in the subjugation of the weaker by the stronger. The scattering of the Jews, the introduction of slavery into America, the conquests of imperialism are examples in point. In these cases the oppressed retained at least the memory of former days; they possessed in common a past, a tradition, sometimes a religion or a culture.

The parallel drawn by Bebel between women and the proletariat is valid in that neither ever formed a minority or a separate collective unit of mankind. And instead of a single historical event it is in both cases a historical development that explains their status as a class and accounts for the membership of *particular individuals* in that class. But proletarians have not always existed, whereas there have always been women. They are women in virtue of their anatomy and physiology. Throughout history they have always been subordinated to men, and hence their dependency is not the result of a historical event or a social change—it was not something that *occurred.* The reason why otherness in this case seems to be an absolute is in part that it lacks the contingent or incidental nature of historical facts. A condition brought about at a certain time can be abolished at some other time, as the Negroes of Haiti and others have proved; but it might seem that a natural condition is beyond the possibility of change. In truth, however, the nature of things is no more immutably given, once for all, than is historical reality. If woman seems to be the inessential which never becomes the essential, it is because she herself fails to bring about this change. Proletarians say "We"; Negroes also. Regarding themselves as subjects, they transform the bourgeois, the whites, into "others." But women do not say "We," except at some congress of feminists or similar formal demonstration; men say "women," and women use the same word in referring to themselves. They do not authentically assume a subjective attitude. The proletarians have accomplished the revolution in Russia, the Negroes in Haiti, the Indo-Chinese are battling for it in Indo-China; but the women's effort has never been anything more than a symbolic agitation. They have gained only what men have been willing to grant; they have taken nothing, they have only received.

The reason for this is that women lack concrete means for organizing themselves into a unit which can stand face to face with the correlative unit. They have no past, no history, no religion of their own; and they have no such solidarity of work and interest as that of the proletariat. They are not even promiscuously herded together in the way that creates community feeling among the American Negroes, the ghetto Jews, the workers of Saint-Denis, or the factory hands of Renault. They live dispersed among the males, attached through residence, housework, economic condition, and social standing to certain men—fathers or husbands—more firmly than they are to other women. If they belong to the bourgeoisie, they feel solidarity with men of that class, not with proletarian women; if they are white, their allegiance is to white men, not to Negro women. The proletariat can propose to massacre the ruling class, and a sufficiently fanatical Jew or Negro might dream of getting sole possession of the atomic bomb and making humanity wholly Jewish or black; but woman cannot even dream of exterminating the males. The bond that unites her to her oppressors is not comparable to any other. The division of the sexes is a biological fact, not an event in human history. Male and female stand opposed within a primordial *Mitsein*, and woman has not broken it. The couple is a fundamental unity with its two halves riveted together, and the cleavage of society along the line of sex is impossible. Here is to be found the basic trait of woman: she is the Other in a totality of which the two components are necessary to one another.

This has always been a man's world; and none of the reasons hitherto brought forward in explanation of this fact has seemed adequate. But we shall be able to understand how the hierarchy of the sexes was established by reviewing the data of prehistoric research and ethnography in the light of existentialist philosophy. I have already stated that when two human categories are together, each aspires to impose its sovereignty upon the other. If both are able to resist this imposition, there is created between them a reciprocal relation, sometimes in enmity, sometimes in amity, always in a state of tension. If one of the two is in some way privileged, has some advantage, this one prevails over the other and undertakes to keep it in subjection. It is therefore understandable that man would wish to dominate woman; but what advantage has enabled him to carry out his will?

The accounts of the primitive forms of human society provided by ethnographers are extremely contradictory, the more so as they are better informed and less systematized. It is peculiarly difficult to form an idea of woman's situation in the pre-agricultural period. We do not even know whether woman's musculature or her respiratory apparatus, under conditions different from those of today, were not as well developed as in man. She had hard work to do, and in particular it was she who carried the burdens. This last fact is of doubtful significance; it is likely that if she was assigned this function, it was because a man kept his hands free on the trail in order to defend himself against possible aggressors, animal or human; his role was the more dangerous and the one that demanded more vigor. It would appear, nevertheless, that in many cases the women were strong and tough enough to take part in the warriors' expeditions. We need recall only the tales of Herodotus and the more recent accounts of the amazons of Dahomey to realize that woman has shared in warfare—and with no less ferocity and cruelty than man; but even so, man's superior strength must have been of tremendous importance in the age of the club and the wild beast. In any case, however strong the women were, the bondage of reproduction was a terrible handicap in the struggle against a hostile world. Pregnancy, childbirth, and menstruation reduced their capacity for work and made them at times wholly dependent upon the men for protection and food. As there was obviously no birth control, and as nature failed to provide women with sterile periods like other mammalian females, closely spaced maternities must have absorbed most of their strength and their time, so that they were incapable of providing for the children they brought into the world. Here we have a first fact heavily freighted with consequences: the early days of the human species were difficult; the gathering, hunting, and fishing peoples got only meager products from the soil and those with great effort; too many children were born for the group's resources; the extravagant fertility of woman prevented her from active participation in the increase of these resources while she created new needs to an indefinite extent. Necessary as she was for the perpetuation of the species, she perpetuated it too generously, and so it was man who had to assure equilibrium between reproduction and production. Even in times when humanity most needed births, when maternity was most venerated, manual labor was the primary necessity, and woman was never permitted to take first place. The primitive hordes had no permanence in property or territory, and hence set no store by posterity; children were for them a burden, not a prized possession. Infanticide was common among the nomads, and many of the newborn that escaped massacre died from lack of care in the general state of indifference.

The woman who gave birth, therefore, did not know the pride of creation; she felt herself the plaything of obscure forces, and the painful ordeal of childbirth seemed a useless or even troublesome accident. But in any case giving birth and suckling are not *activities*, they are natural functions; no project is involved; and that is why woman found in them no reason for a lofty affirmation of her existence—she submitted passively to her biologic fate. The domestic labors that fell to her lot because they were reconcilable with the cares of maternity imprisoned her in repetition and immanence; they were repeated from day to day in an identical form, which was perpetuated almost without change from century to century; they produced nothing new.

Man's case was radically different; he furnished support for the group, not in the manner of worker bees by a simple vital process, through biological behavior, but by means of acts that transcended his animal nature. *Homo faber* has from the beginning of time been an inventor: the stick and the club with which he armed himself to knock down fruits and to slaughter animals became forthwith instruments for enlarging his grasp upon the world. He did not limit himself to bringing home the fish he caught in the sea: first he had to conquer the watery realm by means of the dugout canoe fashioned from a tree-trunk; to get at the riches of the world he annexed the world itself. In this activity he put his power to the test; he set up goals and opened up roads toward them; in brief, he found self-realization as an existent. To maintain, he created; he burst out of the present, he opened the future. This is the reason why fishing and hunting expeditions had a sacred character. Their successes were celebrated with festivals and triumphs, and therein man gave recognition to his human estate. Today he still manifests this pride when he has built a dam or a skyscraper or an atomic pile. He has worked not merely to conserve the world as given; he has broken through its frontiers, he has laid down the foundations of a new future.

Early man's activity had another dimension that gave it supreme dignity: it was often dangerous. If blood were but a nourishing fluid, it would be valued no higher than milk; but the hunter was no butcher, for in the struggle against wild animals he ran grave risks. The warrior put his life in jeopardy to elevate the prestige of the horde, the clan to which he belonged. And in this he proved dramatically that life is not the supreme value for man, but on the contrary that it should be made to serve ends more important than itself. The worst curse that was laid upon woman was that she should be excluded from these warlike forays. For it is not in giving life but in risking life that man is raised above the animal; that is why superiority has been accorded in humanity not to the sex that brings forth but to that which kills.

Here we have the key to the whole mystery. . . .

"To be a woman," says Kierkegaard in *Stages on the Road of Life*, "is something so strange, so confused, so complicated, that no one predicate comes near expressing it and that the multiple predicates that one would like to use are so contradictory that only a woman could put up with it." This comes from not regarding woman positively, such as she seems to herself to be, but negatively, such as she appears to man. For if woman is not the only *Other*, it remains none the less true that she is always defined as the Other. And her ambiguity is just that of the concept of the Other: it is that of the human situation in so far as it is defined in its relation with the Other. As I have already said, the Other is Evil; but being necessary to the Good, it turns into the Good; through it I attain to the Whole, but it also separates me therefrom; it is the gateway to the infinite and the measure of my finite nature. And here lies the reason why woman incarnates no stable concept; through her is made unceasingly the passage from hope to frustration, from hate to love, from good to evil, from evil to good. Under whatever aspect we may consider her, it is this ambivalence that strikes us first. . . .

. . . Man seeks in woman the Other as Nature and as his fellow being. But we know what ambivalent feelings Nature inspires in man. He exploits her, but she crushes him, he is born of her and dies in her; she is the source of his being and the realm that he subjugates to his will; Nature is a vein of gross material in which the soul is imprisoned, and she is the supreme reality; she is contingence and Idea, the finite and the whole; she is what opposes the Spirit, and the Spirit itself. Now ally, now enemy, she appears as the dark chaos from whence life wells up, as this life itself, and as the over-yonder toward which life tends. Woman sums up nature as Mother, Wife, and Idea. . . .

. . . There is a whole world of significance which exists only through woman; she is the substance of men's acts and sentiments, the incarnation of all the values that call out their free activity. It is understandable that, were he condemned to the most cruel disappointments, man would not be willing to relinquish a dream within which all his dreams are enfolded.

. . . [Woman] is all that man desires and all that he does not attain. She is the good mediatrix between propitious Nature and man; and she is the temptation of unconquered Nature, counter to all goodness. She incarnates all moral values, from good to evil, and their opposites; she is the substance of action and whatever is an obstacle to it, she is man's grasp on the world and his frustration; as such she is the source and origin of all man's reflection on his existence and of whatever expression he is able to give to it; and yet she works to divert him from himself, to make him sink down in silence and in death. She is servant and companion, but he expects her also to be his audience and critic and to confirm him in his sense of being; but she opposes him with her indifference, even with her mockery and laughter. He projects upon her what he desires and what he fears, what he loves and what he hates. And if it is so difficult to say anything specific about her, that is because man seeks the whole of himself in her and because she is All. She is All, that is, on the plane of the inessential; she is all the Other. And, as the other, she is other than herself, other than what is expected of her. Being all, she is never quite *this* which she should be; she is everlasting deception, the very deception of that existence which is never successfully attained nor fully reconciled with the totality of existents.

Plato

Plato visualized an ideal society in which each individual was assigned a specific function. These assignments were not considered arbitrary but were, rather, seen as a requirement of nature. By nature some were qualified to rule, others were to be in the guardian class, while still others were to be farmers and artisans. So seriously did Plato take this stratification that he fashioned a

For biographical note on Plato, see p. 135.

prophecy that "ruin will come upon the state" if the ruler is drawn from the class of those composed of "iron or brass" instead of from the offspring of "golden parents." He acknowledged that children do not always possess the quality of their parents. For this reason, the Rulers [those of golden mixture] "must, without the smallest pity," assign their less talented offspring "to the station proper to his nature and thrust him among the craftsmen and farmers." This mobility of children to a lower level occurs also in the opposite direction so that if the parents among the farmers or artisans produce a child more gifted than themselves, the Rulers "will promote [them] according to [their] value. . . ."

How, then, should this argument from nature affect the assignments of women? Plato raises the question using the analogy of watchdogs: "Should the females guard the flock and hunt with the males and take a share in all they do, or should they be kept within doors as fit for no more than bearing and feeding their puppies?" Plato sees no reason why in his society women cannot be equal with men with the exception that some functions might be limited to men because of the difference in strength between the sexes. Accordingly, says Plato, "if we are to set women to the same tasks as men, we must teach them the same things. They must have the same two branches of training for mind and body and also be taught the art of war, and they must receive the same treatment." While expressing these views in his *Republic*, Plato was aware that "if these proposals are carried out, they might be ridiculed as involving a good many breaches of custom."

Reading ───

The Equality of Women
Plato

Let us state his case for him. "Socrates and Glaucon," he will say, "there is no need for others to dispute your position; you yourselves, at the very outset of founding your commonwealth, agreed that everyone should do the one work for which nature fits him." Yes, of course; I suppose we did. "And isn't there a very great difference in nature between man and woman?" Yes, surely. "Does not that natural difference imply a corresponding difference in the work to be given to each?" Yes. "But if so, surely you must be mistaken now and contradicting yourselves when you say that men and women, having such widely divergent natures, should do the same things?" What is your answer to that, my ingenious friend? . . .

Come then, let us see if we can find the way out. We did agree that different natures should have different occupations, and that the natures of man and woman are different; and yet we are now saying that these different natures are to have the same occupations. Is that the charge against us?

Exactly.

. . . but we have altogether neglected to consider what sort of sameness or difference we meant and in what respect these natures and occupations were to be defined as different or the same. Consequently, we might very well be asking one another whether there is not an opposition in nature between bald and long-haired men, and, when that was admitted, forbid one set to be shoemakers, if the other were following that trade.

That would be absurd.

Yes, but only because we never meant any and every sort of sameness or difference in nature, but the sort that was relevant to the occupations in question. We meant, for instance, that a man and a woman have the same nature if both have a talent for medicine; whereas two men have different natures if one is a born physician, the other a born carpenter.

Yes, of course.

If, then, we find that either the male sex or the female is specially qualified for any particular form of occupation, then that occupation, we shall say, ought to be assigned to one sex or the other. But if the only difference appears to be that the male begets and the female brings forth, we shall conclude that no difference between man and woman has yet been produced that is relevant to our purpose. We shall continue to think it proper for our Guardians and their wives to share in the same pursuits.

And quite rightly.

The next thing will be to ask our opponent to name any profession or occupation in civic life for the purposes of which woman's nature is different from man's.

That is a fair question. . . .

Suppose, then, we invite him to follow us and see if we can convince him that there is no occupation concerned with the management of social affairs that is peculiar to women. We will confront him with a question: When you speak of a man having a natural talent for something, do you mean that he finds it easy to learn, and after a little instruction can find out much more for himself; whereas a man who is not so gifted learns with difficulty and no amount of instruction and practice will make him even remember what he has been taught? Is the talented man one whose bodily powers are readily at the service of his mind, instead of being a hindrance? Are not these the marks by which you distinguish the presence of a natural gift for any pursuit?

Yes, precisely.

Now do you know of any human occupation in which the male sex is not superior to the female in all these respects? Need I waste time over exceptions like weaving and watching over saucepans and batches of cakes, though women are supposed to be good at such things and get laughed at when a man does them better?

It is true, he replied, in almost everything one sex is easily beaten by the other. No doubt many women are better at many things than many men; but taking the sexes as a whole, it is as you say.

To conclude, then, there is no occupation concerned with the management of social affairs which belongs either to woman or to man, as such. Natural gifts are to be found here and there in both creatures alike; and every occupation is open to both, so far as their natures are concerned, though woman is for all purposes the weaker.

Certainly.

Is that a reason for making over all occupations to men only?

Of course not.

No, because one woman may have a natural gift for medicine or for music, another may not.

Surely.

Is it not also true that a woman may, or may not, be warlike or athletic?

I think so.

And again, one may love knowledge, another hate it; one may be high-spirited, another spiritless?

True again.

It follows that one woman will be fitted by nature to be a Guardian, another will not; because these were the qualities for which we selected our men Guardians. So for the purpose of keeping watch over the commonwealth, woman has the same nature as man, save in so far as she is weaker.

So it appears.

It follows that women of this type must be selected to share the life and duties of Guardians with men of the same type, since they are competent and of a like nature, and the same natures must be allowed the same pursuits.

Yes.

We come round, then, to our former position, that there is nothing contrary to nature in giving our Guardians' wives the same training for mind and body. The practice we proposed to establish was not impossible or visionary, since it was in accordance with nature. Rather, the contrary practice which now prevails turns out to be unnatural.

So it appears. . . .

Now, for the purpose of producing a woman fit to be a Guardian, we shall not have one education for men and another for women, precisely because the nature to be taken in hand is the same.

True. . . .

Plato, "The Equality of Woman," *The Republic,* trans. F. M. Cornford, Oxford University Press, New York and London, 1953, pp. 150–154.

Joyce Trebilcot

In this article, Joyce Trebilcot, a professor of philosophy at Washington University, asks whether psychological differences between the sexes are relevant to whether there should be sex roles. By a "sex role" she means "a role performed only or primarily by persons of a particular sex." At stake here is the question whether society should direct men and women into certain roles and away from others. The underlying assumption is that there is a correlation between psychological states, on the one hand, and modes of behavior on the other. If there are psychological differences between the sexes, there will also be differences in the behavior between the sexes. Therefore the real question is whether society should enforce this correlation.

Trebilcot deals with three attempts to show that it is appropriate for society to enforce what is assumed to be a natural correlation between certain roles and the sexes, respectively. *First,* there are those who say that if there are certain natural or innate psychological differences between females and males, then different roles are *inevitable.* But does it follow, she asks, that society should enforce this "natural" assignment of roles? Trebilcot cites John Stuart Mill, who in response this question said, "The anxiety of mankind to interfere in behalf of nature, for fear that nature should not succeed in effecting its purpose, is an altogether unnecessary solicitude." *Secondly,* there is the argument from *well-being,* which holds that each sex is happier in certain roles than in others, and that different roles are required to promote the happiness of each sex. If, moreover, the choices of roles were left to each sex, with all roles being openly available, some individuals might choose contrary to their well-being. To avoid such errors, society should encourage each individual to make the "correct" role choice. But does society possess adequate knowledge to ensure the right choice of sex roles? *Finally,* there is the argument from *efficiency,* which says that efficiency is served if socially valuable tasks are assigned to the sex which possesses the greatest innate ability for them. This argument requires various kinds of evidence to show such a correlation between sex and efficiency regarding various tasks.

All three of the above arguments from inevitability, well-being, and efficiency must be considered, says Professor Trebilcot, in relation to other values, including freedom of individual choice, the question of justice, and the value of equal opportunity. She concludes that from her perspective "the question is, after all, not what women and men naturally are, but what kind of society is morally justifiable."

Reading _____

Sex Roles: The Argument from Nature
Joyce Trebilcot

I am concerned here with the normative question of whether, in an ideal society, certain roles should be assigned to females and others to males. In discussions of this issue, a great deal of attention is given to the claim that there are natural psychological differences between the sexes. Those who hold that at least some roles should be sex roles generally base their view primarily on an appeal to such natural differences, while many of those advocating a society without sex roles argue either that the sexes do not differ in innate psychological traits or that there is no evidence that they do. In this paper I argue that whether there are natural psychological differences between females and males has little bearing on the issue of whether society should reserve certain roles for females and others for males.

Let me begin by saying something about the claim that there are natural psychological differences between the sexes. The issue we are dealing with arises, of course, because there are biological differences among human beings which are bases for designating some as females and others as males. Now it is held by some that, in addition to biological differences between the sexes, there are also natural differences in temperament, interests, abilities, and the like. In this paper I am concerned only with arguments which appeal to these psychological differences as bases of sex roles. Thus, I exclude, for example, arguments that the role of jockey should be female because women are smaller than men or that boxers should be male because men are more muscular than women. Nor do I discuss arguments which appeal directly to the reproductive functions peculiar to each sex. If the physiological processes of gestation or of depositing sperm in a vagina are, apart from any psychological correlates they may have, bases for sex roles, these roles are outside the scope of the present discussion.

It should be noted, however, that virtually all those who hold that there are natural psychological differences between the sexes assume that these differences are determined primarily by differences in biology. According to one hypothesis, natural psychological differences between the sexes are due at least in part to differences between female and male nervous systems. As the male fetus develops in the womb, the testes secrete a hormone which is held to influence the growth of the central nervous system. The female fetus does not produce this hormone, nor is there an analogous female hormone which is significant at this stage. Hence it is suggested that female and male brains differ in structure, that this difference is due to the prenatal influence of testicular hormone and that the difference in brains is the basis of some later differences in behavior.

A second view about the origin of allegedly natural psychological differences between the sexes, a view not incompatible with the first, is psychoanalytical. It conceives of feminine or masculine behavior as, in part, the individual's response to bodily structure. On this view, one's more or less unconscious experience of one's own body (and in some versions, of the bodies of others) is a major factor in producing sex-specific personality traits. The classic theories of this kind are, of course, Freud's: penis envy and the castration complex are supposed to arise largely from perceptions of differences between female and male bodies. Other writers make much of the analogies between genitals and genders: the uterus is passive and receptive, and so are females; penises are active and penetrating, and so are males. But here we are concerned not with the etiology of allegedly natural differences between the sexes but rather with the question of whether such differences, if they exist, are grounds for holding that there should be sex roles.

That a certain psychological disposition is natural only to one sex is generally taken to mean in part that members of that sex are more likely to have the disposition, or to have it to a greater degree, than persons of the other sex. The situation is thought to be similar to that of height. In a given population, females are on the average shorter than males, but some females are taller than some males, as suggested by figure 1.

The shortest members of the population are all females, and the tallest are all males, but there is an area of overlap. For psychological traits, it is usually assumed that there is some degree of overlap and that the degree of overlap is different for different characteristics. Because of the difficulty of identifying natural psychological characteristics, we have of course little or no data as to the actual distribution of such traits.

I shall not undertake here to define the concept of role, but examples include voter, librarian, wife, president. A broad concept of role might also comprise, for example, being a joker, a person who walks gracefully, a compassionate person. The genders, femininity and masculinity, may also be conceived as roles. On this view, each of the gender roles includes a number of more specific sex roles, some of which may be essential to it. For example, the concept of femininity may be construed in such a way that it is necessary to raise a child in order to be fully feminine, while other feminine roles—teacher, nurse, charity worker—are not essential to gender. In the arguments discussed below, the focus is on sex roles rather than genders, but, on the assumption that the genders are roles, much of what is said applies, *mutatis mutandis*, to them.

A sex role is a role performed only or primarily by persons of a particular sex. Now if this is all we mean by "sex role," the problem of whether there should be sex roles must be dealt with as two separate issues: "Are sex roles a good thing?" and "Should society enforce sex roles?" One might argue, for example, that sex roles have value but that, even so, the demands of individual autonomy and freedom are such that societal institutions and practices should not enforce correlations between roles and sex. But the debate over sex roles is of course mainly a discussion about the second question, whether society should enforce these correlations. The judgment that there should be sex roles is generally taken to mean not just that sex-exclusive roles are a good thing, but that society should promote such exclusivity.

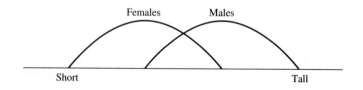

In view of this, I use the term "sex role" in such a way that to ask whether there should be sex roles is to ask whether society should direct women into certain roles and away from others, and similarly for men. A role is a sex role then (or perhaps an "institutionalized sex role") only if it is performed exclusively or primarily by persons of a particular sex *and* societal factors tend to encourage this correlation. These factors may be of various kinds. Parents guide children into what are taken to be sex-appropriate roles. Schools direct students into occupations according to sex. Marriage customs prescribe different roles for females and males. Employers and unions may refuse to consider applications from persons of the "wrong" sex. The media carry tales of the happiness of those who conform and the suffering of the others. The law sometimes penalizes deviators. Individuals may ridicule and condemn role crossing and smile on conformity. Societal sanctions such as these are essential to the notion of sex role employed here.

I turn now to a discussion of the three major ways the claim that there are natural psychological differences between the sexes is held to be relevant to the issue of whether there should be sex roles.

1 INEVITABILITY

It is sometimes held that if there are innate psychological differences between females and males, sex roles are inevitable. The point of this argument is not, of course, to urge that there should be sex roles, but rather to show that the normative question is out of place, that there will be sex roles, whatever we decide. The argument assumes first that the alleged natural differences between the sexes are inevitable; but if such differences are inevitable, differences in behavior are inevitable; and if differences in behavior are inevitable, society will inevitably be structured so as to enforce role differences according to sex. Thus, sex roles are inevitable.

For the purpose of this discussion, let us accept the claim that natural psychological differences are inevitable. We assume that there are such differences and ignore the possibility of their being altered, for example, by evolutionary change or direct biological intervention. Let us also accept the second claim, that behavioral differences are inevitable. Behavioral differences could perhaps be eliminated even given the assumption of natural differences in disposition (for example, those with no natural inclination to a certain kind of behavior might nevertheless learn it), but let us waive this point. We assume then that behavioral differences, and hence also role differences, between the sexes are inevitable. Does it follow that there must be sex roles, that is, that the institutions and practices of society must enforce correlations between roles and sex?

Surely not. Indeed, such sanctions would be pointless. Why bother to direct women into some roles and men into others if the pattern occurs regardless of the nature of society? Mill makes the point elegantly in *The Subjection of Women:* "The anxiety of mankind to interfere in behalf of nature, for fear lest nature should not succeed in effecting its purpose, is an altogether unnecessary solicitude."

It may be objected that if correlations between sex and roles are inevitable, societal sanctions enforcing these correlations will develop because people will expect the sexes to perform different roles and these expectations will lead to behavior which encourages their fulfillment. This can happen, of course, but it is surely not inevitable. One need not act so as to bring about what one expects.

Indeed, there could be a society in which it is held that there are inevitable correlations between roles and sex but institutionalization of these correlations is deliberately avoided. What is inevitable is presumably not, for example, that every woman will perform a certain role and no man will perform it, but rather that most women will perform the role and most men will not. For any individual, then, a particular role may not be inevitable. Now suppose it is a value in the society in question that people should be free to choose roles according to their individual needs and interests. But then there should not be sanctions enforcing correlations between roles and sex, for such sanctions tend to force some individuals into roles for which they have no natural inclination and which they might otherwise choose against.

I conclude then that, even granting the assumptions that natural psychological differences, and therefore role differences, between the sexes are inevitable, it does not follow that there must be sanctions enforcing correlations between roles and sex. Indeed, if individual freedom is valued, those who vary from the statistical norm should not be required to conform to it.

2 WELL-BEING

The argument from well-being begins with the claim that, because of natural psychological differences between the sexes, members of each sex are happier in certain roles than in others, and the roles which tend to promote happiness are different for each sex. It is also held that if all roles are equally available to everyone regardless of sex, some individuals will choose against their own well-being. Hence, the argument concludes, for the sake of maximizing well-being there should be sex roles: society should encourage individuals to make "correct" role choices.

Suppose that women, on the average, are more compassionate than men. Suppose also that there are two sets of roles, "female" and "male," and that because of the natural compassion of women, women are happier in female than in male roles. Now if females and males overlap with respect to compassion, some men have as much natural compassion as some women, so they too will be happier in female than in male roles. Thus, the first premise of the argument from well-being should read: Suppose that, because of natural psychological differences between the sexes, *most* women are happier in female roles and *most* men in male roles. The argument continues: If all roles are equally available to everyone, some of the women who would be happier in female roles will choose against their own well-being, and similarly for men.

Now if the conclusion that there should be sex roles is to be based on these premises, another assumption must be added—that the loss of potential well-being resulting from societally produced adoption of unsuitable roles by individuals in the overlapping areas of the distribution is *less* than the loss that would result from "mistaken" free choices if there were no sex roles. With sex roles, some individuals who would be happier in roles assigned to the other sex perform roles assigned to their own sex, and so there is a loss of potential happiness. Without sex roles, some individuals, we assume, choose against their own well-being. But surely we are not now in a position to compare the two systems with respect to the number of mismatches produced. Hence the additional premise required for the argument, that overall well-being is greater with sex roles than without them, is entirely unsupported.

Even if we grant, then, that because of innate psychological differences between the sexes members of each sex achieve greater well-being in some roles than in others, the argument from well-being does not support the conclusion that there should be sex roles. In our present state of knowledge, there is no reason to suppose that a sex role system which makes no discriminations within a sex would produce fewer mismatches between individuals and roles than a system in which all roles are open equally to both sexes.

3 EFFICIENCY

If there are natural differences between the sexes in the capacity to perform socially valuable tasks, then, it is sometimes argued, efficiency is served if these tasks are assigned to the sex with the greatest innate ability for them. Suppose, for example, that females are naturally better than males at learning foreign languages. This means that, if everything else is equal and females and males are given the same training in a foreign language, females, on the average, will achieve a higher level of skill than males. Now suppose that society needs interpreters and translators and that in order to have such a job one must complete a special training program whose only purpose is to provide persons for these roles. Clearly, efficiency is served if only individuals with a good deal of natural ability are selected for training, for the time and effort required to bring them to a given level of proficiency is less than that required for the less talented. But suppose that the innate ability in question is normally distributed within each sex and that the sexes overlap (see fig. 2). If we assume that a sufficient number of candidates can be recruited by considering only persons in the shaded area, they are the only ones who

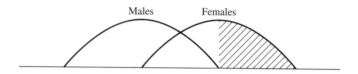

should be eligible. There are no men in this group. Hence, although screening is necessary in order to exclude nontalented women, it would be inefficient even to consider men, for it is known that no man is as talented as the talented women. In the interest of efficiency, then, the occupational roles of interpreter and translator should be sex roles; men should be denied access to these roles but women who are interested in them, especially talented women, should be encouraged to pursue them.

This argument is sound. That is, if we grant the factual assumptions and suppose also that efficiency for the society we are concerned with has some value, the argument from efficiency provides one reason for holding that some roles should be sex roles. This conclusion of course is only prima facie. In order to determine whether there should be sex roles, one would have to weigh efficiency, together with other reasons for such roles, against reasons for holding that there should not be sex roles. The reasons against sex roles are very strong. They are couched in terms of individual rights—in terms of liberty, justice, equality of opportunity. Efficiency by itself does not outweigh these moral values. Nevertheless, the appeal to nature, if true, combined with an appeal to the value of efficiency, does provide one reason for the view that there should be sex roles.

The arguments I have discussed here are not the only ones which appeal to natural psychological differences between the sexes in defense of sex roles, but these three arguments—from inevitability, well-being, and efficiency—are, I believe, the most common and the most plausible ones. The argument from efficiency alone, among them, provides a reason—albeit a rather weak reason—for thinking that there should be sex roles. I suggest, therefore, that the issue of natural psychological differences between women and men does not deserve the central place it is given, both traditionally and currently, in the literature on this topic.

It is frequently pointed out that the argument from nature functions as a cover, as a myth to make patriarchy palatable to both women and men. Insofar as this is so, it is surely worthwhile exploring and exposing the myth. But of course most of those who use the argument from nature take it seriously and literally, and this is the spirit in which I have dealt with it. Considering the argument in this way, I conclude that whether there should be sex roles does not depend primarily on whether there are innate psychological differences between the sexes. The question is, after all, not what women and men naturally are, but what kind of society is morally justifiable. In order to answer this question, we must appeal to the notions of justice, equality, and liberty. It is these moral concepts, not the empirical issue of sex differences, which should have pride of place in the philosophical discussion of sex roles.

From Joyce Trebilcot, "Sex Roles: The Argument from Nature," *Ethics,* vol. 85 (April 1975), 249–255, University of Chicago Press.

QUESTIONS FOR REVIEW AND DISCUSSION

1. What does Simone de Beauvoir mean when she says, "It is not nature that defines woman; it is she who defines herself by dealing with nature on her own account in her emotional life"?
2. Beauvoir speaks of the "other," saying that "otherness is a fundamental category of human thought." But in what way is the otherness of woman different from various other kinds of others, for example, blacks, Chinese, Jews, and the proletariat, according to Beauvoir?
3. How does Beauvoir answer her own question: "Why is it that women do not dispute male sovereignty?"
4. According to Plato's political theory, should women be assigned only to those tasks which are consistent with their nature?
5. How does Joyce Trebilcot respond to the notion that sex roles are determined by nature and that different roles for men and women should be "enforced" by society for three reasons: namely (i) these roles are *inevitable,* (ii) the *well-being* and happiness of each sex is thereby assured, and (iii) *efficiency* is served if socially valuable tasks are assigned to the sex which has the greatest innate ability for them.

10

Natural Law

Aquinas

Saint Thomas Aquinas was born near Naples in A.D. 1225. At the age of five he was placed in the Abbey of Monte Cassino, and for the next nine years he pursued his studies in this Benedictine abbey. He then entered the Dominican order and in A.D. 1245 went to the University of Paris. Here he came under the influence of Albert the Great, who was known as the "Universal Teacher" because of his immense learning. The great achievement of Saint Thomas Aquinas was bringing together the insights of classical philosophy and Christian theology. He "Christianized" the philosophy of Aristotle. At the same time he drew on medieval writers, including Arabian and Jewish philosophers, as well as other Christian fathers, including Saint Augustine. Aquinas was primarily a theologian, but he relied heavily on the philosophy of Aristotle in writing his theological works. His view was that philosophy and theology play complementary roles in man's quest for truth.

To understand Aquinas's views about law and the state, we need to consider his interpretation of the moral dimension of human life. Morality, as Aquinas viewed it, is not an arbitrary set of rules for behavior. The basis of moral obligation, he thought, is found, first of all, in the very nature of man. Built into man's nature are various inclinations, such as the preservation of his life, the propagation of his species, and, because he is rational, the inclination toward the search for truth. The basic moral truth is simply to "do good and avoid evil." As a rational being, then, man is under a basic natural obligation to protect his life and health, in which case suicide and carelessness are wrong. Second, the natural inclination to propagate the species forms the basis of the union of man and wife, and any other basis for this relation would be wrong. And third, because man seeks for truth, he can do this best by living in peace in society with his fellow men, who are also engaged in this quest. To ensure an ordered society, human laws are fashioned for the direction of the community's behavior. Preserving life, propagating the species, forming an ordered society under human laws, and pursuing the quest for truth—all these activities pertain to man at his natural level. The moral law is founded on human nature, on the natural inclinations toward specific modes of

Aquinas, Botticelli. *(New York Public Library Picture Collection)*

behavior, and on the reason's ability to discern the right course of conduct. Because human nature has certain fixed features, the rules for behavior that correspond to these features are called *natural law*.

Much of this theory of natural law was already developed by Aristotle.

In his *Ethics,* Aristotle distinguished between natural justice and *conventional** justice. Some forms of behavior, he said, are wrong only because, and only after, a law has been made to regulate such behavior. To use a modern example, it is wrong to drive a vehicle at certain speeds only because a speed limit has been set, but there is nothing in nature that requires that vehicles travel at that speed. Such a law is therefore not natural but conventional, because before the law was passed, there was nothing wrong with traveling at speeds exceeding the new limit. However, there are some laws the precepts of which are derived from nature, so that the behavior they regulate has always been wrong, as in the case of murder.

Law, says Aquinas, has to do primarily with reason. The rule and measure of acts is the reason, because it belongs to reason to direct a man's whole activity toward his end. Law consists of these rules and measures of human acts and therefore is based on reason. The natural law is dictated by the reason. But Aquinas argues that since God created all things, human nature and the natural law are best understood as the product of God's wisdom or reason. From this standpoint, Aquinas distinguishes four kinds of law.

ETERNAL LAW

This law refers to the fact that "the whole community of the universe is governed by Divine Reason. Therefore, the very notion of the government of things in God, the Ruler of the universe, has the nature of a law. And since the Divine Reason's conception of things is not subject to time but is eternal . . . therefore it is that this kind of law must be called eternal."

NATURAL LAW

For Aquinas, natural law consists of that portion of the eternal law (God's Reason) that pertains particularly to man. His reasoning is that "all things partake in some way of the eternal law . . . from its being imprinted on them," and from this all things "derive their respective inclinations to their proper acts and ends." This is particularly true of man, because his rational capacity "has a share of the Eternal Reason, whereby it has a natural inclination to proper act and end." And, says Aquinas, "this participation of the eternal law in the rational creature is called the natural law," and again, "the natural law is nothing else than the rational creature's participation of the eternal law." We have already indicated the basic precepts of the natural law as being the preservation of life, propagation and education of offspring, and pursuit of truth and a peaceful society. Thus the natural law consists of broad general moral principles that reflect God's intentions for man in creation.

---

*"Conventional" means "established by agreement" as compared with a rule of behavior based on the requirements of nature.

HUMAN LAW

Human law refers to the specific statutes of governments. These statutes or human laws are derived from the general precepts of natural law. Just as "we draw conclusions of the various sciences" from "naturally known indemonstrable principles," so also "from the precepts of the natural law . . . the human reason needs to proceed to the more particular determination of certain matters." And "these particular determinations, devised by human reason, are called human laws. . . ."

What was so far-reaching about this conception of human law was that it repudiated the notion that a law was a law only because it was decreed by a sovereign, by the state. Aquinas argued that what gives a rule the character of law is its moral dimension, its conformity with the precepts of natural law, its agreement with the moral law. Taking Saint Augustine's formula, namely, that "that which is not just seems to be no law at all," Aquinas said that "every human law has just so much of the nature of law, as it is derived from the law of nature." But, he adds, "if in any point it deflects from the law of nature, it is no longer a law but a perversion of law." Such laws no longer bind in conscience, but are sometimes obeyed to prevent an even greater evil. Aquinas went farther than simply denying the character of law to a command of a government that violated the natural moral law; such a command, he said, should not be obeyed. Some laws, he said, "may be unjust through being opposed to the Divine Good: such are the laws of tyrants inducing to idolatry, or to anything else contrary to the Divine Law. . . ." He concluded that "laws of this kind must nowise be observed, because . . . *we ought to obey God rather than men.*"

DIVINE LAW

The function of law, said Aquinas, is to direct man to his proper end. Since man is ordained to an end of eternal happiness, in addition to his temporal happiness, there must be a kind of law that can direct him to that supernatural end. Here, in particular, Aquinas parted company with Aristotle, for Aristotle knew only about man's natural purpose and end, and for this purpose, the natural law known by man's reason was considered a sufficient guide. But the eternal happiness to which man is ordained, said Aquinas, is "in proportion to man's natural faculty." Therefore, "it was necessary that besides the natural and the human law, man should be directed to his end by a law given by God." The divine law, then, is available to man through revelation and is found in the Scriptures. It is not the product of man's reason but is given to man through God's grace to ensure that men know what they must do to fulfill both their natural and, especially, their supernatural ends. The difference between the natural law and divine law is this: The natural law represents man's rational knowledge of the good, by which the intellect directs the will to control man's appetites and passions, leading men to fulfill their natural end by achieving the cardinal virtues of justice, temperance, courage, and prudence. The divine law, on the other hand, comes directly from God through revelation, a gift of God's grace, whereby men are directed to their supernatural ends, having obtained the higher or theological virtues of faith, hope, and love, not through any of man's natural powers, for these virtues are "infused" into man by God's grace. In this way, Aquinas completed and surpassed the naturalistic ethics of Aristotle, showed how the natural desire of man to know God can be ensured, indicated how revelation becomes the guide for reason, and described the manner in which man's highest nature is perfected through God's grace.

THE STATE

The state, said Aquinas, is a natural institution. It is derived from the nature of man. In this view, Aquinas was following the political theory of Aristotle, from whom he had taken the phrase that "man is by nature a social animal." But insofar as Aquinas had a different view of human nature, he was bound to have a somewhat different political philosophy as well. The difference lay in the two conceptions of the role or task of the state. Aristotle supposed that the state could provide for all the needs of man because he knew only about man's natural needs. Aquinas, on the other hand, believed that in addition to his material or natural needs, man also has a supernatural end. The state is not equipped to deal with this more ultimate end of man. It is the church that directs man to this end. But Aquinas did not simply divide these two realms of human concern, giving one to the state and the other to the church. Instead, he looked on the state, and explained its origin, in terms of God's creation.

The state, in this view, is willed by God and has its God-given function. It was required because of the social nature of man. The state is not, for Aquinas, as it was for Augustine, a product of man's sinfulness. On the contrary, Aquinas says that even "in the state of innocence man would have lived in society." But even then, "a common life could not exist, unless there were someone in control, to attend to the common good." The state's function is to secure the common good by keeping the peace, organizing the activities of the citizens into harmonious pursuits, providing for the resources to sustain life, and prevent–ing, as far as possible, obstacles to the good life. This last item concerning threats to the good life gives to the state not only a function tied to man's ultimate end; it also accounts for the state's position in relation to the church.

The state is subordinate to the church. To say this did not mean that Aquinas considered the church a superstate. Aquinas saw no contradiction in saying that the state has a sphere in which it has a legitimate function and that at the same time it must subordinate itself to the church. Within its own sphere the state is autonomous or independent. But insofar as there are aspects of human life that bear on man's supernatural end, the state must not put arbitrary hindrances in the way to frustrate man's spiritual life. The church does not challenge the independence of the state; it only says that the state is not absolutely independent. Within its own sphere, the state is what Aquinas calls a "perfect society," having its own end and the means for achieving it. But the state is like man; neither the state nor man has only a natural end. Man's spiritual end cannot be achieved, as Aquinas says, "by human power, but by divine power." Still, because man's destiny does include attaining to the enjoyment of God, the state must recognize this aspect of human affairs; in providing for the common good of the citizens, the sovereign must pursue his community's end with a consciousness of man's spiritual end. Under these circumstances, the state does not become the church, but it does mean that the sovereign "should order those things which lead to heavenly beatitude and prohibit, as far as possible, their contraries." In this way, Aquinas affirmed the legitimacy of the state and its autonomy in its own sphere, subordinating it to the church only to ensure that the ultimate spiritual end of man be taken into account.

Since the state rules the behavior of its citizens through the agency of law, the state is in turn limited by the requirements of just laws. Nowhere is Aquinas's rejection of the absolute autonomy or independence of the state so clearly stated as when he describes the standards for the making of human or *positive law.** We have already analyzed the different types of law—eternal, natural, human, and divine. The state is particularly the source of human law. Each government is faced with the task of fashioning specific laws or statutes to regulate the behavior of its citizens under the particular circumstances of its own time and place. Lawmaking, however, must not be an arbitrary act, but must be done under the influence of the natural law, which is man's participation in God's eternal law. Positive laws must consist of particular rules derived from the general principles of natural law. Any positive human law that violates the natural law loses its character as law, is a "perversion of law," and loses its binding force in the consciences of men. The lawmaker has his authority to legislate from God, the source of all authority, and to God he is responsible. If the sovereign decrees an unjust law by violating God's divine law, such a law, says Aquinas, "must nowise be observed."

The political sovereign has his authority from God, and the purpose of his authority is to provide for the common good. Authority is never to be used as an end in itself or for selfish ends. Nor must the common good be interpreted in such a way that the individual is lost sight of in the collective whole. The common good must be the good of concrete persons. Thus Aquinas says that "the proper effect of law is to lead its subjects to their proper virtue . . . to make those to whom it is given good. . . ." The only "true ground" of the lawgiver is his intention to secure "the common good regulated according to divine justice," and thus it follows that "the effect of the law is to make men good. . . ." This is to say that the phrase "common good" has no meaning for Aquinas except insofar as it results in the good of individuals. At the same time, Aquinas says that "the goodness of any part is considered in comparison with the whole. . . . Since then every man is a part of the state, it is impossible that a man be good unless he be well proportionate to the common good." The entire scheme of society and its laws

---

*"Positive law" means a law "posited," or laid down, by government without any reference to a "higher source" such as morality or nature.

is characterized by the rational elements in it. Law itself, says Aquinas, is "an ordinance of reason for the common good, made by him who has care of the community, and promulgated." Thus although the sovereign has authority and power, the laws must not reflect this power in a naked sense but as power domesticated by reason and aimed at the common good.

Reading _____

Natural Law

Aquinas

Law is a rule and measure of acts, whereby man is induced to act or is restrained from acting; for *lex* (law) is derived from *ligare* (to bind), because it binds one to act. Now the rule and measure of human acts is the reason, which is the first principle of human acts. . . . For it belongs to the reason to direct to the end, which is the first principle in all matters of action. . . .

Now as reason is a principle of human acts, so in reason itself there is something which is the principle in respect of all the rest. Hence to this principle chiefly and mainly law must needs be referred. Now the first principle in practical matters, which are the object of the practical reason, is the last end: and the last end of human life is happiness or beatitude, as we have stated above. Consequently, law must needs concern itself mainly with the order that is in beatitude. Moreover, since every part is ordained to the whole as the imperfect to the perfect, and since one man is a part of the perfect community, law must needs concern itself properly with the order directed to universal happiness. . . .

ETERNAL LAW

Law is nothing else but a dictate of practical reason emanating from the ruler who governs a perfect community. Now it is evident, granted that the world is ruled by divine providence, as was stated in the First Part, that the whole community of the universe is governed by the divine reason. Therefore the very notion of the government of things in God, the ruler of the universe, has the nature of a law. And since the divine reason's conception of things is not subject to time, but is eternal, according to Prov. viii. 23, therefore it is that this kind of law must be called eternal. . . .

NATURAL LAW

Law being a rule and measure, can be in a person in two ways: in one way, as in him that rules and measures; in another way, as in that which is ruled and measured, since a thing is ruled and measured in so far as it partakes of the rule or measure. Therefore, since all things subject to divine providence are ruled and measured by the eternal law, as was stated above, it is evident that all things partake in some way in the eternal law, in so far as, namely, from its being imprinted on them, they derive their respec‑ tive inclinations to their proper acts and ends. Now among all others, the rational creature is subject to divine providence in a more excellent way, in so far as it itself partakes of a share of providence, by being provident both for itself and for others. Therefore it has a share of the eternal reason, whereby it has a natural inclination to its proper act and end; and this participation of the eternal law in the rational creature is called the natural law. . . . . The light of natural reason, whereby we discern what is good and what is evil, which is the function of the natural law, is nothing else than an imprint on us of the divine light. It is therefore evident that the natural law is nothing else than the rational creature's participation of the eternal law. . . .

HUMAN LAW

As we have stated above, a law is a dictate of the practical reason. Now it is to be observed that the same procedure takes place in the practical and in the speculative reason, for each proceeds from principles to conclusions, as we stated above. Accordingly, we conclude that, just as in the speculative reason, from naturally known indemonstrable principles we draw the conclusions of the various sciences, the knowledge of which is not imparted to us by nature, but acquired by the efforts of reason, so too it is that from the precepts of the natural law, as from common and indemonstrable principles, the human reason needs to proceed to the more particular determination of certain matters. These particular determinations, devised by human reason, are called human laws, provided that the other essential conditions of law be observed. . . .

DIVINE LAW

Besides the natural and the human law it was necessary for the directing of human conduct to have a divine law. And this for four reasons. First, because it is by law that man is directed how to perform his proper acts in view of his last end. Now if man were ordained to no other end than that which is proportionate to his natural ability, there would be no need for man to have any further direction, on the part of his reason, in addition to the natural law and humanly devised law which is derived from it. But since man is ordained to an end of eternal happiness which exceeds man's natural ability, as we have stated above, therefore it was necessary that, in addition to the natural and the human law, man should be directed to his end by a law given by God.

Secondly, because, by reason of the uncertainty of human judgment, especially on contingent and particular matters, different people form different judgments on human acts; whence also different and contrary laws result. In order, therefore, that man may know without any doubt what he ought to do, and what he ought to avoid, it was necessary for man to be directed in his proper acts by a law given by God, for it is certain that such a law cannot err.

Thirdly, because man can make laws in those matters of which he is competent to judge. But man is not competent to judge of interior movements, that are hidden, but only of exterior acts which are observable; and yet for the perfection of virtue it is necessary for man to conduct himself rightly in both kinds of acts. Consequently, human law could not sufficiently curb and direct interior acts, and it was necessary for this purpose that a divine law should supervene.

Fourthly, because, as Augustine says, human law cannot punish or forbid all evil deeds, since, while aiming at doing away with all evils, it would do away with many good things, and would hinder the advance of the common good, which is necessary for human living. In order, therefore, that no evil might remain unforbidden and unpunished, it was necessary for the divine law to supervene, whereby all sins are forbidden. . . .

As we have stated above, man has a natural aptitude for virtue; but the perfection of virtue must be acquired by man by means of some kind of training. Thus we observe that a man is helped by diligence in his necessities, for instance, in food and clothing. Certain beginnings of these he has from nature, viz., his reason and his hands; but he has not the full complement, as other animals have, to whom nature has given sufficiently of clothing and food. Now it is difficult to see how man could suffice for himself in the matter of his training, since the perfection of virtue consists chiefly in withdrawing man from under undue pleasures, to which above all man is inclined, and especially the young, who are more capable of being trained. Consequently a man needs to receive this training from another, whereby to arrive at the perfection of virtue. And as to those young people who are inclined to acts of virtue by their good natural disposition, or by custom, or rather by the gift of God, paternal training suffices, which is by admonitions. But since some are found to be dissolute and prone to vice, and not easily amenable to words, it was necessary for such to be restrained from evil by force and fear, in order that, at least, they might desist from evil-doing, and leave others in peace, and that they themselves, by being habituated in this way, might be brought to do willingly what hitherto they did from fear, and thus become virtuous. Now this kind of training, which compels through fear of punishment, is the discipline of laws. Therefore, in order that man might have peace and virtue, it was necessary for laws to be framed; for as the Philosopher says, *as man is the most noble of animals if he be perfect in virtue, so he is the lowest of all, if he be severed from law and justice.* For man can use his reason to devise means of satisfying his lusts and evil passions, which other animals are unable to do. . . .

UNJUST LAW NOT A LAW

As Augustine says, *that which is not just seems to be no law at all*. Hence the force of a law depends on the extent of its justice. Now in human affairs a thing is said to be just from being right, according to the rule of reason. But the first rule of reason is the law of nature, as is clear from what has been stated above. Consequently, every human law has just so much of the nature of law as it is derived from the law of nature. But if in any point it departs from the law of nature, it is no longer a law but a perversion of law.

But it must be noted that something may be derived from the natural law in two ways: first, as a conclusion from principles; secondly, by way of a determination of certain common notions. The first way is like to that by which, in the sciences, demonstrated conclusions are drawn from the principles; while the second is likened to that whereby, in the arts, common forms are determined to some particular. Thus, the craftsman needs to determine the common form of a house to the shape of this or that particular house. Some things are therefore derived from the common principles of the natural law by way of conclusions: e.g., that *one must not kill* may be derived as a conclusion from the principle that *one should do harm to no man*; while some are derived therefrom by way of determination: e.g., the law of nature has it that the evil-doer should be punished, but that he be punished in this or that way is determination of the human law.

From Aquinas, "Treatise on Law" in *Introduction to Saint Thomas Aquinas*, ed. Anton C. Pegis, The Modern Library, Random House, New York, 1948.

QUESTIONS FOR REVIEW AND DISCUSSION

1. Aquinas refers to four kinds of law. What are they, and how are they related to each other?
2. What is the difference between divine law and eternal law?
3. What should a person do if a human law is contrary to the natural law, according to Aquinas? Are there any exceptions?
4. How would Aquinas respond to the decision of the United States Supreme Court in *Roe v. Wade*, which permits abortion in certain cases?

11

The Social Contract

Hobbes and Locke

Hobbes

Thomas Hobbes was born in England in 1588. He graduated from Oxford in 1608 and became the tutor of the Earl of Devonshire, William Cavendish. In this position he traveled with the Cavendish family extensively on the Continent, where he met leading thinkers of the day, including Galileo. Known especially as a great political thinker, he became one of the most famous Englishmen abroad in his day. He designed a natural philosophy based on the law of motion. In a series of books, *Concerning Body (De Corpore), Concerning Man (De Homine)*, and *Concerning the Citizen (De Cive)*, he tried to show that all behavior, including physical movement, thinking, and political arrangements, represents bodies in motion. In England, Hobbes was much admired by Sir Francis Bacon, who enjoyed conversation with him and frequently dictated his thoughts to Hobbes during "delicious walks at Gorambery." Hobbes became best known for his influential book *Leviathan*. He died in Derbyshire in 1679 at the age of ninety-one.

What strikes one first about Hobbes's theory of state is that he approaches the subject not from an historical point of view, but from the vantage point of logic and analysis. He does not ask "*When* did civil societies emerge?" but rather "*How* do you explain the emergence of society?" He is concerned to discover the *cause* of civil society, and in harmony with his general method, he sets out to explain the cause of the state by describing the motion of bodies. His thought about political philosophy resembles the method of geometry in the sense that from axiomlike premises he deduces all the consequences of his political theory. Most of these premises cluster around his conception of human nature.

THE STATE OF NATURE

Hobbes describes men, first of all, as they appear in what he calls the *state of nature*, which is the condition of men before there is any state or civil society. In this state of nature, all men are equal and equally have the right to whatever they consider necessary for their survival. "Equality" here means simply that anyone is capable of hurting his neighbor and taking what he judges he needs for his own protection. Differences in strength can in time be overcome, and the weak can destroy the strong. The "right of all to all" that prevails in the state of nature does not mean that one man has a right whereas others have corresponding duties. The word "right" in the bare state of nature is a man's *freedom* "to do what he would, and against whom he thought fit, and to possess, use and enjoy all that he would, or could get." The driving force in man is the will to survive, and the psychological mood pervading all men is fear—the fear of death and particularly the fear of violent death. In the state of nature, all men are relentlessly pursuing whatever acts they think will secure their safety. The picture one gets of this state of nature is of men moving against each other, bodies in motion, or the anarchic condition Hobbes called "the war of all against all."

Why do men behave this way? Hobbes analyzes human motivation by saying that all men possess a twofold *endeavor*, namely *appetite* and *aversion*. These two endeavors account for man's motions to and from persons or objects and have the same meanings as the words "love" and "hate." Men are attracted to what they think will help them survive, and they hate whatever they judge to be a threat to them. The words "good" and "evil" have whatever meaning each individual will give them, and each person will call good whatever he loves and evil whatever he hates, "there being nothing simply and absolutely so." Men are fundamentally egotistical in that they are concerned chiefly about their own survival and identify goodness with their own appetites. It would appear therefore that in the state of nature there is no obligation for men to respect others or that there is no morality in the traditional sense of goodness and justice. Given this egotistical view of human nature, it would appear also that men do not possess the capacity to create an ordered and peaceful society.

But Hobbes argued that several logical conclusions or consequences can be deduced from man's concern for his survival, among these being what Hobbes called *natural laws*. Even in the state of nature, men *know* these natural laws, which are logically consistent with man's principal concern for his own safety. A natural law, said Hobbes, "is a precept, or general rule, found out by reason," telling what to do and what not to do. If the major premise is that I want to survive, I can logically deduce, even in the state of nature, certain rules of behavior that will help me to survive. The first law of nature is therefore that every man ought to "seek peace and follow it." Now this law that urges me to seek peace is natural because it is a logical extension of my concern for survival. It is obvious that I have a better chance to survive if I

Thomas Hobbes. *(National Portrait Gallery, London)*

help to create the conditions of peace. My desire for survival therefore impels me to seek peace.

From this first and fundamental law of nature is derived the second law, which states that "a man be willing, when others are so too, as farforth as for peace and defense of himself he shall think it necessary, to lay down his right to all things; and be contented with so much liberty against other men, as he would allow other men against himself. . . ."

OBLIGATION IN THE STATE OF NATURE

If men know these and other natural laws even in the state of nature, do they have an obligation to obey them? Hobbes answers that these laws are always binding, in the state of nature as well as in civil society. But he distinguishes between two ways in which these natural laws are applicable in the state of nature, saying that "the laws of nature oblige *in foro interno* [i.e., in the court of conscience]; that is to say, they bind to a desire they should take place: but *in foro externo* [i.e., in actual practice]; that is, to putting them in act, not always." Thus it isn't as if there were no obligation in the state of nature. Rather, the circumstances for living by these laws in the state of nature are not always present. Men have a right to all things in the state of nature not because there is no obligation, but because if a man were modest, tractable, and kept his promises "in such time and place where no man else should do so, [he] should but make himself a prey to others, and procure his own ruin, contrary to the ground of all laws of nature, which tend to nature's preservations." And even when men act to preserve themselves, they are not free from rational natural laws, for even in the state of nature they ought to act in good faith: ". . . if any man *pretend* somewhat to tend necessarily to his preservation, which yet he himself doth not confidently believe so, he may offend against the laws of nature."

Hobbes was aware that the logical outcome of egotistical individuals all deciding how best to survive would be anarchy, where there were "no arts; no letters; no society; and which is worst of all, continual fear, and danger of violent death; and the life of man, solitary, poor, nasty, brutish, and short. . . ." To avoid such a condition of anarchy, the chief cause of which is the conflict of individual and egotistical judgments of right, men, following the dictates of natural law, seeking peace, renounce some of their rights or freedoms and enter into a Social Contract and thereby create an artificial man, that great leviathan, called a commonwealth or state.

THE SOCIAL CONTRACT

The contract by which men avoid the state of nature and enter civil society is an agreement between individuals, "as if every man should say to every man, *I authorize and give up my right of governing myself, to this man, or to this assembly of men, on this condition, that you give up your right to him, and authorize all his actions in like manner.*" Two things stand out clearly in this contract. First, the parties to the contract are individuals who promise each other to hand over their right to govern themselves to the sovereign; it is not a contract between the sovereign and the citizens. The sovereign has absolute power to govern and is in no way subject to the citizens. Second, Hobbes clearly states that the sovereign can be either "this man" or "this assembly of men," suggesting that, in theory at least, his view of sovereignty was not identified with any particular form of government. It may be that he had a preference for a single ruler with absolute power, but he recognized the possible compatibility of his theory of sovereignty with "democracy." But whatever form the sovereign would take, it is clear that Hobbes saw the transfer of the right to rule from the people to the sovereign as both absolute and irrevocable.

Hobbes was particularly anxious to demonstrate with logical rigor that sovereign power is indivisible. Having shown that in the state of nature anarchy is the logical consequence of independent individual judgments, he concluded that the only way to overcome such anarchy is to make a single body out of the several bodies of the citizens. The only way to transform multiple wills into a single will is to agree that the sovereign's single will and judgment represent the will and judgment of all the citizens. In effect, this is what the contract says when men agree to hand over their right to govern themselves. The sovereign now acts not only on behalf of the citizens but *as if* he embodied the will of the citizens, thereby affirming an identity between the wills of the sovereign and citizens. Resistance against the sovereign by a citizen is therefore illogical on two counts, first because it would amount to resistance to himself, and second, because to resist is to revert to independent judgment, which is to revert to the state of nature or anarchy. The power of the sovereign must therefore be absolute in order to secure the conditions of order, peace, and law.

CIVIL LAW VERSUS NATURAL LAW

Law begins only when there is a sovereign. This is a logical truism, for, in the judicial or *legal* sense, a law is defined as a command of the sovereign. It follows that where there is no sovereign, there is no law. To be sure, Hobbes affirmed that even in the state of nature men have knowledge of the natural law, and in a special sense, the natural law is binding even in the state of nature. But only after there is a sovereign can there be a legal order, because only then is there the apparatus of law in which the power of enforcement is central. Without the power to enforce, said Hobbes, covenants are "mere words." Hobbes identifies law with sovereign command and makes the additional point that "there can be no unjust law."

Nowhere does Hobbes's severe authoritarianism express itself in more startling form than when he argues that there can be no unjust law. It appears that justice and morality begin with the sovereign, that there are no principles of justice and morality that precede and limit the acts of the sovereign. Hobbes affirmed this in a notable passage: "To the care of the sovereign, belongeth the making of good laws. But what is a good law? By good law, I mean not a just law: for no law can be unjust." Hobbes gives two reasons for saying no law can be unjust: first, because justice means obeying the law, and this is why justice comes into being only after a law has been made and cannot itself be the standard for law; second, when a sovereign makes a law, it is as though the people were making the law, and what they agree on cannot be unjust. Indeed, the third natural law Hobbes speaks of is *"that men perform their covenants made,"* and he indicated that this is the "fountain of justice." Hence to keep the contract in which you agreed to obey the sovereign is the essence of Hobbesian justice.

It is evident that Hobbes forces the reader to take each word seriously and ("reckon") all the "consequences" that can be deduced from it. If law means the sovereign's command and if justice means obeying the law, there can be no *unjust* law. But there can be a *bad* law, for Hobbes was enough of an Aristotelian to recognize that a sovereign has a definite purpose "for which he was trusted with the sovereign power, namely, the procuration of *the safety of the people;* to which he is obliged by the law of nature, and to render an account thereof to God. . . ." But even in such a case, where the sovereign has commanded a "bad" law, the citizens are not the ones to judge it as such, nor does this justify their disobedience. The sovereign has the sole power to judge what is for the safety of the people; if the people disagreed with him, they would revert to anarchy. If the sovereign engages in iniquitous acts, this is a matter between the sovereign and God, not between the citizens and the sovereign. And because he feared anarchy and disorder so deeply, Hobbes pushed his logic of obedience to the point of making religion and the church subordinate to the state. To the Christian who felt that the sovereign's command violated the law of God, Hobbes gave no comfort but insisted that if such a person could not obey the sovereign, he must "go to Christ in martrydom. . . ."

Reading _____

The State of Nature
Hobbes

CHAPTER 1

The greatest part of those men who have written aught concerning commonwealths, either suppose, or require us, or beg of us to believe, that man is a creature born fit for society. The Greeks call him *political animal;* and on this foundation they so build up the doctrine of civil society, as if for the preservation of peace, and the government of mankind, there were nothing else necessary, than that men should agree to make certain covenants and conditions together, which themselves should then call laws. Which axiom, though received by most, is yet certainly false, and an error proceeding from our too slight contemplation of human nature. For they who shall more narrowly look into the causes for which men come together, and delight in each other's company, shall easily find that this happens not because naturally it could happen no otherwise, but by accident. For if by nature one man should love another (that is) as man, there could no reason be returned why every man should not equally love every man, as being equally man, or why he should rather frequent those whose society affords him honour or profit.

We do not therefore by nature seek society for its own sake, but that we may receive some honour or profit from it. . . . I hope no body will doubt but that men would much more greedily be carried by nature, if all fear were removed, to obtain dominion, than to gain society. We must therefore resolve, that the original of all great and lasting societies consisted not in the mutual good will men had towards each other, but in the mutual fear they had of each other.

The cause of mutual fear consists partly in the natural equality of men, partly in their mutual will of hurting: whence it comes to pass that we can neither expect from others, nor promise to ourselves the least security. For if we look on men full-grown, and consider how brittle the frame of our human body is, . . . and how easy a matter it is, even for the weakest man to kill the strongest, there is no reason why any man trusting to his own strength should conceive himself made by nature above others: they are equals who can do equal things one against the other; but they who can do the greatest things (namely, kill) can do equal things. All men therefore among themselves are by nature equal; the inequality we now discern, hath its spring from the civil law.

All men in the state of nature have a desire and will to hurt, but not proceeding from the same cause, neither equally to be condemned. For one man, according to that natural equality which is among us, permits as much to others, as he assumes to himself (which is an argument of a temperate man, and one that rightly values his power). Another, supposing himself above others, will have a license to do what he wishes, and challenges respect and honour, as due to him before others (which is an argument of a fiery spirit). This man's will to hurt ariseth from vain glory, and the false esteem he hath of his own strength; the other's, from the necessity of defending himself, his liberty, and his goods, against this man's violence. . . .

But the most frequent reason why men desire to hurt each other, ariseth hence, that many men at the same time have an appetite to the same thing; which yet very often they can neither enjoy in common, nor yet divide it; whence it follows that the strongest must have it, and who is strongest must be decided by the sword.

Among so many dangers therefore, as the natural lusts of men do daily threaten each other withal, to have a care of one's self is not a matter so scornfully to be looked upon, as if so be there had not been a power and will left in one to have done otherwise. For every man is desirous of what is good for him, and shuns what is evil, but chiefly the chiefest of natural evils, which is death; and this he doth, by a certain impulsion of nature, no less than that whereby a stone moves downward. It is therefore neither absurd, nor reprehensible, neither against the dictates of true reason, for a man to use all his endeavours to preserve and defend his body and the members thereof from death and sorrows. . . . Therefore the first foundation of natural right is this, that every man as much as in him lies endeavour to protect his life and members.

But because it is in vain for a man to have a right to the end, if the right to the necessary means be denied him; it follows, that since every man hath a right to preserve himself, he must also be allowed a right to use all the means, and do all the actions, without which he cannot preserve himself.

Now whether the means which he is about to use, and the action he is performing, be necessary to the preservation of his life and members, or not, he himself, by the right of nature, must be judge. . . .

Nature hath given to every one a right to all; that is, it was lawful for every man in the bare state of nature, or before such time as men had engaged themselves by any covenants or bonds, to do what he would, and against whom he thought fit, and to possess, use, and enjoy all what he would, or could get. Now because whatsoever a man would, it therefore seems good to him because he wills it, and either it really doth, or at least seems to him to contribute towards his preservation, it follows, that in the state of nature, to have all, and do all, is lawful for all. And this is that which is meant by that common saying, nature hath given all to all, from whence we understand likewise, that in the state of nature, profit is the measure of right.

But it was the least benefit for men thus to have a common right to all things; for the effects of this right are the same, almost, as if there had been no right at all. For although any man might say of every thing, this is mine, yet could he not enjoy it, by reason of his neighbour, who having equal right, and equal power, would pretend the same thing to be his.

If now to this natural proclivity of men, to hurt each other, which they derive from their passions, but chiefly from a vain esteem of themselves, you add, the right of all to all, wherewith one by right invades, the other by right resists, and whence arise perpetual jealousies and suspicions on all hands, and how hard a thing it is to provide against an enemy invading us, with an intention to oppress, and ruin, though they come with a small number, and no great provision; it cannot be denied but that the natural state of men, before they entered into society, was a mere war, and that not simply, but a war of all men against all men. . . .

But it is easily judged how disagreeable a thing to the preservation either of mankind, or of each single man, a perpetual war is. But it is perpetual in its own nature, because in regard of the equality of those that strive, it cannot be ended by victory; for in this state the conqueror is subject to so much danger, as it were to be accounted a miracle, if any, even the most strong, should close up his life with many years, and old age. . . . Whosoever therefore holds, that it had been best to have continued in that state in which all things were lawful for all men, he contradicts himself. For every man by natural necessity desires that which is good for him: nor is there any that esteems a war of all against all, which necessarily adheres to such a state, to be good for him. And so it happens, that through fear of each other we think it fit to rid ourselves of this condition, and to get some fellows; that if there needs must be war it may not yet be against all men, nor without some helps.

Yet cannot men expect any lasting preservation continuing thus in the state of nature, that is, of war, by reason of that equality of power, and other human faculties they are endued withal. Wherefore to seek peace, where there is any hope of obtaining it, and where there is none, to enquire out for auxiliaries of war, is the dictate of right reason, that is, the law of nature. . . .

CHAPTER II

The first and fundamental law of nature is, that peace is to be sought after, where it may be found; and where not, there to provide ourselves for helps of war. . . .

But one of the natural laws derived from this fundamental one is this: that the right of all men to all things, ought not to be retained, but that some certain rights ought to be transferred, or relinquished. For if every one should retain his right to all things, it must necessarily follow, that some by right might invade, and others, by the same right, might defend themselves against them (for every man, by natural necessity, endeavours to defend his body). Therefore war would follow. He therefore acts against the reason of peace, that is, against the law of nature, whosoever he be, that doth not part with his right to all things. . . .

No man is obliged by any contracts whatsoever not to resist him who shall offer to kill, wound, or any other way hurt his body. For there is in every man a certain high degree of fear, through which he apprehends that evil which is done to him to be the greatest; and therefore by natural necessity he shuns it all he can, and it is supposed he can do no otherwise. When a man is arrived to this degree of fear, we cannot expect but he will provide for himself either by flight or fight. Since therefore no man is tied to impossibilities, they who are threatened either with death (which is the greatest evil to nature) or wounds, or some other bodily hurts, and are not stout enough to bear them, are not obliged to endure them. . . .

Likewise no man is tied by any compacts whatsoever to accuse himself, or any other, by whose damage he is like to procure himself a bitter life. Wherefore neither is a father obliged to bear witness against his son, nor a husband against his wife, nor a son against his father, nor any man against any one by whose means he hath his subsistence; for in vain is that testimony which is presumed to be corrupted from nature. . . .

CHAPTER III

As it was necessary to the conservation of each man, that he should part with some of his rights, so it is no less necessary to the same conservation, that he retain some others, to wit, the right of bodily protection, of free enjoyment of air, water, and all necessaries for life. Since therefore many common rights are retained by those who enter into a peaceable state, and that many peculiar ones are also acquired, hence ariseth this dictate of the natural law, to wit, that what rights soever any man challenges to himself, he also grant the same as due to all the rest. . . .

The laws of nature are immutable and eternal: what they forbid, can never be lawful; what they command, can never be unlawful. For pride, ingratitude, breach of contracts (or injury), inhumanity, contumely, will never be lawful, nor the contrary virtues to these ever unlawful, as we take them for dispositions of the mind, that is, as they are considered in the court of conscience, where only they oblige, and are laws. . . .

CHAPTER V

Since therefore the exercise of the natural law is necessary for the preservation of peace, and that for the exercise of the natural law security is no less necessary, it is worth the considering what that is which affords such a security. For this matter nothing else can be imagined, but that each man provide himself of such meet helps, as the invasion of one on the other may be rendered so dangerous, as either of them may think it better to refrain, than to meddle. But first, it is plain, that the consent of two or three cannot make good such a security; because that the addition but of one, or some few on the other side, is sufficient to make the victory undoubtedly sure, and heartens the enemy to attack us. It is therefore necessary, to the end the security sought for may be obtained, that the number of them who conspire in a mutual assistance be so great, that the accession of some few to the enemy's party may not prove to them a matter of moment sufficient to assure the victory. . . .

Wherefore consent or contracted society, without some common power whereby particular men may be ruled through fear of punishment, doth not suffice to make up that security which is requisite to the exercise of natural justice.

Since therefore the conspiring of many wills to the same end doth not suffice to preserve peace, and to make a lasting defence, it is requisite that, in those necessary matters which concern peace and self-defence, there be but one will of all men. But this cannot be done, unless every man will so subject his will to some other one, to wit, either man or council, that whatsoever his will is in those things which are necessary to the common peace, it be received for the wills of all men in general, and of every one in particular. Now the gathering together of many men who deliberate of what is to be done, or not to be done, for the common good of all men, is that which I call a council.

This submission of the wills of all those men to the will of one man, or one council, is then made, when each one of them obligeth himself by contract to every one of the rest, not to resist the will of that one man, or council, to which he hath submitted himself; that is, that he refuse him not the use of his wealth and strength against any others whatsoever (for he is supposed still to retain a right of defending himself against violence) and this is called union. But we understand that to be the will of the council, which is the will of the major part of those men of whom the council consists. . . .

Now union thus made is called a city, or civil society, and also a civil person; for when there is one will of all men, it is to be esteemed for one

person, and by the word one it is to be known, and distinguished from all particular men, as having its own rights and properties. Insomuch as neither any one citizen, nor all of them together (if except him whose will stands for the will of all), is to be accounted the city. A city therefore (that we may define it) is one person, whose will, by the compact of many men, is to be received for the will of them all; so as he may use all the power and faculties of each particular person, to the maintenance of peace, and for common defence.

From Hobbes, *De Cive*, ed. Sterling P. Lamprecht, Appleton-Century-Crofts, New York, 1949.

Locke

John Locke's life resembled Hobbes's in many ways. Also an Englishman, Locke was born in 1632 and died in 1704. He lived through the Civil War, the Bloodless Revolution, and the Restoration. At Westminster School he developed an early interest in science which was to stay with him for the rest of his life. At Oxford he was particularly influenced by the philosophy of Descartes, which furthered his bent in science. He studied to become a doctor, later becoming associated with the Earl of Shaftesbury and his family as a friend, physician, and adviser. His most famous writings include his *Essay on Human Understanding,* considered by some to have proposed a theory of knowledge so influential that it provided support for the foundations of modern science. His *Two Treatises of Government* was enormously influential and his "Second Treatise," from which the following reading is selected, was especially significant in the development of the American philosophy of democracy. As in the case of Hobbes, Locke drew much of his political philosophy from his interpretation of human nature and from historical events which he witnessed, especially wars. As in the case of Hobbes, Locke also fashioned a theory of the State of Nature and the Social Contract.

THE MORAL BASIS OF SOCIETY

Locke says that "moral good and evil . . . is only the conformity or disagreement of our voluntary actions to some law," and he speaks of three kinds of laws, namely, the *law of opinion,* the *civil law,* and the *divine law.* The law of opinion represents a community's judgment of what kind of behavior will lead to happiness: conformity to this law is called "virtue," though it must be noticed that different communities have different ideas of what virtue consists of. The civil law is set by the commonwealth and enforced by the courts. This law tends to follow the first, for in most societies the courts enforce those laws that embody the opinion of the people. The divine law, which men can know through either their own reason or revelation, is the true rule for human behavior: "That God has given a rule whereby men should govern themselves, I think there is nobody so brutish as to deny." And "this is the only true touchstone of moral rectitude." In the long run, then, the law of opinion and also the civil law should be made to conform to the divine law, the "touchstone of moral rectitude." The reason there is a discrepancy between these three kinds of laws is that men everywhere tend to choose immediate pleasures instead of choosing those that have more lasting value. However ambiguous this moral theory may seem to us, Locke believed that these moral rules were eternally true, and upon the insights derived from the divine law he built his theory of natural rights.

THE STATE OF NATURE

In his *Second Treatise of Government,* Locke begins his political theory as Hobbes did, with a treatment of "the state of nature." But he described this condition in a very different way, even making Hobbes the target of his remarks. For Locke, the state of nature is not the same as Hobbes' "war of all against all." On the contrary, Locke says that "men living together according to reason, without a common superior on earth with authority to judge between them is properly the state of nature." According to Locke's theory of knowledge, men were able even in the state of nature to know the moral law. He said that "reason, which is that law, teaches all mankind who will but consult it, that, being all equal and independent, no one ought to harm another in his life, health, liberty or possessions." This natural moral law is not simply the egotistical law of self-preservation but the positive recognition of each man's value as a person by virtue of his status as a creature of God. This natural law implied natural rights with correlative duties, and among these rights Locke emphasized particularly the right of private property.

PRIVATE PROPERTY

For Hobbes, there could be a right to property only after the legal order had been set up. Locke said that the right to private property precedes the civil law, for it is grounded in the natural moral law. The justification of private ownership is labor. Since a man's labor is his own, whatever he transforms from its original condition by his own labor becomes his, for his labor is now mixed with those things. It is by mixing his labor with something that a man takes what was common property and makes it his private property. There is consequently also a limit to that amount of property one can accumulate, namely, "as much as anyone can make use of to any advantage of life before it spoils, so much he may by his labour fix a property in. . . ." Locke assumed also that as a matter of natural right a person could inherit property, for "every man is born with . . . a right, before any other man, to inherit with his brethren his father's goods."

Locke was critical of those who appeared to be preoccupied with the division of things among the people instead of concentrating upon ways to make sure there would be something to divide. Resources were given, he said, "to the use of the industrious and rational—and labor was to be their title to it—not to the fancy or covetousness of the quarrelsome and contentious."

But how much could the industrious and rational use without amassing so much that it would spoil? Moreover, would the development and accumulation of property by the industrious and rational be available as "an advantage" to the life of man? What concerned Locke was whether in the process of acquiring resources someone would injure another human being. If he used all he acquired, there was no injury, provided "enough and as good (was) left in common for others." If he gave away part to someone else so that it did not spoil and perish in his possession, this also counted as an acceptable moral use. The moral use of things could be extended by other means. For example, plums, which might rot in a week, could be bartered for nuts, which could last a year. No one would be injured by this transaction and there would be no waste as nothing perished uselessly. If someone traded the nuts for a jewel or his sheep for a bright piece of metal he could keep all his life, "he invaded not the right of others; he might heap as much of these durable things as he pleased." It was not the largeness of his possessions that was morally wrong, said Locke, but "the perishing uselessly of it." The final strategy by which the industrious and rational could extend their accumulated property without injuring or invading anyone was through the use of gold and silver: ". . . and thus came in the use of money—some lasting thing that men might keep without spoiling." By mutual consent men began to take money in exchange for the truly useful but perishable supports of life.

If the use of money made possible the accumulation of resources, an even greater vehicle of this accumulation was the possession of land. Who should have the land? Only someone who would productively use it. Otherwise it would be wasted and would lose its usefulness to the life of man. Therefore, whoever appropriates land to himself either by his labor, in exchange for other things, or for money has a moral right to it. Moreover, by fully using the land, he increases mankind's inventory of resources that provide for the support of human life. One acre of land appropriated and worked by someone makes available many more times the resources than 10 acres of equal quality lying waste. The actions of the industrious and the rational are moral as there is no invasion or injury at each transaction. The industrious and the rational also positively increase the standard of living of everyone by efficiently developing the natural resources.

If this is an accurate analysis of how the present distribution of resources came about, except for notorious cases of plunder, it would mean that the inequalities are accounted for in part by the activities of the industrious and the rational. Even Marx acknowledged in the *Communist Manifesto* the extraordinary achievement of this social class, the industrious and rational, when he wrote:

> The bourgeoisie, during its rule of scarce one hundred years, has created more massive and more colossal productive forces than have all the preceeding generations together. Subjection of Nature's forces to man, machinery,

application of chemistry to industry and agriculture, steam navigation, railways, electric telegraphs, clearing of whole continents for cultivation, canalisation of rivers, whole populations conjured out of the ground—what earlier century had even a presentiment that such productive forces slumbered in the lap of social labor?

CIVIL GOVERNMENT

If men have natural rights and also know the moral law, why do they desire to leave the state of nature? To this question Locke answered that "the great and chief end of men's uniting into commonwealths and putting themselves under government is the preservation of their property." By the term *property* Locke meant men's "lives, liberty and estates, which I call by the general name, property." It is true that men know the moral law in the state of nature, or rather they are capable of knowing it if they turn their minds to it. But through indifference and neglect they do not always develop a knowledge of it. Moreover, when disputes arise, every man is his own judge and tends to decide in his own favor. It is desirable therefore to have both a set of written laws and also an independent judge to decide disputes. To achieve those ends, men create a political society.

Locke put great emphasis on the inalienable character of men's rights, and this led him to argue that political society must rest upon the *consent* of men, for "men being . . . by nature all free, equal and independent, no one can be put out of this estate and subjected to the political power of another without his consent." But to what do men consent? They consent to have the laws made and enforced by society, but since "no rational creature can be supposed to change his condition with an intention to be worse," these laws must be framed so as to confirm those rights that men have by nature. They consent also to be bound by the majority, since "it is necessary the body should move that way whither the greater force carries it, which is the consent of the majority." For this reason Locke considered absolute monarchy as "no form of civil government at all." Whether in fact there was a time when men entered a compact is considered by Locke to be of no great consequence, for the important thing is that logically our behavior indicates that we have given our consent, and this Locke calls "tacit consent." For if we enjoy the privilege of citizenship, own and exchange property, rely upon the police and the courts, we have in effect assumed also the responsibilities of citizenship and consent to the rule of the majority. The fact that a person stays in his country, for after all he could leave and go to another one, confirms his act of consent.

SOVEREIGNTY

Locke gives us a different picture of the sovereign power in society from the one we find in Hobbes. Hobbes' sovereign was absolute. Locke agrees that there must be a "supreme power," but he carefully placed this in the hands of the legislature, for all intents the majority of the people. He emphasized the importance of the division of powers chiefly to ensure that those who execute or administer the laws do not also make them, for "they may exempt themselves from obedience to the laws they make, and suit the law, both in its making and execution, to their own private advantage. . . ." The executive is therefore "under the law." Even the legislature is not absolute, although it is "supreme," for legislative power is held as a *trust* and is therefore only a fiduciary power. Consequently, "there remains still in the people a supreme power to remove or alter the legislative when they find the legislative act contrary to the trust reposed in them." Locke would never agree that men had irrevocably transferred their rights to the sovereign. The right to rebellion is retained, though rebellion is justified only when the government is *dissolved*.

Reading _____

Natural Rights and Civil Society
Locke

OF THE STATE OF NATURE

To understand political power aright, and derive it from its original, we must consider what state all men are naturally in, and that is a state of perfect freedom to order their actions and dispose of their possessions and persons as they think fit, within the bounds of the law of nature, without asking leave, or depending upon the will of any other man.

A state also of equality, wherein all the power and jurisdiction is reciprocal, no one having more than another; there being nothing more evident than that creatures of the same species and rank, promiscuously born to all the same advantages of nature, and the use of the same faculties, should also be equal one amongst another without subordination or subjection. . . .

But though this be a state of liberty, yet it is not a state of licence; though man in that state has an uncontrollable liberty to dispose of his person or possessions, yet he has not liberty to destroy himself, or so much as any creature in his possession, but where some nobler use than its bare preservation calls for it. The state of nature has a law of nature to govern it, which obliges every one; and reason, which is that law, teaches all mankind who will but consult it, that, being all equal and independent, no one ought to harm another in his life, health, liberty, or possessions. For men being all the workmanship of one omnipotent and infinitely wise Maker—all the servants of one sovereign Master, sent into the world by His order, and about His business—they are His property, whose workmanship they are, made to last during His, not one another's pleasure; and being furnished with like faculties, sharing all in one community of nature, there cannot be supposed any such subordination among us, that may authorise us to destroy one another, as if we were made for one another's uses, as the inferior ranks of creatures are for ours. Every one, as he is bound to preserve himself, and not to quit his station wilfully, so, by the like reason, when his own preservation comes not in competition, ought he, as much as he can, to preserve the rest of mankind, and not, unless it be to do justice on an offender, take away or impair the life, or what tends to the preservation of the life, the liberty, health, limb, or goods of another.

And that all men may be restrained from invading others' rights, and from doing hurt to one another, and the law of nature be observed, which willeth the peace and preservation of all mankind, the execution of the law on nature is in that state put into every man's hand, whereby every one has a right to punish the transgressors of that law to such a degree as may hinder its violation. For the law of nature would, as all other laws that concern men in this world, be in vain if there were nobody that, in the state of nature, had a power to execute that law, and thereby preserve the innocent and restrain offenders. And if any one in the state of nature may punish another for any evil he has done, every one may do so. For in that state of perfect equality, where naturally there is no superiority or jurisdiction of one over another, what any may do in prosecution of that law, every one must needs have a right to do.

OF POLITICAL OR CIVIL SOCIETY

Man being born, as has been proved, with a title to perfect freedom, and an uncontrolled enjoyment of all the rights and privileges of the law of nature equally with any other man or number of men in the world, hath by nature a power not only to preserve his property—that is, his life, liberty, and estate—against the injuries and attempts of other men, but to judge of and punish the breaches of that law in others as he is persuaded the offence deserves, even with death itself, in crimes where the heinousness of the fact in his opinion requires it. But . . . there, and there only, is political society, where every one of the members hath quitted this natural power, resigned it up into the hands of the community in all cases that exclude him not from appealing for protection to the law established by it; and thus all private judgment of every particular member being excluded, the community comes to be umpire; and . . . decides all the differences that may happen between any members of that society concerning any matter of right, and punishes those offences which any member hath committed against the society with such penalties as the law has established. . . .

Wherever, therefore, any number of men so unite into one society, as to quit every one his executive power of the law of nature, and to resign it to the public, there, and there only, is a political, or civil society. And this is done wherever any number of men, in the state of nature, enter into society to make one people, one body politic, under one supreme government, or else when any one joins himself to, and incorporates with, any government already made. For thereby he authorises the society, or, which is all one, the legislative thereof, to make laws for him, as the public good of the society shall require, to the execution whereof his own assistance . . . is due. And this puts men out of a state of nature into that of a commonwealth, by setting up a judge on earth with authority to determine all the controversies and redress the injuries that may happen to any member of the commonwealth; which judge is the legislative, or magistrates appointed by it. And wherever there are any number of men, however associated, that have no such decisive power to appeal to, there they are still in the state of nature. . . .

The great and *chief End* therefore, of Men's uniting into Commonwealths, and putting themselves under Government, *is the Preservation of their Property.* To which in the State of Nature there are many Things wanting.

First, There wants an establish'd, settled, known Law, received and allow'd by common Consent to be the Standard of Right and Wrong, and the common Measure to decide all Controversies between them. For though the Law of Nature be plain and intelligible to all rational Creatures; yet Men being biassed by their Interest, as well as ignorant for want of Study of it, are not apt to allow of it as a Law binding to them in the Application of it to their particular Cases.

Secondly, In the State of Nature there wants a known and indiffer–ent Judge, with Authority to determine all Differences according to the establish'd Law. For every one in that State, being both Judge and Executioner of the Law of Nature, Men being partial to themselves, Passion and Revenge is very apt to carry them too far, and with too much Heat in their own Cases; as well as Negligence and Unconcernedness, to make them too remiss in other Men's.

Thirdly, In the State of Nature there often wants Power to back and support the Sentence when Right, and to give it due Execution. They who by any Injustice offend, will seldom fail, where they are able, by Force to make good their Injustice; such Resistance many times makes the Punishment dangerous, and frequently destructive to those who attempt it.

Thus Mankind, notwithstanding all the Privileges of the state of Nature, being but in an ill Condition, while they remain in it, are quickly driven into Society. Hence it comes to pass, that we seldom find any Number of Men live any time together in this State. The Inconveniences that they are therein exposed to, by the irregular, and uncertain Exercise of the Power every Man has of punishing the Transgressions of others, make them take Sanctuary under the establish'd Laws of Government, and therein seek the Preservation of their Property. 'Tis this makes them so willingly give up every one his single Power of punishing, to be exercised by such alone, as shall be appointed to it amongst them; and by such Rules as the Community, or those authorized by them to that Purpose, shall agree on. And in this we have the original Right and Rise of both the legislative and executive Power, as well as of the Governments and Societies themselves.

For in the State of Nature, to omit the Liberty he has of innocent Delights, a Man has two Powers:

The first is to do whatsoever he thinks fit for the Preservation of himself and others, within the Permission of the Law of Nature; by which Law, common to them all, he and all the rest of Mankind are of one Community, make up one Society, distinct from all other Creatures. . . .

The other Power a Man has in the State of Nature, is the Power to punish the Crimes committed against that Law. Both these he gives up, when he joins in a private, if I may so call it, or particular political Society, and incorporates into any Common-wealth, separate from the rest of Mankind.

The first Power, . . . he gives up to be regulated by Laws made by the Society, so far forth as the Preservation of himself, and the rest of that Society shall require; which Laws of the Society in many Things confine the Liberty he had by the Law of Nature.

Secondly, the Power of punishing he wholly gives up, and engages his natural Force (which he might before employ in the Execution of the Law of Nature, by his own single Authority, as he thought fit) to assist the executive Power of the Society, as the Law thereof shall require. For being now in a new State, wherein he is to enjoy many conveniences, from the Labour, Assistance, and Society of others in the same Community, as well as Protection from its whole Strength; he is to part also with as much of his natural Liberty in providing for himself, as the Good, Prosperity, and Safety of the Society shall require; which is not only necessary, but just; since the other Members of the Society do the like.

But though Men when they enter into Society, give up the Equality, Liberty, and executive Power they had in the State of Nature, into the Hands of the Society, . . . yet it being only with an Intention in every one the better to preserve himself his Liberty and Property; (For no rational Creature can be supposed to change his Condition with an Intention to be worse) the Power of the Society, or Legislative constituted by them, can never be suppos'd to extend farther than the common Good; but is obliged to secure every ones Property, by providing against those three Defects above-mention'd, that made the State of Nature so unsafe and uneasie. And so whoever has the Legislative or supreme Power of any Common-wealth, is bound to govern by establish'd standing Laws, promulgated and known to the People, and not by extemporary Decrees; by indifferent and upright Judges, who are to decide Controversies by those Laws; and to employ the Force of the Community at Home, only in the Execution of such Laws, or Abroad to prevent or redress foreign Injuries, and secure the Community from Inroads and Invasion. And all this to be directed to no other End, but the Peace, Safety, and publick Good of the People.

From Locke, *Two Treatises of Government.*

QUESTIONS FOR REVIEW AND DISCUSSION

1. How does Hobbes describe the "state of nature"?
2. What does Hobbes mean by the distinction between *"in foro interno"* and *"in foro externo"* regarding when the natural law is to be obeyed?
3. How does Hobbes define the Social Contract, and who are the parties to this contract? Why is it important to understand who the parties are?
4. Why is it illogical to disobey a law, after a civil society is established, if you decide that it is a bad law?
5. What is Hobbes's reason for saying that "there is no such thing as an unjust law"?
6. How would you compare the State of Nature as described by Hobbes and Locke, respectively?
7. The concept of *property* is important for both Hobbes and Locke, but they have different explanations for its foundation. What is this difference?
8. Locke says that there is a limit to the amount of property a person can rightly accumulate, namely, "as much as anyone can make use of to any advantage of life before it spoils." What has made it possible to go well beyond this limit?
9. Both Hobbes and Locke agree that in civil society there has to be a "supreme power." Which of these theories resembles most closely American society's concept of sovereignty?

12

Individualism and Liberty

Bentham and Mill

Both Bentham and Mill applied the principle of utility to the practical concerns of government. For Bentham, two leading questions were "How can the principle of utility clarify the purpose and objectives of law?" and "What is the justification for punishment?" For Mill, the central concern was the matter of human liberty, or "When is it appropriate or inappropriate for the government to interfere with an individual's freedom?" To all these questions, Bentham and Mill provided answers based squarely on the principle of utility. In this way, the foundation of moral philosophy which guides an individual's conduct became for them also the basis for political philosophy which involves the role of government in directing the behavior of citizens.

Bentham

LAW AND PUNISHMENT

It was particularly in connection with law and punishment that Bentham made impressive use of the principle of utility. Since it is the function of the legislator to discourage some acts and encourage others, how shall he classify those which should be discouraged as opposed to those which should be encouraged?

Object of Law

Bentham's method of legislation was first of all to measure the "mischief of an act." This mischief consisted of the consequences, the pain or evil inflicted by

For biographical note on Bentham see p. 72.

Inns of Court, where Bentham studied law. *(New York Public Library Picture Collection)*

the act. Acts that produce evil must be discouraged. There are, says Bentham, both primary and secondary evils that concern the legislator. A robber inflicts an evil on his victim, who loses his money: this is a case of primary evil. But robbery creates a secondary evil because successful robbery suggests that theft is easy. This suggestion is evil because it weakens respect for property, and property becomes insecure. From the point of view of the legislator, the secondary evils are frequently more important than the primary evils because, taking the example of robbery again, the actual loss to the victim may very well be considerably less than the loss in stability and security to the community as a whole.

The law is concerned with augmenting the total happiness of the community, and it must do this by discouraging those acts which would produce evil consequences. A criminal act or offense is by definition one that is clearly detrimental to the happiness of the community, and the only act that ought to be the concern of the law is one that in some specific way does in fact inflict some sort of pain and thereby diminish the pleasure of some specific individual or group. For the most part, the government accomplishes its business of promoting the happiness of society by punishing men who commit offenses that the principle of utility has clearly measured as evil.

It was Bentham's confirmed belief that if the legislator used only the principle of utility in deciding which acts should be considered "offenses," many acts that the laws of his day controlled would have to be considered a matter of private morals to be subject only to the sanction of opinion. Utilitarianism had the effect, then, of requiring a reclassification of behavior to determine what is and is not appropriate for the government to regulate. In addition, the principle of utility provided Bentham with a new and simple theory of punishment, a theory that he thought could not only be justified more readily than the older theories, but could also achieve the purposes of punishment far more effectively.

Punishment

"All punishment," said Bentham, "is in itself evil" because it inflicts suffering and pain. At the same time, the "object which all laws have in common is to augment the total happiness of the community." If punishment is to be justified from a utilitarian point of view, it must be shown, said Bentham, that the pain inflicted by punishment in some way prevents or excludes some greater pain. Punishment must therefore be "useful" in achieving a greater aggregate of pleasure and happiness and has no justification if its effect is simply to add still more units or lots of pain to the community. The principle of utility would clearly call for the elimination of pure "retribution," where someone is made to suffer only because his act caused his victim pain, for no useful purpose is served by adding still more pain to the sum total society suffers.

This is not to say that utilitarianism rejects the category of punishment, but only that the principle of utility, particularly in the hands of Bentham, called for a reopening of the question of why society should punish offenders and urged a reclassification of cases that are "meet" and "unmeet" for punishment. Punishment should not be inflicted (1) where it is *groundless*, where, for example, there is an offense that admits of compensation and where there is virtual certainty that compensation is forthcoming, or (2) where it must be *inefficacious* in that it cannot prevent a mischievous act, such as when a law made after the act is retroactive, or *ex post facto*, or where a law has already been made but not been announced. Punishment would be inefficacious also where an infant, an insane person, or a drunkard was involved, although Bentham admitted that neither infancy nor intoxication was sufficient grounds for "absolute impunity." Nor should punishment be inflicted (3) where it is *unprofitable* or too *expensive*, "where the mischief it would produce would be greater than what it prevented," or (4) where it is *needless*, "where the mischief may be prevented, or cease of itself, without it: that is at a cheaper rate," particularly in cases "which consist in disseminating pernicious principles in matters of duty," since in these cases persuasion is more efficacious than force.

Whether a given kind of behavior should be left to *private ethics* instead of becoming the object of *legislation* was a question Bentham answered by simply applying the principle of utility. If to involve the whole legislative process and the apparatus of punishment does more harm than good, the matter should be left to private ethics. He was convinced that attempts to regulate sexual immorality would be particularly unprofitable, since this would require intricate supervision, as would "such offenses as ingratitude or rudeness, where the definition is so vague that the judge could not safely be entrusted with the power to punish." Duties that we owe to ourselves could hardly be the concern of law and punishment, nor must we be "coerced" to be "benevolent," although we can be liable on certain occasions for failing to help. But the main concern of law must be to encourage those acts which would lead to the greatest happiness of the community. There is, then, a justification for punishment, which is that through punishment the greatest good for the greatest number is most effectively secured.

Besides providing a rationale for punishment, the principle of utility also gives us some clue to what punishment should consist of. Bentham describes the desirable properties of each unit or lot of punishment by considering "the proportion between punishments and offenses," and he gives the following rules: The punishment must be great enough to outweigh the profit that the offender might get from the offense; the greater the offense, the greater the punishment. Where two offenses come in competition, the punishment for the greater offense must be sufficient to induce a man to prefer the less. Punishments should be variable and adaptable to fit the particular circumstances, although each offender should get the same punishment for the same offense. The amount of punishment should never be greater then the minimum required to make it effective. The more uncertain that an offender will be caught, the greater should be the punishment, and if an offense is habitual, the punishment must outweigh not only the profit of the immediate offense but of the undiscovered offenses. These rules led Bentham to conclude that punishment should be *variable* to fit the particular case, *equable* so as to inflict equal pain for similar offenses, *commensurable* in order that punishments for different classes of crimes be proportional, *characteristic* so as to impress the imagination of potential offenders, *frugal* so as not to be excessive, *reformatory* in order to correct faulty behavior, *disabling* in order to deter future offenders, *compensatory* to the sufferer, and, in order not to create new problems, have *popular* acceptance and be capable of *remittance* for sufficient cause.

BENTHAM'S RADICALISM

It was inevitable that Bentham would discover elements in the law and the general social structure of England that did not fit the requirements set by the principle of utility. Bentham wanted the legislative process to operate on the principle of utility with practically the same rigor with which the stars obey the principle of gravitation. To systematic thought he wanted to add systematic action, so that wherever he found a discrepancy between the actual legal and social order on the one hand and the principle of utility on the other, he wanted to press for reforms. He traced most of the evils of the legal system to the judges who, he charged, "made the common law. Do you know how they make it? Just as a man makes laws for his dog. When your dog does anything you want to break him of, you wait till he does it and then beat him . . . this is the way judges make laws for you and me." Having exposed one monstrous evil after another, Bentham was impelled by his zeal to reform these evils and to become an aggressive philosophical radical.

Bentham laid the cause for the breakdown of the principle of utility to the very structure of the aristocratic society of his day. Why should social evils and evils of the legal system persist even after he had demonstrated that certain new modes of behavior would produce the "greatest happiness of the greatest number?" The answer, he thought, was that those in power did not want the "greatest happiness of the greatest number." The rulers were more concerned with their own interests. Bentham was acutely aware that men seek their own happiness. The object of government, however, is to help achieve the greatest happiness of the greatest number. Whenever those in power represent only a class or a small group, their self-interest will be in conflict with the proper end of government. The way to overcome this conflict or contradiction is to identify the rulers and the ruled, or to put the government into the hands of the people. If there is an identity between the rulers and the ruled, their interests will be the same and the greatest happiness of the greatest number will be assured. This identity of interest cannot, by definition, be achieved under a monarchy, for the monarch acts in his own interests or at best aims at the happiness of a special class grouped around him. It is in a democracy that the greatest happiness of the greatest number is most apt to be realized, for the rulers are the people, and representatives of the people are chosen precisely because they promise to serve the greatest good. The application of the principle of utility clearly required, as Bentham saw it, the rejection of monarchy with all its corollaries, and so he would do away with king, house of peers, and the established church and would prefer to construct a democratic order after the model of the United States. Although Bentham rejected the doctrine of natural rights, he found in the principle of utilitarianism a strong argument for democracy. Each person, he said, can achieve his greatest happiness in an environment of freedom, which democracy makes possible. He believed, moreover, that since "all government is in itself one vast evil," its only justification is to apply evil in order to prevent or exclude some greater evil.

Bentham's radicalism consisted of his desire to press for major social reforms in order to put his philosophical principles into practice, and his reforms were required in order to construct the kind of society and legal process that could most likely contribute the greatest happiness to the greatest number.

Mill

Mill was as much concerned with the problems of society as was Bentham. The principle of the greatest happiness inevitably led all utilitarians to consider how the individual and the government should be related. Bentham had put his faith in democracy as the great cure for social evils inasmuch as in a democracy the interests of the rulers and the ruled are the same because the rulers are the ruled. But Mill did not have the same implicit faith in democracy that Bentham had. Although Mill agreed that democracy is the best form of government, he set forth in his essay *On Liberty* certain dangers inherent in the democratic form of government. Principally, he warned that the will of the people is most often the will of the majority, and it is entirely possible for the majority to oppress the minority. In addition, there is in a democracy the tyranny of opinion, a danger as great as oppression. Even in a democracy, therefore, it is necessary to set up safeguards against the forces that would deny men their free and full self-development. In his concern to eliminate clear social evils, Mill reflected Bentham's desire for reform. But Mill was particularly concerned to preserve liberty by setting limits to the actions of government.

Mill argued that "the sole end for which mankind are warranted, individually or collectively, in interfering with the liberty of action of any of their number, is self-protection. That the only purpose for which power can be rightly exercised over any member of a civilized community, against his will, is to prevent harm to others." There is, of course, a legitimate role for government, but, said Mill, no government should interfere with its subjects (1) when the action can be done better by private persons, (2) when, although the government could possibly do the action better than private individuals, it is desirable for the individuals to do it for their development and education, and (3) when there is danger that too much power will unnecessarily accrue to the government. Mill's argument for liberty was, therefore, an argument for individualism. Let each individual pursue his happiness in his own way. Even in the realm of ideas, men must be free to express their thoughts and beliefs, because truth is most quickly discovered when opportunity is given to refute falsehoods. Mill took the position that "there is the greatest difference between

For biographical note on Mill, see p. 81.

John Stuart Mill. *(The Bettmann Archive)*

presuming an opinion to be true because, with every opportunity for contesting it, it has not been refuted, and assuming its truth for the purpose of not permitting its refutation." He assumed, however, that it is important that the truth be known, and his whole concept of liberty, unlike Bentham's, was conceived as the precondition for developing the full possibilities of human nature.

As he considered the ideal goal of man, Mill asked, "What more or better can be said of any condition of human affairs than that it brings human beings themselves nearer to the best thing they can be?" But is it the function of government to make human beings the best thing they can be? Mill had a deep dislike for the totalitarian state even though he lived too early to see its ugliest manifestations. When he set forth the limits beyond which the government must not go, Mill argued forcefully that a man must not, except to prevent harm, be subject to the power of government, and especially "his own good, either physical or moral, is not a sufficient warrant."

Still, Mill had departed sufficiently from Bentham's version of utilitarianism to set in motion subtle forces that moved Mill from his clear individualism to tepid forms of collectivism. If he was concerned with quality instead of quantity in pleasures, and if this quality is based on human beings' being "the best thing they can be," and, finally, if only those persons who have experienced the higher pleasures can know them, there is the natural urge for those who know these qualitatively higher pleasures to want others to have them also. But what is to be done if those who do not know and appreciate the higher values do not want them? It is not surprising that in this situation Mill advocated, for example, compulsory education, thereby reversing his earlier view that men must not interfere with the liberty of any member of mankind even for "his own good." It is most often in the name of man's good that the state moves into the area of man's freedom.

What Mill said about liberty has particular relevance in the twentieth century, which has witnessed the encroachment of government on the actions and thoughts of men everywhere. But the difficulties of stating utilitarianism as a consistent philosophy are nowhere better seen than in Mill's own attempts to defend its principle. A good example of his thought is found in his essay *On Liberty*, a portion of which is found in the following selected reading.

Reading _____

The Limits of State Power
Mill

The object of this essay is to assert one very simple principle, as entitled to govern absolutely the dealings of society with the individual in the way of compulsion and control, whether the means used be physical force in the form of legal penalties or the moral coercion of public opinion. The principle is that the sole end for which mankind are warranted, individually or collectively, in interfering with the liberty of action of any of their number is self-protection. That the only purpose for which power can be rightfully exercised over any member of a civilized community, against his will, is to prevent harm to others. His own good, either physical or moral, is not a sufficient warrant. He cannot rightfully be compelled to do or forbear because it will be better for him to do so, because it will make him happier, because, in the opinions of others, to do so would be wise or even right. These are good reasons for remonstrating with him, or reasoning with him, or persuading him, or entertaining him, but not for compelling him or visiting him with any evil in case he do otherwise. To justify that, the conduct from which it is desired to deter him must be calculated to produce evil to someone else. The only part of the conduct of anyone for which he is amenable to society is that which concerns others. In the part which merely concerns himself, his independence is, of right, absolute. Over himself, over his own body and mind, the individual is sovereign. . . .

It is proper to state that I forego any advantage which could be derived to my argument from the idea of abstract right as a thing independent of utility. I regard utility as the ultimate appeal on all ethical questions; but it must be utility in the largest sense, grounded on the permanent interests of man as a progressive being. Those interests, I contend, authorize the subjection of individual spontaneity to external control only in respect to those actions of each which concern the interest of other people. . . .

. . . This, then, is the appropriate region of human liberty. It comprises, first, the inward domain of consciousness, demanding liberty of conscience in the most comprehensive sense, liberty of thought and feeling, absolute freedom of opinion and sentiment on all subjects, practical or speculative, scientific, moral, or theological. The liberty of expressing and publishing opinions may seem to fall under a different principle, since it belongs to that part of the conduct of an individual which concerns other people, but, being almost of as much importance as the liberty of thought itself and resting in great part on the same reasons, is practically inseparable from it. Secondly, the principle requires liberty of tastes and pursuits, of framing the plan of our life to suit our own character, of doing as we like, subject to such consequences as may follow, without impediment from our fellow creatures, so long as what we do does not harm them, even though they should think our conduct foolish, perverse, or wrong. Thirdly, from this liberty of each individual follows the liberty, within the same limits, of combination among individuals; freedom to unite for any purpose not involving harm to others; the persons combining being supposed to be of full age and not forced or deceived.

No society in which these liberties are not, on the whole, respected is free, whatever may be its form of government; and none is completely free in which they do not exist absolute and unqualified. The only freedom which deserves the name is that of pursuing our own good in our own way, so long as we do not attempt to deprive others of theirs or impede their efforts to obtain it. Each is the proper guardian of his own health, whether bodily *or* mental and spiritual. Mankind are greater gainers by suffering each other to live as seems good to themselves than by compelling each to live as seems good to the rest. . . .

. . . If all mankind minus one were of one opinion, mankind would be more justified in silencing that one person then he, if he had the power, would be justified in silencing mankind. Were an opinion a personal possession of no value except to the owner, if to be obstructed in the enjoyment of it were simply a private injury, it would make some difference whether the injury was inflicted only on a few persons or on many. But the peculiar evil of silencing the expression of an opinion is that it is robbing the human race, posterity as well as the existing generation—those who dissent from the opinion, still more than those who hold it. If the opinion is right, they are deprived of the opportunity of exchanging error for truth; if wrong, they lose, what is almost as great a benefit, the clearer perception and livelier impression of truth produced by its collision with error. . . .

. . . But it is not the minds of heretics that are deteriorated most by the ban placed on all inquiry which does not end in the orthodox conclusions. The greatest harm done is to those who are not heretics, and whose whole mental development is cramped and their reason cowed by the fear of heresy. Who can compute what the world loses in the multitude of promising intellects combined with timid characters, who dare not follow out any bold, vigorous, independent train of thought, lest it should land them in something which would admit of being considered irreligious or immoral?

We have now recognized the necessity to the mental well-being of mankind (on which all their other well-being depends) of freedom of opinion, and freedom of the expression of opinion, on four distinct grounds, which we will now briefly recapitulate:

First, if any opinion is compelled to silence, that opinion may, for aught we can certainly know, be true. To deny this is to assume our own infallibility.

Secondly, though the silenced opinion be an error, it may, and very commonly does, contain a portion of truth; and since the general or prevailing opinion on any subject is rarely or never the whole truth, it is only by the collision of adverse opinions that the remainder of the truth has any chance of being supplied.

Thirdly, even if the received opinion be not only true, but the whole truth; unless it is suffered to be, and actually is, vigorously and earnestly contested, it will, by most of those who receive it, be held in the manner of a prejudice, with little comprehension or feeling of its rational grounds. And not only this, but, fourthly, the meaning of the doctrine itself will be in danger of being lost or enfeebled, and deprived of its vital effect on the character and conduct; the dogma becoming a mere formal profession, inefficacious for good, but cumbering the ground and preventing the growth of any real and heartfelt conviction from reason or personal experience. . . .

Such being the reasons which make it imperative that human beings should be free to form opinions and to express their opinions without reserve; and such the baneful consequences to the intellectual; and through that to the moral nature of man, unless this liberty is either conceded or asserted in spite of prohibition; let us next examine whether the same reasons do not require that men should be free to act upon their opinions—to carry these out in their lives without hindrance, either physical or moral, from their fellow men, so long as it is at their own risk and peril. This last proviso is of course indispensable. No one pretends that actions should be as free as opinions. On the contrary, even opinions lose their immunity when the circumstances in which they are expressed are such as to constitute their expression a positive instigation to some mischievous act. An opinion that corn dealers are starvers of the poor, or that private property is robbery, ought to be unmolested when simply circulated through the press, but may justly incur punishment when delivered orally to an excited mob assembled before the house of a corn dealer, or when handed about among the same mob in the form of a placard. Acts, of whatever kind, which without justifiable cause do harm to others may be, and in the more important cases absolutely require to be, controlled by the unfavorable sentiments, and, when needful, by the active interference of mankind. The liberty of the individual must be thus far limited; he must not make himself a nuisance to other people. But if he refrains from molesting others in what concerns them, and merely acts according to his own inclination and judgment in things which concern himself, the same reasons which show that opinion should be free prove also that he should be allowed, without molestation, to carry his opinions into practice at his own cost. That mankind are not infallible; that their truths, for the most part, are only half-truths; the unity of opinion, unless resulting from the fullest and freest comparison of opposite opinions, is not desirable, and diversity not an evil, but a good, until mankind are much more capable than at present of recognizing all sides of the truth, are principles applicable to men's modes of action not less than to their opinions. As it is useful that while mankind are imperfect there should be different opinions, so it is that there should be different experiments of living; that free scope should be given to varieties of character, short of injury to others; and that the worth of different modes of life should be proved practically, when anyone thinks fit to try them. It is desirable, in short, that in things which do not primarily concern others, individuality should assert itself. Where not the person's own character but the traditions or customs of other people and the rule of conduct, there is wanting one of the principal ingredients of human happiness, and quite the chief ingredient of individual and social progress. . . .

What, then, is the rightful limit to the sovereignty of the individual over himself? Where does the authority of society begin? How much of human life should be assigned to individuality, and how much to society?

Each will receive its proper share if each has that which more particularly concerns it. To individuality should belong the part of life in which it is chiefly the individual that is interested; to society, the part which chiefly interests society.

Though society is not founded on a contract, and though no good purpose is answered by inventing a contract in order to deduce social obligations from it, everyone who receives the protection of society owes a return for the benefit, and the fact of living in society renders it indispensable that each should be bound to observe a certain line of conduct toward the rest. This conduct consists, first, in not injuring the interests of one another, or rather certain interests which, either by express legal provision or by tacit understanding, ought to be considered as rights; and secondly, in each person's bearing his share (to be fixed on some equitable principle) of the labors and sacrifices incurred for defending the society or its members from injury and molestation. These conditions society is justified in enforcing at all costs to those who endeavor to withhold fulfillment. Nor is this all that society may do. The acts of an individual may be hurtful to others or wanting in due consideration for their welfare, without going to the length of violating any of their constituted rights. The offender may then be justly punished by opinion, though not by law. As soon as any part of a person's conduct affects prejudicially the interests of others, society has jurisdiction over it, and the question whether the general welfare will or will not be promoted by interfering with it becomes open to discussion. But there is no room for entertaining any such question when a person's conduct affects the interests of no person besides himself, or needs not affect them unless they like (all the persons concerned being of full age and the ordinary amount of understanding). In all such cases, there should be perfect freedom, legal and social, to do the action and stand the consequences.

It would be a great misunderstanding of this doctrine to suppose that it is one of selfish indifference which pretends that human beings have no business with each other's conduct of life, and that they should not concern themselves about the well-doing or well-being of one another, unless their own interest is involved. Instead of any diminution, there is need of a great increase of disinterested exertion to promote the good of others. But disinterested benevolence can find other instruments to persuade people to their good than whips and scourges, either of the literal or the metaphorical sort. . . .

. . . But neither one person, nor any number of persons, is warranted in saying to another human creature of ripe years that he shall not do with his life for his own benefit what he chooses to do with it. . . .

From John Stuart Mill, *On Liberty*, London, 1859.

QUESTIONS FOR REVIEW AND DISCUSSION

1. Bentham and Mill each give reasons for justifying the use of law to control people's behavior. What are these reasons?
2. How does the principle of utility help to define the purpose which the laws should try to accomplish?
3. According to Mill, what single purpose justifies the government's interfering with a person's liberty of action?
4. How does Mill relate the pursuit of truth and the freedom of speech?
5. According to Bentham and Mill, is it appropriate for the government to require cyclists to wear helmets and to prohibit people from smoking?

13

Class Conflict

Marx

Karl Marx was born in Trier, Germany, in 1818. His father was a lawyer and his grandfather a rabbi. After high school, Marx went to the University of Bonn, where in 1835 at the age of seventeen he began the study of law. A year later he transferred to the University of Berlin, giving up the study of law and pursuing instead the study of philosophy. At the age of twenty-three, he received his doctoral degree from the University of Jena. While at the University of Berlin, he came under the spell of Hegel's philosophy. In time, however, Marx gave up certain aspects of Hegel's thought. Nevertheless, Marx did take from Hegel the notion that there is a process going on in history, a conflict of opposites, or what Hegel called a "dialectic." But whereas Hegel said this dialectic represents ideas in conflict, Marx, under the influence of the philosopher Feuerbach, came to believe that this conflict in history was located in the material conditions of life. That is why Marx developed his central theory of *dialectical materialism* as an explanation of where history is moving. At age twenty-five, Marx went to Paris, then to Brussels, and finally to London. In London, he met Friedrich Engels, with whom he wrote a statement of principles for the international Communist League which was published in 1848 as *The Manifesto of the Communist Party*. Marx became a prolific writer, submitting articles on European affairs to the *New York Daily Tribune*. His most famous work is *Das Kapital*. Karl Marx died in London in 1883 at the age of sixty-five.

In his early writing, namely *The Communist Manifesto*, Marx had formulated his basic doctrine, which he considered in many ways original. "What I did that was new," he said, "was to prove (1) that the *existence of classes* is only bound up with particular historic phases in the development of production; (2) that the class struggle necessarily leads to the dictatorship of the proletariat; (3) that the dictatorship itself only constitutes the transition to the *abolition of all classes* and to a classless society." Later, while in London, he worked out in painstaking detail his argument, which he thought provided scientific support for the more general pronouncements in his *Manifesto*. Accordingly, he stated in the preface to *Das Kapital* that "it is the ultimate aim of this work, to lay bare the economic law of motion of modern society." This law of motion became his theory of *dialectical materialism*.

FIVE EPOCHS

Marx indicated that the class struggle is bound up with "particular historic phases." He distinguished five such phases, dividing history into five separate epochs. These he called (1) the primitive communal, (2) slave, (3) feudal, (4) capitalist, and, as a prediction of things to come, (5) the socialist and communist phases. For the most part, this was a more or less conventional division of Western social history into its major periods. But what Marx wanted to do was to discover the "law of motion," which could explain not only *that* history had produced these various epochs, but also the *reasons why* these particular epochs unfolded as they did. If he could discover history's law of motion, he could not only explain the past but also predict the future. He had assumed that the behavior of individuals and societies is subject to the same kind of analysis as are the objects of physical and biological science. He considered the commodity and value products of economics as being "of the same order as those [minute elements] dealt with in microscopic anatomy."

Marx at age 42. (*Culver Pictures*)

When he analyzed the structure of each historical epoch, he thought he discovered there the fact of class conflict as the decisive force at work.

CHANGE: QUANTITATIVE AND QUALITATIVE

What history shows is that social and economic orders are in a process of change. The effect of Marx's dialectical materialism was to show, also, that since the material order is primary, since it is the basis of what is truly real, there are no stable, fixed points in reality because everything is involved in the dialectic process of change. With this view, Marx had rejected the notion that somewhere there are stable, permanent structures of reality or certain "eternal verities." Materialism meant to Marx that the world as we see it is all there is, that the materialist outlook on the world "is simply the conception of nature as it is, without any reservations." Moreover, with Engels he agreed that all of nature, "from the smallest thing to the biggest, from a grain of sand to the sun . . . to man, is in . . . a ceaseless state of movement and change." History is the process of change from one epoch to another in accordance with the rigorous and inexorable laws of historical motion.

For Marxism, change is not the same as mere growth. A society does not simply mature the way a boy becomes a man. Nor does nature simply move in an eternally uniform and constantly repeated circle. It passes through a real history. Change means the emergence of new structures, novel forms. What causes change is simply the *quantitative* alteration of things, which leads to something *qualitatively* new. For example, as one increases the temperature of water, it not only becomes warmer, but it finally reaches the point at which this quantitative change changes water from a liquid into vapor. Reversing the process, by gradually decreasing the temperature of water, one finally changes it from liquid to a solid, to ice. Similarly, a large pane of glass can be made to vibrate, the range of vibrations increasing as the quantity of force applied to it is increased. But finally, a further addition of force will no longer add to the quantity of vibration but will, instead, cause a qualitative change, the shattering of the glass.

Marx thought that history displays this kind of change by which certain quantitative elements in the economic order finally force a qualitative change in the arrangements of society. This is the process that has moved history from the primitive communal to the slave and in turn to the feudal and capitalist epochs. Indeed, Marx's prediction that the capitalist order would fall was based on this notion that changes in the quantitative factors in capitalism would inevitably destroy capitalism. With the low-key expression of one who was describing how water will turn into steam as the heat is increased, Marx wrote in his *Das Kapital* that "while there is a progressive diminution in the number of capitalist magnates, there is of course a corresponding increase in the mass of poverty, enslavement, degeneration and exploitation, but at the same time a steady intensification of the role of the working class." Then "the centralization of the means of production and the socialization of labor reach a point where they prove incompatible with their capitalist husk. This bursts asunder. The knell of private property sounds. The expropriators are expropriated." This, on the social level, is what Marx describes as the *qualitative leap,* which is "the leap to a new aggregate state . . . where consequently quantity is transformed into quality."

DETERMINISM OR INEXORABLE LAW

There is a basic difference between the transformation of water into steam as a laboratory experiment and the movement of society from feudalism to capitalism and finally from capitalism to socialism. The difference is that one can *choose* to raise or not to raise the temperature of the water. But there are no such hypothetical qualifications surrounding history. Although one can say "*if* the temperature is raised," one cannot say "*if* the social order is thus and so." Marxism holds that there *is* a fundamental "contradiction within the very essence of things" causing the dialectic movement, and although there are ways of delaying or accelerating this inner movement in the nature of things, there is no way to prevent its ultimate unfolding. All things are related to each other *causally*; nothing floats freely. For this reason, there are no isolated events either in physical nature or in human behavior or, therefore, in history. That there is a definite and inexorable process of movement and change at work producing "history" is as certain as the plain fact that nature exists.

END OF HISTORY

For Marx, history would have an end with the emergence of socialism and finally communism. Here, again, he followed Hegel's theory in an inverted way. For Hegel, the dialectic process comes to an end when the idea of freedom is perfectly realized, for by definition this would mean the end of all conflict and struggle. Marx, however, seeing that the dialectic or struggle of opposites is in the material order and therefore in the struggle between the classes, predicted that when the inner contradictions between the classes were resolved, the principle cause of movement and change would disappear, a classless society would emerge where all the forces and interests would be in perfect balance, and this equilibrium would be perpetual. For this reason, there could be no further development in history, inasmuch as there would no longer be any conflict to impel history on to any future epoch.

Marx's theory of the dialectic development of the five epochs of history rested on the distinction between the order of material reality on the one hand and the order of human thought on the other. He was convinced that the only way to achieve a realistic understanding of history, and therefore to avoid errors in the practical program of revolutionary activity, was to assess properly the roles of the material order and the order of human thought. Accordingly, Marx made a sharp distinction between the substructure (i.e., the infrastructure) and the superstructure of society. The *infrastructure* is the material order, containing the energizing force that moves history, whereas the *superstructure* consists of men's ideas and simply reflects the configurations of the material order.

INFRASTRUCTURE: THE MATERIAL ORDER

To Marx materialism meant the sum total of the natural environment, and this included for him all of inorganic nature, the organic world, social life, and human consciousness. Unlike Democritus, who defined matter in terms of irreducible tiny particles, atoms, Marx defines matter as "objective reality existing outside the human mind. . . ." Again, unlike Democritus, who considered atoms as the "bricks of the universe," Marxist materialism did not take this approach of trying to discover a single form of matter in all things. The chief characteristic of Marxist materialism is that it recognizes a wide diversity in the material world without reducing it to any one form of matter. The material order contains everything in the natural world that exists outside our minds; the notion that any spiritual reality, God, for example, exists outside our minds and as something other than nature is denied. That human beings possess minds means only that organic matter has developed to the point where the cerebral cortex has become an organ capable of the intricate process of reflex action called "human thought."

Moreover, the human mind has been conditioned by the labor activity of man as a social being. For this reason, relying on the Darwinian notion of the evolution of man, Marxism affirms the primacy of the material order and regards mental activity as a secondary by-product of matter. The earliest forms of life were without mental activity until man's ancestors developed the use of their forelimbs, learned to walk erect, and began to use natural objects as tools to procure food and to protect themselves against harm. The big transformation from animal to human being came with the ability to fashion and use tools and to control such forces as fire, which, in turn, made possible a wider variety of food and the further development of the brain. Even now the complex material order is the basic reality, whereas the mental realm is derivative from it. In particular, the material order consists of (1) the *factors* of production and (2) the *relations* of production.

Factors of Production

The basic fact of human life is that in order to live, men must secure food, clothing, and shelter, and in order to have these material things, men must produce them. Wherever we find any society of men, there are always at hand those factors of production—the raw materials, instruments, and the experienced labor skill—by which things are produced to sustain life. But these factors or forces of production represent chiefly the way men are related to these material things. Of greater importance is the way men are related to one another in the process of production. What Marx wanted to emphasize was that production always takes place as a social act, where men struggle against and utilize nature not as individuals, but as groups, as societies. The static analysis of what goes into production was for Marx, therefore, not as important as the dynamic relations of men to each other as a producing society. To be sure, the factors of production were seen by Marx as affecting the relations of production, inasmuch as such circumstances as the scarcity of raw materials or the ownership by some of the instruments of production could have a considerable effect on the way men would become related to one another in the process of production. In any case, Marx centered his analysis of the material order on the way men engaged in the act of production, on the *relations of production.*

Relations of Production

Marx considered his analysis of the relations of production to be virtually the core of his social analysis. It was here that he thought he had located the energizing force of the dialectic process. The key to the relations of production was the status of property or its ownership; that is, what determined how men were related to one another in the process of production was their relation to property. Under the slave system, for example, the slave owner owned the means of production, even owning the slave, whom he could purchase or sell. The institution of slavery was a necessary product of the dialectic process, since it arose at a time when advanced forms of tools made possible more stable and sustained agricultural activity and a division of labor. But in the slave epoch, as well as in the subsequent historical epochs, the laborer, slave or hired, was "exploited" in that he shared in neither the ownership nor the fruits of production. The basic struggle between the classes is seen already in the slave system, for the ownership of property divides the society between those who have and those who have not. In the feudal system, the feudal lord owned the means of production. The serf rose above the level of the former slaves, had some share in the ownership of tools, but still worked for the feudal lord and, says Marx, felt exploited and struggled against his exploiter. In capitalism, the workers are free as compared with the slaves and the serfs, but they do not own the means of production, and in order to survive, they must sell their labor to the capitalist.

The shift from slave to feudal to capitalist relations of production is not the result of rational design but a product of the inner movement and logic of the material order. Specifically, the impelling force to survive leads to the creation of tools, and, in turn, the kinds of tools created affect the way men become related to each other. Certain tools, such as the bow and arrow, permit independent existence, while the plough logically implies a division of labor. Similarly, whereas a spinning wheel can be used in the home or in small shops, heavier machinery requires large factories and a new concentration of workers in a given locality. Such is the survey Marx makes of the unfolding of the epochs of history, emphasizing that this process moves in a deterministic way, impelled by basic economic drives whose direction is set by the technological requirements of the moment. The thoughts and behavior of all men are determined by their relations to one another and to the means of production. Although in all periods there is conflict and struggle between the different classes, the class struggle is particularly violent under capitalism.

There are at least three characteristics of the class struggle under capitalism. *First,* the classes have now been reduced basically to two, the owners, or bourgeoisie, and the workers, or proletariat. *Second,* the relation of these classes to each other rests on a fundamental contradiction, namely, that although both classes participate in the act of production, the mode of distribution of the fruits of production does not correspond to the contribution made by each class. The reason for this discrepancy is that the price of labor in the capitalist system is determined by the forces of supply and demand, and the large supply of workers tends to send wages down to a subsistence level. But the products created by labor can be sold for more than it costs to hire the labor force. Marx's analysis assumed the labor theory of value, that the value of the product is created by the amount of labor put into it. form this point of view, since the product of labor could be sold for more than the cost of labor, the capitalist would then reap the difference, which Marx called "surplus value."

The existence of surplus value constituted the contradiction in the capitalistic system for Marx. For this reason, Marx argued that in the capitalistic system exploitation was not merely an isolated occurrence here or there, now or then, but always and everywhere, because of the manner in which the iron law of wages operates. Still, Marx made no moral judgment of this condition, saying that as a matter of fact the worker received what he was worth if determination of the wage through the supply and demand of labor is the norm. "It is true," he said, "that the daily maintenance of labor power costs only half a day's labor, and that nevertheless the labor power can work for an entire working day, with the result that the value which its use creates during a working day is twice the value of a day's labor power. So much the better for the purchaser, but it is nowise an injustice to the seller [worker]."

In a sense, Marx did not "blame" the capitalist for this arrangement any more than he would attribute to the capitalist the organization of the laborers into a self-conscious and powerful group. These are rather the consequences of the material forces of history, which have determined the existence of these arrangements. Labor became a coherent group only because large-scale machinery required large factories, and suddenly the multitude of workers who were required to run the machines found themselves living close together. That history had produced the capitalist system was one thing, but that the system rested on a contradiction was something else. For this reason, Marx "excused" the capitalist but argued that for "scientific reasons" he must say that the class conflict caused by this contradiction of surplus value would force the dialectic movement to the next stage in history, namely, socialism and finally communism.

The *third* characteristic of this class struggle was the prediction that the condition of the workers in capitalism would become progressively more wretched, that the poor would become poorer and more numerous, while the rich would become richer and fewer until the masses would take over all the means of production. As a matter of historic fact, Marx could not have been more wrong than he was on this point, since it is precisely the workers whose condition has improved most dramatically in the highly developed capitalistic economies. Still, Marx argued that as long as the means of production remained in the hands of a few, the class struggle would continue inexorably until the contradiction was resolved, ending the dialectic movement.

With this rigorous view of the nature of the class struggle, Marx had clearly assigned to the infrastructure, to the material order, the supreme significance in the dialectic process of history. What, then, is the status and role of human thought? Do ideas have power and consequences? For Marx, ideas represented a mere reflection of the basic material reality, and for this reason, he described the enterprise of human thought as the *superstructure*.

SUPERSTRUCTURE: THE ORIGIN AND ROLE OF IDEAS

Each epoch, said Marx, has its dominant ideas. Men formulate ideas in the areas of religion, morality, and law. Hegel had argued that men agreed for the most part in their religious, moral, and juristic thought because there was at work in them a universal spirit, the Idea. Marx, on the contrary, said that the ideas of each epoch grow out of and reflect the actual material conditions of the historic period. For this reason, thinking comes *after* the material order has affected men's minds. Thus Marx accounted for the relationship between man's conscious life and his material environment by saying, "It is not the consciousness of men that determines their being, but, on the contrary, their social being that determines their consciousness."

The source of ideas is rooted in the material order. Such ideas as justice and goodness and even religious salvation, says Marx, are only various modes of rationalizing the existing order. Justice, for the most part, represents the will of the economically dominant class and its desire to "freeze" the relations of production as they are. Marx had been impressed during his early years as a law student with the teachings of the jurist Savigny, who had defined law as the "spirit" of each epoch. Savigny argued that law is like language and is therefore different for each society. Like Savigny, but now for different reasons, Marx rejected the notion of a universal and eternal standard of justice. Indeed, he thought it followed with logical rigor that if ideas simply reflect the inner order of the relations of production, each successive epoch will have its own set of ideas, its own dominant philosophy.

The conflict of ideas within a society at a given time is caused by the dynamic nature of the economic order. The dialectic process, which is a struggle of opposites, has its material aspect but also its ideological side. Since members of a society are related to the dialectic process by belonging to different classes, their interests are different, and therefore their ideas are opposed. Moreover, the greatest error, according to Marx, is to fail to realize that ideas that accurately reflected the material order at an earlier time no longer do so because, in the meantime, the substructure of reality has moved on. Those who hold on to old ideas do not realize that there is no longer any reality corresponding to those ideas, and their desire to reverse the order of things to fit these ideas makes them "reactionaries." However, an astute observer can discover the direction in which history is moving and will adjust his thinking and behavior to it. The fact is, says Marx, that the dialectic process involves the disappearance of some things and the birth of new things; that is why one epoch dies and another is born, and there is no way to stop the process. Those who assume the objective reality of "eternal principles" of justice, goodness, and righteousness do not realize that such notions cannot refer to reality since the material order, which is the only reality, is constantly changing. "The sum total of the productive relations," says Marx, "constitutes the economic structure of society—the real foundation on which rise legal and political superstructures . . . [and which] determines the general character of the social, political, and spiritual processes of life."

Because he believed that ideas were chiefly a reflection of the material order, Marx attributed a limited role or function to them. Ideas are particularly useless when they bear no relationship to the economic reality. Marx's impatience with reformers, do-gooders, and utopians was intense. He argued that ideas cannot determine the direction of history, that they can only hinder or accelerate the inexorable dialectic. For this reason, Marx thought that his own ideas about capitalism did not constitute a moral condemnation. He did not say that capitalism was either wicked or due to human folly; it was caused by the "law of motion of society." In the end, Marx assumed that he was proceeding in his analysis as a scientist, limiting his thought to objective reality, abstracting from it the laws of motion.

ALIENATION: MARX'S CONCEPT OF THE CONDITION OF MAN

Marx described the condition of man in industrial society with the word "alienation." Man, he said, is alienated. To be alienated means to be separated, to be estranged. It is especially the worker, the laborers, who is alienated. What is he alienated or separated from and why?

The cause of man's alienation, said Marx, is the very organization of the world of work. The existence of private property means that the worker invests his labor in materials and things which are not his. The finished product which results from his labor does not belong to the laborer. The worker is used as a means to produce objects and is paid a wage. But the worker is separated or alienated from the things he produces because they are

London, Cheapside, a place familiar to Marx. *(Culver Pictures)*

not the things *he* wants to make. Also, in the process of working on things, the worker cannot use his own ideas but must do what others tell him to do and do it in the way others direct or order him. In many respects, the workers begin to take on the characteristics of machines. Even more serious is the reduction of human beings to extensions or even slaves of machines.

All this leads Marx to say that man is alienated from his humanity, from what it truly means to be a human being. The worker's labor is put into the objects he makes. This is what Marx means when he says that labor is "objectified" or when he speaks of the "objectification of labor." His labor, and therefore a part of himself, has been put into the objects of his work. And since the finished objects are not his, that part of himself which is now in the object has been separated, alienated, from himself.

The very process of working represents a special form of alienation. This is so because a person's work is no longer an expression of his own creative powers. Work ceases to express a worker's individual feelings and ideas or even his unique nature. As a result, the worker as Marx says, "does not fulfill himself in his work but denies himself, has a feeling of misery rather than well-being, does not develop fully his mental and physical energies but is physically exhausted and mentally debased." For this reason, the worker "feels himself at home only during leisure time, whereas at work he feels homeless."

Marx's chief criticism of industrial society is that it transforms human beings into things. In addition to the exploitation of the working class by capitalists, which results in the unfair distribution of wealth, Marx was even more concerned with the gradual degradation of all men by the demands of the industrial system. The ultimate result of the process of alienation, he said, was that the joy of life was destroyed. Men now failed to become what their human nature could under better circumstances lead them to be. Everywhere human beings are reduced, even in their own sight and experience, to a level of life far below their capacity or their hopes. This represents not only a loss of personal power, but also a reduction of personal dignity and a serious absence of the sense of meaning and purpose to life. In the end, the worker sees many objects around him, but they are alien to him, they are not his. So he reflects on himself, he sees that he too is alien to himself. He is alienated from himself in that he can see the difference between what his actual daily life consists of as compared with what his life could or even ought to be. The reality is that his life is dominated by objects and people external to and alienated from himself. His internal life—the life of feelings, of spontaneous and creative choices, in short his very personal and individual life directed toward self-fulfillment and higher values—remains virtually undeveloped and unfulfilled.

As Marx points out in the selected reading which follows, the only time men feel that they are acting freely is when they are expressing their animal functions, namely, eating, drinking, and procreating. To be sure, says Marx, these are human as well as animal functions, but under the circumstances of alienation in all the rest of life, they are reduced to animal functions.

Reading _____

Alienated Labor

Marx

We proceed from a *present* fact of political economy.

The worker becomes poorer the more wealth he produces, the more his production increases in power and extent. The worker becomes a cheaper commodity the more commodities he produces. The *increase in value* of the world of things is directly proportional to the *decrease in value* of the human world. Labor not only produces commodities. It also produces itself and the worker as a *commodity,* and indeed in the same proportion as it produces commodities in general.

This fact simply indicates that the object which labor produces, its product, stands opposed to it as an *alien thing,* as a *power independent* of the producer. The product of labor is labor embodied and made objective in a thing. It is the *objectification* of labor. The realization of labor is its objectification. In the viewpoint of political economy this realization of labor appears as the *diminution* of the worker, the objectification as the *loss of and subservience to the object,* and the appropriation as *alienation* as externalization.

So much does the realization of labor appear as diminution that the worker is diminished to the point of starvation. So much does objectification appear as loss of the object that the worker is robbed of the most essential objects not only of life but also of work. Indeed, work itself becomes a thing of which he can take possession only with the greatest effort and with the most unpredictable interruptions. So much does the appropriation of the object appear as alienation that the more objects the worker produces, the fewer he can own and the more he falls under the domination of his product, of capital.

All these consequences follow from the fact that the worker is related to the *product of his labor* as to an *alien* object. For it is clear according to this premise: The more the worker exerts himself, the more powerful becomes the alien objective world which he fashions against himself, the poorer he and his inner world become, the less there is that belongs to him. It is the same in religion. The more man attributes to God, the less he retains in himself. The worker puts his life into the object; then it no longer belongs to him but to the object. The greater this activity, the poorer is the worker. What the product of his work is, he is not. The greater this product is, the smaller he is himself. The *externalization* of the worker in his product means not only that his work becomes an object, an *external* existence, but also that it exists *outside him* independently, alien, an autonomous power, opposed to him. The life he has given to the object confronts him as hostile and alien. . . .

Let us now consider more closely the *objectification,* the worker's production and with it the *alienation* and *loss* of the object, his product.

The worker can make nothing without *nature,* without the *sensuous external world.* It is the material wherein his labor realizes itself, wherein it is active, out of which and by means of which it produces.

But as nature furnishes to labor the *means of life* in the sense that labor cannot *live* without objects upon which labor is exercised, nature also furnishes the *means of life* in the narrower sense, namely, the means of physical subsistence of the *worker* himself.

The more the worker *appropriates* the external work and sensuous nature through his labor, the more he deprives himself of the *means of life* in two respects: first, that the sensuous external world gradually ceases to be an object belonging to his labor, a *means of life* of his work; secondly, that it gradually ceases to be a *means of life* in the immediate sense, a means of physical subsistence of the worker.

In these two respects, therefore, the worker becomes a slave to his objects; first, in that he receives an *object of labor,* that is, he receives *labor,* and secondly that he receives the *means of subsistence.* The first enables him to exist as a *worker* and the second as a *physical subject.* The terminus of this slavery is that he can only maintain himself as a *physical subject* so far as he is a *worker* and only as a *physical subject* is he a worker.

(The alienation of the worker in his object is expressed according to the laws of political economy as follows: the more the worker produces, the less he has to consume; the more values he creates the more worthless and unworthy he becomes; the better shaped his product, the more misshapen is he; the more civilized his product, the more barbaric is the worker; the more powerful the work, the more powerless becomes the worker; the more intelligence the work has, the more witless is the worker and the more he becomes a slave of nature.)

Political economy conceals the alienation in the nature of labor by ignoring the direct relationship between the worker (labor) *and production.* To be sure, labor produces marvels for the wealthy but it produces deprivation for the worker. It produces palaces, but hovels for the worker. It produces beauty, but mutilation for the worker. It displaces labor through machines, but it throws some workers back into barbarous labor and turns others into machines. It produces intelligence, but for the worker it produces imbecility and cretinism. . . .

Up to now we have considered the alienation, the externalization of the worker only from one side: his *relationship to the products of his labor.* But alienation is shown not only in the result but also in the *process of production,* in the *producing activity* itself. How could the worker stand in an alien relationship to the product of his activity if he did not alienate himself from himself in the very act of production? After all, the product is only the résumé of activity, of production. If the product of work is externalization, production itself must be active externalization, externalization of activity, activity of externalization. Only alienation—and externalization in the activity of labor itself—is summarized in the alienation of the object of labor.

What constitutes the externalization of labor?

First is the fact that labor is *external* to the laborer—that is, it is not part of his nature—and that the worker does not affirm himself in his work but denies himself, feels miserable and unhappy, develops no free physical and mental energy but mortifies his flesh and ruins his mind. The worker, therefore feels at ease only outside work, and during work he is outside himself. He is at home when he is not working and when he is working he is not at home. His work, therefore, is not voluntary, but coerced, *forced labor.* It is not the satisfaction of a need but only a *means* to satisfy other needs. Its alien character is obvious from the fact that as soon as no physical or other pressure exists, labor is avoided like the plague. External labor, labor in which man is externalized, is labor of self-sacrifice, of penance. Finally, the external nature of work for the worker appears in the fact that it is not his own but another person's, that in work he does not belong to himself but to someone else. In religion the spontaneity of human imagination, the spontaneity of the human brain and heart, acts independently of the individual as an alien, divine or devilish activity. Similarly, the activity of the worker is not his own spontaneous activity. It belongs to another. It is the loss of his own self.

The result, therefore, is that man (the worker) feels that he is acting freely only in his animal functions—eating, drinking, and procreating, or at most in his shelter and finery—while in his human functions he feels only like an animal. The animalistic becomes the human and the human the animalistic.

To be sure, eating, drinking, and procreation are genuine human functions. In abstraction, however, and separated from the remaining sphere of human activities and turned into final and sole ends, they are animal functions.

We have considered labor, the act of alienation of practical human activity, in two aspects: (1) the relationship of the worker to the *product of labor* as an alien object dominating him. This relationship is at the same time the relationship to the sensuous external world, to natural objects as an alien world hostile to him; (2) the relationship of labor to the *act of production in labor*. This relationship is that of the worker to his own activity as alien and not belonging to him, activity as passivity, power as weakness, procreation as emasculation, the worker's *own* physical and spiritual energy, his personal life—for what else is life but activity—as an activity turned against him, independent of him, and not belonging to him. *Self-alienation*, as against the alienation of the *object*, stated above.

We have now to derive a third aspect of *alienated labor* from the two previous ones.

Man is a species-being *[Gattungswesen]* not only in that he practically and theoretically makes his own species as well as that of other things his object, but also—and this is only another expression for the same thing—in that as present and living species he considers himself to be a *universal* and consequently free being.

The life of the species in man as in animals is physical in that man (like the animal) lives by inorganic nature. And as man is more universal than the animal, the realm of inorganic nature by which he lives is more universal. As plants, animals, minerals, air, light, etc., in theory form a part of human consciousness, partly as objects of natural science, partly as objects of art—his spiritual inorganic nature or spiritual means of life which he first must prepare for enjoyment and assimilation—so they also from in practice a part of human life and human activity. Man lives physically only by these products of nature; they may appear in the form of food, heat, clothing, housing, etc. The universality of man appears in practice in the universality which makes the whole of nature his *inorganic* body: (1) as a direct means of life, and (2) as the matter, object, and instrument of his life activity. Nature is the *inorganic body* of man, that is, nature insofar as it is not the human body. Man *lives* by nature. This means that nature is his *body* with which he must remain in perpetual process in order not to die. That the physical and spiritual life of man is tied up with nature is another way of saying that nature is linked to itself, for man is a part of nature.

In alienating (1) nature from man, and (2) man from himself, his own active function, his life activity, alienated labor also alienated the *species* from him; it makes *species-life* the means of individual life. In the first place it alienates species-life and the individual life, and secondly it turns the latter in its abstraction into the purpose of the former, also in its abstract and alienated form.

For labor, *life activity,* and *productive life* appear to man at first only as a *means* to satisfy a need, the need to maintain physical existence. Productive life, however, is species-life. It is life begetting life. In the mode of life activity lies the entire character of a species, its species-character; and free conscious activity is the species-character of man. Life itself appears only as a *means of life.*

The animal is immediately one with its life activity, not distinct from it. The animal is *its life activity.* Man makes his life activity itself into an object of will and consciousness. He has conscious life activity. It is not a determination with which he immediately identifies. Conscious life activity distinguishes man immediately from the life activity of the animal. Only thereby is he a species-being. Or rather, he is only a conscious being—that is, his own life is an object for him—since he is a species-being. Only on that account is his activity free activity. Alienated labor reverses the relationship in that man, since he is a conscious being, makes his life activity, his *essence,* only a means for his *existence.*

The practical creation of an *objective world,* the *treatment* of inorganic nature, is proof that man is a conscious species-being, that is, a being which is related to its species as to its own essence or is related to itself as a species-being. To be sure animals also produce. They build themselves nests, dwelling places, like the bees, beavers, ants, etc. But the animal produces only what is immediately necessary for itself or its young. It produces in a one-sided way while man produces universally. The animal produces under the domination of immediate physical need while man produces free of physical need and only genuinely so in freedom from such need. The animal only produces itself while man reproduces the whole of nature. The animal's product belongs immediately to its physical body while man is free when he confronts his product. The animal builds only according to the standard and need of the species to which it belongs while man knows how to produce according to the standard of any species and at all times knows how to apply an intrinsic standard to the object. Thus man creates also according to the laws of beauty.

In the treatment of the objective world, therefore, man proves himself to be genuinely a *species-being.* This production is his active species-life. Through it nature appears as *his* work and his actuality. The object of labor is thus the *objectification of man's species-life;* he produces himself not only intellectually, as in consciousness, but also actively in a real sense and sees himself in a world he made. In taking from man the object of his production, alienated labor takes from his *species-life,* his actual and objective existence as a species. It changes his superiority to the animal to inferiority, since he is deprived of nature, his inorganic body.

By degrading free spontaneous activity to the level of a means, alienated labor makes the species-life of man a means of his physical existence.

The consciousness which man has from his species is altered through alienation, so that species-life becomes a means for him.

(3) Alienated labor hence turns the *species-existence of man,* and also nature as his mental species-capacity, into an existence *alien* to him, into the *means* of his *individual existence.* It alienates his spiritual nature, his *human essence,* from his own body and likewise from nature outside him.

(4) A direct consequence of man's alienation from the product of his work, from his life activity, and from his species-existence, is the *alienation of man* from *man.* When man confronts himself, he confronts *other* men. What holds true of man's relationship to his work, to the product of his work, and to himself, also holds true of man's relationship to other men, to their labor, and the object of their labor.

In general, the statement that man is alienated from his species-existence means that one man is alienated from another just as each man is alienated from human nature.

The alienation of man, the relation of man to himself, is realized and expressed in the relation between man and other men.

Thus in the relation of alienated labor every man sees the others according to the standard and the relation in which he finds himself as a worker.

We began with an economic fact, the alienation of the worker and his product. We have given expression to the concept of this fact: *alienated, externalized* labor. We have analyzed this concept and have thus analyzed merely a fact of political economy.

Let us now see further how the concept of alienated, externalized labor must express and represent itself in actuality.

If the product of labor is alien to me, confronts me as an alien power, to whom then does it belong?

If my own activity does not belong to me, if it is an alien and forced activity, to whom then does it belong?

To a being *other* than myself?

Who is this being?

Gods? To be sure, in early times the main production, for example, the building of temples in Egypt, India, and Mexico, appears to be in the service of the gods, just as the product belongs to the gods. But gods alone were never workmasters. The same is true of *nature.* And what a contradiction it would be if the more man subjugates nature through his work and the more the miracles of gods are rendered superfluous by the marvels of industry, man should renounce his joy in producing and the enjoyment of his product for love of these powers.

The *alien* being who owns labor and the product of labor, whom labor serves and whom the product of labor satisfies can only be *man* himself.

That the product of labor does not belong to the worker and an alien power confronts him is possible only because this product belongs to *a man other than the worker*. If his activity is torment for him, it must be the *pleasure* and the life-enjoyment for another. Not gods, not nature, but only man himself can be this alien power over man.

Let us consider the statement previously made, that the relationship of man to himself is *objective* and *actual* to him only through his relationship to other men. If man is related to the product of his labor, to his objectified labor, as to an *alien*, hostile, powerful object independent of him, he is so related that another alien, hostile, powerful man independent of him is the lord of this object. If he is unfree in relation to his own activity, he is related to it as bonded activity, activity under the domination, coercion, and yoke of another man.

Every self-alienation of man, from himself and from nature, appears in the relationship which he postulates between other men and himself and nature. Thus religious self-alienation appears necessarily in the relation of laity to priest, or also to a mediator, since we are here now concerned with the spiritual world. In the practical real world self-alienation can appear only in the practical real relationships to other men. The means whereby the alienation proceeds is a *practical* means. Through alienated labor man thus not only produces his relationship to the object and to the act of production as an alien man at enmity with him. He also creates the relation in which other men stand to his production and product, and the relation in which he stands to these other men. Just as he begets his own production as loss of his reality, as his punishment; just as he begets his own product as a loss, a product not belonging to him, so he begets the domination of the nonproducer over production and over product. As he alienates his own activity from himself, he confers upon the stranger an activity which is not his own.

From *Writings of the Young Marx on Philosophy and Society,* ed. trans. Loyd D. Easton and Kurt H. Guddat. Copyright © 1967 by Loyd D. Easton and Kurt H. Guddat. Reprinted by permission of Doubleday and Company, Inc., New York.

QUESTIONS FOR REVIEW AND DISCUSSION

1. Marx says that there is an "inexorable law of change" in history. What are the significant stages which describe these historical changes?
2. How does Marx describe the difference between "quantitative" and "qualitative" change?
3. According to Marx, when would the process of historical change end and why?

4. How does Marx account for human thought, for ideas people have about ethics, religion, and law?
5. Marx predicted that in capitalism the conditions of the workers would become progressively more wretched until they would revolt and take over the means of production. Has this happened?
6. What does Marx mean by the "alienation of labor"?
7. Given that Marxism provided the basis for communism in several countries during most of the twentieth century, how do you account for its ultimate failure in these countries?

14

Justice as Fairness

Rawls

John Rawls, the author of *A Theory of Justice,* has been professor of philosophy at Harvard University since 1962. He was educated at Kent School and Princeton University, and earned his doctorate at Cornell University. Earlier, he taught at Princeton and at the Massachusetts Institute of Technology, and was a Fulbright Fellow at Oxford University. It has been said that Rawls's book "descends straight from Kant, Mill, and Sidgwick" (Rorty), which means, among other things, that its author bypassed the issues and influences of positivism and analytic philosophy* which dominated philosophy during the years of the development of Rawls's landmark book.

Imagine yourself in what Rawls describes as "the original position," a time when you are about to establish an organized society. You, and everybody else, will have to decide how to create a good society, one in which everyone is treated in a fair way. What should each person's place or situation, job, class position, and social status be? How should questions of this kind be answered? To make sure that the answers, and therefore each person's position and status, are decided on fairly, Rawls ask us to forget what our present situation is. To make sure that the principles of justice we are about to agree to are fair and objective, it is necessary for us, says Rawls, to step behind a "veil of ignorance." This veil of ignorance simply means that none of us knows (that is, we act as though we do not know) what our special circumstances are. We are to suppose that the slate is wiped clean and we are starting all over. No one knows what his or her special talents are. The purpose, then, of the veil of ignorance is to eliminate from our minds any prejudice based on our special circumstances so that we can approach the task of formulating the principles of justice from as objective a point of view as possible. Under these circumstances, how should we go about devising an arrangement among people which would amount to justice?

Rawls assumes that everyone has a sense of justice. This does not mean that everybody always agrees with a particular definition of justice. It does

*For a discussion of these types of philosophy, see chap. 20.

mean, however, that all people have a certain rational ability through which they understand what is and what is not fair. Moreover, rational human beings also know which principles will be respected. Rational persons know, for example, that it is not fair to achieve the good life for some at the expense of others.

From his ideas about the "original position" and the "veil of ignorance," Rawls arrives at "two principles of justice." The first principal is based on the special way in which each person is assumed to be equal. Hence Rawls says, "First: each person is to have an equal right to the most extensive basic liberty compatible with a similar liberty for others." This form of liberty is basically political liberty. It includes the right to vote and to be eligible for public office as well as freedom of speech and assembly, freedom of conscience, and freedom to hold property.

The second principle of justice, says Rawls, recognizes certain inequalities among people. People are, after all, different in many ways. These differences are reflected in the distribution of wealth and income. Recognizing these differences, Rawls describes this principle as follows: "Social and economic inequalities are to be arranged so that they are both (a) reasonably expected to be to everyone's advantage, and (b) attached to positions and offices open to all." What Rawls is attempting to accomplish in this second principle is, first, to recognize the facts of inequality and differences among individuals, and second, to make sure that these differences do not lead to injustice. Justice, says Rawls, does not require that wealth and income should be divided equally. However, an unequal division is justified only if everyone is better off, that is, if such an unequal division results in everyone's advantage.

These two principles must be arranged in a special sequence that Rawls calls "a serial order." The first principle deals with political freedom. The second principle deals with social and economic arrangements. Justice requires that political freedoms should always remain the highest priority and that the social and economic arrangements should be adapted to these political freedoms. Accordingly, it would be a violation of justice if a society sacrificed personal and political freedoms, the basic liberties, in exchange for some additional social and economic benefits.

The following brief selection from Rawls's *A Theory of Justice* will provide a further elaboration of some of these central elements of his political philosophy.

Reading _____

The Principles of Fairness

Rawls

THE MAIN IDEA OF THE THEORY OF JUSTICE

My aim is to present a conception of justice which generalizes and carries to a higher level of abstraction the familiar theory of the social contract. . . . In order to do this we are not to think of the original contract as one to enter a particular society or to set up a particular form of government. Rather, the guiding idea is that the principles of justice for the basic structure of society are the object of the original agreement. They are the principles that free and rational persons concerned to further their own interests would accept in an initial position of equality as defining the fundamental terms of their association. These principles are to regulate all further agreements' they specify the kinds of social cooperation that can be entered into and the forms of government that can be established. This way of regarding the principles of justice I shall call justice as fairness.

Thus we are to imagine that those who engage in social cooperation choose together, in one joint act, the principles which are to assign basic rights and duties and to determine the division of social benefits. Men are to decide in advance how they are to regulate their claims against one another and what is to be the foundation charter of their society. Just as each person must decide by rational reflection what constitutes his good, that is, the system of ends which it is rational for him to pursue, so a group of persons must decide once and for all what is to count among them as just and unjust. The choice which rational men would make in this hypothetical situation of equal liberty, assuming for the present that this choice problem has a solution, determines the principles of justice.

In justice as fairness the original position of equality corresponds to the state of nature in the traditional theory of the social contract. This original position is not, of course, thought of as an actual historical state of affairs, much less as a primitive condition of culture. It is understood as a purely hypothetical situation characterized so as to lead to a certain conception of justice. Among the essential features of this situation is that no one knows his place in society, his class position or social status, nor does any one know his fortune in the distribution of natural assets and abilities, his intelligence, strength, and the like. I shall even assume that the parties do not know their conceptions of the good or their special psychological propensities. The principles of justice are chosen behind a veil of ignorance. This ensures that no one is advantaged or disadvantaged in the choice of principles by the outcome of natural chance or the contingency of social circumstances. Since all are similarly situated and no one is able to design principles to favor his particular condition, the principles of justice are the result of a fair agreement or bargain. For given the circumstances of the original position, the symmetry of everyone's relations to each other, this initial situation is fair between individuals as moral persons, that is, as rational beings with their own ends and capable, I shall assume, of a sense of justice. The original position is, one might say, the appropriate initial status quo, and thus the fundamental agreements reached in it are fair. This explains the propriety of the name "justice as fairness": it conveys the idea that the same principles of justice are agreed to in an initial situation that is fair. The name does not mean that the concepts of justice and fairness are the same, any more than the phrase "poetry as metaphor" means that the concepts of poetry and metaphor are the same. . . .

One feature of justice as fairness is to think of the parties in the initial situation as rational and mutually disinterested. This does not mean that the parties are egoists, that is, individuals with only certain kinds of interests, say in wealth, prestige, and domination. But they are conceived as not taking an interest in one another's interests. They are to presume that even their spiritual aims may be opposed, in the way that the aims of those of different religions may be opposed. Moreover, the concept of rationality must be interpreted as far as possible in the narrow sense, standard in economic theory, of taking the most effective means to given ends. . . .

I maintain instead that the persons in the initial situation would choose two rather different principles: the first requires equality in the assignment of basic rights and duties, while the second holds that social and economic inequalities, for example inequalities of wealth and authority, are just only if they result in compensating benefits for everyone, and in particular for the least advantaged members of society. The principles rule out justifying institutions on the grounds that the hardships of some are offset by a greater good in the aggregate. It may be expedient but it is not just that some should have less in order that others may prosper. But there is no injustice in the greater benefits earned by a few provided that the situation of persons not so fortunate is thereby improved. The intuitive idea is that since everyone's well-being depends upon a scheme of cooperation without which no one could have a satisfactory life, the division of advantages should be such as to draw forth the willing cooperation of everyone taking part in it, including those less well situated. Yet this can be expected only if reasonable terms are proposed. The two principles mentioned seem to be a fair agreement on the basis of which those better endowed, or more fortunate in their social position, neither of which we can be said to deserve, could expect the willing cooperation of others when some workable scheme is a necessary condition of the welfare of all. . . .

THE ORIGINAL POSITION

The Veil of Ignorance

The idea of the original position is to set up a fair procedure so that any principles agreed to will be just. The aim is to use the notion of pure procedural justice as a basis of theory. Somehow we must nullify the effects of specific contingencies which put men at odds and tempt them to exploit social and natural circumstances to their own advantage. Now in order to do this I assume that the parties are situated behind a veil of ignorance. They do not know how the various alternatives will affect their own particular case and they are obliged to evaluate principles solely on the basis of general considerations.

It is assumed, then, that the parties do not know certain kinds of particular facts. First of all, no one knows his place in society, his class position or social status; nor does he know his fortune in the distribution of natural assets and abilities, his intelligence and strength, and the like. Nor, again, does anyone know his conception of the good, the particulars of his rational plan of life, or even the special features of his psychology such as his aversion to risk or liability to optimism or pessimism. More than this, I assume that the parties do not know the particular circumstances of their own society. That is, they do not know its economic or political situation, or the level of civilization and culture it has been able to achieve. The persons in the original position have no information as to which generation they belong. These broader restrictions of knowledge are appropriate in part because questions of social justice arise between generations as well as within them, for example, the question of the appropriate rate of capital saving and of the conservation of natural resources and the environment of nature. There is also, theoretically anyway, the question of a reasonable genetic policy. In these cases too, in order to carry through the idea of the original position, the parties must not know the contingencies that set them in opposition. They must choose principles the consequences of which they are prepared to live with whatever generation they turn out to belong to.

As far as possible, then, the only particular facts which the parties know is that their society is subject to the circumstances of justice and whatever this implies. It is taken for granted, however, that they know the general facts about human society. They understand political affairs and the principles of economic theory; they know the basis of social organization and the laws of human psychology. Indeed, the parties are presumed to know whatever general facts affect the choice of the principles of justice. . . .

The veil of ignorance makes possible a unanimous choice of a particular conception of justice. Without these limitations on knowledge the bargaining problem of the original position would be hopelessly complicated. . . .

Now the reasons for the veil of ignorance go beyond mere simplicity. We want to define the original position so that we get the desired solution. If a knowledge of particulars is allowed, then the outcome is biased by arbitrary contingencies. As already observed, to each according to his threat advantage is not a principle of justice. If the original position is to yield agreements that are just, the parties must be fairly situated and treated equally as moral persons. The arbitrariness of the world must be corrected for by adjusting the circumstances of the initial contractual situation. . . .

The Rationality of the Parties

There is one further assumption to guarantee strict compliance. The parties are presumed to be capable of a sense of justice and this fact is public knowledge among them. This condition is to insure the integrity of the agreement made in the original position. . . . In reaching an agreement, then, they know that their undertaking is not in vain: their capacity for a sense of justice insures that the principles chosen will be respected. It is essential to observe, however, that this assumption still permits the consideration of men's capacity to act on the various conceptions of justice. . . . The assumption only says that the parties have a capacity for justice in a purely formal sense: taking everything relevant into account, including the general facts of moral psychology, the parties will adhere to the principles eventually chosen. They are rational in that they will not enter into agreements they know they cannot keep, or can do so only with great difficulty.

The Maximin Rule

The term "maximin" means the *maximum minimorum;* and the rule directs our attention to the worst that can happen under any proposed course of action, and to decide in the light of that. . . .

The maximin rule tells us to rank alternatives by their worst possible outcomes: we are to adopt the alternative the worst outcome of which is superior to the worst outcomes of the others. . . .

TWO PRINCIPLES OF JUSTICE

I shall now state in a provisional form the two principles of justice that I believe would be chosen in the original position.

The first statement of the two principles reads as follows.

First: each person is to have an equal right to the most extensive basic liberty compatible with a similar liberty for others.

Second: social and economic inequalities are to be arranged so that they are both (a) reasonably expected to be to everyone's advantage, and (b) attached to positions and offices open to all. There are two ambiguous phrases in the second principle, namely "everyone's advantage" and "open to all."

By way of general comment, these principles primarily apply, as I have said, to the basic structure of society. They are to govern the assignment of rights and duties and to regulate the distribution of social and economic advantages. As their formulation suggests, these principles presuppose that the social structure can be divided into two more or less distinct parts, the first principle applying to the one, the second to the other. They distinguish between those aspects of the social system that define and secure the equal liberties of citizenship and those that specify and establish social and economic inequalities. The basic liberties of citizens are, roughly speaking, political liberty (the right to vote and to be eligible for public office) together with freedom of speech and assembly; liberty of conscience and freedom of thought; freedom of the person along with the right to hold (personal) property; and freedom from arbitrary arrest and seizure as defined by the concept of the rule of law. These liberties are all required to be equal by the first principle, since citizens of a just society are to have the same basic rights.

The second principle applies, in the first approximation, to the distribution of income and wealth and to the design of organizations that make use of differences in authority and responsibility, or chains of command. While the distribution of wealth and income need not be equal, it must be to everyone's advantage, and at the same time, positions of authority and offices of command must be accessible to all. One applies the second principle by holding positions open, and then, subject to this constraint, arranges social and economic inequalities so that everyone benefits.

These principles are to be arranged in a serial order with the first principle prior to the second. This ordering means that a departure from the institutions of equal liberty required by the first principle cannot be justified by, or compensated for, by greater social and economic advantages. The distribution of wealth and income, and the hierarchies of authority, must be consistent with both the liberties of equal citizenship and equality of opportunity.

It is clear that these principles are rather specific in their content, and their acceptance rests on certain assumptions that I must eventually try to explain and justify. A theory of justice depends upon a theory of society in ways that will become evident as we proceed. For the present, it should be observed that the two principles (and this holds for all formulations) are a special case of a more general conception of justice that can be expressed as follows.

All social values—liberty and opportunity, income and wealth, and the bases of self-respect—are to be distributed equally unless an unequal distribution of any, or all, of these values is to everyone's advantage. Injustice, then, is simply inequalities that are not to the benefit of all. Of course, this conception is extremely vague and requires interpretation.

As a first step, suppose that the basic structure of society distributes certain primary goods, that is, things that every rational man is presumed to want. These goods normally have a use whatever a person's rational plan of life. For simplicity, assume that the chief primary goods at the disposition of society are rights and liberties, powers and opportunities, income and wealth. These are the social primary goods. Other primary goods such as health and vigor, intelligence and imagination, are natural goods; although their possession is influenced by the basic structure, they are not so directly under its control. Imagine, then, a hypothetical initial arrangement in which all the social primary goods are equally distributed: everyone has similar rights and duties, and income and wealth are evenly shared. This state of affairs provides a benchmark for judging improvements. If certain inequalities of wealth and organizational powers would make everyone better off than in this hypothetical starting situation, then they accord with the general conception.

Now it is possible, at least theoretically, that by giving up some of their fundamental liberties men are sufficiently compensated by the resulting social and economic gains. The general conception of justice imposes no restrictions on what sort of inequalities are permissible; it only requires that everyone's position be improved. We need not suppose anything so drastic as consenting to a condition of slavery. Imagine instead that men forego certain political rights when the economic returns are significant and their capacity to influence the course of policy by the exercise of these rights would be marginal in any case. It is this kind of exchange which the two principles as stated rule out: being arranged in serial order they do not permit exchanges between basic liberties and economic and social gains. The serial ordering of principles expresses an underlying preference among primary social goods. When this preference is rational so likewise is the choice of these principles in this order.

From John Rawls, *A Theory of Justice,* Belknap Press of Harvard University Press, Cambridge, Mass., 1971. Reprinted by permission of the publishers from *A Theory of Justice* by John Rawls, Cambridge, MA: The Belknap Press of Harvard University Press. Copyright © 1971 by the President and Fellows of Harvard College.

QUESTIONS FOR REVIEW AND DISCUSSION

1. What does Rawls mean by the "original position"?
2. Why is it important for those who want to create a just society to consider themselves as being behind a "veil of ignorance"?
3. What are Rawls's two principles of justice?
4. Does Rawls think that justice requires that all wealth should be divided equally? If not, what would justify differences in wealth?
5. What is meant by the "serial order" of the two principles of justice? Would this notion be convincing to people in China or in some third-world country?

In Praise of Dialectic, Magritte. The search for knowledge leads to a window, and when you open it, you see new things, but also you confront another window which you must open, and that will lead to yet another window; and so on. *(Reproduced by permission of the National Galley of Victoria, Melbourne)*

PART THREE

Knowledge
What Can I Know?

There is the fact that I am here, seated by the fire, attired in a dressing gown, having this paper in my hands. . . . And how could I deny that these hands and this body are mine. [But] how often has it happened to me that in the night I dreamt that I found myself in this particular place, that I was dressed and seated near the fire, while in reality I was lying undressed in bed! . . . I remind myself that on occasions I have in sleep been deceived by similar illusions and in dwelling carefully on this reflection I see no certain indications by which we may clearly distinguish wakefulness from sleep. . . .

Descartes
Meditations (1640)

It may seem strange to ask the question "What can I know?" Common sense tells us that we know a great deal and that what we do not know may be discovered in the future. But the philosophical question "What can I know?" is a way of challenging the commonsense attitude toward knowledge. Our common sense leads us to believe that our knowledge will help us live through the events of each day successfully. We know that the sun will rise in the morning, that the food we eat will nourish our bodies, that the aspirin we swallow will cause our headache to disappear, that gasoline will make our automobiles move, and that our calculations will accurately guide a vehicle to the moon. But even though we seem to have knowledge about these things, it turns out that we do not really have a clear idea of what it means *to know*. When we try to describe *how* we know something, we discover that the process of knowing is full of surprises. How, for example, can we be absolutely sure that we are not dreaming? Descartes said we could never be sure because there are "no certain indications," no clear way to distinguish wakefulness from sleep. We may, moreover, think that seeing a physical object will give us reliable knowledge about it. But when we see a stick in the water which looks bent, we discover when we remove it from the water that it is not bent. If we can be mistaken about the exact shape of the stick in the water, does that not raise doubts in our minds about other experiences we once thought would give us exact knowledge? When, therefore, philosophers ask the question "What can I know?" they are really asking what we can know about which no reasonable person would raise any doubt. In order to deal with these questions, we need to consider a series of problems which cluster around the process of knowing, and we will call these problems the "elements of knowing."

THE ELEMENTS OF KNOWING

Appearance and Reality

Nothing seems more obvious to us than the presence and existence of a physical object which we see. But when we look, for example, at an apple, what do we see and what do we know about it? We say it is red, has a round shape, and has a certain texture and taste. Is it really red or has an artificial light or plastic bag made it look red? Is it round or is it that my looking at it from an angle makes it appear round? Is it sweet or has its taste been affected by the candy I ate earlier? More important, is the redness in the apple or is that color in my eye or brain? To see an apple, or any other physical object, is to perceive it through my sense of sight. In short, I have a sensation of it. The content of this sensation is, for example, the color red. This sensation is inside of me.

We now have three parts of my experience of seeing the apple: (1) myself, who has the sensation, (2) the content of the sensation, namely, the color and shape, or what are called "sense data," and (3) the apple, upon which my sensation depends. What, then, do we know about the apple? There is no doubt that I have a sensation of color, but can I be sure that the redness is in, or is part of, the apple? Is the apple *really* what it *appears* to be? Similarly, we saw earlier that the stick in the water does appear to be bent; there is no doubt that we have a sensation of a bent stick. But is the stick really bent? Is it *true* that the stick is bent, even though it is true that I perceive the stick to be bent? It is clear that appearance can differ from reality. The information we get from our sensation does not always tell us the truth about the object. We cannot be sure whether other qualities such as hardness or weight belong to things that appear to have them. Even hardness and weight might not be a part of the apple. These qualities might instead depend on other circumstances, such as, for example, altitude and gravity. We discover that we know less about the apple and the stick than we originally thought we did. In any case, the information we get directly from our senses does not necessarily tell us the truth about an object, the truth about what an object is really like. In the picture on the next page we think we see cupboards, bookshelves, books, other objects, and benches against the wall. Actually, that is all merely appearance created by the clever use of inlaid wood of different colors. The reality is that the wall is perfectly flat.

Duke of Urbino's study, fifteenth century. The wall is perfectly flat. The arrangement of inlaid wood of different shades gives the appearance of shelves, books, and benches. *(The Metropolitan Museum of Art, Roger Fund, 1939)*

Building Knowledge Upon Experience

Just as Descartes raised the astonishing question of whether we can ever tell the difference between wakefulness and sleep, so David Hume asked in all seriousness whether we could be sure that the sun will rise tomorrow. How could there be any question over whether the sun will rise? Hume put the question the other way around, namely, how could you be certain, that is, how do you *know* that the sun will rise? Common sense tells us that we can expect the sun to rise because it has always risen before. But how can our knowledge of a past event give us any assurance that the same event will occur in the future? We think we have solid knowledge about the future because we build our knowledge on our experience of the past. From the past, we infer the future. We employ what is called the "principle of induction," which is defined as reasoning from a particular instance to a general rule. From our experience of seeing an apple fall, we reason that all bodies fall. But is this knowledge? What more do we know than that we are in the *habit* of expecting certain events to happen and *until now* they have happened? We cannot say with certainty that they will happen in the future. If we say we know that they will happen in the future because there is a *uniformity in nature*, we are back where we started because the phrase "uniformity of nature" is exactly what we are trying to prove in the first place when we say that we can be sure that the sun will rise because it has always risen before. Although the "laws of motion" are working today, how can we be sure that they will be working tomorrow?

We can ask the same kind of question about the relation of certain events to each other that we call "cause" and "effect." What more do we know than that so far event *A* has always been followed by event *B*, that after swallowing aspirin my headache disappears? There is really no reason why *B* should follow *A* in the future. But even though we cannot have exact knowledge with certainty about the future, because we never know when the future will be different, we do nevertheless have a *kind* of knowledge which is called "probable knowledge." Our knowledge, to the extent that it is built on our experience of particular instances or experiments, does not *prove* that the future will continue to be the same as the past. Nevertheless, the *probability* that the future will be what we expect it to be makes it possible for us to go about our daily affairs confident that certain causes will be followed by certain effects and that the sun will rise in the morning.

Knowledge Prior to Experience

We have another kind of knowledge which does not require experience to prove that it is true. Moreover, it is true not only with respect to the past, but is always and everywhere true. This knowledge is called "a priori knowledge" because it is prior to or independent of experience. Examples are commonly found in mathematics. We know that two plus two equals four under any and all circumstances. It may be that at one time we learned to count with marbles or apples, but we quickly discovered that we could clearly think of the relations between two and two no matter two of what. We do not have to assume that we are born with these ideas, although it is fair to assume that the human mind has a certain capacity to obey various "laws of thought." As soon as we understand what is meant by "two" and "plus," we are able to move accurately to "four."

One of the laws of thought is the "law of contradiction," which states that a thing cannot both be and not be at the same time. We know, therefore, that bachelors are not married or that a thing cannot be all white and all green at the same time. Merely by the operation of the mind we arrive at conclusions which necessarily must be true.

Two reasons account for the necessity of the truth of a priori knowledge. First, in an a priori statement, the subject (bachelor) already contains the predicate (not married) so that to say that a bachelor is married would be to commit a contradiction. The consistent use of language guarantees the truth of the a priori statement. Second, a priori statements are true also because the law of contradiction refers not only to words but to things, so that to say a bachelor is married is not only an example of an inconsistent use of language but a contradiction of the actual condition (unmarried) of a person (bachelor). A priori knowledge is independent of experience only in the sense that once we understand such concepts as "bachelor" or "two and two," we can by mere thinking see the truth of a statement. No further observation or experience could deny the necessary truth of some statements, such as, for example, that if A is bigger than B and B is bigger than C, then A is bigger than C.

The World of Ideas

It is fascinating to discover how much of our knowledge is contained in words which do not refer to any particular thing. You know what I mean when I say "tree" or "triangle" or "man" or "woman" even before I say "that oak" or "this right triangle" or "John" or "Mary." It may be that after seeing several trees, our mind is able to discover something common in all of them and draw out, or *abstract*, that common element. We came upon a similar way of knowing when we referred to mathematics: after seeing two oranges, two people, or two houses, the mind can grasp the concept of "two" without further reference to two this or two that. When we look at a tree, we *see* an oak but *think* a tree. Similarly, we can speak of qualities such as white without necessarily referring to any white thing. We can think whiteness in the same way that we can think triangularity. More important, when we try to prove something about triangles, we do not think of any particular triangle but rather about what is common, or universally applicable, to all of them.

We can think of such ideas as "beauty" or "justice" without referring to any specific beautiful object or example of justice. Do we have the ideas of beauty and justice before we experience examples of them? How would we ever know whether we are experiencing a beautiful object or that a government acts justly? What impresses us about the world of ideas is its stability, its permanence. Trees change and disappear, but the idea of "tree" continues. Actually, all particular things come and go, but the ideas of "triangularity," "whiteness," "man," "woman," "beauty," and "justice" remain. This contrast between particular things and the world of ideas (or universals) is reflected in the way we know. If we limit our knowledge to particular things, we cannot know as much as when we also focus our thinking on ideas or universals. The question we will want to ask is how these two worlds of knowledge are related to each other.

Using the Word "Truth"

Our common sense tells us how to use the word "truth" most of the time. When a mother says to her child "tell me the truth," having in mind the disappearance of the cookies, the child knows exactly what is called for. If he took the cookies, the truth is "I took them." If he did not and does not know who did, the truth is "I don't know who took them." Truth can be defined, then, as the proper relation between a statement and a fact. This relation is usually called "correspondence," so that a statement is true if it is based on a corresponding fact. This example of the cookies happens to be an easy one because the statement "I took them" corresponds, that is, "fits," perfectly with the fact that the child took the cookies out of the jar. Complications arise, however, if we ask, for example, if it is true that we see a bent stick in the water. If we use our language carefully, we will discover what is and what is not true in this case. It is true that we see (have an impression of) a bent stick. It is also true that the stick is straight. It is false to say I see a bent stick if I mean that I believe the stick is actually bent. In this case, there are two facts, namely, the impression of bentness and the actual straightness. It happens that we can easily *verify* whether in fact the stick is bent or straight by simply taking the stick out of the water. But not all questions can be settled or verified this easily.

Place yourself back several centuries and imagine how the truth about the sun was discussed. Some people believed it to be true that the sun rises, that is, that the sun moves around the earth. Other scientists thought this could not be true because it did not fit with other knowledge they had about astronomy. For them, the standard of truth was *coherence,* which means that something is true if it is consistent with other valid knowledge. Observations made possible by the invention of the telescope and new mathematical calculations showed that planets, including the earth, revolve around the sun. It appears, then, that the truth is that the sun does not rise in the literal sense.

There is still another theory of truth, namely, the "pragmatic theory." Unlike the correspondence theory, which says that a statement is true if it fits or copies some reality, or the coherence theory, which says that a statement is true if it is consistent with all other knowledge, the pragmatic theory states the radical notion that a belief is true if it "works," if it provides a workable or reliable basis for practical behavior. Such a "truth" has "cash value" if it makes a practical or successful difference in the life of a person. For this reason, says William James, truth is what *happens* to an idea; truth is *made* by events.

The Linguistic Turn

A dramatic shift in what philosophers considered their most important activity occurred during the twentieth century, a shift which has been called "the linguistic turn." As the name implies, the linguistic turn represented a shift to the analysis of language and away from a search for what the world is like. As Gustav Bergman says, "All linguistic philosophers talk about the world by means of talking about a suitable language. This is the linguistic turn. . . ."

Those philosophers who chose to take this "turn" were for the most part influenced by the successes of the sciences and the clarity of mathematics. By contrast, they were frustrated by the various problems of philosophy for which they could find no solutions. Most philosophers from Plato through Hegel had devised systems of thought which gave the impression that they contained accurate information about human nature, the world about us, and the way our minds function in the pursuit of truth. As we have seen, classical philosophers had distinguished between the worlds of appearance and reality, urged a distinction between mind and body, sought to find truth in the essential nature of things, and assumed that it is possible to discover the essence of such notions as justice, goodness, and God. All these major subjects obviously had to be formulated in words, in language. The linguistic turn occurred when some philosophers began to ask whether this language could be tested, verified, for its accuracy. Their test would be whether the grand systems of philosophy are formulated in sentences which conform to those conditions under which alone words can have literal meaning. For this reason, A. J. Ayer concluded that "the propositions of philosophy are not factual, but linguistic in character—that is, they do not describe the behavior of physical, or even mental, objects; they express definitions, or the formal consequences of definitions. Accordingly, we may say that philosophy is a department of logic." This is how Wittgenstein also viewed the enterprise of philosophy when he said that "the result of philosophy is the logical clarification of thoughts," so that, "the result of philosophy is not a number of philosophical propositions (i.e. a new body of knowledge) but to make propositions clear."

What would it take to make a statement or proposition clear? For those who took the linguistic turn, the clarity of propositions would depend on whether the language used could be directly connected to something in our experience. Statements about such things as consciousness, reason, knowledge, or the "essence of human nature" need to be translated into propositions about objects we directly experience or of which we have "direct perceptual acquaintance." This act of translating philosophical language into a language based on elements of our actual experience raised the possibility of constructing an "ideal language," a good example of which is Bertrand Russell's theory of "logical atomism." According to Russell, the things in the world have various characteristics, and all things have relationships to each other. "That they have these properties and relations are *facts.*" If a language could be constructed in which each sentence refers to a fact, then, says Russell, there would be a perfect fit between language and the objects of knowledge. Such a language would make it possible to exhibit the structure of the world because the structure of such an ideal language for which each word corresponds to an atomic fact would represent the structure of the world. Russell warned however that one would have to be careful not to apply this linguistic method too naively, for that would result, he says, in the "fallacy of verbalism . . . the fallacy that consists in mistaking the properties of words for the properties of things."

The impact of the method of linguistic analysis has been pervasive, and its practitioners have become known as "analytic philosophers." For some of these philosophers, this method meant that it was meaningless to try to solve certain problems, since they were now considered to be "pseudo problems" produced by the imprecise use of language. What made this language imprecise is that it had no clear connection with factual experience. Moreover, as Richard Rorty has pointed out, some philosophers "have not used English. They have formulated their problems in what *looks* like ordinary English, but have in fact misused the language by using terms jargonistically while relying on the ordinary connotations of these terms." But would an ideal language, based solely on empirical observation, solve the problem of speaking meaningfully about all our experiences? How would it be possible, for example, to translate a statement about "consciousness" (which cannot be experienced by "direct perceptual acquaintance") into an ideal language? Could it be that we would still have to talk about consciousness as though we know what we are talking about? It may be that an ideal language is not strictly speaking an empiricist language, and therefore, says Rorty, "the linguistic turn may, for all we know now, lead us back to rationalism and to idealism."

We have discovered that in the process of knowing we encounter several problems, namely, that appearance is not always the same as reality; that most of our knowledge is built on experience, but the fact that something has happened in the past does not guarantee that it will also happen in the future; that although objects and events outside us provide most of the raw material of our knowledge, there is nevertheless something in our minds which we bring to these objects to make our knowledge possible; that we need to understand how the world of ideas and the world of things are related to each other; that there are various ways of defining truth, namely, as the correspondence of a statement with a fact, as the coherence of one piece of knowledge with other valid knowledge, or as a practical idea which works; finally, that the linguistic turn changed the definition of meaningful statements by limiting them to those statements which are based on direct perceptual acquaintance, thus limiting the statements that can be considered "true." These are some of the elements of knowledge we will encounter as we consider the thought of some philosophers who sought to answer the question "What can I know?"

SOME APPROACHES TO PHILOSOPHIES OF KNOWLEDGE

Plato was especially concerned to make sense out of the confused world of everyday experience. He thought he discovered a world of *ideas* above the world of things. Things, he said, are only a pale copy of ideas. This helped him explain the difference between appearance and reality. Ideas, he said, are more real than things, and for this reason he is called an "idealist."

Descartes wondered whether we could ever achieve intellectual certainty.

He was bothered by doubt because he thought it is possible to doubt everything we experience or can think of. And so he deliberately pushed his method of doubt in every conceivable direction and to every subject until he discovered something he could not doubt, namely, that he was doubting. Upon the certainty of this knowledge that he was doubting he built a full system of thought using only his rational powers each step of the way; for this reason he is called a "rationalist."

Hume disagreed with Descartes and denied that human reason has the power to produce the kind of knowledge Descartes claimed it could. On the contrary, Hume said that we can never know anything more than what we experience with our senses. All our ideas, he said, can be traced back to our impressions of things. Moreover, past knowledge does not guarantee how future events will occur. Because his theory put such severe limits on what we can know, Hume is called an empiricist and a "skeptic."

Kant took Hume seriously but also thought that Descartes had something important to say about how we know. Therefore, Kant tried to harmonize the rationalism of Descartes and the skepticism of Hume and in the process developed his own theory of knowledge, which is called "critical idealism."

William James was impatient with the endless technical discussions about theories of knowledge. He emphasized the practical aspects of philosophy and said that the way to test a theory or an idea is to try it and see if it makes a difference in life. For this reason, he is called a "pragmatist."

The *analytic philosophers* were twentieth-century thinkers who sought to limit the task of philosophy to the analysis of language in order to distinguish between those propositions which make sense because they can be verified and those which are meaningless because they do not refer to verifiable aspects of our experience. We will refer to Bertrand Russell, Rudolph Carnap, Ludwig Wittgenstein, and Richard Rorty.

15

Opinion versus Knowledge

Plato

Plato describes how the human mind achieves knowledge and indicates what knowledge consists of, by means of (1) his allegory of the *cave*, (2) his metaphor of the *divided line,* and (3) his doctrine of the *forms.*

THE CAVE

Plato asks us to imagine some men living in a large cave where from childhood they have been chained by the leg and by the neck so that they cannot move. Because they cannot even turn their heads, they can see only what is in front of them. Behind them is an elevation that rises abruptly from the level where the prisoners are seated. On this elevation there are persons walking back and forth carrying artificial objects, including the figures of animals and human beings made out of wood and stone and various other materials. Behind these walking persons is a fire, and farther back still is the entrance to the cave. The chained prisoners can look only forward against the wall at the end of the cave and can see neither one another or the moving persons nor the fire behind them. All that the prisoners can ever see are the shadows on the wall in front of them, which are projected as persons walking in front of the fire. They never see the objects or the men carrying them, nor are they aware that the shadows are the shadows of other things. When they see a shadow and hear a person's voice echo from the wall, they assume that the sound is coming from the shadow, since they are not aware of the existence of anything else. These prisoners, then, recognize as reality only the shadows formed on the wall.

    What would happen asks Plato, if one of these prisoners were released from his chains, were forced to stand up, turn around, and walk with eyes lifted up toward the light of the fire? All his movements would be exceedingly

For biographical note on Plato, see p. 135.

Plato. *(The Bettmann Archive)*

painful. Suppose he were forced to look at the objects being carried, the shadows of which he had become accustomed to seeing on the wall. Would he not find these actual objects less congenial to his eyes, and less meaningful, than the shadows? And would not his eyes ache if he looked straight at the light from the fire itself? At this point he would undoubtedly try to escape from his liberator and turn back to the things he could see with clarity, being convinced that the shadows were clearer than the objects he was forced to look at in the firelight.

Suppose this prisoner could not turn back, but were instead dragged forcibly up the steep and rough passage to the mouth of the cave and released only after he had been brought out into the sunlight. The impact of the radiance of the sun on his eyes would be so painful that he would be unable to see any of the things that he was now told were real. It would take some time before his eyes became accustomed to the world outside the cave. He would first of all recognize some shadows and would feel at home with them. If one were the shadow of a man, he would have seen that shape before as it appeared on the wall of the cave. Next, he would see the reflections of men and things in the water, and this would represent a major advance in his knowledge, for what he once knew only as a solid dark blur would now be seen in more precise detail of line and color. A flower makes a shadow which gives very little, if any, indication of what a flower really looks like, but its image as reflected in the water provides the eyes with a clearer vision of each petal and its various colors. In time, he would see the flower itself. As he lifted his eyes skyward, he would find it easier at first to look at the heavenly bodies at night, looking at the moon and the stars instead of the sun in daytime. Finally, he would look right at the sun in its natural positions in the sky and not at its reflection from or through anything else.

This extraordinary experience would gradually lead this liberated prisoner to conclude that the sun is what makes things visible. It is the sun, too, that accounts for the seasons of the year, and for that reason the sun is the cause of life in the spring. Now he would understand what he and his fellow prisoners saw on the wall, how shadows and reflections differ from things as they really are in the visible world, and that without the sun there would be no visible world.

How would such a person feel about his previous life in the cave? He would recall what he and his fellow prisoners there took to be wisdom, how they had a practice of honoring and commending each other, giving prizes to the one who had the sharpest eye for the passing shadows and the best memory for the order in which they followed each other so that he could make the best guess as to which shadow would come next. Would the released prisoner still think such prizes were worth having, and would he envy the men who received honors in the cave? Instead of envy, he would have only sorrow and pity for them.

If he went back to his former seat in the cave, he would at first have great difficulty, for going suddenly from daylight into the cave would fill his eyes with darkness. He could not, under these circumstances, compete very effectively with the other prisoners in making out the shadows on the wall. While his eyesight was still dim and unsteady, those who had their permanent residence in the darkness could win every round of competition with him. They would at first find this situation very amusing and would taunt him by saying that his sight was perfectly all right before he went up out of the cave and that now he has returned with his sight ruined. Their conclusion would be that it is not worth trying to go up out of the cave. Indeed, says Plato, "if they could lay hands on the man who was trying to set them free and lead them up, they would kill him."

Most people, this allegory would suggest, dwell in the darkness of the cave. They have oriented their thoughts around the blurred world of shadows. It is the function of *education* to lead men out of the cave into the world of light. Education is not simply a matter of putting knowledge into the soul of a person who does not possess it, any more than vision is putting sight into blind eyes. Knowledge is like a vision in that it requires an organ capable of receiving it. Just as the prisoner had to turn his whole body around in order that his eyes could see the light instead of the darkness, so also it is necessary for the entire soul to turn away from the deceptive world of change and appetite that causes a blindness of the soul. Education, then, is a matter of *conversion*, a complete turning around from the world of appearance to the world of reality. "The conversion of the soul," says Plato, "is not to put the power of sight in the soul's eye, which already has it, but to insure that, instead of looking in the wrong direction, it is turned the way it ought to be." But looking in the right direction does not come easily. Even the "noblest natures" do not always want to look that way, and so Plato says that the rulers must "bring compulsion to bear" upon them to ascent upward from darkness to light. Similarly, when those who have been liberated from the cave achieve the highest knowledge, they must not be allowed to remain in the higher world of contemplation, but must be made to come back down into the cave and take part in the life and labors of the prisoners.

Plato said that there are two worlds, the dark world of the cave and the bright world of light. For Plato knowledge was not only possible: it was virtually infallible. What made knowledge infallible was that it was based on what is most *real*. The dramatic contrast between the shadows, reflections, and the actual objects was for Plato the decisive clue to the different degrees to which human beings could be enlightened. Plato saw the counterparts of shadows in all of human life and discourse. Disagreements between men concerning the meaning of justice, for example, were the result of each one's looking at a different aspect of the reality of justice. One person might take justice to mean whatever the rulers in fact command the people to do, on the assumption that justice has to do with rules of behavior laid down by the ruler. Just as a shadow bears some relation to the object of which it is the shadow, so this conception of justice has some measure of truth to it, for justice does have some connection with the ruler. But different rulers command different modes of behavior, and there could be no single coherent concept of justice if men's knowledge of justice were derived from the wide variety of examples of it.

The Sophists were skeptical about the possibility of true knowledge because they were impressed by the variety and constant change in things, and, they argued, since our knowledge comes from our experience, our knowledge will reflect this variety and will therefore be relative to each person. Plato agreed that such knowledge as is based on our sense experiences would be relative and not absolute, but he would not accept the Sophists' notion that *all* knowledge is relative. "The ignorant," writes Plato, "have no single mark before their eyes at which they must aim in all the conduct of their lives. . . ." If all we could know were the shadows, we could never have reliable knowledge, for these shadows would always change in size and shape depending on the, to us, unknown motions of the real objects. Plato was convinced that the human mind is able to discover that "single mark," that "real" object behind all the multitude of shadows, which is to attain true knowledge. There is, Plato believed, a true Idea of Justice, an Idea that can be blurred by rulers, and communities. This line of reasoning lay behind his distinction between the world of sense and the world of thought, between the visible world and the intelligible world.

Whereas the allegory of the cave illustrates these distinctions in dramatic terms, Plato's metaphor of the divided line sets forth the stages or levels of knowledge in more systematic form.

THE DIVIDED LINE

In the process of discovering true knowledge, the mind, says Plato, moves through four stages of development. At each stage, there is a parallel between the kind of object presented to the mind and the kind of thought this object makes possible. These objects and their parallel modes of thought can be diagramed as follows:

	Objects	y	Modes of Thought	
(The Good) Intelligible World	[Forms]		Knowledge	Knowledge
	Mathematical Objects		Thinking	
(The Sun) Visible World	Things		Belief	Opinion
	Images		Imagining	

The vertical line from x to y is a continuous one, suggesting that there is some degree of knowledge at every point. But as the line passes through the lowest forms of reality to the highest, there is a parallel progression from the lowest degree of truth to the highest. The line is divided, first of all, into two unequal parts. The upper and larger part represents the intelligible world and the smaller, lower part the visible world. This unequal division symbolizes the lower degree of reality and truth found in the visible world as compared with the greater reality and truth in the intelligible world. Each of these parts is then subdivided in the same proportion as the whole line, producing four parts, each one representing a clearer and more certain mode of thought than the one below. Recalling the allegory of the cave, we can think of this line as beginning in the dark and shadowy world at x and moving up to the bright light at y. Going from x to y represents a continuous process of the mind's enlightenment. The objects presented to the mind at each level are not four different kinds of real objects: rather, they represent four different ways of looking at the same object.

Imagining

The most superficial form of mental activity is found at the lowest level of the line. Here the mind confronts images, or the least amount of reality. The word "imagining" could, of course, mean the activity of penetrating beyond the mere appearances of things to their deeper reality. But here Plato means by imagining simply the sense experience of appearances wherein these appearances are taken as true reality. An obvious example is a shadow, which can be mistaken for something real. Actually, the shadow *is* something real; it is a real shadow. But what makes imagining the lowest form of knowing is that at this stage the mind does not know that it *is* a shadow or an image that it has confronted. If a person knew that it was a shadow, he would not be in the state of imagining or illusion. The prisoners in the cave are trapped in the deepest ignorance because they are unaware that they are seeing shadows.

Besides shadows, there are other kinds of images which Plato considered deceptive. These are the images fashioned by the artist and the poet. The artist presents images that are at least two steps removed from true reality. Suppose an artist paints a portrait of Socrates. Socrates represents a specific or concrete version of the Ideal Man. Moreover, the portrait represents only the artist's own view of Socrates. The three levels of reality here are, then, (1) the Idea of Man, (2) the embodiment of this Idea in Socrates, and (3) the image of Socrates as represented on canvas. Plato's criticism of art is that it produces images that, in turn, stimulate illusory ideas in the observer. Again, it is when the image is taken as a perfect version of something real that illusion is produced. For the most part, men know that an artist puts on canvas his own way of seeing a subject. Still, artistic images do shape men's thoughts, and if men restrict their understanding of things to these images with all their distortions and exaggerations, they will certainly lack an understanding of things as they really are.

What concerned Plato most were the images fashioned by the art of using words. Poetry and rhetoric were for him the most serious sources of illusion. Words have the power of creating images before the mind, and the poet and rhetorician have great skill in using words to create such images. Plato was particularly critical of the Sophists, whose influence came from this very skill in the use of words. They could make either side of an argument *seem* as good as the other. In a discussion of justice, for example, the Sophist, or any other artist with words, could create the same distortion that we found in the portrait. Justice as understood in Athens could be taken by a pleader and distorted in favor of a special client. This special pleader's version of justice could be a distortion of the Athenian view; also, the Athenian view might very well be a distortion of the Ideal Justice. If someone heard only the special pleader's version of justice, he would be at least twice removed from the true Idea of Justice. There is no illusion if the special pleader's distortions of Athenian justice are recognized as such. Moreover, it would be possible for some citizens to recognize that Athenian law itself represented some deviations from the true concept of Justice. Everything depends on what the mind has access to as its object. The special pleader does present some degree of truth about Justice but in a very distorted form, just as a shadow gives some evidence of some reality. Imagining, however, implies that a person is not aware that he is observing an image; therefore, imagining amounts to illusion and ignorance.

Belief

The next stage after imagining is belief. It may strike one as strange that Plato should use the word "believing" instead of "knowing" to describe the state of mind induced by seeing actual objects. We tend to feel a strong sense of certainty when we observe visible and tangible things. Still, for Plato, seeing constitutes only believing, because visible objects depend on their context for many of their characteristics. There is, then, a degree of certainty that seeing gives us, but this is not absolute certainty. If the water of the Mediterranean looks blue from the shore but turns out to be clear when taken from the sea, one's certainty about its color or composition is at least open to question. That all bodies have weight because we see them fall may seem a certainty, but we now know that this testimony of our vision must also be adjusted to the fact of the weightlessness of bodies in space at certain altitudes. Plato says, therefore, that believing, even if it is based on seeing, is still in the stage of opinion.

The state of mind produced by visible objects is clearly on a level higher than imagining, because it is based on a higher form of reality. But although actual things possess greater reality than their shadows, they do not by themselves give us all the knowledge we want to have about them. Again, justice may be seen in a particular context, but to find justice defined in a different way in another culture does raise the question about the true nature of Justice. Whether it be color, weight, or justice, these properties of things and acts are experienced under particular circumstances. For this reason, our knowledge about them is limited to these particular circumstances. But the mind is unsatisfied with this kind of knowledge, knowing that its certainty could very well be shaken if the circumstances were altered. The scientist and the jurist, therefore, do not want to confine their understanding to these particular cases, but look for principles behind the behavior of things.

Thinking

When a person moves from believing to thinking, he moves from the visible world to the intelligible world, from the realm of opinion to the realm of knowledge. The state of mind that Plato calls "thinking" is particularly characteristic of the scientist. The scientist deals with visible things, but not simply with his vision of them. For him, visible things are symbols of a reality that can be thought but not seen. Plato illustrates this kind of mental activity by referring to the mathematician. The mathematician engages in the act of "abstraction," of drawing out from the visible thing what this thing symbolizes. When a mathematician sees the diagram of a triangle, he thinks about *triangularity* or triangle-in-itself. He distinguishes between the *visible* triangle and the *intelligible* triangle. By using visible symbols, science provides a bridge from the visible to the intelligible world.

Science forces one to think, because the scientist is always searching for laws or principles. Although the scientist may look at a particular object, a triangle or a brain, he goes beyond this particular triangle or brain and thinks about *the* Triangle or *the* Brain. Science requires that we "let go" our senses and rely instead on our intellects. The mind knows that two and two equals four no matter two of what. It knows also that the angles of an equilateral triangle are all equal, regardless of the size of the triangle. Thinking, therefore, represents the power of the mind to abstract from a visible object that property which is the same in all objects in that class even though each such actual object will have other variable properties. We can, in short, think the Idea *Man* whether we observe small, large, dark, light, young, or old persons.

Thinking is characterized not only by its treatment of visible objects as symbols, but also by reasoning from *hypotheses*. By an "hypothesis" Plato meant a truth which is taken as self-evident but which depends on some higher truth. "You know," says Plato, "how students of subjects like geometry and arithmetic begin by postulating odd and even numbers, or the various figures and the three kinds of angle. . . . These data they take as known, and having adopted them as assumptions, they do not feel called upon to give any account of them to themselves or to anyone else but treat them as self-evident." Using hypothesis, or "starting from these assumptions, they go on until they arrive, by a series of consistent steps, at all the conclusions they set out to investigate." For Plato, then, an hypothesis did not mean what it means to us, namely, a temporary truth. Rather, he meant by it a firm truth but one that is related to a larger context. The special sciences and mathematics treat their subjects as if they were independent truths. All Plato wants to say here is that if we could view all things as they really are, we should discover that all things are related or connected. Thinking or reasoning from hypotheses gives us knowledge of the truth, but it does bear this limitation, that it isolates some truths from others, thereby leaving the mind still to ask *why* a certain truth is true.

Perfect Intelligence

The mind is never satisfied as long as it must still ask for a fuller explanation of things. But to have perfect knowledge would require that the mind should grasp the relation of everything to everything else, that it should see the unity of the whole of reality. Perfect intelligence represents the mind as completely released from sensible objects. At this level, the mind is dealing directly with the *Forms.* The Forms are those intelligible objects, such as Triangle and Man, which have been abstracted from the actual objects. The mind is now dealing with these pure Forms without any interference from even the symbolic character of visible objects. Here, also, the mind no longer uses hypotheses, because they represent limited and isolated truths. This highest level of knowledge is approached to the extent that the mind is able to move beyond the restrictions of hypotheses toward the unity of all Forms. It is by the faculty of power of *dialectic* that the mind moves toward its highest goal, for this is the power of seeing at once the relation of all divisions of knowledge to each other. Perfect intelligence therefore means the *synoptic* view of reality, and this, for Plato, implies the unity of knowledge.

Plato concludes his discussion of the divided line with the summary statement "Now you may take, as corresponding to the four sections, these four states of mind: *intelligence* for the highest, *thinking* for the second, *belief* for the third and for the last *imagining.* These you may arrange as the terms in a proportion, assigning to each a degree of clearness and certainty corresponding to the measure in which their objects possess truth and reality." The highest degree of reality, he argues, was possessed by the Forms, as compared with shadows, reflections, and even visible objects. What he meant by the Forms we must now explore in greater detail.

THE PLATONIC DOCTRINE OF FORMS OR IDEAS

Plato's theory of the Forms or Ideas represents his most significant philosophical contribution. However obscure and unsatisfactory his theory may be to us, it gathers around itself the novel insights that led Plato's philosophy beyond anything that had been thought before him. Basically, the Forms or Ideas are those changeless, eternal, and nonmaterial essences or patterns of which the actual visible objects we see are only poor copies. There is the Form of *the* Triangle, and all the triangles we see are mere copies of that Form. This description of the Forms as nonmaterial realities indicates what was so novel about the Platonic doctrine: Whereas the pre-Socratic philosophers thought of reality as material stuff of some sort, Plato now designated the nonmaterial Ideas or Forms as the true reality. Similarly, whereas the Sophists thought that all knowledge is relative because the material order, which is all they knew, is constantly shifting and changing, Plato argued that knowledge is absolute because the true object of thought is not the material order but the changeless and eternal order of the Ideas or

Forms. Although Socrates anticipated this view by holding that there is an absolute Good, which makes possible our judgments of particular goods, Plato went beyond Socrates's ethical concern by adding to the concept of Good a theory of metaphysics, an explanation of the whole structure of reality and the place of morality in it.

The doctrine of Forms represents a serious attempt to explain the nature of existence. We have certain kinds of experiences that raise the question about existence for us. For example, we make judgments about things and behavior, saying about a thing that it is beautiful and about an act that it is good. This suggests that there is somewhere a standard of beauty which *is* different from the things we are judging and that there *is* a standard of good which is somehow separate from the person or his act that we judge. Moreover, visible things change—they come and go, generate and perish. Their existence is brief. Compared with things, Ideas such as Good and Beautiful seem timeless. They have more *being* than things. Plato concluded, therefore, that the real world is not the visible world but rather the intelligible world. The intelligible world is most real, said Plato, because it consists of the eternal Forms.

KNOWLEDGE AS RECOLLECTION

According to Plato, the soul, that is, the human mind, before it is united with the body, is acquainted with the intelligible world or the world of Forms. In this prior existence, the soul has true knowledge. After its union with a human body, a person's mind contains its original knowledge deep in its memory. True knowledge in this world consists of remembering, in reminiscence or recollection. For Plato, then, the human mind is not originally an empty vessel into which knowledge is poured by teaching a person information. On the contrary, what the mind or soul once knew is raised to present awareness by a process of recollection aided by the technique of *dialectic* or the Socratic method. In his dialogue entitled *Meno*, Plato illustrates how Socrates is able to show that even a young uneducated slave boy "knows" some truths of geometry not because somebody taught him that subject but because he naturally knows the relationship of various ideas to each other.

Reading _____

Allegories of Line and Cave
Plato

THE LINE

Conceive, then, that there are these two powers I speak of, the Good reigning over the domain of all that is intelligible, the Sun over the visible world—or the heaven as I might call it; only you would think I was showing off my skill in etymology. At any rate you have these two orders of things clearly before your mind: the visible and the intelligible?

I have.

Now take a line divided into two unequal parts, one to represent the visible order, the other the intelligible; and divide each part again in the same proportion, symbolizing degrees of comparative clearness or obscu-rity. Then (A) one of the two sections in the visible world will stand for images. By images I mean first shadows, and then reflections in water or in close-grained, polished surfaces, and everything of that kind, if you understand.

Yes, I understand.

Let the second section (B) stand for the actual things of which the first are likenesses, the living creatures about us and all the works of nature or of human hands.

So be it.

Will you also take the proportion in which the visible world has been divided as corresponding to degrees of reality and truth, so that the likeness shall stand to the original in the same ratio as the sphere of appearances and belief to the sphere of knowledge?

Certainly.

Now consider how we are to divide the part which stands for the intelligible world. There are two sections. In the first (C) the mind uses as images those actual things which themselves had images in the visible world; and it is compelled to pursue its inquiry by starting from assumptions and travelling, not up to a principle, but down to a conclusion. In the second (D) the mind moves in the other direction, from an assumption up towards a principle which is not hypothetical; and it makes no use of the images employed in the other section, but only of Forms, and conducts its inquiry solely by their means.

I don't quite understand what you mean.

Then we will try again; what I have just said will help you to understand. (C) You know, of course, how students of subjects like geometry and arithmetic begin by postulating odd and even numbers, or the various figures and the three kinds of angle, and other such data in each subject. These data they take as known; and, having adopted them as assumptions, they do not feel called upon to give any account of them to themselves or to anyone else, but treat them as self-evident. Then, starting from these assumptions, they go on until they arrive, by a series of consistent steps, at all the conclusions they set out to investigate.

Yes, I know that.

You also know how they make use of visible figures and discourse about them, though what they really have in mind is the originals of which these figures are images: they are not reasoning, for instance, about this particular square and diagonal which they have drawn, but about *the* Square and *the* Diagonal; and so in all cases. The diagrams they draw and the models they make are actual things, which may have their shadows or images in water; but now they serve in their turn as images, while the student is seeking to behold those realities which only thought can apprehend.[1]

True.

This, then, is the class of things that I spoke of as intelligible, but with two qualifications: first, that the mind, in studying them, is compelled to employ assumptions, and, because it cannot rise above these, does not travel upwards to a first principle; and second, that it uses as images those actual things which have images of their own in the section below them and which, in comparison with those shadows and reflections, are reputed to be more palpable and valued accordingly.

I understand: you mean the subject-matter of geometry and of the kindred arts.

(D) Then by the second section of the intelligible world you may understand me to mean all that unaided reasoning apprehends by the power of dialectic, when it treats its assumptions, not as first principles, but as *hypotheses* in the literal sense, things "laid down" like a flight of steps up which it may mount all the way to something that is not hypothetical, the first principle of all; and having grasped this, may turn back and, holding on to the consequences which depend upon it, descend at last to a conclusion, never making use of any sensible object, but only of Forms, moving through Forms from one to another, and ending with Forms.

I understand, he said, though not perfectly; for the procedure you describe sounds like an enormous undertaking. But I see that you mean to distinguish the field of intelligible reality studied by dialectic as having a greater certainty and truth than the subject-matter of the "arts," as they are called, which treat their assumptions as first principles. The students of these arts are, it is true, compelled to exercise thought in contemplating objects which the senses cannot perceive; but because they start from assumptions

---

[1]Conversely, the fact that the mathematician can use visible objects as illustrations indicates that the realities and truths of mathematics are embodied, though imperfectly, in the world of visible and tangible things; whereas the counterparts of the moral Forms can only be beheld by thought.

without going back to a first principle, you do not regard them as gaining true understanding about those objects, although the objects themselves, when connected with a first principle, are intelligible. And I think you would call the state of mind of the students of geometry and other such arts, not intelligence, but thinking, as being something between intelligence and mere acceptance of appearances.

You have understood me quite well enough, I replied. And now you may take, as corresponding to the four sections, these four states of mind: *intelligence* for the highest, *thinking* for the second, *belief* for the third, and for the last *imagining*. These you may arrange as the terms in a proportion, assigning to each a degree of clearness and certainty corresponding to the measure in which their objects possess truth and reality.

THE ALLEGORY OF THE CAVE

The progress of the mind from the lowest state of unenlightenment to knowledge of the Good is now illustrated by the famous parable comparing the world of appearance to an underground Cave. . . .

One moral of the allegory is drawn from the distress caused by a too sudden passage from darkness to light. The earlier warning against plunging untrained minds into the discussion of moral problems, as the Sophists and Socrates himself had done, is reinforced by the picture of the dazed prisoner dragged out into the sunlight. Plato's ten years' course of pure mathematics is to habituate the intellect to abstract reasoning before moral ideas are called in question.

Next, said I, here is a parable to illustrate the degrees in which our nature may be enlightened or unenlightened. Imagine the condition of men living in a sort of cavernous chamber underground, with an entrance open to the light and a long passage all down the cave.[2] Here they have been from childhood, chained by the leg and also by the neck, so that they cannot move and can see only what is in front of them, because the chains will not let them turn their heads. At some distance higher up is the light of a fire burning behind them; and between the prisoners and the fire is a track[3] with a parapet built along it, like the screen at a puppet-show, which hides the performers while they show their puppets over the top.

I see, said he.

Now behind this parapet imagine persons carrying along various artificial objects, including figures of men and animals in wood or stone or

[2]The *length* of the "way in" (*eisodos*) to the chamber where the prisoners sit is an essential feature, explaining why no daylight reaches them.

[3]The track crosses the passage into the cave at right angles, and is *above* the parapet built along it.

other materials, which project above the parapet. Naturally, some of these persons will be talking, others silent.[4]

It is a strange picture, he said, and a strange sort of prisoners.

Like ourselves, I replied; for in the first place prisoners so confined would have seen nothing of themselves or of one another, except the shadows thrown by the fire-light on the wall of the Cave facing them, would they?

Not if all their lives they had been prevented from moving their heads.

And they would have seen as little of the objects carried past.

Of course.

Now, if they could talk to one another, would they not suppose that their words referred only to those passing shadows which they saw?[5]

Necessarily.

And suppose their prison had an echo from the wall facing them? When one of the people crossing behind them spoke, they could only suppose that the sound came from the shadow passing before their eyes.

No doubt.

In every way, then, such prisoners would recognize as reality nothing but the shadows of those artificial objects.

Inevitably.

Now consider what would happen if their release from the chains and the healing of their unwisdom should come about in this way. Suppose one of them set free and forced suddenly to stand up, turn his head, and walk with eyes lifted to the light; all these movements would be painful, and he would be too dazzled to make out the objects whose shadows he had been used to see. What do you think he would say, if someone told him that what he had formerly seen was meaningless illusion, but now, being somewhat nearer to reality and turned towards more real objects, he was getting a truer view? Suppose further that he were shown the various objects being carried by and were made to say, in reply to questions, what each of them was. Would he not be perplexed and believe the objects now shown him to be not so real as what he formerly saw?

Yes, not nearly so real.

And if he were forced to look at the fire-light itself, would not his eyes ache, so that he would try to escape and turn back to the things which he could see distinctly, convinced that they really were clearer than these other objects now being shown to him?

---

[4]A modern Plato would compare his Cave to an underground cinema, where the audience watch the play of shadows thrown by the film passing before a light at their backs. The film itself is only an image of "real" things and events in the world outside the cinema. For the film Plato has to substitute the clumsier apparatus of a procession of artificial objects carried on their heads by persons who are merely part of the machinery, providing for the movement of the objects and the sounds whose echo the prisoners hear. The parapet prevents these persons' shadows from being cast on the wall of the Cave.

[5]Adam's text and interpretation. The prisoners, having seen nothing but shadows, cannot think their words refer to the objects carried past behind their backs. For them shadows (images) are the only realities.

Yes.

And suppose someone were to drag him away forcibly up the steep and rugged ascent and not let him go until he had hauled him out into the sunlight, would he not suffer pain and vexation at such treatment, and, when he had come out into the light, find his eyes so full of its radiance that he could not see a single one of the things that he was now told were real?

Certainly he would not see them all at once.

He would need, then, to grow accustomed before he could see things in that upper world.[6] At first it would be easiest to make out shadows, and then the images of men and things reflected in water, and later on the things themselves. After that, it would be easier to watch the heavenly bodies and the sky itself by night, looking at the light of the moon and stars rather than the Sun and the Sun's light in the day-time.

Yes, surely.

Last of all, he would be able to look at the Sun and contemplate its nature, not as it appears when reflected in water or any alien medium, but as it is in itself in its own domain.

No doubt.

And now he would begin to draw the conclusion that it is the Sun that produces the seasons and the course of the year and controls everything in the visible world, and moreover is in a way the cause of all that he and his companions used to see.

Clearly he would come at last to that conclusion.

Then if he called to mind his fellow prisoners and what passed for wisdom in his former dwelling-place, he would surely think himself happy in the change and be sorry for them. They may have had a practice of honouring and commending one another, with prizes for the man who had the keenest eye for the passing shadows and the best memory for the order in which they followed or accompanied one another, so that he could make a good guess as to which was going to come next.[7] Would our released prisoner be likely to covet those prizes or to envy the men exalted to honour and power in the Cave? Would he not feel like Homer's Achilles, that he would far sooner "be on earth as a hired servant in the house of a landless man"[8] or endure anything rather than go back to his old beliefs and live in the old way?

Yes, he would prefer any fate to such a life.

Now imagine what would happen if he went down again to take his former seat in the Cave. Coming suddenly out of the sunlight, his eyes would be filled with darkness. He might be required once more to deliver his opinion on those shadows, in competition with the prisoners who had never been

---

[6]Here is the moral—the need of habituation by mathematical study before discussing moral ideas and ascending through them to the Form of the Good.

[7]The empirical politician, with no philosophic insight, but only a 'knack of remembering what usually happens' (*Gorg.* 501 A). He has *eikasia* = conjecture as to what is likely (*eikos*).

[8]This verse, being spoken by the ghost of Achilles, suggests that the Cave is comparable with Hades.

released, while his eyesight was still dim and unsteady; and it might take some time to become used to the darkness. They would laugh at him and say that he had gone up only to come back with his sight ruined; it was worth no one's while even to attempt the ascent. If they could lay hands on the man who was trying to set them free and lead them up, they would kill him.[9]

Yes, they would.

Every feature in this parable, my dear Glaucon, is meant to fit our earlier analysis. The prison dwelling corresponds to the region revealed to us through the sense of sight, and the fire-light within it to the power of the Sun. The ascent to see the things in the upper world you may take as standing for the upward journey of the soul into the region of the intelligible; then you will be in possession of what I surmise, since that is what you wish to be told. Heaven knows whether it is true; but this, at any rate, is how it appears to me. In the world of knowledge, the last thing to be perceived and only with great difficulty is the essential Form of Goodness. Once it is perceived, the conclusion must follow that, for all things, this is the cause of whatever is right and good; in the visible world it gives birth to light and to the lord of light, while it is itself sovereign in the intelligible world and the parent of intelligence and truth. Without having had a vision of this Form no one can act with wisdom, either in his own life or in matters of state.

So far as I can understand, I share your belief.

Then you may also agree that it is no wonder if those who have reached this height are reluctant to manage the affairs of men. Their souls long to spend all their time in that upper world—naturally enough, if here once more our parable holds true. Nor, again, is it at all strange that one who comes from the contemplation of divine things to the miseries of human life should appear awkward and ridiculous when, with eyes still dazed and not yet accustomed to the darkness, he is compelled, in a law-court or elsewhere, to dispute about the shadows of justice or the images that cast those shadows, and to wrangle over the notions of what is right in the minds of men who have never beheld Justice itself.[10]

It is not at all strange.

No; a sensible man will remember that the eyes may be confused in two ways—by a change from light to darkness or from darkness to light; and he will recognize that the same thing happens to the soul. When he sees it troubled and unable to discern anything clearly, instead of laughing thoughtlessly, he will ask whether, coming from a brighter existence, its unaccustomed vision is obscured by the darkness, in which case he will think its condition enviable and its life a happy one; or whether, emerging from the depths of ignorance, it is dazzled by excess of light. If so, he will rather feel sorry for it; or, if he were inclined to laugh, that would be less ridiculous than to laugh at the soul which has come down from the light.

[9] An allusion to the fate of Socrates.

[10] In the *Gorgias* 486 A, Callicles, forecasting the trial of Socrates, taunts him with the philosopher's inability to defend himself in a court.

That is a fair statement.

If this is true, then, we must conclude that education is not what it is said to be by some, who profess to put knowledge into a soul which does not possess it, as if they could put sight into blind eyes. On the contrary, our own account signifies that the soul of every man does possess the power of learning the truth and the organ to see it with; and that, just as one might have to turn the whole body round in order that the eye should see light instead of darkness, so the entire soul must be turned away from this changing world, until its eye can bear to contemplate reality and that supreme splendour which we have called the Good. Hence there may well be an art whose aim would be to effect this very thing, the conversion of the soul, in the readiest way; not to put the power of sight into the soul's eye, which already has it, but to ensure that, instead of looking in the wrong direction, it is turned the way it ought to be.

Yes, it may well be so.

From Plato, *The Republic of Plato*, F. M. Cornford, Oxford University Press, Oxford, Eng., 1962. Reprinted by permission of the publisher.

QUESTIONS FOR REVIEW AND DISCUSSION

1. Show how the "allegory of the cave" illustrates the different levels of the "divided line" in Plato's dialogue. Give some details.
2. In your judgment, why did Plato develop his theory of "forms"; that is, what problem about knowledge did he try to solve by this theory?
3. Have you ever had the experience of saying, "I knew that even before I learned it or heard it for the first time"? Is this what Plato talked about in his theory of knowledge as "recollection"?

16

Power of Reason

Descartes

René Descartes was born in France in 1596 and died in Sweden in 1650. He had gone to Sweden at the invitation of Queen Christina, who was impressed by his enormous intellectual achievements and wanted to receive instruction from him. The queen could see him only at five o'clock in the morning, and the unaccustomed exposure to the bitter cold at this early hour made him an easy prey to illness. Within a few months he suffered from fever and died at the age of fifty-four. Earlier he had left France and settled in Holland, where he wrote his celebrated books, including his *Discourse on Method* and *Meditations on First Philosophy*. Descartes was concerned chiefly with the problem of intellectual certainty. He had been educated, as he says, "at one of the most celebrated schools in Europe," and yet, "I found myself embarrassed with . . . many doubts and errors. . . ." The philosophy he learned left him confused and uncertain, for "no single thing is to be found in it which is not subject to dispute, and in consequence which is not dubious. . . ." He was most impressed by the exactness of mathematics and wondered whether it might be possible for the human mind to achieve this same exactness and certainty on all subjects. Descartes is usually called the "father of modern philosophy" because he set out to establish a new way of approaching philosophy. Instead of quoting earlier philosophers and theologians as, for example, Aquinas did, or relying on the authority of past traditions, he sought to build the foundation of knowledge simply on the powers of human reason.

Descartes broke with the past by deciding that he would no longer rely on previous philosophers for his ideas. Instead, he set out to build all knowledge on his own rational powers. Nor would he accept an idea as true only because it was expressed by someone with authority. Neither the authority of Aristotle's great reputation nor the authority of the church could suffice to produce the kind of certainty he sought. Descartes was determined to discover the basis of intellectual certainty in his own reason. He therefore gave philosophy a fresh start by using only those truths he could know through his own powers as the foundation for all other knowledge. He was well aware of his unique place in the history of philosophy, for he writes that "although all the truths which I class among my principles have been known from all time and by all men, there has been no one up to the present, who, so far as I know, has adopted them as the principles of philosophy. . . . as the sources from which may be derived a knowledge of all things else in the world. This is why it here remains to me to prove that they are such."

His ideal was to arrive at a system of thought whose various principles were true and were related to each other in such a clear way that the mind could move easily from one true principle to another. But in order to achieve such an organically connected set of truths, Descartes felt that he must make these truths "conform to a rational scheme." With such a scheme he could not only organize present knowledge but could "direct our reason in order to discover those truths of which we are ignorant." His first task therefore was to work out his "rational scheme," his *method*.

DESCARTES'S METHOD

Descartes's method consists of harnessing the powers of the mind with a special set of rules. He insisted on the *necessity* of method, on systematic and orderly thinking. He was appalled at scholars who sought aimlessly for truth, comparing them to men who, "burning with an unintelligent desire to find treasure continuously roam the streets, seeking to find something that a passerby might have chanced to drop. . . . It is very certain that unregulated inquiries and confused reflections of this kind only confound the natural light and bind our mental powers." Our minds naturally possess two powers, namely, *intuition* and *deduction*, "mental powers by which we are able, entirely without fear of illusion, to arrive at the knowledge of things." But by themselves these powers can lead us astray unless they are carefully regulated. Method consists, therefore, in those rules by which our powers of intuition and deduction are guided in an orderly way.

THE EXAMPLE OF MATHEMATICS

Descartes looked to mathematics for the best example of clear and precise thinking. "My method," he writes, "contains everything which gives certainty to the rules of arithmetic." Indeed, Descartes wanted to make all knowledge a "universal mathematics." For he was convinced that mathematical certainty is the result of a special *way of thinking*, and if he could discover this way, he would have a method for discovering true knowledge "of whatever lay within the compass of my powers." Mathematics is not *itself* the method but merely exhibits the method Descartes is searching for; geometry and arithmetic, he says, are only "examples" or "the outer covering" and not "the constituents" of his new method. What is there about mathematics that led Descartes to find in it the basis of his own method?

In mathematics, Descartes discovered something fundamental about the operation of the human mind. Specifically, he fastened on the mind's ability to

René Descartes. *(New York Public Library Picture Collection)*

apprehend directly and clearly basic truths. He was not so much concerned with explaining the mechanics of the formation of our ideas from experience as he was with affirming the fact that our minds are capable of knowing some ideas with absolute clarity and distinctness. Moreover, mathematical reasoning showed him that we are able to discover what we do not know by progressing in an orderly way from what we do know. If we can discover the mathematical values of certain terms (for example, the degree of an angle) from our knowledge of other terms (for example, the length of lines and degrees of other angles in a triangle), why can we not use this same method of reasoning in other fields as well? Descartes was convinced that we could, for he claimed that his method contained "the primary rudiments of human reason" and that with it he could elicit the "truths in every field whatsoever." To him all the various sciences are merely different ways in which the same powers of reasoning and the same method are used. In each case, the method is the orderly use of intuition and deduction.

INTUITION AND DEDUCTION

Descartes placed the whole edifice of knowledge on the foundation of intuition and deduction, saying that "these two methods are the most certain routes to knowledge," adding that any other approach should be "rejected as suspect of error and dangerous. . . ." By "intuition," Descartes means an intellectual activity or vision of such clarity that it leaves no doubt in the mind. Whereas the fluctuating testimony of our senses and the imperfect creations of our imaginations leave us confused, intuition provides "the conception which an unclouded and attentive mind gives us so readily and distinctly that we are wholly freed from doubt about that which we understand. . . ." Intuition gives us not only clear notions but also some truths about reality, such as, for example, that I *think,* that I *exist,* and that a *sphere has a single surface,* truths that are basic, simple, and irreducible. Moreover, it is by intuition that we grasp the connection between one truth and another: for example, that two things equal to a thing are equal to each other (if $A = B$ and $C = B$, then $A = C$) is made clear to us by intuition.

By "deduction," Descartes means something similar to intuition, describing it as "all necessary inference from facts that are known with certainty." What makes intuition and deduction similar is that both involve truth: by intuition we grasp a simple truth completely and immediately, whereas by deduction we arrive at a truth by a process, a "continuous and uninterrupted action of the mind. . . ." By tying deduction so closely to intuition, Descartes gave a new interpretation of deduction, which up to his time had been identified with a mode of reasoning called the "syllogism." Deduction, as Descartes described it, is different from a syllogism, for whereas a syllogism indicates the relationship of *concepts* to each other, deduction for Descartes indicates the relation of *truths* to each other. It is one thing to move from a fact that is known with certainty to a conclusion that that fact implies, as Descartes indicates we must do by deduction. But it is something different to go from a *premise* to a conclusion as one does in a syllogism. Descartes was aware that one can reason *consistently* from a premise, but he argued that the value of the conclusion would depend on whether the premise was *true* or not. His quarrel with earlier philosophy and theology was that conclusions were drawn logically from premises that were either untrue or else based only on authority. Descartes wanted to rest knowledge on a starting point that had absolute certainty in the individual's own mind. Knowledge requires the use, therefore, of intuition and deduction, where "first principles are given by intuition alone while the remote conclusions . . . are furnished only by deduction." Still, Descartes's *method* does not consist only of intuition and deduction, but also of the rules he formulated for their guidance.

RULES OF METHOD

The chief point of Descartes's rules is to provide a clear and orderly procedure for the operation of the mind. It was his conviction that "method consists entirely in the order and disposition of the objects toward which our mental vision must be directed if we would find out any truth." The mind must begin with a simple and absolutely clear truth and must move step by step without losing clarity and certainty along the way. Descartes spent many years at the task of formulating rules for helping the mind choose appropriate starting points for reasoning and to direct the mind in the ordered process of reasoning. Of the twenty-one rules found in his *Rules for the Direction of the Mind,* the following are among the most important:

Rule III When we propose to investigate a subject, "our inquiries should be directed, not to what others have thought, nor to what we ourselves conjecture, but to what we can clearly and perspicuously behold and with certainty deduce. . . ."

Rule IV This is a rule requiring that other rules be adhered to strictly, for "if a man observe them accurately, he shall never assume what is false as true, and will never spend his mental efforts to no purpose"

Rule V We shall comply with the method exactly if we "reduce involved and obscure propositions step by step to those that are simpler, and then starting with the intuitive apprehension of all those that are absolutely simple, attempt to ascend to the knowledge of all others by precisely similar steps. . . ."

Rule VIII "If in the matters to be examined we come to a step in the series of which our understanding is not sufficiently well able to have an intuitive cognition, we must stop short there."

In a similar way, Descartes formulated four precepts in his *Discourse on Method* which he believed were perfectly sufficient, "provided I took the firm and unwavering resolution never in a single instance to fail in observing them."

> The *first* was never to accept anything for true which I did not clearly know to be such; . . . to comprise nothing more in my judgment than what was presented to my mind so clearly and distinctly as to exclude all ground of doubt. The *second,* to divide each of the difficulties under examination into as many parts as possible, and as might be necessary for its adequate solution. The *third,* to conduct my thoughts in such order that by commencing with objects the simplest and easiest to know, I might ascend by little and little, and, as it were, step by step, to the knowledge of the more complex. . . . And the *last,* in every case to make enumerations so complete, and reviews so general, that I might be assured that nothing was omitted.

Descartes puts very little emphasis in his method on sense experience and experiment in achieving knowledge. How is it that we know the essential qualities, for example, of a piece of wax, Descartes asks? At one time a piece of wax is hard, has a certain shape, color, size, and fragrance. But when we bring it close to the fire, its fragrance vanishes, its shape and color are lost, and its size increases. What remains in the wax that permits us still to know it is wax? "It cannot," says Descartes "be anything that I observed by means of the senses, since everything in the field of taste, smell, sight, touch, and hearing are changed, and still the same wax nevertheless remains." It is "nothing but my understanding alone which does conceive it . . . solely an inspection by the mind," which enables me to know the true qualities of the wax. And, says Descartes, "what I have said here about the wax can be applied to all other things external to me." He relies for the most part on the truths contained in the mind, "deriving them from no other source than certain germs of truth which exist naturally in our souls." Descartes was confident that he could start from the beginning and rethink and rebuild all of philosophy by having recourse solely to his own rational powers and directing them in accordance with his rules. He therefore set out to show that we can have certainty of knowledge not only about mathematical concepts but also about the nature of reality.

METHODIC DOUBT

Descartes used the method of doubt in order to find an absolutely certain starting point for building up our knowledge. Having set out in his *Rules* that we should never accept anything about which we can entertain any doubt, Descartes now tries to doubt everything, saying that "because I wished to give myself entirely to the search after truth, I thought it was necessary for me . . . to reject as absolutely false everything concerning which I could imagine the least ground of doubt. . . ." His intention is clear, for he wants to sweep away all his former opinions, "so that they might later on be replaced, either by others which were better, or by the same, when I had made them conform to the uniformity of a rational scheme."

By this method of doubt, Descartes shows how uncertain our knowledge is, even of what seems most obvious to us. What can be clearer than "that I am here, seated by the fire . . . holding this paper in my hands. . . ." But when I am asleep, I dream that I am sitting by the fire, and this makes me realize that "there are no conclusive indications by which waking life can be distinguished from sleep. . . ." Nor can I be sure that *things* exist, for I cannot tell when I am imagining or really knowing, for "I have learned that [my] senses sometimes mislead me." But surely arithmetic, geometry, or sciences that deal with things must contain some certainty, for "whether I am awake or asleep, two and three together will always make the number five." Here Descartes refers to his long-held belief that there is a God who can do anything: but "how can I be sure that [God] has brought it about that there is no earth, no sky, no extended

bodies . . . and that nevertheless I have impressions of these things. . . . And
. . . that I am always mistaken when I add two and three. . . ." We cannot be
certain that God is supremely good, for "He may be an evil genius not less
powerful than deceitful," so that all things I experience "are nothing but
illusions and dreams." Descartes is therefore "constrained to confess that there
is nothing in what I formerly believed to be true which I cannot somehow
doubt."

REVERSAL OF DOUBT

At this point Descartes says that "if I am fortunate enough to find a single
truth which is certain and indubitable," that will suffice to reverse doubt and
establish a philosophy. Like Archimedes, who demanded only an immovable
fulcrum to move the earth from its orbit, Descartes searched for his one truth
and found it in the very act of doubting.

COGITO AND THE SELF

Although I can doubt that my body exists, or that I am awake, or that I am
being deceived, in short that all is illusion or false, one thing remains about
which I can have no doubt at all—that *I think*. To doubt is to think, said
Descartes, and "it must necessarily be that I who [think am] something; and
remarking that this truth, *I think, therefore I am [cogito ergo sum]*, was so solid
and so certain that all the most extravagant suppositions of the skeptics were
incapable of upsetting it, I judged that I could receive it without scruple as the
first principle of the philosophy that I sought." So clear was the truth of his
own existence that again Descartes says, "This conclusion, *I think, therefore I
am*, is the first and most certain of all which occur to one who philosophizes in
an orderly way." Accordingly, Descartes employed this basic truth for
reversing his doubts about the self, things, true ideas, and God.

At first, nothing more is proved by this truth, "I think, therefore I am,"
than the existence of my thinking self. My doubts still remain about the
existence of my own body and about anything else that is other than my
thinking. To say *Cogito ergo sum* is to affirm *my* existence: "But what then am I?
A thing which thinks. What is a thing which thinks? It is a thing which doubts,
understands, affirms, denies, wills, refuses and which also imagines and
feels." Throughout, Descartes assumes that because thinking is a fact, there
must also be a thinker, "a thing which thinks." This "thing" is not the body,
for "I knew that I was a substance the whole nature of which is to think, and
that for its existence there is no need of any place, nor does it depend on any
material thing." This much then seems absolutely certain, namely, that I, an
ego, exist, "for it is certain that no thought can exist apart from a thing which
thinks. . . ." But so far the thinker is alone, a Robinson Crusoe, enclosed in
his ideas.

CRITERION OF TRUTH

To go beyond the certainty of his own existence as a thinking being, Descartes asks again how we know something to be true: "What," he asks, "is required in a proposition for it to be true and certain?" What is there about the proposition *Cogito ergo sum* that makes it certain? "I came to the conclusion that I might assume as a general rule that the things which we conceive very *clearly* and *distinctly* are all true." In this context "clear means "that which is present and apparent to an attentive mind," in the same way that objects are clear to our eyes, and "distinct" refers to "that which is so precise and different from all other objects that it contains within itself nothing but what is clear." The reason, then, that the proposition I think, therefore I am is true is simply that it is clear and distinct to my mind. This is the reason, too, that mathematical propositions are true, for they are so clear and distinct that we cannot help accepting them. But to guarantee the truth of our clear and distinct ideas, Descartes had to prove that God exists and that He is not a deceiver who makes us think that false things are true.

THE EXISTENCE OF GOD

Descartes cannot use Aquinas's proofs for the existence of God because those proofs are based on the very facts which are still subject to Descartes's doubt, namely, facts about the external world such as *motion* and *cause* among physical things. Instead, Descartes must prove God's existence solely in terms of his rational awareness of his own existence and internal thoughts. He therefore begins his proof by examining the various ideas that pass through his mind.

Two things strike him about these ideas, that they are caused and that according to their content they differ markedly from each other. Ideas are effects, and their causes must be discovered. Some of our ideas seem to be "born with me," some "invented" by me, whereas others "come from without." Our reason tells us that "something cannot be derived from nothing" and also that "the more perfect . . . cannot be a consequence of . . . the less perfect." Our ideas possess different degrees of reality, but "it is manifest by natural light that there must be at least as much reality in the efficient and total cause as in the effect." Some of our ideas, judging by the degree of their reality, could have their origin in myself. But the idea of God contains so much "objective reality" that I wonder whether I could have produced that idea by myself. For "by the name God I understand a substance which is infinite, independent, all-knowing, all-powerful and by which I myself and everything else, if anything else exists, have been created." How can I, a finite substance, produce the idea of an infinite substance? Indeed, how could I know that I am finite unless I could compare myself with the idea of a perfect being? The idea of perfection is so clear and distinct that I am convinced that it could not proceed from my imperfect nature. Even if I were

Classroom, University of Paris, during the lifetime of Descartes. *(Snark International/Art Resource)*

potentially perfect, the idea of perfection could not come from that potentiality, for an actual effect must proceed from a being that *actually* exists. For these reasons, Descartes concludes that since ideas have causes, and since the cause must have at least as much reality as the effect, and finally since he is finite and imperfect, it must be that the cause of his idea of a perfect and infinite Being comes from outside himself, from a perfect Being who exists, from God. In addition, Descartes concludes that God cannot be a deceiver, "since the light of nature teaches us that fraud and deception necessarily proceed from some defect," which could hardly be attributed to a perfect Being.

In addition to this argument from causation, by which he proved the existence of God, Descartes, following Augustine and Anselm, offered his version of the ontological argument. Whereas in the argument from causation he reasoned that his idea of a perfect Being could not have come from himself because of his own known imperfection, in the ontological argument Descartes sought to demonstrate the existence of God by exploring what the very idea of God implies. He says that if "all which I know clearly and distinctly as pertaining to this object really does belong to it, may I not derive from this an argument demonstrating the existence of God?" How is it possible to move from an analysis of an idea to the certainty that God exists?

Some of our ideas, says Descartes, are so clear and distinct that we immediately perceive what they imply. One cannot, for example, think of a triangle without at once thinking of its lines and angles. Although one cannot think about a triangle without also thinking about its attributes of lines and angles, it does not follow that to think about a triangle implies that it exists. But just as the idea of a triangle implies certain attributes, so also the idea of God implies attributes, specifically the attribute of existence. The idea of God signifies a perfect Being. But the very idea of perfection implies existence. To speak of a nonexistent perfection is to engage in contradiction. One cannot coherently conceive of a Being who is supremely perfect in all respects and at the same time nonexistent. Just as one cannot think the idea of triangle without recognizing its attributes, so also one cannot think the idea God, says Descartes, without recognizing that this idea clearly implies the attribute of existence. Descartes says, "That which we clearly and distinctly understand to belong to the true and immutable nature of anything, its essence or form, can be truly affirmed of that thing. But after we have with sufficient accuracy investigated the nature of God, we clearly and distinctly understand that to exist belongs to His true nature. Therefore we can with truth affirm of God that He exists."

Against this line of reasoning, Descartes's critic Gassendi said that perfection does not imply existence, since existence is not a necessary attribute of perfection. To lack existence, he said, implies no impairment of perfection, only the lack of reality. Kant, as we have seen, went into considerably greater detail in his criticism of these attempts to prove the existence of God.

EXISTENCE OF THINGS

From his own existence, Descartes has proved God's existence. Along the way he has also established the criterion of truth and provided thereby the foundation for mathematical thought and for all rational activity. Now Descartes takes another look at the physical world, at his own body and other things, and asks whether he can be certain that they exist. To be a thinking thing does not of itself prove that my body exists, for my thinking self "is entirely and absolutely distinct from my body and can exist without it." How then can I know that my body and other physical things exist?

Descartes answers that we all have the clear and distinct experiences of changing our position and moving about, activities that imply a body, or what he calls "an extended substance." We also receive sense impressions, of sight, sound, and touch, frequently even against our will, and these lead us to believe that they come from bodies other than our own. This overwhelming inclination to believe that these impressions "are conveyed to me by corporeal objects" must come from God; otherwise He could not "be defended from the accusation of deceit if these ideas were produced by causes other than corporeal objects. Hence we must allow that corporeal objects exist." For Descartes, then, knowledge of the self is prior to knowledge of God, and both the self and God are prior to our knowledge of the external world.

Descartes has now reversed all his doubts and has satisfied himself absolutely that the self, things, and God exist. He has concluded that there are thinking things and things that are extended, have dimension.

Reading _____

Certainty and the Limits of Doubt
Descartes

FIRST MEDITATION: WHAT CAN BE CALLED INTO DOUBT

Some years ago I was struck by the large number of falsehoods that I had accepted as true in my childhood, and by the highly doubtful nature of the whole edifice that I had subsequently based on them. I realized that it was necessary, once in the course of my life, to demolish everything completely and start again right from the foundations if I wanted to establish anything at all in the sciences that was stable and likely to last. But the task looked an enormous one, and I began to wait until I should reach a mature enough age to ensure that no subsequent time of life would be more suitable for tackling such inquiries. This led me to put the project off for so long that I would now be to blame if by pondering over it any further I wasted the time still left for carrying it out. So today I have expressly rid my mind of all worries and arranged for myself a clear stretch of free time. I am here quite alone, and at last I will devote myself sincerely and without reservation to the general demolition of my opinions.

But to accomplish this, it will not be necessary for me to show that all my opinions are false, which is something I could perhaps never manage. Reason now leads me to think that I should hold back my assent from opinions which are not completely certain and indubitable just as carefully as I do from those which are patently false. So, for the purpose of rejecting all my opinions, it will be enough if I find in each of them at least some reason for doubt. And to do this I will not need to run through them all individually, which would be an endless task. Once the foundations of a building are undermined, anything built on them collapses of its own accord; so I will go straight for the basic principles on which all my former beliefs rested.

Whatever I have up till now accepted as most true I have acquired either from the senses or through the senses. But from time to time I have found that the senses deceive, and it is prudent never to trust completely those who have deceived us even once.

Yet although the senses occasionally deceive us with respect to objects which are very small or in the distance, there are many other beliefs about which doubt is quite impossible, even though they are derived from the senses—for example, that I am here, sitting by the fire, wearing a winter dressing-gown, holding this piece of paper in my hands, and so on. Again, how could it be denied that these hands or this whole body are mine? Unless perhaps I were to liken myself to madmen, whose brains are so damaged by the persistent vapours of melancholia that they firmly maintain they are kings when they are paupers, or say they are dressed in purple when they are naked, or that their heads are made of earthenware, or that they are pumpkins, or made of glass. But such people are insane, and I would be thought equally mad if I took anything from them as a model for myself.

A brilliant piece of reasoning! As if I were not a man who sleeps at night, and regularly has all the same experiences while asleep as madmen do when awake—indeed sometimes even more improbable ones. How often, asleep at night, am I convinced of just such familiar events—that I am here in my dressing-gown, sitting by the fire—when in fact I am lying undressed in bed! Yet at the moment my eyes are certainly wide awake when I look at this piece of paper; I shake my head and it is not asleep; as I stretch out and feel my hand I do so deliberately, and I know what I am doing. All this would not happen with such distinctness to someone asleep. Indeed! As if I did not remember other occasions when I have been tricked by exactly similar thoughts while asleep! As I think about this more carefully, I see plainly that there are never any sure signs by means of which being awake can be distinguished from being asleep. The result is that I begin to feel dazed, and this very feeling only reinforces the notion that I may be asleep.

Suppose then that I am dreaming, and that these particulars—that my eyes are open, that I am moving my head and stretching out my hands—are not true. Perhaps, indeed, I do not even have such hands or such a body at all. Nonetheless, it must surely be admitted that the visions which come in sleep are like paintings, which must have been fashioned in the likeness of things that are real, and hence that at least these general kinds of things—eyes, head, hands and the body as a whole—are things which are not imaginary but are real and exist. For even when painters try to create sirens and satyrs with the most extraordinary bodies, they cannot give them natures which are new in all respects; they simply jumble up the limbs of different animals. Or if perhaps they manage to think up something so new that nothing remotely similar has ever been seen before—something which is therefore completely fictitious and unreal—at least the colours used in the composition must be real. By similar reasoning, although these general kinds of things—eyes, head; hands and so on—could be imaginary, it must at least be admitted that certain other even simpler and more universal things are real. These are as it were the real colours from which we form all the images of things, whether true or false, that occur in our thought.

This class appears to include corporeal nature in general, and its extension; the shape of extended things; the quantity, or size and number of these things; the place in which they may exist, the time through which they may endure, and so on.

So a reasonable conclusion from this might be that physics, astronomy, medicine, and all other disciplines which depend on the study of composite things, are doubtful; while arithmetic, geometry and other subjects of this kind, which deal only with the simplest and most general things, regardless of whether they really exist in nature or not, contain something certain and indubitable. For whether I am awake or asleep, two and three added together are five, and a square has no more than four sides. It seems impossible that such transparent truths should incur any suspicion of being false.

And yet firmly rooted in my mind is the long-standing belief that there is an omnipotent God who made me the kind of creature that I am. How do I know that he has not brought it about that there is no earth, no sky, no extended thing, no shape, no size, no place, while at the same time ensuring that all these things appear to me to exist just as they do now? Moreover, since I sometimes consider that others go astray in cases where they think they have the most perfect knowledge, may I not similarly go wrong every time I add two and three or count the sides of a square, or in some even simpler matter, if that is imaginable? But perhaps God would not have wished me to be deceived in this way, since he is said to be supremely good. But if it were inconsistent with his goodness to have created me such that I am deceived all the time, it would seem equally foreign to his goodness to allow me to be deceived even occasionally; yet this last assertion cannot be made.

Perhaps there may be some who would prefer to deny the existence of so powerful a God rather than believe that everything else is uncertain. Let us not argue with them, but grant them that everything said about God is a fiction. According to their supposition, then, I have arrived at my present state by fate or chance or a continuous chain of events, or by some other means; yet since deception and error seem to be imperfections, the less powerful they make my original cause, the more likely it is that I am so imperfect as to be deceived all the time. I have no answer to these arguments, but am finally compelled to admit that there is not one of my former beliefs about which a doubt may not properly be raised; and this is not a flippant or ill-considered conclusion, but is based on powerful and well thought-out reasons. So in future I must withhold my assent from these former beliefs just as carefully as I would from obvious falsehoods, if I want to discover any certainty.

But it is not enough merely to have noticed this; I must make an effort to remember it. My habitual opinions keep coming back, and, despite my wishes, they capture my belief, which is as it were bound over to them as a result of long occupation and the law of custom. I shall never get out of the habit of confidently assenting to these opinions, so long as I suppose them to be what in fact the are, namely highly probable opinions—opinions which, despite the fact that they are in a sense doubtful, as has just been shown, it is still much more reasonable to believe than to deny. In view of this, I think it will be a good plan to turn my will in completely the opposite direction and deceive myself, by pretending for a time that these former opinions are utterly false and imaginary. I shall do this until the weight of preconceived opinion is counter-balanced and the distorting influence of habit no longer prevents my judgement from perceiving things correctly. In the meantime, I know that no danger or error will result from my plan, and that I cannot possibly go too far in my distrustful attitude. This is because the task now in hand does not involve action but merely the acquisition of knowledge.

I will suppose therefore that not God, who is supremely good and the source of truth, but rather some malicious demon of the utmost power and cunning has employed all his energies in order to deceive me. I shall think that the sky, the air, the earth, colours, shapes, sounds and all external things are merely the delusions of dreams which he has devised to ensnare my judgement. I shall consider myself as not having hands or eyes, or flesh, or blood or senses, but as falsely believing that I have all these things. I shall stubbornly and firmly persist in this mediation; and, even if it is not in my power to know any truth, I shall at least do what is in my power, that is, resolutely guard against assenting to any falsehoods, so that the deceiver, however powerful and cunning he may be, will be unable to impose on me in the slightest degree. . . .

SECOND MEDITATION: THE NATURE OF THE HUMAN MIND, AND HOW IT IS BETTER KNOWN THAN THE BODY

So serious are the doubts into which I have been thrown as a result of yesterday's meditation that I can neither put them out of my mind nor see any way of resolving them. It feels as if I have fallen unexpectedly into a deep whirlpool which tumbles me around so that I can neither stand on the bottom nor swim up to the top. Nevertheless I will make an effort and once more attempt the same path which I started on yesterday. Anything which admits of the slightest doubt I will set aside just as if I had found it to be wholly false; and I will proceed in this way until I recognize something certain, or, if nothing else, until I at least recognize for certain that there is no certainty. Archimedes used to demand just one firm and immovable point in order to shift the entire earth; so I too can hope for great things if I manage to find just one thing, however slight, that is certain and unshakeable.

I will suppose then, that everything I see is spurious. I will believe that my memory tells me lies, and that none of the things that it reports ever happened. I have no senses. Body, shape, extension, movement and place are chimeras. So what remains true? Perhaps just the one fact that nothing is certain.

Yet apart from everything I have just listed, how do I know that there is not something else which does not allow even the slightest occasion for doubt? Is there not a God, or whatever I may call him, who puts into me the thoughts I am now having? But why do I think this, since I myself may perhaps be the author of these thoughts? In that case am not I, at least, something? But I have just said that I have no senses and no body. This is the sticking point: what follows from this? Am I not so bound up with a body and with senses that I cannot exist without them? But I have convinced myself that there is absolutely nothing in the world, no sky, no earth, no minds, no bodies. Does it now follow that I too do not exist? No: if I convinced myself of something then I certainly existed. But there is a deceiver of supreme power and cunning who is deliberately and constantly deceiving me. In that case I too undoubtedly exist, if he is deceiving me; and let him deceive me as much as he can, he will never bring it about that I am nothing so long as I think that I am something. So after considering everything very thoroughly, I must finally conclude that this proposition, *I am, I exist*, is necessarily true whenever it is put forward by me or conceived in my mind.

But I do not yet have a sufficient understanding of what this "I" is, that now necessarily exists. So I must be on my guard against carelessly taking something else to be this "I," and so making a mistake in the very item of knowledge that I maintain is the most certain and evident of all. I will therefore go back and meditate on what I originally believed myself to be, before I embarked on this present train of thought. I will then subtract anything capable of being weakened, even minimally, by the arguments now introduced, so that what is left at the end may be exactly and only what is certain and unshakeable.

What then did I formerly think I was? A man. But what is a man? Shall I say "a rational animal"? No; for then I should have to inquire what an animal is, what rationality is, and in this way one question would lead me down the slope to other harder ones, and I do not now have the time to waste on subtleties of this kind. Instead I propose to concentrate on what came into my thoughts spontaneously and quite naturally whenever I used to consider what I was. Well, the first thought to come to mind was that I had a face, hands, arms and the whole mechanical structure of limbs which can be seen in a corpse, and which I called the body. The next thought was that I was nourished, that I moved about, and that I engaged in sense-perception and thinking; and these actions I attributed to the soul. But as to the nature of this soul, either I did not think about this or else I imagined it to be something tenuous, like a wind or fire or ether, which permeated my more solid parts. As to the body, however, I had no doubts about it, but thought I knew its nature distinctly. If I had tried to describe the mental conception I had of it, I would have expressed it as follows: by a body I understand whatever has a determinable shape and a definable location and can occupy a space in such a way as to exclude any other body; it can be perceived by touch, sight, hearing, taste or smell, and can be moved in various ways, not by itself but by whatever else comes into contact with it. For, according to my judgement, the power of self-movement, like the power of sensation or of thought, was quite foreign to the nature of a body; indeed, it was a source of wonder to me that certain bodies were found to contain faculties of this kind.

But what shall I now say that I am, when I am supposing that there is some supremely powerful and, if it is permissible to say so, malicious deceiver, who is deliberately trying to trick me in every way he can? Can I now assert that I possess even the most insignificant of all the attributes which I have just said belong to the nature of a body? I scrutinize them, think about them, go over them again, but nothing suggests itself; it is tiresome and pointless to go through the list once more. But what about the attributes I assigned to the soul? Nutrition or movement? Since now I do not have a body, these are mere fabrications. Sense-perception? This surely does not occur without a body, and besides, when asleep I have appeared to perceive through the senses many things which I afterwards realized I did not perceive through the senses at all. Thinking? At last I have discovered it—thought; this alone is inseparable from me. I am, I exist—that is certain. But for how long? For as long as I am thinking. For it could be that were I totally to cease from thinking, I should totally cease to exist. At present I am not admitting anything except what is necessarily true. I am, then, in the strict sense only a thing that thinks, that is, I am a mind, or intelligence, or intellect, or reason—words whose meaning I have been ignorant of until now. But for all that I am a thing which is real and which truly exists. But what kind of a thing? As I have just said—a thinking thing.

What else am I? I will use my imagination. I am not that structure of limbs which is called a human body. I am not even some thin vapour which permeates the limbs—a wind, fire, air, breath, or whatever I depict in my imagination; for these are things which I have supposed to be nothing. Let this supposition stand, for all that I am still something. . . .

But what then am I? A thing that thinks. What is that? A thing that doubts, understands, affirms, denies, is willing, is unwilling, and also imagines and has sensory perceptions.

This is a considerable list, if everything on it belongs to me. But does it? Is it not one and the same "I" who is now doubting almost everything, who nonetheless understands some things, who affirms that this one thing is true, denies everything else, desires to know more, is unwilling to be deceived, imagines many things even involuntarily, and is aware of many things which apparently come from the senses? Are not all these things just as true as the fact that I exist, even if I am asleep all the time, and even if he who created me is doing all he can to deceive me? Which of all these activities is distinct from my thinking? Which of them can be said to be separate from myself? The fact that it is I who am doubting and understanding and willing is so evident that I see no way of making it any clearer. But it is also the case that the "I" who imagines is the same "I." For even if, as I have supposed, none of the objects of imagination are real, the power of imagination is something which really exists and is part of my thinking. Lastly, it is also the same "I" who has sensory perceptions, or is aware of bodily things as it were through the senses. For example, I am now seeing light, hearing a noise, feeling heat. But I am asleep, so all this is false. Yet I certainly *seem* to see, to hear, and to be warmed. This cannot be false; what is called "having a sensory perception" is strictly just this, and in this restricted sense of the term it is simply thinking.

From all this I am beginning to have a rather better understanding of what I am. But it still appears—and I cannot stop thinking this—that the corporeal things of which images are formed in my thought, and which the senses investigate, are known with much more distinctness than this puzzling "I" which cannot be pictured in the imagination. And yet it is surely surprising that I should have a more distinct grasp of things which I realize are doubtful, unknown and foreign to me, than I have of that which is true and known—my own self. But I see what it is: my mind enjoys wandering off and will not yet submit to being restrained within the bounds of truth. Very well then; just this once let us give it a completely free rein, so that after a while, when it is time to tighten the reins, it may more readily submit to being curbed.

Let us consider the things which people commonly think they understand most distinctly of all; that is, the bodies which we touch and see. I do not mean bodies in general—for general perceptions are apt to be somewhat more confused—but one particular body. Let us take, for example, this piece of wax. It has just been taken from the honeycomb; it has not yet quite lost the taste of the honey; it retains some of the scent of the flowers from which it was gathered; its colour, shape and size are plain to see; it is hard, cold and can be handled without difficulty; if you rap it with your knuckle it makes a sound. In short, it has everything which appears necessary to enable a body to be known as distinctly as possible. But even as I speak, I put the wax by the fire, and look: the residual taste is eliminated, the smell goes away, the colour changes, the shape is lost, the size increases; it becomes liquid and hot; you can hardly touch it, and if you strike it, it no longer makes a sound. But does the same wax remain? It must be admitted that it does; no one denies it, no one thinks otherwise. So what was it in the wax that I understood with such distinctness? Evidently none of the features which I arrived at by means of the senses; for whatever came under taste, smell, sight, touch or hearing has now altered—yet the wax remains.

Perhaps the answer lies in the thought which now comes to my mind; namely, the wax was not after all the sweetness of the honey, or the fragrance of the flowers, or the whiteness, or the shape, or the sound, but was rather a body which presented itself to me in these various forms a little while ago, but which now exhibits different ones. But what exactly is it that I now imagining? Let us concentrate, take away everything which does not belong to the wax, and see what is left: merely something extended, flexible and changeable. But what is meant here by "flexible" and "changeable"? Is it what I picture in my imagination: that this piece of wax is capable of changing from a round shape to a square shape, or from a square shape to a triangular shape? Not at all; for I can grasp that the wax is capable of countless changes of this kind, yet I am unable to run through this immeasurable number of changes in my imagination, from which it follows that it is not the faculty of imagination that gives me my grasp of the wax as flexible and changeable. And what is meant by "extended"? Is the extension of the wax also unknown? For it increases if the wax melts, increases again if it boils, and is greater still if the heat is increased. I would not be making a correct judgement about the nature of wax unless I believed it capable of being extended in many more different ways than I will ever encompass in my imagination. I must therefore admit that the nature of this piece of wax is in no way revealed by my imagination, but is perceived by the mind alone. (I am speaking of this particular piece of wax; the point is even clearer with regard to wax in general.) But what is this wax which is perceived by the mind alone? It is of course the same wax which I see, which I touch, which I picture in my imagination, in short the same wax which I thought it to be from the start. And yet, and here is the point, the perception I have of it is a case not of vision or touch or imagination—nor has it ever been, despite previous appearances—but of purely mental scrutiny; and this can be imperfect and confused, as it was before, or clear and distinct as it is now, depending on how carefully I concentrate on what the wax consists in.

But as I reach this conclusion I am amazed at how [weak and] prone to error my mind is. For although I am thinking about these matters within myself, silently and without speaking, nonetheless the actual words bring me up short, and I am almost tricked by ordinary ways of talking. We say that we see the wax itself, if it is there before us, not that we judge it to be there from its colour or shape; and this might lead me to conclude without more ado that knowledge of the wax comes from what the eye sees, and not from the scrutiny of the mind alone. But then if I look out of the window and see men crossing the square, as I just happen to have done, I normally say that I see the men themselves, just as I say that I see the wax. Yet do I see any more than hats and coats which could conceal automatons? I *judge* that they are men. And so something which I thought I was seeing with my eyes is in fact grasped solely by the faculty of judgement which is in my mind.

However, one who wants to achieve knowledge above the ordinary level should feel ashamed at having taken ordinary ways of talking as a basis for doubt. So let us proceed, and consider on which occasion my perception of the nature of the wax was more perfect and evident. Was it when I first looked at it, and believed I knew it by my external senses, or at least by what they call the "common" sense—that is, the power of imagination? Or is my knowledge more perfect now, after a more careful investigation of the nature of the wax and of the means by which it is known? Any doubt on this issue would clearly be foolish; for what distinctness was there in my earlier perception? Was there anything in it which an animal could not possess? But when I distinguish the wax from its outward forms—take the clothes off, as it were, and consider it naked—then although my judgement may still contain errors, at least my perception now requires a human mind.

But what am I to say about this mind, or about myself? (So far, remember, I am not admitting that there is anything else in me except a mind.) What, I ask, is this "I" which seems to perceive the wax so distinctly? Surely my awareness of my own self is not merely much truer and more certain than my awareness of the wax, but also much more distinct and evident. For if I judge that the wax exists from the fact that I see it, clearly this same fact entails much more evidently that I myself also exist. It is possible that what I see is not really the wax; it is possible that I do not even have eyes with which to see anything. But when I see, or think I see (I am not here distinguishing the two), it is simply not possible that I who am now thinking am not something. By the same token, if I judge that the wax exists from the fact that I touch it, the same result follows, namely that I exist. If I judge that it exists from the fact that I imagine it, or for any other reason, exactly the same thing follows. And the result that I have grasped in the case of the wax may be applied to everything else located outside me. Moreover, if my perception of the wax seemed more distinct after it was established not just by sight or touch but by many other considerations, it must be admitted that I now know myself even more distinctly. This is because every consideration whatsoever which contributes to my perception of the wax, or of any other body, cannot but establish even more effectively the nature of my own mind. But besides this, there is so much else in the mind itself which can serve to make my knowledge of it more distinct, that it scarcely seems worth going through the contributions made by considering bodily things.

I see that without any effort I have now finally got back to where I wanted. I now know that even bodies are not strictly perceived by the senses or the faculty of imagination but by the intellect alone, and that this perception derives not from their being touched or seen but from their being understood; and in view of this I know plainly that I can achieve an easier and more evident perception of my own mind than of anything else.

From René Descartes, *Selected Philosophical Writings*, trans. J. Cottingham, R. Stoothoff, and D. Murdoch, Cambridge University Press, Cambridge, Eng., 1990. Reprinted with the permission of Cambridge University Press.

QUESTIONS FOR REVIEW AND DISCUSSION

1. Descartes speaks of *intuition, deduction,* and the *syllogism* (i.e., a major premise: minor premise:: and a conclusion). In what way are these notions similar, and how do they differ?
2. Descartes tries to achieve certainty of knowledge by first doubting everything he has ever known. This he called the "method of doubt." What in fact did he doubt, and what was it impossible for him to doubt?
3. Descartes says that we have the idea of God. How does Descartes proceed from this idea to prove the existence of God?
4. What did Descartes propose as the standard by which to determine if an idea is "true"?

17

Limits of Knowledge

Hume

David Hume was born in Edinburgh in 1711 of Scottish parents. He attended the University of Edinburgh but did not graduate. His parents wanted him to be a lawyer, but he rejected their wishes, regarding, as he said, "every object as contemptible except the improvement of my talents in literature." His first book, *A Treatise of Human Nature* (1739), was not an immediate success, and Hume expressed his disappointment by saying that "never literary attempt was more unfortunate, [for the book] fell deadborn from the press." His next book *Essays Moral and Political* (1741) was an immediate success. Hume then revised his first book and gave it a new title, *An Enquiry concerning Human Understanding.* He wrote several other books, including *Dialogues on Natural Religion.* Hume became very famous. For a while he was secretary to the British Ambassador in France and was for two years Under-Secretary of State. He returned in 1769 to Edinburgh, where his house became the gathering place of distinguished persons. By now he was wealthy and lived his last seven years quietly among his friends and admirers, among whom Adam Smith was included. He died in 1776 at the age of sixty-five. He became the most influential member of the group (which also included Locke and Berkeley) known as the British Empiricists, who said that knowl–edge is limited to experience ("empiricism": the practice of emphasizing experience or observation rather than intuition or speculation in the pursuit of knowledge).

The only way, says Hume, to solve the problem of disagreements and speculations regarding "abstruse questions" is to "enquire seriously into the nature of human understanding, and show from an exact analysis of its powers and capacity, that it is by no means fitted for such remote and abstruse subjects." Accordingly, Hume carefully analyzed a series of topics that led him to his skeptical conclusion, beginning with an account of the contents of the mind.

CONTENTS OF THE MIND

Nothing seems more unbounded, says Hume, than man's thought. Although our body is confined to one planet, our mind can roam instantly into the most

David Hume. *(New York Public Library Picture Collection)*

distant regions of the universe. Nor, it may seem, is the mind bound by the limits of nature or reality, for without difficulty the imagination can conceive the most unnatural and incongruous appearances, such as flying horses and gold mountains. But, although the mind seems to possess this wide freedom, it is, says Hume, "really confined within very narrow limits." In the last analysis, the contents of the mind can all be reduced to the materials given us by the senses and experience, and those materials Hume calls "perceptions." The perceptions of the mind take two forms, which Hume distinguishes as *impressions* and *ideas*.

Impressions and *ideas* make up the total content of the mind. The original stuff of thought is an *impression*, and an *idea* is merely a copy of an impression. The difference between an impression and an idea is only the degree of their vividness. The original perception is an impression, such as when we hear, see, feel, love, hate, desire, or will. These impressions are "lively" and clear when we have them. When we reflect on these impressions, we have ideas of them, and those ideas are less lively versions of the original impressions. To feel pain is an impression, whereas the memory of this sensation is an idea. In every particular, impressions and their corresponding ideas are alike, differing only in their degree of vivacity.

Besides distinguishing between impressions and ideas, Hume argues that without impressions there can be no ideas. For if an idea is simply a copy of an impression, it follows that for every idea there must be a prior impression. Not every idea, however, reflects a corresponding impression, for we have never seen a flying horse or a golden mountain even though we have ideas of them. But Hume explains such ideas as being the product of the mind's "faculty of compounding, transposing, or diminishing the materials afforded us by the senses and experience." When we think of a flying horse, our imagination joins two ideas, wings and horse, which we originally acquired as impressions through our senses. If we have any suspicion that a philosophical term is employed without any meaning or idea, we need, says Hume, "but enquire, *from what impression is that supposed idea derived?* And if it be impossible to assign any, this will serve to confirm our suspicion." Hume subjected even the idea of God to this test and concluded that it arises from reflecting on the operations of our own minds "augmenting without limit" the qualities of goodness and wisdom that we experience among human beings. But if all our ideas follow from impressions, how can we explain what we call *thinking*, or the patterns by which ideas group themselves in our minds?

ASSOCIATION OF IDEAS

It is not by mere chance that our ideas are related to each other. There must be, says Hume, "some bond of union, some associating quality, by which one idea naturally introduces another." Hume calls it "a gentle force, which commonly prevails . . . pointing out to everyone those simple ideas, which are most proper to be united in a complex one." It is not a special faculty of the mind that associates one idea with another, for Hume has no impression of the structural equipment of the mind. But by observing the actual patterns of our thinking and analyzing the groupings of our ideas, Hume thought he discovered the explanation of the association of ideas.

His explanation was that whenever there are certain qualities in ideas, these ideas are associated with one another. These qualities are three in number: resemblance, contiguity in time or place, and cause and effect. Hume believed that the connections of all ideas to one another could be explained by these qualities and gave the following examples of how they work: "A picture naturally leads our thoughts to the original [*resemblance*]: the mention of one apartment in the building naturally introduces an enquiry . . . concerning the others [*contiguity*]: and if we think of a wound, we can scarcely forebear reflecting on the pain which follows it [*cause and effect*]." There are no operations of the mind that differ in principle from one of these three examples of the association of ideas. But of these, the notion of cause and effect was considered by Hume to be the central element in knowledge. He took the position that the causal principle is the foundation upon which the validity of all knowledge depends. If there is any flaw in the causal principle, we can have no certainty of knowledge.

CAUSALITY

Hume's most original and influential ideas deal with the problem of causality. For Hume, the very idea of causality is suspect, and he approaches the problem by asking the question "What is the origin of the idea of causality?" Since ideas are copies of impressions, Hume asks what impression gives us the idea of causality. His answer is that there is no impression corresponding to this idea. How then does the idea of causality arise in the mind? It must be, says Hume, that the idea of causality arises in the mind when we experience certain relations between objects. When we speak of cause and effect, we mean to say that *A* causes *B*. But what kind of a relation does this indicate between *A* and *B*? Experience furnishes us three relations: first, there is the relation of *contiguity*, for *A* and *B* are always close together; second, there is *priority in time*, for *A*, the "cause," always precedes *B*, the "effect"; and third, there is *constant conjunction*, for we always see *A* followed by *B*. But there is still another relation that the idea of causality suggests to common sense, namely, that between *A* and *B* there is a "necessary connection." But neither contiguity, priority, nor constant conjunction implies "necessary" connection between objects. There is no object, says Hume, that implies the existence of another when we consider objects individually. No amount of observation of oxygen can ever tell us that when mixed with hydrogen it will give us water. We know this only after we have seen the two together: "It is therefore by *experience* only that we can infer the existence of one object from another." While we do have impressions of contiguity, priority, and constant conjunction, we do *not* have any impression of *necessary connections*. Thus causality is not a quality in the objects we observe, but is rather a "habit of association" in the mind produced by the repetition of instances of *A* and *B*.

Insofar as Hume assumed that the causal principle is central to all kinds of knowledge, his attack on this principle undermined the validity of all knowledge. He saw no reason for accepting the principle that *whatever begins to exist must have a cause of existence* as either intuitive or capable of demonstration. In the end, Hume considered thinking or reasoning "as species of sensation," and as such, our thinking cannot extend beyond our immediate experiences.

WHAT EXISTS EXTERNAL TO US?

Hume's extreme empiricism led him to argue that there is no rational justification for saying that bodies or things have a continued and independent existence external to us. Our ordinary experience suggests that things outside of us do exist. But if we take seriously the notion that our ideas are copies of impressions, the philosophical conclusion must be that all we know are impressions. Impressions are internal subjective states and are not clear proof of an external reality. To be sure, we always act as though there is a real external world of things, and Hume was willing to "take for granted in all our reasonings" that things do exist. But he wanted to inquire into the reason why we think there is an external world.

Our senses do not tell us that things exist independent of us, for how do we know that they continue to exist even when we interrupt our sensation of them? And even when we sense something, we are never given a double view of it whereby we can distinguish the thing from our impression of it; we have only the impression. There is no way for the mind to reach beyond impressions or the ideas they make possible: ". . . let us chase our imagination to the heavens, or to the utmost limits of the universe; we never advance a step beyond our selves, nor can we conceive any kind of existence, but those perceptions which have appeared in that narrow compass. This is the universe of the imagination, nor have we any idea but what is there produced."

CONSTANCY AND COHERENCE

Our belief that things exist external to us, says Hume, is the product of our imagination as it deals with two special characteristics of our impres– sions. From impressions our imagination becomes aware of both *constancy* and *coherence*. There is a constancy in the arrangement of things when, for example, I look out of my window: there are the mountain, the house, and the trees. If I shut my eyes or turn away and then later look at the same view again, the arrangement is still the same, and it is this constancy in the contents of my impressions that leads my imagination to conclude that the mountain, house, and trees exist whether I think of them or not. Similarly, I put a log on the fire before I leave the room, and when I return it is almost in ashes. But even though a great change has taken place in the fire, I am accustomed to find this kind of change under similar circum– stances: "this coherence . . . in their changes is one of the characteristics of external objects. . . ." In the case of the mountain, there is a constancy of our impressions, whereas with respect to the fire our impressions have a coherent relation to the processes of change. For these reasons, the imagination leads us to believe that certain things continue to have an independent existence external to us. But this is a *belief* and not a rational proof, for the assumption that our impressions are connected with things is "without any foundation in reasoning." Hume extends this skeptical line of reasoning beyond objects or things to consider the existence of the *self, substance,* and *God.*

THE SELF

Hume denied that we have any idea of *self*. This may seem paradoxical, that *I* should say that I do not have an idea of myself, yet here again Hume wants to test what we mean by a self by asking "From what impression could this idea be deriv'd?" Is there any continuous and identical reality which forms our ideas of the self? Do we have any one impression that is invariably associated with our idea of *self*? "When I enter most intimately into what I call *myself*," says Hume, "I always stumble on some particular perception or other, of heat or cold, love or hatred, pain or pleasure. I never can catch *myself* at any time without a perception and never can observe anything but the perception." Hume denies the existence of a continuous self-identity and says about the rest of mankind that "they are nothing but a bundle or collection of different perceptions." How then do we account for what we think is the self? It is our power of memory that gives the impression of our continuous identity. Hume compares the mind to "a kind of theatre where several perceptions successively make their appearance," but adds that "we have not the most distant notion of the place where these scenes are represented. . . ."

SUBSTANCE

What led Hume to deny the existence of a continuous self that in some way retains its identity through time was his thorough denial of the exis– tence of any form of *substance*. Locke retained the idea of substance as that *something* which has color or shape, and other qualities, although he spoke of it as "something we know not what." Berkeley denied the existence of substance underlying qualities but retained the idea of spiritual sub– stances. Hume denied that substance in any form exists or has any coherent meaning. If what is meant by the *self* is some form of substance, Hume argued that no such substance can be derived from our impressions of sensation. If the idea of substance is conveyed to us by our senses, Hume asked, ". . . which of them; and after what manner? If it be perceiv'd by the eyes, it must be a colour; if by the ears, a sound; if by the palate, a taste. . . . We have therefore no idea of substance, distinct from that of a collection of particular qualities. . . ."

GOD

It was inevitable that Hume's rigorous premise that "our ideas reach no further than our experience" would lead him to raise skeptical questions about the existence of God. Most attempts to demonstrate the existence of God rely on some version of causality. Among these, the argument from design has always made a powerful impact on the mind. Hume is aware of the power of this argument, but he quickly sorts out the elements of the problem, leaving the argument with less than its usual force.

The argument from design begins with the observance of a beautiful order in nature. This order resembles the kind of order the human mind is able to impose on unthinking materials. From this preliminary observation, the mind concludes that unthinking materials do not contain the principle of orderliness within themselves: "Throw several pieces of steel together, without shape or form; they will never arrange themselves so as to com–pose a watch. . . ." Order, it is held, requires activity of a mind, an orderer. Our experience tells us that neither a watch nor a house can come into being without a watchmaker or an architect. From this it is inferred that the natural order bears an analogy to the order fashioned by human effort and that just as the watch requires an ordering cause, so the natural order of the universe requires one. But such an inference, says Hume, "is uncertain; because the subject lies entirely beyond the reach of human experience."

If the whole argument from design rests on the proposition *"that the cause or causes of order in the universe probably bear some remote analogy to human intelligence,"* then, says Hume, the argument cannot prove as much as it claims. Hume's criticism of the idea of causality has particular force here. Since we derive the idea of cause from repeated observations of the contiguity, priority, and constant conjunction of two things, how can we assign a cause to the universe when we have never experienced the universe as related to anything we might consider a cause? The use of analogy does not solve the problem, since the analogy between a watch and the universe is not exact. Why not consider the universe the product of a vegetative process instead of a rational designer? And even if the cause of the universe is something like an intelligence, how can moral characteristics be ascribed to such a being? Moreover, if analogies are to be used, which one should be selected? Houses and ships are frequently designed by a group of designers: Should we say there are many gods? Sometimes experimental models are built with no present knowledge of what the finished form will be like: Is the universe a trial model or the final design? By this way of probing, Hume wished to emphasize that the order of the universe is simply an empirical fact and that we cannot infer from it the existence of God. Again, this does not, however, make Hume an atheist. He is simply testing our idea of God the way he had tested our ideas of the self and substance by his rigorous principle of empiricism. He ends, to be sure, as a skeptic, but finally makes the telling point that "to whatever length any one may push his speculative principles of scepticism, he must act and live and converse like other men. . . . It is impossible for him to persevere in total scepticism, or make it appear in his conduct for a few hours."

Empiricism and the Limits of Knowledge

Hume

All the objects of human reason or enquiry may naturally be divided into two kinds, to wit, *Relations of Ideas,* and *Matters of Fact.* Of the first kind are the sciences of Geometry, Algebra, and Arithmetic; and in short, every affirmation which is either intuitively or demonstratively certain. *That the square of the hypotenuse is equal to the square of the two sides,* is a proposition which expresses a relation between these figures. *That* three times five is equal to the half of thirty, expresses a relation between these numbers. Propositions of this kind are discoverable by the mere operation of thought, without dependence on what is anywhere existent in the universe. Though there never were a circle or triangle in nature, the truths demonstrated by Euclid would for ever retain their certainty and evidence.

Matters of fact, which are the second objects of human reason, are not ascertained in the same manner; nor is our evidence of their truth, however great, of a like nature with the foregoing. The contrary of every matter of fact is still possible; because it can never imply a contradiction, and is conceived by the mind with the same facility and distinctness, as if ever so conformable to reality. *That the sun will not rise tomorrow* is no less intelligible a proposition, and implies no more contradiction than the affirmation, *that it will rise.* We should in vain, therefore, attempt to demonstrate its falsehood. Were it demonstratively false, it would imply a contradiction, and could never be distinctly conceived by the mind.

It may, therefore, be a subject worthy of curiosity, to enquire what is the nature of that evidence which assures us of any real existence and matter of fact, beyond the present testimony of our senses, or the records of our memory. This part of philosophy, it is observable, has been little cultivated, either by the ancients or moderns; and therefore our doubts and errors, in the prosecution of so important an enquiry, may be the more excusable; while we march through such difficult paths without any guide or direction. They may even prove useful, by exciting curiosity, and destroying that implicit faith and security, which is the bane of all reasoning and free enquiry. The discovery of defects in the common philosophy, if any such there be, will not, I presume, be a discouragement, but rather an incitement, as is usual, to attempt something more full and satisfactory than has yet been proposed to the public.

All reasonings concerning matters of fact seem to be founded on the relation of *Cause and Effect.* By means of that relation alone we can go beyond the evidence of our memory and senses. If you were to ask a man, why he believes any matter of fact, which is absent; for instance, that his friend is in the country, or in France; he would give you a reason; and this reason would be some other fact; as a letter received from him, or the knowledge of his former resolutions and promises. A man finding a watch or any other machine in a desert island, would conclude that there had once been men in that island.

All our reasonings concerning fact are of the same nature. And here it is constantly supposed that there is a connexion between the present fact and that which is inferred from it. Were there nothing to bind them together, the inference would be entirely precarious. The hearing of an articulate voice and rational discourse in the dark assures us of the presence of some person: Why? because these are the effects of the human make and fabric, and closely connected with it. If we anatomize all the other reasonings of this nature, we shall find that they are founded on the relation of cause and effect, and that this relation is either near or remote, direct or collateral. Heat and light are collateral effects of fire, and the only effect may justly be inferred from the other.

If we would satisfy ourselves, therefore, concerning the nature of that evidence, which assures us of matters of fact, we must enquire how we arrive at the knowledge of cause and effect.

Old Edinburgh, where Hume lived and walked. (*New York Public Library Picture Collection*)

I shall venture to affirm, as a general proposition, which admits of no exception, that the knowledge of this relation is not, in any instance, attained by reasonings *a priori* [that is, prior to experience]; but arises entirely from experience, when we find that any particular objects are constantly conjoined with each other. Let an object be presented to a man of ever so strong natural reason and abilities; if that object be entirely new to him, he will not be able, by the most accurate examination of its sensible qualities, to discover any of its causes or effects. Adam, though his rational faculties be supposed, at the very first, entirely perfect, could not have inferred from the fluidity and transparency of water that it would suffocate him, or from the light and warmth of fire that it would consume him. No object ever discovers, by the qualities which appear to the senses, either the causes which produced it, or the effects which will arise from it; nor can our reason, unassisted by experience, ever draw any inference concerning real existence and matter of fact.

This proposition, *that causes and effects are discoverable, not by reason but by experience,* will readily be admitted with regard to such objects, as we remember to have once been altogether unknown to us; since we must be conscious of the utter inability, which we then lay under, of foretelling what would arise from them. Present two smooth pieces of marble to a man who has no tincture of natural philosophy; he will never discover that they will adhere together in such a manner as to require great force to separate them in a direct line, while they make so small a resistance to a lateral pressure. Such events, as bear little analogy to the common course of nature, are also readily confessed to be known only by experience; nor does any man imagine that the explosion of gunpowder, or the attraction of a loadstone, could ever be discovered by arguments *a priori*. In like manner, when an effect is supposed to depend upon an intricate machinery or secret structure of parts, we make no difficulty in attributing all our knowledge of it to experience. Who will assert that he can give the ultimate reason, why milk or bread is proper nourishment for a man, not for a lion or a tiger?

But the same truth may not appear, at first sight, to have the same evidence with regard to events, which have become familiar to us from our first appearance in the world, which bear a close analogy to the whole course of nature, and which are supposed to depend on the simple qualities of objects, without any secret structure of parts. We are apt to imagine that we could discover these effects by the mere operation of our reason, without experience. We fancy, that were we brought on a sudden into this world, we could at first have inferred that one Billiard-ball would communicate motion to another upon impulse; and that we needed not to have waited for the event, in order to pronounce with certainty concerning it. Such is the influence of custom, that, where it is strongest, it not only covers our natural ignorance, but even conceals itself, and seems not to take place, merely because it is found in the highest degree.

But to convince us that all the laws of nature, and all the operations of bodies without exception, are known only by experience, the following reflections may, perhaps, suffice. Were any object presented to us, and were we required to pronounce concerning the effect, which will result from it, without consulting past observation; after what manner, I beseech you, must the mind proceed in this operation? It must invent or imagine some event, which it ascribes to the object as its effect; and it is plain that this invention must be entirely arbitrary. The mind can never possibly find the effect in the supposed cause, by the most accurate scrutiny and examination. For the effect is totally different from the cause, and consequently can never be discovered in it. Motion in the second Billiard-ball is a quite distinct event from motion in the first; nor is there anything in the one to suggest the smallest hint of the other. A stone or piece of metal raised into the air, and left without any support, immediately falls: but to consider the matter *a priori,* is there anything we discover in this situation which can beget the idea of a downward, rather than an upward, or any other motion, in the stone or metal?

It is certain that the most ignorant and stupid peasants—nay infants, nay even brute beasts—improve by experience, and learn the qualities of natural objects, by observing the effects which result from them. When a child has felt the sensation of pain from touching the flame of a candle, he will be careful not to put his hand near any candle; but will expect a similar effect from a cause which is similar in its sensible qualities and appearance. If you assert, therefore, that the understanding of the child is led into this conclusion by any process of argument or ratiocination, I may justly require you to produce that argument; nor have you any pretence to refuse so equitable a demand. You cannot say that the argument is abstruse, and may possibly escape your enquiry; since you confess that it is obvious to the capacity of a mere infant. If you hesitate, therefore, a moment, or if, after reflection, you produce any intricate or profound argument, you, in a manner, give up the question, and confess that it is not reasoning which engages us to suppose the past resembling the future, and to expect similar effects from causes which are, to appearance, similar. This is the proposition which I intended to enforce in the present section.

From David Hume, *An Enquiry concerning Human Understanding,* 1748.

QUESTIONS FOR REVIEW AND DISCUSSION

1. According to Hume, what constitutes the whole contents of the mind?
2. If all our ideas are based on sense impressions, where do we get the idea of a winged horse or a gold mountain?
3. What is Hume's explanation for what are called "necessary connections," or, cause and effect?
4. Why did Hume deny that we have any idea of a "self"? Does Hume's theory fit your own experience?

18

How Knowledge Is Possible

Kant

Immanuel Kant was impressed by Hume's theory of knowledge. "I openly confess," he said, "that the suggestion of David Hume was the very thing which many years ago first interrupted my dogmatic slumber and gave my investigations in the field of speculative philosophy quite a new direction." But Kant said, "I was far from following [Hume] in the conclusions at which he arrived." Kant rejected Hume's final skepticism. He decided that Hume had not completed the task of explaining how knowledge is acquired. Also, Kant saw some value in Descartes's rationalism. He was fascinated by the way our minds work when thinking about mathematics.

Here, then, Kant faced two extreme theories of knowledge, rationalism on the one hand and empiricism on the other. He realized that both rationalism and empiricism were ignored by the most successful method of thought in his day, namely, the science of physics, especially as formulated by Sir Isaac Newton. Rationalism, because it followed the model of mathematics, seemed to consist merely of relating ideas to one another without making contact with things as they really are. Physics did make this contact successfully. Empiricism as formulated by Hume raised skeptical doubts about *causality*, saying that we cannot be sure a certain effect will always follow a particular cause. Yet physics is built on the reliability of cause and effect. Therefore, Kant set out to discover how the mind works when it is thinking scientifically. In this process he was able to take what he considered important from both rationalism and empiricism to develop his own theory of knowledge, which is known as "critical idealism."

For biographical note on Kant, see p. 58.

THE WAY OF CRITICAL PHILOSOPHY

Kant's *critical* philosophy consists of an analysis of the powers of human reason, by which he meant "a critical inquiry into the faculty of reason with reference to all the knowledge which it may strive to attain independently of all experience." The way of critical philosophy is, therefore, to ask the question "What and how much can understanding and reason know, apart from all experience?" Thus, whereas earlier metaphysicians engaged in disputes about the nature of the supreme being and other subjects that took them beyond the realm of immediate experience, Kant asked the critical question whether the human reason possesses the powers to undertake such inquiries. From this critical point of view Kant thought it foolish for metaphysicians to engage in attempts to construct systems of knowledge even before they had inquired into whether by pure reason alone one can apprehend what is not given to him in experience. Critical philosophy for Kant was therefore not the negation of metaphysics, but rather a preparation for it. If metaphysics has to do with knowledge that is developed by reason alone, that is, prior to experience, or *a priori,** the critical question is how is such a priori knowledge possible.

The Nature of a priori Knowledge

Kant affirmed that we possess a faculty that is capable of giving us knowledge without an appeal to experience. He agreed with the empiricists that our knowledge begins with experience, but he added that "though our knowledge begins with experience, it does not follow that it all arises out of experience." This was the point that Hume had missed, for Hume had said that all our knowledge consists of a series of impressions, which we derive through our senses. Yet we clearly possess a kind of knowledge that does not come *out of* experience even though it begins *with* experience. Hume was right that we do not, for example, experience or sense *causality*, but Kant rejected his explanation that causality is simply a psychological habit of connecting two events that we call cause and effect. Kant believed that we have knowledge about causality and that we get this knowledge not from sense experience but directly from the faculty of rational judgment and, therefore, a priori.

What, more specifically, is a priori knowledge? Kant replies that "if one desires an example from the sciences, one needs only to look at any proposition in mathematics. If one desires an example from the commonest operations of the understanding, the proposition that every change must have a cause can serve one's purposes." What makes a proposition of mathematics, or the proposition that every change must have a cause, a priori knowledge? It is, says Kant, that this kind of knowledge cannot be derived from experience. Experience cannot show us that *every* change must have a cause, since we have not yet experienced every change. Nor can experience show us that connections between events are *necessary*, for the most experience can tell us is

*a priori knowledge is knowledge prior to experience.

Immanuel Kant. (*New York Public Library Picture Collection*)

"that a thing is so and so, but not that it cannot be otherwise." Experience, then, cannot give us knowledge about *necessary* connections or about the *universality* of propositions. Yet we do in fact have this kind of knowledge about causality and universality, for these are the notions that characterize mathematics and scientific knowledge. We confidently say that all heavy objects will fall in space or that all instances of five added to seven will equal twelve. That there is such a priori knowledge is clear, but what concerned Kant was how such knowledge can be accounted for. How, in short, can Hume's skepticism be answered?

Kant's Copernican Revolution

It was clear to Kant that if we assume, as Hume did, that the mind, in forming its concepts, must conform to its objects, there could be no solution to the problem of how knowledge is possible. Hume's theory would work for our ideas of things we have actually experienced. If I ask "How do I know that the chair is brown?" my answer is that I can see it; and if my assertion is challenged, I refer to my experience. When I thus refer to my experience, that settles the question, because we all agree that experience gives us a kind of knowledge that conforms to the nature of things.

But we also have a kind of knowledge which cannot be validated by experience; if I say, for example, that every straight line is the shortest way between two points, I certainly cannot say that I have had experience of every possible straight line. What makes it possible for me to make judgments about events before they even occur, judgments that are universally true and can always be verified? If, as Hume believed, the mind is passive and simply receives its information from the objects, it follows that the mind would have information only about that particular object. But the mind makes judgments about all objects, even those which it has not yet experienced, and in addition, objects do in fact behave in the future according to these judgments we make about them. This scientific knowledge gives us reliable information about the nature of things. But since this knowledge could not be explained on the assumption that the mind conforms to its objects (how could it conform to every straight line, every change?), Kant was forced to try a new hypothesis regarding the relation between the mind and its objects.

Kant's new hypothesis was that it is the objects that conform to the operations of the mind, and not the other way around. He came to this hypothesis with a spirit of experimentation, consciously following the example of Copernicus, who "failing of satisfactory progress in explaining the movements of the heavenly bodies on the supposition that they all revolved round the spectator, . . . tried whether he might not have better success if he made the spectator to revolve and the stars to remain at rest." Seeing an analogy here with his own problem, Kant says that

> hitherto it has been assumed that all our knowledge must conform to objects. But all our attempts to extend our knowledge of objects by establishing something in regard to them *a priori* by means of concepts, have, on this assumption, ended in failure. We must, therefore, make trial whether we may not have more success in the tasks of metaphysics, if we suppose that objects must conform to our knowledge. . . . If intuition must conform to the constitution of the objects, I do not see how we could know anything of the latter *a priori;* but if the object (as object of the senses) must conform to the constitution of our faculty of intuition, I have no difficulty in conceiving such a possibility.

Kant did not mean to say that the mind creates objects, nor did he mean that the mind possesses innate ideas. His Copernican revolution consisted rather in his saying that the mind brings something to the objects it experiences. With Hume, Kant agreed that our knowledge begins with experience, but unlike Hume, Kant saw the mind as an active agent doing something with the objects it experiences. The mind, says Kant, is structured in such a way that it imposes its way of knowing on its objects. By its very nature, the mind actively organizes our experiences. That is, thinking involves not only receiving impressions through our senses but also making judgments about what we experience. Just as a person who wears colored glasses sees everything in that color, so every human being, having the faculty of thought, inevitably thinks about things in accordance with the natural structure of the mind.

THE STRUCTURE OF RATIONAL THOUGHT

Kant says that "there are two sources of human knowledge, which perhaps spring from a common but to us unknown root, namely sensibility and understanding. Through the former objects are *given* to us; through the latter they are *thought*." Knowledge is, therefore, a cooperative affair between the knower and the thing known. But, although I am able to distinguish the difference between myself as a knower and the thing I know, I can never know that thing as it is in itself, for the moment I know it, I know it as my structured mind permits me to know it. If colored glasses were permanently fixed to my eyes, I should always see things in that color and could never escape the limitations placed on my vision by those glasses. Similarly, my mind always brings certain ways of thinking to things, and this always affects my understanding of them. What, we may ask, does the mind bring to the *given* raw materials of our experience?

The Categories of Thought and the Forms of Intuition

The distinctive activity of the mind is to synthesize and to unify our experience. It achieves this synthesis first by imposing on our various experiences in the *"sensible manifold"** certain forms of intuition: space and time. We inevitably perceive things as being in *space* and *time*. But space and time are not ideas derived from the things we experience, nor are they concepts. Space and time are encountered immediately in intuition and are, at the same time, a priori or, to speak figuratively, lenses through which we always see objects of experience.

In addition to space and time, which deal particularly with the way we sense things, there are certain categories of thought which deal more specifically with the way the mind unifies or synthesizes our experience. The mind achieves this unifying act by making various kinds of judgments as we engage in the act of interpreting the world of sense. The manifold of experience is judged by us through certain fixed forms or concepts such as *quantity, quality, relation,* and *modality.* When we assert *quantity,* we have in

---

*The "sensible manifold" is simply everything we experience with our senses—objects, colors, sounds, etc.

mind one or many. When we make a judgment of *quality*, we make either a positive or negative statement. When we make a judgment of *relation*, we think of cause and effect on the one hand or of the relation of subject and predicate on the other. And when we make a judgment of *modality*, we have in mind that something is either possible or impossible. All these ways of thinking are what constitute the act of synthesis through which the mind strives to make a consistent single world out of the manifold of sense impressions.

The Self and the Unity of Experience

What makes it possible for us to have a unified grasp of the world about us? From his analysis of the way our minds work, Kant's answer is that it is the mind that transforms the raw data given to our senses into a coherent and related set of elements. But this leads Kant to say that the unity of our experience must imply a unity of the self, for unless there be a unity between the several operations of the mind, there can be no knowledge of experience. To have such knowledge involves, in various sequences, sensation, imagination, and memory, as well as the powers of intuitive synthesis. Thus it must be the same self that at once senses an object, remembers its characteristics, imposes on it the forms of space and time and the category of cause and effect. All these activities must occur in some single subject; otherwise there could be no knowledge, for if one subject had only sensations, another only memory, and so on, the sensible manifold could never be unified.

Where and what is this single subject that accomplishes this unifying activity? Kant calls it the "transcendental unity of apperception,"* what we should call the *self*. He uses the term "transcendental" to indicate that we do not experience the self directly even though such a unity, or self, is implied by our actual experience. Thus the idea of this self is a priori as a necessary condition for our experience of having knowledge of a unified world of nature. In the act of unifying all the elements of experience, we are conscious of our own unity, so that our consciousness of a unified world of experience and our own self-consciousness occur simultaneously. Our self-consciousness, however, is affected by the same faculties that affect our perception of external objects. I bring to the knowledge of myself the same apparatus and, therefore, impose on myself as an object of knowledge the same "lenses" through which I see everything. Just as I do not know things as they are apart from the perspective from which I see them, so also I do not know the nature of this "transcendental unity of apperception," myself, except as I am aware of the

*The "transcendental unity of apperception" is my conscious self as it brings together, that is, synthesizes, all the things I see and experience and organizes everything in accordance with the faculties of my mind such as space and time and cause and effect. My mind can bring all these elements together into a unity because the human mind is more than just a camera taking individual shots without "understanding" them. The camera is not a conscious self that can simultaneously *sense* and *know* things.

knowledge I have of the unity of the field of experience. What I am sure of is that a unified self is implied by any knowledge of experience.

Phenomenal and Noumenal Reality

A major impact of Kant's critical philosophy was his insistence that human knowledge is forever limited in its scope. This limitation takes two forms. In the first place, knowledge is limited to the world of experience. Second, our knowledge is limited by the manner in which our faculties of perception and thinking organize the raw data of experience. Kant did not doubt that the world as it appears to us is not the ultimate reality. He distinguished between *phenomenal* reality, or the world as we experience it, and *noumenal* reality, which is purely intelligible, or nonsensual, reality. When we experience a thing, we inevitably perceive it through the "lenses" of our a priori categories of thought. But what is a thing like when it is not being perceived? What is a thing-in-itself *(Ding an sich)?* We can obviously never have an experience of a nonsensuous perception. All objects we know are sensed objects. Still we know that the existence of our world of experience is not produced by the mind. The mind, rather, imposes its ideas on the manifold of experience, which is derived from the world of things-in-themselves. This means that there is a reality external to us that exists independently of us but which we can know only as it appears to us and is organized by us. The concept of a thing-in-itself does not, then, increase our knowledge but reminds us of the limits of our knowledge.

Reading _____

How Knowledge Is Possible
Kant

I. THE DISTINCTION BETWEEN PURE AND EMPIRICAL KNOWLEDGE

There can be no doubt that all our knowledge begins with experience. For how should our faculty of knowledge be awakened into action did not objects affecting our senses partly of themselves produce representations, partly arouse the activity of our understanding to compare these representations and, by combining or separating them, work up the raw material of the sensible impressions into that knowledge of objects which is entitled experience? In the order of time, therefore, we have no knowledge antecedent to experience, and with experience all our knowledge begins.

But though all our knowledge begins with experience, it does not follow that it all arises out of experience. For it may well be that even our empirical knowledge is made up of what we receive through impressions and of what our own faculty of knowledge (sensible impressions serving merely as the occasion) supplies from itself. If our faculty of knowledge makes any such addition, it may be that we are not in a position to distinguish it from the raw material, until with long practice of attention we have become skilled in separating it.

This, then, is a question which at least calls for closer examination, and does not allow of any off-hand answer:—whether there is any knowledge that is thus independent of experience and even of all impressions of the senses. Such knowledge is entitled *a priori*, and distinguished from the *empirical*, which has its sources *a posteriori*, that is, in experience.

The expression "*a priori*" does not, however, indicate with sufficient precision the full meaning of our question. For it has been customary to say, even of much knowledge that is derived from empirical sources, that we have it or are capable of having it *a priori*, meaning thereby that we do not derive it immediately from experience, but from a universal rule—a rule which is itself, however, borrowed by us from experience. Thus we would say of a man who undermined the foundations of his house, that he might have known *a priori* that it would fall, that is, that he need not have waited for the experience of its actual falling. But still he could not know this completely *a priori*. For he had first to learn through experience that bodies are heavy, and therefore fall when their supports are withdrawn.

In what follows, therefore, we shall understand by *a priori* knowledge, not knowledge independent of this or that experience, but knowledge absolutely independent of all experience. Opposed to it is empirical knowledge, which is knowledge possible only *a posteriori*, that is, through experience. *A priori* modes of knowledge are entitled pure when there is no admixture of anything empirical. Thus, for instance, the proposition, "every alteration has its cause," while an *a priori* proposition, is not a pure proposition, because alteration is a concept which can be derived from experience.

II. WE ARE IN POSSESSION OF CERTAIN MODES OF A PRIORI KNOWLEDGE, AND EVEN THE COMMON UNDERSTANDING IS NEVER WITHOUT THEM

What we here require is a criterion by which to distinguish with certainty between pure and empirical knowledge. Experience teaches us that a thing is so and so, but not that it cannot be otherwise. First, then, if we have a proposition which in being thought is thought as *necessary*, it is an *a priori* judgment; and if, besides, it is not derived from any proposition except one which also has the validity of a necessary judgment, it is an absolutely *a priori* judgment. Secondly, experience never confers on its judgments true or strict, but only assumed and comparative *universality*, through induction. We can properly only say, therefore, that, so far as we have hitherto observed, there is no exception to this or that rule. If, then, a judgment is thought with strict universality, that is, in such manner that no exception is allowed as possible, it is not derived from experience, but is valid absolutely *a priori*. Empirical universality is only an arbitrary extension of a validity holding in most cases to one which holds in all, for instance, in the proposition, "all bodies are heavy." When, on the other hand, strict universality is essential to a judgment, this indicates a special source of knowledge, namely, a faculty of *a priori* knowledge. Necessity and strict universality are thus sure criteria of *a priori* knowledge, and are inseparable from one another. But since in the employment of these criteria the contingency of judgments is sometimes more easily shown than their empirical limitation, or, as sometimes also happens, their unlimited universality can be more convincingly proved than their necessity, it is advisable to use the two criteria separately, each by itself being infallible.

Now it is easy to show that there actually are in human knowledge judgments which are necessary and in the strictest sense universal, and which are therefore pure *a priori* judgments. If an example from the sciences be desired, we have only to look to any of the propositions of mathematics; if we seek an example from the understanding in its quite ordinary employment, the proposition, "every alteration must have a cause," will serve our purpose. In the latter case, indeed, the very concept of a cause so manifestly contains the concept of a necessity of connection with an effect and of the strict universality of the rule, that the concept would be altogether lost if we attempted to derive it, as Hume has done, from a repeated association of that which happens with that which precedes, and from a custom of connecting representations, a custom originating in this repeated association, and constituting therefore a merely subjective necessity. Even without appealing to such examples, it is possible to show that pure *a priori* principles are indispensable for the possibility of experience, and so to prove their existence *a priori*. For whence could experience derive its certainty, if all the rules, according to which it proceeds, were always themselves empirical, and therefore contingent? Such rules could hardly be regarded as first principles. At present, however, we may be content to have established a pure employment, and to have shown what are the criteria of such an employment.

Such *a priori* origin is manifest in certain concepts, no less than in judgments. If we remove from our empirical concept of a body, one by one, every feature in it which is (merely) empirical, the colour, the hardness or softness, the weight, even the impenetrability, there still remains the space which the body (now entirely vanished) occupied, and this cannot be removed. Again, if we remove from our empirical concept of any object, corporeal or incorporeal, all properties which experience has taught us, we yet cannot take away that property through which the object is thought as substance or as inhering in a substance (although this concept of substance is more determinate than that of an object in general). Owing, therefore, to the necessity with which this concept of substance forces itself upon us, we have no option save to admit that it has its seat in our faculty of *a priori* knowledge. . . .

IV. THE DISTINCTION BETWEEN ANALYTIC AND SYNTHETIC JUDGMENTS

In all judgments in which the relation of a subject to the predicate is thought (I take into consideration affirmative judgments only, the subsequent application to negative judgments being easily made), this relation is possible in two different ways. Either the predicate B belongs to the subject A, as something which is (covertly) contained in this concept A; or B lies outside the concept A, although it does indeed stand in connection with it. In the one case I entitled the judgment analytic, in the other synthetic. Analytic judgments (affirmative) are therefore those in which the connection of the predicate with the subject is thought through identity; those in which this connection is thought without identity should be entitled synthetic. The former, as adding nothing through the predicate to the concept of the subject, but merely breaking it up into those constituent concepts that have all along been thought in it, although confusedly, can also be entitled explicative. The latter, on the other hand, add to the concept of the subject a predicate which has not been in any wise thought in it, and which no analysis could possibly extract from it; and they may therefore be entitled ampliative. If I say, for instance, "All bodies are extended," this is an analytic judgment. For I do not require to go beyond the concept which I connect with "body" in order to find extension as bound up with it. To meet with this predicate, I have merely to analyse the concept, that is, to become conscious to myself of the manifold which I always think in that concept. The judgment is therefore analytic. But when I say, "All bodies are heavy," the predicate is something quite different from anything that I think in the mere concept of body in general; and the addition of such a predicate therefore yields a synthetic judgment.

Judgments of experience, as such, are one and all synthetic. For it would be absurd to found an analytic judgment on experience. Since, in framing the judgment, I must not go outside my concept, there is no need to appeal to the testimony of experience in its support. That a body is extended is a proposition that holds *a priori* and is not empirical. For, before appealing to experience, I have already in the concept of body all the conditions required for my judgment, I have only to extract from it, in accordance with the principle of contradiction, the required predicate, and in so doing can at the same time become conscious of the necessity of the judgment—and that is what experience could never have taught me. On the other hand, though I do not include in the concept of a body in general the predicate "weight," none the less this concept indicates an object of experience through one of its parts, and I can add to that part other parts of this same experience, as in this way belonging together with the concept. From the start I can apprehend the concept of body analytically through the characters of extension, impenetrability, figure, etc., all of which are thought in the concept. Now, however, looking back on the experience from which I have derived this concept of body, and finding weight to be invariably connected with the above characters, I attach it as a predicate to the concept; and in doing so I attach it synthetically, and am therefore extending my knowledge. The possibility of the synthesis of the predicate "weight" with the concept of "body" thus rests upon experience. While the one concept is not contained in the other, they yet belong to one another, though only contingently, as parts of a whole, namely, of an experience which is itself a synthetic combination of intuitions.

But in *a priori* synthetic judgments this help is entirely lacking. (I do not here have the advantage of looking around in the field of experience.) Upon what, then, am I to rely, when I seek to go beyond the concept A, and to know that another concept B is connected with it? Through what is the synthesis made possible? Let us take the proposition, "Everything which happens has its cause." In the concept of "something which happens," I do indeed think an existence which is preceded by a time, etc., and from this concept analytic judgments may be obtained. But the concept of a "cause" lies entirely outside the other concept, and signifies something different from "that which happens," and is not therefore in any way contained in this latter representation. How come I then to predicate of that which happens something quite different, and to apprehend that the concept of cause, though not contained in it, yet belongs, and indeed necessarily belongs, to it? What is here the unknown = X which gives support to the understanding when it believes that it can discover outside the concept A a predicate B foreign to this concept, which it yet at the same time considers to be connected with it? It cannot be experience, because the suggested principle has connected the second representation with the first, not only with greater universality, but also with the character of necessity, and therefore completely *a priori* and on the basis of mere concepts. Upon such synthetic, that is, ampliative principles, all our *a priori* speculative knowledge must ultimately rest; analytic judgments are very important, and indeed necessary, but only for obtaining that clearness in the concepts which is requisite for such a sure and wide synthesis as will lead to a genuinely new addition to all previous knowledge.

From Immanuel Kant, *Critique of Pure Reason*, trans. Norman Kemp Smith, St. Martin's, Macmillan, London, 1929.

QUESTIONS FOR REVIEW AND DISCUSSION

1. Why is Kant's philosophy called "critical philosophy"?
2. In simple terms, what is meant by a priori knowledge? Give an example.
3. Concerning the notion of cause and effect, how does Kant differ from Hume in explaining how we arrive at the idea of cause and effect?
4. What is meant by Kant's Copernican revolution?
5. Kant says that all knowledge *begins* with experience but that it does not follow that it all *arises* out of experience. What does he mean by that?
6. In what way does Kant's distinction between the *phenomenal* world and the *noumenal* world indicate the limits of human knowledge? (Consider here his theory of the *ding an sich*.)

19

Thinking and Doing

James

William James was born in New York City in 1842. He was the brother of the renowned novelist Henry James. He received his M.D. from the Harvard Medical School and soon joined that faculty as an instructor in physiology. From medicine he moved to psychology and philosophy, producing in 1890 his famous book *Principles of Psychology*. He became a member of the illustrious Harvard department of philosophy which included George Santayana and Josiah Royce. His published essays were widely influential, and as collections in book form, they were and still are read around the world. By the time he died in 1910 at the age of sixty-eight he had created a new approach to philosophy and had managed to communicate his principles of *pragmatism* to an unusually wide audience. James did not believe that the human mind can achieve a single, unified concept of the world. Nor did he think it was important to have such a concept. All we can know, he said, is certain parts of the universe. Moreover, these parts look different to different people. These many parts and views provide the basis for a *pluralistic** view of the world. And the main thing about these plural views, he said, is not whether they are consistent with one another but whether they lead to successful action, that is, whether they work or not.

PRAGMATISM AS A METHOD

William James thought that "the whole function of philosophy ought to be to find out what difference it will make to you and me, at definite instants of our lives, if this world-formula or that world-formula be the true one." His emphasis was on the concrete concerns of life, on facts, on action as it affects and displays power, and on power and action as they affect *my* life *now* and in the determinate future. But pragmatism as such contains no substance or content, no special information about human purpose or destiny. As a philosophy, pragmatism does not have its own creed; it does not offer a world-formula.

*Pluralism is the view that there are not one (monism), not two (dualism), but many ultimate substances and truths.

"Pragmatism," said James, "is a method only." Still, as a method, pragmatism assumes that human life has a purpose and that rival theories about man and the world would have to be tested against this purpose. There is in fact no single definition of man's purpose; the understanding of human purpose is part of the activity of thinking. Philosophical thinking arises when human beings want to understand things and the setting in which they live; purpose derives its meaning from a sense of being at home in the universe. As a method, pragmatism rejected rationalism chiefly because, said James, it was dogmatic and presumed to give conclusive answers about the world in terms that frequently left the issues of life untouched. By contrast, pragmatism hovered close to life, refusing to close the process of thought prematurely, taking its cue from the proved facts of life, willing to be led to new conceptions of purpose as deeper facets of human emotion and expectations were discovered. Again, as a method, pragmatism did not specify any *particular* results,

William James. (*Culver Pictures*)

although it did orient thinking around results, fruits, and consequences. No formulation either in science, theology, or philosophy should be taken as final; all formulations of theory are only approximations. In the last analysis, the meanings of all these theories are to be found not in their internal verbal consistency, but in their capacity to solve problems.

Instead of mere consistency, said James, "you must bring out of each word its practical cash value." Although pragmatism stands for no particular results, as a method in practice its essence is precisely to ensure *results*. When it finds a theory that does not *make* a difference one way or another for practical life, such a theory is abandoned. If, for example, there is a dispute over whether God exists, pragmatism has no preconceived creed to offer, but it does ask whether it makes a difference to believe in God's existence. To raise that question could very well lead one to see the "truth" in the claim of God's existence even though the same person might have rejected a "rational proof" of the existence of God. By asking always what difference an idea makes, James virtually reduced the pragmatic method to the formula "Does it work?" But supporting that formula was the combined methodological apparatus, as James said, of "nominalism—in always appealing to particulars; [of] utilitarianism in emphasizing practical aspects; [of] positivism in its disdain for verbal solutions, useless questions and metaphysical abstractions." It was inevitable that such a method should raise the question whether to say about an idea that "it works" is the same as saying that "it is true."

THE PRAGMATIC THEORY OF TRUTH

James made the startling statement that "truth *happens* to an idea." What was so startling about this statement was that the more traditional theories of truth took virtually the opposite view, namely, that truth is a property or quality of an idea. James was rejecting what he called the "copy-view" of truth. This theory assumes that an idea "copies" reality and an idea is therefore true if it copies what is "out there" accurately. Truth is that quality an idea has when it copies accurately. The assumption of the "intellectualists" who hold this theory, said James, is that "truth means essentially an inert static relation. When you've got your true idea of anything, there's an end of the matter. You're in possession; you *know*. . . ." Against this theory, James brought the whole arsenal of his pragmatism. Truth must be the cash value of an idea. What other motive could there be for saying that something is true or not true than to provide workable guides to practical behavior? James would ask, "What concrete difference will its being true make in anyone's actual life?"

By tying truth to life, to action, James rejected the view that truth is a *stagnant* property in ideas. Ideas *become* true; they are *made* true by events. That is why he wanted to say that truth *happens* to ideas. In addition, to say that truth happens to ideas is to make truth a part of experience. Whereas the copy-view of truth assumes that ideas really do copy what is out there, pragmatism says that there rarely is exact copying. Consider, he says, a clock on the wall. We consider it to be a clock not because we have a copy-view of it; we see only its face and hands, but not its internal mechanism, which makes it a clock. Still, our notion of it passes for true, not because our idea of it is an accurate copy, but because we *use* it as a clock and as such it *works*, enabling us to end a lecture "on time" and to catch the train. To be sure, we could check our idea to verify whether it is indeed a clock; but *verifiability* is as good as verification. We do not in fact verify every idea. Indeed, says James, "for one truth-process completed there are a million in our lives that function in this state of nascency." For this reason, truth lives "on a credit system." We do not require in every instance of truth that we should, as it were, see the wheels of the clock. What more would be added to the truth of our idea that that is a clock than we already have in the successful regulation of our behavior?

Ideas become true insofar as they help us to make successful connections between various parts of our experience. Truth is therefore part of the process of experience, of *living*. As part of a process, truth is *made* by the process of successful experience; successful experience *is* the verification process. To say that a truth always is, that it absolutely obtains, would mean that the clock on the wall is a clock whether any one sees it or not. But what James wants to show is that the question about the "truth" of the clock arises only in actual life when we live "as if" that thing on the wall is a clock, and the truth that it is a clock is *made* by our successful behavior. On this theory, says James, there are many *plural* truths, as many truths as there are concrete successful actions. Moreover, James would say that truth is bound up with the personal interests of concrete individuals. By this he meant that truth is not something *capricious*. As bound up with personal interests, the "truth" must lead to successful action; it must *work*. In the long run, a true belief must work beneficially, just as an "untrue" one will work destructively.

If the pragmatist is asked why anyone *ought* to seek the truth. James answers that "our obligation to seek the truth is part of our general obligation to do what pays," just as one ought to seek health because it pays to be healthy. Above all, James thought that the pragmatic theory of truth could render a desperately needed service to philosophy by providing a means for settling disputes. Some disputes cannot be resolved if each party simply affirms that his views are true. James would ask "Which theory fits the facts of real life?" One such dispute, which has exercised philosophers through the ages, is the question of freedom versus determinism.

ROLE AND STATUS OF THE WILL

William James was convinced that it is not possible to "prove" by any rational mode of argument that the will of man is either free or determined. Apparently equally good arguments could be given for each case. But he was nevertheless convinced that he could put the problem in a new light by applying the pragmatic method, by asking what difference it makes in actual life to accept one or the other side of the dispute. And the dispute was worth undertaking because it implied something momentous about life—either men were driven by external forces or they possessed "freedom" to choose their mode of behavior and therefore possessed the power to shape their lives and, thus, history.

The central issue in this dispute, said James, "relates solely to the existence of possibilities," of things that may, but need not, be. The determinist says that there are no possibilities, that what will be will be: ". . . those parts of the universe already laid down absolutely appoint and decree what the other parts shall be. The future has no ambiguous possibilities in its womb. . . ." However, the indeterminist says that there is a certain amount of "loose play" in the universe, so that the present existence of certain facts and arrangements does not necessarily determine what the future shall be; he says that there are genuine alternatives in the future from which an actual choice can be made. Here, then, are two contradictory points of view. "What divides us into *possibility* men and *antipossibility* men?" asks James. It is, he says, the postulates of rationality. For some men it seems more rational to say that all events are set down from eternity, whereas for others it seems more rational to assume that men can engage in genuine choice. If both these points of view seem equally rational to their respective proponents, how can the dispute be resolved?

This was not for James simply an interesting puzzle. His whole philosophical orientation revolved around this problem of the role and status of the will. With his basic concern about action and choosing those ideas and modes of behavior with the highest cash value, he inevitably saw philosophy in terms of human striving, and this, he was convinced, implied a certain kind of universe. His solution of the problem, therefore, was to ask the simple pragmatic question "What does a deterministic world imply?" If, that is, one says that all events without exception are rigorously determined from the beginning of time so that they could not have happened in any other way, what kind of universe must this be? Using a metaphor, one could only answer that such a universe is like a machine, where each part fits tightly and all the gears are interlocked, so that the slightest motion of one part causes a motion of every other part. There is no loose play in the machine.

"How can such a metaphor be applied to men?" James asks. A man is different from a mechanical part in a machine. What makes a man different is his consciousness. For one thing, a man is capable of a "judgment of regret." But how can one "regret" what could not have been otherwise? The determinist must define the world as a place where what "ought to be" is impossible. Still we are always making judgments not only of regret but of approval and disapproval. Moreover, we seek to persuade others to do or refrain from doing certain actions. In addition, men are punished or rewarded for certain actions. All these forms of judgment imply that a man is constantly facing genuine choices; a "forced" or "determined" act is not a *choice*.

The capacity of choice involves the capacity to recognize alternative influences on one, to hold these alternatives in momentary suspense, and then select one or the other. If one denies such a capacity for choice, the only alternative is the mechanical explanation. But no human beings ever consciously act as if this were a mechanically determined universe. Most of our language and thought processes suggest just the opposite; they suggest that at many points each person in fact faces genuine possibilities, options, real choices.

James did not want to deny the reality of causal relations. Indeed, his pragmatism rested on the operational formula that "*if* we do *A, B* will happen." But the word "if" is the clue; we are not forced to do *A,* and therefore *B* will happen only if we decide to choose *A.* James realized that if the determinist charged that his (James's) ideas about free will were determined, and that his assumptions about genuine possibilities were part of the block universe, such charges would indeed bring an end to rational discourse and the problem could no longer be discussed. What would remain, however, would be human beings with hopes, fears, and regrets. In the arena of daily life the assumptions of mechanical determinism would be abandoned, and the pragmatic question would come to the forefront, namely, "What should I do?" or "Which alternative would be better or wiser for me?"

In actual practical life, we see ourselves and others as vulnerable. Men are capable of lying, stealing, and murdering. We judge these to be wrong, not only in retrospect, but wrong because they were not rigorously inevitable when they were done; persons doing these things "could have" done otherwise. James concludes, in this vein, by saying that this problem is finally a "personal" one, that he simply cannot conceive of the universe as a place where murder *must* happen; it is a place where murder *can* happen and *ought not.* In short, for James, the truth about the freedom of the will is decided by the practical consequences of this idea for human behavior.

Reading _____

Pragmatism and the Enterprise of Knowing
James

Some years ago, being with a camping party in the mountains, I returned from a solitary ramble to find every one engaged in a ferocious metaphysical dispute. The *corpus* of the dispute was a squirrel—a live squirrel supposed to be clinging to one side of a tree-trunk; while over against the tree's opposite side a human being was imagined to stand. This human witness tries to get sight of the squirrel by moving rapidly round the tree, but no matter how fast he goes, the squirrel moves as fast in the opposite direction, and always keeps the tree between himself and the man, so that never a glimpse of him is caught. The resultant metaphysical problem now is this: *Does the man go round the squirrel or not?* He goes round the tree, sure enough, and the squirrel is on the tree; but does he go round the squirrel? In the unlimited leisure of the wilderness, discussion had been worn threadbare. Every one had taken sides, and was obstinate; and the numbers on both sides were even. Each side, when I appeared, therefore appealed to me to make it a majority. Mindful of the scholastic adage that whenever you meet a contradiction you must make a distinction, I immediately sought and found one, as follows: "Which party is right," I said, "depends on what you *practically mean* by 'going round' the squirrel. If you mean passing from the north of him to the east, then to the south, then to the west, and then to the north of him again, obviously the man does go round him, for he occupies these successive positions. But if on the contrary you mean being first in front of him, then on the right of him, then behind him, then on his left, and finally in front again, it is quite as obvious that the man fails to go round him, for by the compensating movements the squirrel makes, he keeps his belly turned towards the man all the time, and his back turned away. Make the distinction, and there is no occasion for any further dispute. You are both right and both wrong according as you conceive the verb 'to go round' in one practical fashion or the other."

Although one or two of the hotter disputants called my speech a shuffling evasion, saying they wanted no quibbling or scholastic hair-splitting, but meant just plain honest English "round," the majority seemed to think that the distinction had assuaged the dispute.

I tell this trivial anecdote because it is a peculiarly simple example of what I wish now to speak of as *the pragmatic method*. The pragmatic method is primarily a method of settling metaphysical disputes that otherwise might be interminable. Is the world one or many?—fated or free?—material or spiritual?—here are notions either of which may or may not hold good of the world; and disputes over such notions are unending. The pragmatic method in such cases is to try to interpret each notion by tracing its respective practical consequences. What difference would it practically make to any one if this notion rather than that notion were true? If no practical difference whatever can be traced, then the alternatives mean practically the same thing, and all dispute is idle. Whenever a dispute is serious, we ought to be able to show some practical difference that must follow from one side or the other's being right.

A glance at the history of the idea will show you still better what pragmatism means. The term is derived from the same Greek word *pragma*, meaning action, from which our words "practice" and "practical" come. It was first introduced into philosophy by Mr. Charles Peirce in 1878. In an article entitled "How to Make Our Ideas Clear," in the *Popular Science Monthly* for January of that year Mr. Peirce, after pointing out that our beliefs are really rules for action, said that, to develop a thought's meaning, we need only determine what conduct it is fitted to produce: that conduct is for us its sole significance. And the tangible fact at the root of all our thought-distinctions, however subtle, is that there is no one of them so fine as to consist in anything but a possible difference of practice. To attain perfect clearness in our thoughts of an object, then, we need only consider what conceivable effects of a practical kind the object may involve—what sensations we are to expect from it, and what reactions we must prepare. Our conception of these effects, whether immediate or remote, is then for us the whole of our conception of the object, so far as that conception has positive significance at all.

This is the principle of Peirce, the principle of pragmatism. It lay entirely unnoticed by any one for twenty years, until I, in an address before Professor Howison's Philosophical Union at the University of California, brought it forward again and made a special application of it to religion. By that date (1898) the times seemed ripe for its reception. The word "pragmatism" spread, and at present it fairly spots the pages of the philosophic journals. On all hands we find the "pragmatic movement" spoken of, sometimes with respect, sometimes with contumely, seldom with clear understanding. It is evident that the term applies itself conveniently to a number of tendencies that hitherto have lacked a collective name, and that it has "come to stay."

To take in the importance of Peirce's principle, one must get accustomed to applying it to concrete cases. I found a few years ago that Ostwald, the illustrious Leipzig chemist, had been making perfectly distinct use of the principle of pragmatism in his lectures on the philosophy of science, though he had not called it by that name.

"All realities influence our practice," he wrote me, "and that influence is their meaning for us. I am accustomed to put questions to my classes in this way: In what respects would the world be different if this alternative to that were true? If I can find nothing that would become different, then the alternative has no sense."

That is, the rival views mean practically the same thing, and meaning, other than practical, there is for us none. Ostwald in a published lecture gives this example of what he means. Chemists have long wrangled over the inner constitution of certain bodies called "tautomerous." Their properties seemed equally consistent with the notion that an instable hydrogen atom oscillates inside of them, or that they are instable mixtures of two bodies. Controversy raged, but never was decided. "It would never have begun," says Ostwald, "if the combatants had asked themselves what particular experimental fact could have been made different by one or the other view being correct. For it would then have appeared that no difference of fact could possibly ensue; and the quarrel was as unreal as if, theorizing in primitive times about the raising of dough by yeast, one party should have invoked a 'brownie,' while another insisted on an 'elf' as the true cause of the phenomenon."

It is astonishing to see how many philosophical disputes collapse into insignificance the moment you subject them to this simple test of tracing a concrete consequence. There can *be* no difference anywhere that doesn't *make* a difference elsewhere—no difference in abstract truth that doesn't express itself in a difference in concrete fact and in conduct consequent upon that fact, imposed on somebody, somehow, somewhere, and somewhen. The whole function of philosophy ought to be to find out what definite difference it will make to you and me, at definite instants of our life, if this world-formula or that world-formula be the true one.

There is absolutely nothing new in the pragmatic method. Socrates was an adept at it. Aristotle used it methodically. Locke, Berkeley, and Hume made momentous contributions to truth by its means. Shadworth Hodgson keeps insisting that realities are only what they are "known as." But these forerunners of pragmatism used it in fragments: they were preluders only. Not until in our time has it generalized itself, become conscious of a universal mission, pretended to a conquering destiny. I believe in that destiny, and I hope I may end by inspiring you with my belief.

Pragmatism represents a perfectly familiar attitude in philosophy, the empiricist attitude, but it represents it, as it seems to me, both in a more radical and in a less objectionable form than it has ever yet assumed. A pragmatist turns his back resolutely and once for all upon a lot of inveterate habits clear to professional philosophers. He turns away from abstraction and insufficiency, from verbal solutions, from bad *a priori* reasons, from fixed principles, closed systems, and pretended absolutes and origins. He turns towards concreteness and adequacy, towards facts, towards action and towards power. That means the empiricist temper regnant and the rationalist temper sincerely given up. It means the open air and possibilities of nature, as against dogma, artificiality, and the pretence of finality in truth.

At the time it does not stand for any special results. It is a method only. But the general triumph of that method would mean an enormous change in what I called in my last lecture the "temperament" of philosophy. Teachers of the ultra-rationalistic type would be frozen out, much as the courtier type is frozen out in republics, as the ultramontane type of priest is frozen out in protestant lands. Science and metaphysics would come much nearer together, would in fact work absolutely hand in hand.

Metaphysics has usually followed a very primitive kind of quest. You know how men have always hankered after unlawful magic, and you know what a great part in magic *words* have always played. If you have his name, or the formula of incantation that binds him, you can control the spirit, genie, afrite, or whatever the power may be. Solomon knew the names of all the spirits, and having their names, he held them subject to his will. So the universe has always appeared to the natural mind as a kind of enigma, of which the key must be sought in the shape of some illuminating or power-bringing word or name. That word names the universe's *principle*, and to possess it is after a fashion to possess the universe itself. "God," "Matter," "Reason," "the Absolute," "Energy" are so many solving names. You can rest when you have them. You are at the end of your metaphysical quest.

But if you follow the pragmatic method, you cannot look on any such word as closing your quest. You must bring out of each word its practical cash-value, set it at work within the stream of your experience. It appears less as a solution, then, than as a program for more work, and more particularly as an indication of the ways in which existing realities may be *changed.*

Theories thus become instruments, not answers to enigmas, in which we can rest. We don't lie back upon them, we move forward, and, on occasion, make nature over again by their aid. Pragmatism unstiffens all our theories, limbers them up and sets each one at work. Being nothing essentially new, it harmonizes with many ancient philosophic tendencies. It agrees with nominalism, for instance, in always appealing to particulars; with utilitarianism in emphasizing practical aspects; with positivism in its disdain for verbal solutions, useless questions and metaphysical abstractions.

All these, you see, are *anti-intellectualist* tendencies. Against rationalism as a pretension and a method pragmatism is fully armed and militant. But, at the outset, at least, it stands for no particular results. It has no dogmas, and no doctrines save its method. As the young Italian pragmatist Papini has well said, it lies in the midst of our theories, like a corridor in a hotel. Innumerable chambers open out of it. In one you may find a man writing an atheistic volume; in the next some one on his knees praying for faith and strength; in a third a chemist investigating a body's properties. In a fourth a system of idealistic metaphysics is being excogitated; in a fifth the impossibility of metaphysics is being shown. But they all own the corridor, and all must pass through it if they want a practicable way of getting into or out of their respective rooms.

No particular results then, so far, but only an attitude of orientation, is what the pragmatic method means. *The attitude of looking away from first things, principles, "categories," supposed necessities; and of looking towards last things, fruits, consequences, facts.*

So much for the pragmatic method! You may say that I have been praising it rather than explaining it to you, but I shall presently explain it abundantly enough by showing how it works on some familiar problems. Meanwhile the word pragmatism has come to be used in a still wider sense, as meaning also a certain *theory of truth.*

From William James, "What Pragmatism Means," 1907.

Reading _____

Pragmatism's Conception of Truth

James

Truth, as any dictionary will tell you, is a property of certain of our ideas. It means that their "agreement," as falsity means their "disagreement," with "reality." Pragmatists and intellectualists both accept this definition as a matter of course. They begin to quarrel only after the question is raised as to what may precisely be meant by the term "agreement," and what by the term "reality," when reality is taken as something for our ideas to agree with.

The popular notion is that a true idea must copy its reality. Like other popular views, this one follows the analogy of the most usual experience. Our true ideas of sensible things do indeed copy them. Shut your eyes and think of yonder clock on the wall, and you get just such a true picture or copy of its dial. But your idea of its "works" (unless you are a clockmaker) is much less of a copy, yet it passes muster, for it in no way clashes with the reality. Even though it should shrink to the mere word "works," that word still serves you truly; and when you speak of the "time-keeping function" of the clock, or its spring's "elasticity," it is hard to see exactly what your ideas can copy.

You perceive that there is a problem here. Where our ideas cannot copy definitely their object, what does agreement with that object mean? Some idealists seem to say that they are true whenever they are what God means that we ought to think about that subject. Others hold the copyview all through, and speak as if our ideas possessed truth just in proportion as they approach to being copies of the Absolute's eternal way of thinking.

These views, you see, invite pragmatistic discussion. But the great assumption of the intellectualists is that truth means essentially an inert static relation. When you've got your true idea of anything, there's an end of the matter. You're in possession; you *know*; you have fulfilled your thinking destiny. You are where you ought to be mentally; you have obeyed your categorical imperative; and nothing more need follow on that climax of your rational destiny. Epistemologically you are in stable equilibrium.

Pragmatism, on the other hand, asks its usual question. "Grant an idea or belief to be true," it says, "what concrete difference will its being true make in any one's actual life? How will the truth be realized? What experiences will be different from those which would obtain if the belief were false? What, in short, is the truth's cash-value in experiential terms?"

The moment pragmatism asks this question, it sees the answer: *True ideas are those that we can assimilate, validate, corroborate and verify. False ideas are those that we cannot.* That is the practical difference it makes to us to have true ideas; that, therefore, is the meaning of truth, for it is all that truth is known as.

This thesis is what I have to defend. The truth of an idea is not a stagnant property inherent in it. Truth *happens* to an idea. It *becomes* true, is *made* true by events. Its verity *is* in fact an event, a process: the process namely of its verifying itself, is veri-*fication*. Its validity is the process of its valid-*ation*.

Take, for instance, yonder object on the wall. You and I consider it to be a "clock," although no one of us has seen the hidden works that make it one. We let our notion pass for true without attempting to verify. If truths mean verification-process essentially, ought we then to call such unverified truths as this abortive? No, for they form the overwhelmingly large number of the truths we live by. Indirect as well as direct verifications pass muster. Where circumstantial evidence is sufficient, we can go without eye-witnessing. Just as we here assume Japan to exist without ever having been there, because it *works* to do so, everything we know conspiring with the belief, and nothing interfering, so we assume that thing to be a clock. We *use* it as a clock, regulating the length of our lecture by it. The verification of the assumption here means its leading to no frustration or contradiction. Verifi *ability* of wheels and weights and pendulum is as good as verification. For one truth-process completed there are a million in our lives that function in this state of nascency. They turn us *towards* direct verification; lead us into the *surroundings* of the objects they envisage; and then, if everything runs on harmoniously, we are so sure that verification is possible that we omit it, and are usually justified by all that happens.

Truth lives, in fact, for the most part on a credit system. Our thoughts and beliefs "pass," so long as nothing challenges them, just as banknotes pass so long as nobody refuses them. But this all points to direct face-to-face verifications somewhere, without which the fabric of truth collapses like a financial system with no cash-basis whatever. You accept my verification of one thing, I yours of another. We trade on each other's truth. But beliefs verified concretely by *somebody* are the posts of the whole superstructure. . . .

Our account of truth is an account of truths in the plural, of processes of leading, realized *in rebus,* and having only this quality in common, that they *pay.* They pay by guiding us into or towards some part of a system that dips at numerous points into sense-percepts, which we may copy mentally or not, but with which at any rate we are now in the kind of commerce vaguely designated as verification. Truth for us is simply a collective name for verification-processes, just as health, wealth, strength, etc., are names for other processes connected with life, and also pursued because it pays to pursue them. Truth is *made,* just as health, wealth, and strength are made, in the course of experience.

From William James, "Pragmatism's Conception of Truth," 1907.

QUESTIONS FOR REVIEW AND DISCUSSION

1. What are the chief characteristics of pragmatism as described by James?
2. James said that "truth happens to an idea." What did he mean by that description of truth, and what rival theory of truth was he thereby rejecting?

20

Words and the World: The Linguistic Turn

The Analytic Philosophers: Russell, Carnap, Wittgenstein, and Rorty

The dominant movement of philosophical activity in the contemporary English-speaking world is known as "analytic philosophy," although it has not been universally accepted. To call it a *movement* rather than a *school* underscores the fact that although analytic philosophy has certain clear distinguishing characteristics, the sources out of which it emerged, the changes it has undergone, and the variety of ways in which it is pursued are many. What unifies all analytic philosophers is their agreement concerning the central task of philosophy. The task of philosophy, they say, is to clarify the meaning of language. In his early work, the *Tractatus Logico-Philosophicus*, Wittgenstein said that "the object of philosophy is the logical clarification of thoughts" so that "the result of philosophy is not a number of philosophical propositions, but to make propositions clear."

To say that the philosopher does not formulate "philosophical propositions" meant for the early analysts that there must be a self-imposed limit on the scope of philosophical activity. Specifically, this meant that, in contrast to the immediately past tradition of nineteenth-century idealism, especially Hegelianism, whose practitioners engaged in constructing complete systems of thought regarding the whole universe, the analysts would now undertake the more modest task of working on individual problems. Not only would these problems be single and manageable, they would all fit into a single class; they would all be problems revolving around the meanings and usages of language. For this reason, it would no longer be the task of the philosopher to investigate the nature of reality, to build complete systems that seek to explain the universe, or to fashion moral, political, and religious philosophies of behavior. Philosophy, in this new key, "is not a doctrine but an activity," and as such, it can produce "no ethical propositions," said Wittgenstein. The philosopher is no longer to consider himself capable of discovering unique forms of information about the world and man. The discovery of facts is the task of the scientist. There are no facts left over for the philosophers after all the sciences have done their work.

The new assumption was that the philosopher can render a genuine service by carefully unpacking complex problems whose origin is found in the imprecise use of language. Scientists themselves, it was felt, had discussed their findings in language that was often misleading and in certain ways ambiguous. That is, scientific language contained ambiguities of logic, not of physical discovery, and the clarification of these logical ambiguities was required. It was assumed, also, that rigorous linguistic analysis could *prevent* the use or abuse of language in ways that would cause us, as A. J. Ayer said, "to draw false inferences, or ask spurious questions, or make nonsensical assumptions." What concerned Ayer was that we often use propositions about nations as though nations were persons, we talk about material things as though we believed in a physical world "beneath" or "behind" visible phenomena, and we use the word "is" in relation to things whose existence we could not possibly want to infer. Philosophy is called on to remove these dangers from our use of language, said Ayer. In a somewhat similar vein, Gilbert Ryle wrote about "Systematically Misleading Expressions," saying that although he would rather allot to philosophy "a sublimer task than the detection of the sources in linguistic idioms of recurrent misconstructions and absurd theories," still, philosophical analysis consists in inquiring about "what it really means to say so and so." In this way, the new philosophy became closely related to the enterprises of science, not as a rival discipline offering propositions of what reality is like but as the proofreader of the scientists' expressions, checking the literature of science for its clarity and logical meaningfulness. It would no longer be the function of the philosopher either to propound vast systems of thought after the manner of Plato, Aristotle, and Hegel or to tell people how they ought to behave. He would instead analyze statements or propositions to discover the causes of ambiguities and the foundations of meaning in language.

What caused this dramatic shift in the enterprise of philosophy? At Cambridge, Bertrand Russell and G. E. Moore had reacted in the early decades of the twentieth century against the system-building of the Hegelian philosophers such as F. H. Bradley, Bernard Bosanquet, and J. E. McTaggart, who had been engaged in ambitious metaphysical speculation. Although Moore did not necessarily want to give up metaphysics, he was especially disturbed by the contrast between metaphysical language and so-called common sense. To him certain statements, such as, for example, McTaggart's famous notion that "time is unreal," seemed "perfectly monstrous." Moore was inspired to analyze language particularly to clarify ordinary language and to make language fit the test of common sense in its meaning. Bertrand Russell, however, was a brilliant mathematician, trained in precise thought, and in comparison with the language of mathematics, metaphysical language seemed to him loose and obscure. He did not want to reject metaphysics any more than Moore did, but he did want to tighten up the language of metaphysics. While Moore set out to analyze commonsense language, Russell tried to analyze "facts" for the purpose of inventing a new language, "logical atomism," which would have the exactness and rigor of mathematics because it would be made to correspond exactly to the "facts." Although neither Moore nor Russell gave up the attempt to understand reality, the way they went about their task emphasized the fact that philosophy is concerned not with discovery but with clarification and, therefore, in a sense, not with truth but with meaning.

Across the channel, a group of mathematicians, scientists, and philosophers formed a group in Vienna in the 1920s, describing themselves as "logical positivists"* and known as the "Vienna Circle." Their orientation was rigorously empirical, and they proceeded to reject the whole enterprise of metaphysics. Their ideal for philosophy was the unification of the sciences, hoping thereby to produce a unified system of meaningful and valid knowledge. Among this group were such men as Moritz Schlick, Rudolph Carnap, Friedrich Waismann, Herbert Feigl, Otto Neurath, and Kurt Gödel. A young former student of Bertrand Russell's, Ludwig Wittgenstein, lived nearby, and although he was not a member of the Circle, he had conversations with its members, and his early book, *Tractatus Logico-Philosophicus* (1919), was considered by the Vienna Circle to express its philosophical point of view with great accuracy. Not only had Wittgenstein said that "whatever can be said at all can be said clearly," he concluded his book by saying that "whereof one cannot speak, thereof one must be silent." This dictum was less harsh than Hume's rigorous conclusion in his *Enquiry,* where, following the implicit logic of his principles of empiricism, he wrote:

> When we run over libraries, persuaded of these principles, what havoc we must make? If we take in our hand any volume; of divinity or school metaphysics, for instance; let us ask, Does it contain any abstract reasoning concerning quantity or number? No. Does it contain any experimental reasoning concerning matter of fact and existence? No. Commit it then to the flames: for it can contain nothing but sophistry and illusion.

The Vienna Circle philosophers thought of themselves as the twentieth-century heirs of Hume's empirical tradition. To this tradition they now sought to apply the rigorous apparatus of mathematics and science. If their ideal was to clarify the language of science and the sciences, their first task would have to be the formulation of a standard for clarity, and this resulted in their famous *verification principle.*** This principle would in time be shown to suffer from certain defects and require attempts at modification. These internal difficulties with their central principle as well as with other aspects of their philosophical concerns, and the scattering of the members to British and American universities in the 1930s, dissolved the Vienna Circle and gradually led to the decline of logical positivism.

What followed next in the history of analytic philosophy was the decisive work of the "new" Wittgenstein. Between his *Tractatus Logico-Philosophi-*

*See p. 327.

**See pp. 329–332.

cus (1919) and the posthumous publication of his famed *Philosophical Investigations* (1953), his thought had acquired a radically new character, and it is this version of his way of doing philosophy that has dominated the contemporary philosophical scene in the English-speaking world. The major facets of analytic philosophy are to be found, then, in Bertrand Russell's *logical atomism,* the Vienna Circle's *logical positivism,* and the later Wittgenstein's *philosophical analysis.*

LOGICAL ATOMISM

Bertrand Russell's* point of departure in philosophy was his admiration for the precision of mathematics. Accordingly, he announced that "the kind of philosophy that I wish to advocate, which I call logical atomism, is one which has forced itself upon me in the course of thinking about the philosophy of mathematics." He wanted to set forth "a certain kind of logical doctrine and on the basis of this a certain kind of metaphysics." Russell thought that since it was possible to construct a logic by which the whole of mathematics could be derived from a small number of logical axioms, as he had already done with A. N. Whitehead in their *Principia Mathematica,* then why could not this logic form the basis of a language that could accurately express everything that could be clearly stated? His assumption was, recalling that in the quotation above he connected "logical atomism" and "a certain kind of metaphysics," that the world would correspond to his specially constructed logical language. The vocabulary of the new logic would, for the most part, correspond to particular objects in the world. To accomplish this task of creating a new language, Russell set out first of all to analyze certain "facts," which he differentiated from "things."

"The things in the world," said Russell, "have various properties, and stand in various relations to each other. That they have these properties and relations are *facts. . . .*" Facts constitute for Russell the complexity of the relations of things to each other, and therefore "it is with the analysis of *facts* that one's consideration of the problem of complexity must begin." Russell's basic assumption was that "facts, since they have components, must be in some sense complex, and hence must be susceptible of analysis." The complexity of facts is matched by the complexity of language. For this reason, the aim of analysis is to make sure that every statement represents an adequate picture of the reality, of the facts, of the world.

Language, according to Russell, consists of a unique arrangement of words, and the meaningfulness of language is determined by the accuracy with which these words represent facts. Words, in turn, are formulated into propositions. "In a logically perfect language," said Russell, "the words in a proposition would correspond one by one with the components of the corre-

*For biographical note on Russell, see p. 361.

Bertrand Russell. (*UPI/Bettman Newsphotos*)

sponding facts." By analysis, certain *simple* words are discovered. These are words that cannot be further analyzed into something more primary and can therefore be understood only by knowing what they symbolize. The word "red," for example, is not capable of further analysis and is therefore understood as a simple *predicate*. Other words, similarly simple, refer to particular things, and as symbols of these things they are *proper names*. Language consists in part, then, of words, which in their simplest form refer to a particular thing and its predicate, as for example a *red rose*. A proposition states a fact. When a fact is of the simplest kind, it is called an "atomic fact." Propositions that state atomic facts are called "atomic propositions." If our language consisted only of such atomic propositions, it would amount only to a series of reports regarding atomic facts. This is what Wittgenstein said in his *Tractatus,* when he wrote that "the world is everything that is the case. . . . What is the case, the fact, is the existence of atomic facts."

It is clear that in our language atomic propositions are put together into more complex propositions. When two or more atomic propositions are linked together with such words as "and" and "or," the result is what Russell calls a "molecular proposition." However, there are no "molecular" *facts,* only atomic facts. For this reason, molecular propositions cannot correspond to molecular facts. How can one test the truth or falsity, then, of molecular propositions? Their truth depends on the truth or falsity of the atomic propositions of which they are made up. Language, on this account, consists of an indefinite number of atomic propositions, whose correspondence with actual facts is settled by empirical methods and techniques. Nothing can be said about the world that is not analyzable down to an atomic proposition, which, in turn, corresponds to an atomic fact. The grammatical independence of each atomic proposition indicates the metaphysical independence of each atomic fact. Again, in an ideal language, words and propositions would correspond to facts. Moreover, it was assumed that after a careful analysis of words and propositions and their corresponding atomic facts, one would arrive at the basic character of language and of the world, and that apart from these facts there would be no residue. Thus the ideal language would express all there is to say about the world. All of reality, on this theory, could be described in statements such as "That is green."

Difficulties developed in the program of logical atomism first of all when Russell and others tried to account for *general* facts. It is one thing to say "That is a white horse," the truth or falsity of which is checked by connecting the *words* "white" and "horse" with the atomic *facts* of this white color and this animal, the horse. It is another thing to say "All horses are white." How would one test the truth or falsity of such a statement? According to logical atomism, one should analyze this statement into its atomic propositions and test *their* truth or falsity. There is no atomic fact corresponding to "all horses . . . ," for this means more than just this horse and that horse, namely, all horses, and this is a *general* fact. But the whole argument of logical atomism was that only atomic facts exist, and the theory had no way of dealing adequately with so-called general facts unless general facts were accepted as a form of atomic facts. Still, if one were disposed to consider only the particular things recorded by our senses as the basis of our language, as Hume did, singular atomic facts would be the only facts available for human discourse, and language would therefore consist solely of atomic and molecular propositions.

The young Wittgenstein became more and more convinced that philosophy must reject the metaphysical elements in logical atomism. The right method of philosophy would be "to say nothing except what can be said clearly, i.e., the propositions of science. . . ." This became the basic theme of logical positivism.

LOGICAL POSITIVISM

The men who formed the Vienna Circle were by temperament attracted to the methods of science and mathematics. They were disposed to reject metaphysics, as had the earlier positivists, who considered metaphysics as outdated by science. Now they had the additional argument, because of Russell's work in logic and Wittgenstein's powerful formulation of the relation of logic and language in the *Tractatus*, that metaphysics is impossible as shown by the logical and essential character of language. They called themselves "logical positivists," or sometimes "logical empiricists." For the English-speaking world, A. J. Ayer, in his brilliantly lucid and powerfully argued book *Language, Truth and Logic* (1936), did, as he later said with considerable understatement, "something to popularize what may be called the classic position of the Vienna Circle."

This position called for a blanket rejection of metaphysics, and the grounds for this rejection were to be found in the Vienna Circle's famous *verification principle*.

Logical Analysis

Among the foremost members of the Vienna Circle was the eminent positivist Rudolph Carnap. Born in Germany in 1891, he taught in Vienna and Prague from 1926 to 1935. After arriving in the United States in 1936, he taught for many years at the University of Chicago, and from 1954 until his death in 1970 he was associated with the University of California at Los Angeles. "The only proper task of Philosophy," Carnap wrote in his *Philosophy and Logical Syntax*, "is Logical Analysis."

The function of logical analysis, Carnap said, is to analyze all knowledge, all assertions of science and of everyday life, in order to make clear the sense of each such assertion. The purpose of logical analysis is to discover how we can become certain of the truth or falsehood of any proposition. One of the principal tasks of the logical analysis of a given proposition is, therefore, to discover the method of verification of that proposition.

For Carnap, the method of verification of a proposition is either direct or indirect. These two forms of verification are central to scientific method, for in the field of science every proposition, says Carnap, either asserts something about present perceptions or about future perceptions. In both cases, verification is either through direct perception (direct verification) or by the logical connection of already verified propositions (indirect verification). Thus if a scientist were to make an assertion from which no proposition verified by perception could be deduced, it would be no assertion at all. To say, for example, that there is not only a gravitational field but also a *levitational field* cannot be verified. While propositions concerning gravity can be verified by observable effects on bodies, there are no observable effects or laws describing levitation. Assertions about levitation are, says Carnap, no assertions at all because they do not speak about anything. They are nothing but a series of empty words—expressions with no sense.

When logical analysis is applied to metaphysics, Carnap concludes that metaphysical propositions are not verifiable. In Chapter I of his *Philosophy and Logical Syntax*, he says,

> Metaphysical propositions are neither true nor false, because they assert nothing, they contain neither knowledge nor error, they lie completely outside the field of knowledge, of theory, outside the discussion of truth or falsehood. But they are, like laughing, lyrics, and music, expressive. They express not so much temporary feelings as permanent emotional or volitional dispositions. . . . The danger lies in the *deceptive* character of metaphysics; it gives the illusion of knowledge without actually giving any knowledge. This is the reason why we reject it.

Normative ethics* and value judgments in general belong, according to Carnap, to the realm of metaphysics. When he applies his method of logical analysis to the propositions of normative ethics, these propositions predictably turn out to be meaningless for him. There can of course be a science of ethics in the form of psychological or sociological or other empirical investigations about the actions of human beings and their effects on other people. But the philosophy of moral values or moral norms does not rest on any facts, since its purpose is to state norms for human action or for making judgments about moral values. The value statement "Killing is evil" has the grammatical form of an assertive proposition. But, says Carnap, "a value statement is nothing else than a command in a misleading grammatical form. It may have effects upon the actions of men, and these effects may be in accordance with our wishes or not; but it is neither true nor false. It does not assert anything and can neither be proved nor disproved."

Carnap was convinced that the propositions of psychology belong to the region of empirical science in just the same way as do the propositions of biology and chemistry. He was aware that many would consider it an offensive presumption to place psychology, "hitherto robed in majesty as the theory of spiritual events," into the domain of the physical sciences. Yet that is what he proceeded to do, saying in his essay on "Psychology and Physical Language" that *"every sentence of psychology may be formulated in physical language."* What he meant by this was that "all sentences of psychology describe physical occurrences, namely, the physical behavior of humans and other animals." This is an extension of the general thesis of physicalism, which Carnap described as holding that "physical language is a universal language, that is, a language into which every sentence may be translated." In effect, Carnap would make psychology an aspect of physics, since all science would become physics and the various domains of science would become parts of unified science. In this manner, propositions in psychology were to be tested by the criterion of verifiability by translating them into physical language. Thus the statement "John is in pain" is translated into a statement describing the observable state S of John's body. This process of translation requires only that there be a scientific law stating that someone is in pain if and only if his bodily condition

---

*A theory of ethics which prescribes specific standards of behavior, how we "ought" to behave.

is in a particular state S. It is then meaningful to say that "John is in pain" and "John's body is in state S" since, while not equivalent, these are interchangeable translations. Only those statements which could be verified or translated into verifiable statements were thought to have meaning. Neither metaphysics, some aspects of psychology, theories of "reality," nor the philosophy of normative values could satisfy the criterion of verifiability and were therefore rejected as meaningless.

The Principle of Verification

If the charge against metaphysics was that its language, its propositions or sentences, was *meaningless* or, as Wittgenstein said in the *Tractatus, senseless,* such a charge required the use of some criterion by which to test which sentences did and which did not express a genuine proposition about a matter of fact. Accordingly, the logical positivists formulated the verification principle as the basic criterion for the meaningfulness or the literal significance of a proposition. If a proposition fulfilled the requirements of this criterion, it was considered meaningful, and if a proposition failed to do so, it was considered meaningless.

The *verification principle* consisted of the notion that *the meaning of a statement is the method of its verification.* The assumption behind this principle was that verification must always rest on empirical observation, that is, in sense experience. Any proposition, therefore, that could not be verified by the method of observation would be said to have no meaning. The case of mathematical propositions was treated in a special way, but it was clear that with such a rigorous criterion, metaphysical language could not pass the test of meaningfulness.

The positivists, following the tradition of Hume and Kant, distinguished two types of statements, namely, *analytic* and *synthetic.* Each of these types has a different ground for its meaningfulness. Analytic statements derive their meaningfulness from the definitions of their words or symbols. To say that "all men are mortals" has literal significance because the word "men" is defined in such a way as to include the idea "mortals." In general, in analytic statements the subject already contains or implies the predicate. For the most part, analytic statements do not increase our knowledge, and for this reason they are *tautologies.** Moreover, their meaning does not depend on experience, only on the consistent use of their clearly defined terms. If words with clearly defined terms are used inconsistently, the result is a *contradiction.* A statement, then, that is necessarily true, true because of the meanings of its terms, is a tautology, whereas a statement that is necessarily false is a contradiction. An analytic proposition that is also a tautology is always and in every case necessarily true, because its only test is the meanings of the terms. Thus the truth or falsity of an analytic proposition turns on the logical analysis of meanings. However, *synthetic* propositions are either true or false in each case, and their

*"Tautology"—two phrases in an expression meaning the same thing, for example, "a beginner just starting," as in "he is a . . ."

truth or falsity can be discovered only by reference to some nonlogical or non-linguistic datum, a fact. Unlike analytic statements, which are *necessarily* either tautologies or contradictions, synthetic statements may be either true or false. Synthetic statements require some sense experience of the object that such a statement refers to in order to advance from its possible to its actual truth.

From this distinction between analytic and synthetic propositions, the positivists formulated their conception of *cognitive meaning* or *literal signifi-cance*. Analytic propositions, they said, have a *formal* meaning, since their meaning derives not from facts but from the logical implications of words and ideas, as in mathematics, logic, and the formal sciences. However, synthetic propositions have a factual meaning, because their meaning is based on the empirical observation of the objects referred to in these statements. Synthetic statements are the language of the factual sciences, physics, biology, psycholo-gy, and so on. It was at this point that the principle of verification had its deci-sive application. For now the positivists concluded that there could be only two kinds of statements that could have any meaning at all, namely, *analytic* statements, which are universally and necessarily true because the consistent use of words would never allow them to be anything else, and *synthetic* state-ments, which are judged as true or false by using the verification principle. Statements that are neither analytic nor synthetic have no cognitive meaning or literal significance; they are simply *emotive*. It takes only brief reflection to realize that into this category of emotive or *noncognitive* language would fall not only metaphysics but also ethics, aesthetics, and religion.

But the verification principle encountered some difficulties. Among these difficulties was, first of all, the serious question of what constituted verifica-tion. To answer "sense experience" raised the further question "Whose experi-ence?" The assumption behind the verification principle was that whatever could be said meaningfully would be stated in atomic or elementary state-ments. Scientific language would be reducible ultimately to *observational state-ments*. But what is the "fact" that an observation statement reports? Is it a sub-jective experience about a physical object, or is it a pure picture of that object? The technical problem was whether it is ever possible to translate a person's internal experience into a statement about a physical object, or vice versa. This is the problem of solipsism, the view that the self is the only object of real knowledge and that therefore the experiences of one person cannot be the same as those of another. Each person's experience is different, and all of their experiences are different from the objectively real world. If this is the case, what does the verification principle amount to in the end? Verification state-ments would mean one thing to one person and something else to others.

In the second place, it was in the very area where this principle was pre-sumed to have its greatest relevance, in the sciences, that its greatest difficulty arose. Scientific knowledge is frequently expressed in the form of universal laws. These "laws" are the basis for scientific *prediction*. But the problem the positivists faced was whether to consider scientific statements meaningful. How can a statement that makes a prediction be verified? Can my present experience, or experiment, tell me anything about the future? Obviously, literal significance or meaning is one thing when we verify the statement "There is a black cow in Smith's barn" and quite another thing when we say, as the scientist does, for example, that when a moving body is not acted on by external forces, its direction will remain constant. The first case is specific and verifiable. The second involves an indefinite number of cases, and any single case in the future can falsify that statement. Since there is no single fact that can verify *now* the future truth of a general scientific statement, such a statement, by a rigorous application of the verification principle, would be meaningless. Moritz Schlick (1882–1936), who became famous as the founder and leader of the Vienna Circle, had said of certain utterances, "If not conclusively verifiable in principle, then not propositions." This would have to apply to scientific as well as other forms of language. For this reason, a compromise in the rigorous application of the principle was proposed, thus giving rise to the distinction between the *strong* and *weak* forms of the verification principle. The weak form said simply that a statement must be at least "verifiable in principle" or *capable* of verification, that is, confirmed in some degree by the observation of something physical.

In the third place, it turned out that the verification principle was not itself verifiable. Critics asked why it should be that the criterion of meaning should be sense experience. The Vienna Circle did not answer this question in any formal way. It may be that for them the verification principle was clearly suggested by the difference between scientific procedures on the one hand and metaphysical speculation on the other. Being oriented chiefly to science, the positivists assumed that only language that referred to physical objects and their interrelationships could have cognitive meaning. Moreover, the techniques of logic as they understood them implied the correspondence between words and facts and between the logical structure of language and the logical relation of facts. The positivists assumed, furthermore, that through *physicalism*, their doctrine that called for the coupling of all statements to physical facts, they could achieve the *unity of science,* and that such a unified knowledge would give sciences a common language and tell us all there is to say.

There was, however, this internal defect in the verification principle, namely, the impossibility of verifying general scientific statements. Gradually, this led not only to a weak form of verification but also to the recognition that statements reflect many forms of experience. For this reason, the initial intensity of positivism was toned down. The blanket rejection of metaphysics and morals was reversed. Instead, analysts began to ask what kind of problem the metaphysicians and moralists were driving at. Ayer described this new temper by saying that "the metaphysician is treated no longer as a criminal but as a patient: there may be good reasons why he says the strange things he does." Ethics, in this view, is no longer nonsense but a discipline whose language is analyzed both for its relation to fact and for its value in pointing to a problem. As it turns out, ethical language is, as R. M. Hare has argued, not *descriptive* but rather *imperative*. C. L. Stevenson has also elaborated the emotive theory of ethics, showing that ethical statements express approval and disapproval and are used particularly for purposes of persuasion. What positivism came ultimately to say about ethics was that it is not possible to derive normative state-ments, what *ought* to be done, from a description of facts, from what *is.* But even though the analyst still holds that it is not his function as a philosopher to *prescribe* or *exhort* any particular form of behavior, he does accept the task of creatively analyzing moral language for the purpose of clarifying it. That he reserves the right to make value judgements as a *person* underscores the grow-ing recognition that there are modes of human experience besides simply the observation of physical objects and their interrelationships that have meaning and literal significance. Although logical positivism in its classical form dis-solved from the weight of its inner difficulties, its impact continues in the ana-lytic movement, which is still concerned overwhelmingly with the usages and analysis of language.

THE "NEW" WITTGENSTEIN

Ludwig Wittgenstein was born in Vienna in 1889. His wealthy family provid-ed a highly creative environment during Ludwig's early years. His father was a successful engineer, and his mother had many artistic interests. Young Wittgenstein studied engineering in Berlin and also became an accomplished musician. He went to England and became acquainted with Bertrand Russell's *Principles of Mathematics* and ultimately became Russell's student at Cam-bridge University, both as an undergraduate and as an "advanced student." After military service in the First World War, he returned to Vienna, where he completed his first book, *Tractatus Logico-Philosophicus,* which made a strong impression on the Vienna Circle. Earlier, when his father died in 1912, Ludwig inherited a great fortune. When he returned from the war, he took immediate steps to give away all his money. From that time he lived with exceptional fru-gality. His interest in philosophy was unique, having no precise forerunners. His book, the *Tractatus,* influenced the spread of logical positivism. He eventu-ally rejected and surpassed, as "grave errors," some of the basic ideas of the *Tractatus,* especially the picture-theory of language. His *Philosophical Investiga-tions* became even more influential through its creative impact on the analytic or linguistic movement. In 1937 he succeeded G. E. Moore to the chair of phi-losophy at Cambridge, where his lectures were "highly unacademic." It is said that he *thought* before his class! One of his colleagues, G. H. von Wright has written "On 29 April 1951 there died at Cambridge, England, one of the most famous and influential philosophers of our time, Ludwig Wittgenstein."

With the appearance of Ludwig Wittgenstein's *Philosophical Investigations* (1953), analytic philosophy adjusted itself to a new point of view. It was still concerned with language, as were logical atomism and logical positivism. But now the analyst would see the nature of language in a different light. Wittgen-stein, who had provided the most impressive systematic statement of logical atomism in his *Tractatus Logico-Philosophicus* (1919), had shortly thereafter repudiated a considerable portion of that book on the grounds that his theory of language on which it was based was now seen as inadequate. It was inade-

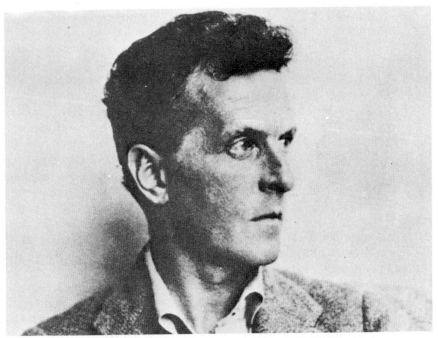

Ludwig Wittgenstein. *(The McGraw-Hill Encyclopedia of World Biography)*

quate because it assumed that language has really only one function, namely, to state facts. It was further assumed that sentences for the most part derive their meanings from stating facts. More seriously, Wittgenstein had assumed, as did also Carnap, that the skeleton of all language is a logical one. What struck him now was the somewhat obvious point that language has *many* functions besides simply "picturing" objects. Language always functions in a *context* and therefore has as many purposes as there are contexts.

Words, said Wittgenstein, are like "tools in a tool-box; there is a hammer, pliers, a saw, a screwdriver, a rule, a glue-pot, glue, nails and screws.—The function of words is as diverse as the functions of these objects." What made him think earlier that language had only one function? He had been "held captive" by a "picture" of language as being the giving of names, as if by Adam, to all things. We are all the victims, he said, of "the bewitchment of our intelligence by means of language." Our incorrect picture of language is "produced by grammatical illusions." To analyze grammar might lead one to discover some logical structure in language. But would that justify the conclusion that all language has essentially the same rules, functions, and meanings? It occurred to Wittgenstein that the assumption that all language states facts and contains a logical skeleton was derived not by observation but by "thought." It was simply assumed that all language, despite certain superficial differences, is alike, the way all games are alike.

Wittgenstein uncovered the flaw in this analogy by taking the case of games and asking "What is common to them all?—Don't say: There *must* be something common, or they would not be called 'games'—but *look and see* whether there is anything common at all.—For if you look at them you will not see something that is common to *all*, but similarities, relationships, and a whole series of them at that. To repeat: don't think, but look." He was apparently saying that logical atomism was the product of thought, of theory, and not of careful observation of the way in fact language operates and is used. Wittgenstein therefore shifted the program of analysis from a preoccupation with logic and the construction of a "perfect" language to a study of the ordinary usages of language. He moved away from what Russell and Carnap were doing and turned now in the direction of G. E. Moore's earlier emphasis on the analysis of ordinary language, testing it by the criterion of "common sense." Wittgenstein was now of the opinion that language does not contain one single pattern alone, that it is as variable as life itself. Indeed, he said that "to imagine a language means to imagine a form of life." For this reason, analysis should consist not of the *definition* of language or its meanings but rather of a careful *description* of its uses: "We must do away with all explanation, and *description alone* must take its place." We must, said Wittgenstein, "stick to the subjects of everyday thinking, and not go astray and imagine that we have to describe extreme subtleties." Confusions arise not when our language is "doing work," but only when it is "like an engine idling."

By recognizing the diversity of the functions of language, Wittgenstein inevitably altered the task of philosophy. For one thing, unlike the positivists, he would not reject the statements of metaphysics outright. Since the new mood was to consider the metaphysician a patient instead of a criminal, the function of philosophy could now be considered as "therapeutic." Metaphysical language can indeed create confusion, and the central concern of philosophy is to deal with problems that baffle and confuse us because of the lack of clarity. Philosophy is a "battle against the bewitchment of our intelligence by means of language." Bewitchment causes confusion, and so "a philosophical problem has the form: 'I don't know my way about.'" Philosophy helps one to find his way, to survey the scene. "What we do," said Wittgenstein, "is to bring words back from their metaphysical to their everyday usage." His aim in philosophy, he said, was "to show the fly the way out of the fly-bottle." When the fly is out of the bottle, and when words are brought back from metaphysics to their everyday usage, and when the person who didn't know his way about now does know the way, what has happened? Wittgenstein says that philosophy "leaves everything as it is."

Philosophy does not provide men with new or more information, but adds clarity by a careful description of language. It is as though one could see all the parts of a jigsaw puzzle but was baffled by how to put it together; he is actually looking at everything he needs to solve the problem. Philosophical puzzlement is similar and can be removed by a careful description of language as we ordinarily use it. What makes us feel trapped as a fly in a bottle is the use of language in ways other than their ordinary use. Hence "the results of philosophy are the uncovering of one or another piece of plain nonsense." By "nonsense" Wittgenstein did not necessarily mean the language of metaphysics, for, again, he had a basic sympathy for what some metaphysicians were trying to do. If metaphysics displayed resistance or a prejudice that obscures the ordinary usage of words, he agreed that this is "not a *stupid* prejudice." He saw in the confusions of metaphysics a deep human condition, saying that "the problems arising through a misinterpretation of our forms of language have the character of *depth*. They are deep disquietudes; their roots are as deep in us as the forms of our language and their significance is as great as the importance of our language."

How, more specifically, does one who doesn't know his way about find it, or how does the fly escape from the fly-bottle? One must not expect from Wittgenstein any single systematic answer to this question. He is too sensitive to the suppleness and variability of life and language to force on them the straitjacket of a single method. "There is not *a* philosophical method," he says, "though there are indeed methods, like different therapies." Because philosophical problems grow out of language, it is necessary to acquire a basic familiarity with the usages of the language out of which each problem arises. Since there are many kinds of games, there are many sets of rules of the games. Similarly, since there are many languages (that is, the many forms of ordinary language of work, play, worship, science, and so forth), there are many *usages*. Under these circumstances, "the work of the philosopher consists in *assembling reminders* for a particular purpose." In his *Philosophical Investigations*, Wittgenstein "does philosophy" by taking many problems and assembling many reminders of the way language is used as a means of clarifying these problems. But the philosopher, in addition to assembling these uses of language, selects and arranges them in order to get a picture of the landscape. In other words, philosophy does not consist in giving crisp abstract answers to questions. A person who has lost his way wants, rather, a map of the terrain, and this is supplied by the selection and arrangement of concrete examples of the actual use of language in ordinary experience.

But it is not enough to just look at these examples of usage, any more than it is sufficient simply to look at the pieces of the jigsaw puzzle. There must be selection and rearrangement. Then everything is before one that one needs for solving the problem. Still, says Wittgenstein, we frequently "fail to be struck by what, once seen, is *most* striking and most powerful." The most important things are hidden "because of their simplicity and familiarity." But what does it mean to "fail to be struck"? There is no sure method according to Wittgenstein to guarantee that one will "be struck" and thereby find one's way. Apparently the fly can frequently pass the opening of the jar without escaping. In any case, what Wittgenstein sought to do was to shift philosophy's concern from meanings, from the assumption that words carried in them as so much freight "pictures" of objects in the world. Instead, he directed attention, through the assembling, selecting, and arranging of relevant examples, to the actual usages of words. Because most *philosophical* problems were assumed to arise from puzzlements about words, the scrupulous description of their ordinary uses would, it was assumed, eliminate this puzzlement.

RICHARD RORTY'S PRAGMATIC TURN

How Revolutionary Is Analytical Philosophy?

The emergence of analytic philosophy gave the impression that the linguistic turn had produced a major revolution in the aims, limits, and practice of philosophy. Ever since Plato, traditional philosophers had sought to discover the foundations of knowledge, to know exactly what is "out there"—outside the mind—to distinguish between mind and body, between appearance and reality, and to provide a "grounding" for absolutely certain truth.

By contrast, analytic philosophers scaled down the enterprise of philosophy to the more modest objective of discovering the foundations of meaningful language. Sentences or propositions would be considered meaningful only if they corresponded to objective and verifiable facts. In this way, philosophy would resemble the rigor of scientific knowledge.

But did this shift in the concerns of philosophy represent a major revolution? To be sure, linguistic analysis clarified some philosophical problems by demonstrating the frequent misuse of language. More dramatically, by requiring that language, to be meaningful, must accurately represent facts, it simply eliminated several "problems" from the agenda of philosophy. What "facts" could be "represented" by language when talking about the "good" or the "beautiful" or the "just" or "God"? If there were no such facts, philosophy could no longer speak confidently, or meaningfully, about ethics, aesthetics, religion, justice, and metaphysics. Surely this represented a revolutionary departure from the traditional concerns of philosophy.

However, in a very significant way, analytic philosophy did not usher in a major change in the assumptions of philosophy, according to Richard Rorty. In his provocative book *Philosophy and the Mirror of Nature* Rorty argues that analytic philosophy is not something new but is rather a variation of what Descartes and Kant had done, namely, provide a "foundation" for knowledge. What is new in analytic philosophy, says Rorty, is the conviction that knowledge is represented by what is linguistic and not by what is mental. But to say this is to leave unchanged the assumption that as human beings we possess by our very nature some framework within which the activity of inquiry takes place. We still have, in analytic philosophy, (1) a "knowing subject," (2) "reality out there," and (3) a "theory of representation" which describes how reality is represented to the knowing subject. The old account of how we know is still the same, namely, that the mind is like a great mirror containing representations of nature, some accurate and some inaccurate which we then study by purely "rational" methods. Analytic philosophy does not remove the assumption that the mind is like a mirror. It simply tries to increase the accuracy of the representations captured by the mind, as Rorty says, by "inspecting, repairing and polishing the mirror." Moreover, to engage in repairing and polishing the mirror implies the presence of another old assumption, namely, that there is something, "reality," which is "out there" (eternally out there) but which for some reason is inaccurately represented to the mind. For these reasons, Rorty believes that a truly revolutionary move in philosophy would

Richard Rorty. *(David Burnett/Contact Press Images)*

require the final rejection of several assumptions, including the traditional mirror imagery, the assumption that human beings are equipped with a structural framework which dictates how human inquiry must proceed, and the assumption that even before there is thinking or history, there is an "essence" to reality, which to know is to know the truth.

Evolution of Rorty's Pragmatism

Richard Rorty was himself an analytic philosopher as a young professor at Princeton University. He was born in 1931 and reared in New York City as an only child whose parents were free-lance journalists and whose maternal grandfather, Walter Raschenbusch, was an eminent liberal Protestant theologian. At age 14, Rorty entered the University of Chicago and later completed his graduate studies in philosophy at Yale. After a brief teaching assignment at Wellesley, he joined the faculty at Princeton, whose department at that time was strongly oriented toward analytic philosophy. For a few years, Rorty immersed himself in "doing" analytic philosophy but finally grew dissatisfied with the piecemeal task of unraveling linguistic and logical puzzles. After a brief period of professional crisis during the early 1970s, and to the considerable surprise of his colleagues, Rorty chose a new direction for his studies, a direction he found in the pragmatism of John Dewey.

John Dewey had delivered a lecture in 1909 on "The Influence of Darwinism on Philosophy" on the occasion of the celebration of the fiftieth anniversary of Darwin's *Origin of Species* (1859). The influence it had, said Dewey, was that it introduced a new mode of thinking, a mode that influenced Dewey himself. The theory of biological evolution, Dewey said, emphasized that change is fundamental to everything that exists. And this change represents not only, as Whitehead would say later, simple rearrangements of bits of matter. The biological dimension focused on the presence of "organic systems" and their creativity with respect to the environment.

Darwin had "laid his hand upon the sacred ark of absolute permanency," writes John Randall. This meant that knowledge could no longer aim at realities lying behind any notion of the mathematical Order of Nature or any vestige of Platonic "eternality." There is no "givenness" about the world. Philosophy would no longer enquire about absolute origins and absolute final ends, as in Hegel's gradual realization of the Idea of freedom or Marx's final phase of human society. Philosophy would no longer, in some quarters, seek to prove that our life necessarily must have certain qualities or values as a result of an earlier cause, such as creation, or a specific goal. The world, in this view, is not described as reflecting an eternal pattern, out there, abstractly.

Instead, philosophical thinking would begin with our immediate concrete experiences of *life*. Human life would be seen at least in one respect as it was by Aristotle, namely, that although we are a part of nature and behave in certain mechanical ways as described by science, we are nevertheless *human*. And although we partake of some characteristics of other animals, we are nevertheless unique. What makes us unique is that we are aware of the processes of nature and we can know how we *function*. We know where some forms of behavior lead, what values or ends they support or frustrate. Experience tells us what things are "necessary for," or "better for" and "worse for," other things. We can evaluate things not in terms of some remote and abstract standards but rather in terms of some more obvious "ends" built into the very natural functions of our organisms. Human life in this view reveals a close relationship between the functions of human nature and the various simultaneous functions of the larger natural environment, thus providing wide choices of ends and values.

It is easy to see how this "new mode of knowledge" influenced Dewey in the direction of pragmatism. Instead of pursuing a single ultimate truth about reality, the emphasis shifted to a pluralism of truths, many truths, and their characteristic that they are ideas or notions that are true because they "work."

Rorty was drawn to Dewey's pragmatism for these and several other reasons. For one thing, it gave him an avenue of escape from the severe limitations which linguistic analysis had placed on the scope of philosophic activity. Pragmatism provided for him a basis for finally rejecting the idea that the mind is a reliable mirror reflecting reality, a notion that assumed that only those thoughts and language are true which faithfully represent the real world. Since there is no way to be absolutely certain that a thought or statement accurately corresponds to reality, it is, he thought, better to think that a statement is true if it leads to successful behavior, if, that is, it "works." Statements should be looked upon as "tools" whose truth is based on their usefulness. Since there are several types of statements, there are correspondingly several kinds of truths. To look upon truth in this manner is to bring back to philosophy the subject matter of many fields. From this point of view, science has no special claim on truth, since it is only one among many areas of practical human concerns, such as politics, ethics, art, literature, history, and religion. Scientific method cannot therefore provide the sole criterion for truth, since there are several particular kinds of truth.

What especially attracted Rorty to pragmatism was that its pluralistic view of truth opened wide areas of legitimate philosophical discussion. In addition to the analysis of language, it now became philosophically useful to study novels and poetry to find there insights into human problems which philosophy had virtually abandoned. Moreover, Anglo-American philosophers could more comfortably engage in discourse with their continental counterparts, where the darker themes of dread, *angst*, and solitude permeate the works of such writers as Nietzsche, Kierkegaard, and Heidegger. Rorty discovered that while analytic philosophy had isolated itself from some of the deepest concerns of life, it is possible to overcome this isolation by expanding the range and type of literature as worthy subjects of study. Almost inevitably, Rorty is no longer in a department of philosophy but has, since 1983, held the title of University Professor of Humanities at the University of Virginia. Here, his mode of philosophy relies heavily on literary and cultural criticism and acknowledges the morally illuminating power of novelists and poets. Rorty has no interest in nor does he think it is useful to engage in "systematic" philosophy. More and more, he believes, the emphasis will be on "edifying" philosophy, whose practitioners will be concerned with culture and self-transformation.

"Contingency"

If there is one theme that captures the truly radical aspect of Rorty's philosophical point of view, it is his conviction that there are no eternal "essences," as for example, "human nature," the "true nature of the self," or "universal moral law," discoverable by human reason. Instead of a timeless and stable structure in reality, what we find, says Rorty, is that everywhere we are confronted by "contingency," by the ever-presence of "chance." If everything is "contingent," how can there be any meaning to life? If there is no timeless truth, how can we know whether our lives fall short of their intended purpose or value? Rorty is aware of these consequences of his pragmatism, but instead of being intimidated by this bewildering world of chance, he sees in it wide opportunities for overcoming contingency by constant self-transformation or self-creation. Still, he insists that it is philosophically important to recognize that contingency, chance, characterizes such fundamental aspects of our experience as our *language,* our idea of our *selfhood,* and our conception of human society, or *community.*

The Contingency of Language We normally think of language as a means by which our vocabulary represents reality to the mind. How can a vocabulary represent, be the medium of, something "out there"? One way is to use the metaphor of a jigsaw puzzle. By the use of words, it is assumed that we can describe various pieces of the puzzle so that as the vocabulary changes and evolves, our language comes closer and closer to what exists out there. But this assumes that out there are to be found fixed and stable realities capable of being described.

Take, for example, the language of science. Galileo created a new vocabulary when he described the behavior of the earth and the sun in relation to each other. What does this history of the change in scientific language illustrate? Does it show that Galileo's new description represents a deeper insight into the intrinsic nature of the natural world? Rorty does not think so. "We must," he says, "resist the temptation to think that the redescriptions of reality offered by contemporary physical or biological sciences are somehow closer to 'the things themselves.'" It is not as though more of the jigsaw puzzle has been filled in by the new language. Rather, we should instead use the metaphor of language as a "tool" so that the new vocabulary of science simply enables those who create the new language to accomplish new objectives. There is no necessary line of development in language any more than there is a necessary line of evolution in nature. We cannot return to the way of thinking about nature and its purposes before the time of Darwin. Contingency, chance, that is, the more or less random behavior of things, explains the changes in nature and in language. Physical evolution did not have to occur precisely as it did. Was it necessary or only by chance that orchids came upon the scene—and didn't Mendel, says Rorty, "let us see mind as something which just happened rather than as something which was the whole point of the process"? To say the opposite, namely, that the world has an intrinsic nature which the physicist or poet has glimpsed, is, he says, "a remnant of the idea that the world is a divine creation, the work of someone who had something in mind, who Himself spoke some language in which He described His own project."

Because our language is the product of random choices made by those who sought to describe the world, there is no reason now to be bound by that inherited language. That the language of the past has influenced the way we think is not a sufficient reason to assume that we should not create our own new vocabulary if that would be more useful in solving our problems. "It is essential to my view," says Rorty, "that we have no prelinguistic consciousness to which language needs to be adequate, no deep sense of how things are which it is the duty of philosophers to spell out in language." Truth, says Rorty, is no more than what Nietzsche called "a mobile army of metaphors."

The Contingency of Selfhood Plato gave us the metaphor of two worlds, the world of time, appearance, and change, on the one hand, and the world of enduring, changeless truth on the other. A person's life represents the attempt to escape from the distractions of the flesh and dominant opinions of a particular time and place in order to enter the real world of reason and contemplation. With this vocabulary, Plato created a language designed to describe the essence of human nature, implying that there is only one true description of our human situation. As we face the contingent events of our life, we are to control our affections by the use and power of our reason and thereby achieve moral and intellectual virtue. Theologians offered basically this same metaphor, urging human beings to strive toward our "true nature." Similarly, Kant described the difference between our daily experiences with their local influences on our choices, on the one hand, and our internal moral consciousness, which reveals for all human beings our timeless and universal moral laws, on the other. These versions of the two worlds which we encounter represent the true world as compared with the deceptive world which we must try to escape.

Rorty believes that the language of Plato, the theologians, and Kant has imposed labels and descriptions of "the self" on our consciousness as if these were absolutely true descriptions. There are, after all, alternative ways of defining the self. If, for example, Nietzsche says that "God is dead," he implies that there is nothing more to reality than the flow of events, the flux of chance. Nor is there any universal moral law nor a "true self." This skepticism leaves the question of how to provide a meaning for human life. There is no other choice, says Nietzsche, and Rorty agrees, than for each of us to give meaning to our own lives by writing our own language, describing our own objectives. In a real sense, each of us must be involved in transforming our "self," not by seeking the truth but by overcoming the old self, by choosing, willing a new self. According to Rorty, "we create ourselves by telling our own story."

Plato tried to describe human nature in some specific detail when he spoke of the tripartite aspect of the self, including the physical body, the passions and affections, and, highest of all, the mind. He assumed that the mind had a "clear shot" at the truth and could overcome the contingent events encountered in daily life. But Rorty finds that quite different descriptions of consciousness have been offered without assuming a realm of eternal truth. On the contrary, he finds in the writings of Freud a tripartite description of the self as nothing but the product of contingent events. The sense of guilt is explained not by an innate knowledge of the moral law. Rather, as Freud says, "a regressive degrading of the libido takes place, the super-ego becomes exceptionally severe and unkind, and the ego, in obedience to the super-ego, produces strong reaction-formations in the shape of conscientiousness, pity and cleanliness. . . ." It may be that the metaphor of the two worlds has been too powerful to overcome. But Freud replies that "If one considers chance to be unworthy of determining our fate, it is simply a relapse into the pious view of the universe which Leonardo himself was on the way of overcoming when he wrote that the sun does not move . . . we are all too ready to forget that in fact everything to do with our life is chance, from our origin out of the meeting of spermatozoon and ovum onwards. . . . Everyone of us human beings corresponds to one of the countless experiments in which [the countless causes] of nature force their way into experience."

The Contingency of Community How shall human beings live together, or how can human beings achieve solidarity and community? Here, again, Plato drew a tight connection between "the essential nature of man" and the social and political arrangement of the community. The three classes of Plato's society were thought by him to be the necessary extensions of the three parts of the human soul, or self. The artisans embody the physical element of man, the guardians express the spirited passions, and the rulers are the incarnation of the mind, reason. Plato also argued that there must first be a harmony of the three parts of the private individual if the collective harmony of the community is to be achieved. All the elements of the self must be subject to and governed by the highest faculty, by reason. Similarly, all the classes of society must be subordinate to the ruler. This whole arrangement is dictated by the structure of human nature.

Rorty disagrees with this notion that the public life of mankind must be based on the antecedent facts of human nature. Theologians have also offered their versions of the Platonic account of the origin and justification of political authority, especially in their theory of the divine rights of kings, while Karl Marx drew from his description of history, and from the relation of human beings to the material order of nature, a theory of a classless society. These various vocabularies or languages describing the good society are contingent on the special perspectives of each author. Each account focuses on a different concept of "ultimate reality," a different view of the essential nature of man. It is not surprising then, says Rorty, that there can be no single concept of community which is required by some true description of human nature.

For his part, Rorty holds that since there is no absolutely true account available about human nature, there is no point in looking in that direction for some moral basis of society. The contingency of language and the contingency of the self mean that there is no reliable objective information which can lead to the "right" kind of community. There is no theory of knowledge that can guarantee the just society—neither "rationality, the love of God, or the love of truth." Instead, Rorty agrees with the insights of Dewey as reflected by John Rawls in his Dewey lectures:

> What justifies a conception of justice is not its being true to an order antecedent and given to us, but its congruence with our deeper understanding of ourselves and our aspirations, and our realization that, given our history and the traditions embedded in our public life, it is the most reasonable doctrine for us.

The central value on which to build a community is the value of freedom and equality, the ideal of liberal democracy. It is not helpful, says Rorty, to ask at this point the question "How do you *know* that freedom is the chief goal of social organization?" any more than it is to ask "How do you *know* that Jones is worthy of your friendship?" The preference for freedom and equality and the desire to eliminate suffering are not discovered by reason but by chance. These values were not always obvious nor always chosen. They were not always options, for example, for the Egyptians, nor can they be defended rationally against those who refuse to accept them. The social glue that holds a liberal society together consists in a consensus, says Rorty, in which everybody has an opportunity at self-creation to the extent of his or her abilities. From the point of view of his pragmatism, Rorty says that what matters most is the widely shared conviction that "what we call 'good' or 'true' [is] whatever is the outcome of free discussion," for if we take care of political freedom, "truth and goodness will take care of themselves."

Reading ———————————————————————————————

Truth and Pragmatism
Richard Rorty

TRUTH

We need to make a distinction between the claim that the world is out there and the claim that truth is out there. To say that the world is out there, that it is not our creation, is to say, with common sense, that most things in space and time are the effects of causes which do not include human mental states. To say that truth is not out there is simply to say that where there are no sentences there is no truth, that sentences are elements of human languages, and that human languages are human creations.

Truth cannot be out there—cannot exist independently of the human mind—because sentences cannot so exist, or be out there. The world is out there, but descriptions of the world are not. Only descriptions of the world can be true or false. The world on its own—unaided by the describing activities of human beings—cannot. . . . To say that there is no such thing as intrinsic nature is not to say that the intrinsic nature of reality has turned out, surprisingly enough, to be extrinsic. It is to say that the term "intrinsic nature" is one which it would pay us not to use, an expression which has caused more trouble than it has been worth. To say that we should drop the idea of truth as out there waiting to be discovered is not to say that we have discovered that, out there, there is no truth. It is to say that our purposes would be served best by ceasing to see truth as a deep matter, as a topic of philosophical interest, or "true" as a term which repays "analysis." "The nature of truth" is an unprofitable topic, resembling in this respect "the nature of man" and "the nature of God," and differing from "the nature of the positron," and "the nature of Oedipal fixation." . . . Interesting philosophy is rarely an examination of the pros and cons of a thesis. Usually it is, implicitly or explicitly, a contest between an entrenched vocabulary which has become a nuisance and a half-formed new vocabulary which vaguely promises great things. . . .

PRAGMATISM

"Pragmatism" is a vague, ambiguous, and overworked word. Nevertheless, it names the chief glory of our country's intellectual tradition. No other American writers have offered so radical a suggestion for making our future different from our past, as have James and Dewey. At present, however, these two writers are neglected. . . The great pragmatists should [be understood] . . . as breaking with the Kantian epistemological tradition altogether. As long as we see James or Dewey as having "theories of truth" or "theories of knowledge" or "theories of morality" we shall get them wrong. We shall ignore their criticisms of the assumption that there ought to *be* theories about such matters. We shall not see how radical their thought was— . . . to make philosophy into a foundational discipline.

James and Dewey rejected neither the Enlightenment's choice of the scientist as moral example, nor the technological civilization which science had created. They wrote, as Nietzsche and Heidegger did not, in a spirit of social hope. They asked us to liberate our new civilization by giving up the notion of "grounding" our culture, our moral lives, our politics, our religious beliefs, upon "philosophical bases." They asked us to give up the neurotic Cartesian quest for certainty which had been one result of Galileo's frightening new cosmology, the quest for "enduring spiritual values" which had been one reaction to Darwin, and the aspiration of academic philosophy to form a tribunal of pure reason which had been the neo-Kantian response to Hegelian historicism. They asked us to think of the Kantian project of grounding thought or culture in a permanent ahistorical matrix as *reactionary*. They viewed Kant's idealization of Newton, and Spencer's of Darwin, as just as silly as Plato's idealization of Pythagoras, and Aquinas' of Aristotle.

Emphasizing this message of social hope and liberation, however, makes James and Dewey sound like prophets rather than thinkers. This would be misleading. They had things to say about truth, knowledge, and morality, even though they did not have *theories* of them, in the sense of sets of answers to the textbook problems. In what follows, I shall offer three brief sloganistic characterizations of what I take to be their central doctrine.

My first characterization of pragmatism is that it is simply antiessentialism applied to notions like "truth," "knowledge," "language," "morality," and similar objects of philosophical theorizing. Let me illustrate this by James's definition of "the true" as "what is good in the way of belief." This has struck his critics as not to the point, as unphilosophical, as like the suggestion that the essence of aspirin is that it is good for headaches. James's point, however, was that there *is* nothing deeper to be said: truth is not the sort of thing which *has* an essence . . . Those who want truth to have an essence want knowledge, or rationality, or inquiry, or the relation between thought and its object, to have an essence. Further, they want to be able to use their knowledge of such essences to criticize views they take to be false, and to point the direction of progress toward the discovery of more truths. James thinks these hopes are vain. There are no essences anywhere in the area. There is no wholesale, epistemological way to direct, or criticize, or underwrite, the course of inquiry.

Rather, the pragmatists tell us, it is the vocabulary of practise rather than of theory, of action rather than contemplation, in which one can say something useful about truth. Nobody engages in epistemology or semantics because he wants to know how "This is red" pictures the world. Rather, we want to know in what sense Pasteur's views of disease picture the world accurately and Paracelsus' inaccurately, or what exactly it is that Marx pictured more accurately than Machiavelli.

So a second characterization of pragmatism might go like this: there is no epistemological difference between truth about what ought to be and truth about what is, nor any metaphysical difference between facts and values, nor any methodological difference between morality and science. Even nonpragmatists think Plato was wrong to think of moral philosophy as discovering the essence of goodness, and Mill and Kant wrong in trying to reduce moral choice to rule. But every reason for saying that they were wrong is a reason for thinking the epistemological tradition wrong in looking for the essence of science, and in trying to reduce rationality to rule. For the pragmatists, the pattern of all inquiry—scientific as well as moral—is deliberation concerning the relative attractions of various concrete alternatives. The idea that in science or philosophy we can substitute "method" for deliberation between alternative results of speculation is just wishful thinking. It is like the idea that the morally wise man resolves his dilemmas by consulting his memory of the Idea of the Good, or by looking up the relevant article of the moral law. It is the myth that rationality consists in being constrained by rule. According to this Platonic myth, the life of reason is not the life of Socratic conversation but an illuminated state of consciousness in which one never needs to ask if one has exhausted the possible descriptions of, or explanations for, the situation. One simply arrives at true beliefs by obeying mechanical procedures.

Let me sum up by offering a third and final characterization of pragmatism: it is the doctrine that there are no constraints on inquiry save conversational ones—no wholesale constraints derived from the nature of the objects, or of the mind, or of language, but only those retail constraints provided by the remarks of our fellow-inquirers. The way in which the properly-programmed speaker cannot help believing that the patch before him is red has *no* analogy for the more interesting and controversial beliefs which provoke epistemological reflection. The pragmatist tells us that it is useless to hope that objects will constrain us to believe the truth about them, if only they are approached with an unclouded mental eye, or a rigorous method, or a perspicuous language. He wants us to give up the notion that God, or evolution, or some other underwriter of our present world-picture, has programmed us as machines for accurate verbal picturing, and that philosophy brings self-knowledge by letting us read our own program.

QUESTIONS FOR REVIEW AND DISCUSSION

1. Rorty argues that the linguistic turn (analytic philosophy) did not radically alter the basic assumptions of classical philosophy regarding the theory of

knowledge, even though it dramatically reduced the scope of philosophy. Which assumptions is he referring to? In your answer, compare Carnap's theory of "verification" with Rorty's notion of truth.

2. What does Rorty mean by "contingency" as applied to the events, or even the structure, of the world?

3. Describe briefly Rorty's notion of the contingency of language by comparing it with Bertrand Russell's logical atomism.

4. How would you compare Rorty's notion of how to choose the most desirable society or community with Plato's approach to the good society?

5. What is Rorty's attitude toward the pursuit of truth? Is his approach closer to Descartes or William James?

6. If you asked Rorty why he looks for valid insights about life in novels, poetry, and other literature, what would be his answer?

Cathedral of St. Etienne de Bourges, begun in the thirteenth century and completed about 1300. *(Tudor Publishing Co., New York)*

PART FOUR

Religious Knowledge and the Existence of God

What Can I Believe?

Love God and do as you please.
Saint Augustine
Homilies on Saint John's Epistle (A.D. 407)

If God did not exist, then everything would be permitted.
Fyodor Dostoevski
The Brothers Karamazov (1880)

There is no human nature since there is no God to conceive it. . . . [M]an is only what he wills himself to be.

Jean-Paul Sartre
Existentialism and Humanism (1946)

We have often heard the statement that "money is his religion." What makes this an appropriate comment is that it comes very close to an accurate definition of what religion is about. Not that religion has anything to do with money; rather, it is that religion describes a relationship. "Religion" can be defined as the way a person relates himself to what he considers most important, or to what he considers ultimate reality. There is also the statement that in one way or another every person is religious. This is so because everybody has some idea of what is most important or what constitutes ultimate reality. Why is it that everybody is concerned with ultimate reality? The concern with what is most important or ultimately real grows out of three aspects of human experience. First, every human being has a certain sense of physical insecurity. We are vulnerable to accident, disease, hunger, war, and death. How do we protect ourselves against a series of disasters which threaten our physical existence? The threat to our survival raises the second question about the meaning of our existence. Is our life, as Thomas Hobbes said, "solitary, poor, nasty, brutish, and short?" Or is there some deeper

meaning to it which makes life important and full of purpose? Third, there is
the sense of moral duty. Should we do whatever we please? Are we willing for
others to do anything they please? At its highest levels, religion has brought
all these concerns together by referring to God as the source of man's
existence, the source of man's nature and destiny, and the guide to man's scale
of values and daily conduct.

SOME ELEMENTS OF RELIGION

The Nature of Religious Knowledge

Religion is a form of experience which is difficult to put into words. Religious
experience is frequently a matter of feeling or emotion rather than intellectual
knowledge. In religion one is more apt to ask "What can I believe?" instead of
"What can I know?" This implies that to believe something is different from
knowing something. All knowledge is not of the same kind. If knowledge is
limited to what we can see, touch, and measure, then we can never have
knowledge of God, who is not available to the sense of sight and touch. Some
religious people claim that their feelings, emotions, and their beliefs provide
for them a kind of knowledge, just as when a person who loves another has a
special knowledge of that relationship. Besides personal feelings or emotions,
religious knowledge is based on the experience of a community of people who
are witnesses to religious ideas. Moreover, religious wisdom is preserved in
literature and continues to appear valid from one generation to another.
Others claim a special source of religious knowledge that they call
"revelation." God is said to reveal significant knowledge through special
persons, such as prophets and writers of sacred scriptures. For some, nature is
a source of revelation: Saint Augustine said that when he looked at flowers
they said to him, "God made us." Most of these sources of religious
knowledge seem to be either private with individuals or limited to a special
community.

Philosophers, however, seek to provide a broader, even universal,
rational basis for religious knowledge. They try to discover in nature or
human experience some clear grounds for the claims of religion. Some
philosophers conclude that there cannot be any exact knowledge either
for or against religion; they call themselves "agnostics." Still others are
certain that religious knowledge about God is not valid; such persons call
themselves "atheists." All these various attitudes toward religious knowledge
become apparent especially when we consider the problem of the existence
of God.

The Existence of God

Most religions are based on ideas about a supreme being. Also, most religious
people believe in the existence of this supreme being as the major element in
their religious commitment. Religious leaders do not question the existence of

God. They assume that God exists, and they build the rest of their teachings on this belief. Philosophers, however, try to find reasons to show that a belief in God can be defended intellectually. Using certain logical procedures, they develop what are called "proofs" for the existence of God. Instead of relying on tradition, custom, literature, or revelation, philosophers have tried to construct their "proofs" by relying solely on the operation of human reason. These so-called proofs are designed not only to provide a rational support for what people already believe. Rather, some philosophers consider the existence of God a necessary part of any complete understanding of the natural world and of human destiny. Without the existence of God, they feel, we cannot fully explain many of our experiences. One experience we all have is the impression that nature seems to work with almost clock-work precision. The seasons come and go on time, the planets move in their regular orbits, the parts of our bodies carry out their specific functions, and the various species reproduce themselves through intricate procedures. Surely, some say, this natural order resembles the inner workings of a clock. And just as a clock has a maker, so also the natural order must be the product of some mind, a supreme designer.

As another example, consider the question raised by a boy who asks his father where that log came from as he throws it into the fireplace. It may be that he simply wants to know whether his father bought it or had cut down one of the trees on their land. But the boy's question could be more philosophical. He may want to know what caused the tree to come into existence. To this question his father may give him a series of answers referring to a series of causes. This is like answering the question about where a child came from by referring to parents, grandparents, and those farther back through a long series of generations. But however far this series of causes can be traced, one must still ask about the earliest cause. How did the series of causes get started? There must be, it is argued, a first cause whose nature is such that it did not itself need to be caused, and this first cause some philosophers call God. Not all philosophers agree with the so-called proofs of this kind, and we will consider the views for and against these arguments.

SOME APPROACHES TO RELIGION

Our aim in this section is to provide alternative views on the nature of religious knowledge and the proofs for God's existence.

The claim for religious knowledge has its defenders and its critics. *Saint Thomas Aquinas* combined elements of the Christian faith with Aristotle's philosophy to show how faith and reason participate in religious knowledge. *William James* approached religious knowledge from a pragmatic point of view, saying that the willingness to believe can under certain circumstances determine what we can know, even in matters of religion. *Bertrand Russell* insisted that if language is to contain meaningful information, its words and phrases must refer to something with which we are acquainted in our experience. Otherwise language does not increase our knowledge, as is the case, he thought, with the language of religion. For *Sigmund Freud,* religion appeared to be the product of a deep and primal wish.

Two of the most significant attempts to prove the existence of God were made by *Anselm* and *Aquinas.* Anselm employed a purely intellectual argument known as the "ontological argument." By contrast, Aquinas chose certain aspects of our experience, such as the movement of things or the appearance of order and design, upon which he constructed his five proofs. *William Paley* also proposed an argument from design, using the analogy of the watch and the watchmaker. *David Hume,* the empiricist, rejected these arguments; in particular, with respect to the argument from design, he said that there is as much evidence of disorder as there is of design to refute the argument. While *Kant* had reasons for finding the concept of God significant, he did not agree that there is any rational way to prove God's existence.

21

The Nature of Religious Knowledge

Aquinas, James, Russell, and Freud

Aquinas

According to Thomas Aquinas, religious knowledge is possible in two different ways. One way is through faith and the other through reason. Faith is what theology is concerned about, while reason is the way of philosophy. What is the difference between these two? The most notable difference between theology and philosophy is that each begins from a different starting point. Although they both have something to say about God, they do so for different reasons. The philosopher begins with the simplest object of sense experience and through a process of reasoning moves beyond that object to more general principles. By thinking about a tree, it is possible to raise the most profound questions about existence. How does the tree come into existence? What does it mean for anything to be? Is everything that exists the same, on principle, as a tree, namely, that at one time it did not exist, then it exists, and finally it ceases to exist? Must not there be a being which always is? The human mind can know certain truths that seem eternal, as, for example, that 7 and 3 always make 10. The permanence, the eternity of these truths, is in sharp contrast to the limited span of existence of a tree.

As we shall see later, Aquinas reasons his way from simple things, as did Aristotle, to the highest forms of being, ending with the idea of God. Theology, however, begins with a faith in God and considers all things we find in nature as being the creatures of God. The theologian's faith comes from the tradition of his religious community. And that tradition is assumed to be the product of God's revelation to man. There is, then, a sharp difference in the starting point and the method of theology and philosophy. The philosopher

For biographical note on Aquinas, see p. 172.

Saint Thomas Aquinas. (*Culver Pictures*)

draws his conclusions from his rational interpretations of the things in nature, whereas the theologian rests the demonstrations of his conclusions on the authority of revealed knowledge.

Aquinas took great pains to point out that philosophy and theology do not necessarily contradict each other. Theology, however, is far more concerned with what is urgent for man's religious life and destiny, while philosophy deals with matters that are not always significant for man's religious end. Some truths available to theology can never be discovered by natural reason, as for example the doctrine of the trinity. Some truths can be discovered by reason, as for example that God exists; these truths are also revealed in order to make sure that they are known. There is, said Aquinas, some overlapping between philosophy and theology. For the most part, however, philosophy and theology are two separate disciplines. Wherever reason is capable of knowing something, faith, strictly speaking, is not necessary. Also, what faith uniquely knows through revelation cannot be known by natural reason alone. Philosophy can only infer that God exists as the first cause of things. But philosophy cannot, by studying the objects of experience, understand what God is like. Nevertheless, both theology and philosophy are concerned with truth: both affirm the existence of God as the truth about the created world, but they do this in different ways.

Reading _____

How God Is Known

Aquinas

GOD CAN BE KNOWN BY NATURAL REASON

Our natural knowledge begins from sense. Hence, our natural knowledge can go as far as it can be led by sensible things. But our intellect cannot be led by sense so far as to see the essence of God; because sensible creatures are effects of God which do not equal the power of God, their cause. Hence from the knowledge of sensible things the whole power of God cannot be known; nor therefore can His essence be seen. But because they are His effects and depend on their cause, we can be led from them so far as to know of God *whether* He *exists*, and to know of Him what must necessarily belong to Him, as the first cause of all things, exceeding all things caused by Him.

Hence, we know His relationship with creatures, that is, that He is the cause of all things; also that creatures differ from Him, inasmuch as He is not in any way part of what is caused by Him; and that His effects are removed from Him, not by reason of any defect on His part, but because He superexceeds them all.

BY GRACE A HIGHER KNOWLEDGE OF GOD CAN BE KNOWN THAN BY NATURAL REASON

We have a more perfect knowledge of God by grace than by natural reason. Which is proved thus. The knowledge which we have by natural reason requires two things: images derived from the sensible things, and a natural intelligible light enabling us to abstract intelligible conceptions from them.

Now in both of these, human knowledge is assisted by the revelation of grace. For the intellect's natural light is strengthened by the infusion of gratuitous light, and sometimes also the images in the imagination are divinely formed, so as to express divine things better than do those which we receive naturally from sensible things, as appears in prophetic visions; while sometimes sensible things, or even voices, are divinely formed to express some divine meaning. . . .

From Aquinas, *Summa Theologica*, Question XII, art. 12 & 13, in *The Basic Writings of Saint Thomas Aquinas*, ed. Anton C. Pegis, Random House, New York, 1944.

James

William James raised this question "Can our will either help or hinder our intellect in its perceptions of truth?" In answering this question, James did not intend to propose the fanciful thesis that "wishing will make it true." His intention was to give a defense of "our right" to believe something of which our purely logical intellect may not have been persuaded. Religious questions in particular have a way of running ahead of evidence. But if the evidence for God's existence is lacking, there is, nevertheless, the fact of human behavior. James put great store in the concrete fact that men engage in moral discourse and also religious practice. It is necessary to recognize this fact of religious behavior when considering the issue of religious truth. Moreover, pragmatism recognizes the close relation between thinking and doing and therefore between belief and action. This makes belief an important element in life, and what James wanted to do was to discover just how relevant the will to believe is in relation to truth.

James said that the will to believe is relevant only under highly restricted conditions. One cannot will to believe just anything under any and all circumstances. First of all, there must be a clear *hypothesis* that is proposed for our belief. Such a hypothesis must be *live* rather than *dead*; that is, it must, like an electric wire, make a connection with my life. If an American Protestant is asked to believe in the Mahdi, this makes no connection with him and arouses no credibility at all and could, therefore, be only a dead hypothesis. Further, there must be an *option*. James argued that a genuine option requires that both alternative hypotheses be *live* and not dead; the option must be *forced* and not avoidable; and it must be *momentous* and not trivial. The will to believe, then, is relevant and can operate only when we are confronted with an option that (1) is *forced* upon us, in that it is impossible not to choose one way or the other, (2) is a *living* option because both hypotheses make a genuine appeal, and (3) is a *momentous* option because the opportunity to choose might not present itself again. Moreover, a belief is relevant only where reason alone cannot settle the matter.

For biographical note on James, see p. 309.

Having stated these conditions, James then argues that it is frequently the case that our wills influence our convictions. The clearest example, he thought, was our postulate that there is truth and that our minds can attain it. How do we know there is truth? We don't, says James; our belief that there is truth is but a "passionate affirmation of desire." We want to have truth, and we want to believe that our experiments will unfold more truth, and in this desire we have the support of the community. For these reasons, James says that "our passionate nature not only lawfully may, but must, decide an option between propositions, whenever it is a genuine option that cannot by its nature be decided on intellectual grounds; for to say, under such circumstances, 'Do not decide, but leave the question open,' is itself a passional decision . . . and is attended with the . . . risk of losing the truth."

James argues that certain kinds of truths become possible only when we put ourselves in the position for the truth fully to materialize itself. If we fail to make ourselves "available," we risk losing the truth. Suppose a young man wants to know whether a certain young woman loves him. Let us also suppose that objectively it is a fact that she loves him but he does not *know* it. If he assumes that she does not, if, that is, he does not will to believe that she loves him, his doubt will prevent him from saying or doing what would cause her to reveal her love. In this case, he would "lose the truth." His will to believe would not necessarily create the love; that is already there. Belief has the effect of making what is already there become known. If the young man required evidence before he could know the truth, he would never know it, because the evidence he is looking for can become available only after he wills to believe it is true. In this case, the will to believe would have discovered a fact that already existed. Projecting this method deeper into the realm of religious experience, James did not want to argue that the will to believe would "create" the existence of God as the product of mere wish. He rather thought that the truth of religion and the power of God in human experience is the discovery, through the will to believe, of what is in fact "there." Some truths will forever escape us until we plunge into the stream of experience.

Besides *discovering* facts, the will to believe can *create* facts. An individual, says James, frequently gains a promotion chiefly because he believed he could achieve it and acted resolutely on that belief. Taking his own estimate of his powers as true, such a person *lives* by it, sacrifices for its sake, and takes risks. His faith *creates* its own verification. In a political campaign, the will to believe can provide the psychic energy for creating a majority for a candidate. When one person is impressed by the optimism of another, he is energized to express the same optimism about the outcome of the election, and this *energy* can eventually create the majority vote. James gives the illustration of passengers on a train, all of whom are individually brave, but when held up by robbers, each one is afraid that if he resists he will be shot. If they believe that the others would arise, resistance could begin. The robbers know that they can count on one another. The passengers, however, are paralyzed. Although they possess superior force, they are not *sure* their fellows would support their resistance. But if one passenger actually arose, that evidence of resolve could influence the others, and this will to believe would help to create the fact of total resistance.

In the end, religious experience was for James a fact that is both *discovered* and *created* through the will to believe. His pragmatism led him to distinguish between organized religion and that firsthand religion whose "cash value" could be realized only when a person put himself into a position to be affected by it. Religion grows out of the deep personal experience of the fragmentary or broken character of life, and this awareness leads one to discover a power that can overcome this sense of incompleteness. James thought of God in these terms, as a power able to reconstruct human life. For this reason, James concluded that "the universe is no longer a mere *It* to us, but a *Thou*, if we are religious; any relation that may be possible from person to person might be possible here."

Reading _____

The Will to Believe

James

The thesis I defend is, briefly stated, this: *Our passional nature not only lawfully may, but must, decide an option between propositions, whenever it is a genuine option that cannot by its nature be decided on intellectual grounds; for to say, under such circumstances, "Do not decide, but leave the question open," is itself a passional decision—just like deciding yes or no—and is attended with the same risk of losing the truth.* The thesis thus abstractly expressed will, I trust, soon become quite clear. But I must first indulge in a bit more of preliminary work.

It will be observed that for the purposes of this discussion we are on "dogmatic" ground—ground, I mean, which leaves systematic philosophical scepticism altogether out of account. The postulate that there is truth, and that it is the destiny of our minds to attain it, we are deliberately resolving to make, though the sceptic will not make it. We part company with him, therefore, absolutely, at this point. But the faith that truth exists, and that our minds can find it, may be held in two ways. We may talk of the *empiricist* way and of the *absolutist* way of believing in truth. The absolutists in this matter say that we not only can attain to knowing truth, but we can *know* when we have attained to knowing it; while the empiricists think that although we may attain it, we cannot infallibly know when. To *know* is one thing, and to know for certain *that* we know is another. One may hold to the first being possible without the second; hence the empiricists and the absolutists, although neither of them is a sceptic in the usual philosophic sense of the term, show very different degrees of dogmatism in their lives. . . .

In truths dependent on our personal action, then, faith based on desire is certainly a lawful and possibly an indispensable thing.

But now, it will be said, these are all childish human cases, and have nothing to do with great cosmical matters, like the question of religious faith. Let us then pass on to that. Religions differ so much in their accidents that in discussing the religious question we must make it very generic and broad. What then do we now mean by the religious hypothesis? Science says things are; morality says some things are better than other things; and religion says essentially two things.

First, she says that the best things are the more eternal things, the overlapping things, the things in the universe that throw the last stone, so to speak, and say the final word. "Perfection is eternal"—this phrase of Charles Secrétan seems a good way of putting this first affirmation of religion, an affirmation which obviously cannot yet be verified scientifically at all.

The second affirmation of religion is that we are better off even now if we believe her first affirmation to be true.

Now, let us consider what the logical elements of this situation are *in case the religious hypothesis in both its branches be really true.* (Of course, we must admit that possibility at the outset. If we are to discuss the question at all, it must involve a living option. If for any of you religion be a hypothesis that cannot, by any living possibility, be true, then you need go no farther. I speak to the "saving remnant" alone.) So proceeding, we see, first, that religion offers itself as a *momentous* option. We are supposed to gain, even now, by our belief, and to lose by our non-belief, a certain vital good. Secondly, religion is a *forced* option, so far as that good goes. We cannot escape the issue by remaining sceptical and waiting for more light, because, although we do avoid error in that way *if religion be untrue,* we lose the good, *if it be true,* just as certainly as if we positively chose to disbelieve. It is as if a man should hesitate indefinitely to ask a certain woman to marry him because he was not perfectly sure that she would prove an angel after he brought her home. Would he not cut himself off from that particular angel-possibility as decisively as if he went and married some one else? Scepticism, then, is not avoidance of option; it is option of a certain particular kind of risk. *Better risk loss of truth than chance of error*—that is your faith-vetoer's exact position. He is actively playing his stake as much as the believer is; he is backing the field against the religious hypothesis, just as the believer is backing the religious hypothesis against the field. To preach scepticism to us as a duty until "sufficient evidence" for religion be found, is tantamount therefore to telling us, when in presence of the religious hypothesis, that to yield to our fear of its being error is wiser and better than to yield to our hope that it may be true. It is not intellect against all passions, then; it is only intellect with one passion laying down its law. And by what, forsooth, is the supreme wisdom of this passion warranted? Dupery for dupery, what proof is there that dupery through hope is so much worse than dupery through fear? I, for one, can see no proof; and I simply refuse obedience to the scientist's command to imitate his kind of option, in a case where my own stake is important enough to give me the right to choose my own form of risk. If religion be true and the evidence for it be still insufficient, I do not wish, by putting your extinguisher upon my nature (which feels to me as if it had after all some business in this matter), to forfeit my sole chance in life of getting upon the winning side—that chance depending, of course, on my willingness to run the risk of acting as if my passional need of taking the world religiously might be prophetic and right.

All this is on the supposition that it really may be prophetic and right, and that, even to us who are discussing the matter, religion is a live hypothesis which may be true. Now, to most of us religion comes in a still further way that makes a veto on our active faith even more illogical. The more perfect and more eternal aspect of the universe is represented in our religions as having personal form. The universe is no longer a mere *It* to us, but a *Thou*, if we are religious; and any relation that may be possible from person to person might be possible here. For instance, although in one sense we are passive portions of the universe, in another we show a curious autonomy, as if we were small active centers on our own account. We feel, too, as if the appeal of religion to us were made to our own active good-will, as if evidence might be forever withheld from us unless we met the hypothesis half-way. To take a trivial illustration: just as a man who in a company of gentlemen made no advances, asked a warrant for every concession, and believed no one's word without proof, would cut himself off by such churlishness from all the social rewards that a more trusting spirit would earn—so here, one who should shut himself up in snarling logicality and try to make the gods extort his recognition willy-nilly, or not get it at all, might cut himself off forever from his only opportunity of making the gods' acquaintance. This feeling, forced on us we know not whence, that by obstinately believing that there are gods (although not to do so would be so easy both for our logic and out life) we are doing the universe the deepest service we can, seems part of the living essence of the religious hypothesis. If the hypothesis *were* true in all its parts, including this one, then pure intellectualism, with its veto on our making willing advances, would be an absurdity; and some participation of our sympathetic nature would be logically required. I, therefore, for one, cannot see my way to accepting the agnostic rules for truth-seeking, or willfully agree to keep my willing nature out of the game. I cannot do so for this plain reason, that a *rule of thinking which would absolutely prevent me from acknowledging certain kinds of truth if those kinds of truth were really there, would be an irrational rule.* That for me is the long and short of the formal logic of the situation, no matter what the kinds of truth might materially be.

From William James, "The Will to Believe," 1896.

Russell

Born in England in 1872, Bertrand Russell was ninety-eight years old when he died in north Wales in 1970. As an orphan, he was reared by his grandparents; he inherited his title of 3d Earl Russell from his grandfather. His brilliance became apparent at an early age, and at Cambridge University he won a long list of honors. He eventually wrote more than forty books and became one of the most influential philosophers of the twentieth century. As an *empiricist*,* he sought to define the limits of human knowledge. He also sought to give all thinking the rigor of mathematics. In particular, he analyzed language to its most basic elements, namely, its "atomic facts,"** making sure in this way that language and the world to which it refers are related to each other accurately. Russell wrote on all subjects, including philosophy, politics, mathematics, and religion.

In his late teens, just before he went to Cambridge University, Bertrand Russell wrote down his "beliefs" and "unbeliefs." He wrote, for example, "I may say to begin with that I do believe in God, and that I shall call myself a theist if I had to give my creed a name." In setting forth his reasons for believing in God, Russell said, "I shall take account of scientific arguments." He found in the orderly behavior of nature a strong reason for believing in "a cause which regulates the action of force on nature" and this cause can be attributed, he said, only "to a divine controlling power which I accordingly call God." As his interest in mathematics grew, Russell developed a desire to make philosophical language as clear and accurate as the language of mathematics. Indeed, Russell eventually became known for his attempt to invent a new language which he called "logical atomism." This language of logical atomism would, he thought, have the exactness and rigor of mathematics because it was supposed to correspond exactly to "facts." As we shall see, in order to make language fit the "facts" of experience, only certain kinds of facts could be admitted for consideration. Russell concluded, as did the empiricists, that only that language which refers to things we all experience can be meaningful. Clearly, discussions about God could not pass this test of meaningfulness.

Russell wondered whether he could devise a way to construct a language that could accurately express everything that could be stated clearly. In the beginning, he made a major assumption, namely, that the world could and would correspond to his specially constructed language. The vocabulary of his language would correspond to the particular objects in the world. What kind of "facts" would form the basis of this language? "The things in the world," said Russell, "have various properties, and stand in various relations to each other. That they have these properties and relations are facts. . . ." Language, according to Russell, consists of a unique arrangement of words, and the

---

*An empiricist is one who believes that the only source of knowledge is experience.

**See p. 324.

meaningfulness of language is determined by the accuracy with which the words represent facts.

A fact is either simple or complex. Words match facts. If there is no fact to match a word, then the word is meaningless. Words are arranged in the form of propositions; the words in a proposition must correspond one by one with corresponding facts. Words and propositions must be analyzed to discover what they symbolize. The simplest word or proposition symbolizes the simplest fact, which is called an "atomic fact." When two or more atomic propositions are linked together with such words as "and" and"or," the result is what Russell calls "molecular propositions." But no matter how complex a proposition is, it can be analyzed into its parts, and each part must correspond to a fact. These facts must be contained in our actual experience. Or, as Russell says, "Every proposition which we can understand must be composed wholly of constituents with which we are acquainted."

Once again, this puts Russell squarely in the camp of empiricism, which says that all knowledge is based on experience. Propositions which cannot be traced back to facts with which we are actually acquainted cannot be considered meaningful propositions. For this reason, Russell comes to the conclusion that many of the propositions of traditional religious language could not meet the test of logical atomism. There is no way, for example, to relate the proposition that "God is all-powerful" with any facts with which we are acquainted. Russell was not prepared to say that God does not exist, which is the position of the atheist. Instead, he called himself an *agnostic*, saying that "the agnostic suspends judgment, saying that there are not sufficient grounds either for affirmation or for denial."

Reading _____

What Is an Agnostic?
Russell

ARE AGNOSTICS ATHEISTS?

NO. AN ATHEIST, like a Christian, holds that we *can* know whether or not there is a God. The Christian holds that we can know there is a God; the atheist, that we can know there is not. The agnostic suspends judgment, saying that there are not sufficient grounds either for affirmation or for denial. At the same time, an agnostic may hold that the existence of God, though not impossible, is very improbable; he may even hold it so improbable that it is not worth considering in practice. In that case, he is not far removed from atheism. His attitude may be that which a careful philosopher would have toward the gods of ancient Greece. If I were asked to *prove* that Zeus and Poseidon and Hera and the rest of the Olympians do not exist, I should be at a loss to find conclusive arguments. An agnostic may think the Christian God as improbable as the Olympians; in that case, he is, for practical purposes, at one with the atheists.

SINCE YOU DENY "GOD'S LAW," WHAT AUTHORITY DO YOU ACCEPT AS A GUIDE TO CONDUCT?

An agnostic does not accept any "authority" in the sense in which religious people do. He holds that a man should think out questions of conduct for himself. Of course, he will seek to profit by the wisdom of others, but he will have to select for himself the people he is to consider wise, and he will not regard even what they say as unquestionable. He will observe that what passes as "God's law" varies from time to time. The Bible says both that a woman must not marry her deceased husband's brother, and that, in certain circumstances, she must do so. If you have the misfortune to be a childless widow with an unmarried brother-in-law, it is logically impossible for you to avoid disobeying "God's law."

Cambridge, where Bertrand Russell studied and taught. (*Culver Pictures*)

DOES AN AGNOSTIC DO WHATEVER HE PLEASES?

In one sense, no; in another sense, everyone does whatever he pleases. Suppose, for example, you hate some one so much that you would like to murder him. Why do you not do so? You may reply: "Because religion tells me that murder is a sin." But as a statistical fact, agnostics are not more prone to murder than other people, in fact, rather less so. They have the same motives for abstaining from murder as other people have. Far and away the most powerful of these motives is the fear of punishment. In lawless conditions, such as a gold rush, all sorts of people will commit crimes, although in ordinary circumstances they would have been law-abiding. There is not only actual legal punishment; there is the discomfort of dreading discovery, and the loneliness of knowing that, to avoid being hated, you must wear a mask even with your closest intimates. And there is also what may be called "conscience": If you ever contemplated a murder, you would dread the horrible memory of your victim's last moments or lifeless corpse. All this, it is true, depends upon your living in a law-abiding community, but there are abundant secular reasons for creating and preserving such a community.

I said that there is another sense in which every man does as he pleases. No one but a fool indulges every impulse, but what holds a desire in check is always some other desire. A man's anti-social wishes may be restrained by a wish to please God, but they may also be restrained by a wish to please his friends, or to win the respect of his community, or to be able to contemplate himself without disgust. But if he has no such wishes, the mere abstract precepts of morality will not keep him straight.

CAN AN AGNOSTIC BE A CHRISTIAN?

The word "Christian" has had various different meanings at different times. Throughout most of the centuries since the time of Christ, it has meant a person who believed in God and immortality and held that Christ was God. But Unitarians call themselves Christians, although they do not believe in the divinity of Christ, and many people nowadays use the word God in a much less precise sense than that which it used to bear. Many people who say they believe in God no longer mean a person, or a trinity of persons, but only a vague tendency or power or purpose imminent in evolution. Others, going still further, mean by "Christianity" merely a system of ethics which, since they are ignorant of history, they imagine to be characteristic of Christians only.

When, in a recent book, I said that what the world needs is "love, Christian love, or compassion," many people thought this showed some change in my views, although, in fact, I might have said the same thing at any time. If you mean by a "Christian" a man who loves his neighbor, who has wide sympathy with suffering and who ardently desires a world freed from the cruelties and abominations which at present disfigure it, then, certainly, you will be justified in calling me a Christian. And, in this sense, I think you will find more "Christians" among agnostics than among the orthodox. But, for my part, I cannot accept such a definition. Apart from other objections to it, it seems rude to Jews, Buddhists, Mohammedans and other non-Christians, who, so far as history shows, have been at least as apt as Christians to practice the virtues which some modern Christians arrogantly claim as distinctive of their own religion.

I think also that all who called themselves Christians in an earlier time, and a great majority of those who do so at the present day, would consider that belief in God and immortality is essential to a Christian. On these grounds, I should not call myself a Christian, and I should say that an agnostic cannot be a Christian. But, if the word "Christianity" comes to be generally used to mean merely a kind of morality, then it will certainly be possible for an agnostic to be a Christian.

DOES AN AGNOSTIC DENY THAT MAN HAS A SOUL?

This question has no precise meaning unless we are given a definition of the word "soul." I suppose what is meant is, roughly, something nonmaterial which persists throughout a person's life and even, for those who believe in immortality, throughout all future time. If this is what is meant, an agnostic is not likely to believe that man has a soul. But I must hasten to add that this does not mean that an agnostic must be a materialist. Many agnostics (including myself) are quite as doubtful of the body as they are of the soul, but this is a long story taking one into difficult metaphysics. Mind and matter alike, I should say, are only convenient symbols in discourse, not actually existing things.

ARE YOU NEVER AFRAID OF GOD'S JUDGMENT IN DENYING HIM?

Most certainly not. I also deny Zeus and Jupiter and Odin and Brahma, but this causes me no qualms. I observe that a very large portion of the human race does not believe in God and suffers no visible punishment in consequence. And if there were a God, I think it very unlikely that He would have such an uneasy vanity as to be offended by those who doubt His existence.

HOW DO AGNOSTICS EXPLAIN THE BEAUTY AND HARMONY OF NATURE?

I do not understand where this "beauty" and "harmony" are supposed to be found. Throughout the animal kingdom, animals ruthlessly prey upon each other. Most of them are either cruelly killed by other animals or slowly die of hunger. For my part, I am unable to see any very great beauty or harmony in the tapeworm. Let it not be said that this creature is sent as a punishment for our sins, for it is more prevalent among animals than among humans. I suppose the questioner is thinking of such things as the beauty of the starry heavens. But one should remember that stars every now and again explode and reduce everything in their neighborhood to a vague mist. Beauty, in any case, is subjective and exists only in the eye of the beholder.

IS NOT FAITH IN REASON ALONE A DANGEROUS CREED? IS NOT REASON IMPERFECT AND INADEQUATE WITHOUT SPIRITUAL AND MORAL LAW?

No sensible man, however agnostic, has "faith in reason alone." Reason is concerned with matters of fact, some observed, some inferred. The question whether there is a future life and the question whether there is a God concern matters of fact, and the agnostic will hold that they should be investigated in the same way as the question, "Will there be an eclipse of the moon tomorrow?" But matters of fact alone are not sufficient to determine action, since they do not tell us what ends we ought to pursue. In the realm of ends, we need something other than reason. The agnostic will find his ends in his own heart and not in an external command. Let us take an illustration: Suppose you wish to travel by train from New York to Chicago; you will use reason to discover when the trains run, and a person who thought that there was some faculty of insight or intuition enabling him to dispense with the timetable would be thought rather silly. But no timetable will tell him that it is wise to travel to Chicago. No doubt, in deciding that it is wise, he will have to take account of further matters of fact; but behind all the matters of fact, there will be the ends that he thinks fitting to pursue, and these, for an agnostic as for other men, belong to a realm which is not that of reason, though it should be in no degree contrary to it. The realm I mean is that of emotion and feeling and desire.

DO AGNOSTICS THINK THAT SCIENCE AND RELIGION ARE IMPOSSIBLE TO RECONCILE?

The answer turns upon what is meant by "religion." If it means merely a system of ethics, it can be reconciled with science. If it means a system of dogma, regarded as unquestionably true, it is incompatible with the scientific spirit, which refuses to accept matters of fact without evidence, and also holds that complete certainty is hardly ever attainable.

WHAT KIND OF EVIDENCE COULD CONVINCE YOU THAT GOD EXISTS?

I think that if I heard a voice from the sky predicting all that was going to happen to me during the next twenty-four hours, including events that would have seemed highly improbable, and if all these events then proceeded to happen, I might perhaps be convinced at least of the existence of some superhuman intelligence. I can imagine other evidence of the same sort which might convince me, but so far as I know, no such evidence exists.

Freud

Sigmund Freud was born in Freiberg in Moravia in 1856 and died in London in 1939 at the age of eighty-three. He began his medical studies at the University of Vienna in 1873. In 1882 he studied at the General Hospital of Vienna to qualify for private practice. There he served in the department of internal medicine and later in the psychiatric clinic. He pursued his advanced studies with distinguished medical scientists in the fields of anatomy, neurology, and psychiatry. After further study in Paris, Freud returned to Vienna, where in collaboration with the famous physician Joseph Brewer he published in 1893 a significant article, "The Psychical Mechanism of Hysterical Phenomena." Out of this research, involving the cure of symptoms of hysteria by helping the patient recall under hypnosis the circumstances of the development of these symptoms, there emerged the beginnings of psychoanalysis. His books became widely influential. His first, in 1900, was *The Interpretation of Dreams.* His last book, entitled *Moses and Monotheism,* was published in 1939. His other works include the *General Introduction to Psychoanalysis* (1920), *Civilization and Its Discontents* (1929), and *The Future of an Illusion* (1927).

Freud approached religion from the point of view of a psychoanalyst. He was aware of the strong support for religion found in tradition, in the widespread practice of religion, and in the genuine consolation provided by religion. Nevertheless, Freud concluded that "religious ideas are illusions." These illusions, he said, grow out of deep-rooted wishes. The strength of these wishes provides the power of illusions. The origin of these wishes is traced back to early experiences of childhood. "We know," says Freud, "that the terrifying effect of infantile helplessness aroused the need for protection—protection through love—which the father relieved. . . ." As we grow older, says Freud, we discover that the same helplessness we experienced as a child continues throughout life. Before human beings developed scientific knowledge and abilities, they tried to overcome the sense of helplessness by use of the "illusion" that behind nature there exists a strong father, God, and that God provides protection against life's dangers. God also provides the conditions for a moral world order where justice will finally triumph. Moreover, religion promises the continuation of life beyond the short span on earth. All these ideas, says Freud, are the product of wish-fulfillment, a projection of the father-image on the world scene, and are no more than illusions.

Freud emphasized that an illusion is not necessarily an error. After all, a poor girl may have an illusion that a prince will come after her and take her away with him. Although this may be an illusion, it is not an error and it need not necessarily be false, since this experience is possible and indeed has happened. But certain beliefs are illusions because they have no relationship with reality. As Freud says, "We call a belief an illusion when wish-fulfillment is a prominent factor in its motivation. . . ." There is no scientific proof for the claims of religion, says Freud. He realizes that science does not have an answer for everything. Freud admits moreover that neither can science disprove the ideas of religion. Nevertheless, Freud concludes that religion is based overwhelmingly on the wish for security and that this wish results in the development of illusions. These illusions prevent the development of intelligence because they encourage attempts to solve problems through uncritical emotions instead of through the use of reason. The solution to this problem, according to Freud, is for people to "grow up, " so that just as children ultimately learn how to take care of themselves after they leave home, so, also, mankind can learn how to achieve brotherly love and morality without a cosmic father.

Reading ————————————————————————————————————

The Future of an Illusion
Freud

If we fix our attention on the psychical origin of religious ideas, we will find [that these ideas] which profess to be dogmas, are not the residue of experience or the final result of reflection; they are illusions, fulfilments of the oldest, strongest and most insistent wishes of mankind; the secret of their strength is the strength of these wishes. We know already that the terrifying effect of infantile helplessness aroused the need for protection—protection through love—which the father relieved, and that the discovery that this helplessness would continue through the whole of life made it necessary to cling to the existence of a father—but this time a more powerful one. Thus the benevolent rule of divine providence allays our anxiety in face of life's dangers, the establishment of a moral world order ensures the fulfilment of the demands of justice, which within human culture have so often remained unfulfilled, and the prolongation of earthly existence by a future life provides in addition the local and temporal setting for these wish-fulfilments. Answers to the questions that tempt human curiosity, such as the origin of the universe and the relation between the body and the soul, are developed in accordance with the underlying assumptions of this system; it betokens a tremendous relief for the individual psyche if it is released from the conflicts of childhood arising out of the father complex, which are never wholly overcome, and if these conflicts are afforded a universally accepted solution.

Sigmund Freud. (*Library of Congress*)

When I say that they are illusions, I must define the meaning of the word. An illusion is not the same as an error, it is indeed not necessarily an error. Aristotle's belief that vermin are evolved out of dung, to which ignorant people still cling, was an error; so was the belief of a former generation of doctors that *tabes dorsalis* was the result of sexual excess. It would be improper to call these errors illusions. On the other hand, it was an illusion on the part of Columbus that he had discovered a new sea-route to India. The part played by his wish in this error is very clear. One may describe as an illusion the statement of certain nationalists that the Indo-Germanic race is the only one capable of culture, or the belief, which only psycho-analysis destroyed, that the child is a being without sexuality. It is characteristic of the illusion that it is derived from men's wishes; in this respect it approaches the psychiatric delusion, but it is to be distinguished from this, quite apart from the more complicated structure of the latter. In the delusion we emphasize as essential the conflict with reality; the illusion need not be necessarily false, that is to say, unrealizable or incompatible with reality. For instance, a poor girl may have an illusion that a prince will come and fetch her home. It is possible; some such cases have occurred. That the Messiah will come and found a golden age is much less probable; according to one's personal attitude one will classify this belief as an illusion or as analogous to a delusion. Examples of illusions that have come true are not easy to discover, but the illusion of the alchemists that all metals can be turned into gold may prove to be one. The desire to have lots of gold, as much gold as possible, has been considerably damped by our modern insight into the nature of wealth, yet chemistry no longer considers a transmutation of metals into gold as impossible. Thus we call a belief an illusion when wish-fulfilment is a prominent factor in its motivation, while disregarding its relations to reality, just as the illusion itself does.

If after this survey we turn again to religious doctrines, we may reiterate that they are all illusions, they do not admit of proof, and no one can be compelled to consider them as true or to believe in them. Some of them are so improbable, so very incompatible with everything we have laboriously discovered about the reality of the world, that we may compare them—taking adequately into account the psychological differences—to delusions. Of the reality value of most of them we cannot judge; just as they cannot be proved, neither can they be refuted. We still know too little to approach them critically. The riddles of the universe only reveal themselves slowly to our enquiry, to many questions science can as yet give no answer; but scientific work is our only way to the knowledge of external reality. Again, it is merely illusion to expect anything from intuition or trance; they can give us nothing but particulars, which are difficult to interpret, about our own mental life, never information about the questions that are so lightly answered by the doctrines of religion. It would be wanton to let one's own arbitrary action fill the gap, and according to one's personal estimate declare this or that part of the religious system to be more or less acceptable. These questions are too momentous for that; too sacred, one might say.

At this point it may be objected: well, then, if even the crabbed sceptics admit that the statements of religion cannot be confuted by reason, why should not I believe in them, since they have so much on their side—tradition, the concurrence of mankind, and all the consolation they yield? Yes, why not? Just as no one can be forced into belief, so no one can be forced into unbelief. But do not deceive yourself into thinking that with such arguments you are following the path of correct reasoning. If ever there was a case of facile argument, this is one. Ignorance is ignorance; no right to believe anything is derived from it. No reasonable man will behave so frivolously in other matters or rest content with such feeble grounds for his opinions or for the attitude he adopts; it is only in the highest and holiest things that he allows this. In reality these are only attempts to delude one-self or other people into the belief that one still holds fast to religion, when one has long cut oneself loose from it. Where questions of religion are concerned people are guilty of every possible kind of insincerity and intellectual misdemeanour. Philosophers stretch the meaning of words until they retain scarcely anything of their original sense;

by calling "God" some vague abstraction which they have created for themselves, they pose as deists, as believers, before the world; they may even pride themselves on having attained a higher and purer idea of God, although their God is nothing but an insubstantial shadow and no longer the mighty personality of religious doctrine. Critics persist in calling "deeply religious" a person who confesses to a sense of man's insignificance and impotence in face of the universe, although it is not this feeling that constitutes the essence of religious emotion, but rather the next step, the reaction to it, which seeks a remedy against this feeling. He who goes no further, he who humbly acquiesces in the insignificant part man plays in the universe, is, on the contrary, irreligious in the truest sense of the word.

QUESTIONS FOR REVIEW AND DISCUSSION

1. How does Aquinas distinguish between faith and reason, between theology and philosophy?
2. Did James say that "the will to believe" is something like "wishing will make it true"? Can you think of an example in which an act of will can create a fact?
3. Why did Bertrand Russell move from his earlier ideas of God to his later position as an "agnostic"?
4. Freud calls religion an "illusion." What does he mean by that?

22

Proving the Existence of God

Anselm, Aquinas, Paley, Hume, Kant, and Pascal

Anselm

Anselm was born in 1033 in Aosta, a town in northwest Italy. His parents came from noble families and had hoped that their son would pursue a political career. He received an excellent classical education and soon showed powers of considerable intellectual ability. He disappointed his parents when he decided to enter the Benedictine monastery at Bec, in Normandy, France. There he studied with the renowned scholar Lanfranc. In time, Anselm succeeded Lanfranc as Abbot at the monastery and later as Archbishop of Canterbury in England. He was one of the most significant thinkers between Augustine (354–430) and Aquinas (1225–1274) and became famous for his "ontological argument" for the existence of God, which he set forth in his book *Proslogium.* He insisted on the need for precise logical philosophy, not as a substitute for faith, but as a means for making faith mature. He died in 1109 at Canterbury at the age of seventy-six.

ANSELM'S ONTOLOGICAL ARGUMENT

For Anselm, there was no clear line between philosophy and theology. As Augustine before him, he was particularly concerned with providing rational support for the doctrines of Christianity, which he already accepted as a matter of faith. He was convinced that faith and reason lead to the same conclusions. Moreover, Anselm believed that human reason can create a natural theology that is rationally coherent and does not depend on any authority other than rationality. This did not mean, however, that Anselm denied any connection between natural theology and faith. On the contrary, his view was that natural theology consists of giving a rational version of what is believed. He was not trying to *discover* the truth about God through reason alone, but wanted rather to employ reason in order to *understand* what he was believing. His method therefore was *faith seeking understanding;* "I do not seek to understand

372

in order that I may believe," he said, "but I believe in order that I may under-stand." He made it particularly clear that his enterprise of proving God's exis-tence could not even begin unless he had already believed in His existence. The human mind cannot penetrate into the profundity of God, "for I deem my intellect in no way sufficient thereunto. . . ." From the rational proof of God's existence, Anselm had a limited expectation, as he said that "I desire only a lit-tle understanding of the truth which my heart believes and loves."

The first thing to notice about this proof is that Anselm's thought pro-ceeds from within his mind, and in that way he is unlike Aquinas, who starts with the assumption that each proof must begin with some empirical evidence from which the mind can then move logically to God. Anselm followed Augustine's doctrine of divine illumination, which gave him direct access to certain truths. Indeed, Anselm asks the reader, before beginning the ontologi-cal argument, to "enter the inner chamber of your mind" and to "shut out all things save God and whatever may aid you in seeking God." Clearly, Anselm is assured of the existence of God before he begins, saying, again, that "unless I believe, I shall not understand."

The argument itself moves swiftly. We believe, says Anselm, that God is "something than which nothing greater can be thought." The question then is "Does this something, than which nothing greater can be thought, really exist?" There are those who would deny God's existence. Anselm quotes Psalm 13:1, where it says, "The fool has said in his heart: There is no God." What is meant by the word "fool" in this context? It means that one who denies God's existence is involved in a flat contradiction. For when the fool hears the phrase "something than which nothing greater can be thought," he understands what he hears, and what he understands can be said to be in his intellect. But it is one thing for something to be in the intellect; it is another to understand that something actually exists. A painter, for example, thinks in advance what he is about to portray. At this point, there is in his intellect an understanding of what he is about to make, although not an understanding that the portrait, which is still to be made, actually exists. But when he has finally painted it, he both has in his understanding and understands as exist-ing the portrait he has finally made. This proves that something can be in the intellect even before the intellect knows it to exist. There is, then, in the fool's intellect an understanding of what is meant by the phrase "something than which nothing greater can be thought."

This brings Anselm to the crux of his argument, which is this: Anyone, even the fool, can think of something greater than a being which is only in the intellect as an *idea,* and this something is the *actual existence* of that than which there is no greater. The contradiction in which the fool finds himself is in understanding what is meant by the word "God," namely, a being than which nothing greater can be thought, realizing that its actual existence is greater than just having an idea of it in the intellect, and still denying that God exists. Therefore, says Anselm, "there exists beyond doubt something than which a greater cannot be thought, both in understanding and in reality." In a conclud-ing prayer, Anselm thanks God "because through your divine illumination I now so understand that which, through your generous gift, I formerly believed. . . ."

Gaunilon's Rebuttal

In the Abbey of Marmontier near Tours, another Benedictine monk, Gaunilon, came to the defense of the "fool." Gaunilon did not want to deny God's existence but simply to argue that Anselm had not constructed an adequate proof. For one thing, Gaunilon argued that the first part of the "proof" is impossible to achieve: It requires that there be in the understanding an idea of God, that upon hearing this word the fool is expected to have a conception of that than which there is no greater. But, says Gaunilon, the fool cannot form a concept of such a being since there is nothing among other realities he experiences from which this concept can be formed, in addition to which Anselm has already argued that there is no reality like Him. Actually, if the human mind could form such a concept, no "proof" would be necessary, for one would then already connect existence as an aspect of a perfect being. Gaunilon's other major objection is that we often think of things that in fact do not exist. We can imagine a perfect island, an island than which no greater can exist, but there is no way to prove that such a perfect island exists.

Anselm's Reply to Gaunilon

Anselm gave two replies. First, he said that we, along with the fool, are able to form a concept of that than which there is no greater. We do this whenever we compare different degrees of perfection in things and move upward to the maximum perfection, than which there is no more perfect. Second, he thought Gaunilon's reference to a perfect island showed that he had missed the point of the argument. Anselm points out that we can move from an idea to its necessary existence in only one case, namely, in the case of that Being whose nonexistence cannot be thought. An island does not *have to be*, it is a *possible* or *contingent* kind of being. This would be similarly true of every finite thing. There is only one something through which everything else has its being but that is itself not derived from anything else but has its existence necessarily from itself, and this is God.

Reading ————————————————————————————

That God Truly Exists
Anselm

After I had published, at the pressing entreaties of several of my brethren, a certain short tract [the *Monologium*] as an example of mediation on the meaning of faith from the point of view of one seeking, through silent reasoning within himself, things he knows not—reflecting that this was made up of a connected chain of many arguments, I began to wonder if perhaps it might be possible to find one single argument that for its proof required no other save itself, and that by itself would suffice to prove that God really exists, that He is the supreme good needing no other and is He whom all things have need of for their being and well-being, and also to prove whatever we believe about the Divine Being. . . .

Judging, then, that what had given me such joy to discover would afford pleasure, if it were written down, to anyone who might read it, I have written the following short tract dealing with this question as well as several others, from the point of view of one trying to raise his mind to contemplate God and seeking to understand what he believes. . . .

Well then, Lord, You who give understanding to faith, grant me that I may understand, as much as You see fit, that You exist as we believe You to exist, and that You are what we believe You to be. Now we believe that You are something than which nothing greater can be thought. Or can it be that a thing of such a nature does not exist, since "the Fool has said in his heart, there is no God" [Ps. xiii. 1, lii. 1]? But surely, when this same Fool hears what I am speaking about, namely, "something-than-which-nothing-greater-can-be-thought," he understands what he hears, and what he understands is in his mind, even if he does not understand that it actually exists. For it is one thing for an object to exist in the mind, and another thing to understand that an object actually exists. Thus, when a painter plans beforehand what he is going to execute, he has [the picture] in his mind, but he does not yet think that it actually exists because he has not yet executed it. However, when he has actually painted it, then he both has it in his mind and understands that it exists because he has now made it. Even the Fool, then, is forced to agree that something-than-which-nothing-greater-can-be-thought exists in the mind, since he understands this when he hears it, and whatever is understood is in the mind. And surely that-than-which-a-greater-cannot-be-thought cannot exist in the mind alone. For if it exists solely in the mind even, it can be thought to exist in reality also, which is greater. If then that-than-which-a-greater-cannot-be-thought exists in the mind alone, this same that-than-which-a-greater-*cannot*-be-thought is that-than-which-a-greater-*can*-be-thought. But this is obviously impossible. Therefore there is absolutely no doubt that something-than-which-a-greater-cannot-be-thought exists both in the mind and in reality.

From St. Anselm, *Proslogium*, trans. M. J. Charlesworth, Clarendon Press, Oxford, Eng., 1965.

Aquinas

AQUINAS'S FIVE WAYS

Aquinas formulated five *proofs* or ways of demonstrating the existence of God. His approach was the opposite of Anselm's. Anselm began his proof with the *idea* of a perfect being "than which no greater can be conceived," from which he inferred the existence of that being inasmuch as the actual existence of it is greater than the mere idea of a perfect being. By contrast, Aquinas said that all knowledge must begin with our experience of sense objects. Instead of beginning with innate ideas of perfection, Aquinas rested all five of his proofs on the ideas derived from a rational understanding of the ordinary objects that we experience with our senses. The chief characteristic of all sense objects is that their existence requires a *cause*. That every event or every object requires a cause is something the human intellect knows as a principle whenever, but not until, it comes in contact with experience. By the light of natural reason, the intellect knows, by experiencing events, that for every effect there must be a cause, that *ex nihilo nihil fit*, nothing comes from nothing. To demonstrate that God exists, Aquinas relied, then, first on his analysis of sense objects and second on his notion that the existence of these objects requires a finite series of causes and ultimately a First Cause, or God.

Proof from Motion

We are certain, because it is evident to our senses, that in the world some things are in motion. It is equally clear to us that whatever is in motion was moved by something else. If a thing is at rest, it is only potentially in motion. Motion occurs when something potentially in motion is moved and is then actually in motion; motion is the transformation of *potentiality* into *actuality*. Imagine a series of dominoes standing next to each other. When they are set up in a row, it can be said that they are all potentially in motion, although actually at rest. Consider a particular domino. Its potentiality is that it will not move until it is knocked over by the one next to it. It will move only if it is moved by something actually moving. From this fact, Aquinas drew the general conclusion that nothing can be transformed from a state of potentiality by something that is also in a mere state of potentiality. A domino cannot be knocked over by another domino that is standing still. "Potentiality" means the absence of something and is therefore, in this case, the absence of motion; for this reason, potential motion in the neighboring domino cannot move the next one because potential motion is nonmotion, and you cannot derive motion from nonmotion. As Aquinas says, "nothing can be reduced from potentiality to actuality except by something in a state of actuality." Moreover, it is not possible for the same thing, for example, a domino, to be *at the same time* in actuality and potentiality regarding motion. What is actually at rest

For biographical note on Aquinas, see p. 172.

cannot be simultaneously in motion. This means that the particular domino cannot be simultaneously the thing that is moved and also the mover. Something potentially in motion cannot move itself. Whatever is moved must be moved by another. The last domino to fall was potentially in motion, but so was the next to the last. Each domino could become a *mover* only after it had been moved by the one prior to it. Here we come to Aquinas's decisive point: If we are to account for motion, we cannot do so by going back in an infinite regress. If we must say about each mover in this series that it in turn was moved by a prior mover, we would never discover the source of motion, because every mover would then be only potentially in motion. Even if such a series went back infinitely, each one would still be only potential, and from that no actual motion could ever emerge. The fact is, however, that there *is* motion. There must therefore be a mover which is able to move things but which does not itself have to be moved, and this, says Aquinas, "everyone understands to be God."

Two things need to be noticed about this proof. First, Aquinas does not limit his concept of motion to things such as dominoes, that is, to locomotion. He has in mind the broadest meaning of motion so as to include the idea of generation and creation. Second, for Aquinas, the First Mover is not simply the first member of a long series of causes, as though such a mover were just like the others, its only distinction being that it is the first. Clearly, this could not be the case, for then this mover would also be only potentially in motion. The First Mover must therefore be pure actuality without potentiality and is therefore first not in the series but in actuality.

Proof from Efficient Cause

We experience various kinds of effects, and in every case we assign an efficient cause to each effect. The efficient cause of the statue is the work of the sculptor. If we took away the activity of the sculptor, we should not have the effect, the statue. But there is an order of efficient causes; the parents of the sculptor are his efficient cause. Workers in the quarry are the efficient cause of this particular piece of marble's availability to the sculptor. There is, in short, an intricate order of efficient causes traceable in a series. Such a series of causes is demanded because no event can be its own cause; the sculptor does not cause himself, and the statue does not cause itself. A cause is prior to an effect. Nothing, then, can be prior to itself; hence events demand a prior cause. Each prior cause must itself have its own cause, as parents must have their own parents. But it is impossible to go backward to infinity, because all the causes in the series depend on a first efficient cause that has made all the other causes to be actual causes. There must then be a first efficient cause "to which everyone gives the name of God."

Proof from Necessary versus Possible Being

In nature we find that things are possible to be and not to be. Such things are *possible* or *contingent* because they do not always exist; they are *generated* and are *corrupted*. There was a time when a tree did not exist; it exists, and finally it goes out of existence. To say, then, that it is *possible* for the tree to exist must mean that it is also possible for it *not* to exist. The possibility for the tree *not* to exist must be taken two ways; first, it is possible for the tree *never* to come into existence, and second, once the tree is in existence, there is the possibility that it will go out of existence. To say, then, that something is *possible* must mean that at both ends of its being, that is, before it comes into being and after it goes out of being, it does not exist. *Possible* being has this fundamental characteristic, namely, that it can *not-be*. It can not-be not only after having existed but more important *before* it is generated, caused, or moved. For this reasons, something that is possible, which can not-be, in fact "at some time is not."

All *possible* beings, therefore, at one time did not exist, will exist for a time, and will finally pass out of existence. Once possible things *do* come into existence, they can cause other similar possible beings to be generated, such as when parents beget children, and so on. But Aquinas is making the argument that possible beings do not have their existence in themselves or from their own essence, and if *all* things in reality were only *possible*, that is, if about *everything* one could say that it could not-be *both* before it is and after it is, then at one time there was nothing in existence. But if there was a time when nothing existed, then nothing could start to be and even now there would be nothing in existence, "because that which does not exist begins to exist only through something already existing." But since our experience clearly shows us that things do exist, this must mean that not all beings are *merely possible*. Aquinas concludes from this that "there must exist something the existence of which is necessary." We must therefore admit, he says, "the existence of some being having of itself its own necessity, and not receiving it from another, but rather causing in others this necessity. This all men speak of as God."

Proof from the Degrees of Perfection

In our experience we find that some beings are more and some less good, true, and noble. But these and other ways of comparing things are possible only because things resemble in their different ways something that is the maximum. There must be something that is truest, noblest, and best. Similarly, since it can be said about things that they have more or less being, or a lower or higher form of being, such as when we compare a stone with a rational creature, there must also be "something which is most being." Aquinas then argues that the maximum in any genus is the cause of everything in that genus, as fire, which is the maximum of heat, is the cause of all hot things. From this Aquinas concludes that "there must also be something which is to all beings the cause of their being, goodness, and every other perfection; and this we call God."

Proof from the Order of the Universe

We see that things which do not possess intelligence, such as parts of the natural world or parts of the human body, behave in an orderly manner. They act in special and predictable ways to achieve certain ends or functions. Because these things act to achieve ends always, or nearly always, in the same way and to achieve the best results, "it is plain that they achieve their end, not fortuitously, but designedly." But things that lack intelligence, such as an ear or a lung, cannot carry out a function unless they are directed by something that does have intelligence, as the arrow is directed by the archer. Aquinas concludes, therefore, that "some intelligent being exists by whom all natural things are directed to their ends; and this being we call God."

The two major characteristics of these five proofs are (1) their foundation in sense experience and (2) their reliance on the notion of causality. In addition, the first three proofs do not as obviously lead to the idea of what all men call God, a personal being. These are, however, proofs that Aquinas considered philosophical corroborations of the religious notion of God, and they, it must be remembered, were composed in the context of his theological task. Moreover, many of Aquinas's illustrations, such as, for example, that fire is the maximum of heat, and his assumptions, that order, for example, presupposes an intelligence independent of the natural process, raise for the modern mind critical questions. Still, Aquinas was deliberately employing the insights he had derived from Aristotle, Maimonides, and Albert the Great in order, by means of these philosophical arguments, to make the religious claim of God's existence intellectually defensible. His own view was that the argument from motion was the most obvious of all. The third one, comparing possible and necessary being, appears, however, to contain the most philosophical rigor and the basic assumption of all the other proofs, namely, that possible beings must derive their existence from something that has its existence necessarily in itself.

Reading _____

The Five Ways

Aquinas

The existence of God can be proved in five ways. The first and more manifest way is the argument from motion. It is certain, and evident to our senses, that in the world some things are in motion. Now whatever is moved is moved by another, for nothing can be moved except it is in potentiality to that towards which it is moved; whereas a thing moves inasmuch as it is in act. For motion is nothing else than the reduction of something from potentiality to actuality. But nothing can be reduced from potentiality to actuality, except by something in a state of actuality. Thus that which is actually hot, as fire, makes wood, which is potentially hot, to be actually hot, and thereby moves and changes it. Now it is not possible that the same thing should be at once in actuality and potentiality in the same respect, but only in different respects. For what is actually hot cannot simultaneously be potentially hot; but it is simultaneously potentially cold. It is therefore impossible that in the same respect and in the same way a thing should be both mover and moved, i.e., that it should move itself. Therefore, whatever is moved must be moved by another. If that by which it is moved be itself moved, then this also must needs be moved by another, and that by another again. But this cannot go on to infinity, because then there would be no first mover, and consequently, no other mover, seeing that subsequent movers move only inasmuch as they are moved by the first mover; as the staff moves only because it is moved by the hand. Therefore it is necessary to arrive at a first mover, moved by no other; and this everyone understands to be God.

The second way is from the nature of efficient cause. In the world of sensible things we find there is an order of efficient causes. There is no case known (neither is it, indeed, possible) in which a thing is found to be the efficient cause of itself; for so it would be prior to itself, which is impossible. Now in efficient causes it is not possible to go on to infinity, because in all efficient causes following in order, the first is the cause of the intermediate cause, and the intermediate is the cause of the ultimate cause, whether the intermediate cause be several, or one only. Now to take away the cause is to take away the effect. Therefore, if there be no first cause among efficient causes, there will be no ultimate, nor any intermediate, cause. But if in efficient causes it is possible to go on to infinity, there will be no first efficient cause, neither will there be an ultimate effect, nor any intermediate efficient causes; all of which is plainly false. Therefore it is necessary to admit a first efficient cause, to which everyone gives the name of God.

The third way is taken from possibility and necessity, and runs thus. We find in nature things that are possible to be and not to be, since they are found to be generated, and to be corrupted, and consequently, it is possible for them to be and not to be. But it is impossible for these always to exist, for that which can not-be at some time is not. Therefore, if everything can not-be, then at one time there was nothing in existence. Now if this were true, even now there would be nothing in existence, because that which does not exist begins to exist only through something already existing. Therefore, if at one time nothing was in existence, it would have been impossible for anything to have begun to exist; and thus even now nothing would be in existence—which is absurd. Therefore, not all beings are merely possible, but there must exist something the existence of which is necessary. But every necessary thing either has its necessity caused by another, or not. Now it is impossible to go on to infinity in necessary things which have their necessity caused by another, as has been already proved in regard to efficient causes. Therefore we cannot but admit the existence of some being having of itself its own necessity, and not receiving it from another, but rather causing in others their necessity. This all men speak of as God.

The fourth way is taken from the gradation to be found in things. Among beings there are some more and some less good, true, noble, and the like. But *more* and *less* are predicated of different things according as they resemble in their different ways something which is the maximum, as a thing is said to be hotter according as it more nearly resembles that which is hottest;

so that there is something which is truest, something best, something noblest, and, consequently, something which is most being, for those things that are greatest in truth are greatest in being, as it is written in *Metaph.* ii. Now the maximum in any genus is the cause of all in that genus, as fire, which is the maximum of heat, is the cause of all hot things, as is said in the same book. Therefore there must also be something which is to all beings the cause of their being, goodness, and every other perfection; and this we call God.

The fifth way is taken from the governance of the world. We see that things which lack knowledge, such as natural bodies, act for an end, and this is evident from their acting always, or nearly always, in the same way, so as to obtain the best result. Hence it is plain that they achieve their end, not fortuitously, but designedly. Now whatever lacks knowledge cannot move towards an end, unless it be directed by some being endowed with knowledge and intelligence; as the arrow is directed by the archer. Therefore some intelligent being exists by whom all natural things are directed to their end; and this being we call God.

From Aquinas, *Summa Theologica,* in *The Basic Writings of Saint Thomas Aquinas,* ed. Anto C. Pegis, Random House, New York, 1944.

Paley

William Paley (1743–1805) was born in England, where he was a utilitarian philosopher and an Anglican priest. He was the author of several influential books, including *The Principles of Moral and Political Philosophy* (1785), the contents of which represented his lectures at Cambridge University; *A View of the Evidence of Christianity* (1794), which was required reading for entrance to Cambridge University until the twentieth century; and *Natural Theology* (1802), in which he presented his argument for the existence of God using the analogy that a watch requires a watchmaker.

THE WATCH AND THE WATCHMAKER

Because a watch performs such a specific function and has a clear purpose, which is grasped by the human mind, Paley concludes that "the inference . . . is inevitable; that the watch must have a maker." The fact that we have not seen the watch made does not lessen or weaken the conclusion, says Paley. Nor does the argument fall if for some reason the watch does not work accurately. Even if the watch contains some parts whose usefulness is not at all obvious in the functioning of the watch, it still requires a maker. Paley even asks, what if the watch possessed the power to create another watch, would that not eliminate the need for some intelligent creator? But this question would still have to be asked about the first watch. (Since the watch is only an analogy, the same questions could be asked about the intricate arrangement of the human body and its organs regarding their specific functions; that human beings can reproduce their own natures does not settle the question about the origin of human nature.) No matter how far one goes into the past, the question about an orderer would still remain. That order or design requires a designer; Paley says the "conclusion is invincible." Similarly, Paley says that when we compare the human eye to a telescope, how can we say that the telescope was designed (contrived) but contend that the eye was not?

THE ARGUMENT FROM DESIGN: HUME AND PALEY

The ideas of Paley provide a striking statement of the *argument from design* (otherwise known as the "teleological argument": *telos* is the Greek word for "purpose"). As we will see in the next section, David Hume had earlier written a strong denial of the argument from design, in response to earlier advocates of this popular view, including Aquinas. Although written in 1802, long after Hume had died (in 1776), Paley's treatise serves as an excellent vantage point from which to appreciate the force of Hume's rejection of the argument from design.

Reading _____

The Analogy of the Watch and the Eye
William Paley

In crossing a heath, suppose I pitched my foot against a *stone*, and were asked how the stone came to be there; I might possibly answer, that, for anything I knew to the contrary, it had lain there forever: nor would it perhaps be very easy to show the absurdity of this answer. But suppose I had found a *watch* upon the ground, and it should be inquired how the watch happened to be in that place: I should hardly think of the answer which I had before given, that, for anything I knew, the watch might have always been there. Yet why should not this answer serve for the watch as well as for the stone? Why is it not as admissible in the second case, as in the first? For this reason, and for no other, viz. that, when we come to inspect the watch, we perceive (what we could not discover in the stone) that its several parts are framed and put together for a purpose, e.g., that they are so formed and adjusted as to produce motion, and that motion so regulated as to point out the hour of the day; that if the different parts had been differently shaped from what they are, of a different size from what they are, or placed after any other manner, or in any other order, that that in which they are placed, either no motion at all would have been carried on in the machine, or none which would have answered the use that is now served by it. . . . This mechanism being observed (it requires indeed an examination of the instrument, and perhaps some previous knowledge of the subject, to perceive and understand it; but being once, as we have said, observed and understood), the inference, we think, is inevitable; that the watch must have had a maker; that there must have existed, at sometime, and at some place or other, an artificer or artificers, who formed it for the purpose which we find it actually to answer; who comprehended its construction, and designed its use.

Nor would it, I apprehend, weaken the conclusion, that we had never seen a watch made, that we had never known an artist capable of making one; that we were altogether incapable of executing such a piece of workmanship ourselves, or of understanding in what manner it was performed; all this being no more than what is true of some exquisite remains of ancient art, of some lost arts, and, to the generality of mankind, of the more curious productions of modern manufacture. Does one man in a million know how oval frames are turned? Ignorance of this kind exalts our opinion of the artist's skill, if he be unseen and unknown, but raises no doubt in our minds of the existence and agency of such an artist, at some former time, and in some place or other. Nor can I perceive that it varies at all the inference, whether the question arise concerning a human agent, or concerning an agent of a different species, or an agent possessing, in some respects, a different nature.

Neither, secondly, would it invalidate our conclusion, that the watch sometimes went wrong, or that it seldom went exactly right. The purpose of the machinery, the design and the designer, might be evident, and in the case supposed would be evident, in whatever way we accounted for the irregularity of the movement, or whether we could account for it or not. It is not necessary that a machine be perfect, in order to show with what design it was made: still less necessary, where the only question is, whether it were made with any design at all.

Nor, thirdly, would it bring any uncertainty into the argument, if there were a few parts of the watch, concerning which we could not discover, or had not yet discovered, in what manner they conduced to the general effect; or even some parts, concerning which we could not ascertain whether they conduced to that effect in any manner whatever. For, as to the first branch of the case; if by the loss, or disorder, or decay of the parts in question, the movement of the watch were found in fact to be stopped, or disturbed, or retarded, no doubt would remain in our minds as to the utility or intention of these parts, although we should be unable to investigate the manner according to which, or the connexion by which, the ultimate effect depended upon their action or assistance; and the more complex is the machine, the more likely is this obscurity to arise. Then, as to the second thing supposed, namely, that there were parts which might be spared, without prejudice to the movement of the watch, and that we had proved this by experiment—these superfluous parts, even if we were completely assured that they were such, would not vacate the reasoning which we had instituted concerning other parts. The indication of contrivance remained, with respect to them, nearly as it was before.

Nor, fourthly, would any man in his senses think the existence of the watch, with its various machinery, accounted for, by being told that it was one out of possible combinations of material forms; that whatever he had found in the place where he found the watch, must have contained some internal configuration or other; and that this configuration might be the structure now exhibited, viz. of the works of a watch, as well as a different structure.

Nor, fifthly, would it yield to his inquiry more satisfaction to be answered, that there existed in things a principle of order, which had disposed the parts of the watch into their present form and situation. He never knew a watch made by the principle of order; nor can he even form to himself an idea of what is meant by a principle of order distinct from the intelligence of the watchmaker.

Sixthly, he would be surprised to hear that the mechanism of the watch was no proof of contrivance, only a motive to induce the mind to think so. . . .

Neither, lastly, would our observer be driven out of his conclusion, or from his confidence in its truth, by being told that he knew nothing at all about the matter. He knows enough for his argument. He knows the utility of the end: he knows the subserviency and adaptation of the means to the end. These points being known, his ignorance of other points, affect not the certainty of his reasoning. The consciousness of knowing little need not beget a distrust of that which he does know.

Suppose, in the next place, that the person who found the watch, should, after sometime, discover, that, in addition to all the properties which he had hitherto observed in it, it possessed the unexpected property of producing, in the course of its movement, another watch like itself (the thing is conceivable), that it contained within it a mechanism, a system of parts, a mould for instance, or a complex adjustment of lathes, files, and other tools, evidently and separately calculated for this purpose; let us inquire, what effect ought such a discovery to have upon his former conclusion.

The first effect would be to increase his admiration of the contrivance, and his conviction of the consummate skill of the contriver. Whether he regarded the object of the contrivance, the distinct apparatus, the intricate, yet in many parts intelligible mechanism, by which it was carried on, he would perceive in this new observation, nothing but an additional reason for doing what he had already done,—for referring the construction of the watch to design, and to supreme art. If that construction *without* this property, or which is the same thing, before this property had been noticed, proved intention and art to have been employed about it, still more strong would the proof appear, when he came to the knowledge of this farther property, the crown and perfection of all the rest. . . .

Though it be now no longer probable, that the individual watch which our observer had found was made immediately by the hand of an artificer, yet doth not this alteration in anywise affect the inference, that an artificer had been originally employed and concerned in the production. The argument from design remains as it was. Marks of design and contrivance are no more accounted for now than they were before. In the same thing, we may ask for the cause of different properties. We may ask for the cause of the color of a body, of its hardness, of its heat; and these causes may be all different. We are now asking for the cause of that subserviency to a case, that relation to an end, which we have remarked in the watch before us. No answer is given to this question by telling us that a preceding watch produced it. There cannot be design without a designer; contrivance, without a contriver; order, without choice; arrangement, without anything capable of arranging; subserviency and relation to a purpose, without that which could intend a purpose; means suitable to an end, and executing their office in accomplishing that end, without the end ever having been contemplated, or the means accommodated to it. Arrangement, disposition of parts, subserviency of means to an end, relation of instruments to a use, imply the presence of intelligence and mind. No one, therefore, can rationally believe, that the insensible, inanimate watch, from which the watch before us issued, was the proper cause of the mechanism we so much admire in it;—could be truly said to have constructed the instrument, disposed its parts, assigned their office, determined their order, action, and mutual dependency, combined their several motions into one result, and that also a result connected with the utilities of other beings. All these properties, therefore, are as much unaccounted for as they were before.

Nor is anything gained by running the difficulty farther back, i.e., by supposing the watch before us to have been produced from another watch, that from a former, and so on indefinitely. Our going back ever so far brings us no nearer to the last degree of satisfaction upon the subject. Contrivance is still unaccounted for. We still want a contriver. A designing mind is neither supplied by this supposition, nor dispensed with. If the difficulty were diminished the farther we went back, by going back indefinitely we might exhaust it. And this is the only case to which this sort of reasoning applies. Where there is a tendency, or, as we increase the number of terms, a continual approach towards a limit, *there*, by supposing the number of terms to be what is called infinite, we may conceive the limit to be attained: but where there is no such tendency, or approach, nothing is effected by lengthening the series. There is no difference, as to the point in question (whatever there may be as to many points), between one series and another; between a series which is finite, and a series which is infinite. A chain, composed of an infinite number of links, can no more support itself, than a chain composed of a finite number of links. And of this we are assured (though we never *can* have tried the experiment), because, by increasing the number of links, from ten, for instance, to a hundred, from a hundred to a thousand, etc., we make not the smallest approach, we observe not the smallest tendency, towards self-support. There is no difference in this respect (yet there may be a great difference in several respects) between a chain of a greater or less length, between one chain and another, between one that is finite and one that is infinite. This very much resembles the case before us. The machine which we are inspecting demonstrates, by its construction, contrivance and design. Contrivance must have had a contriver; design, a designer; whether the machine immediately proceeded from another machine or not. That circumstance alters not the case.

That other machine may, in like manner, have proceeded from a former machine: nor does that alter the case; contrivance must have had a contriver. That former one from one preceding it: no alteration still; a contriver is still necessary.

Our observer would farther also reflect, that the maker of the watch before him, was, in truth and reality, the maker of every watch produced from it; there being no difference (except that the latter manifests a more exquisite skill) between the making of another watch with his own hands, by the mediation of files, lathes, chisels, etc., and the disposing, fixing, and inserting of these instruments, or of others equivalent to them, in the body of the watch already made, in such a manner as to form a new watch in the course of the movements which he had given to the old one. It is only working by one set of tools instead of another.

The conclusion which the *first* examination of the watch, of its works, construction, and movement, suggested, was, that it must have had, for the cause and author of that construction, an artificer, who understood its mechanism, and designed its use. This conclusion is invincible. A *second* examination presents us with a new discovery. The watch is found, in the course of its movement, to produce another watch, similar to itself: and not only so, but we perceive in it a system or organization, separately calculated for that purpose. What effect would this discovery have or ought it to have, upon our former inference? What, as hath already been said, but to increase, beyond measure, our admiration of the skill which had been employed in the formation of such a machine! Or shall it, instead of this, all at once turn us round to an opposite conclusion, viz. that no art or skill whatever has been concerned in the business, although all other evidences of art and skill remain as they were, and this last and supreme piece of art be now added to the rest? Can this be maintained without absurdity? Yet this is atheism.

This is atheism: for every indication of contrivance, every manifestation of design, which existed in the watch, exists in the works of nature; with the difference, on the side of nature, of being greater and more, and that in a degree which exceeds all computation. I mean, that the contrivances of nature surpass the contrivances of art, in the complexity, subtlety, and curiosity of the mechanism; and still more, if possible, do they go beyond them in number and variety: yet, in a multitude of cases, are not less evidently mechanical, not less evidently contrivances, not less evidently accommodated to their end, or suited to their office, than are the most perfect productions of human ingenuity.

THE ANALOGY OF THE EYE

I know no better method of introducing so large a subject, than that of comparing a single thing with a single thing; an eye, for example, with a telescope. As far as the examination of the instrument goes, there is precisely the same proof that the eye was made for vision, as there is that the telescope was made for assisting it. They are made upon the same principles; both being adjusted to the laws by which the transmission and reflection of rays of light are regulated. I speak not of the origin of the laws themselves; but such laws being fixed, the construction in both cases, is adapted to them. For instance; these laws require, in order to produce the same effect, that the rays of light, in passing from water into the eye, should be refracted by a more convex surface than when it passes out of air into the eye. Accordingly we find, that the eye of a fish, in that part of it called the crystalline lens, is much rounder than the eye of terrestrial animals. What plainer manifestation of design can there be than this difference? What could a mathematical instrument-maker have done more, to show his knowledge of his principle, his application of that knowledge, his suiting of his means to his end; I will not say to display the compass or excellence of his skill and art, for in these all comparison is indecorous, but to testify counsel, choice, consideration, purpose?

To some it may appear a difference sufficient to destroy all similitude between the eye and the telescope, that the one is a perceiving organ, the other an unperceiving instrument. The fact is, that they are both instruments. And as to the mechanism, at least as to mechanism being employed, and even as to the kind of it, this circumstance varies not the analogy at all. . . . The lenses of the telescope, and the humours of the eye, bear a complete resemblance to one another, in their figure, their position, and in their power over the rays of light, viz. in bringing each pencil to a point at the right distance from the lens; namely in the eye, at the exact place where the membrane is spread to receive it. How is it possible, under circumstances of such close affinity, and under the operation of equal evidence, to exclude contrivance from the one, yet to acknowledge the proof of contrivance having been employed, as the plainest and clearest of all propositions, in the other?

From William Paley, *Evidences of the Existence and Attributes of the Deity*, published in 1802.

Hume

HUME AND THE ARGUMENT FROM DESIGN

It was inevitable that Hume's rigorous premise that "our ideas reach no further than our experience" would lead him to raise skeptical questions about the existence of God. Most attempts to demonstrate the existence of God rely on some version of causality. Among these, the argument from *design* has always made a powerful impact on the mind. Hume was aware of the power of this argument, but he quickly sorted out the elements of the problem, leaving the argument with less than its usual force.

For biographical note on Hume, see p. 287.

The argument from design begins with the observance of a beautiful order in nature. This order resembles the kind of order the human mind is able to impose on unthinking materials. From this preliminary observation, the mind concludes that unthinking materials do not contain the principles of orderliness within themselves: "Throw several pieces of steel together, without shape or form; they will never arrange themselves so as to compose a watch. . . ." Order, it is held, requires the activity of mind, an orderer. Our experience tells us that neither a watch nor a house can come into being without a watchmaker or an architect. From this it is inferred that the natural order bears an analogy to the order fashioned by human effort and that just as the watch requires an ordering cause, so the natural order of the universe requires one. But such an inference, says Hume, "is uncertain, because the subject lies entirely beyond the reach of human experience."

If the whole argument from design rests on the proposition *"that the cause or causes of order in the universe probably bear some remote analogy to human intelligence,"* then, says Hume, the argument cannot prove as much as it claims. Hume's criticism of the idea of causality has particular force here. Since we derive the idea of cause from repeated observations of the contiguity, priority, and constant conjunction of two things, how can we assign a cause to the universe when we have never experienced the universe as related to anything we might consider a cause? The use of analogy does not solve the problem, since the analogy between a watch and the universe is not exact. Why not consider the universe the product of a vegetative process instead of a rational designer? And even if the cause of the universe is something like an intelligence, how can moral characteristics be ascribed to such a being? Moreover, if analogies are to be used, which one should be selected? Houses and ships are frequently designed by a group of designers: Should we say there are many gods? Sometimes experimental models are built with no present knowledge of what the finished form will be like: Is the universe a trial model or the final design? By this line of probing, Hume wished to emphasize that the order of the universe is simply an empirical fact and that we cannot infer from it the existence of God. This does not make Hume an atheist. He is simply testing our idea of God the way he had tested our ideas of the *self* and *substance* by his rigorous principle of empiricism. He ends, to be sure, as a skeptic, but finally makes the telling point that "to whatever length any one may push his speculative principles of scepticism, he must act and live and converse like other men. . . . It is impossible for him to persevere in total scepticism, or make it appear in his conduct for a few hours."

Reading _____

Evil and the Proof from Design

Hume

If a person whom we shall suppose utterly unacquainted with the universe were assured that it were the production of a very good, wise, and powerful Being, however finite, he would, from his conjectures, form *beforehand* a different notion of it from what we find it to be by experience; nor would he ever imagine, merely from these attributes of the cause of which he is informed, that the effect could be so full of vice and misery and disorder, as it appears in this life. Supposing now that this person were brought into the world, still assured that it was the workmanship of such a sublime and benevolent Being, he might, perhaps, be surprised at the disappointment, but would never retract his former belief if founded on any very solid argument, since such a limited intelligence must be sensible of his own blindness and ignorance, and must allow that there may be many solutions of those phenomena which will forever escape his comprehension. But supposing, which is the real case with regard to man, that this creature is not antecedently convinced of a supreme intelligence, benevolent, and powerful, but is left to gather such a belief from the appearances of things—this entirely alters the case, nor will he ever find any reason for such a conclusion. He may be fully convinced of the narrow limits of his understanding, but this will not help him in forming an inference concerning the goodness of superior powers, since he must form that inference from what he knows, not from what he is ignorant of. The more you exaggerate his weakness and ignorance, the more diffident you render him, and give him the greater suspicion that such subjects are beyond the reach of his faculties. You are obliged, therefore, to reason with him merely from the known phenomena, and to drop every arbitrary supposition or conjecture.

Did I show you a house or palace where there was not one apartment convenient or agreeable, where the windows, doors, fires, passages, stairs, and the whole economy of the building were the source of noise, confusion, fatigue, darkness, and the extremes of heat and cold, you would certainly blame the contrivance, without any further examination. The architect would in vain display his subtilty, and prove to you that, if this door or that window were altered, greater ills would ensue. What he says may be strictly true: the alteration of one particular, while the other parts of the building remain, may only augment the inconveniences. But still you would assert in general that, if the architect had had skill and good intentions, he might have formed such a plan of the whole, and might have adjusted the parts in such a manner as would have remedied all or most of these inconveniences. His ignorance, or even your own ignorance of such a plan, will never convince you of the impossibility of it. If you find any inconveniences and deformities in the building, you will always, without entering into any detail, condemn the architect.

In short, I repeat the question: Is the world, considered in general and as it appears to us in this life, different from what a man or such a limited being would, *beforehand,* expect from a very powerful, wise, and benevolent Deity? It must be strange prejudice to assert the contrary. And from thence I conclude that, however consistent the world may be, allowing certain suppositions and conjectures with the idea of such a Deity, it can never afford us an inference concerning his existence. . . .

Look round this universe. What an immense profusion of beings, animated and organized, sensible and active! You admire this prodigious variety and fecundity. But inspect a little more narrowly these living existences, the only beings worth regarding. How hostile and destructive to each other! How insufficient all of them for their own happiness! How contemptible or odious to the spectator! The whole presents nothing but the idea of a blind nature, impregnated by a great vivifying principle, and pouring forth from her lap, without discernment or parental care, her maimed and abortive children! . . .

Epicurus' old questions are yet unanswered.

Is he [God] willing to prevent evil, but not able? then is he impotent. Is he able, but not willing? then is he malevolent. Is he both able and willing? whence then is evil?

From David Hume, *Dialogues concerning Natural Religion,* published 1779.

Kant

KANT'S CRITICISM OF TRADITIONAL PROOFS

With his critical estimate of the powers and scope of human reason, it was inevitable that Kant would reject the traditional proofs for the existence of God, namely, the *ontological, cosmological,* and *teleological* proofs. His argument against the *ontological* proof is that it is all a verbal exercise, for the essence of this proof is the assertion that since we have the idea of a most perfect being, it would be contradictory to say that such a being does not exist. Such a denial would be contradictory because the concept of a perfect being necessarily includes the predicate of *existence.* That is, a being that does not exist can hardly be considered a perfect being. But Kant argues that this line of reasoning is "taken from judgments, not from things and their existence," that the idea of God is made to have the predicate of existence by simply fashioning the concept in such a way that existence is made to be included in the idea of a perfect being. This argument nowhere indicates why it is necessary to have the subject, *God.* There would be a contradiction if a perfect being did exist and we denied that such a being was omnipotent. But to say that we avoid a contradiction by agreeing that a supreme being is omnipotent does not by itself demonstrate that such a being exists. Moreover, to deny that God exists is not

For biographical note on Kant, see p. 58.

Immanuel Kant. (*New York Public Library Picture Collection*)

simply to deny a predicate but to abandon the subject and thereby all the predicates that go with it, and "if we reject subject and predicate alike, there is no contradiction; for nothing is then left to be contradicted." Kant concluded, therefore, that "all the trouble and labour bestowed on the famous ontological or cartesian proof of the existence of a supreme being from concepts alone is trouble and labour wasted. A man might as well expect to become richer in knowledge by the aid of mere ideas as a merchant to increase his wealth by adding some noughts to his cash account."

Whereas the ontological proof begins with an idea (of a perfect being), the *cosmological* proof "takes its stand on experience" for it says that "I exist, therefore, an absolutely necessary being exists," on the assumption that if anything exists, an absolutely necessary being must also exist. The error of this argument, according to Kant, is that while it begins with experience, it soon moves beyond experience. Within the realm of sense experience it is legitimate to infer a cause for each event, but "the principle of causality has no meaning and no criterion for its application save only in the sensible world." Here is the direct application of Kant's critical method, for he argues that we cannot employ certain categories of the mind in trying to describe realities beyond sense experience. The cosmological argument cannot, therefore, securely lead us to a first cause of all things, for the most we can infer from our experience of things is a regulative idea of God. Whether there actually is such a being, a ground of all contingent things, raises the same question posed by the ontological argument, namely, whether we can successfully bridge the gap between our idea of a perfect being and demonstrative proof of its existence.

Similarly, the *teleological* argument begins with considerable persuasiveness, for it says that "in the world we everywhere find clear signs of an order in accordance with a determinate purpose. . . . The diverse things could not of themselves have cooperated, by so great a combination of diverse means, to the fulfillment of determinate final purposes, had they not been chosen and designed for these purposes by an ordering rational principle in conformity with underlying ideas." To this argument Kant replies that it may well be that our experience of order in the universe suggests an orderer, but order in the world does not demonstrate that the material stuff of the world could not exist without an orderer. The most this argument from design can prove, says Kant, "is an *architect* of the world who is always very much hampered by the adaptability of the material in which he works, not a *creator* of the world to whose idea everything is subject." To prove the existence of a creator leads us back to the cosmological argument with its idea of causality, but since we cannot use the category of causality beyond the things in experience, we are left simply with an idea of a first cause or creator, and this takes us back to the ontological argument, with its deficiencies. Kant's conclusion, therefore, is that we cannot use theoretical principles, which have no application beyond the field of sense experience, to demonstrate the existence of God.

It follows from Kant's critical remarks about the "proofs," however, that just as we cannot demonstrate God's existence, neither can we demonstrate that God does not exist. By pure reason alone we can neither prove nor disprove God's existence. If, therefore, the existence of God cannot be effectively dealt with by the theoretical reason, which Kant has gone to such lengths to show has relevance only in the realm of sense experience, some other aspect of reason must be considered as the source of the idea of God. Thus despite the inability of human reason to prove the existence of God, the idea of God has importance in Kant's philosophy.

Reading _____

Critique of Pure Reason
Kant

THE IMPOSSIBILITY OF THE PHYSICO-THEOLOGICAL [TELEOLOGICAL] PROOF

The chief points of the physico-theological proof are as follows: (1) In the world we everywhere find clear signs of an order in accordance with a determinate purpose, carried out with great wisdom; and this in a universe which is indescribably varied in content and unlimited in extent. (2) This purposive order is quite alien to the things of the world, and only belongs to them contingently; that is to say, the diverse things could not of themselves have co-operated, by so great a combination of diverse means, to the fulfilment of determinate final purposes, had they not been chosen and designed for these purposes by an ordering rational principle in conformity with underlying ideas. (3) There exists, therefore, a sublime and wise cause (or more than one), which must be the cause of the world not merely as a blindly working all-powerful nature, by *fecundity*, but as intelligence, through *freedom*. (4) The unity of this cause may be inferred from the unity of the reciprocal relations existing between the parts of the world, as members of an artfully arranged structure—inferred with certainty in so far as our observation suffices for its verification, and beyond these limits with probability, in accordance with the principles of analogy. . . .

The inference, therefore, is that the order and purposiveness everywhere observable throughout the world may be regarded as a completely contingent arrangement, and that we may argue to the existence of a cause *proportioned* to it. But the concept of this cause must enable us to know something quite *determinate* about it, and can therefore be no other than the concept of a being who possesses all might, wisdom, etc. in a word, all the perfection which is proper to an all-sufficient being. For the predicates—"very great," "astounding," "immeasurable" in power and excellence—give no determinate concept at all, and do not really tell us what the thing is in itself. They are only relative representations of the magnitude of the object, which the observer, in contemplating the world, compares with himself and with his capacity of comprehension, and which are equally terms of eulogy whether we be magnifying the object or be depreciating the observing subject in relation to that object. Where we are concerned with the magnitude (of the perfection) of a thing, there is no determinate concept except that which comprehends all possible perfection; and in that concept only the allness (*omnitudo*) of the reality is completely determined.

Now no one, I trust, will be so bold as to profess that he comprehends the relation of the magnitude of the world as he has observed it (alike as regards both extent and content) to omnipotence, of the world order to supreme wisdom, of the world unity to the absolute unity of its Author, etc. Physico-theology is therefore unable to give any determinate concept of the supreme cause of the world, and cannot therefore serve as the foundation of a theology which is itself in turn to form the basis of religion.

To advance to absolute totality by the empirical road is utterly impossible. None the less this is what is attempted in the physico-theological proof. What, then, are the means which have been adopted to bridge this wide abyss?

The physico-theological argument can indeed lead us to the point of admiring the greatness, wisdom, power, etc., of the Author of the world, but can take us no further. Accordingly, we then abandon the argument from empirical grounds of proof, and fall back upon the contingency which, in the first steps of the argument, we had inferred from the order and purposiveness of the world. With this contingency as our sole premise, we then advance, by means of transcendental concepts alone, to the existence of an absolutely necessary being, and (as a final step) from the concept of the absolute necessity of the first cause to the completely determinate or determinable concept of that necessary being, namely, to the concept of an all-embracing reality. Thus the physico-theological proof, failing in its undertaking, has in face of this difficulty suddenly fallen back upon the cosmological proof; and since the latter is only a disguised ontological proof, it has really achieved its purpose by pure reason alone—although at the start it disclaimed all kinship with pure reason and professed to establish its conclusions on convincing evidence derived from experience.

Thus the physico-theological proof of the existence of an original or supreme being rests upon the cosmological proof, and the cosmological upon the ontological. And since, besides these three, there is no other path open to speculative reason, the ontological proof from pure concepts of reason is the only possible one, if indeed any proof of a proposition so far exalted above all empirical employment of the understanding is possible at all.

From Immanuel Kant, *Critique of Pure Reason,* trans. Norman Kemp Smith, St. Martin's, Macmillan, London, 1969.

Pascal

BETTING WITHOUT REALLY LOSING

Born in France, Blaise Pascal (1623–1662) was a brilliant and inventive thinker whose scientific work has relevance even today in some areas. He is considered the founder of the modern theory of probability, an outgrowth of his genius in mathematics. In physics, his experimentation with vacuums and atmospheric pressure led to his invention of the syringe and the hydraulic press. He designed and helped to construct a workable calculating machine. But in spite of these and other extraordinary achievements, he is most widely known as a religious philosopher and the author of the celebrated book *Pensées*. He became caught up in some theological controversies of his time to which he contributed some spirited arguments which can be found in his other nonscientific book called *The Provincial Letters*. Pascal was chronically in bad health and eventually entered the Convent of Port Royal in 1654. His *Pensées* is a sustained exploration of the inner spiritual life of human beings, and it is in this book that his well-known argument for the existence of God, which he called "The Wager," is found. After a long and painful illness, Pascal died in 1662 at the early age of thirty-nine.

Pascal did not believe that it is possible to arrive at a rational proof for the existence of God. He nevertheless had a profound religious faith. He sought to make the most of his conviction that "the heart has its reasons of which the reason knows nothing." His argument is relatively simple in spite of his speaking of the odds of winning or losing as measured by infinity and finitude, respectively. Whatever you say about God's existence, you are already committed to a wager, one way or another. What, then, is the best way to bet? He says, "You have two things to lose [if you bet against the existence of God]: the true and the good. . . . If you win [that is, if you bet that God exists] you win everything; if you lose you lose nothing." Why is it that you cannot lose and that you win everything? Pascal's answer is that if you believe that God exists and this turns out to be true, you will achieve eternal happiness. Moreover, what harm can you suffer if you bet this way? By doing so, "you will," says Pascal, "be faithful, honest, humble, grateful, full of good works, a sincere, true friend." You will win all this even if it turns out that God does not exist. Therefore, in this sense you lose nothing, not even your integrity of "reason," because "since you must necessarily choose, your reason is no more affronted by choosing one rather than the other."

QUESTIONS FOR REVIEW AND DISCUSSION

1. What is the major difference between the way Anselm and Aquinas go about trying to prove the existence of God?

2. In what way did Hume criticize the proof for the existence of God that is based on the notion that the orderly universe obviously requires a "designer." (Refer to Paley's analogy of the watchmaker.)
3. What, in simple terms, is Kant's criticism of any of the traditional proofs for the existence of God. (Refer to Kant's distinction between the phenomenal and noumenal worlds.)
4. In what way did Pascal argue that a person cannot really lose the wager that God exists?

Elementary particles. (*Argonne National Laboratory*)

P A R T   F I V E

Metaphysics
What Is There?

There is an infinite number of atoms and they are invisible on account of their size. The material of the atoms is packed entirely close and can be called what is. . . . .

Leucippus (fifth century B.C.)
From Simplicius, *Commentary on Aristotle*

It seems probable to me that God in the beginning formed matter in solid, massy, hard, impenetrable, moveable particles [atoms] so very hard, as never to wear or break in pieces; no ordinary power being able to divide what God Himself made one. . . . .

Sir Isaac Newton
Mathematical Principles (1686)

Modern experimental physics has developed methods of breaking up the nucleus of the atom. . . . .

Albert Einstein
Evolution of Physics (1938)

The term "metaphysics" is the title which an ancient editor gave to a collection of Aristotle's essays. Because this book of essays, which Aristotle had called *First Philosophy*, came after his other books covering the biological and physical sciences, the editor labeled it *meta* (the Greek word meaning "after") physics. But *meta* also means "beyond," and so the term "metaphysics" came to refer to the subject matter or reality beyond physical nature or beyond the things we see. Actually, the distinction between science and metaphysics is not always a sharp one. Both science and metaphysics seek knowledge. But metaphysics pursues a kind of knowledge that is not limited to any one particular science. Instead, the metaphysician turns his attention to broad questions which are raised in his mind by our daily experiences. What every metaphysician tries to do is to form a comprehensive view of the whole world and then organize this view into a system of ideas or concepts. Just why anyone would want to engage in constructing such vast systems of thought will become clearer as we consider the major elements of metaphysics.

THE ELEMENTS OF METAPHYSICS

Knowledge for Its Own Sake

Most of our knowledge has some practical application. The study of ethics helps us lead a good life, religion attempts to provide our lives with meaning, politics enables our communities to flourish, and the sciences help us to control nature and produce things for our health, safety, and survival. But what about metaphysics? There is a deep human urge to understand how we fit into the universe. Indeed, in the first sentence of his *Metaphysics* Aristotle says that "all men by nature desire to know." And we want to know things which do not have immediate practical use, "for even apart from their usefulness, they are loved for themselves."

We enjoy the things we see. The variety of things in nature is a matter of fascination to us. Animals see things too, but their reaction to these things is different from ours. We want not only to sense things, but also to understand everything about them. That is why we pursue a special kind of knowledge, because, as Aristotle says, "we do not regard any of the senses as Wisdom; yet surely these [senses] give the most authoritative knowledge of particulars. But they do not tell us the 'why' of anything—e.g., why fire is hot; they only say *that* it is hot." It could be argued that to discover why something happens and not only that it happens can have practical applications; for example, the discovery of why atoms behave the way they do can lead to harnessing atomic energy. But the motivation to pursue metaphysical knowledge is simply a quest for knowledge for its own sake. This pursuit satisfies man's wonder "in order to know, and not for any utilitarian end," for this knowledge, says Aristotle, "alone exists for its own sake."

What Is There?

From the earliest times, philosophers reflected on the question "What is there?" Sometimes they rephrased the question to ask "What is real?" or "What really is?" Their concern was not simply to make a list, an inventory, of all the things in nature. They were puzzled by the fact that things come and go, that they come into being, exist, and then cease to be. But even before asking where things come from and where they go, the question of what anything really is had to be faced. For example, Lucretius describes in his poem *On the Nature of Things* how our senses deceive us when we look on a solid white mass on a distant hill: "Often the fleecy flocks cropping the glad pasture on a hill creep on whither each is called and tempted by the grass bejewelled with fresh dew, and the lambs fed full gambol and butt playfully; yet all this seems blurred to us from afar, and to lie like a white mass on a green hill." What appears to be a white mass from a distance turns out to be a flock of sheep.

Could this also be the case with everything which to our senses appears to be solid? What is a lump of sugar? It can be described as white, hard, and sweet. It may be said that the lump of sugar *is* all these adjectives. But would you have sugar if you put together white, hard, and sweet? These adjectives do not exist as such by themselves. They are adjectives requiring a subject, or, as metaphysicians say, they are secondary qualities requiring a primary quality. *Something* must be white, hard, and sweet. This would mean that secondary qualities do not exist in the same way as primary qualities do. If the sheep were scattered, let's say by a wolf, the solid white mass on the hill would disappear. If the sugar lump were melted, its color and hardness would disappear. In these cases, would the sheep and the sugar disappear or only some of the qualities and adjectives? If, now, we ask "What is there?" or "What really is?" the answer is not all that obvious. Metaphysics focuses finally on the question "What does it mean for something to be?" What, in short, is being? Metaphysics is the study of being and its principles or causes.

One and the Many

Another way to address the question "What is there?" is to consider the relationship between the one and the many. We see many human beings, but they all share one thing in common, namely, their *humanness*. There are many trees, but they all share in what we know as *tree*. We have seen in an earlier chapter that Plato thought he solved this problem of the one and the many by saying that the many are temporary and pale copies of the One, which he called "Idea" or "Form." Only the Forms have real being, while the many have a temporary existence. According to this view, there are two worlds, the world of the many, which is the world we move around in, and the world of Ideas and Forms.

Earlier philosophers, in the fifth century B.C., such as Leucippus and Democritus, took quite a different view. They said that the many, by which they meant every conceivable thing in nature, were made of one thing, namely, matter, which they described as small irreducible particles that they called "atoms." In this view, the many are simply a wide variety of combinations or arrangements of the one. Everything in nature is reducible to these constituent particles. So, although there are many things in the world, they are all reducible to one kind of thing, namely, atoms, or matter. This seemed to be too simple an explanation for some, who thought, as Descartes did, that there are at least two basic substances at the heart of reality. Descartes called these two substances "thought" and "extension," or mind and body. His view further complicated matters, for the problem now was how to explain the relationship between mind and body or between soul and body.

Earlier, Aristotle had dealt with this problem in a somewhat different way when he spoke of form and matter. Unlike the first atomists, Aristotle said that we never find matter by itself, nor do we (and here he disagreed with Plato) find form by itself. There can be no form, he said, without matter, nor matter without form. In the Middle Ages, Aquinas took this teaching of Aristotle to mean that when describing man we must account for both body and soul. The soul, said Aquinas, is the form of the body. There cannot be what we call "man" without both body and soul. Body, or matter, is what makes any particular person this specific individual, while the soul is what makes this individual a human being. The one, humanness, is in the many, that is, in each person; in metaphysical terms this means the universal (Man) is in each particular (James and Mary). The conclusion metaphysicians wish to draw from the discussion of the one and the many is that while the many do exist (briefly), only the one (the permanent reality) possesses true being.

Change

One of the earliest concerns of metaphysicians was how to account for change. We experience the fact of change in a wide variety of ways. Things change in quantity, in quality, and in their location. There is also change through generation, that is, being born or coming into being. There is also the change from an acorn to an oak tree, from a child to an adult. These are various forms of change, and each one requires a special explanation. But there was one major form of change that puzzled and still puzzles philosophers, and that is how anything comes to be. One philosopher, Parmenides, held the radical view that there cannot be any change or that what we call change is an illusion. His reasoning was actually very simple. True change, he said, must mean that something that was not at one time later comes into being. But how can something come into being? Only in one of two ways: either from something else or out of nothing. If it comes out of something else, it already existed; if out of nothing, then "nothing" must be treated as though it had some being; otherwise it would be absurd to think that something could come out of nothing, or out of nonbeing. Either way, then, the phrase "comes into being" must mean that what we call change refers to what already exists, in which case there is no real change. While this may be logically clear, it defies common sense.

There is, however, according to Aristotle, a way to account for change. The process of change, he said, expresses the movement from *potentiality* to *actuality*. We say, for example, that a great change takes place when a child grows up and is able to speak and play the piano. At one time the child could not do these things. Aristotle explains this mode of change by saying that the capacity to do these things was in the child as potentiality, just as the capacity to be a parent is potentially in the child. The child comes into being from other beings, from parents. He possesses potentially all the abilities he will eventually fulfill or bring into actuality. Change, for Aristotle, does not mean that something comes into being out of nothing; it simply means that in some way something can at one time be absent (Aristotle calls this "privation") but later come into full being, like the acorn "changing" into an oak. But this movement, or change, from potentiality to actuality requires further explanation. How is this change achieved? How can something which is only potential become actual? This leads us to consider further the causes of being.

The Causes of Being

One answer to the question of how things become what they are is to say that they are the product of *chance*. Or one can say, as Sir Isaac Newton did, that God created all the atoms in such a way as to make them function in an orderly manner. Or in a more philosophical vein one can say with Aristotle that the simple example of the creation of a statue can best explain how things come to be. He spoke of four "causes" which we will discuss more fully later. For the present, we will simply list them. First, there has to be the *idea* of something that you want to make; this is the pattern or form of the statue. Second, there must be some *material* out of which to make the statue. Third, there is the *activity* by which the sculptor actually carves out the pattern or form. Fourth, there is the *purpose* or end for which the statue is made. By itself, the marble would never become a statue; without the carving by the sculptor the marble would remain only potentially a statue. Some act is necessary to bring what is potential in the marble into actuality. Whether nature has "purposes" in the broad sense is debated by metaphysicians and scientists. But that some active power or cause is needed to explain motion or change in general seemed obvious to Aristotle, and this led him to his celebrated theory of the Unmoved Mover.

APPROACHES TO METAPHYSICS

Aristotle was the first philosopher to organize the subject of metaphysics into its systematic form. He provided a system of concepts by which to study the nature of Being, the nature of things and their causes. He spoke of *substance* as the primary essence of things, but also about *matter* and *form,* the phenomenon of *change* in terms of his famous "four causes," the significant differences between *potentiality* and actuality, and his notion of the "unmoved mover."

Lucretius, the Latin poet, took the ideas of *Leucippus* and *Democritus* and composed an impressive poem, *On the Nature of Things,* in which he tries to show in considerable detail that everything, including mind as well as body, consists of matter, or *atoms.* He describes the atoms as hard, indivisible, and eternal. They come in different shapes and sizes, and this is what accounts for the difference between the mind (composed of the smallest, smoothest, and swiftest atoms) and the body and other things (composed of larger and more jagged atoms with hooks which form the larger things). There is no purpose in the universe, since all things come into being through random collision of atoms caused by a "swerve" as the atoms fall in space. In the twentieth century, *Sir Arthur Eddington* of Cambridge University described all things in essentially the same manner as Democritus did, but instead of speaking of atoms or matter, he refers to "electric charges moving about with great speed." What makes this interesting is that today matter and energy are thought by scientists to be interchangeable ways of accounting for the basic stuff of reality.

By contrast, *Bishop Berkeley* proposed the astonishing theory that matter does not exist, that consciousness, idea, is the basic reality. For something to be, it is necessary for it to be perceived by some conscious being. But what if you are at some time away from your library and not perceiving your books— do they still exist? Yes, says Berkeley, because God perceives them. Here, then, is the contrast between Democritus and Berkeley, between materialism and idealism. Some wag pointed out that the idealist says, "No matter" while the materialist says, "Never mind."

23

Causes of Being

Aristotle

Aristotle's answer to the question "What is there?" represents an interesting contrast to his predecessors. The earliest philosophers said that what "really is" is matter. While they defined matter in various ways, Democritus offered the most influential version of this theory with his notion of atoms moving in space. Plato, Aristotle's teacher, argued that Ideas, or Forms, are the true reality. In Book I of his *Metaphysics* Aristotle traces the development of the various conceptions of matter and of Plato's Forms and concludes that although these earlier theories had some plausible insights, they were, nevertheless, inadequate. They were inadequate primarily because they did not offer a full enough explanation of the process of *change*. In particular, Aristotle felt that they had overlooked the causes of motion, that is, how things come into being and why they behave the way they do. By "motion" Aristotle meant change, and change, he thought, must be explained in terms of "causes" or "becauses." Aristotle concluded that it is not enough to say that all things consist of matter and possess form; what needs to be added, he said, is how things in nature become what they are and for what purpose they strive.

KNOWLEDGE FOR ITS OWN SAKE

In his work entitled *Metaphysics* (a term that indicates the position of this work among his other writings, namely, *beyond*, or coming after, *Physics*) Aristotle develops what he called the science of "first philosophy." Throughout his *Metaphysics*, he is concerned with a type of knowledge that he thought could be rightly called "wisdom." He begins this work with the statement "All men by nature desire to know." This innate desire, says Aristotle, is not only a desire to know in order to do or make something. In addition to these pragmatic motives, there is in man a desire to know certain kinds of things simply

For biographical note on Aristotle, see p. 29.

Aristotle. (*Culver Productions*)

for the sake of knowing. An indication of this, says Aristotle, is "the delight
we take in our senses; for even apart from their usefulness they are loved for
themselves" inasmuch as our seeing "makes us know and brings to light
many differences between things."

There are different levels of knowledge. Some men know only what they experience through their senses, as, for example, when they know that fire is hot. But, says Aristotle, we do not regard what we know through the senses as wisdom. To be sure, our most authoritative knowledge of particular things is acquired through our senses. Still, this kind of knowledge tells us only the "that" of anything and not the "why"; it tells us, for example, *that* fire is hot but not *why*. Similarly, in medicine, some men know only *that* medicines heal certain illnesses. This knowledge, based on specific experiences, is, according to Aristotle, on a lower level than the knowledge of the medical scientist who knows not only *that* a medicine will heal but knows also the reason *why*. In the various crafts, the master craftsmen "know in a truer sense and are wiser than the manual workers, because they know the *causes* of the things that are done."

Wisdom is therefore more than that kind of knowledge obtained from sensing objects and their qualities. It is even more than knowledge acquired from repeated experiences of the same kinds of things. Wisdom is similar to the knowledge possessed by the scientist who begins by looking at something, then repeats these sense experiences, and finally goes beyond sense experience by thinking about the causes of the objects of his experiences. There are as many sciences as there are definable areas of investigation, and Aristotle deals with many of them, including physics, ethics, politics, and aesthetics. In each case, the respective science is concerned with discovering the causes or reasons or principles underlying the activity of its special subject matter; thus, for example, in physics one asks what causes material bodies to move, in ethics what causes the good life, in politics what causes the good state, and in aesthetics what causes a good poem. Sciences differ not only in their subject matter but also in their relation to one another. Some sciences depend on others, such as when the physicist must rely on the science of mathematics. In the hierarchy of sciences, Aristotle says that "the science which knows to what end each thing must be done is the most authoritative of the sciences, and more authoritative than any ancillary science." In addition to the specific sciences, then, there is another science, first philosophy, or what we now call "metaphysics," which goes beyond the subject matter of the other sciences and is concerned with "first principles and causes." These "first principles and causes" are the true foundation of *wisdom,* for they give us knowledge not of any particular object or activity, but rather knowledge of true reality.

Metaphysics deals with knowledge at the highest level of abstraction. This knowledge is abstract because it is about what is universal instead of what is particular. Every science has its own level of abstraction inasmuch as it deals with the first principles and causes of its subject matter, such as when the physicist talks about the principles of motion in general as distinguished from describing the motion of this planet or that pendulum. Wisdom has to do, then, with the abstract levels of knowledge and not with the levels of visible things, for, as Aristotle says, "sense-perception is common to all, and therefore easy and no mark of Wisdom." True wisdom, first philosophy, or metaphysics is the most abstract and also the most exact of all the sciences because it tries to discover the truly first principles from which even the first principles of the various sciences are derived. True knowledge is therefore found in what is most knowable, and, says Aristotle, "the first principles and the causes are most knowable . . . and from these, all other things come to be known . . ." We are led, then, to consider more specifically the subject matter of metaphysics.

THE PROBLEM OF METAPHYSICS DEFINED

The various sciences seek to find the first principles and causes of specific kinds of things, such as material bodies, the human body, the state, a poem, and so on. Unlike these sciences, which ask "What is such-and-such a thing like and why?" metaphysics asks a far more general question, a question that each science must ultimately take into account, namely, "What does it mean to be anything whatsoever?" What, in short, does it mean *to be?* It was precisely this question that concerned Aristotle in his *Metaphysics*, making metaphysics for him "the science of any existent, as existent." The problem of metaphysics as he saw it was therefore the study of being and its "principles" and "causes."

Aristotle's metaphysics was to a considerable extent an outgrowth of his views on logic and his interest in biology. From the viewpoint of his logic, "to be" meant for him to be something that could be accurately defined and that could therefore become the subject of discourse. From the point of view of his interest in biology, he was disposed to think of "to be" as something implicated in a dynamic process. "To be,"as Aristotle saw the matter, always meant to be *something*. Hence all existence is individual and has a determinate nature. All the categories Aristotle dealt with in his logical works, categories (or predicates) such as *quality, relation, posture, place,* and so on, presuppose some subject to which these predicates can apply. This subject to which all the categories apply Aristotle called "substance" *(ouisa).* To be, then, is to be a particular kind of substance. Also, "to be" means to be a substance as the product of a dynamic process. In this way, metaphysics is concerned with *being* (that is, existing substances) and its *causes* (that is, the processes by which substances come into being).

SUBSTANCE AS THE PRIMARY ESSENCE OF THINGS

A major clue to what is meant by substance is discovered, Aristotle thought, in the way we know a thing. Having in mind again the categories or predicates, he says that we know a thing better when we know *what it is* than when we know the color, size, or posture it has. The mind separates a thing from all its qualities and focuses on what a thing really is, on its *essential nature*. We recognize that all *men* are men in spite of their different sizes, colors, or ages. *Something* about each concretely different man makes him a man in spite of the unique characteristics that make him this particular man. At this point, Aristotle would readily agree that these special characteristics (categories, predicates) also exist, have some kind of being. But the being of these characteristics is not the central object of metaphysical inquiry.

The central concern of metaphysics is the study of substance, the essential nature of a thing. In this view, substance means "that which is not asserted of a subject but of which everything else is asserted." Substance is what we know as basic about something, *after* which we can say other things about *it*. Whenever we define something, we get at its essence *before* we can say anything about it, such as when we speak of a large table or a healthy man. Here table and man are understood in their "essence," in what makes them a table or a man, before they are understood as large or healthy. To be sure, we can know only specific and determinate things, actual individual tables and men. At the same time, the essence, or substance, of a table or a man has its existence separate from its categories or its qualities. This does not mean that a substance is ever in fact found existing separately from its qualities. Still, if we can know the essence of a thing, "tableness" let us say, as "separable" from these particular qualities, round, small, and brown, there must be some universal essence that is found wherever one sees a table, and this essence or substance must be independent of its particular qualities inasmuch as the essence is the same even though in the case of each actual table the qualities are different.

What Aristotle seems to be saying is that a thing is more than the sum of its particular qualities. There is something "beneath" *(sub stance)* all the qualities; thus any specific thing is a combination of qualities, on the one hand, and a substratum to which the qualities apply, on the other. With these distinctions in mind, Aristotle was led, as was Plato before him, to consider just how this essence, or universal, was related to the particular thing. What, in short, makes a substance a substance; is it *matter* as a substratum or is it *form?*

MATTER AND FORM

Although Aristotle distinguished between matter and form, he nevertheless said that we never find matter without form or form without matter in nature. Everything that exists is some concrete individual thing, and every *thing* is a unity of matter and form. Substance, therefore, is a composite of form and matter.

Plato, it will be recalled, argued that Ideas or Forms, such as Man or Table, have a separate existence. Similarly, he treated *space* as the material substratum or the stuff out of which individual things were made. For Plato, then, this primary stuff of space was molded by the eternally existing Forms into individual shapes. This was Plato's way of explaining how there could be many individual things that all have one and the same, that is, universal, nature or essence while still being individual. This universal, Plato said, is the Form, which exists eternally and is separate from any particular thing and is found in each thing only because the thing (this table) *participates* in the Form (tableness, or Ideal Table).

Aristotle rejected Plato's explanation of the universal Forms, rejecting specifically the notion that the Forms existed separately from individual things. Of course, Aristotle did agree that there are universals, that universals such as Man and Table are more than merely subjective notions. Indeed, Aristotle recognized that without the theory of universals, there could be no scientific knowledge, for then there would be no way of saying something about all members of a particular class. What makes scientific knowledge effective is that it discovers classes of objects (for example, a certain form of human disease), so that whenever an individual falls into this class, other facts can be assumed also to be relevant. These classes, then, are not merely mental fictions but do in fact have objective reality. But, said Aristotle, their reality is to be found nowhere else than in the individual things themselves. What purpose, he asked, could be served by assuming that the universal Forms existed separately? If anything, this would complicate matters, inasmuch as everything, that is, not only individual things but also their relationships, would have to be reduplicated in the world of Forms.

Moreover, Aristotle was not convinced that Plato's theory of Forms could help us know things any better, saying that "they help in no wise towards the knowledge of other things. . . ." Since presumably the Forms are motionless, Aristotle concluded that they could not help us understand things as we know them, which are full of motion, nor could they, being immaterial, explain objects of which we have sense impressions. Again, how could the immaterial Forms be related to any particular thing? That things *participate* in the Forms was not a satisfactory explanation for Aristotle, leading him to conclude that "to say that they are patterns and that other things share in them, is to use empty words and poetical metaphors."

When we use the words "matter" and "form" to describe any specific thing, we seem to have in mind the distinction between what something is made of and what it is made into. This, again, disposes our minds to assume that what things are made of, matter, exists in some primary and unformed state until it is made into a thing. But again Aristotle argues that we shall not find anywhere such a thing as "primary matter," that is, matter without form. Consider the sculptor who is about to make a statue of Venus out of marble. He will never find marble without some form; it will always be this marble or that, a square piece or an irregular one, but he will always work with a piece in which form and matter are already combined. That he will give it a different form is another question. The question here is "How does one thing become another thing?" What, in short, is the nature of *change?*

THE PROCESS OF CHANGE: THE FOUR CAUSES

In the world around us we see things constantly changing. Change is one of the basic facts of our experience. For Aristotle, the word "change" means many things, including motion, growth, decay, generation, and corruption. Some of these changes are *natural*, whereas others are the products of *human art.* Things are always taking on new form; new life is born and statues are made. Because change always involves taking on new form, several questions can be asked concerning the process of change. Of anything, says Aristotle, we can ask four questions, namely, (1) What is it? (2) What is it made of? (3) By what is it made? and (4) For what end is it made? The responses to these four questions represent Aristotle's four *causes.* Although the word "cause" refers in modern use primarily to an event prior to an effect, for Aristotle it meant an explanation. His four causes represent therefore a broad pattern or framework for the total explanation of anything or everything. Taking an object of art, for example, four causes might be (1) a statue (2) of marble (3) by a sculptor (4) for a decoration. Distinguished from objects produced by human art, there are those things which are produced by *by nature.* Although nature does not, according to Aristotle, have "purposes" in the sense of "the reason for," it does always and everywhere have "ends" in the sense of having built-in ways of behaving. For this reason, seeds sprout and roots go down (not up!) and plants grow and in this process of change move toward their "end," that is, their distinctive function or way of being. In nature, then, change will involve these same four elements. Aristotle's *four causes* are therefore (1) the *formal* cause, which determines what a thing is, (2) the *material* cause, or that out of which it is made, (3) the *efficient* cause, by what a thing is made, and (4) the *final* cause, the "end" for which it is made.

Aristotle looked at life through the eyes of a biologist. For him, nature is *life.* All things are in motion, in the process of becoming and dying away. The process of reproduction was for him a clear example of the power inherent in all living things to initiate change and to reproduce their kind. Summarizing his causes, Aristotle said that "all things that come to be come to be by some agency and from something, and come to be something." From this biological viewpoint, Aristotle was able to elaborate his notion that form and matter never exist separately. In nature, generation of new life involves, according to Aristotle, first of all an individual who already possesses the specific form which the offspring will have (the male parent); there must then be the matter capable of being the vehicle for this form (this matter being contributed by the female parent); from this comes a new individual with the same specific form. In this example, Aristotle indicates that change does not involve bringing together formless matter with matterless form. On the contrary, change occurs always in and to something that is already a combination of form and matter and that is on its way to becoming something new or different.

POTENTIALITY AND ACTUALITY

All things, said Aristotle, are involved in processes of change. Each thing possesses a power to become what its form has set as its end. There is in all things a dynamic power of striving toward their "end." Some of this striving is toward external objects, such as when a man builds a house. But there is also the striving to achieve ends that pertain to one's internal nature, such as when a man fulfills his nature as a man by the act of thinking. This self-contained end of anything Aristotle called its "entelechy."

That things have ends led Aristotle to consider the distinction between *potentiality* and *actuality*. This distinction is used by Aristotle to explain the processes of change and development. If the *end* of an acorn is to be a tree, in some way the acorn is only potentially a tree but not actually so at this time. A fundamental mode of change, then, is the change from potentiality to actuality. But the chief significance of this distinction is that Aristotle argues for the priority of actuality over potentiality. That is, although something actual emerges from the potential, there could be no movement from potential to actual if there were not first of all something actual. A boy is potentially a man, but before there could be a boy with that potentiality there had to be prior to him an actual man.

Since all things in nature are similar to the relation of a boy to a man or an acorn to a tree, Aristotle was led to see in nature different levels of being. If everything were involved in change, in generation and corruption, everything would partake of potentiality. But, as we have seen, for there to be something potential, there must already be something actual. To explain the existence of the world of potential things, Aristotle thought it was necessary to assume the existence of some actuality at a level above potential or perishing things. He was led to the notion of a Being that is pure actuality, without any potentiality, at the highest level of being. Since change is a kind of motion, Aristotle saw the visible world as one composed of things in motion. But motion, a mode of change, involves potentiality. Things are potentially in motion but must be moved by something that is actually in motion. Again, to explain motion ultimately led Aristotle to speak of the "Unmoved Mover."

THE UNMOVED MOVER

For Aristotle, the Unmoved Mover did not mean the same thing as a *first* mover, as though motion could be traced back to a *time* when motion began. Nor was the Unmoved Mover considered by him a *creator* in the sense of later theology. From his previous distinction between potentiality and actuality, Aristotle concluded that the only way to explain how motion or change can occur is to assume that something actual is *logically* prior to whatever is potential. The fact of change must imply the existence of something actual, something *purely* actual without any mixture of potentiality. This Mover is not, according to Aristotle, an *efficient* cause in the sense of exerting a power or force, or as expressing a *will*. Such acts would imply potentiality, such as when one says that God "willed" to create the world. This would mean that *before* God created the world, he was potentially capable or intended to create it.

Aristotle did not think of the Unmoved Mover as a Being that *thinks* or prescribes *purposes* for the world. In a sense, the Unmoved Mover does not know anything precisely because it is not a kind of being as much as it is a way of explaining the fact of motion. All nature is full of striving toward fulfilling all its particular entelechies. Each thing is aiming at perfecting its possibilities and its *end*, aiming, that is, at becoming the perfect tree, the perfectly good man, and so on. The aggregate of all these strivings constitutes the large-scale processes of the world order so that it can be said that all reality is in the process of change, moving from its potentialities and possibilities to the ultimate perfection of these potentialities. To explain this comprehensive or general motion, to make it intelligible, Aristotle referred to the Unmoved Mover as the "reason for" or the "principle of" motion. For this reason, the Unmoved Mover stood for him as the actual and, because there is here no potentiality, the *eternal* principle of motion. Since this explanation of motion implies an eternal activity, then, there was never a "time" when there was not a world of things in process. For this reason, too, Aristotle denied that there was a "creation" in time.

Although there are passages in Aristotle that have a distinctly religious and theistic flavor, the dominant mood of his thought on this matter is less religious than it is scientific. Still, to speak of an Unmoved Mover involved Aristotle in certain metaphorical language. In explaining how an Unmoved Mover can "cause" motion, he compared it to a beloved who "moves" the lover just by being the object of love, by the power of attraction and not by force. In a more technical way, Aristotle considered the Unmoved Mover as the *form* and the world as the substance. From the point of view of his four causes, Aristotle considered the Mover as the *final* cause, in the way that the form of man is in the boy, directing the motion of his change toward a final, that is, fixed or appropriate, natural end. By being a final cause, the Unmoved Mover thereby, in relation to the world, becomes also *efficient* cause, through the power of attraction, by being desired and loved, by inspiring the striving toward natural ends, a process that goes on eternally.

What in Aristotle's thought was the unconscious principle of motion and immanent form of the world, the Unmoved Mover, became, especially at the hands of Aquinas in the thirteenth century, the philosophical description of the God of Christianity. Aristotle's Unmoved Mover could be said to be pure understanding, pure *nous*, and since it must think the best, it "thinks itself . . . and its thinking is a thinking of thinking . . . throughout all eternity." Such a "God" is not the religious God who becomes involved in the affairs of man. Aristotle's "God" is immanent in the world, making the world an intelligible order.

Reading

Causes and Purpose in Nature
Aristotle

WISDOM THE KNOWLEDGE OF CAUSES

All men by their very nature feel the urge to know. That is clear from the pleasure we take in our senses, for their own sake, irrespective of their utility.
Above all, we value sight; disregarding its practical uses, we prefer it, I
believe, to every other sense, even when we have no material end in view.
Why? Because sight is the principal source of knowledge and reveals many
differences between one object and another.

Animals are endowed with sense-perception, from which some of them
derive memory; others do not, and are therefore less intelligent and less able
to learn than the former. Some animals, though possessed of memory, are
unable to hear sounds and therefore cannot be taught; these creatures, which
include bees and suchlike, are said to have instinct.

Brute beasts live by sense-impression and memory with but a small share
in connected experience, whereas the human race lives by art and science.
Man derives experience through memory: his several acts of memory give rise
to a single effect which we call experience. The latter is easily confused with
art and science, which are, however, its results; for as Polus rightly says:
"Experience produced science, inexperience chance." You have art where from
many notions of experience there proceeds one universal judgment applying
in all similar cases. Thus, the judgment that a certain remedy was good for
Callias, Socrates, and various other persons suffering from a particular disease
is a matter of experience; but the judgment that such and such a remedy is
good for all men of similar constitution (e.g., phlegmatic or bilious) suffering
from such and such a disease (a burning fever, for instance) belongs to science.

From a practical point of view, certainly, there is little to choose between
art and experience: an experienced man, in fact, is more successful than one
who has theory alone. Knowledge and proficiency, however, are thought to
belong more properly to art than to experience, and artists are considered
wiser than those who are limited to experience. This suggests that Wisdom is
always proportionate to the degree of knowledge; for an artist knows the
cause of a thing, while the other does not. He who has only experience knows
that a thing *is* so, but not *why* it is so, whereas an artist knows the why and
wherefore. This is why a master craftsman in any trade is more highly
esteemed, is considered to know more, and therefore to be wiser than an artisan, because he understands the reason for what is done. He is said to be
wiser, not indeed for what he can do, but on account of his theoretical knowledge. The artisan's work may be compared in one sense with the unconscious
activity of certain inanimate agents like fire, excepting that the latter operate
according to their nature whereas the artisan does so by habit.

Generally speaking, the proof of a man's knowledge or ignorance is his ability or inability to teach; and we therefore hold that knowledge consists in art rather than in experience, for the artist is capable of transmitting his knowledge to others, whereas the man of simple experience cannot.

Wisdom, again, is not to be identified with sense-perception which, though it is our primary source of knowledge, can never tell us *why* anything is so (e.g., why fire is hot), but only that it *is* so. In the early stages of civilization a pioneer in any field which required the exercise of something more than sense-perception was probably admired by his fellow men not so much because his discovery was useful as because he appeared a wise man and superior to themselves. It is also probable that, as the horizons of knowledge were gradually enlarged, exponents of the fine arts were invariably considered wiser than those of the useful arts, whose knowledge was directed to mere utility; and it was only when these two kinds of art had been established that there arose others which aimed neither at utility nor at sensible satisfaction. These theoretical arts, moreover, were evolved in places where men had plenty of free time: mathematics, for example, originated in Egypt, where a priestly caste enjoyed the necessary leisure.

The difference between art, science, and kindred mental activities has already been explained in the *Ethics*. My present point is that all agree that what we ordinarily call Wisdom is concerned with first causes or principles. Hence, as I said earlier, we consider an experienced man wiser than one who has only sensation, an artist than a merely experienced man, a mastercraftsman than an artisan, and the speculative sciences as more learned than the productive. Thus it is clear that Wisdom is the knowledge of certain principles and causes.

From *Aristotle's Metaphysics*, ed. trans. John Warrington, intro. by Sir David Ross, Everyman's Library, E. P. Dutton, New York, 1956.

Reading ———————————————————————————

Physics
Aristotle

THE FOUR CAUSES (OR "BECAUSES")

We have next to consider in how many senses "because" may answer the question "why." For we aim at understanding, and since we never reckon that we understand a thing till we can give an account of its "how and why," it is clear that we must look into the "how and why" of things coming into existence and passing out of it, or more generally into the essential constituents of physical change, in order to trace back any object of our study to the principles so ascertained.

Well then, (1) the existence of *material* for the generating process to start from (whether specifically or generically considered) is one of the essential factors we are looking for. Such is the bronze for the statue, or the silver for the phial. (Material *aitia*.) Then, naturally, (2) the thing in question cannot be there unless the material has actually received the *form* or characteristics of the type, conformity to which brings it within the definition of the thing we say it is, whether specifically or generically. (Formal *aitia*.) Then again, (3) there must be something to initiate the process of the change or its cessation when the process is completed, such as the act of a voluntary agent (of the smith, for instance), or the father who begets a child; or more generally the prime, conscious or unconscious, *agent* that produces the effect and starts the material on its way to the product, changing it from what it was to what it is to be. (Efficient *aitia*.) And lastly, (4) there is the *end* or purpose, for the sake of which the process is initiated, as when a man takes exercise for the sake of his health. "Why does he take exercise?" we ask. And the answer "Because he thinks it good for his health" satisfies us. (Final *aitia*.) Then there are all the intermediary agents, which are set in motion by the prime agent and make for the goal, as means to the end. Such are the reduction of superfluous flesh and purgation, or drugs and surgical instruments, as means to health. For both actions and tools may be means, or "media," through which the efficient cause reaches the end aimed at.

This is a rough classification of the causal determinants (*aitiai*) of things; but it often happens that, when we specify them, we find a number of them coalescing as joint factors in the production of a single effect, and that not merely incidentally; for it is *qua* statue that the statue depends for its existence alike on the bronze and on the statuary. The two, however, do not stand on the same footing, for one is required as the material and the other as initiating the change.

Also, it can be said of certain things indifferently that either of them is the cause or the effect of the other. Thus we may say that a man is in fine condition "because" he has been in training, or that he has been in training "because" of the good condition he expected as the result. But one is the cause as aim (final *aitia*) and the other as initiating the process (efficient *aitia*).

Again, the same cause is often alleged for precisely opposite effects. For if its presence causes one thing, we lay the opposite to its account if it is absent. Thus, if the pilot's presence would have brought the ship safe to harbour, we say that he caused its wreck by his absence.

But in all cases the essential and causal determinants we have enumerated fall into four main classes. For letters are the causes of syllables, and the material is the cause of manufactured articles, and fire and the like are causes of physical bodies, and the parts are causes of the whole, and the premises are causes of the conclusion, in the sense of that out of which these respectively are made; but of these things some are causes in the sense of the *substratum* (e.g., the parts stand in this relation to the whole), others in the sense of the essence—the whole or the synthesis or the form. And again, the fertilizing sperm, or the physician, or briefly the voluntary or involuntary *agent* sets going or arrests the transformation or movement. And finally, there is the goal or *end* in view, which animates all the other determinant factors as the best they can attain to; for the attainment of that "for the sake of which" anything exists or is done is its final and best possible achievement (though of course "best" in this connexion means no more than "taken to be the best").

PURPOSE AS "FINAL CAUSE" IN NATURE

We must now consider why Nature is to be ranked among causes that are final, that is to say purposeful; and further we must consider what is meant by "necessity" when we are speaking of Nature. For thinkers are forever referring things to necessity as a cause, and explaining that, since hot and cold and so forth are what they are, this or that exists or comes into being "of necessity"; for even if one or another of them alleges some other cause, such as "Sympathy and Antipathy" or "Mind," he straight away drops it again, after a mere acknowledgement.

So here the question rises whether we have any reason to regard Nature as making for any goal at all, or as seeking any one thing as preferable to any other. Why not say, it is asked, that Nature acts as Zeus drops the rain, not to make the corn grow, but of necessity (for the rising vapour must needs be condensed into water by the cold, and must then descend, and incidentally, when this happens, the corn grows), just as, when a man loses his corn on the threshing-floor, it did not rain on purpose to destroy the crop, but the result was merely incidental to the raining? So why should it not be the same with natural organs like the teeth? Why should it not be a coincidence that the front teeth come up with an edge, suited to dividing the food, and the back ones flat and good for grinding it, without there being any design in the matter? And so with all other organs that seem to embody a purpose. In cases where a coincidence brought about such a combination as might have been arranged on purpose, creatures, it is urged, having been suitably formed by the operation of chance, survived; otherwise they perished, and still perish, as Empedocles says of his "man-faced oxen."

Such and suchlike are the arguments which may be urged in raising this problem; but it is impossible that this should really be the way of it. For all these phenomena and all natural things are either constant or normal, and this is contrary to the very meaning of luck or chance. No one assigns it to chance or to a remarkable coincidence if there is abundant rain in the winter, though he would if there were in the dog-days; and the other way about, if there were parching heat. Accordingly, if the only choice is to assign these occurrences either to coincidence or to purpose, and if in these cases chance coincidence is out of the question, then it must be purpose. But, as our opponents themselves would admit, these occurrences are all natural. There is purpose, then, in what is, and in what happens, in Nature.

Further, in any operation of human art, where there is an end to be achieved, the earlier and successive stages of the operation are performed for the purpose of realizing that end. Now, when a thing is produced by Nature, the earlier stages in every case lead up to the final development in the same way as in the operation of art, and *vice versa,* provided that no impediment balks the process. The operation is directed by a purpose; we may, therefore, infer that the natural process was guided by a purpose to the end that is realized. Thus, if a house were a natural product, the process would pass through the same stages that it in fact passes through when it is produced by art; and if natural products could also be produced by art, they would move along the same line that the natural process actually takes. We may therefore say that the earlier stages are for the purpose of leading to the later. Indeed, as a general proposition, the arts either, on the basis of Nature, carry things further than Nature can, or the imitate Nature. If, then, artificial processes are purposeful, so are natural processes too; for the relation of antecedent to consequent is identical in art and in Nature.

This principle comes out most clearly when we consider the other animals. For their doings are not the outcome of art (design) or of previous research or deliberation; so that some raise the question whether the works of spiders and ants and so on should be attributed to intelligence or to some similar faculty. And then, descending step by step, we find that plants too produce organs subservient to their perfect development—leaves, for instance, to shelter the fruit. Hence, if it is by nature and also for a purpose that the swallow makes her nest and the spider his web, and that plants make leaves for the sake of the fruit and strike down (and not up) with their roots in order to get their nourishment, it is clear that causality of the kind we have described is at work in things that come about or exist in the course of Nature.

Also, since the term "nature" is applied both to material and to form, and since it is the latter that constitutes the goal, and all else; is for the sake of that goal, it follows that the form is the final cause.

Now there are failures even in the arts (for writers make mistakes in writing and physicians administer the wrong dose); so that analogous failures in Nature may evidently be anticipated as possible. Thus, if in art there are cases in which the correct procedure serves a purpose, and attempts that fail are aimed at a purpose but miss it, we may take it to be the same in Nature, and monstrosities will be like failures of purpose in Nature. So if, in the primal combinations, such "ox-creatures" as could not reach an equilibrium and goal should appear, it would be by the miscarriage of some principle, as monstrous births are actually produced now by abortive developments of sperm. Besides, the sperm must precede the formation of the animal, and Empedocles' "primal all-generative" is no other than such sperm.

In plants, too, though they are less elaborately articulated, there are manifest indications of purpose. Are we to suppose, then, that as there were "ox-creatures man-faced" so also there were "vine-growths olive-bearing"? Incongruous as such a thing seems, it ought to follow if we accept the principle in the case of animals. Moreover, it ought still to be a matter of chance what comes up when you sow this seed or that.

In general, the theory does away with the whole order of Nature, and indeed with Nature's self. For natural things are exactly those which do move continuously, in virtue of a principle inherent in themselves, towards a determined goal; and the final development which results from any one such principle is not identical for any two species, nor yet is it any random result; but in each, there is always a tendency towards an identical result, if nothing interferes with the process. A desirable result and the means to it may also be produced by chance, as for instance we say it was "by luck" that the stranger came and ransomed the prisoner before he left, where the ransoming is done as if the man had come for that purpose, though in fact he did not. In this case the desirable result is incidental; for, as we have explained, chance is an incidental cause. But when the desirable result is effected invariably or normally, it is not an incidental or chance occurrence; and in the course of Nature the result always is achieved either invariably or normally, if nothing hinders. It is absurd to suppose that there is no purpose because in Nature we can never detect the moving power in the act of deliberation. Art, in fact, does not deliberate either, and if the shipbuilding art were incorporate in the timber, it would proceed by nature in the same way in which it now proceeds by art. If purpose, then, is inherent in art, so is it in Nature also. The best illustration is the case of a man being his own physician, for Nature is like that—agent and patient at once.

That Nature is a cause, then, and a goal-directed cause, is above dispute.

From Aristotle, *The Physics*, trans. Philip P. Wicksteed and Francis M. Cornford, vol. I, Loeb Classical Library, Harvard University Press.

QUESTIONS FOR REVIEW AND DISCUSSION

1. How did Aristotle describe the four causes?
2. Aristotle speaks of "matter" and "form." What does he mean by these terms, and how does he relate the two to each other? How does this relationship of form and matter differ from Plato's theory of Forms?
3. Aristotle tries to account for the process of change, either locomotion, that is, from here to there, or generation, as when bringing something into being, like a child's being born. Here Aristotle refers to "potentiality" and "actuality." Describe the process from potentiality to actuality. Having in mind this distinction, what is the relation between an acorn and an oak, or a fetus and a person?
4. What does Aristotle mean by the "Unmoved Mover," and why did he find it necessary to propose this idea?

24

Atoms and Space

Leucippus, Democritus and Eddington

Leucippus and Democritus

Leucippus and Democritus are renowned for their theory that all nature consists of *atoms* and the *void* (space). Although it is difficult to disentangle their individual contributions, it is agreed that Leucippus was the founder of the atomist theory and that Democritus supplied much of the elaboration of it. These two Greek philosophers lived in the fifth century B.C.; the life of Democritus spanned one hundred years (460–360) B.C.). In time, Democritus, because of his great learning, overshadowed Leucippus, to whom, nevertheless, goes the credit for the insight that everything is made of atoms moving in space. But since only some fragments of their writings are available, our selected reading will be taken from a poem written by the Roman philosopher Lucretius (98–55 B.C.) based on the atomic theory of Democritus and his successor Epicurus.

ATOMS AND THE VOID

The philosophy of atomism originated, according to Aristotle, as an attempt to overcome the logical consequences of the denial of space by earlier philosophers. Parmenides denied that there could be separate and discrete things because everywhere there was *being*, in which case the total reality would be One. Specifically, he denied the existence of nonbeing or the void, because to say that there *is* the void is to say that there *is something*. It is impossible, he thought, to say that there *is* nothing. Yet, in order to prove that there is motion and change, it is necessary to assume that there is empty space in which things can move. But empty space is nothing; yet to say that it *is* meant for Parmenides that space is part of the total *Is*. By arguing that there is only the One, since there could be no areas of nonbeing between things to give things separate spheres of existing, Parmenides thought he had proved that there could be no motion or change. It was precisely to reject this treatment of space or the void that Leucippus formulated his new theory.

Leucippus affirmed the reality of space and thereby prepared the way for a coherent theory of motion and change. What had complicated Parmenides's concept of space was his thought that whatever exists must be *material*, wherefore space, if it existed, must also be material. Leucippus, however, thought it possible to affirm that space exists without having to say at the same time that it is material. Thus he described space as something like a receptacle that could be empty in some places and full in others. As a receptacle, space, or the void, could be the place where objects move, and Leucippus apparently saw no reason for denying this characteristic of space. Without this concept of space, it would have been impossible for Leucippus and Democritus to develop that part of their philosophy for which they are best known, namely, that all things consist of atoms.

According to Leucippus and Democritus, things consist of an infinite number of particles or units called "atoms." To these atoms both Leucippus and Democritus ascribed the characteristics that Parmenides had ascribed to the One, namely, indestructibility and, therefore, eternity. Whereas Parmenides had said reality consists of a single One, the atomists now said that there are an infinite number of atoms, each one being completely full, containing no empty spaces, therefore being completely hard and indivisible. These

Democritus. (*Napoli, [proveniente da Ercolano], Museo Nazionale/Alinari/Art Resource*)

atoms exist in space and differ from one another in shape and size, and because of their small size, they are invisible. Since these atoms are eternal, they did not have to be created. Nature consists, therefore, of two things only: namely, *space,* which is a vacuum, and *atoms.* The atoms move about in space, and their motion leads them to form the objects we experience.

The atomists did not think it was necessary to account for the origin of this motion of the atoms in space. The original motion of these atoms, they thought, was similar to the motion of dust particles as they dart off in all directions in a sunbeam even when there is no wind to impel them. Democritus said that there is no absolute "up" or "down," and since he did not ascribe *weight* to atoms, he thought atoms could move in any and all directions. Things as we know them have their origin in the motion of the atoms. Moving in space, the atoms originally were single, individual units, but inevitably they began to collide with each other, and in cases where their shapes were such as to permit them to interlock, they began to form clusters, or what Anaxagoras (500–428 B.C.) called "vortices." In this the atomists resembled the Pythagoreans (ca. 525–500 B.C.), who had said that all things are numbers. Things, like numbers, are made up of combinable units, and things, for the atomists, were simply combinations of various kinds of atoms. Mathematical figures and physical figures were, therefore, thought to be similar.

In the beginning, then, there were atoms in space. Each atom is like the Parmenidean One, but although they are indestructible, they are in constant motion. The stuff about which some earlier philosophers (Thales, Anaximenes, Heraclitus, and Empedocles) spoke—namely, water, air, fire, and earth—the atomists described as different clusters of changeless atoms, the product of the movement of originally single atoms. The four elements were not the primeval "roots" of all other things but were themselves the product of the absolutely original stuff, the atoms.

The atomists produced a mechanical conception of the nature of things. For them, everything was the product of the collision of atoms moving in space. Their theory had no place in it for the element of *purpose* or *design,* and their materialistic reduction of all reality to atoms left no place, and in their minds no need, for a creator or designer. They saw no need to account either for the origin of the atoms or for the original motion impelling the atoms, since the question of origins could always be asked, even about God. For them, to ascribe eternal existence to the material atoms seemed as satisfactory as any other solution.

So formidable was this atomistic theory that although it went into a decline after Aristotle and during the Middle Ages, it was revived and provided science with its working model for centuries to come. Sir Isaac Newton (1642–1727) still thought in atomistic terms when he wrote his famous *Principia,* in which, having deduced the motion of the planets, the comets, the moon, and the sea, he wrote in 1686:

> I wish we could devise the rest of the phenomena of Nature by the same kind of reasoning from mechanical principles, for I am induced by many reasons to

suspect that they may all depend upon certain forces by which the particles of bodies, by some causes hitherto unknown, are either mutually impelled towards one another and cohere in regular figures, or are repelled and recede from one another.

This theory of bodies in motion as the explanation of nature held sway until the quantum theory and Einstein gave the twentieth century a new conception of matter, denying the attribute of indestructibility to the atoms.

Democritus was concerned with two other philosophical problems besides describing the structure of nature: namely, the problem of knowledge and the problem of human conduct. Being a thorough materialist, Democritus held that *thought* can be explained in the same way that any other phenomenon can, namely, as the movement of atoms. He distinguished between two different kinds of perception, one of the senses and one of the understanding, both of these being physical processes. When the eye sees something, this something is an "effluence" or the shedding of atoms by the object, forming an "image." These atomic images of things enter the eyes (and other organs of sense) and make an impact on the soul, which is itself made up of atoms. Whereas Protagoras said that our senses are all equally reliable, that everything we sense really is what we sense it to be, Democritus disagreed, saying that "there are two forms of knowledge, the trueborn and the bastard. To the bastard belong all these: sight, hearing, smell, taste, touch. The trueborn is quite apart from these."

What distinguishes these two modes of thought is that whereas "trueborn" knowledge depends only on the object, "bastard" knowledge is affected by the particular conditions of the body of the person involved. This is why two persons can agree that what they have tasted is an apple (trueborn) and still disagree about the taste (bastard knowledge), one saying the apple is sweet and the other saying it is bitter, so that, concludes Democritus, "by the senses we know in truth nothing sure, but only something that changes according to the disposition of the body and of the things that enter into it or resist it." Still Democritus had to say that both sensation and thought are the same type of mechanical process.

When Democritus came to the other problem, however, the problem of ethics, he appears to have departed from his mechanical view of things. For one thing, if all reality is mechanically interlocked, there would hardly be any point in giving advice on how to behave, since each person's movements would be determined by the movement of other things, and conduct would not be within a person's control. Despite this technical contradiction in his philosophy, Democritus developed a very lofty set of rules for human behavior, urging moderation in all things along with the cultivation of culture as the surest way of achieving the most desirable goal of life, namely, cheerfulness.

Reading _____

Atoms Moving in Space
Lucretius

LUCRETIUS DESCRIBES HOW ATOMS PRODUCE ALL THINGS INCLUDING THINKING AND SENSATION

All nature then, as it is of itself, is built of these two things: for there are *bodies* and the *void*, in which they are placed and where they move hither and thither. For that body exists is declared by the sensation which all share alike; and unless faith in this sensation be firmly grounded at once and prevail, there will be nought to which we can make appeal about things hidden, so as to prove ought by the reasoning of the mind. And next, were there not room and empty space, which we call void, nowhere could bodies be placed, nor could they wander at all hither and thither in any direction. . . . Besides these there is nothing which you could say is parted from all body and sundered from void, which could be discovered as it were a third nature in the list. And so besides void and bodies no third nature by itself can be left in the list of things, which might either at any time fall within the purview of our senses, or be grasped by anyone through reasoning of the mind. . . .

ATOMS ARE SOLID AND EVERLASTING

First, since we have found existing a twofold nature of two things far differing, the nature of body and of space, in which all things take place, it must needs be that each exists alone by itself and unmixed. For wherever space lies empty, which we call the void, body is not there; moreover, wherever body has its station, there is by no means empty void. Therefore the first bodies are solid and free from void. . . . These cannot be broken up when hit by blows from without, nor again can they be pierced to the heart and undone, nor by any other way can they be assailed and made to totter; all of which I have above shown to you but a little while before. For it is clear that nothing could be crushed in without void, or broken or cleft in twain by cutting, nor admit moisture nor likewise spreading cold or piercing flame, whereby all things are brought to their end. And the more each thing keeps void within it, the more is it assailed within by these things and begins to totter. Therefore, if the first bodies are solid and free from void, as I have shown, they must be everlasting. Moreover, if matter had not been everlasting, ere this all things had wholly passed away to nothing, and all that we see had been born again from nothing. But since I have shown above that nothing can be created from nothing, nor can what has been begotten be summoned back to nothing, the first-beginnings must needs be of immortal body, into which at their last day all things can be dissolved, that there may be matter enough for renewing things. Therefore the first-beginnings are of solid singleness. . . .

SPACE AND ATOMS ARE INFINITE, THAT IS, SPACE WITHOUT LIMIT AND ATOMS BEYOND COUNTING

But since I have taught that the most solid bodies of matter fly about for ever unvanquished through the ages, come now, let us unfold, whether there be a certain limit to their full sum or not; and likewise the void that we have discovered, or room or space, in which all things are carried on, let us see clearly whether it is all altogether bounded or spreads out limitless and immeasurably deep.

The whole universe then is bounded in no direction of its ways; for then it would be bound to have an extreme edge. Now it is seen that nothing can have an extreme edge, unless there be something beyond to bound it, so that there is seen to be a spot farther than which the nature of our sense cannot follow it. As it is, since we must admit that there is nothing outside the whole sum, it has not an extreme point, it lacks therefore bound and limit. Nor does it matter in which quarter of it you take your stand; so true is it that, whatever place every man takes up, he leaves the whole boundless just as much on every side. Moreover, suppose now that all space were created finite, if one were to run on to the end, to its farthest coasts, and throw a flying dart, would you have it that dart, hurled with might and main, goes on whither it is sped and flies afar, or do you think that something checks and bars its way? For one or the other you must needs admit and choose. Yet both shut off your escape and constrain you to grant that the universe spreads out free from limit. . . .

THE "SWERVE" AS ATOMS MOVE IN SPACE: THE RANDOM CAUSE OF ALL THINGS

When first-bodies are being carried downwards straight through the void by their own weight, at times quite undetermined and at undetermined spots they push a little from their path: yet only just so much as you could call a change of trend. But if they were not used to swerve, all things would fall downwards through the deep void like drops of rain, nor could collision come to be, nor a blow brought to pass for the first-beginnings: so nature would never have brought ought to being. [The swerve of atoms causes collisions leading to the formation of clusters, and these clusters constitute the beginning of the things we know.]

But if perchance anyone believes that heavier bodies, because they are carried more quickly straight through the void, can fall from above on the lighter, and so bring about the blows which can give creative motions, he wanders far away from true reason. For all things that fall through the water and thin air, these things must needs quicken their fall in proportion to their weights, just because the body of water and the thin nature of air cannot check each thing equally, but give place more quickly when overcome by heavier bodies. But, on the other hand, the empty void [i.e., a vacuum] cannot on any side or any time support anything, but rather, as its own nature desires, it continues to give place; wherefore all things must needs be borne on through the calm void moving at equal rate with unequal weights. The heavier will not then ever be able to fall on the lighter from above, nor of themselves bring about the blows, which make diverse the movements, by which nature carries things on. Wherefore, again and again, it must needs be that the first-bodies *swerve* a little; yet not more than the very least, lest we seem to be imagining a sideways movement, and the truth refute it. For this we see plain and evident, that bodies, as far as in them lies, cannot travel sideways, since they fall headlong from above, as far as you can descry. But that nothing at all makes itself swerve from the straight direction of its path, who is there who can descry? [Hence, the "swerve" and not "creation" is the cause of all things.]

Herein we need not wonder why it is that, when all the first-beginnings of things [atoms] are in motion, yet the whole seems to stand wholly at rest, except when anything starts moving with its own body. For all the nature of the first-bodies lies far away from our senses, below their purview; wherefore, since you cannot reach to look upon them, they must needs steal away their motions from you too; above all, since such things as we can look upon, yet often hide their motions, when withdrawn from us on some distant spot. For often the fleecy flocks cropping the glad pasture on a hill creep on whither each is called and tempted by the grass bejewelled with fresh dew, and the lambs fed full gambol and butt playfully; yet all this seems blurred to us from afar, and to lie like a white mass on a green hill.

DIFFERENT KINDS OF ATOMS

Now come, next in order learn of what kind are the beginnings of all things and how far differing in form, and how they are made diverse with many kinds of shapes; not that but a few are endowed with a like form, but that they are not all alike smooth. . . . Other particles there are, moreover, which cannot rightly be thought to be smooth nor altogether hooked with bent points, but rather with tiny angles standing out a little. . . .

Or, again, things which seem to us hard and compact, these, it must needs be, are made of particles more hooked one to another, and are held together close-fastened at their roots, as it were by branching particles. First of all in this class diamond stones stand in the forefront of the fight, well used to despise all blows, and stubborn flints and the strength of hard iron, and brass sockets, which scream aloud as they struggle. . . .

MATTER: THE ORIGIN OF SENSATION AND THOUGHT

Next then, what is it, that strikes on the very mind, which stirs and constrains it to utter diverse thoughts, that you may not believe that the sensible is begotten of the insensible? We may be sure it is that stones and wood and earth mixed together yet cannot give out vital sense. Herein it will be right to remember this, that I do not say that sensations are begotten at once from all and every of the things which give birth to sensible things, but that it is of great matter, first of what size are these bodies, which create the sensible, and with what form they are endowed.

First of all, no body at all can have sensation before the nature of the living thing is itself begotten, because, we may be sure, its substance is scattered abroad and is kept in air, in streams, in earth and things sprung from earth, nor has it come together yet and combined the appropriate vital motions with one another, whereby the all-seeing senses are kindled and see to the safety of each living thing.

A BLOW ON THE HEAD SCATTERS THE ATOMS, DESTROYING SENSATION AND THOUGHT

Moreover, a heavier blow than its nature can endure, of a sudden fells any living creature, and hastens to stun all the sensations of its body and mind. For the positions of the first-beginnings are broken up and the vital motions are checked deep within, until the substance, after the shock throughout all the limbs, loosens the vital clusters of the soul from the body, scatters it abroad and drives it out through every pore. For what else are we to think that a blow can do when it meets each thing, but shake it to pieces and break it up? . . .

THERE MUST BE OTHER WORLDS LIKE OURS

We find that in every direction everywhere, and on either side, above and below, through all the universe, there is no limit. . . .

[And] when there is much matter ready to hand, when space is there, and neither matter nor any cause delays, things must, we may be sure, be carried on and completed. As it is, if there is so great a store of seeds as the whole life of living things could not number, and if the same force and nature abides which could throw together the seeds of things, each into their place in like manner as they are thrown together here, it must needs be that you confess that there are other worlds in other regions, and diverse races of men and tribes of wild beasts. . . .

And since I have shown of what kind are the beginnings of all things, with what diverse shapes they differ, and how of their own accord they fly on, impelled by everlasting motion, and in what manner each several thing can be

created out of them; next after this it seems that the nature of the mind and the
soul must now be displayed in my verses. . . .

THE NATURE OF THE HUMAN MIND

First I say that the mind, which we often call the understanding, in which is
placed the reasoning and guiding power of life, is a part of a man no whit the
less than hand and foot and eyes are created parts of the whole living being.
Now that you may be able to learn that the soul too is in the limbs, it comes to
pass that when a great part of the body is removed yet often the life lingers on
in our limbs.

Now I say that mind and soul are held in union one with the other, and
form of themselves a single nature, but that the head, as it were, and lord in
the whole body is the reason, which we call mind or understanding, and it is
firmly seated in the middle region of the breast. For here it is that fear and terror throb, around these parts are soothing joys; here then is the understanding
and the mind. The rest of the soul, spread abroad throughout the body, obeys
and is moved at the will and inclination of the understanding. The mind alone
by itself has understanding for itself, it rejoices for itself, when no single thing
stirs either soul or body. And just as, when head or eye hurts within us at the
attack of pain, we are not tortured at the same time in all our body; so the
mind sometimes feels pain by itself or waxes strong with joy, when all the rest
of the soul through the limbs and frame is not roused by any fresh feeling.

This same reasoning shows that the nature of mind and soul is bodily.
For when it is seen to push on the limbs, to pluck the body from sleep, to
change the countenance, and to guide and turn the whole man—none of
which things we see can come to pass without touch, nor touch in its turn
without body—must we not allow that mind and soul are formed of bodily
nature? Moreover, you see that our mind suffers along with the body, and
shares our feelings together in the body.

Now of what kind of body this mind is, and of what parts it is formed, I
will go on to give account to you in my discourse. First of all I say that it is
very fine in texture, and is made and formed of very tiny particles. [The modern encephalograph measures the impact of tiny particles, or electrical impulses, emitted by the brain.] That this is so, if you give attention, you may be able
to learn from this. Nothing is seen to come to pass so swiftly as what the mind
pictures to itself coming to pass and starts to do itself. Therefore the mind
bestirs itself more quickly than any of the things whose nature is manifest for
all to see. But because it is so very nimble . . . it must needs be formed of bodies exceeding small and smooth and round. And this truth, when known to
you, will in many things, good friend, prove useful, and will be reckoned of
service. This fact, too, shows the nature of the mind, of how thin a texture it is
formed, and in how small a place it might be contained, could it be gathered
in a mass; that as soon as the unruffled peace of death has laid hold on a man,
and the nature of mind and soul has passed away, you could discern nothing

there, that sight or weight can test, stolen from the entire body; death preserves all save the feeling of life, and some warm heat. And so it must needs be that the whole soul is made of very tiny seeds, and is linked on throughout veins, flesh, and sinews; inasmuch as, when it is all already gone from the whole body, yet the outer contour of the limbs is preserved unbroken, nor is a jot of weight wanting. Even so it is, when the flavour of wine has passed away or when the sweet breath of a perfume is scattered to the air, or when its savour is gone from some body; still the thing itself seems not a whit smaller to the eyes on that account.

We feel that the understanding is begotten along with the body, and grows together with it, and along with it comes to old age. For as children totter with feeble and tender body, so a weak judgment of mind goes with. Then when their years are ripe and their strength hardened, greater is their sense and increased their force of mind. Afterwards, when now the body is shattered by the stern strength of time, and the frame has sunk with its force dulled, then the reason is maimed, the tongue raves, the mind stumbles, all things give way and fail at once. And so it is natural that all the nature of the mind should also be dissolved, even as is smoke, into the high breezes of the air; inasmuch as we see that it is born with the body, grows with it, and, as I have shown, at the same time becomes weary and worn with age.

From *Lucretius De Rerum Natura*, ed. trans. Cyril Bailey, Clarendon Press, Oxford, Eng., 1947. By permission of the Oxford University Press.

Eddington

Reading _____

Two Tables
Sir Arthur Eddington

I have settled down to the task of writing these lectures and have drawn up my chairs to my two tables. Two tables! Yes; there are duplicates of every object about me—two tables, two chairs, two pens.

This is not a very profound beginning to a course which ought to reach transcendent levels of scientific philosophy. But we cannot touch bedrock immediately; we must scratch a bit at the surface of things first. And whenever I begin to scratch; the first thing I strike is—my two tables.

One of them has been familiar to me from earliest years. It is a commonplace object of that environment which I call the world. How shall I describe

Sir Arthur Eddington (1882–1944) was a writer on science and philosophy of science and professor of astronomy at Cambridge University, England.

it? It has extension; it is comparatively permanent; it is colored; above all it is *substantial*. By substantial I do not merely mean that it does not collapse when I lean up on it; I mean that it is constituted of "substance," and by that word I am trying to convey to you some conception of its intrinsic nature. It is a *thing;* not like space, which is a mere negation; nor like time, which is—Heaven knows what! But that will not help you to my meaning because it is the distinctive characteristic of a "thing" to have this substantiality, and I do not think substantiality can be described better than by saying that it is the kind of nature exemplified by an ordinary table. And so we go round in circles. After all if you are a plain commonsense man, not too much worried with scientific scruples, you will be confident that you understand the nature of an ordinary table. I have even heard of plain men who had the idea that they could better understand the mystery of their own nature if scientists would discover a way of explaining it in terms of the easily comprehensible nature of a table.

Table no. 2 is my scientific table. It is a more recent acquaintance and I do not feel so familiar with it. It does not belong to the world previously mentioned—that world which spontaneously appears around me when I open my eyes, though how much of it is objective and how much subjective I do not here consider. It is part of a world which in more devious ways has forced itself on my attention. My scientific table is mostly emptiness. Sparsely scattered in that emptiness are numerous electric charges rushing about with great speed; but their combined bulk amounts to less than a billionth of the bulk of the table itself. Notwithstanding its strange construction it turns out to be an entirely efficient table. It supports my writing paper as satisfactorily as table no. 1; for when I lay the paper on it the little electric particles with their headlong speed keep on hitting the underside, so that the paper is maintained in shuttlecock fashion at a nearly steady level. If I lean upon this table I shall not go through; or, to be strictly accurate, the chance of my scientific elbow going through my scientific table is so excessively small that it can be neglected in practical life. Reviewing their properties one by one, there seems to be nothing to choose between the two tables for ordinary purposes; but when abnormal circumstances befall, then my scientific table shows to advantage. If the house catches fire my scientific table will dissolve quite naturally into scientific smoke, whereas my familiar table undergoes a metamorphosis of its substantial nature which I can only regard as miraculous.

There is nothing *substantial* about my second table. It is nearly all empty space—space pervaded, it is true, by fields of force, but these are assigned to the category of "influences," not of "things." Even in the minute part which is not empty we must not transfer the old notion of substance. In dissecting matter into electric charges we have travelled far from that picture of it which first gave rise to the conception of substance, and the meaning of that conception—if it ever had any—has been lost by the way. The whole trend of modern scientific views is to break down the separate categories of "things," "influences," "forms," etc., and to substitute a common background of all experience. Whether we are studying a material object, a magnetic field, a geometrical figure, or a duration of time, our scientific information is summed up in measures; neither the apparatus of measurement nor the mode of using it suggests that there is anything essentially different in these problems. The measures themselves afford no ground for a classification by categories. We feel it necessary to concede some background to the measures—an external world; but the attributes of this world, except insofar as they are reflected in the measures, are outside scientific scrutiny. Science has at last revolted against attaching the exact knowledge contained in these measurements to a traditional picture-gallery of conceptions which convey no authentic information of the background and obtrude irrelevancies into the scheme of knowledge.

I will not here stress further the nonsubstantiality of electrons, since it is scarcely necessary to the present line of thought. Conceive them as substantially as you will, there is a vast difference between my scientific table with its substance (if any) thinly scattered in specks in a region mostly empty and the table of everyday conception which we regard as the type of solid reality—an incarnate protest against Berkeleian subjectivism.* It makes all the difference in the world whether the paper before me is poised as it were on a swarm of flies and sustained in shuttlecock fashion by a series of tiny blows from the swarm underneath, or whether it is supported because there is substance below it, it being the intrinsic nature of substance to occupy space to the exclusion of other substance; all the difference in conception at least, but no difference to my practical task of writing on the paper.

I need not tell you that modern physics has by delicate test and remorseless logic assured me that my second scientific table is the only one which is really there—wherever "there" may be. On the other hand I need not tell you that modern physics will never succeed in exorcising that first table—strange compound of external nature, mental imagery, and inherited prejudice—which lies visible to my eyes and tangible to my grasp. We must bid good-bye to it for the present, for we are about to turn from the familiar world to the scientific world revealed by physics. This is, or is intended to be, a wholly external world.

"You speak paradoxically of two worlds. Are they not really two aspects or two interpretations of one and the same world?"

Yes, no doubt they are ultimately to be identified after some fashion. But the process by which the external world of physics is transformed into a world of familiar acquaintance in human consciousness is outside the scope of physics. And so the world studied according to the methods of physics remains detached from the world familiar to consciousness, until after the physicist has finished his labors upon it. Provisionally, therefore, we regard the table which is the subject of physical research as altogether separate from the familiar table, without prejudging the question of their ultimate identification. It is true that the whole scientific inquiry starts from the familiar world and in the end it must return to the familiar world; but the part of the journey over which the physicist has charge is in foreign territory.

*As we will see in the next reading, Bishop Berkeley thought that these tables, and all other things, were sets of ideas.

Until recently there was a much closer linkage; the physicist used to borrow the raw material of his world from the familiar world, but he does so no longer. His raw materials are ether, electrons, quanta, potentials, Hamiltonian functions, etc., and he is nowadays scrupulously careful to guard these from contamination by conceptions borrowed from the other world. There is a familiar table parallel to the scientific table, but there is no familiar electron, quantum, or potential parallel to the scientific electron, quantum, or potential. We do not even desire to manufacture a familiar counterpart to these things or, as we should commonly say, to "explain" the electron. After the physicist has quite finished his world-building, a linkage or identification is allowed; but premature attempts at linkage have been found to be entirely mischievous.

From Sir Arthur Eddington, *The Nature of the Physical World*, Cambridge University Press, Cambridge, Eng., 1928. Used with permission of Cambridge University Press.

QUESTIONS FOR REVIEW AND DISCUSSION

1. Democritus said that the whole world consists solely of atoms and the void (space). Using our information from Lucretius, how did this atomist theory account for:
   a. The beginning of things as we now know them
   b. Living things—vegetation, animals, people
   c. Feelings and thinking
2. Sir Arthur Eddington speaks of "two tables." In what way is Eddington's theory of the objects we physically see and feel similar to the theory of Democritus, and in what specific way is it different? Can you think of an explanation suggesting that these two theories are in fact not really different?

25

Mind, the True Reality

Berkeley

George Berkeley was born in Ireland in 1685. At the age of fifteen he entered Trinity College, where he studied mathematics, logic, language, and philosophy. After taking his B.A. degree, he became a clergyman in the Church of England, rising to Bishop in 1734. He became famous as an author; his books include *Essays toward a New Theory of Vision* (1709), *A Treatise concerning Principles of Human Knowledge* (1710), and *Three Dialogues between Hylas and Philonous*. He traveled in France, Italy, and America, where he hoped to create a college (one of the colleges at Yale is named after him). He influenced American philosophy through his frequent associations with Jonathan Edwards. From America he returned to Ireland, where he was Bishop of Cloyne until age sixty-eight, when he retired to Oxford; he died there a year later in 1753. He is buried in Christ Church Chapel in Oxford.

George Berkeley was a member of that group known today as the "British Empiricists," who also included Locke and Hume. John Locke had developed a theory of knowledge which Berkeley accepted, namely, that all our knowledge depends on our sense experience. This was a radical change from earlier theories as developed, for example, by such rationalists as Descartes, Leibniz, and Spinoza. As compared with the more grandiose ideas of the rationalists, Locke's theory of knowledge seemed to agree with the ordinary experience of common sense. Berkeley was influenced by John Locke's new theories. But it is ironic that Locke's commonsense approach to philosophy should have influenced Berkeley to formulate a philosophical position that at first seems so much at odds with common sense. Berkeley became the object of severe criticism and ridicule for denying what seemed most obvious to anyone. Berkeley had set out to deny the existence of matter. Dr. Samuel Johnson must have expressed the reaction of many when he kicked a large stone and said about Berkeley, "I refute him thus."

Berkeley's startling and provocative formula was that "to be is to be perceived," *esse est percipi*. Clearly this would mean that if something were not perceived, it would not exist. Berkeley was perfectly aware of the potential nonsense involved in this formula, for he says, "Let it not be said that I take

George Berkeley (right). (*Yale University Art Gallery, Gift of Isaac Lothrop of Plymouth, Massachusetts*)

away Existence. I only declare the meaning of the word so far as I comprehend it." Still, to say that the existence of something depends on its being perceived does raise for us the question whether it exists when it is not being perceived. For Berkeley the whole problem turned on how we interpret or understand the word "exists": "The table I write on I say exists; that is, I see and feel it: and if I were out of my study I should say it existed; meaning thereby that if I were in my study I might perceive it, or that some other spirit actually does perceive it." Here Berkeley is saying that the word "exists" has no other meaning than the one contained in his formula, for we can know no instance where the term "exists" is used without at the same time assuming that a mind is perceiving something. To those who argued that material things have some kind of *absolute* existence without any relation to their being perceived, Berkeley replied, "That is to me unintelligible." To be sure, he said, "the horse is in the stable, the books in the study as before, even if I am not there. But since we know of no instance of anything's existing without being perceived, the table, horse, and books *exist* even when I do not perceive them because someone does perceive them."

How did Berkeley come upon this novel view? In his *New Theory of Vision* he argued that all our knowledge depends on actual vision and other sensory experiences. In particular, Berkeley argued that we never sense *space* or *magnitude;* we only have different visions or perceptions of things when we see them from different perspectives. Nor do we *see* distance; the distance of objects is *suggested* by our experience. All that we ever see is the qualities of an object that our faculty of vision is capable of sensing. We do not see the *closeness* of an object; we only have a different vision of it when we move toward or away from it. The more Berkeley considered the workings of his own mind and wondered how his ideas were related to objects outside of his mind, the more certain he was that he could never discover any object independent of his ideas. "When we do our utmost to conceive the existence of external bodies," he said, "we are all the while contemplating our own ideas." Nothing seems easier for us than to imagine trees in a park or books in a closet without anyone's looking at them. But what is all this, says Berkeley, except "framing in your mind certain ideas which you call *books* and *trees* . . . But do not *you* yourself perceive or think of them all the while?" It is impossible, he concluded, ever to think of *anything* except as related to a mind. We never experience something that exists outside of us and separate from us as our ideas of "close" and "far" might suggest. There is nothing *out there* of which we do not have some perception.

It was Locke's philosophy that had raised doubts in Berkeley's mind about the independent existence of things, about the reality of matter. Locke had failed to push his own theory of knowledge to conclusions that to Berkeley seemed inevitable. When Locke spoke of substance as "something we know not what," he was only a short step from saying that it was nothing, which Berkeley did say. Locke's treatment of the relation between ideas and things assumes there is a real difference between primary and secondary qualities, between an object's size and shape on the one hand and its color, taste, and smell on the other. He assumed that whereas color exists only as an idea in the mind, size has to do with an object's *substance*, that reality that exists "behind" or "under" such secondary qualities as color and is therefore independent of a mind, is inert matter.

Berkeley, however, argued that size, shape, and motion, "abstracted from all other qualities, are inconceivable." What, for example, is a cherry? It is soft, red, round, sweet, and fragrant. All these qualities are ideas in the mind that the cherry has the power to produce through the senses, so that the softness is felt, the color is seen, the roundness is either felt or seen, the sweetness is tasted, and the fragrance is smelled. Again, the very existence of all these qualities consists in their being perceived. And, apart from these qualities, there is no sensed reality—in short, nothing else. The cherry, then, consists of all the qualities we perceive; the cherry (and all things) represents a complex of sensations. To say that besides the qualities perceived by the senses there are more primary qualities, such as shape and size, is to assume, says

Berkeley, that primary and secondary qualities can be divided. It is impossible, he said, even to conceive of shape or size as independent of perception and therefore independent of secondary qualities. Is it possible, he asks, to separate primary and secondary qualities "even in thought?" He adds, "I might as easily divide a thing from itself. . . . In truth, the object and the sensation are the same thing, and cannot therefore be abstracted from each other." A thing *is*, therefore, the sum of its perceived qualities, and it is for this reason that Berkeley argued that to be is to be perceived. Since substance, or matter, is never perceived or sensed, it cannot be said to exist. If substance does not exist and if only sensed qualities are real, then only thinking or, as Berkeley says, *spiritual* beings exist.

Besides leading Locke's empirical philosophy to what he thought were obvious conclusions, Berkeley was also contending with a complex of problems, to which he referred in his *Principles of Human Knowledge* as ". . . the chief causes of error and difficulty in the Sciences, with the grounds of Scepticism, Atheism and Irreligion, . . . inquired into." It was the notion of *matter* that caused all the difficulties, for if an inert material substance is admitted as really existing, where is there any place for spiritual or immaterial substances in such a universe? Also, would not scientific knowledge, based on general ideas drawn from the behavior of things, give us a complete philosophy without requiring the idea of God, leading to "the monstrous systems of atheists?" This is not to say that Berkeley arbitrarily denounced the idea of matter because of these theological consequences, but that he had additional reasons for pressing his views, which, he was convinced, were intrinsically right.

MATTER, A MEANINGLESS TERM

Locke had said that substance, or matter, supports or acts as a *substrate* to the qualities we sense. In Berkeley's *First Dialogue between Hylas and Philonous*, Hylas expresses Locke's view: ". . . I find it necessary to suppose a material *substratum*, without which [qualities] cannot be conceived to exist." Philonous replies that the word "substratum" has no clear meaning for him and that he would want to "know any sense, literal or not literal, that you understand in it." But Hylas admits that he cannot assign any definite meaning to the term "substratum," saying "I declare I know not what to say." From this the conclusion is drawn that "The *absolute* existence of unthinking things [matter] are words without meaning." This is not to say that sensible things do not possess reality, but only that sensible things exist only insofar as they are perceived. This of course implies that only ideas exist, but Berkeley adds that "I hope that to call a thing 'idea' makes it no less real." Aware that his idealism can be ridiculed, Berkeley writes: "What therefore becomes of the sun, moon, and stars? What must we think of houses, rivers, mountains, trees, stones; nay even of our own bodies? Are all these so many chimeras and illusions of fancy?" By his principles, he says, "we are not deprived of any one thing in nature. Whatever we see, feel, hear, or any wise conceive or understand, remains as secure as ever, and is as real as ever. There is a *rerum natura,* and the distinction between realities and chimeras retains its full force." If this is the case, why say that only *ideas,* instead of *things,* exist? In order, says Berkeley, to eliminate the useless concept of matter: "I do not argue against the existence of any one thing that we can apprehend, either by sense or reflexion. . . . The only thing whose existence we deny, is that which philosophers call matter or corporeal substance. And in doing of this, there is no damage done to the rest of mankind, who, I dare say, will never miss it."

SCIENCE AND ABSTRACT IDEAS

Since it was the science of his day, particularly physics, that relied so heavily on the notion of matter, Berkeley had to come to terms with its assumptions and methods. Science had assumed that we can, and must, distinguish between appearance and reality. The sea appears blue but is really not. Berkeley challenged the scientist to show whether there is any other reality than the sensible world. In this analysis Berkeley was pursuing the principle of empiricism and was trying to refine it. Physicists, he said, were obscuring science by including metaphysics in their theories: They used such words as "force," "attraction," "gravity" and thought they referred to some real physical entity. Even to speak of minute particles whose motions cause the quality of color is to engage in a rational and not empirical analysis. What disturbed Berkeley most was that scientists used general or abstract terms as though these terms accurately referred to real entities, particularly to an underlying material substance in nature. Nowhere, Berkeley argues, do we ever come upon such a substance, for substance is an abstract idea. Only sensed qualities really exist, and the notion of substance is a misleading inference drawn from observed qualities: "As several of these [qualities] are observed to accompany each other, they come to be marked by one name, and so to be reputed as one *thing.* Thus, for example, a certain colour, taste, smell, figure, and consistence having been observed to go together, are accounted one distinct thing, signified by the name apple; other collections of ideas constitute a stone, a tree, a book and the like sensible things." Similarly, when scientists observe the operations of things, they use such abstract terms as "force" or "gravity" as though these were things or had some real existence in things. But "force" is simply a word describing our sensation of the behavior of things and gives us no more knowledge than our senses and reflections give us.

Berkeley did not mean to destroy science any more than he wanted to deny the existence of the "nature of things." What he did want to do was to clarify what scientific language was all about. Terms such as "force," "gravity," and "causality" refer to nothing more than clusters of ideas which our minds derive from sensation. We experience that heat melts wax, but all we know from this experience is that what we call "melting wax" is always accompanied by what we call "heat." We have no knowledge of any single thing for which the word "cause" stands. Indeed, the only knowledge we have is of particular experiences. But even though we do not have firsthand knowledge of the causes of all things, we do know the order of things. We experience order, that A is followed by B, even though we have no experience of *why* this occurs. Science gives us a description of physical behavior, and many mechanical principles can be accurately formulated from our observations that are useful for purposes of prediction. Thus Berkeley would leave science intact, but he would clarify its language so that nobody would think that science was giving us more knowledge than we can derive from the sensible world. And the sensible world shows us neither substance nor causality.

GOD AND THE EXISTENCE OF THINGS

Since Berkeley did not deny the existence of things or their order in nature, it was necessary for him to explain how things external to our minds exist even when *we* don't perceive them and how they achieve their order. Thus, elaborating his general thesis that to be is to be perceived, Berkeley says that "when I deny sensible things an existence out of the mind, I do not mean my mind in particular, but all minds. Now it is plain they have an existence exterior to my mind, since I find them by experience to be independent of it. There is therefore some other mind wherein they exist, during the intervals between the time of my perceiving them." And because all human minds are intermittently diverted from things, "there is an *omnipresent eternal Mind,* which knows and comprehends all things, and exhibits them to our view in such a manner and according to such rules as he himself hath ordained, and are by us termed the *Laws of Nature.*" The existence of things therefore depends on the existence of God, and God is the cause of the orderliness of things in nature.

Again, Berkeley did not want to deny, for example, that even if I left the room, the candle would still be there, and that when I returned after an interval of time, it would have burned down. But this meant for Berkeley only that experience has a certain regularity that makes it possible for us to predict what our future experiences will be. To say that candles burn even when *I* am not in the room still does not prove that material substance exists independently from a mind. It seemed a matter of common sense to Berkeley to say that we can know about the candle only because we actually experience a perception of it. In a similar way, we know that we exist because we have an awareness of our mental operations.

If, then, I try to describe or interpret reality in terms of my experience, I come first to the conclusion that there are other persons like myself who have minds. From this it can be assumed that since I have ideas, other persons likewise have ideas. Apart from my finite mind and the finite minds of others, there is a greater mind analogous to mine, and this is God's mind. God's ideas constitute the regular order of nature. The ideas that exist in men's minds are God's ideas, which He communicates to men so that the objects or things that we perceive in daily experience are caused not by *matter* or *substance,* but by God. It is God, too, who coordinates all experiences of finite minds, ensuring regularity and dependability in experience, which, in turn, enables us to think in terms of the "laws of nature." Thus the orderly arrangement of ideas in God's mind is communicated to the finite minds or spirits of human beings, allowance being made for the differences in competence between the Divine and finite minds. The ultimate reality, then, is spiritual, God, and not material, and the continued existence of objects when *we* are not perceiving them is explained by God's continuous perception of them.

To say, as Berkeley does, that men's ideas come from God implies a special interpretation of causation. Again, Berkeley did not deny that we have an insight into causation; he insisted only that our sense data do not disclose to us a unique causal power. We do not, for example, when considering how and why water freezes, discover any power in cold that forces water to become solid. We do, however, understand causal connections through our mental operations. We are, for example, aware of our volition: we can will to move our arm, or, what is more important here, we can produce imaginary ideas in our minds. Our power to produce such ideas suggests that perceived ideas are also caused by a mental power. But whereas imaginary ideas are produced by finite minds, perceived ideas are created and caused to be in us by an infinite mind.

Berkeley was confident that through his treatment of the formula *esse est percipi* he had effectively undermined the position of philosophical materialism and religious skepticism. Locke's empiricism inevitably implied skepticism insofar as he insisted that knowledge is based on sense experience and that substance, or the reality behind appearances, could never be known. Whether Berkeley's arguments for the reality of God and spiritual beings successfully refuted materialism and skepticism remains a question, for his arguments contained some of the flaws he held against the materialists. His influence was nevertheless significant, but it was his empiricism and not his idealism that had lasting influence. Building on Locke's empiricism, Berkeley made the decisive point that the human mind reasons only and always about particular sense experiences, that abstract ideas refer to no equivalent reality. Hume, who carried empiricism to its fullest expression, spoke of Berkeley as "a great philosopher [who] has disputed the received opinion in this particular, and has asserted that all general ideas are nothing but particular ones. . . . I look upon this to be one of the greatest and most valuable discoveries that has been made of late years in the republic of letters."

Reading _____

No Such Thing as Matter
Berkeley

HYLAS: You were represented in last night's conversation, as one who maintained the most extravagant opinion that ever entered into the mind of man, to wit, that that there is no such thing as *material substance* in the world.

PHILONOUS: That there is no such thing as what Philosophers call *material substance,* I am seriously persuaded: but, if I were made to see anything absurd or sceptical in this, I should then have the same reason to renounce this that I imagine I have now to reject the contrary opinion.

HYLAS: What! can anything be more fantastical, more repugnant to common sense, or a more manifest piece of Scepticism, than to believe there is no such thing as *matter?*

PHILONOUS: Softly, good Hylas. What if it should prove, that you, who hold there is, are, by virtue of that opinion, a greater sceptic, and maintain more paradoxes and repugnances to common sense, than I who believe no such thing?

HYLAS: You may as soon persuade me, the part is greater than the whole, as that, in order to avoid absurdity and Scepticism, I should ever be obliged to give up my opinion in this point.

PHILONOUS: Well then, are you content to admit that opinion for true, which, upon examination, shall appear most agreeable to common sense, and remote from Scepticism?

HYLAS: With all my heart. Since you are for raising disputes about the plainest things in nature, I am content for once to hear what you have to say. . . .

PHILONOUS: Make me to understand the differences between what is immediately perceived, and a sensation.

HYLAS: The sensation I take to be an act of the mind perceiving; besides which, there is something perceived; and this I call the *object.* For example, there is red and yellow on that tulip. But then the act of perceiving those colours is in me only, and not in the tulip.

PHILONOUS: What tulip do you speak of? Is it that which you see?

HYLAS: The same.

PHILONOUS: And what do you see beside colour, figure, and extension?

HYLAS: I acknowledge, Philonous, that, upon a fair observation of what passes in my mind, I can discover nothing else but that I am a thinking being, affected with variety of sensations; neither is it possible to conceive how a sensation should exist in an unperceiving substance. But then, on the other hand, when I look on sensible things in a different view, considering them as so many modes and qualities, I find it necessary to suppose a material substratum, without which they cannot be conceived to exist.

PHILONOUS: *Material substratum* call you it? Pray, by which of your senses came you acquainted with that being?

HYLAS: It is not itself sensible; its modes and qualities only being perceived by the senses.

PHILONOUS: I presume then it was by reflection and reason you obtained the idea of it?

HYLAS: I do not pretend to any proper positive idea of it. However, I conclude it exists, because qualities cannot be conceived to exist without a support.

PHILONOUS: It seems then you have only a relative notion of it, or that you conceive it not otherwise than by conceiving the relation it bears to sensible qualities?

HYLAS: Right.

PHILONOUS: Be pleased therefore to let me know wherein that relation consists.

HYLAS: Is it not sufficiently expressed in the term *substratum* or *substance?*

PHILONOUS: If so, the word *substratum* should import that it is spread under the sensible qualities or accidents?

PHILONOUS: How say you, Hylas, can you see a thing which is at the same time unseen?

HYLAS: No, that were a contradiction.

PHILONOUS: Is it not as great a contradiction to talk of *conceiving* a thing which is unconceived?

HYLAS: It is.

PHILONOUS: The tree or house therefore which you think of is *conceived* by you?

HYLAS: How should it be otherwise?

PHILONOUS: And what is conceived is surely in the mind?

HYLAS: Without question, that which is conceived is in the mind.

PHILONOUS: How then came you to say, you conceived a house or tree existing independent and out of all minds whatsoever?

HYLAS: That was I own an oversight; but stay, let me consider what led me into it.—It is a pleasant mistake enough. As I was thinking of a tree in a solitary place where no one was present to see it, methought that was to conceive a tree as existing unperceived or unthought of—not considering that I myself conceived it all the while. But now I plainly see that all I can do is to frame ideas in my own mind. I may indeed conceive in my own thoughts the idea of a tree, or a house, or a mountain, but that is all. And this is far from proving that I can conceive them *existing out of the minds of all Spirits.*

PHILONOUS: You acknowledge then that you cannot possibly conceive how any one corporeal sensible thing should exist otherwise than in a mind?

HYLAS: I do.

PHILONOUS: And yet you will earnestly contend for the truth of that which you cannot so much as conceive?

HYLAS: I profess I know not what to think; but still there are some scruples remain with me. Is it not certain I see things at a distance? Do we not perceive the stars and moon, for example, to be a great way off? Is not this, I say, manifest to the senses?

PHILONOUS: Do you not in a dream too perceive those or the like objects?

HYLAS: I do.

PHILONOUS: And have they not then the same appearance of being distant?

HYLAS: They have.

PHILONOUS: But you do not thence conclude the apparitions in a dream to be without the mind?

HYLAS: By no means.

PHILONOUS: You ought not therefore to conclude that sensible objects are without the mind, from their appearance or manner wherein they are perceived.

HYLAS: I acknowledge it. But doth not my sense deceive me in those cases?

PHILONOUS: By no means. The idea or thing which you immediately perceive, neither sense nor reason informs you that it actually exists without the mind. By sense you only know that you are affected with such certain sensations of light and colours, &c. And these you will not say are without the mind.

HYLAS: True: but, beside all that, do you not think the sight suggests something of *outness* or *distance?*

PHILONOUS: Upon approaching a distant object, do the visible size and figure change perpetually, or do they appear the same at all distances?

HYLAS: They are in a continual change.

PHILONOUS: Sight therefore doth not suggest or any way inform you that the visible object you immediately perceive exists at a distance or will be perceived when you advance farther onward; there being a continued series of visible objects succeeding each other during the whole time of your approach.

HYLAS: It doth not; but still I know, upon seeing an object, what object I shall perceive after having passed over a certain distance: no matter whether it be exactly the same or no: there is still something of distance suggested in the case.

PHILONOUS: Good Hylas, do but reflect a little on the point, and then tell me whether there be any more in it than this:—From the ideas you actually perceive by sight, you have by experience learned to collect what other ideas you will (according to the standing order of nature) be affected with, after such a certain succession of time and motion.

HYLAS: Upon the whole, I take it to be nothing else.

PHILONOUS: Now, is it not plain that if we suppose a man born blind was on a sudden made to see, he could at first have no experience of what may be suggested by sight?

HYLAS: It is.

PHILONOUS: He would not then, according to you, have any notion of distance annexed to the things he saw; but would take them for a new set of sensations existing only in his mind?

HYLAS: It is undeniable.

PHILONOUS: But, to make it still more plain: is not *distance* a line turned endwise to the eye?

HYLAS: It is.

PHILONOUS: And can a line so situated be perceived by sight?

HYLAS: It cannot.

PHILONOUS: Doth it not therefore follow that distance is not properly and immediately perceived by sight?

HYLAS: It should seem so.

PHILONOUS: Again, is it your opinion that colours are at a distance?

HYLAS: It must be acknowledged they are only in the mind.

PHILONOUS: But do not colours appear to the eye as coexisting in the same place with extension and figures?

HYLAS: They do.

PHILONOUS: How can you then conclude from sight that figures exist without, when you acknowledge colours do not; the sensible appearance being the very same with regard to both?

HYLAS: I know not what to answer.

PHILONOUS: But, allowing that distance was truly and immediately perceived by the mind, yet it would not thence follow it existed out of the mind. For, whatever is immediately perceived is an idea: and can any idea *exist* out of the mind?

HYLAS: To suppose that were absurd: but, inform me, Philonous, can we perceive or know nothing beside our ideas?

PHILONOUS: As for the rational deducing of causes from effects, that is beside our inquiry. And, by the senses you can best tell whether you perceive anything which is not immediately perceived. And I ask you, whether the things immediately perceived are other than your own sensations or ideas? You have indeed more than once, in the course of this conversation, declared yourself on those points; but you seem, by this last question, to have departed from what you then thought.

HYLAS: To speak the truth, Philonous, I think there are two kinds of objects—the one perceived immediately, which are likewise called *ideas;* the other are real things or external objects, perceived by the mediation of ideas, which are their images and representations. Now, I own ideas to not exist without the mind; but the latter sort of objects do. I am sorry I did not think of this distinction sooner; it would probably have cut short your discourse.

PHILONOUS: Are those external objects perceived by sense, or by some other faculty?

HYLAS: They are perceived by sense.

PHILONOUS: How! is there anything perceived by sense which is not immediately perceived?

HYLAS: Yes, Philonous, in some sort there is. For example, when I look on a picture or statue of Julius Caesar, I may be said after a manner to perceive him (though not immediately) by my senses.

PHILONOUS: It seems then you will have our ideas, which alone are immediately perceived to be pictures of external things, and that these also are perceived by sense, inasmuch as they have a conformity or resemblance to our ideas?

HYLAS: That is my meaning.

PHILONOUS: And, in the same way that Julius Caesar, in himself invisible, is nevertheless perceived by sight; real things, in themselves imperceptible, are perceived by sense.

HYLAS: In the very same.

PHILONOUS: Tell me, Hylas, when you behold the picture of Julius Caesar, do you see with your eyes any more than some colours and figures, with a certain symmetry and composition of the whole?

HYLAS: Nothing else.

PHILONOUS: And would not a man who had never known anything of Julius Caesar see as much?

HYLAS: He would.

PHILONOUS: Consequently he hath his sight, and the use of it, in as perfect a degree as you?

HYLAS: I agree with you.

PHILONOUS: Whence comes it then that your thoughts are directed to the Roman emperor, and his are not? This cannot proceed from the sensations or ideas of sense by you then perceived; since you acknowledge you have no advantage over him in that respect. It should seem therefore to proceed from reason and memory: should it not?

HYLAS: It should.

PHILONOUS: Consequently, it will not follow from that instance that anything is perceived by sense which is not immediately perceived. Though I grant we may, in one acceptation, be said to perceive sensible things mediately by sense—that is, when, from a frequently perceived connexion, the immediate perception of ideas by one sense suggest to the mind others, perhaps belonging to another sense, which we wont to be connected with them. For instance, when I hear a coach drive along the streets, immediately I perceive only the sound; but, from the experience I have had that such a sound is connected with a coach, I am said to hear the coach. It is nevertheless evident that, in truth and strictness, nothing can be *heard* but *sound;* and the coach is not then properly perceived by sense, but suggested from experience. So likewise when we are said to see a red-hot bar of iron; the solidity and heat of the iron are not the objects of sight, but suggested to the imagination by the colour and figure which are properly perceived by that sense. In short, those things alone are actually and strictly perceived by any sense, which would have been perceived in case that same sense had then been first conferred on us. As for other things, it is plain they are only suggested to the mind by experience, grounded on former perceptions. But, to return to your comparison of Caesar's picture, it is plain, if you keep to that, you must hold the real things or archetypes of our ideas are not perceived by sense, but by some internal faculty of the soul, as reason or memory. I would therefore fain know what arguments you can draw from reason for the existence of what you call *real things* or *material objects*. Or, whether you remember to have seen them formerly as they are in themselves; or, if you have heard or read of any one that did.

HYLAS: I see, Philonous, you are disposed to raillery; but that will never convince me.

PHILONOUS: My aim is only to learn from you the way to come at the knowledge of *material beings*. Whatever we perceive is perceived immediately or mediately: by sense; or by reason and reflection. But, as you have excluded sense, pray show me what reason you have to believe their existence; or what *medium* you can possibly make use of to prove it, either to mine or your own understanding.

HYLAS: To deal ingenuously, Philonous, now I consider the point, I do not find I can give you any good reason for it. But, thus much seems pretty plain, that it is at least possible such things may really exist. And, as long as there is no absurdity in supposing them, I am resolved to believe as I did, till you bring good reasons to the contrary.

PHILONOUS: What! is it come to this, that you only believe the existence of material objects, and that your belief is founded barely on the possibility of its being true? Then you will have me bring reasons against it: though another would think it reasonable the proof should lie on him who holds the affirmative. And, after all, this very point which you are now resolved to maintain, without any reason, is in effect what you have more than once during this discourse seen good reason to give up. But, to pass over all this; if I understand you rightly, you say our ideas do not exist without the mind; but that they are copies, images, or representatives, of certain originals that do?

HYLAS: You take me right.

PHILONOUS: They are then like external things?

HYLAS: They are.

PHILONOUS: Have those things a stable and permanent nature, independent of our senses; or are they in a perpetual change, upon our producing any motions in our bodies, suspending, exerting, or altering, our faculties or organs of sense?

HYLAS: Real things, it is plain, have a fixed and real nature, which remains the same notwithstanding any change in our sense, or in the posture and motion of our bodies; which indeed may affect the ideas in our minds, but it were absurd to think they had the same effect on things existing without the mind.

PHILONOUS: How then is it possible that things perpetually fleeting and variable as our ideas should be copies or images of anything fixed and constant? Or, in other words, since all sensible qualities, as size, figure, colour, &c., that is, our ideas, are continually changing upon every alteration in the distance, medium, or instruments of sensation; how can any determinate material objects be properly represented or painted forth by several distinct things, each of which is so different from and unlike the rest? Or, if you say it resembles some one only of our ideas, how shall we be able to distinguish the true copy from all the false ones?

HYLAS: I profess, Philonous, I am at a loss. I know not what to say to this.

PHILONOUS: But neither is this all. Which are material objects in themselves— perceptible or imperceptible?

HYLAS: Properly and immediately nothing can be perceived but ideas. All material things, therefore, are in themselves insensible, and to be perceived only by our ideas.

PHILONOUS: Ideas then are sensible, and their archetypes or originals insensible?

HYLAS: Right.

PHILONOUS: But how can that which is sensible be like that which is insensible? Can a real thing, in itself *invisible*, be like a *colour;* or a real thing, which is not *audible*, be like a *sound?* In a word, can anything be like a sensation or idea, but another sensation or idea?

HYLAS: I must own, I think not.

PHILONOUS: Is it possible there should be any doubt on the point? Do you not perfectly know your own ideas?

HYLAS: I know them perfectly; since what I do not perceive or know can be no part of my idea.

PHILONOUS: Consider, therefore, and examine them, and then tell me if there be anything in them which can exist without the mind? or if you can conceive anything like them existing without the mind?

HYLAS: Upon inquiry, I find it is impossible for me to conceive or understand how anything but an idea can be like an idea. And it is most evident that *no idea can exist without the mind.*

PHILONOUS: You are therefore, by our principles, forced to deny the reality of sensible things; since you made it to consist in an absolute existence exterior to the mind. That is to say, you are a downright sceptic. So I have gained my point, which was to show your principles led to Scepticism.

HYLAS: For the present I am, if not entirely convinced, at least silenced.

From George Berkeley, *Three Dialogues between Hylas and Philonous*, First Dialogue, 1713.

QUESTIONS FOR REVIEW AND DISCUSSION

1. Berkeley made the astonishing statement that there is no such thing as matter. How did he arrive at that conclusion? Refer here to Berkeley's example of the cherry.
2. Dr. Samuel Johnson was so outraged by Berkeley's denial of matter that he must have expressed the attitude of many when he kicked a large stone and said about Berkeley's theory, "I refute him thus." But did kicking the stone amount to a refutation? What did kicking the stone prove?
3. Berkeley said that "to be is to be perceived" *(esse est percipi).* You see books in your library: are the books still there when you walk out and are no longer perceiving the books? How does Berkeley deal with this question?

Picasso, *Girl Before a Mirror*. Woman looking into mirror for her identity. (*Pablo Picasso. "Girl Before a Mirror." March 1932. Oil on canvas. 64 × 51 1/4" [162.6 × 130.2 cm.] Collection The Museum of Modern Art, New York. Gift of Mrs. Simon Guggenheim.*)

P A R T   S I X

Personal Identity
What Am I?

I am a thing that thinks. . . . Nature also teaches me . . . that I am not lodged in my body as a pilot in a ship, but so intimately conjoined, and as it were intermingled with it, that with it I form a unitary whole.

René Descartes
Meditations (1640)

When I enter most intimately into what I call myself, I always stumble on some particular perception or other, of heat or cold, light or shade, love or hatred, pain or pleasure. I never can catch myself at any time without a perception and never can observe anything but the perception.

[Someone] may perhaps perceive something simple and continued which he calls himself; tho' I am certain there is no such principle in me.

David Hume
The Treatise of Human Nature (1739)

WHAT AM I?

Are you the same person you were five years ago? Your body is now different, but you have memories of those earlier days. Why should there even be a question about your identity? As it turns out, our clearest experience is that we possess a body, and at the same time we are conscious of a time when both our body and our thinking were in many respects different. Are we the same, that is, the identical person we were earlier in spite of several obvious changes in us? It appears that what makes it possible even to raise the question of personal identity is the fact of our "consciousness," our ability to think about ourselves as possessing a peculiar continuity, a persistence, in spite of continuous change.

Of the many aspects of this question about personal identity there is the underlying question "What am I?" One reason for this question is that the scientific conception of the physical world views this world as unthinking. We find ourselves as conscious beings in a world that is presumably made up of unthinking particles. As conscious beings, we have feelings, emotion, pains, and various mental states including beliefs and desires. How can there be consciousness or thinking if our bodies are composed of simple particles, of matter? It is no wonder that the pursuit of answers to this question led to the assumption that in addition to the body, there must be another substance, another form of being, the mind or soul, which together with the body constitutes the identity of a person. But to say that a person is a mind and body is to face a very complicated question about (1) whether there is such a thing as a mind and (2) how, if there is a mind, it is possible to relate these two, mind and body, into what we call a person. This will be the limited question on which the following readings will focus.

APPROACHES TO THE MIND-BODY PROBLEM

It was *René Descartes* who set the stage for this discussion by formulating his famous dualism between mind and body. He defined the"self" as "a thing that thinks." This has been the dominant view of many other thinkers since Descartes, but even for Descartes himself there were problems with this theory. In particular, there was the question of how the mind and the body are related to each other.

While Descartes tried to account for this relationship by saying that the mind is connected to the brain through a special gland, other philosophers concluded that Descartes had made a terrible mistake in his description of the mind. In particular, *Gilbert Ryle* of Oxford wrote a major book, *The Concept of Mind,* in which he charged that Descartes had made a "category mistake."

Other thinkers have wondered whether it is necessary to assume the existence of anything in addition to the body, saying that experiences of sensations and consciousness can be accounted for by the workings of the body alone. A related issue is whether machines have what we call minds—a fair question in a time of enormously sophisticated computers and robots. On the other hand, if what we call minds are something quite different from bodies, what happens to them when the body dies? This question was addressed by *Plato, Hume,* and *Kierkegaard* among others.

Finally *John Searle* of the University of California provides us with an analysis of the mind-body question in which he tries to solve this problem by employing a twentieth-century vocabulary in order to overcome the limitations of the seventeenth-century language which made the problem unsolvable.

26

The Separation of Mind and Body

Descartes

In modern philosophy, it was René Descartes who formulated the notion that the soul, or mind, and body are two distinct substances. This theory of dualism has been subjected to a contemporary critical analysis by Oxford's Gilbert Ryle, who has called Descartes's theory the myth of the "Ghost in the Machine."

The whole drift of Descartes's thought is in the direction of dualism, that is, the notion that there are two different kinds of substances in nature. We know a substance by its attribute, and since we clearly and distinctly know two quite different attributes, namely, *thought* and *extension*, there must be two different substances, the spiritual and the corporeal, mind and body. Because Descartes defines a substance as "an existent thing which requires nothing but itself to exist," he considers each substance as thoroughly independent of the other. To know something about the mind, therefore, we need make no reference to the body, and similarly, the body can be thoroughly understood without any reference to mind. One of the consequences of this dualism was that Descartes hereby separated theology and science and assumed that there need be no conflict between them. Science would study physical nature in isolation of any other discipline, since material substance possessed its own sphere of operation and could be understood in terms of its own laws.

If thought and extension are so distinct and separate, how can one account for living things? Descartes reasoned that because living bodies partake of extension, they are part of the material world. Consequently, living bodies operate according to the same mechanical and mathematical laws that govern other things in the material order. Speaking, for example, of animals, Descartes considered them to be *automata*, which behave automatically like machines, saying, "The greatest of all prejudices we have retained from infan-

For biographical note on Descartes, see p. 268.

451

Descartes and Queen Christina of Sweden. The queen invited Descartes to Sweden to learn and discuss his philosophy. (*Culver Pictures*)

cy is that of believing that brutes think." We assume animals think, says Descartes, only because we see them act as humans do on occasion, as when dogs do acrobatic tricks. Because *men* have two principles of motion, one physical and the other mental, we assume that when animals perform human-like acts their physical movements are caused by their mental powers. But Descartes saw no reason for attributing mental powers to animals, because all their motions, or actions, can be accounted for by mechanical considerations alone, since it is "nature which acts in them according to the disposition of their organs, just as a clock, which is only composed of wheels and weights. . . ." Thus animals are machines or automata. But what about human beings?

   Many activities of the human body, said Descartes, are as mechanical as those of animals. Such physical acts as respiration, circulation of the blood, and digestion are automatic. The workings of the human body could be reduced, he thought, to physics. Every physical event can be adequately accounted for by a consideration of mechanical or efficient causes; there is no need to consider a final cause when describing the physical processes of the body. Moreover, since Descartes believed that the total quantity of motion in the universe is constant, he was led to conclude that the movements of the human body could not *originate* in the human mind or soul; the soul, he said, could only affect or alter the direction of the motion in certain elements and parts of the body. Just how the mind could do this was difficult to explain precisely, because thought and extension, mind and body, were for Descartes such different and separate substances. He said that the soul does not move the various parts of the body directly, but having "its principal seat in the brain," in the pineal gland, it comes first of all in contact with the "vital spirits" and through these interacts with the body. Clearly, Descartes tried to give the human body a mechanical explanation and at the same time preserve the possibility of the soul's influence, through the activity of the will, on human behavior. Man, therefore, unlike an animal, is capable of several kinds of activities; he can engage in pure thought, his mind can be influenced by physical sensations and perceptions, his body can be directed by his mind, and his body is moved by purely mechanical forces.

But Descartes's strict dualism made it difficult for him to describe how the mind and body could interact on each other. If each substance is completely independent, the mind must dwell in the body as a pearl in an oyster, or, to use Descartes's own metaphor, as a pilot in a ship. Scholastic philosophy had described man as a unity, in which mind is the form and body is the matter, and said that without one there could not be the other. Hobbes had reduced mind to bodies in motion and achieved the unity of man in that way.

But Descartes aggravated the separation of mind and body by his novel definition of "thinking." For Descartes included in the act of thinking some experiences that had traditionally been referred to the body, namely, the whole sphere of sense perceptions, for example, "feeling." When Descartes defines "what I am" as "a thing which thinks," he makes no mention of the body, for everything is included in "thinking": a thinking thing "is a thing which doubts, understands, affirms, denies, wills, refuses, and which also imagines and *feels*. " Presumably the self could feel heat without a body. But here Descartes cannot, apparently, accept his own dualism, for he admits that "nature also teaches me by these sensations of pain, hunger, thirst, etc., that I am not lodged in my body as a pilot in a vessel, but that I am very closely united to it, and, so to speak, so intermingled with it that I seem to compose with it one whole." He attempted to locate the mind in the pineal gland, although even there the technical problem of interaction remains, for if there is interaction, there would have to be contact, and so mind would have to be extended. Concerning this problem, his rules of method did not lead him to any clear and distinct conclusion.

Reading _____

On the Relation between Mind and Body
Descartes

Simply from knowing that I exist, and that, meantime, I do not observe any other thing as evidently pertaining to my nature, i.e., to my essence, except this only, that I am a thinking thing, I rightly conclude that my essence consists in this alone, that I am a thinking thing (i.e., a substance, the whole nature or essence of which consists in thinking). And although possibly (or rather certainly, as I shall shortly be declaring) I have a body with which I am very closely conjoined, yet since on the one hand I have a clear and distinct idea of myself, in so far as I am only a thinking unextended thing, and on the other hand a distinct idea of the body, in so far as it is only an extended unthinking thing, it is certain that I am truly distinct from my body, and can exist without it.

I am also aware in me of certain faculties, such as the power of changing location, of assuming diverse postures, and the like, which cannot be thought, and cannot therefore exist, any more than can the preceding, apart from some substance in which they reside. But evidently, since the clear and distinct apprehension of these faculties involves the feature of extension, but not any intellection, they must, if they indeed exist, belong to some substance which is corporeal, i.e., extended and unthinking.

Now there is nothing which nature teaches me more expressly, or more sensibly, than that I have a body which is adversely affected when I sense pain, and stands in need of food and drink when I suffer hunger or thirst, etc.; and consequently I ought not to doubt there being some truth in all this.

Nature also teaches me by these sensings of pain, hunger, thirst, etc., that I am not lodged in my body merely as a pilot in a ship, but so intimately conjoined, and as it were intermingled with it, that with it I form a unitary whole. Were not this the case, I should not sense pain when my body is hurt, being, as I should then be, merely a thinking thing, but should apprehend the wound in a purely cognitive manner, just as a sailor apprehends by sight any damage to his ship; and when my body has need of food and drink I should apprehend this expressly, and not be made aware of it by confused sensings of hunger, thirst, pain, etc. For these sensings of hunger, thirst, pain, etc., are in truth merely confused modes of thinking, arising from and dependent on the union, and, as it were, the intermingling of mind and body.

Besides this, nature teaches me that my body exists as one among other bodies, some of which are to be sought after and others shunned. And certainly on sensing colors, sounds, odors, tastes, heat, hardness, and the like, I rightly conclude that in the bodies from which these various sensory apprehensions proceed, there are variations corresponding to them, though not perhaps resembling them; and since among these sense-apprehensions some are pleasing to me, and others displeasing, there can be no doubt that my body, or rather my entire self, inasmuch as I am composed of body and mind, can be variously affected, beneficially or harmfully, by surrounding bodies. Many things included in that totality of mind and body belong to the mind alone, e.g., the notion I have of the truth that what has once taken place can no longer not have taken place, and all these other truths which are known by the natural light, without the aid of the body, of these latter I am not here speaking. The term nature likewise extends to many things which pertain only to body, such as its having weight, and the like, and with these also I am not here dealing, but only with what God has given me as a being composed of body as well as of mind. Nature, taken in this special [restricted] sense, does indeed teach me to shun whatever causes me to sense pain, or to pursue what causes me to sense pleasure, and other things of that sort; but I do not find that it teaches me, by way of sensory apprehensions, that we should, without previous careful and mature mental examination of them, likewise draw conclusions regarding things located in the world outside us; for, as would seem, it is the task of the mind alone, not of the composite mind-body, to discern truth in questions of this kind.

In this inquiry, what I first note is the great difference between mind and body, in that body, from its very nature, is always divisible, and mind altogether indivisible. For truly, when I consider the mind, that is to say, my self in so far only as I am a thinking thing, I can distinguish in myself no parts; I apprehend myself to be a thing single and entire. Although the whole mind may seem to be united to the whole body, yet if a foot, an arm, or any other part of the body, is cut off, I know that my mind is not thereby diminished. Nor can its faculties of willing, sensing, understanding, etc., be spoken of as being its parts; it is one and the same mind which wills, which senses, which understands. The opposite holds in respect of a corporeal, i.e., of an extended, thing. I cannot think of it save as readily divisible into parts, and therefore recognize it as being divisible. This, of itself, would suffice to convince me that the mind is altogether different from the body, even if I had not already so decided on other grounds.

From René Descartes, "Meditations" in Descartes: *Philosophical Writings,* ed. trans. Norman Kemp Smith, Modern Library, Random House, New York, 1958.

QUESTIONS FOR REVIEW AND DISCUSSION

1. How did Descartes arrive at the conclusion that there are two substances, mind and body?
2. One problem Descartes had to solve was how to explain the relationship between mind and body. What was his answer?
3. What has been your experience concerning the relationship between your mind and your body?

27

Descartes' Category-Mistake

Ryle

Gilbert Ryle was born in 1900 and died in October of 1976. He spent most of his life at Oxford University. At age twenty-four he became a lecturer, and shortly after World War II he was appointed Oxford's Waynefleet Professor of Metaphysical Philosophy. His writings, including *Philosophical Arguments, Dilemmas,* and his influential article *"Systematically Misleading Expressions,"* established him as a significant figure in the world of philosophy. His book *The Concept of Mind,* published in London in 1949, is recognized as a classic. Our discussion of the main argument of this book and our brief selected reading from it will provide not only a provocative analysis of the mind-body problem but also a sample of Ryle's novel style of analytical philosophy.

As early as 1932, Ryle had already established his commitment to a new style in philosophy in his vigorous essay "Systematically Misleading Expressions." In this essay he wrote that to enquire "what it means to say so and so . . . is what philosophical analysis is, and . . . this is the sole and whole function of philosophy." Philosophy, says Ryle in the introduction to *The Concept of Mind,* does not give new information about minds, or for that matter about any other subject. "The philosophical arguments which constitute this book," he writes, "are not intended to increase what we know about minds, but to rectify the logical geography of the knowledge which we already possess."

THE GHOST IN THE MACHINE

Ryle contends that the "official doctrine" about the nature and the place of minds is unsound and contradicts virtually everything we know about minds. In its simplest form, the official doctrine holds that every human being has both a mind and a body, that these two are coordinated, but that upon the death of the body, the mind may continue both to exist and exert its powers. Not only is this basic theory of mind-body incorrect, says Ryle, but it also leads to many other serious errors as one elaborates the implications of this doctrine.

456

Gilbert Ryle at Magdalen College, Oxford University. (*Stumpf*)

It must follow from the official doctrine that each person has two collateral histories, one consisting of the events of his body and the other consisting of what transpires in and happens to his mind. Whereas human bodies are in space and are governed by mechanical physical laws, minds do not exist in space and are not subject to mechanical laws. A person's bodily life is publicly observable, while the activities of the mind are not accessible to external observers and are therefore private.

At this point a rather serious difficulty is encountered, because the contrast between the public character of the body and the private status of the mind requires one to say that the workings of the body are external whereas the workings of the mind are internal. It is then a short step to say that the mind is *in* the body. Although this language describing the place of the mind may be "metaphorical," since the mind which occupies no space could hardly be in any particular place, it is Ryle's contention that for the most part the contrast between the outer and inner realms is taken literally. Theorists in various disciplines take this contrast between "inner" and "outer" for granted. Stimuli are assumed to come from "outside" and from far distances generating responses inside the skull. Activity of the mind is said to produce external events such as a motion of the hand or eye; smiles suggest activities of the mind. All this suggests, too, some mode of transaction between the mind and body, but there is no method for either observing or reporting just how these transactions between mind and body take place. No laboratory experiment can discover this relationship.

Self-analysis and introspection are special modes of perception requiring no physical eye and are so private as to be a special privilege of the mind itself, to which no one else has direct access. Even though one were to assume that minds similar to one's own are located in other human bodies, there is no way to discover what they do or undergo. And so, says Ryle, "absolute solitude is on this showing the ineluctable destiny of the soul. Only our bodies can meet." Accordingly, our language, which presumes to describe someone's mental activities such as knowing, hoping, dreading, or intending, must be construed as signifying special events in the secret histories of people. No one has direct access to these mental operations, neither biographer, teacher, critic, or friend. But because we know how to use mental-conduct words and to use them with general correctness, earlier philosophers constructed their theories of the nature and place of minds in conformity with the official doctrine. They sought to identify the logical geography of their mental-conduct concepts, and thus arose what Ryle has called the basically incorrect "dogma of the Ghost in the Machine."

THE CATEGORY MISTAKE

What Ryle finds wrong with the official doctrine of the Ghost in the Machine is not that some details here and there are ambiguous, but that the very principle on which the theory rests is false. It is not even a series of particular mistakes. It is, says Ryle, one big mistake of a unique kind; this he calls a *category-mistake*. The big mistake consists in representing the facts of mental life as if they belonged to one and the same logical category, whereas in fact they belong to quite different and separate ones. The official doctrine is therefore a "myth," and it is necessary to "rectify the logic of mental-conduct concepts."

To indicate what is meant by a category-mistake, Ryle describes the imaginary visit of a foreigner to Oxford for the first time. The visitor is shown the playing fields, museums, scientific laboratories, and some of the colleges. Having seen these various places, the visitor asks, "But where is the University?" The question assumes that the University is yet another institution, a counterpart to the colleges and laboratories, another entity that can be seen in the same way as the others. Actually, the University is simply the way all he has already seen is coordinated. Thus the visitor's mistake consists in his assumption that one can correctly speak of the Bodleian Library, the Ashmolean Museum, All Souls College, *and* the University as if the University were the same kind of member in the class to which the others belong. In

High Street, Oxford, where Ryle walked to his lecture hall. (*Culver Pictures*)

short, the visitor mistakenly placed the University into the wrong category, a category in which it does not belong. In a similar illustration, Ryle speaks of the mistake made by a child watching a military parade in which a division is marching by. Having been told that he was seeing battalions, batteries, and squadrons, the child wanted to know when the division was going to appear. Again, he assumed that the division is another unit similar to the others, not realizing that in seeing the battalions, batteries, and squadrons, he had already seen the division. His mistake was in thinking it correct to speak of battalions, batteries, squadrons, *and* a division. He placed the division in the wrong category. The category-mistake indicates an inability to use certain elements in the English language correctly. What is more significant, says Ryle, is that people who are perfectly capable of applying concepts are nevertheless liable in their abstract thinking to allocate these concepts to logical categories to which they do not belong.

What Ryle has sought to do through these illustrations is to show, as he says, that "a family of radical category-mistakes is the source of the double-life theory." The notion that a person is a ghost mysteriously ensconced in a machine is a consequence of thinking that because a person's feeling, thinking, and purposive activity cannot be described solely in terms of physics, it must be described as something similar to or having bodily characteristics, even though the mind is not a body. Moreover, because mental conduct differs so from bodily activities, the official theory sought to invest mind with its own status, although made of a different stuff and having a different structure, and possessing its own complex organization. Body and mind were thought to be separate fields of causes and effects, the body's being mechanical and the mind's nonmechanical.

How did this category-mistake originate? Although Ryle designates Descartes as the major culprit of this error, it is obvious that the mind-body dualism has a history extending very much farther back than the seventeenth century. Still, Descartes's special formulation of this official doctrine for modern philosophy, says Ryle, followed Galileo's assertion that his methods of scientific discovery were capable of providing a mechanical theory which would be applicable to every occupant in space. From a strictly scientific point of view, Descartes was impressed with the mechanical description of nature, but as a religious and moral person, he was reluctant to agree with the claim that human nature in its mental aspects differs only in degree of complexity from a machine. Consequently, Descartes and subsequent philosophers wrongly construed mental-conduct words to signify nonmechanical processes and concluded that nonmechanical laws must explain the nonspatial workings of minds. But what this explanation retained was the assumption that mind, although different from body, was nevertheless a member of the categories of "thing," "stuff," "state," "process," "cause," and "effect." Thus, just as the visitor expected the University to be another extra unit, so Descartes and his heirs treated minds as additional, although special, centers of the causal process.

From these conclusions a host of theoretical difficulties arose. How are the mind and body related? How do they cause effects in each other? If the mind is governed by strict laws analogous to the law governing the body, does this not imply a determinism, in which case such notions as responsibility, choice, merit, and freedom make no sense? Worst of all, only negative terms could be used to speak of the mind as compared with the body, since minds are not in space, have no motions, are not aspects of matter, and are not capable of observation. For these and others reasons, Ryle concludes that the entire argument of the Ghost in the Machine is "broken-backed."

In a sustained and careful analysis of several assertions "about the mind," Ryle seeks to clarify the assertions by arguing in each case that mental-conduct words do indeed refer to mental acts but not to minds. The acts of knowing, exercising intelligence, understanding, willing, feeling, imagining, and the like, according to the official theory, were considered as being unconnected with the body and as occurring, when referred to in the present tense, in the mind. Refuting this, Ryle holds that in virtually every assertion about the mind some facts about bodily behavior are relevant. For example, in speaking of human emotions, one does not infer the working of some interior and obscure forces. In favorable circumstances, says Ryle, "I find out your inclinations and your moods more directly than this. I hear and understand your conversational avowals, your interjections and your tones of voice; I see and understand your gestures and facial expressions." Or, if we consider that the act of theorizing is the distinctive act of human intelligence and that this supports the dogma of the Ghost in the Machine, Ryle gives various rejoinders, including the following: "To find that most people have minds . . . is simply to find that they are able and prone to do certain sorts of things, and this we do by witnessing the sorts of things they do." Or, "overt intelligent performances are not clues to the workings of minds; they are those workings." Ryle says, further, that "in opposition to this entire dogma, I am arguing that in describing the workings of a person's mind we are not describing a second set of shadowy operations. We are describing his one career; namely we are describing the ways in which parts of his conduct are managed." And again, in speaking about the act of *understanding,* Ryle says, "It is being maintained throughout this book that when we characterize people by mental predicates, we are not making untestable inferences to, say, ghostly processes occurring in streams of consciousness which we are debarred from visiting; we are describing the ways in which those people conduct parts of their predominantly public behavior." Things we say about the mind are therefore made true or false not by inner private events but by what has happened or will happen publicly. To say of someone that he is intelligent appears to be an assertion about his mind, but Ryle argues that it is rather a statement of our knowledge about him and a description of his public performance.

What Ryle has sought to achieve through his analysis is a new theory of mind. It may appear that he is arguing that only bodies exist, that mental-conduct words are really statements about bodily behavior, and that there is no independent private inner life. It was his intention in his *The Concept of Mind* to "dissipate the contrast between Mind and Matter," not by reducing the one to the other, but by demonstrating that the polar opposition between mind and matter can be solved by rejecting the assumption that they are terms of the same logical type.

Reading _____

Descartes' Myth: A Category-Mistake
Ryle

(1) THE OFFICIAL DOCTRINE

There is a doctrine about the nature and place of minds which is so prevalent among theorists and even among laymen that it deserves to be described as the official theory. Most philosophers, psychologists and religious teachers subscribe, with minor reservations, to its main articles and, although they admit certain theoretical difficulties in it, they tend to assume that these can be overcome without serious modifications being made to the architecture of the theory. It will be argued here that the central principles of the doctrine are unsound and conflict with the whole body of what we know about minds when we are not speculating about them.

The official doctrine, which hails chiefly from Descartes, is something like this. With the doubtful exceptions of idiots and infants in arms every human being has both a body and a mind. Some would prefer to say that every human being is both a body and a mind. His body and his mind are ordinarily harnessed together, but after the death of the body his mind may continue to exist and function.

Human bodies are in space and are subject to the mechanical laws which govern all other bodies in space. . . .

But minds are not in space, nor are their operations subject to mechanical laws. The workings of one mind are not witnessable by other observers; its career is private. Only I can take direct cognisance of the states and processes of my own mind. A person therefore lives through two collateral histories, one consisting of what happens in and to his body, the other consisting of what happens in and to his mind. The first is public, the second private. The events in the first history are events in the physical world, those in the second are events in the mental world. . . .

It is customary to express this bifurcation of his two lives and of his two worlds by saying that the things and events which belong to the physical world, including his own body, are external, while the workings of his own mind are internal. This antithesis of outer and inner is of course meant to be construed as a metaphor, since minds, not being in space, could not be described as being spatially inside anything else, or as having things going on spatially inside themselves. But relapses from this good intention are common and theorists are found speculating how stimuli, the physical sources of which are yards or miles outside a person's skin, can generate mental responses inside his skull, or how decisions framed inside his cranium can set going movements of his extremities.

Even when "inner" and "outer" are construed as metaphors, the problem how a person's mind and body influence one another is notoriously charged with theoretical difficulties. What the mind wills, the legs, arms and the tongue execute; what affects the ear and the eye has something to do with what the mind perceives; grimaces and smiles betray the mind's moods and bodily castigations lead, it is hoped, to moral improvement. But the actual transactions between the episodes of the private history and those of the public history remain mysterious, since by definition they can belong to neither series. . . .

Underlying this partly metaphorical representation of the bifurcation of a person's two lives there is a seemingly more profound and philosophical assumption. It is assumed that there are two different kinds of existence or status. What exists or happens may have the status of physical existence, or it may have the status of mental existence. Somewhat as the faces of coins are either heads or tails, or somewhat as living creatures are either male or female,

Magdalen College, Oxford, where Ryle's study was located. (*Alfred Savage, Ltd.*)

so, it is supposed, some existing is physical existing, other existing is mental existing. It is a necessary feature of what has physical existence that it is in space and time; it is a necessary feature of what has mental existence that it is in time but not in space. What has physical existence is composed of matter, or else is a function of matter; what has mental existence consists of consciousness, or else is a function of consciousness. . . .

What sort of knowledge can be secured of the workings of a mind? On the one side, according to the official theory, a person has direct knowledge of the best imaginable kind of the workings of his own mind. Mental states and processes are (or are normally) conscious states and processes, and the consciousness which irradiates them can engender no illusions and leaves the door open for no doubts. A person's present thinkings, feelings and willings, his perceivings, rememberings and imaginings are intrinsically "phosphorescent"; their existence and their nature are inevitably betrayed to their owner. The inner life is a stream of consciousness of such a sort that it would be absurd to suggest that the mind whose life is that stream might be unaware of what is passing down it.

True, the evidence adduced recently by Freud seems to show that there exist channels tributary to this stream, which run hidden from their owner. People are actuated by impulses the existence of which they vigorously disavow; some of their thoughts differ from the thoughts which they acknowledge; and some of the actions which they think they will to perform they do not really will. They are thoroughly gulled by some of their own hypocrisies and they successfully ignore facts about their mental lives which on the official theory ought to be patent to them. Holders of the official theory tend, however, to maintain that anyhow in normal circumstances a person must be directly and authentically seized of the present state and workings of his own mind.

On the other side, one person has no direct access of any sort to the events of the inner life of another. He cannot do better than make problematic inferences from the observed behaviour of the other person's body to the states of mind which, by analogy from his own conduct, he supposes to be signalised by that behaviour. Direct access to the workings of a mind is the privilege of that mind itself; in default of such privileged access, the workings of one mind are inevitably occult to everyone else. For the supposed arguments from bodily movements similar to their own to mental workings similar to their own would lack any possibility of observational corroboration. Not unnaturally, therefore, an adherent of the official theory finds it difficult to resist this consequence of his premises, that he has no good reason to believe that there do exist minds other than his own. Even if he prefers to believe that to other human bodies there are harnessed minds not unlike his own, he cannot claim to be able to discover their individual characteristics, or the particular things that they undergo and do. Absolute solitude is on this showing the ineluctable destiny of the soul. Only our bodies can meet. . . .

(2) THE ABSURDITY OF THE OFFICIAL DOCTRINE

Such in outline is the official theory. I shall often speak of it, with deliberate abusiveness, as "the dogma of the Ghost in the Machine." I hope to prove that it is entirely false, and false not in detail but in principle. It is not merely an assemblage of particular mistakes. It is one big mistake and a mistake of a special kind. It is, namely, a category-mistake. It represents the facts of mental life as if they belonged to one logical type or category (or range of types or categories), when they actually belong to another. The dogma is therefore a philosopher's myth. In attempting to explode the myth I shall probably be taken to be denying well-known facts about the mental life of human beings, and my plea that I aim at doing nothing more than rectify the logic of mental-conduct concepts will probably be disallowed as mere subterfuge.

[An illustration of category-mistake.] A foreigner watching his first game of cricket learns what are the functions of the bowlers, the batsmen, the fielders, the umpires and the scores. He then says, "But there is no one left on the field to contribute to the famous element of team-spirit. I see who does the bowling, the batting and the wicket-keeping; but I do not see whose role it is to exercise *esprit de corps.*" It would have to be explained that he was looking for the wrong type of thing. Team-spirit is not another cricketing-operation supplementary to all of the other special tasks. It is, roughly, the keenness with which each of the special tasks is performed, and performing a task keenly is not performing two tasks. Certainly exhibiting team-spirit is not the same thing as bowling or catching, but nor is it a third thing such that we can say that the bowler first bowls *and* then exhibits team-spirit or that a fielder is at a given moment *either* catching *or* displaying *esprit de corps.*

Illustrations of category-mistakes have a common feature which must be noticed. The mistakes were made by people who did not know how to wield the concepts *University, division* and *team-spirit.* Their puzzles arose from inability to use certain items in the English vocabulary. . . .

My destructive purpose is to show that a family of radical category-mistakes is the source of the double-life theory. The representation of a person as a ghost mysteriously ensconced in a machine derives from this argument. Because, as is true, a person's thinking, feeling and purposive doing cannot be described solely in the idioms of physics, chemistry and physiology, therefore they must be described in counterpart idioms. As the human body is a complex organised unit, so the human mind must be another complex organised unit, though one made of a different sort of stuff and with a different sort of structure. Or, again, as the human body, like any other parcel of matter, is a field of causes and effects, so the mind must be another field of causes and effects, though not (Heaven be praised) mechanical causes and effects.

QUESTIONS FOR REVIEW AND DISCUSSION

1. Ryle uses the phrase "Ghost in the Machine" to describe Descartes' concept of the mind. Why do you suppose Ryle uses the word "Ghost"?
2. Ryle's major criticism is that Descartes has committed a serious "category-mistake." How would you describe this mistake?
3. How, in contrast to Descartes, does Ryle describe his own theory of what "mental-conduct words" represent; they do in fact represent "mental acts," but do they refer to a mind? What in short is the best explanation of "knowing," "willing," "feeling," "imagining," and exercising "intelligence"?
4. Do Ryle's examples or analogies of "Oxford University" or "military divisions" help you to understand the relationship between mind and body and between mental and bodily acts?

28

Do Minds Survive Death of the Body?

Plato, Hume, and Kierkegaard

Our discussion of mind and body leaves open the question of what happens to the mind upon death. Three philosophers who were specifically concerned with the question of immortality were Plato, Hume, and Kierkegaard. Each had a different notion of human nature. Consequently, each had a quite different view of life after death.

We have already seen that Plato believed that the body is the prison house of the soul. Moreover, Plato believed that the soul exists even before it enters the body. Bodily existence is an unhappy and discouraging experience because the body tends to drag the soul down from its higher or purer form of life. The pleasures of the body and of wealth are incapable of providing lasting happiness. Also, the senses such as sight, touch, hearing, and taste are deceptive because they are never accurate. Man's pursuit of truth and true pleasure is always frustrated by the body, which is an obstacle to the clear working of the soul or mind. Our best thinking and our longest-lasting pleasures come when the mind is functioning independently of the body. Daily life is complicated by the passions and appetites of the body, against which the soul must constantly struggle. Most important of all, says Plato, is the fact that we cannot achieve through our bodily faculties the objectives we long for most of all, namely, the highest in everything, of beauty, goodness, justice, and truth. Plato asks, "Did you ever reach with bodily senses . . . absolute greatness, health, and strength and the essence or true nature of everything? Has the reality of them ever been perceived by you through the bodily organs?" The body is the "source of endless trouble," says Plato, because "it fills us full of loves and lusts, and fears, and fancies of all kinds, and endless foolery, and in fact, as men say, takes away from us the power of thinking at all."

This whole line of reasoning is not a proof of immortality. It is rather a

For biographical note on Plato, see p. 135; on Hume, p. 287; and on Kierkegaard, p. 552.

way of saying that one should not fear death. Life in bodily form is not so great. Death means the liberation of the soul from the body. What makes this analysis possible for Plato is his view that the soul or mind is more real than the body. Ideas and the mind are eternal. The separation of the soul from the body at death represents a purification of the soul.

Hume, however, denied that man has a soul. Nor does man have a *self*. We do not even have an idea of a self. It may be paradoxical that *I* should say that I do not have an idea of myself. But Hume asks, "From what impression could this idea be derived?" Is there any continuous and identical reality which forms our ideas of self? Do we have any one impression that is invariably associated with our ideas of *self*? "When I enter most intimately into what I call *myself*," says Hume, "I always stumble on some particular perception or other, of heat, cold, love, or hatred, pain, or pleasure. I never catch *myself* at any time without a perception and never can observe anything but the perception." Hume therefore denies the existence of a continuous self-identity and says about the rest of mankind that "they are nothing but a bundle or collection of different perceptions." How then do we account for what we think is the self? It is, says Hume, our power of memory that gives the impression of our continuous identity. Hume compares the mind to "a kind of theatre where several perceptions successively make their appearance" but adds that "we have not the most distant notion of the place where these scenes are represented. . . ."

If there is no self, then there is nothing that can have immortality. Earlier philosophers, including Plato, described the self, or mind, as a form of *substance*. Hume denied the existence of substance. Substance was supposed to be the reality which *has* certain qualities: the statement "the apple is red" suggests that the color red is one thing while the apple, which has the color, is the reality underneath the color and is therefore a different thing. Similarly, thinking suggests, as Descartes said, that there is a thing that thinks. In this view, mind or soul is a substance. But Hume denied the self for the same reason that he denied substance. He saw no way philosophically to prove that there is any self that could have immortality.

In the reading that concludes this section, Kierkegaard has some provocative things to say about death and immortality. The most important point he wants to drive home is the difference between general subjects, on the one hand, and intensely personal subjects, on the other. It is one thing, for example, to talk about world, or what he calls universal, history. It is even one thing to talk about death or immortality *in general*. It is quite a different thing to talk about death as *my* death or immortality as *my* immortality.

Reading _____

The Immortality of the Soul
Plato

I desire to prove to you that the real philosopher has reason to be of good cheer when he is about to die, and that after death he may hope to obtain the greatest good in the other world. And how this may be, Simmias and Cebes, I will endeavour to explain. For I deem that the true votary of philosophy is likely to be misunderstood by other men; they do not perceive that he is always pursuing death and dying; and if this be so, and he has had the desire of death all his life long, why when his time comes should he repine at that which he has been always pursuing and desiring?

Simmias said laughingly: Though not in a laughing humour, you have made me laugh, Socrates; for I cannot help thinking that the many when they hear your words will say how truly you have described philosophers, and our people at home will likewise say that the life which philosophers desire is in reality death, and that they have found them out to be deserving of the death which they desire.

And they are right, Simmias, in thinking so, with the exception of the words "they have found them out"; for they have not found out either what is the nature of that death which the true philosopher deserves, or how he deserves or desires death. But enough of them:—let us discuss the matter among ourselves. Do we believe that there is such a thing as death?

To be sure, replied Simmias.

Is it not the separation of soul and body? And to be dead is the completion of this; when the soul exists in herself, and is released from the body and the body is released from the soul, what is this but death?

Just so, he replied.

There is another question, which will probably throw light on our present inquiry if you and I can agree about it:—Ought the philosopher to care about the pleasures—if they are to be called pleasures—of eating and drinking?

Certainly not, answered Simmias.

And what about the pleasures of love—should he care for them?

By no means.

And will he think much of the other ways of indulging the body, for example, the acquisition of costly raiment, or sandals, or other adornments of the body? Instead of caring about them, does he not rather despise anything more than nature needs? What do you say?

I should say that the true philosopher would despise them.

Would you not say that he is entirely concerned with the soul and not with the body? He would like, as far as he can, to get away from the body and to turn to the soul.

Quite true.

In matters of this sort philosophers, above all other men, may be observed in every sort of way to dissever the soul from the communion of the body.

Very true.

Whereas, Simmias, the rest of the world are of opinion that to him who has no sense of pleasure and no part in bodily pleasure, life is not worth having; and that he who is indifferent about them is as good as dead.

That is also true.

What again shall we say of the actual acquirement of knowledge?—is the body, if invited to share in the enquiry, a hinderer or a helper? I mean to say, have sight and hearing any truth in them? Are they not, as the poets are always telling us, inaccurate witnesses? and yet, if even they are inaccurate and indistinct, what is to be said of the other senses?—for you will allow that they are the best of them?

Certainly, he replied.

Then when does the soul attain truth?—for in attempting to consider anything in company with the body she is obviously deceived.

True.

Then must not true existence be revealed to her in thought, if at all?

Yes.

And thought is best when the mind is gathered into herself and none of these things trouble her—neither sounds nor sights nor pain nor any pleasure—when she takes leave of the body, and has as little as possible to do with it, when she has no bodily sense or desire, but is aspiring after true being?

Certainly.

And in this the philosopher dishonours the body; his soul runs away from his body and desires to be alone and by herself?

That is true.

Well, but there is another thing, Simmias: Is there or is there not an absolute justice?

Assuredly there is.

And an absolute beauty and absolute good?

Of course.

But did you ever behold any of them with your eyes?

Certainly not.

Or did you ever reach them with any other bodily sense?—and I speak not of these alone, but of absolute greatness, and health, and strength, and of the essence or true nature of everything. Has the reality of them ever been perceived by you through the bodily organs? or rather, is not the nearest approach to the knowledge of their several natures made by him who so orders his intellectual vision as to have the most exact conception of the essence of each thing which he considers?

Certainly.

And he attains to the purest knowledge of them who goes to each with the mind alone, not introducing or intruding in the act of thought sight or any other sense together with reason, but with the very light of the mind in her own clearness searches into the very truth of each; he who has got rid, as far as he can, of eyes and ears and, so to speak, of the whole body, these being in his opinion distracting elements which when they infect the soul hinder her from acquiring truth and knowledge—who, if not he, is likely to attain to the knowledge of true being?

What you say has a wonderful truth in it, Socrates, replied Simmias.

And when real philosophers consider all these things, will they not be led to make a reflection which they will express in words something like the following? "Have we not found," they will say, "a path of thought which seems to bring us and our argument to the conclusion, that while we are in the body, and while the soul is infected with the evils of the body, our desire will not be satisfied? and our desire is of the truth. For the body is a source of endless trouble to us by reason of the mere requirement of food; and is liable also to diseases which overtake and impede us in the search after true being: it fills us full of loves, and lusts, and fears, and fancies of all kinds, and endless foolery, and in fact, as men say, takes away from us the power of thinking at all. Whence come wars, and fightings, and factions? whence but from the body and the lusts of the body? Wars are occasioned by the love of money, and money has to be acquired for the sake and in the service of the body; and by reason of all these impediments we have no time to give to philosophy; and, last and worst of all, even if we are at leisure and betake ourselves to some speculation, the body is always breaking in upon us, causing turmoil and confusion in our enquiries, and so amazing us that we are prevented from seeing the truth. It has been proved to us by experience that if we would have pure knowledge of anything we must be quit of the body—the soul in herself must behold things in themselves: and then we shall attain the wisdom which we desire, and of which we say that we are lovers; not while we live, but after death; for if while in company with the body, the soul cannot have pure knowledge, one of two things follows—either knowledge is not to be attained at all, or, if at all, after death. For then, and not till then, the soul will be parted from the body and exist in herself alone. In this present life, I reckon that we make the nearest approach to knowledge when we have the least possible intercourse or communion with the body, and are not surfeited with the bodily nature, but keep ourselves pure until the hour when God himself is pleased to release us. And thus having got rid of the foolishness of the body we shall be pure and hold converse with the pure, and know of ourselves the clear light everywhere, which is no other than the light of truth." For the impure are not permitted to approach the pure. These are the sort of words, Simmias, which the true lovers of knowledge cannot help saying to one another, and thinking. You would agree; would you not?

Undoubtedly, Socrates.

But, O my friend, if this be true, there is great reason to hope that, going whither I go, when I have come to the end of my journey, I shall attain that which has been the pursuit of my life. And therefore I go on my way rejoicing, and not I only, but every other man who believes that his mind has been made ready and that he is in a manner purified.

Certainly, replied Simmias.

And what is purification but the separation of the soul from the body, as I was saying before; the habit of the soul gathering and collecting herself into herself from all sides out of the body; the dwelling in her own place alone, as in another life, so also in this, as far as she can;—the release of the soul from the chains of the body?

Very true, he said.

And this separation and release of the soul from the body is termed death?

To be sure, he said.

And the true philosophers, and they only, are ever seeking to release the soul. Is not the separation and release of the soul from the body their especial study?

That is true.

And, as I was saying at first, there would be a ridiculous contradiction in men studying to live as nearly as they can in a state of death, and yet repining when it comes upon them.

Clearly.

And the true philosophers, Simmias, are always occupied in the practice of dying, wherefore also to them least of all men is death terrible. Look at the matter thus:—if they have been in every way the enemies of the body, and are wanting to be alone with the soul, when this desire of theirs is granted, how inconsistent would they be if they trembled and repined, instead of rejoicing at their departure to that place where, when they arrive, they hope to gain that which in life they desired—and this was wisdom—and at the same time to be rid of the company of their enemy. Many a man has been willing to go to the world below animated by the hope of seeing there an earthly love, or wife, or son, and conversing with them. And will he who is a true lover of wisdom, and is strongly persuaded in like manner that only in the world below he can worthily enjoy her, still repine at death? Will he not depart with joy? Surely he will, O my friend, if he be a true philosopher. For he will have a firm conviction that there, and there only, he can find wisdom in her purity. And if this be true, he would be very absurd, as I was saying, if he were afraid of death.

From Plato, "Phaedo," in *Dialogues of Plato,* trans. Benjamin Jowett, Oxford University Press, Eng., 1920.

Reading _____

Concerning the Immortality of the Soul
Hume

The physical arguments from the analogy of nature are strong for the mortality of the soul: and these are really the only philosophical arguments, which ought to be admitted with regard to this question, or indeed any question of fact.

Hume's lodgings, Edinburgh. (*New York Public Library Picture Collection*)

Where any two objects are so closely connected, that all alterations, which we have seen in the one, are attended with proportionable alterations in the other: we ought to conclude, by all rules of analogy, that, when there are still greater alterations produced in the former, and it is totally dissolved, there follows a total dissolution of the latter.

Sleep, a very small effect on the body, is attended with a temporary extinction: at least, a great confusion in the soul.

The weakness of the body and that of the mind in infancy are exactly proportioned; their vigour in manhood, their sympathetic disorder in sickness, their common gradual decay in old age. The step further seems unavoidable; their common dissolution in death.

The last symptoms, which the mind discovers, are disorder, weakness, insensibility, and stupidity; the forerunners of its annihilation. The further progress of the same causes, increasing the same effects, totally extinguish it.

Judging by the usual analogy of nature, no form can continue, when transferred to a condition of life very different from the original one, in which it was placed. Trees perish in the water; fishes in the air; animals in the earth. Even so small a difference as that of climate is often fatal. What reason then to imagine, that an immense alteration, such as is made on the soul by the dissolution of its body, and all its organs of thought and sensation, can be effected without the dissolution of the whole?

Everything is in common betwixt soul and body. The organs of the one are all of them the organs of the other. The existence therefore of the one must be dependent on the other.

The souls of animals are allowed to be mortal: and these bear so near a resemblance to the souls of men, that the analogy from one to the other forms a very strong argument. Their bodies are not more resembling: yet no one rejects the argument drawn from comparative anatomy.

Nothing in this world is perpetual; Everything, however seemingly firm, is in continual flux and change: The world itself gives symptoms of frailty and dissolution: How contrary to analogy, therefore, to imagine, that one single form, seeming the frailest of any, and subject to the greatest disorders is immortal and indissoluble! What a daring theory is that! How lightly, not to say how rashly, entertained!

How to dispose of the infinite number of posthumous existences ought also to embarrass the religious theory. Every planet, in every solar system, we are at liberty to imagine peopled with intelligent, mortal beings: At least we can fix on no other supposition. For these, then, a new universe must, every generation, be created beyond the bounds of the present universe: or one must have been created at first so prodigiously wide as to admit of this continual influx of beings. Ought such bold suppositions to be received by philosophy: and that merely on the pretext of a bare possibility?

When it is asked, whether *Agamemnon, Thersites, Hannibal, Nero,* and every stupid clown, that ever existed in *Italy, Scythia, Bactria,* or *Guinea,* are now alive; can any man think, that a scrutiny of nature will furnish arguments strong enough to answer so strange a question in the affirmative? The want of argument, without revelation, sufficiently establishes the negative. . . .

Were our horrors of annihilation an original passion, not the effect of our general love of happiness, it would rather prove the mortality of the soul: For as nature does nothing in vain, she would never give us a horror against an impossible event. She may give us a horror against an unavoidable event, provided our endeavours, as in the present case, may often remove it to some distance. Death is in the end unavoidable; yet the human species could not be preserved, had not nature inspired us with an aversion towards it. All doctrines are to be suspected which are favoured by our passions. And the hopes and fears which give rise to this doctrine are very obvious.

'Tis an infinite advantage in every controversy, to defend the negative. If the question be out of the common experienced course of nature, this circumstance is almost, if not altogether, decisive. By what arguments or analogies can we prove any state of existence, which no one ever saw, and which no way resembles any that ever was seen? Who will repose such trust in any pretended philosophy, as to admit upon its testimony the reality of so marvelous a scene? Some new species of logic is requisite for that purpose; and some new faculties of the mind, that they may enable us to comprehend that logic.

Nothing could set in a fuller light the infinite obligations which mankind have to Divine revelation; since we find, that no other medium could ascertain this great and important truth.

From David Hume, "Of the Immortality of the Soul," written 1755.

Reading _____

Death and Immortality Are *My* Death and Immortality

Kierkegaard

Christianity protests every form of objectivity; it desires that the subject should be infinitely concerned about himself. It is subjectivity that Christianity is concerned with, and it is only in subjectivity that its truth exists, if it exists at all; objectively, Christianity has absolutely no existence. If its truth happens to be in only a single subject, it exists in him alone; and there is greater Christian joy in heaven over this one individual than over universal history and the System, which as objective entities are incommensurable for that which is Christian. . . .

For example, the problem of *What it means to die*. I know that I shall die if I take a dose of sulphuric acid, and also if I drown myself, or go to sleep in an atmosphere of coal gas, and so forth. I know that Napoleon always went about with poison ready to hand, and that Juliet in Shakespeare poisoned herself. I know that the Stoics regarded suicide as a courageous deed, and that others consider it a cowardly act. I know that death may result from so ridiculous and trivial a circumstance that even the most serious-minded of men cannot help laughing at death; I know that it is possible to escape what appears to be certain death, and so forth. I know that the tragic hero dies in the fifth act of the drama, and that death here has an infinite significance in pathos; but that when a bartender dies, death does not have this significance. I know that the poet can interpret death in a diversity of moods, even to the limit of the comical; I pledge myself to produce the same diversity of effects in prose. I know furthermore what the clergy are accustomed to say on this subject, and I am familiar with the general run of themes treated at funerals. If nothing else stands in the way of my passing over to world-history, I am ready; I need only purchase black cloth for a ministerial gown, and I shall engage to preach funeral sermons as well as any ordinary clergyman. I freely admit that those who wear a velvet inset in their gowns do it more elegantly; but this distinction is not essential any more than the difference between five dollars and ten dollars for the hearse.

Nevertheless, in spite of this almost extraordinary knowledge or facility in knowledge, I can by no means regard death as something I have understood. Before I pass over to universal history—of which I must always say: "God knows whether it is any concern of yours"—it seems to me that I had better think about this, lest existence mock me, because I had become so learned and highfalutin that I had forgotten to understand what will some time happen to me as to every human being—sometime, nay, what am I saying: suppose death were so treacherous as to come tomorrow! Merely this one uncertainty, when it is to be understood and held fast by an existing individual, and hence enter into every thought, precisely because it is an uncertainty entering into my beginning upon universal history even, so that I make it clear to myself whether if death comes tomorrow, I am beginning upon something that is worth beginning—merely this one uncertainty generates inconceivable difficulties, difficulties that not even the speaker who treats of death is always aware of, in that he thinks that he apprehends the uncertainty of death, while nevertheless forgetting to think it into what he says about it, so that he speaks movingly and with emotion about the uncertainty of death, and yet ends by encouraging his hearers to make a resolution for the whole of life. This is essentially to forget the uncertainty of death, since otherwise the enthusiastic resolve for the whole of life must be made commensurable with the uncertainty of death. To think about it once for all, or once a year at matins of New Year's morning, is of course nonsense, and is the same as not thinking about it at all.

If, on the other hand, the uncertainty of death is merely something in general, then my own death is itself only something in general. Perhaps this is also the case for systematic philosophers, for absent-minded people. For the late Herr Soldin, his own death is supposed to have been such a something in general: "when he was about to get up in the morning he was not aware that he was dead." But the fact of my own death is not for me by any means such a something in general, although for others, the fact of my death may indeed be something of that sort. Nor am I for myself such a something in general, although perhaps for others I may be a mere generality. But if the task of life is to become subjective, then every subject will for *himself* become the very opposite of such a something in general. And it would seem to be a somewhat embarrassing thing to be significant for universal history, and then at home, in company with oneself, to be merely a something in general. It is already embarrassing enough for a man who is an extraordinarily important figure in the public assembly to come home to his wife, and then to be for her only such a something in general; or to be a world-historical Diedrich Menschenschreck, and then at home to be—aye, I do not care to say anything more. But it is still more embarrassing to have so low a standing with oneself, and it is most embarrassing of all to remain unaware of the fact that this is so.

The question then arises as to what death is, and especially as to what it is for the living individual. We wish to know how the conception of death will transform a man's entire life, when in order to think its uncertainty he has to think it in every moment, so as to prepare himself for it. We wish to know what it means to prepare for death, since here again one must distinguish between its actual presence and the thought of it. This distinction appears to make all my preparation insignificant, if that which really comes is not that for which I prepared myself; and if it is the same, then my preparation is in its perfection identical with death itself. And I must take into account the fact that death may come in the very moment that I begin my preparation. The question must be raised of the possibility of finding an ethical expression for the significance of death, and a religious expression for the victory over death; one needs a solving word which explains its mystery, and a binding word by which the living individual defends himself against the ever recurrent conception; for surely we dare scarcely recommend mere thoughtlessness and forgetfulness as wisdom.

When death thus becomes something to be related to the entire life of the subject, I must confess I am very far indeed from having understood it, even if it were to cost me my life to make this confession. Still less have I realized the task existentially. And yet I have thought about this subject again and again; I have sought for guidance in books—and I have found none.

For example, what does it mean to be immortal? In this respect, I know what people generally know. I know that some hold a belief in immortality, that others say they do not hold it; whether they actually do not hold it I know not; it does not occur to me therefore to want to combat them, for such an undertaking is so dialectically difficult that I should need a year and a day before it could become dialectically clear to me whether there is any reality in such a contest; whether the dialectic of communication, when it is properly understood, would approve of such a proceeding or transform it into a mere beating of the air; whether the consciousness of immortality is a doctrinal topic which is appropriate as a subject for instruction, and how the dialectic of instruction must be determined with relation to the learner's presuppositions; whether these presuppositions are not so essential that the instruction becomes a

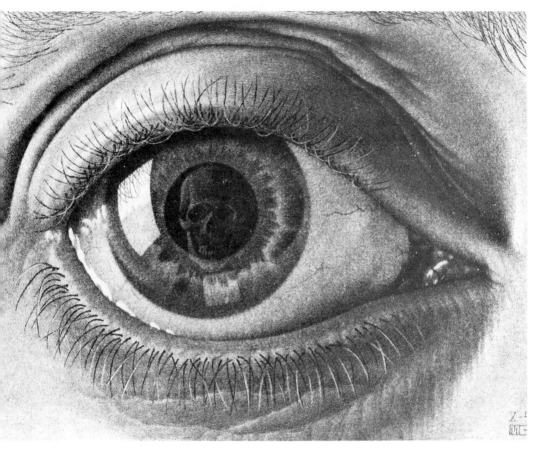

The Eye, Escher. Each person must visualize his own death. (© 1946 M. C. Escher/Cordon Art-Baarn-Holland.)

deception in case one is not at once aware of them, and in that event the instruction is transformed into non-instruction. A book raises the question of the immortality of the soul. The contents of the book constitute the answer. But the contents of the book, as the reader can convince himself by reading it through, are the opinions of the wisest and best men about immortality, all neatly strung on a thread. Oh! thou great Chinese god! Is this immortality? So then the question about immortality is a learned question. All honor to learning! All honor to him who can handle learnedly the learned question of immortality! But the question of immortality is essentially not a learned question, rather it is a question of inwardness, which the subject by becoming subjective must put to himself. Objectively the question cannot be answered, because objectively it cannot be put, since immortality precisely is the potentiation and highest development of the developed subjectivity. Only by really willing to become subjective can the question properly emerge, therefore how could it be answered objectively? The question cannot be answered in social terms, for in social terms it cannot be expressed, inasmuch as only the subject who wills to become subjective can conceive the question and ask rightly, "Do I become immortal, or am I immortal?" Of course, people can combine for many things; thus several families can combine for a box at the theater, and three single gentlemen can combine for a riding horse, so that each of them rides every third day. But it is not so with immortality; the consciousness of my immortality belongs to me alone, precisely at the moment when I am conscious of my immortality I am absolutely subjective, and I cannot become immortal in partnership with three single gentlemen in turn. People who go about with a paper soliciting the endorsement of numerous men and women, who feel a need in general to become immortal, get no reward for their pains, for immortality is not a possession which can be extorted by a list of endorsements. Systematically, immortality cannot be proved at all. The fault does not lie in the proofs, but in the fact that people will not understand that viewed systematically the whole question is nonsense, so that instead of seeking outward proofs, one had better seek to become a little subjective. Immortality is the most passionate interest of subjectivity; precisely in the interest lies the proof. When for the sake of objectivity (quite consistently from the systematic point of view), one systematically ignores the interest, God only knows in this case what immortality is, or even what is the sense of wishing to prove it, or how one could get into one's head the fixed idea of bothering about it.

Quite simply therefore the existing subject asks, not about immortality in general, for such a phantom has no existence, but about his immortality, about what it means to become immortal, whether he is able to contribute anything to the accomplishment of this end, or whether he becomes immortal as a matter of course, or whether he is that and can become it. . . .

The question is raised, how he, while he exists, can hold fast his consciousness of immortality, lest the metaphysical conception of immortality proceed to confuse the ethical and reduce it to an illusion; for ethically, everything culminates in immortality, without which the ethical is merely use and wont, and metaphysically, immortality swallows up existence, yea, the seventy years of existence, as a thing of naught, and yet ethically this naught must be of infinite importance. The question is raised, how immortality practically transforms his life; in what sense he must have the consciousness of it always present to him, or whether perhaps it is enough to think this thought once for all.

And the fact of asking about his immortality is at the same time for the existing subject who raises the question a deed—as it is not, to be sure, for absent-minded people who once in a while ask about the matter of being immortal quite in general, as if immortality were something one has once in a while, and the question were some sort of thing in general. So he asks how he is to behave in order to express in existence his immortality, whether he is really expressing it; and for the time being, he is satisfied with this task, which surely must be enough to last a man a lifetime since it is to last for an eternity. And then? Well, then, when he has completed this task, then comes the turn for world-history. In these days, to be sure, it is just the other way round: now people apply themselves first to world-history, and therefore there comes out of this the ludicrous result (as another author has remarked), that while people are proving and proving immortality quite in general, faith in immortality is more and more diminishing.

From *Either/Or* by Søren Kierkegaard, Vol. II, translated by Walter Lowrie with revisions and a foreword by Howard A. Johnson (copyright 1944 © 1955 by Princeton University Press). Reprinted by permission of Princeton University Press.

QUESTION FOR REVIEW AND DISCUSSION

1. Referring to the earlier chapters dealing with their philosophies, could you have anticipated how Plato and Hume would approach the concept of death? Why? Does Kierkegaard add a useful perspective to the discussion about death?

29

The Mind-Body Problem

Searle

Reading _____

Minds, Brains and Science

John Searle

For thousands of years, people have been trying to understand their relationship to the rest of the universe. For a variety of reasons many philosophers today are reluctant to tackle such big problems. Nonetheless, the problems remain, and in this book I am going to attack some of them.

At the moment, the biggest problem is this: We have a certain commonsense picture of ourselves as human beings which is very hard to square with our overall "scientific" conception of the physical world. We think of ourselves as *conscious, free, mindful, rational* agents in a world that science tells us consists entirely of mindless, meaningless physical particles. Now, how can we square these two conceptions? How, for example, can it be the case that the world contains nothing but unconscious physical particles, and yet that it also contains consciousness? How can a mechanical universe contain intentionalistic human beings—that is, human beings that can represent the world to themselves? How, in short, can an essentially meaningless world contain meanings?

Such problems spill over into other more contemporary-sounding issues: How should we interpret recent work in computer science and artificial intelligence—work aimed at making intelligent machines? Specifically, does the digital computer give us the right picture of the human mind? And why is it that the social sciences in general have not given us insights into ourselves comparable to the insights that the natural sciences have given us into the rest of nature? What is the relation between the ordinary, commonsense explanations we accept of the way people behave and scientific modes of explanation?

John Searle (1932–) is professor of philosophy at the University of California at Berkeley. He was born in Denver, Colorado, in 1932 and was educated at Oxford University, where he was also a Rhodes Scholar.

480

In this first chapter, I want to plunge right into what many philosophers think of as the hardest problem of all: What is the relation of our minds to the rest of the universe? This, I am sure you will recognise, is the traditional mind-body or mind-brain problem. In its contemporary version it usually takes the form: how does the mind relate to the brain?

I believe that the mind-body problem has a rather simple solution, one that is consistent both with what we know about neurophysiology and with our commonsense conception of the nature of mental states—pains, beliefs, desires and so on. But before presenting that solution, I want to ask why the mind-body problem seems so intractable. Why do we still have in philosophy and psychology after all these centuries a "mind-body problem" in a way that we do not have, say, a "digestion-stomach problem"? Why does the mind seem more mysterious than other biological phenomena?

I am convinced that part of the difficulty is that we persist in talking about a twentieth-century problem in an outmoded seventeenth-century vocabulary. When I was an undergraduate, I remember being dissatisfied with the choices that were apparently available in the philosophy of mind: you could be either a monist or a dualist. If you were a monist, you could be either a materialist or an idealist. If you were a materialist, you could be either a behaviorist or a physicalist. And so on. One of my aims in what follows is to try to break out of these tired old categories. Notice that nobody feels he has to choose between monism and dualism where the "digestion-stomach problem" is concerned. Why should it be any different with the "mind-body problem"?

But, vocabulary apart, there is still a problem or family of problems. Since Descartes, the mind-body problem has taken the following form: how can we account for the relationships between two apparently completely different kinds of things? On the one hand, there are mental things, such as our thoughts and feelings; we think of them as subjective, conscious, and immaterial. On the other hand, there are physical things; we think of them as having mass, as extended in space, and as causally interacting with other physical things. Most attempted solutions to the mind-body problem wind up by denying the existence of, or in some way downgrading the status of, one or the other of these types of things. Given the successes of the physical sciences, it is not surprising that in our stage of intellectual development the temptation is to downgrade the status of mental entities. So, most of the recently fashionable materialist conceptions of the mind—such as behaviorism, functionalism, and physicalism—end up by denying, implicitly or explicitly, that there are any such things as minds as we ordinarily think of them. That is, they deny that we do really *intrinsically* have subjective, conscious, mental states and that they are as real and as irreducible as anything else in the universe.

Now, why do they do that? Why is it that so many theorists end up denying the intrinsically mental character of mental phenomena? If we can answer that question, I believe that we will understand why the mind-body problem has seemed so intractable for so long.

There are four features of mental phenomena which have made them seem impossible to fit into our "scientific" conception of the world as made up of material things. And it is these four features that have made the mind-body problem really difficult. They are so embarrassing that they have led many thinkers in philosophy, psychology, and artificial intelligence to say strange and implausible things about the mind.

The most important of these features is consciousness. I, at the moment of writing this, and you, at the moment of reading it, are both conscious. It is just a plain fact about the world that it contains such conscious mental states and events, but it is hard to see how mere physical systems could have consciousness. How could such a thing occur? How, for example, could this grey and white gook inside my skull be conscious?

I think the existence of consciousness ought to seem amazing to us. It is easy enough to imagine a universe without it, but if you do, you will see that you have imagined a universe that is truly meaningless. Consciousness is the central fact of specifically human existence because without it all of the other specifically human aspects of our existence—language, love, humour, and so on—would be impossible. I believe it is, by the way, something of a scandal that contemporary discussions in philosophy and psychology have so little of interest to tell us about consciousness.

The second intractable feature of the mind is what philosophers and psychologists call "intentionality," the feature by which our mental states are directed at, or about, or refer to, or are of objects and states of affairs in the world other than themselves. "Intentionality," by the way, doesn't just refer to intentions, but also to beliefs, desires, hopes, fears, love, hate, lust, disgust, shame, pride, irritation, amusement, and all of those mental states (whether conscious or unconscious) that refer to, or are about, the world apart from the mind. Now the question about intentionality is much like the question about consciousness. How can this stuff inside my head be *about* anything? How can it *refer* to anything? After all, this stuff in the skull consists of "atoms in the void," just as all of the rest of material reality consists of atoms in the void. Now how, to put it crudely, can atoms in the void represent anything?

The third feature of the mind that seems difficult to accommodate within a scientific conception of reality is the subjectivity of mental states. This subjectivity is marked by such facts as that I can feel my pains, and you can't. I see the world from my point of view; you see it from your point of view. I am aware of myself and my internal mental states, as quite distinct from the selves and mental states of other people. Since the seventeenth century we have come to think of reality as something which must be equally accessible to all competent observers—that is, we think it must be objective. Now, how are we to accommodate the reality of *subjective* mental phenomena with the scientific conception of reality as totally *objective*?

Finally, there is a fourth problem, the problem of mental causation. We all suppose, as part of common sense, that our thoughts and feelings make a real difference to the way we behave, that they actually have some *causal* effect on the physical world. I decide, for example, to raise my arm and—lo and behold—my arm goes up. But if our thoughts and feelings are truly mental, how can they affect anything physical? How could something mental make a physical difference? Are we supposed to think that our thoughts and feelings can somehow produce chemical effects on our brains and the rest of our nervous system? How could such a thing occur? Are we supposed to think that thoughts can wrap themselves around the axons or shake the dendrites or sneak inside the cell wall and attack the cell nucleus?

But unless some such connection takes place between the mind and the brain, aren't we just left with the view that the mind doesn't matter, that it is as unimportant causally as the froth on the wave is to the movement of the wave? I suppose if the froth were conscious, it might think to itself: "What a tough job it is pulling these waves up on the beach and then pulling them out again, all day long!" But we know the froth doesn't make any important difference. Why do we suppose our mental life is any more important than a froth on the wave of physical reality?

These four features, consciousness, intentionality, subjectivity, and mental causation are what make the mind-body problem seem so difficult. Yet, I want to say, they are all real features of our mental lives. Not every mental state has all of them. But any satisfactory account of the mind and of mind-body relations must take account of all four features. If your theory ends up by denying any one of them, you know you must have made a mistake somewhere.

The first thesis I want to advance toward "solving the mind-body problem" is this:

Mental phenomena, all mental phenomena whether conscious or unconscious, visual or auditory, pains, tickles, itches, thoughts, indeed, all of our mental life, are caused by processes going on in the brain.

To get a feel for how this works, let's try to describe the causal processes in some detail for at least one kind of mental state. For example, let's consider pains. Of course, anything we say now may seem wonderfully quaint in a generation, as our knowledge of how the brain works increases. Still, the *form* of the explanation can remain valid even though the *details* are altered. On current views, pain signals are transmitted from sensory nerve endings to the spinal cord by at least two types of fibres—there are Delta A fibres, which are specialised for prickling sensations, and C fibres, which are specialised for burning and aching sensations. In the spinal cord, they pass through a region called the tract of Lissauer and terminate on the neurons of the cord. As the signals go up the spine, they enter the brain by two separate pathways: the prickling pain pathway and the burning pain pathway. Both pathways go through the thalamus, but the prickling pain is more localised afterwards in the somato-sensory cortex, whereas the burning pain pathway transmits signals, not only upwards into the cortex, but also laterally into the hypothalamus and other regions at the base of the brain. Because of these differences, it is much easier for us to localise a prickling sensation—we can tell fairly accurately where someone is sticking a pin into our skin, for example—whereas burning and aching pains can be more distressing because they activate more of the nervous system. The actual sensation of pain appears to be caused both by the stimulation of the basal regions of the brain, especially the thalamus, and the stimulation of the somato-sensory cortex.

Now for the purposes of this discussion, the point we need to hammer home is this: our sensations of pains are caused by a series of events that begin at free nerve endings and end in the thalamus and in other regions of the brain. Indeed, as far as the actual sensations are concerned, the events inside the central nervous system are quite sufficient to cause pains—we know this both from the phantom-limb pains felt by amputees and the pains caused by artificially stimulating relevant portions of the brain. I want to suggest that what is true of pain is true of mental phenomena generally. To put it crudely, and counting all of the central nervous system as part of the brain for our present discussion, everything that matters for our mental life, all of our thoughts and feelings, are caused by processes inside the brain. As far as causing mental states is concerned, the crucial step is the one that goes on inside the head, not the external or peripheral stimulus. And the argument for this is simple. If the events outside the central nervous system occurred, but nothing happened in the brain, there would be no mental events. But if the right things happened in the brain, the mental events would occur even if there was no outside stimulus. (And that, by the way, is the principle on which surgical anaesthesia works: the outside stimulus is prevented from having the relevant effects on the central nervous system.)

But if pains and other mental phenomena are caused by processes in the brain, one wants to know: what are pains? What are they really? Well, in the case of pains, the obvious answer is that they are unpleasant sorts of sensations. But that answer leaves us unsatisfied because it doesn't tell us how pains fit into our overall conception of the world.

Once again, I think the answer to the question is obvious, but it will take some spelling out. To our first claim—that pains and other mental phenomena are caused by brain processes, we need to add a second claim:

Pains and other mental phenomena just are features of the brain (and perhaps the rest of the central nervous system).

One of the primary aims of this chapter is to show how *both* of these propositions can be true together. How can it be both the case that brains cause minds and yet minds just are features of brains? I believe it is the failure to see how both these propositions can be true together that has blocked a solution to the mind-body problem for so long. There are different levels of confusion that such a pair of ideas can generate. If mental and physical phenomena have cause and effect relationships, how can one be a feature of the other? Wouldn't that imply that the mind caused itself—the dreaded doctrine of *causa sui*? But at the bottom of our puzzlement is a misunderstanding of causation. It is tempting to think that whenever A causes B there must be two discrete events, one identified as the cause, the other identified as the effect; that all causation functions in the same way as billiard balls hitting each other. This crude model of the causal relationships between the brain and the mind inclines us to accept some kind of dualism; we are inclined to think that events in one material realm, the "physical," cause events in another insubstantial realm, the "mental." But that seems to me a mistake. And the way to remove the mistake is to get a more sophisticated concept of causation. To do this, I will turn away from the relations between mind and brain for a moment to observe some other sorts of causal relationships in nature.

A common distinction in physics is between micro- and macro-properties of systems—the small and large scales. Consider, for example, the desk at which I am now sitting, or the glass of water in front of me. Each object is composed of micro-particles. The micro-particles have features at the level of molecules and atoms as well as at the deeper level of subatomic particles. But each object also has certain properties such as the solidity of the table, the liquidity of the water, and the transparency of the glass, which are surface or global features of the physical systems. Many such surface or global properties can be causally explained by the behaviour of elements at the micro-level. For example, the solidity of the table in front of me is explained by the lattice structure occupied by the molecules of which the table is composed. Similarly, the liquidity of the water is explained by the nature of the interactions between the H_2O molecules. Those macro-features are causally explained by the behavior of elements at the micro-level.

I want to suggest that this provides a perfectly ordinary model for explaining the puzzling relationships between the mind and the brain. In the case of liquidity, solidity, and transparency, we have no difficulty at all in supposing that the surface features are *caused by* the behavior of elements at the micro-level, and at the same time we accept that the surface phenomena *just are* features of the very systems in question. I think the clearest way of stating this point is to say that the surface feature is both *caused by* the behaviour of micro-elements, and at the same time is *realised in* the system that is made up of the micro-elements. There is a cause and effect relationship, but at the same time the surface features are just higher level features of the very system whose behavior at the micro-level causes those features.

In objecting to this someone might say that liquidity, solidity, and so on are identical with features of the micro-structure. So, for example, we might just define solidity as the lattice structure of the molecular arrangement, just as heat often is identified with the mean kinetic energy of molecule movements. This point seems to me correct but not really an objection to the analysis that I am proposing. It is a characteristic of the progress of science that an expression that is originally defined in terms of surface features, features accessible to the senses, is subsequently defined in terms of the micro-structure that causes the surface features. Thus, to take the example of solidity, the table in front of me is solid in the ordinary sense that it is rigid, it resists pressure, it supports books, it is not easily penetrable by most other objects such as other tables, and so on. Such is the commonsense notion of solidity. And in a scientific vein one can define solidity as whatever micro-structure causes these gross observable features. So one can then say either that solidity just is the lattice structure of the system of molecules and that solidity so defined causes, for example, resistance to touch and pressure. Or one can say that solidity consists of such high level features as rigidity and resistance to touch and pressure and that it is caused by the behavior of elements at the micro-level.

If we apply these lessons to the study of the mind, it seems to me that there is no difficulty in accounting for the relations of the mind to the brain in terms of the brain's functioning to cause mental states. Just as the liquidity of the water is caused by the behavior of elements at the micro-level, and yet at the same time it is a feature realised in the system of micro-elements, so in exactly that sense of "caused by" and "realised in" mental phenomena are caused by processes going on in the brain at the neuronal or modular level, and at the same time they are realised in the very system that consists of neurons. And just as we need the micro/macro distinction for any physical system, so for the same reasons we need the micro/macro distinction for the brain. And though we can say of a system of particles that it is 10°C or it is solid or it is liquid, we cannot say of any given particle that this particle is solid, this particle is liquid, this particle is 10°C. I can't for example reach into this glass of water, pull out a molecule and say: "This one's wet."

In exactly the same way, as far as we know anything at all about it, though we can say of a particular brain: "This brain is conscious," or: "This brain is experiencing thirst or pain," we can't say of any particular neuron in the brain: "This neuron is in pain, this neuron is experiencing thirst." To repeat this point, though there are enormous empirical mysteries about how the brain works in detail, there are no logical or philosophical or metaphysical obstacles to accounting for the relation between the mind and the brain in terms that are quite familiar to us from the rest of nature. Nothing is more common in nature than for surface features of a phenomenon to be both caused by and realised in a micro-structure, and those are exactly the relationships that are exhibited by the relation of mind to brain.

Let us now return to the four problems that I said faced any attempt to solve the mind-brain problem.

First, how is consciousness possible?

The best way to show how something is possible is to show how it actually exists. We have already given a sketch of how pains are actually caused by neurophysiological processes going on in the thalamus and the sensory cortex. Why is it then that many people feel dissatisfied with this sort of answer? I think that by pursuing an analogy with an earlier problem in the history of science we can dispel this sense of puzzlement. For a long time many biologists and philosophers thought it was impossible, in principle, to account for the existence of *life* on purely biological grounds. They thought that in addition to the biological processes some other element must be necessary, some *élan vital* must be postulated in order to lend life to what was otherwise dead and inert matter. It is hard today to realise how intense the dispute was between vitalism and mechanism even a generation ago, but today these issues are no longer taken seriously. Why not? I think it is not so much because mechanism won and vitalism lost, but because we have come to understand better the biological character of the processes that are characteristic of living organisms. Once we understand how the features that are characteristic of living beings have a biological explanation, it no longer seems mysterious to us that matter should be alive. I think that exactly similar considerations should apply to our discussions of consciousness. It should seem no more mysterious, in principle, that this hunk of matter, this grey and white oatmeal-textured substance of the brain, should be conscious than it seems mysterious that this other hunk of matter, this collection of nucleo-protein molecules stuck onto a calcium frame, should be alive. The way, in short, to dispel the mystery is to understand the processes. We do not yet fully understand the processes, but we understand their general *character*, we understand that there are certain specific electro-chemical activities going on among neurons or neuron-modules and perhaps other features of the brain and these processes cause consciousness.

Our second problem was, how can atoms in the void have intentionality? How can they be about something?

As with our first question, the best way to show how something is possible is to show how it actually exists. So let's consider thirst. As far as we know anything about it, at least certain kinds of thirst are caused in the hypothalamus by sequences of nerve firings. These firings are in turn caused by the action of angiotensin in the hypothalamus, and angiotensin, in turn, is synthesised by renin, which is secreted by the kidneys. Thirst, at least of these kinds, is caused by a series of events in the central nervous system, principally the hypothalamus, and it is realised in the hypothalamus. To be thirsty is to have, among other things, the desire to drink. Thirst is therefore an intentional state: it has content; its content determines under what conditions it is satisfied, and it has all the rest of the features that are common to intentional states.

As with the "mysteries" of life and consciousness, the way to master the mystery of intentionality is to describe in as much detail as we can how the phenomena are caused by biological processes while being at the same time realised in biological systems. Visual and auditory experiences, tactile sensations, hunger, thirst, and sexual desire, are all caused by brain processes and they are realised in the structure of the brain, and they are all intentional phenomena.

I am not saying we should lose our sense of the mysteries of nature. On the contrary, the examples I have cited are all in a sense astounding. But I am saying that they are neither more nor less mysterious than other astounding features of the world, such as the existence of gravitational attraction, the process of photosynthesis, or the size of the Milky Way.

Our third problem: how do we accommodate the subjectivity of mental states within an objective conception of the real world?

It seems to me a mistake to suppose that the definition of reality should exclude subjectivity. If "science" is the name of the collection of objective and systematic truths we can state about the world, then the existence of subjectivity is an objective scientific fact like any other. If a scientific account of the world attempts to describe how things are, then one of the features of the account will be the subjectivity of mental states, since it is just a plain fact about biological evolution that it has produced certain sorts of biological systems, namely human and certain animal brains, that have subjective features. My present state of consciousness is a feature of my brain, but its conscious aspects are accessible to me in a way that they are not accessible to you. And your present state of consciousness is a feature of your brain and its conscious aspects are accessible to you in a way that they are not accessible to me. Thus the existence of subjectivity is an objective fact of biology. It is a persistent mistake to try to define "science" in terms of certain features of existing scientific theories. But once this provincialism is perceived to be the prejudice it is, then any domain of facts whatever is a subject of systematic investigation. So, for example, if God existed, then that fact would be a fact like any other. I do not know whether God exists, but I have no doubt at all that subjective mental states exist, because I am now in one and so are you. If the fact of subjectivity runs counter to a certain definition of "science," then it is the definition and not the fact which we will have to abandon.

Fourth, the problem of mental causation for our present purpose is to explain how mental events can cause physical events. How, for example, could anything as "weightless" and "ethereal" as a thought give rise to an action?

The answer is that thoughts are not weightless and ethereal. When you have a thought, brain activity is actually going on. Brain activity causes bodily movements by physiological processes. Now, because mental states are features of the brain, they have two levels of description—a higher level in mental terms, and a lower level in physiological terms. The very same causal powers of the system can be described at either level.

Once again, we can use an analogy from physics to illustrate these relationships. Consider hammering a nail with a hammer. Both hammer and nail have a certain kind of solidity. Hammers made of cottonwool or butter will be quite useless, and hammers made of water or steam are not hammers at all. Solidity is a real causal property of the hammer. but the solidity itself is caused by the behavior of particles at the micro-level and it is realised in the system which consists of micro-elements. The existence of two causally real levels of description in the brain, one a macro-level of mental processes and the other a micro-level of neuronal processes is exactly analogous to the existence of two causally real levels of description of the hammer. Consciousness, for example, is a real property of the brain that can cause things to happen. My conscious attempt to perform an action such as raising my arm causes the movement of the arm. At the higher level of description, the intention to raise my arm causes the movement of the arm. But at the lower level of description, a series of neuron firings starts a chain of events that results in the contraction of the muscles. As with the case of hammering a nail, the same sequence of events has two levels of description. Both of them are causally real, and the higher level causal features are both caused by and realised in the structure of the lower level elements.

To summarise: on my view, the mind and the body interact, but they are not two different things, since mental phenomena just are features of the brain. One way to characterise this position is to see it as an assertion of both physicalism and mentalism. Suppose we define "naive physicalism" to be the view that all that exists in the world are physical particles with their properties and relations. The power of the physical model of reality is so great that it is hard to see how we can seriously challenge naive physicalism. And let us define "naive mentalism" to be the view that mental phenomena really exist. There really are mental states; some of them are conscious; many have intentionality; they all have subjectivity; and many of them function causally in determining physical events in the world. The thesis of this first chapter can now be stated quite simply. Naive mentalism and naive physicalism are perfectly consistent with each other. Indeed, as far as we know anything about how the world works, they are not only consistent, they are both true.

QUESTIONS FOR REVIEW AND DISCUSSION

Searle says that the difficulty in discussing the mind-body problem is in part a result of "talking about a twentieth-century problem in an outmoded seventeenth-century vocabulary." According to Searle, here is the old way (since Descartes) the mind-body problem was stated: how can we account for the relationships between two apparently completely different kinds of things— (1) mental things, our thoughts and feelings, immaterial and conscious and (2) physical things, having mass, extending into space, and interacting with other physical things?

What follows here is not so much a question as an outline for a review of Searle's proposed solution of the mind-body problem.

- Searle's two theses: (1) All mental phenomena, all thoughts, conscious seeing and hearing, are caused by process going on in the brain; (2) pains and other mental phenomena are just features of the brain.
- Consider Searle's distinction between macro and micro: the same "stuff," i.e., micro particles, have features at the level of molecules and atoms as well as at the subatomic levels. In other words, the single substance, particles, explains various macro features of these particle arrangements; for example the solidity of a table, the transparency of glass, and the liquidity of water. These macro features are causally explained by the behavior of elements at the micro level.
- Searle says "I want to suggest that this provides a perfectly ordinary model for explaining the puzzling relationships between the mind and the brain."

Now, with this background, review Searle's answers to the following four questions:

1. How is consciousness possible?
2. How can atoms have intentionality, a set purpose?
3. How can we accommodate subjectivity (i.e., *my* thoughts about the world) with an objective conception of the real world?
4. How can mental acts cause physical events?

Albrecht Dürer, *Adam and Eve*. Could they have chosen not to eat the forbidden fruit?
(*The Bettmann Archive*)

P A R T S E V E N

Freedom of the Will
Is My Will Free?

We talk about free will, and say for example the person is free to do so-and-so if he wants to and we forget that his wanting is caught up in the stream of determinism, that unconscious forces drive him into wanting to do the thing in question. The analogy of the puppet whose motions are manipulated from behind by invisible wires . . . is a telling one at almost every point.

John Hospers
Meaning and Free Will (1950)

For reasons I don't really understand, evolution has given us a form of experience of voluntary action where the experience of freedom, that is to say, the experience of the sense of alternative possibilities, is built into the very structure of conscious, voluntary, intentional human behaviour.

John Searle
Minds, Brains and Science (1984)

The judgment of regret calls [a] murder bad. Calling a thing bad means, if it means anything at all, that the thing ought not to be, that something else ought to be in its stead. Determinism, in denying that anything else can be in its stead, virtually defines the universe as a place in which what ought to be is impossible. . . .

William James
The Dilemma of Determinism (1884)

DETERMINISM VERSUS INDETERMINISM

From the earliest philosophers to present-day thinkers who want to know what the world is like and how human beings fit into it, one issue continues to raise a perplexing question, namely: Is the will free? Why should this be a problem? Our common sense or intuition tells us that we constantly face choices or that we make mistakes or that we are undecided about some matter and are still thinking about it—we are deliberating. To face a choice implies that the will is free to move us in different directions. To say that you made a mistake means that you not only should have but that you could have behaved in a different way. The act of taking your time to think out your course of action, the act of deliberation, implies that you are situated not only in a physical sense in a particular place with physical forces at work in your being or personality but that you are also situated in a special condition of freedom, as if there were a limit to the power of, or an insulation from, the various forces upon you, giving you a chance to choose your direction of behavior.

The problem is not all that simple however. There are many things about you that you are not free to choose. You did not choose to be born, to have brown eyes, to be six feet tall, to have blond hair, or even to have a particular disease. All this has been determined genetically—a rather obvious point. Even many ways of thinking or of accepting certain moral values have been programmed by your family and culture. Beyond that, there are forms of behavior that are not considered to be free, as when someone hits another automobile while driving under the influence of drugs or alcohol. What all this suggests is that much of our life and behavior is determined and could be no other way. The question is, how much is determined?

The determinist argues that everything, that is, every event and every aspect of nature is determined and could be no other way. For example, Baron d'Holbach (in *System of Values*, 1770) wrote that a person is

> born without his consent; his organization does in nowise depend upon himself; his ideas come to him involuntarily; his habits are in the power of those who cause him to contract them; he is unceasingly modified by causes whether visible or concealed, over which he has no control, which necessarily regulate his mode of existence, give the hue to his way of thinking and determine his manner of acting. He is good or bad, happy or miserable, wise or foolish, reasonable or irrational, without his will being for anything in these various states. Nevertheless, in spite of the shackles by which he is bound, it is pretended he is a free agent or that independent of these causes by which he moved, he determines his own will, and regulates his own condition.

We are faced, then, with two opposite points of view regarding the human will. The *determinist* argues that in no way is the will free, and the *indeterminist* argues that human experience is incomprehensible without the assumption that the will is free. The determinist is mostly influenced by the notion that every event has a *cause*, that scientific laws of nature define how all things work and are interrelated. For the determinist all of reality, including human nature, functions as a machine. Consider the engine of any automobile: All of its parts are connected to one another. The generator causes the spark plug to ignite the gasoline in the cylinder, the impact of the explosion pushes down the piston which, being connected to the cam shaft, causes the next piston to move up—all this is connected to the drive shaft that in turn is connected to the gears which finally make the wheels turn. For the determinist, all of human existence can be explained according to this mechanical model. All attempts to reduce the severity of this analogy by devising various forms of "soft" determinism are understandable says the indeterminist, but when that is done, when exceptions to the rigor are made, there no longer remains the true determinist point of view.

By contrast, the indeterminist is willing to concede the various valid /elements of determinism in human existence. Moreover, he argues that whereas the scientist has powerful methods of verifying his causal laws of behavior, there appears to be no way to prove that the will is free. Instead, the indeterminist questions whether it is possible to think coherently, in short, to make sense of various human experiences if one adopts the determinist point of view. What, for example does it mean to say that you *must* do something if in fact you are already programmed in a different direction? Although he could not prove that his will was free, Immanuel Kant said, "Because I must, I can." Also, if determinism is the proper view, what is the point of praising or rewarding a person for any particular behavior? Even more serious is the question of whether we should ever punish someone for a crime?

APPROACHES TO THE PROBLEM OF THE FREEDOM OF THE WILL

The following readings reflect the variety of perspectives regarding the question of whether the will is free.

Prof. John Hospers takes the point of view of psychoanalysis and argues that what appears to be a free choice of behavior has been from an early age set in motion and that the individual can in no way avoid that behavior.

Even the ancient philosophy of India as recorded in the *Upanishads* describes how the past has a causal effect on a person's present behavior. In this case however, it is our past choices which produce our present behavior. This cause of our behavior is known as "karma," which says that "we reap what we sow." But unlike a hard determinism, the doctrine of karma provides an escape from the most rigid determinism. In the words of *Radhakrishnan*, "when we perform disinterested work we reach freedom. 'While thus you live there is no way by which karma clings to you.'" In other words, says Radhakrishnan, "what looms over us is no dark fate but our own past."

By contrast, the famed Harvard psychologist *B. F. Skinner* describes the many ways our behavior is controlled, most of these ways being variations of the theme of "stimulus and response." So intricate, says Skinner, is the system of stimuli coming not only from our internal impulses but also from external agents including parents, teachers, police, peers, and advertising, that there is no room left for what could be considered our own free actions.

For *William James,* a profound human experience is our "judgment of regret." What other meaning can such a personal experience have than my feeling that "I could have done something else" or that "it should not have happened." What kind of world is it in which what should not happen must happen, that murder, theft, and lying are a fixed part of a person's life?

A helpful contemporary analysis of the freedom of the will problem is found in *John Searle*'s *Minds, Brains and Science*. Here he concludes that "for reasons I don't really understand, evolution has given us a form of experience of voluntary action where the experience of freedom, that is to say, the experience of the sense of alternative possibilities, is built into the very structure of conscious, voluntary, intentional human behavior. For that reason, I believe, neither this discussion nor any other will ever convince us that our behavior is unfree."

30

Human Beings as Controlled Puppets

Hospers

Reading ───

Free Will and Psychoanalysis

John Hospers

. . . When a metropolitan newspaper headlines an article with the words "Boy Killer Is Doomed Long before He Is Born," and then goes on to describe how a twelve-year-old boy has been sentenced to prison for the murder of a girl, and how his parental background includes records of drunkenness, divorce, social maladjustment, and paresis, are we still to say that his act, though voluntary and assuredly not done at the point of a gun, is free? The boy has early displayed a tendency toward sadistic activity to hide an underlying masochism and "prove that he's a man"; being coddled by his mother only worsens this tendency, until, spurned by a girl in his attempt on her, he kills her—not simply in a fit of anger, but calculatingly, deliberately. Is he free in respect of his criminal act, or for that matter in most of the acts of his life? Surely to ask this question is to answer it in the negative. . . . Though not everyone has criminotic tendencies, everyone has been molded by influences which in large measure at least determine his present behavior; he is literally the product of these influences, stemming from periods prior to his "years of discretion," giving him a host of character traits that he cannot change now even if he would. So obviously does what a man is depend upon how a man comes to be, that it is small wonder that philosophers and sages have considered man far indeed from being the master of his fate. It is not as if man's will were standing high and serene above the flux of events that have molded him; it is itself caught up

John Hospers is a professor of philosophy at the University of Southern California. Professor Hospers is also the author of the book *Human Conduct* (1961).

in this flux, itself carried along on the current. An act is free when it is determined by the man's character, say moralists; but what if the most decisive
aspects of his character were already irrevocably acquired before he could do
anything to mold them? What if even the degree of will power available to
him in shaping his habits and disciplining himself now to overcome the influence of his early environment is a factor over which he has no control? What
are we to say of this kind of "freedom"? Is it not rather like the freedom of the
machine to stamp labels on cans when it has been devised for just that purpose? Some machines can do so more efficiently than others, but only because
they have been better constructed.

It is not my purpose here to establish this thesis in general, but only in
one specific respect which has received comparatively little attention, namely,
the field referred to by psychiatrists as that of unconscious motivation. In what
follows I shall restrict my attention to it because it illustrates as clearly as anything the points I wish to make.

Let me try to summarize very briefly the psychoanalytic doctrine on this
point.[1] The conscious life of the human being, including the conscious decisions and volitions, is merely a mouthpiece for the unconscious—not directly
for the enactment of unconscious drives, but of the compromise between
unconscious drives and unconscious reproaches. There is a Big Three behind
the scenes which the automation called the conscious personality carries out:
the id, an "eternal gimme," presents its wish and demands its immediate satisfaction; the super-ego says no to the wish immediately upon presentation, and
the unconscious ego, the mediator between the two, tries to keep peace by
means of compromise.

To go into examples of the functioning of these three "bosses" would be
endless; psychoanalytic case books supply hundreds of them. The important
point for us to see in the present context is that *it is the unconscious that determines what the conscious impulse and the conscious action shall be*. Hamlet, for
example, had a strong Oedipus wish, which was violently counteracted by
super-ego reproaches; these early wishes were vividly revived in an unusual
adult situation in which his uncle usurped the coveted position from Hamlet's
father and won his mother besides. This situation evoked strong strictures on
the part of Hamlet's super-ego, and it was this that was responsible for his
notorious delay in killing his uncle. A dozen times Hamlet could have killed
Claudius easily; but every time Hamlet "decided" not to: a free choice, moralists would say—but no, listen to the super-ego: "What you feel such hatred
toward your uncle for, what you are plotting to kill him for, is precisely the
crime which you yourself desire to commit: to kill your father and replace him

---

[1]I am aware that the theory presented below is not accepted by all practicing psychoanalysts.
Many non-Freudians would disagree with the conclusions presented. But I do not believe that this
fact affects my argument, as long as the concept of unconscious motivation is accepted. I am
aware, too, that much of the language employed in the following descriptions is animistic and
metaphorical; but as long as I am presenting a view I would prefer to "go the whole hog" and present it in its most dramatic form. The theory can in any case be made clearest by the use of such
language, just as atomic theory can often be made clearest to students with the use of models.

in the affections of your mother. Your fate and your uncle's are bound up together." This paralyzes Hamlet into inaction. Consciously all he knows is that he is unable to act; this conscious inability he rationalizes, giving a different excuse each time.[2]

We have always been conscious of the fact that we are not masters of our fate in every respect—that there are many things which we cannot do, that nature is more powerful than we are, that we cannot disobey laws without danger of reprisals, etc. We have become "officially" conscious, too, though in our private lives we must long have been aware of it, that we are not free with respect to the emotions that we feel—whom we love or hate, what types we admire, and the like. More lately still we have been reminded that there are unconscious motivations for our basic attractions and repulsions, our compulsive actions or inabilities to act. But what is not welcome news is that our very acts of volition, and the entire train of deliberations leading up to them, are but facades for the expression of unconscious wishes, or rather, unconscious compromises and defenses.

A man is faced by a choice: shall he kill another person or not? Moralists would say, here is a free choice—the result of deliberation, an action consciously entered into. And yet, though the agent himself does not know it, and has no awareness of the forces that are at work within him, his choice is already determined for him: his conscious will is only an instrument, a slave, in the hands of a deep unconscious motivation which determines his action. If he has a great deal of what the analyst calls "free-floating guilt," he will not; but if the guilt is such as to demand immediate absorption in the form of self-damaging behavior, this accumulated guilt will have to be discharged in some criminal action. The man himself does not know what the inner clockwork is; he is like the hands on the clock, thinking they move freely over the face of the clock.

A woman has married and divorced several husbands. Now she is faced with a choice for the next marriage: shall she marry Mr. A, or Mr. B, or nobody at all? She may take considerable time to "decide" this question, and her decision may appear as a final triumph of her free will. Let us assume that A is a normal, well-adjusted, kind, and generous man, while B is a leech, an impostor, one who will become entangled constantly in quarrels with her. If she belongs to a certain classifiable psychological type, she will inevitably choose B, and she will do so even if her previous husbands have resembled B, so that one would think that she "had learned from experience." Consciously, she will of course "give the matter due consideration," etc., etc. To the psychoanalyst all this is irrelevant chaff in the wind—only a camouflage for the inner workings about which she knows nothing consciously. If she is of a certain kind of masochistic strain, as exhibited in her previous set of symptoms, she *must* choose B: her super-ego, always out to maximize the torment in the situation, seeing what dazzling possibilities for self-damaging behavior are

---

[2]See *The Basic Writings of Sigmund Freud*, Modern Library Edition, p. 310. (In *The Interpretation of Dreams*.) Cf. also the essay by Ernest Jones, "A Psycho-analytical Study of Hamlet."

promised by the choice of B, compels her to make the choice she does, and even to conceal the real basis of the choice behind an elaborate facade of rationalizations.

. . . A man has wash-compulsion. He must be constantly washing his hands—he uses up perhaps 400 towels a day. Asked why he does this, he says, "I need to, my hands are dirty"; and if it is pointed out to him that they are not really dirty, he says, "They feel dirty anyway, I feel better when I wash them." So once again he washes them. He "freely decides" every time; he feels that he must wash them, he deliberates for a moment perhaps, but always ends by washing them. What he does not see, of course, are the invisible wires inside him pulling him inevitably to do the thing he does: the infantile id-wish concerns preoccupation with dirt, the super-ego charges him with this, and the terrified ego must respond, "No, I don't like dirt, see how clean I like to be, look how I wash my hands!"

Let us see what further "free acts" the same patient engages in (this is an actual case history): he is taken to a concentration camp, and given the worst of treatment by the Nazi guards. In the camp he no longer chooses to be clean, does not even try to be—on the contrary, his choice is now to wallow in filth as much as he can. All he is aware of now is a disinclination to be clean, and every time he must choose he chooses not to be. Behind the scenes, however, another drama is being enacted: the super-ego, perceiving that enough torment is being administered from the outside, can afford to cease pressing its charges in this quarter—the outside world is doing the torturing now, so the super-ego is relieved of the responsibility. Thus the ego is relieved of the agony of constantly making terrified replies in the form of washing to prove that the super-ego is wrong. The defense no longer being needed, the person slides back into what is his natural predilection anyway, for filth. This becomes too much even for the Nazi guards: they take hold of him one day, saying, "We'll teach you how to be clean!" drag him into the snow, and pour bucket after bucket of icy water over him until he freezes to death. . . .

Let us take a less colorful, more everyday example. A student at a university, possessing wealth, charm, and all that is usually considered essential to popularity, begins to develop the following personality pattern: although well taught in the graces of social conversation, he always makes a *faux pas* somewhere, and always in the worst possible situation; to his friends he makes cutting remarks which hurt deeply—and always apparently aimed in such a way as to hurt the most: a remark that would not hurt A but would hurt B he invariably makes to B rather than to A, and so on. None of this is conscious. Ordinarily he is considerate of people, but he contrives always (unconsciously) to impose on just those friends who would resent it most, and at just the times when he should know that he should not impose: at 3 o'clock in the morning, without forewarning, he phones a friend in a near-by city demanding to stay at his apartment for the weekend; naturally the friend is offended, but the person himself is not aware that he has provoked the grievance ("common sense" suffers a temporary eclipse when the neurotic pattern sets in, and one's intelligence, far from being of help in such a situation, is used in the interest of the neurosis), and when the friend is cool to him the next time they meet, he wonders why and feels unjustly treated. Aggressive behavior on his part invites resentment and aggression in turn, but all that he consciously sees is others' behavior towards him—and he considers himself the innocent victim of an unjustified "persecution."

Each of these acts is, from the moralist's point of view, free: he chose to phone his friend at 3 A.M.; he chose to make the cutting remark that he did, etc. What he does not know is that an ineradicable masochistic pattern has set in. His unconscious is far more shrewd and clever than is his conscious intellect; it sees with uncanny accuracy just what kind of behavior will damage him most, and unerringly forces him into that behavior. Consciously, the student "doesn't know why he did it"—he gives different "reasons" at different times, but they are all, once again, rationalizations cloaking the unconscious mechanism which propels him willy-nilly into actions that his "common sense" eschews.

The more of this sort of thing one observes, the more he can see what the psychoanalyst means when he talks about *the illusion of freedom*. And the more of a psychiatrist one becomes, the more he is overcome with a sense of what an illusion this free will can be. In some kinds of cases most of us can see it already: it takes no psychiatrist to look at the epileptic and sigh with sadness at the thought that soon this person before you will be as one possessed, not the same thoughtful intelligent person you knew. But people are not aware of this in other contexts, for example when they express surprise at how a person to whom they have been so good could treat them so badly. Let us suppose that you help a person financially or morally or in some other way, so that he is in your debt; suppose further that he is one of the many neurotics who unconsciously identify kindness with weakness and aggression with strength, then he will unconsciously take your kindness to him as weakness and use it as the occasion for enacting some aggression against you. He can't help it, he may regret it himself later; still, he will be driven to do it. If we gain a little knowledge of psychiatry, we can look at him with pity, that a person otherwise so worthy should be so unreliable—but we will exercise realism too, and be aware that there are some types of people that you cannot be good to; in "free" acts of their conscious volition, they will use your own goodness against you.

Sometimes the persons themselves will become dimly aware that "something behind the scenes" is determining their behavior. The divorcee will sometimes view herself with detachment, as if she were some machine (and indeed the psychoanalyst does call her a "repeating-machine"): "I know I'm caught in a net, that I'll fall in love with this guy and marry him and the whole ridiculous merry-go-round will start all over again."

We talk about free will, and we say, for example, the person is free to do so-and-so if he can do so *if* he wants to—and we forget that his wanting to is itself caught up in the stream of determinism, that unconscious forces drive him into the wanting or not wanting to do the thing in question. The analogy of the puppet whose motions are manipulated from behind by invisible wires, or better still, by springs inside, is a telling one at almost every point.

And the glaring fact is that it all started so early, before we knew what was happening. The personality structure is inelastic after the age of five, and comparatively so in most cases after the age of three. Whether one acquires a neurosis or not is determined by that age—and just as involuntarily as if it had been a curse of God. . . . To speak of human beings as "puppets" in such a context is no idle metaphor but a stark rendering of a literal fact; only the psychiatrist knows what puppets people really are; and it is no wonder that the protestations of philosophers that "the act which is the result of a volition, a deliberation, a conscious decision, is free" leave these persons, to speak mildly, somewhat cold.

. . . Now, what of the notion of responsibility? What happens to it in our analysis?

Let us begin with an example, not a fictitious one. A woman and her two-year-old baby are riding on a train to Montreal in midwinter. The child is ill. The woman wants badly to get to her destination. She is, unknown to herself, the victim of a neurotic conflict whose nature is irrelevant here except for the fact that it forces her to behave aggressively toward the child, partly to spite her husband whom she despises and who loves the child, but chiefly to ward off super-ego charges of masochistic attachment. Consciously she loves the child, and when she says this she says it sincerely, but she must behave aggressively toward it nevertheless, just as many children love their mothers but are nasty to them most of the time in neurotic pseudo-aggression. The child becomes more ill as the train approaches Montreal; the heating system of the train is not working, and the conductor pleads with the woman to get off the train at the next town and get the child to a hospital at once. The woman refuses. Soon after, the child's condition worsens, and the mother does all she can to keep it alive, without, however, leaving the train, for she declares that it is absolutely necessary that she reach her destination. But before she gets there the child is dead. After that, of course, the mother grieves, blames herself, weeps hysterically, and joins the church to gain surcease from the guilt that constantly overwhelms her when she thinks of how her aggressive behavior has killed her child.

Was she responsible for her deed? In ordinary life, after making a mistake, we say, "Chalk it up to experience." Here we should say, "Chalk it up to the neurosis." *She* could not help it if her neurosis forced her to act this way—she didn't even know what was going on behind the scenes, her conscious self merely acted out its assigned part. This is far more true than is generally realized: criminal actions in general are not actions for which their agents are responsible; the agents are passive, not active—they are victims of a neurotic conflict. Their very hyperactivity is unconsciously determined.

To say this is, of course, not to say that we should not punish criminals. Clearly, for our own protection, we must remove them from our midst so that they can no longer molest and endanger organized society. And, of course, if we use the word "responsible" in such a way that justly to hold someone responsible for a deed is by definition identical with being justified in punishing him, then we can and do hold people responsible. But this is like the sense of "free" in which free acts are voluntary ones. It does not go deep enough. In a deeper sense we cannot hold the person responsible: we can hold his neurosis responsible, but *he is not responsible for his neurosis,* particularly since the age at which its onset was inevitable was an age before he could even speak.

The neurosis is responsible—but isn't the neurosis a part of *him?* We have been speaking all the time as if the person and his unconscious were two separate beings; but isn't he one personality, including conscious and unconscious departments together?

I do not wish to deny this. But it hardly helps us here; for what people want when they talk about freedom, and what they hold to when they champion it, is the idea that the *conscious* will is the master of their destiny. "I am the master of my fate, I am the captain of my soul"—and they surely mean their conscious selves, the self that they can recognize and search and introspect. Between an unconscious that willy-nilly determines your actions, and an external force which pushes you, there is little if anything to choose. The unconscious is just *as if* it were an outside force; and indeed, psychiatrists will assert that the inner Hitler (your super-ego) can torment you far more than any external Hitler can. Thus the kind of freedom that people want, the only kind they will settle for, is precisely the kind that psychiatry says that they cannot have.

Heretofore it was pretty generally thought that, while we could not rightly blame a person for the color of his eyes or the morality of his parents, or even for what he did at the age of three, or to a large extent what impulses he had and whom he fell in love with, one *could* do so for other of his adult activities, particularly the acts he performed voluntarily and with premeditation. Later this attitude was shaken. Many voluntary acts came to be recognized, at least in some circles, as compelled by the unconscious. Some philosophers recognized this too—Ayer talks about the kleptomaniac being unfree, and about a person being unfree when another person exerts a habitual ascendancy over his personality. But this is as far as he goes. The usual examples, such as the kleptomaniac and the schizophrenic, apparently satisfy most philosophers, and with these exceptions removed, the rest of mankind is permitted to wander in the vast and alluring fields of freedom and responsibility. So far the inroads upon freedom left the vast majority of humanity untouched; they began to hit home when psychiatrists began to realize, though philosophers did not, that the domination of the conscious by the unconscious extended, not merely to a few exceptional individuals, but to all human beings, that the "big three behind the scenes" are not respecters of persons, and dominate us all, even including that *sanctum sanctorum* of freedom, our conscious will. To be sure, the domination by the unconscious in the case of "normal" individuals is somewhat more benevolent than the tyranny and despotism exercised in neurotic cases, and therefore the former have evoked less comment; but the principle remains in all cases the same: the unconscious is the master of every fate and the captain of every soul.

From John Hospers, "Meaning and Free Will", in *Philosophy and Phenomenological Research*, vol. 10, no. 3 (March 1950). Reprinted by permission, *Philosophy and Phenomenological Research*.

QUESTIONS FOR REVIEW AND DISCUSSION

1. Hospers summarizes the psychoanalytic doctrine he will rely on to show that human behavior, even a person's "conscious decisions," are expressions of the unconscious. In short, "it is the unconscious that determines what the conscious impulse and the conscious action shall be." Behind the scenes of each person's life are the big three, namely, the id, the super-ego, and the unconscious ego. How do these three explain human behavior?

2. Hospers gives several examples of questionable behavior, including a woman who has married and divorced several husbands and is faced with a "choice" for the next marriage; a man with a "wash-compulsion"; a charming university student who in spite of an excellent background always does something wrong—for example, he calls a friend at 3 o'clock in the morning demanding to stay at his apartment for the weekend. Hospers concludes, "the more of this sort of thing one observes, the more he can see what the psychoanalyst means when he talks about *'the illusion of freedom'.*" Do you agree?

3. The glaring fact is, says Hospers, that it all started so early. "The personality structure is inelastic after age five. . . . and in most cases after the age of three." If this is true, what influence can education have on the development of a person?

4. Given the assumptions of psychoanalysis, can a person be held responsible for his or her behavior?

31

The Impact of Our Past on Our Present

Radhakrishnan

Reading ———————————————————————————

Karma

Sarvepalli Radhakrishnan

The law of karma is the counter-part in the moral world of the physical law of uniformity. It is the law of the conservation of moral energy. The vision of law and order is revealed in the Rta of the Rg-Veda. According to the principle of karma there is nothing uncertain or capricious in the moral world. We reap what we sow. The good seed brings a harvest of good, the evil of evil. Every little action has its effect on character. Man knows that some of the tendencies to action which now exist in him are the result of conscious or intelligent choice on his part. Conscious actions tend to become unconscious habits, and not unnaturally the unconscious tendencies we find in ourselves were regarded as the result of past conscious actions. We cannot arrest the process of moral evolution any more than we can stay the sweep of the tides or the course of the stars. The attempt to overleap the law of karma is as futile as the attempt to leap over one's shadow. It is the psychological principle that our life carries within it a record that time cannot blur or death erase. To remedy the defects of the old Vedic idea, that redemption from sin could be had by sacrifices to gods, great emphasis is laid on the law of karma. It proclaims the awful doom, the soul that sinneth, it shall die. Not through sacrifices, but through good deeds does a man become good. "A man becomes good by good deeds and bad by bad deeds." Again, "Man is a creature of will. According as he believes in this world, so will he be when he is departed." So we are asked

Sarvepalli Radhakrishnan was professor of eastern religions and ethics at Oxford University (1936–1952) and president of India (1962–1967).

Radhakrishnan. (*UPI/Bettmann Newsphotos*)

to will the good and do the good. "Whatever world he covets by his mind, and whatever objects he wishes, for the man of pure mind, he gains those worlds and those objects; therefore let him who longs for bhūti, manifested power, worship him who knows the Ātman." The requital of action makes saṁsāra with birth and death, beginningless and endless. The karma theory embraces in its sweep men and gods, animals and plants.

Since the sense of individual responsibility is emphasised, there are critics who think that the karma doctrine is inconsistent with social service. It is said that there is no emphasis on the bearing of one another's burdens. As a matter of fact, the Upaniṣads hold that we can be free from karma only by social service. So long as we perform selfish work we are subject to the law of bondage. When we perform disinterested work we reach freedom. "While thus you live there is no way by which karma clings to you." What binds us to the chain of birth and death is not action as such but selfish action. In an age when the individual was ever ready to shirk responsibility for what he did by throwing the burden on providence or stars or some other being than his own self, the doctrine of karma urged that a man "fetters himself by himself, like a bird by its nest." What looms over us is no dark fate but our own past. We are not the victims of a driving doom. Suffering is the wages of sin. There is no question that such an idea is a great incentive to good conduct. It only says that there are some limiting conditions of human action. We did not make ourselves. When we come up against the impossible, we realise that we cannot do anything we please. Karma rightly understood does not discourage moral effort, does not fetter the mind or chain the will. It only says that every act is the inevitable outcome of the preceding conditions. There is a tendency of the cause to pass into the effect. If the spirit, which is on a higher plane than nature, does not assert its freedom, past conduct and present environment will account completely for the actions of man. Man is not a mere product of nature. He is mightier than his karma. If the law is all, then there is no real freedom possible. Man's life is not the working of merely mechanical relations. There are different levels—the mechanical, the vital, the sentient, the intellectual and the spiritual—these currents cross and recross and inter-penetrate each other. The law of karma, which rules the lower nature of man, has nothing to do with the spiritual in him. The infinite in man helps him to transcend the limitations of the finite. The essence of spirit is freedom. By its exercise man can check and control his natural impulses. That is why his life is something more than a succession of mechanically determined states. His acts to be free must not be expressive of the mere force of habit or shock of circumstance, but of the freedom of the inner soul. The spiritual nature is the basis of his initiative and endeavour. The mechanical part is under constraint. Were man merely the sum of natural conditions, he would be completely subject to the law of karma. But there is a soul in him which is the master. Nothing external can compel it. We are sure that the material forces of the world must bend to the spiritual rule, and so can the law of karma be subjected to the freedom of spirit. Man can have the highest freedom only when he becomes one with God. "He who departs from this world, without having known the soul or those true desires, his part in all worlds is a life of constraint. But he who departs from this world after having known the soul and those true desires, his part in all worlds is a life of freedom." Becoming one with God is the attainment of the highest freedom. The more we live in the presence of God, the more we assert the rights of spirit, the more free we are; the more we lose our grip on the whole to which we belong, the more selfish we are, the more is our bondage to karma. Man oscillates between nature and spirit, and so is subject to both freedom and necessity.

Karma has a cosmic as well as a psychological aspect. Every deed must produce its natural effect in the world; at the same time it leaves an impression on or forms a tendency in the mind of man. It is this tendency or saṁskāra or vāsana that inclines us to repeat the deed we have once done. So all deeds have their fruits in the world and effects on the mind. So far as the former are concerned, we cannot escape them, however much we may try. But in regard to mental tendencies we can control them. Our future conduct holds all possibilities. By self-discipline we can strengthen the good impulses and weaken the bad ones.

The actions of men are capable of prediction and precalculation. If rational, they will show certain properties: we shall detect in them an inward coherence, an unselfish purpose, and so on. But from that we cannot assume that the acts are determined in any mechanical sense. Every living soul is potentially free. His acts are not a mere unwinding of the thread from a reel.

Man possesses freedom as the focus of spiritual life. God has not granted him freedom from outside. He possesses freedom because he is rooted in God. The more he realises his true divine nature, the more free is he.

It is sometimes argued that the law of karma is inconsistent with theism. Karma is a blind unconscious principle governing the whole universe. It is not subject to the control even of God. We do not require a judge to administer a mechanical law. The principle of karma is not inconsistent with the reality of the absolute Brahman. The moral law of karma is the expression of the nature of the absolute. Anthropomorphically we can say a divine power controls the process. Ṛta is the law in the Vedas. Varuna is the lord of Ṛta. Karma refers to the unchanging action of the gods. It is an expression of the nature of reality. It renders impossible any arbitrary interference with moral evolution. The same conclusion is arrived at by modern theories of scientific law and habit, which are irreconcilable with capricious interference. If miracles are necessary to prove God, then science has killed God for all time. Divine interference is regulated by laws. God does not act by private volitions, as Malebranche would say. Only the karma theory can give us a just conception of the spiritual universe. It brings out the living rational nature of the whole. It is the mechanism by which spirit works. The freedom of the spiritual world is expressed in the world of nature by the iron law of mechanical necessity. Freedom and karma are the two aspects of the same reality. If God is immanent in the cosmos, then His spirit resides in the machine. The divine expresses itself in law, but law is not God. The Greek fate, the Stoic reason, and the Chinese Tao, are different names for the primary necessity of law.

There is no doctrine that is so valuable in life and conduct as the karma theory. Whatever happens to us in this life we have to submit in meek resignation, for it is the result of our past doings. Yet the future is in our power, and we can work with hope and confidence. Karma inspires hope for the future and resignation to the past. It makes men feel that the things of the world, its fortunes and failures, do not touch the dignity of the soul. Virtue alone is good, not rank or riches, not race or nationality. Nothing but goodness is good.

From Sarvepalli Radhakrishnan, "Karma" in *Indian Philosophy,* vol. I, George Allen & Unwin, London; Humanities Press, New York, 1971; now Unwin Hyman, an imprint of HarperCollins Publishers Limited.

QUESTIONS FOR REVIEW AND DISCUSSION

1. What is meant by the law of karma?
2. If the law of karma holds that all behavior has consequences, is there any room for human freedom? How does Radhakrishnan explain this question?

32

A Personal Exemption from Complete Determinism

Skinner

The problem of determinism versus indeterminism is a major concern among psychologists as well as for philosophers. One of the foremost advocates of determinism is B. F. Skinner (1904–1990) the eminent Harvard psychologist and influential exponent of behaviorism. Among the early influences in Skinner's career were the theories of the Russian physiologist Pavlov and the ideas of J. B. Watson, the founder of behaviorism. After receiving his Ph.D. at Harvard, he taught at the University of Minnesota, Indiana University, and from 1948 until his retirement in 1974, Harvard University.

Skinner is famous for his experiments with animals, for several scholarly publications, and for his two widely read books, *Walden Two* (1948) and *Beyond Freedom and Dignity* (1971). During World War II, Skinner trained pigeons to pilot torpedoes, although this technique was never put to use. He also taught pigeons to play table tennis. From such experiments Skinner sought to discover a scientific basis for understanding behavior, not only animal behavior but, more significantly human behavior. His conclusion was that human behavior is best understood as determined by genetic inheritance and as the psychological response to the environment.

It was clear to Skinner that the renowned Sigmund Freud was a determinist, but he noticed that many Freudians did not follow Freud along this determinist path. They had no hesitation in assuring their patients that not all their behavior was determined, that they were free to choose among different courses of action. These patients were led to believe that they were the architects of their own destinies. Skinner rejected this notion of freedom, saying that "personal exemption from a complete determinism is revoked as a scientific analysis progresses . . . in accounting for the behavior of the individual."

Here is how Skinner describes the difference between indeterminism (freedom) and determinism:

B.F. Skinner. (*Christopher Johnson*)

Indeterminism "In what we may call the prescientific view . . . a person's behavior is at least to some extent his own achievement. He is free to deliberate, decide, and act, possibly in original ways. . . ."

Determinism "In the scientific view . . . a person's behavior is determined by a genetic endowment traceable to the evolutionary history of the species and by environmental circumstances to which as an individual he has been exposed."

In explaining his understanding of human behavior, Skinner focused on the many ways in which behavior is determined. There is, first of all, the familiar notion of "stimulus" and "response," in which a particular stimulus can produce a predictable response. Then there are what Skinner calls "reinforcers," by which he means that "when a bit of behavior is followed by a certain kind of consequence [for example, praise or reward], that behavior is more likely to occur again" because the praise or reward reinforces that behavior. Skinner also speaks of "operant conditioning," which he defines as the use of stimuli to create behavior designed to "reduce threats to the individual or species." A major item in Skinner's theory is that everywhere we are influenced by "controllers" of our behavior. Controllers are natural, such as fire, poison, and ill health from overeating, and their consequences direct and redirect our behavior. There are also personal controllers such as parents, teachers, and police officers, all of whom provide stimuli to behavior.

Up to this point, what Skinner has described is a series of relatively straightforward examples of cause and effect—"if this, then that." The philosophical question about Skinner's science of behavior, however, is whether his conclusions have anything to do with the question of "complete determinism." Skinner insisted that individuals cannot have a "personal exemption from a complete determinism." What creates questions about whether Skinner is advocating what he himself calls a "complete determinism" is his description of the "designers" of culture. The function of the designer is to deliberate about what values to aim for, and to fashion stimuli and reinforcers to control the environment and individual behavior in order to achieve those ends or values. There is no doubt that designers can in fact do these things. But are the designers free to choose between alternative cultures any more than Freudians' patients could choose their own course of action? It appears that Skinner gives to the designers a personal exemption from a complete determinism.

According to Skinner, the real issue concerning the control of human behavior is the effectiveness of the techniques of control. For example, he says that "we shall not solve the problem of alcoholism and juvenile delinquency by increasing the sense of responsibility. It is the environment which is 'responsible' for the objectionable behavior, and it is the environment, not some attribute of the individual which must be changed."

To document this point, Skinner refers to the most pervasive program of human control in the twentieth century where he considers Pavlovian techniques as successful. He says:

> Communist Russia provided an interesting case history in the relation between environmentalism and personal responsibility. . . . Immediately after the revolution the government could argue that if many Russians were uneducated, unproductive, badly behaved, and unhappy, it was because their environment had made them so. The new government would change the environment, making use of Pavlov's work on conditioned reflexes, and all would be well. But by the early thirties the government had had its chance, and many Russians were still not conspicuously better informed, more productive, better behaved, or happier. The official line was then changed, and Pavlov went out of favor. A strongly purposive psychology was substituted: it was up to the Russian citizen to get an education, work productively, behave well, and be happy. The Russian educator was to make sure that he would accept this responsibility, but not by conditioning him. The successes of the Second World War restored confidence in the earlier principle, however; the government had been successful after all. It might not yet be completely effective, but it was moving in the right direction. Pavlov came back into favor.

One can concede that such a system of controlled behavior can work, at least for a while, since the techniques of control employed involve such severe constraints. Still, the "designers" of the Russian environment appeared to be "free" to employ the Pavlovian techniques, to step back and wonder whether it really worked, and then conclude after the war that maybe it did. In any case, they could choose between alternatives because they appeared to have a personal exemption from a complete determinism.

What is meant by a "complete determinism?" William James gives a clear definition of determinism that has no exemptions:

> [Determinism] professes that those parts of the universe already laid down absolutely appoint and decree what the other parts shall be. The future has no ambiguous possibilities hidden in its womb: the part we call the present is compatible with only one totality. Any other future complement than the one fixed from eternity is impossible. The whole is in each and every part, and welds it with the rest into an absolute unity, an iron block, in which there can be no equivocation or shadow of turning.

To aim for a better culture, we would have to deliberate about at least two major questions: "Who should be the designers and controllers?" and "To what end should the designers aim?" This requires not only deliberation but also choice, two activities which Skinner has already said are not available in a completely determined world.

Again, if all behavior is determined by the very nature of things throughout the universe, how is it possible for someone to step outside of this strictly determined nexus of cause and effect? How can someone achieve an independent or super perspective in order to analyze how things are going and to consider options, alternatives? Instead of determinism, is not the proposed behavior of the designers better described by Skinner's own description of indeterminism (freedom)? Clearly, the designer would have to be "free to deliberate, decide, and act, possibly in original ways," as Skinner says.

The determinist says that "the future has no ambiguous possibilities in its womb" so that "the part we call the present is compatible with only one [future]." Karl Marx stuck doggedly to his theory of determinism when he argued that historical or dialectical materialism was moving in a fixed direction that could not be altered. Each stage in history is, he said, the inevitable next stage after its predecessors. Skinner argues that such a strict theory of historical movement "misses the chance to change the order in which stages succeed one another." He says, "We cannot change the age of the earth or of a child, but in the case of the child, we need not wait for time to pass in order to change the things that happen in time." Marx saw no contradiction between his theory of determinism and the call for revolution, for the revolution was not supposed to change the fixed course of history but only to "lessen and shorten the birth pangs." Skinner, by contrast, departs from determinism in his call for changing the environment and behavior, "in order to change things that happen in time."

Skinner says that "the designer of culture is not an interloper or a meddler. He does not step in to disturb the natural process." In that case, the designer, as a part of the natural process, must be a product of strict determinism. But if the designer is to alter present behavior and to face such questions as "Who shall be the controller and to what end shall this control be directed?"

the assumption must be that there is some "loose play" in nature providing a measure of freedom to choose between alternatives. It is one thing to trace the color of a person's eyes to genetic inheritance, a form of determinism. But that a person faces alternatives, options, choices in behavior appears to be incompatible with a theory of *complete* determinism.

To design an ideal society does not in any way require a commitment to a theory of determinism. One could proceed to craft such a design and indeed implement and enforce it without being a determinist. Whether one is or is not a determinist will not affect the practical outcome. It would be possible for both a determinist and indeterminist to work together on the design of society and come to similar conclusions without ever referring to the question of determinism. What is most fascinating is that we are supposed to *choose* between being a determinist or indeterminist.

Reading _____

Walden Two

B. F. Skinner

"Mr. Castle," said Frazier very earnestly, "let me ask you a question. I warn you, it will be the most terrifying question of your life. *What would you do if you found yourself in possession of an effective science of behavior?* Suppose you suddenly found it possible to control the behavior of men as you wished. What would you do?"

"That's an assumption?"

"Take it as one if you like. *I* take it as a fact. And apparently you accept it as a fact too. I can hardly be as despotic as you claim unless I hold the key to an extensive practical control."

"What would I do?" said Castle thoughtfully. "I think I would dump your science of behavior in the ocean."

"And deny men all the help you could otherwise give them?"

"And give them the freedom they would otherwise lose forever!"

"How could you give them freedom?"

"By refusing to control them!"

"But you would only be leaving the control in other hands."

"Whose?"

"The charlatan, the demagogue, the salesman, the ward heeler, the bully, the cheat, the educator, the priest—all who are now in possession of the techniques of behavioral engineering."

"A pretty good share of the control would remain in the hands of the individual himself."

"That's an assumption, too, and it's your only hope. It's your only possible chance to avoid the implications of a science of behavior. If man is free, then a technology of behavior is impossible. But I'm asking you to consider the other case."

"Then my answer is that your assumption is contrary to fact and any further consideration idle."

"And your accusations—?"

"—were in terms of intention, not of possible achievement."

Frazier sighed dramatically.

"It's a little late to be proving that a behavioral technology is well advanced. How can you deny it? Many of its methods and techniques are really as old as the hills. Look at their frightful misuse in the hands of the Nazis! And what about the techniques of the psychological clinic? What about education? Or religion? Or practical politics? Or advertising and salesmanship? Bring them all together and you have a sort of rule-of-thumb technology of vast power. No, Mr. Castle, the science is there for the asking. But its techniques and methods are in the wrong hands—they are used for personal aggrandizement in a competitive world or, in the case of the psychologist and educator, for futilely corrective purposes. My question is, have you the courage to take up and wield the science of behavior for the good of mankind? You answer that you would dump it in the ocean!"

"I'd want to take it out of the hands of the politicians and advertisers and salesmen, too."

"And the psychologists and educators? You see, Mr. Castle, you can't have that kind of cake. The fact is, we not only *can* control human behavior, we *must*. But who's to do it, and what's to be done?"

"So long as a trace of personal freedom survives, I'll stick to my position," said Castle, very much out of countenance.

"Isn't it time we talked about freedom?" I said. "We parted a day or so ago on an agreement to let the question of freedom ring. It's time to answer, don't you think?"

"My answer is simple enough," said Frazier. "I deny that freedom exists at all. I must deny it—or my program would be absurd. You can't have a science about a subject matter which hops capriciously about. Perhaps we can never *prove* that man isn't free; it's an assumption. But the increasing success of a science of behavior makes it more and more plausible."

"On the contrary, a simple personal experience makes it untenable," said Castle. "The experience of freedom. I *know* that I'm free."

"It must be quite consoling," said Frazier.

"And what's more—you do, too," said Castle hotly. "When you deny your own freedom for the sake of playing with a science of behavior, you're acting in plain bad faith. That's the only way I can explain it." He tried to recover himself and shrugged his shoulders. "At least you'll grant that you *feel* free."

"The 'feeling of freedom' should deceive no one," said Frazier. "Give me a concrete case."

"Well, right now," Castle said. He picked up a book of matches. "I'm free to hold or drop these matches."

"You will, of course, do one or the other," said Frazier. "Linguistically or logically there seem to be two possibilities, but I submit that there's only one in fact. The determining forces may be subtle but they are inexorable. I suggest that as an orderly person you will probably hold—ah! you drop them! Well, you see, that's all part of your behavior with respect to me. You couldn't resist the temptation to prove me wrong. It was all lawful. You had no choice. The deciding factor entered rather late, and naturally you couldn't foresee the result when you first held them up. There was no strong likelihood that you would act in either direction, and so you said you were free."

"That's entirely too glib," said Castle. "It's easy to argue lawfulness after the fact. But let's see you predict what I will do in advance. Then I'll agree there's law."

"I didn't say that behavior is always predictable, any more than the weather is always predictable. There are often too many factors to be taken into account. We can't measure them all accurately, and we couldn't perform the mathematical operations needed to make a prediction if we had the measurements. The legality is usually an assumption—but none the less important in judging the issue at hand."

"Take a case where there's no choice, then," said Castle. "Certainly a man in jail isn't free in the sense in which I am free now."

"Good! That's an excellent start. Let us classify the kinds of determiners of human behavior. One class, as you suggest, is physical restraint—handcuffs, iron bars, forcible coercion. These are ways in which we shape human behavior according to our wishes. They're crude, and they sacrifice the affection of the controllee, but they often work. Now, what other ways are there of limiting freedom?"

Frazier had adopted a professional tone and Castle refused to answer.

"The threat of force would be one," I said.

"Right. And here again we shan't encourage any loyalty on the part of the controllee. He has perhaps a shade more of the feeling of freedom, since he can always `choose to act and accept the consequences,' but he doesn't feel exactly free. He knows his behavior is being coerced. Now what else?"

I had no answer.

"Force or the threat of force—I see no other possibility," said Castle after a moment.

"Precisely," said Frazier.

"But certainly a large part of my behavior has no connection with force at all. There's my freedom!" said Castle.

"I wasn't agreeing that there was no other possibility—merely that *you* could see no other. Not being a good behaviorist—or a good Christian, for that matter—you have no feeling for a tremendous power of a different sort."

"What's that?"

"I shall have to be technical," said Frazier. "But only for a moment. It's what the science of behavior calls 'reinforcement theory.' The things that can happen to us fall into three classes. To some things we are indifferent. Other things we like—we want them to happen, and we take steps to make them happen again. Still other things we don't like—we don't want them to happen and we take steps to get rid of them or keep them from happening again.

"*Now,*" Frazier continued earnestly, "if it's in our power to create any of the situations which a person likes or to remove any situation he doesn't like, we can control his behavior. When he behaves as we want him to behave, we simply create a situation he likes, or remove one he doesn't like. As a result, the probability that he will behave that way again goes up, which is what we want. Technically it's called 'positive reinforcement.'

"The old school made the amazing mistake of supposing that the reverse was true, that by removing a situation a person likes or setting up one he doesn't like—in other words by punishing him—it was possible to *reduce* the probability that he would behave in a given way again. That simply doesn't hold. It has been established beyond question. What is emerging at this critical stage in the evolution of society is a behavioral and cultural technology based on positive reinforcement alone. We are gradually discovering—at an untold cost in human suffering—that in the long run punishment doesn't reduce the probability that an act will occur. We have been so preoccupied with the contrary that we always take 'force' to mean punishment. We don't say we're using force when we send shiploads of food into a starving country, though we're displaying quite as much *power* as if we were sending troops and guns."

"I'm certainly not an advocate of force," said Castle. "But I can't agree that it's not effective."

"It's *temporarily* effective, that's the worst of it. That explains several thousand years of bloodshed. Even nature has been fooled. We 'instinctively' punish a person who doesn't behave as we like—we spank him if he's a child or strike him if he's a man. A nice distinction! The immediate effect of the blow teaches us to strike again. Retribution and revenge are the most natural things on earth. But in the long run the man we strike is no less likely to repeat his act."

"But he won't repeat it if we hit him hard enough," said Castle.

"He'll still *tend* to repeat it. He'll *want* to repeat it. We haven't really altered his potential behavior at all. That's the pity of it. If he doesn't repeat it in our presence, he will in the presence of someone else. Or it will be repeated in the disguise of a neurotic symptom. If we hit hard enough, we clear a little place for ourselves in the wilderness of civilization, but we make the rest of the wilderness still more terrible.

"Now, early forms of government are naturally based on punishment. It's the obvious technique when the physically strong control the weak. But we're in the throes of a great change to positive reinforcement—from a competitive society in which one man's reward is another man's punishment, to a cooperative society in which no one gains at the expense of anyone else.

"The change is slow and painful because the immediate, temporary effect of punishment overshadows the eventual advantage of positive reinforcement. We've all seen countless instances of the temporary effect of force, but clear evidence of the effect of not using force is rare. That's why I insist that Jesus, who was apparently the first to discover the power of refusing to punish, must have hit upon the principle by accident. He certainly had none of the experimental evidence which is available to us today, and I can't conceive that it was possible, no matter what the man's genius, to have discovered the principle from casual observation."

"A touch of revelation, perhaps?" said Castle.

"No, accident. Jesus discovered one principle because it had immediate consequences, and he got another thrown in for good measure."

I began to see light.

"You mean the principle of 'love your enemies'?" I said.

"Exactly! To 'do good to those who despitefully use you' has two unrelated consequences. You gain the peace of mind we talked about the other day. Let the stronger man push you around—at least you avoid the torture of your own rage. *That's* the immediate consequence. What an astonishing discovery it must have been to find that in the long run you could *control the stronger man* in the same way!"

"It's generous of you to give so much credit to your early colleague," said Castle, "but why are we still in the throes of so much misery? Twenty centuries should have been enough for one piece of behavioral engineering."

"The conditions which made the principle difficult to discover made it difficult to teach. The history of the Christian Church doesn't reveal many cases of doing good to one's enemies. To inoffensive heathens, perhaps, but not enemies. One must look outside the field of organized religion to find the principle in practice at all. Church governments are devotees of *power*, both temporal and bogus."

"But what has all this got to do with freedom?" I said hastily.

Frazier took time to reorganize his behavior. He looked steadily toward the window, against which the rain was beating heavily.

"Now that we *know* how positive reinforcement works and why negative doesn't," he said at last, "we can be more deliberate, and hence more successful, in our cultural design. We can achieve a sort of control under which the controlled, though they are following a code much more scrupulously than was ever the case under the old system, nevertheless *feel free*. They are doing what they want to do, not what they are forced to do. That's the source of the tremendous power of positive reinforcement—there's no restraint and no revolt. By a careful cultural design, we control not the final behavior, but the *inclination* to behave—the motives, the desires, the wishes.

"The curious thing is that in that case *the question of freedom never arises.* Mr. Castle was free to drop the matchbook in the sense that nothing was preventing him. If it had been securely bound to his hand he wouldn't have been free. Nor would he have been quite free if I'd covered him with a gun and threatened to shoot him if he let it fall. The question of freedom arises when there is restraint—either physical or psychological.

"But restraint is only one sort of control, and absence of restraint isn't freedom. It's not control that's lacking when one feels 'free,' but the objectionable control of force. Mr. Castle felt free to hold or drop the matches in the sense that he felt no restraint—no threat of punishment in taking either course of action. He neglected to examine his positive reasons for holding or letting go, in spite of the fact that these were more compelling in this instance than any threat of force.

"We have no vocabulary of freedom in dealing with what we want to do," Frazier went on. "The question never arises. When men strike for freedom, they strike against jails and the police, or the threat of them—against oppression. They never strike against forces which make them want to act the way they do. Yet, it seems to be understood that governments will operate only through force or the threat of force, and that all other principles of control will be left to education, religion, and commerce. If this continues to be the case, we may as well give up. A government can never create a free people with the techniques now allotted to it.

"The question is: Can men live in freedom and peace? And the answer is: Yes, if we can build a social structure which will satisfy the needs of everyone and in which everyone will want to observe the supporting code. But so far this has been achieved only in Walden Two. Your ruthless accusations to the contrary, Mr. Castle, this is the freest place on earth. And it is free precisely because we make no use of force or the threat of force. Every bit of our research, from the nursery through the psychological management of our adult membership, is directed toward that end—to exploit every alternative to forcible control. By skillful planning, by a wise choice of techniques we *increase* the feeling of freedom.

"It's not planning which infringes upon freedom, but planning which uses force. A sense of freedom was practically unknown in the planned society of Nazi Germany, because the planners made a fantastic use of force and the threat of force.

"No, Mr. Castle, when a science of behavior has once been achieved, there's no alternative to a planned society. We can't leave mankind to an accidental or biased control. But by using the principle of positive reinforcement—carefully avoiding force or the threat of force—we can preserve a personal sense of freedom."

QUESTIONS FOR REVIEW AND DISCUSSION

1. How does Skinner describe the difference between determinism and indeterminism?
2. Can there be any question about Skinner's analysis, which says that virtually all behavior is influenced by "controllers"? Name some controllers.
3. Skinner insists that individuals cannot have a "personal exemption from a

complete determinism." Is his theory of the design of an ideal society consistent with his basic notion of no exemption from a complete determinism?

4. Is it necessary for Skinner to insist upon a rigorous, hard determinism to accomplish his objective of a new form of society? What would be different in his Walden Two if he retained his notion of "control" but dropped the idea of complete determinism? Or, what, if anything, does the theory of complete determinism add to the distinctiveness of his program?

33

How Can We Explain Judgments of Regret?

James

Reading _____

The Dilemma of Determinism

William James

What does determinism profess?

It professes that those parts of the universe already laid down absolutely appoint and decree what the other parts shall be. The future has no ambiguous possibilities hidden in its womb: the part we call the present is compatible with only one totality. Any other future complement than the one fixed from eternity is impossible. The whole is in each and every part, and welds it with the rest into an absolute unity, an iron block, in which there can be no equivocation or shadow of turning.

With earth's first clay they did the last man knead,
And there of the last harvest sowed the seed.
And the first morning of creation wrote
What the last dawn of reckoning shall read.

Indeterminism, on the contrary, says that the parts have a certain amount of loose play on one another, so that the laying down of one of them does not necessarily determine what the others shall be. It admits that possibilities may be in excess of actualities, and that things not yet revealed to our knowledge may really in themselves be ambiguous. Of two alternative futures which we conceive, both may now be really possible; and the one become

For biographical note on James, see p. 309.

518

impossible only at the very moment when the other excludes it by becoming real itself. Indeterminism thus denies the world to be one unbending unit of fact. It says there is a certain ultimate pluralism in it; and, so saying, it corroborates our ordinary unsophisticated view of things. To that view, actualities seem to float in a wider sea of possibilities from out of which they are chosen; and, *somewhere*, indeterminism says, such possibilities exist, and form a part of truth.

Determinism, on the contrary, says they exist *nowhere*, and that necessity on the one hand and impossibility on the other are the sole categories of the real. Possibilities that fail to get realized are, for determinism, pure illusions: they never were possibilities at all. There is nothing inchoate, it says, about this universe of ours, all that was or is or shall be actual in it having been from eternity virtually there. The cloud of alternatives our minds escort this mass of actuality withal is a cloud of sheer deceptions, to which "impossibilities" is the only name that rightfully belongs.

The issue, it will be seen, is a perfectly sharp one, which no eulogistic terminology can smear over or wipe out. The truth *must* lie with one side or the other, and its lying with one side makes the other false.

The question relates solely to the existence of possibilities, in the strict sense of the term, as things that may, but need not, be. Both sides admit that a volition, for instance, has occurred. The indeterminists say another volition might have occurred in its place: the determinists swear that nothing could possibly have occurred in its place. Now, can science be called in to tell us which of these two point-blank contradicters of each other is right? Science professes to draw no conclusions but such as are based on matters of fact, things that have actually happened; but how can any amount of assurance that something actually happened give us the least grain of information as to whether another thing might or might not have happened in its place? Only facts can be proved by other facts. With things that are possibilities and not facts, facts have no concern. If we have no other evidence than the evidence of existing facts, the possibility-question must remain a mystery never to be cleared up.

And the truth is that facts practically have hardly anything to do with making us either determinists or indeterminists. Sure enough, we make a flourish of quoting facts this way or that; and if we are determinists, we talk about the infallibility with which we can predict one another's conduct; while if we are indeterminists, we lay great stress on the fact that it is just because we cannot foretell one another's conduct, either in war or statecraft or in any of the great and small intrigues and businesses of men, that life is so intensely anxious and hazardous a game. But who does not see the wretched insufficiency of this so-called objective testimony on both sides? What fills up the gaps in our minds is something not objective, not external. What divides us into *possibility* men and *antipossibility* men is different faiths or postulates—postulates of rationality. To this man the world seems more rational with possibilities in it—to that man more rational with possibilities excluded; and talk as we will about having to yield to evidence, what makes us monists or pluralists, determinists or indeterminists, is at bottom always some sentiment like this.

The stronghold of the deterministic sentiment is the antipathy to the idea of chance. As soon as we begin to talk indeterminism to our friends, we find a number of them shaking their heads. This notion of alternative possibility, they say, this admission that any one of several things may come to pass, is, after all, only a round-about name for chance; and chance is something the notion of which no sane mind can for an instant tolerate in the world. What is it, they ask, but barefaced crazy unreason, the negation of intelligibility and law? And if the slightest particle of it exist anywhere, what is to prevent the whole fabric from falling together, the stars from going out, and chaos from recommencing her topsy-turvy reign?

Remarks of this sort about chance will put an end to discussion as quickly as anything one can find. I have already told you that "chance" was a word I wished to keep and use. Let us then examine exactly what it means, and see whether it ought to be such a terrible bugbear to us. I fancy that squeezing the thistle boldly will rob it of its sting.

The sting of the word "chance" seems to lie in the assumption that it means something positive, and that if anything happens by chance, it must needs be something of an intrinsically irrational and preposterous sort. Now, chance means nothing of the kind. It is a purely negative and relative term, giving us no information about that of which it is predicated, except that it happens to be disconnected with something else—not controlled, secured, or necessitated by other things in advance of its own actual presence.

As this point is the most subtile one of the whole lecture, and at the same time the point on which all the rest hinges, I beg you to pay particular attention to it. What I say is that it tells us nothing about what a thing may be in itself to call it "chance." It may be a bad thing, it may be a good thing. It may be lucidity, transparency, fitness incarnate, matching the whole system of other things, when it has once befallen, in an unimaginably perfect way. All you mean by calling it "chance" is that this is not guaranteed, that it may also fall out otherwise. For the system of other things has no positive hold on the chance-thing. Its origin is in a certain fashion negative: it escapes, and says, Hands off! coming, when it comes, as a free gift, or not at all. . . .

Nevertheless, many persons talk as if the minutest dose of disconnectedness of one part with another, the smallest modicum of independence, the faintest tremor of ambiguity about the future, for example, would ruin everything, and turn this goodly universe into a sort of insane sand-heap or nulliverse—no universe at all. Since future human volitions are as a matter of fact the only ambiguous things we are tempted to believe in, let us stop for a moment to make ourselves sure whether their independent and accidental character need be fraught with such direful consequences to the universe as these.

What is meant by saying that my choice of which way to walk home after the lecture is ambiguous and matter of chance as far as the present moment is concerned? It means that both Divinity Avenue and Oxford Street are called; but that only one, and that one *either* one, shall be chosen. Now, I ask you seriously to suppose that this ambiguity of my choice is real; and then to make the impossible hypothesis that the choice is made twice over, and each time falls on a different street. In other words, imagine that I first walk through Divinity Avenue, and then imagine that the powers governing the universe annihilate ten minutes of time with all that it contained, and set me back at the door of this hall just as I was before the choice was made. Imagine then that, everything else being the same, I now make a different choice and traverse Oxford Street. You, as passive spectators, look on and see the two alternative universes—one of them with me walking through Divinity Avenue in it, the other with the same me walking through Oxford Street. Now, if you are determinists you believe one of these universes to have been from eternity impossible: you believe it to have been impossible because of the intrinsic irra- tionality or accidentality somewhere involved in it. But looking outwardly at these universes, can you say which is the impossible and accidental one, and which the rational and necessary one? I doubt if the most iron-clad determin- ist among you could have the slightest glimmer of light on this point. In other words, either universe *after the fact* and once there would, to our means of observation and understanding, appear just as rational as the other. . . .

We have seen what determinism means: we have seen that indetermin- ism is rightly described as meaning chance; and we have seen that chance, the very name of which we are urged to shrink from as from a metaphysical pesti- lence, means only the negative fact that no part of the world, however big, can claim to control absolutely the destinies of the whole. But although, in dis- cussing the word "chance," I may at moments have seemed to be arguing for its real existence, I have not meant to do so yet. We have not yet ascertained whether this be a world of chance or no; at most, we have agreed that it seems so. And I now repeat what I said at the outset, that, from any strict theoretical point of view, the question is insoluble. To deepen our theoretic sense of the *difference* between a world with chances in it and a deterministic world is the most I can hope to do; and this I may now at last begin upon, after all our tedious clearing of the way.

I wish first of all to show you just what the notion that this is a determin- istic world implies. The implications I call your attention to are all bound up with the fact that it is a world in which we constantly have to make what I shall, with your permission, call judgments of regret. Hardly an hour passes in which we do not wish that something might be otherwise. . . . Even from the point of view of our own ends, we should probably make a botch of remod- elling the universe. How much more then from the point of view of ends we cannot see! Wise men therefore regret as little as they can. But still some regrets are pretty obstinate and hard to stifle—regrets for acts of wanton cruel- ty or treachery, for example, whether performed by others or by ourselves. Hardly any one can remain *entirely* optimistic after reading the confession of the murderer at Brockton the other day: how, to get rid of the wife whose con- tinued existence bored him, he inveigled her into a desert spot, shot her four times, and then, as she lay on the ground and said to him, "You didn't do it on purpose, did you, dear?" replied, "No, I didn't do it on purpose," as he raised a rock and smashed her skull. Such an occurrence, with the mild sentence and self-satisfaction of the prisoner, is a field for a crop of regrets, which one need not take up in detail. We feel that, although a perfect mechanical fit to the rest of the universe, it is a bad moral fit, and that something else would really have been better in its place.

But for the deterministic philosophy the murder, the sentence, and the prisoner's optimism were all necessary from eternity; and nothing else for a moment had a ghost of a chance of being put into their place. To admit such a chance, the determinists tell us, would be to make a suicide of reason; so we must steel our hearts against the thought. And here our plot thickens, for we see the first of those difficult implications of determinism and monism which it is my purpose to make you feel. If this Brockton murder was called for by the rest of the universe, if it had to come at its preappointed hour, and if nothing else would have been consistent with the sense of the whole, what are we to think of the universe? Are we stubbornly to stick to our judgment of regret, and say, though it *couldn't* be, yet it *would* have been a better universe with something different from this Brockton murder in it? That, of course, seems the natural and spontaneous thing for us to do; and yet it is nothing short of delibertely espousing a kind of pessimism. The judgment of regret calls the murder bad. Calling a thing bad means, if it mean anything at all, that the thing ought not to be, that something else ought to be in its stead. Determinism, in denying that anything else can be in its stead, virtually defines the universe as a place in which what ought to be is impossible—in other words, as an organism whose constitution is afflicted with an incurable taint, an irremediable flaw. The pessimism of a Schopenhauer says no more than this—that the murder is a symptom; and that it is a vicious symptom because it belongs to a vicious whole, which can express its nature no otherwise than by bringing forth just such a symptom as that at this particular spot. Regret for the murder must transform itself, if we are determinists and wise, into a larger regret. It is absurd to regret the murder alone. Other things being what they are, *it* could not be different. What we should regret is that whole frame of things of which the murder is one member. I see no escape whatever from this pessimistic conclusion if, being determinists, our judgment of regret is to be allowed to stand at all.

The only deterministic escape from pessimism is everywhere to abandon the judgment of regret. That this can be done, history shows to be not impossible. The devil, *quoad existentiam*, may be good. That is, although he be a *principle* of evil, yet the universe, with such a principle in it, may practically be a better universe than it could have been without. On every hand, in a small way, we find that a certain amount of evil is a condition by which a higher form of good is brought. There is nothing to prevent anybody from generalizing this view, and trusting that if we could but see things in the largest of all ways, even such matters as this Brockton murder would appear to be paid for by the uses that follow in their train. An optimism *quand même*, a systematic and infatuated optimism like that ridiculed by Voltaire in his *Candide,* is one of the possible ideal ways in which a man may train himself to look on life. Bereft of dogmatic hardness and lit up with the expression of a tender and pathetic hope, such an optimism has been the grace of some of the most religious characters that ever lived.

Throb thine with Nature's throbbing breast,
And all is clear from east to west.

Even cruelty and treachery may be among the absolutely blessed fruits of time, and to quarrel with any of their details may be blasphemy. The only real blasphemy, in short, may be that pessimistic temper of the soul which lets it give way to such things as regrets, remorse, and grief.

Thus, our deterministic pessimism may become a deterministic optimism at the price of extinguishing our judgments of regret.

But does not this immediately bring us into a curious logical predicament? Our determinism leads us to call our judgments of regret wrong, because they are pessimistic in implying that what is impossible yet ought to be. But how then about the judgments of regret themselves? If they are wrong, other judgments, judgments of approval presumably, ought to be in their place. But as they are necessitated, nothing else *can* be in their place; and the universe is just what it was before—namely, a place in which what ought to be appears impossible. We have got one foot out of the pessimistic bog, but the other one sinks all the deeper. We have rescued our actions from the bonds of evil, but our judgments are now held fast. When murders and treacheries cease to be sins, regrets are theoretic absurdities and errors. The theoretic and the active life thus play a kind of see-saw with each other on the ground of evil. The rise of either sends the other down. Murder and treachery cannot be good without regret being bad: regret cannot be good without treachery and murder being bad. Both, however, are supposed to have been foredoomed; so something must be fatally unreasonable, absurd, and wrong in the world. It must be a place of which either sin or error forms a necessary part. From this dilemma there seems at first sight no escape. Are we then so soon to fall back into the pessimism from which we thought we had emerged? And is there no possible way by which we may, with good intellectual consciences, call the cruelties and the treacheries, the reluctances and the regrets, *all* good together? . . .

The only consistent way of representing a pluralism and a world whose parts may affect one another through their conduct being either good or bad is the indeterministic way. What interest, zest, or excitement can there be in achieving the right way, unless we are enabled to feel that the wrong way is also a possible and a natural way—nay, more, a menacing and an imminent way? And what sense can there be in condemning ourselves for taking the wrong way, unless we need have done nothing of the sort, unless the right way was open to us as well? I cannot understand the willingness to act, no matter how we feel, without the belief that acts are really good and bad. I cannot understand the belief that an act is bad, without regret at its happening. I cannot understand regret without the admission of real, genuine possibilities in the world. Only *then* is it other than a mockery to feel, after we have failed to do our best, that an irreparable opportunity is gone from the universe, the loss of which it must forever after mourn. . . .

From William James, "The Dilemma of Determinism," 1884. An address delivered to the Harvard divinity students and published in the *Unitarian Review* for September 1884.

QUESTIONS FOR REVIEW AND DISCUSSION

1. How, specifically, does William James define determinism?
2. Why do some people find it bothersome to define the world as a place where there is such a thing as "chance"?
3. William James puts great emphasis on our experience of expressing "regret" concerning certain events in our own personal life as well as in the behavior of others. How does he use the fact of such experiences of regret to deal with the question of determinism versus indeterminism?

34

Minds, Brains and Science

Searle

Reading ───────────────────────────────────

The Freedom of the Will

John R. Searle

In these pages, I have tried to answer what to me are some of the most worrisome questions about how we as human beings fit into the rest of the universe. Our conception of ourselves as free agents is fundamental to our overall self-conception. Now, ideally, I would like to be able to keep both my commonsense conceptions and my scientific beliefs. In the case of the relation between mind and body, for example, I was able to do that. But when it comes to the question of freedom and determinism, I am—like a lot of other philosophers—unable to reconcile the two.

One would think that after over 2000 years of worrying about it, the problem of the freedom of the will would by now have been finally solved. Well, actually most philosophers think it has been solved. They think it was solved by Thomas Hobbes and David Hume and various other empirically-minded philosophers whose solutions have been repeated and improved right into the twentieth century. I think it has not been solved. In this lecture I want to give you an account of what the problem is, and why the contemporary solution is not a solution, and then conclude by trying to explain why the problem is likely to stay with us.

On the one hand we are inclined to say that since nature consists of particles and their relations with each other, and since everything can be accounted for in terms of those particles and their relations, there is simply no room for freedom of the will. As far as human freedom is concerned, it doesn't matter whether physics is deterministic, as Newtonian physics was, or whether it

From John R. Searle, *Minds, Brains Science*, Harvard University Press, Cambridge, Mass., 1984.
For biographical note on Searle, see p. 480

allows for an indeterminacy at the level of particle physics, as contemporary quantum mechanics does. Indeterminism at the level of particles in physics is really no support at all to any doctrine of the freedom of the will; because first, the statistical indeterminacy at the level of particles does not show any indeterminacy at the level of the objects that matter to us—human bodies, for example. And secondly, even if there is an element of indeterminacy in the behaviour of physical particles—even if they are only statistically predictable—still, that by itself gives no scope for human freedom of the will; because it doesn't follow from the fact that particles are only statistically determined that the human mind can force the statistically-determined particles to swerve from their paths. Indeterminism is no evidence that there is or could be some mental energy of human freedom that can move molecules in directions that they were not otherwise going to move. So it really does look as if everything we know about physics forces us to some form of denial of human freedom.

The strongest image for conveying this conception of determinism is still that formulated by Laplace: If an ideal observer knew the positions of all the particles at a given instant and knew all the laws governing their movements, he could predict and retrodict the entire history of the universe. Some of the predictions of a contemporary quantum-mechanical Laplace might be statistical, but they would still allow no room for freedom of the will.

So much for the appeal of determinism. Now let's turn to the argument for the freedom of the will. As many philosophers have pointed out, if there is any fact of experience that we are all familiar with, it's the simple fact that our own choices, decisions, reasonings, and cogitations seem to make a difference to our actual behaviour. There are all sorts of experiences that we have in life where it seems just a fact of our experience that though we did one thing, we feel we know perfectly well that we could have done something else. We know we could have done something else, because we chose one thing for certain reasons. But we were aware that there were also reasons for choosing something else, and indeed, we might have acted on those reasons and chosen that something else. Another way to put this point is to say: it is just a plain empirical fact about our behaviour that it isn't predictable in the way that the behaviour of objects rolling down an inclined plane is predictable. And the reason it isn't predictable in that way is that we could often have done otherwise than we in fact did. Human freedom is just a fact of experience. If we want some empirical proof of this fact, we can simply point to the further fact that it is always up to us to falsify any predictions anybody might care to make about our behaviour. If somebody predicts that I am going to do something, I might just damn well do something else. Now, that sort of option is simply not open to glaciers moving down mountainsides or balls rolling down inclined planes or the planets moving in their elliptical orbits.

This is a characteristic philosophical conundrum. On the one hand, a set of very powerful arguments force us to the conclusion that free will has no place in the universe. On the other hand, a series of powerful arguments based on facts of our own experience inclines us to the conclusion that there must be some freedom of the will because we all experience it all the time. . . .

One way to examine a philosophical thesis, or any other kind of a thesis for that matter, is to ask, "What difference would it make? How would the world be any different if that thesis were true as opposed to how the world would be if that thesis were false?" Part of the appeal of determinism, I believe, is that it seems to be consistent with the way the world in fact proceeds, at least as far as we know anything about it from physics. That is, if determinism were true, then the world would proceed pretty much the way it does proceed, the only difference being that certain of our beliefs about its proceedings would be false. Those beliefs are important to us because they have to do with the belief that we could have done things differently from the way we did in fact do them. And this belief in turn connects with beliefs about moral responsibility and our own nature as persons. But if libertarianism, which is the thesis of free will, were true, it appears we would have to make some really radical changes in our beliefs about the world. In order for us to have radical freedom, it looks as if we would have to postulate that inside each of us was a self that was capable of interfering with the causal order of nature. That is, it looks as if we would have to contain some entity that was capable of making molecules swerve from their paths. I don't know if such a view is even intelligible, but it's certainly not consistent with what we know about how the world works from physics. And there is not the slightest evidence to suppose that we should abandon physical theory in favour of such a view.

So far, then, we seem to be getting exactly nowhere in our effort to resolve the conflict between determinism and the belief in the freedom of the will. Science allows no place for the freedom of the will, and indeterminism in physics offers no support for it. On the other hand, we are unable to give up the belief in the freedom of the will. Let us investigate both of these points a bit further.

Why exactly is there no room for the freedom of the will on the contemporary scientific view? Our basic explanatory mechanisms in physics work from the bottom up. That is to say, we explain the behaviour of surface features of a phenomenon such as the transparency of glass or the liquidity of water, in terms of the behaviour of microparticles such as molecules. And the relation of the mind to the brain is an example of such a relation. Mental features are caused by, and realised in neurophysiological phenomena. . . . But we get causation from the mind to the body, that is we get top-down causation over a passage of time; and we get top-down causation over time because the top level and the bottom level go together. So, for example, suppose I wish to cause the release of the neurotransmitter acetylcholine at the axon end-plates of my motorneurons, I can do it by simply deciding to raise my arm and then raising it. Here, the mental event, the intention to raise my arm, causes the physical event, the release of acetylcholine—a case of top-down causation if ever there was one. But the top-down causation works only because the mental events are grounded in the neurophysiology to start with. So, corresponding to the description of the causal relations that go from the top to the bottom, there is another description of the same series of events where the causal relations bounce entirely along the bottom, that is, they are entirely a matter of neurons and neuron firings at synapses, etc. As long as we accept this conception of how nature works, then it doesn't seem that there is any scope for the freedom of the will because on this conception the mind can only affect nature in so far as it is a part of nature. But if so, then like the rest of nature, its features are determined at the basic microlevels of physics.

This is an absolutely fundamental point in this chapter, so let me repeat it. The form of determinism that is ultimately worrisome is not psychological determinism. The idea that our states of mind are sufficient to determine everything we do is probably just false. The worrisome form of determinism is more basic and fundamental. Since all of the surface features of the world are entirely caused by and realised in systems of micro-elements, the behaviour of micro-elements is sufficient to determine everything that happens. Such a "bottom up" picture of the world allows for top-down causation (our minds, for example, can affect our bodies). But top-down causation only works because the top level is already caused by and realised in the bottom levels.

Well then, let's turn to the next obvious question. What is it about our experience that makes it impossible for us to abandon the belief in the freedom of the will? If freedom is an illusion, why is it an illusion we seem unable to abandon? The first thing to notice about our conception of human freedom is that it is essentially tied to consciousness. We only attribute freedom to conscious beings. If, for example, somebody built a robot which we believed to be totally unconscious, we would never feel any inclination to call it free. Even if we found its behaviour random and unpredictable, we would not say that it was acting freely in the sense that we think of ourselves as acting freely. If on the other hand somebody built a robot that we became convinced had consciousness, in the same sense that we do, then it would at least be an open question whether or not that robot had freedom of the will.

The second point to note is that it is not just any state of the consciousness that gives us the conviction of human freedom. If life consisted entirely of the reception of passive perceptions, then it seems to me we would never so much as form the idea of human freedom. If you imagine yourself totally immobile, totally unable to move, and unable even to determine the course of your own thoughts, but still receiving stimuli, for example, periodic mildly painful sensations, there would not be the slightest inclination to conclude that you have freedom of the will.

I said earlier that most philosophers think that the conviction of human freedom is somehow essentially tied to the process of rational decision-making. But I think that is only partially true. In fact, weighing up reasons is only a very special case of the experience that gives us the conviction of freedom. The characteristic experience that gives us the conviction of human freedom, and it is an experience from which we are unable to strip away the conviction of freedom, is the experience of engaging in voluntary, intentional human actions. In our discussion of intentionality we concentrated on that form of intentionality which consisted in conscious intentions in action, intentionality which is causal in the way that I described, and whose conditions of satisfaction are that certain bodily movements occur, and that they occur as caused by that very intention in action. It is this experience which is the foundation stone of our belief in the freedom of the will. Why? Reflect very carefully on the character of the experiences you have as you engage in normal, everyday ordinary human actions. You will sense the possibility of alternative courses of action built into these experiences. Raise your arm or walk across the room or take a drink of water, and you will see that at any point in the experience you have a sense of alternative courses of action open to you.

If one tried to express it in words, the difference between the experience of perceiving and the experience of acting is that in perceiving one has the sense: "This is happening to me," and in acting one has the sense: "I am making this happen." But the sense that "I am making this happen" carries with it the sense that "I could be doing something else." In normal behaviour, each thing we do carries the conviction, valid or invalid, that we could be doing something else right here and now, that is, all other conditions remaining the same. This, I submit, is the source of our unshakable conviction of our own free will. It is perhaps important to emphasise that I am discussing normal human action. If one is in the grip of a great passion, if one is in a great rage, for example, one loses this sense of freedom and one can even be surprised to discover what one is doing.

Once we notice this feature of the experience of acting, a great many of the puzzling phenomena I mentioned earlier are easily explained. Why for example do we feel that the man in the case of post-hypnotic suggestion is not acting freely in the sense in which we are, even though he might think that he is acting freely? The reason is that in an important sense he doesn't know what he is doing. His actual intention-in-action is totally unconscious. The options that he sees as available to him are irrelevant to the actual motivation of his action. . . . If somebody tells me to do something at gunpoint, even in such a case I have an experience which has the sense of alternative courses of action built into it. If, for example, I am instructed to walk across the room at gunpoint, still part of the experience is that I sense that it is literally open to me at any step to do something else. The experience of freedom is thus an essential component of any case of acting with an intention.

Again, you can see this if you contrast the normal case of action with the Penfield cases,[1] where stimulation of the motor cortex produces an involuntary movement of the arm or leg. In such a case the patient experiences the movement passively, as he would experience a sound or a sensation of pain. Unlike intentional actions, there are no options built into the experience. To see this point clearly, try to imagine that a portion of your life was like the Penfield experiments on a grand scale. Instead of walking across the room you simply find that your body is moving across the room; instead of speaking you simply hear and feel words coming out of your mouth. Imagine your experiences are those of a purely passive but conscious puppet and you will

[1]Experiments by Wilder Penfield of Montreal: "by electrically stimulating a certain portion of the patient's motor cortex, Penfield could cause the movement of the patient's limbs. Now the patients were invariably surprised at this, and they characteristically said such things as: 'I didn't do it.' In such a case, we have carved off the bodily movement without the intention."

have imagined away the experience of freedom. But in the typical case of intentional action, there is no way we can carve off the experience of freedom. It is an essential part of the experience of acting.

This also explains, I believe, why we cannot give up our conviction of freedom. We find it easy to give up the conviction that the earth is flat as soon as we understand the evidence for the heliocentric theory of the solar system. Similarly when we look at a sunset, in spite of appearances we do not feel compelled to believe that the sun is setting behind the earth, we believe that the appearance of the sun setting is simply an illusion created by the rotation of the earth. In each case it is possible to give up a commonsense conviction because the hypothesis that replaces it both accounts for the experiences that led to that conviction in the first place as well as explaining a whole lot of other facts that the commonsense view is unable to account for. That is why we gave up the belief in a flat earth and literal "sunsets" in favour of the Copernican conception of the solar system. But we can't similarly give up the conviction of freedom because that conviction is built into every normal, conscious intentional action. And we use this conviction in identifying and explaining actions. This sense of freedom is not just a feature of deliberation, but is part of any action, whether premeditated or spontaneous. The point has nothing essentially to do with deliberation; deliberation is simply a special case.

We don't navigate the earth on the assumption of a flat earth, even though the earth looks flat, but we do act on the assumption of freedom. In fact we can't act otherwise than on the assumption of freedom, no matter how much we learn about how the world works as a determined physical system.

We can now draw the conclusions that are implicit in this discussion. First, if the worry about determinism is a worry that all of our behaviour is in fact psychologically compulsive, then it appears that the worry is unwarranted. Insofar as psychological determinism is an empirical hypothesis like any other, then the evidence we presently have available to us suggests it is false. Thus, this does give us a modified form of compatibilism. It gives us the view that psychological libertarianism is compatible with physical determinism.

Secondly, it even gives us a sense of "could have" in which people's behaviour, though determined, is such that in that sense they could have done otherwise: The sense is simply that as far as the *psychological* factors were concerned, they could have done otherwise. The notions of ability, of what we are able to do and what we could have done, are often relative to some such set of criteria. For example, I could have voted for Carter in the 1980 American election, even if I did not; but I could not have voted for George Washington. He was not a candidate. So there is a sense of "could have," in which there were a range of choices available to me, and in that sense there were a lot of things I could have done, all other things being equal, which I did not do. Similarly, because the psychological factors operating on me do not always, or even in general, compel me to behave in a particular fashion, I often, psychologically speaking, could have done something different from what I did in fact do.

But third, this form of compatibilism still does not give us anything like the resolution of the conflict between freedom and determinism that our urge to radical libertarianism really demands. As long as we accept the bottom-up conception of physical explanation, and it is a conception on which the past three hundred years of science are based, then psychological facts about ourselves, like any other higher level facts, are entirely causally explicable in terms of and entirely realised in systems of elements at the fundamental micro-physical level. Our conception of physical reality simply does not allow for radical freedom.

Fourth, and finally, for reasons I don't really understand, evolution has given us a form of experience of voluntary action where the experience of freedom, that is to say, the experience of the sense of alternative possibilities, is built into the very structure of conscious, voluntary, intentional human behaviour. For that reason, I believe, neither this discussion nor any other will ever convince us that our behaviour is unfree.

My aim in this book has been to try to characterise the relationships between the conception that we have of ourselves as rational, free, conscious, mindful agents with a conception that we have of the world as consisting of mindless, meaningless, physical particles. It is tempting to think that just as we have discovered that large portions of common sense do not adequately represent how the world really works, so we might discover that our conception of ourselves and our behaviour is entirely false. But there are limits on this possibility. The distinction between reality and appearance cannot apply to the very existence of consciousness. For if it seems to me that I'm conscious, I *am* conscious. We could discover all kinds of startling things about ourselves and our behaviour; but we cannot discover that we do not have minds, that they do not contain conscious, subjective, intentionalistic mental states; nor could we discover that we do not at least try to engage in voluntary, free, intentional actions. The problem I have set myself is not to prove the existence of these things, but to examine their status and their implications for our conceptions of the rest of nature. My general theme has been that, with certain important exceptions, our commonsense mentalistic conception of ourselves is perfectly consistent with our conception of nature as a physical system.

QUESTIONS FOR REVIEW AND DISCUSSION

1. Searle suggests that a good way to examine a philosophical thesis is to ask "What difference would it make? How would the world be any different if that thesis were true as opposed to how the world would be if the thesis

were false?" For example, can you think of any of your beliefs about why you behave the way you do that would be false if everything, including your behavior, was strictly determined?

2. What makes it possible, according to Searle, even to ask whether we have freedom of the will? Consider the facts of consciousness; the experience that "I could have done something else"; and the difference between the experience of "perceiving" (i.e., receiving signals or impressions) versus the experience of *acting:* that is, the difference between perceiving "This is happening to me" versus "I am making this happen."

Magritte, *La Condition Humaine*. The painting inside the room represents exactly a part of the landscape outside; but there is a larger reality beyond the immediate picture we see in the room. (© *C. Herscovici 1992/ARS, New York. Magritte, René. "La Condition Humaine." 1933. 100 × 80 cm. Private Collection. Charly Herscovici/Art Resource*)

PART EIGHT

The Question of Destiny
What Is the Meaning of Life?

One would not wish to deny that there are very vital and interesting questions [such as "What is the meaning of life?"]. But does it follow that philosophers ought to discuss them?

G. J. Warnock
English Philosophy since 1900 (1958)

For a long time I could not believe that science had no answer to give to the questions of life. The sciences directly ignore the questions of life. They say: "We have no answers to what you are and why you live." Those sciences were very interesting, very attractive, but the definiteness and clearness of those sciences were in inverse proportion to their applicability to the questions of life; the less applicable they are to the questions of life, the more definite and clear they are; the more they attempt to give answers to the questions of life, the more they become dim and unattractive.

L. N. Tolstoy
My Confession (1882)

Man is nothing else but what he makes of himself. . . . Existentialism defines man in terms of action. There is no doctrine more optimistic since man's destiny is within himself. . . . It tells him that the only hope is in his acting and that action is the only thing that enables man to live.

Jean-Paul Sartre
Existentialism (1947)

PURPOSE IN THE UNIVERSE

Whether there is a meaning to any person's life might depend on whether the universe itself has some overall purpose. It is frequently thought that as our scientific knowledge of the immense galaxies in space increases, the significance of an individual person becomes evermore diminished. To look down at the earth from an airplane is to wonder how it is that individuals, which appear from this distance to be infinitesimal, can take themselves so seriously, be full of anxiety about their future, and search earnestly for the meaning of life.

But the infinitude of interstellar space is matched by another equally impressive infinitude which is found in the micro world. This puts human beings between twin infinities, so that what is lost to human significance when viewed from vast outer space is restored when compared with the depth of microscopic reality. Moreover, the overriding fact is that the human mind is capable of grasping the structures of these two worlds so that human calculations can successfully place a machine on the moon and also successfully manipulate the world of microbiology. What this means is that while there is no overwhelming evidence of a purpose to the universe, neither is it surprising that the human mind can raise questions about the meaning of existence.

We have already seen how earlier philosophers tried to give answers to the question of life's meaning. For example, for Aristotle the concept of purpose was fundamental. Everything, he said, strives to fulfill its purpose, and it is not difficult to discover what that purpose is. Purpose and function are closely related. Each part of the body has a function, the eyes to see, the heart to circulate the blood, and the lungs to supply oxygen. Aristotle asks whether it makes sense to say, on the one hand, that every organ of the body has a purpose but, on the other hand, that when all these organs are united into a complete person, such a unified person has no specific function or purpose. Surely, he said, a person's purpose is to fulfill all his natural functions, which include not only his physical capacities but also his passions and ultimately his intellectual powers. To Aristotle's natural philosophy, Thomas Aquinas added the dimension of religion, which connected a person's natural functions and purpose to an eternal destiny of life with God. But the optimism of these philosophical and theological definitions of the meaning of life were ultimately challenged by the impact of science and skepticism. David Hume in particular rejected the notion of cause and effect on which earlier thinkers had relied to prove the existence of God and to argue for a design in the universe as the source of order, purpose, and meaning. While Hume ended his philosophical investigations as a skeptic, he made the significant comment that "to whatever length one may push his speculative principles, he must act and live and converse like other men. . . . It is impossible for him to persevere in total skepticism, or make it appear in his conduct for a few hours."

APPROACHES TO THE MEANING OF LIFE

Not all philosophers deal with the question of the meaning of life. As we have seen in the earlier section of analytic philosophy, there had been a major reduction in the scope of philosophy following what has been called the "linguistic turn." For those who have tried to put philosophy on a scientific footing, the new definition of philosophy rules out much of philosophy's earlier concerns in ethics, aesthetics, religion, and metaphysics. In its more restricted form these reductions have produced a natural, or simply a formal, limitation of what will concern the philosopher. *Geoffrey Warnock* of Oxford describes another kind of limitation, which can be called a "deliberate" limitation; this simply means that even if such questions as the meaning of life are important, most twentieth-century philosophers have deliberately decided to turn their attention to other subjects. But the question about human destiny is such a compelling concern that it is inevitable human beings cannot ignore it.

Lev Tolstoy in his *Confession* describes how it is that whatever detours a person takes away from this question, the question itself will not go away.

Similarly, *Søren Kierkegaard* describes the human condition as requiring that a person move through the various levels along life's way, that is, through aesthetics, ethics, finally to faith, in order to achieve life's meaning.

For *Jean-Paul Sartre,* because there is no God to provide the meaning of life, this meaning must be created by human beings themselves, requiring virtually as much choice and commitment as religion itself.

35

The Deliberate Limitations of Philosophy

Warnock

Sir Geoffrey Warnock (1923–   ) was knighted in 1986 in recognition of his work in philosophy and in the governance of Oxford University. He was born on August 16, 1923, and educated at Oxford. There he was fellow and tutor in philosophy at Magdalen College, the principal of Hertford College, and vice chancellor of Oxford University. His book from which this reading selection is taken is entitled *English Philosophy since 1900*.

Reading ——————————————————————————————————

Philosophy and Belief

G. J. Warnock

It is . . . certain that questions of "belief"—questions of a religious, moral, political, or generally "cosmic" variety—are seldom if at all directly dealt with in contemporary philosophy. Why is this so? The first part of an answer to this question can easily be given: there is a very large number of questions, not of that variety, which philosophers find themselves to be more interested in discussing. But many would go further. They would wish to say that philosophy has nothing to do with questions of *that* kind. Political philosophy involves the study of political concepts, but says nothing of the rights or wrongs of political issues. The moral philosopher examines the "language of morals," but does not as such express moral judgements. The philosopher of religion may be, but by no means need be, a religious believer. They would say, more generally, that philosophy is the study of the concepts that we employ, and not of the facts, phenomena, cases, or events to which those concepts might be or are applied. To investigate the latter is to raise political or moral or religious, but not philosophical, problems or questions. . . .

From this attitude two questions may arise that should be carefully distinguished. It might be objected, first, that matters of "belief," though indeed quite distinct from the problems now classed as philosophical, ought *also* to be made, at least more frequently, subjects of discussion among philosophers. To say simply that these matters are no part of philosophy is, it might be held, to impose an arbitrary and unreasonable restriction upon the scope of the subject, a restriction, moreover, for which there is no historical warrant. Are there not questions of a quite nontechnical sort, questions about life in general and attitudes to life, which historically have been at any rate touched on by most philosophers, and which furthermore are vastly more interesting to people in general than are the highly abstract, highly "professional," and frequently minute disputations in which philosophers currently engage?

This is not, I believe, an impressive point. No doubt one would not wish to deny that there are very vital and interesting questions of this sort. But does it follow that philosophers ought to discuss them? Have they not perhaps, like physicists or philologists, their own special and specialized concerns in which in fact, for what the point is worth, they are evidently more interested? Is it really any use exhorting or instructing them to do something else? Their position after all is not usually such that they have any great interest in pleasing the public or pursuing mass audiences; they would not be much put out if those whom their work did not attract should pay simply no further attention to it. Even if, as in fact is not perfectly clear, their present concerns are somewhat more confined than the concerns of philosophers historically have been, it is not clearly improper nor in the least degree unusual for such progressive specialization to occur. Finally, is it certain that those philosophers who have dealt largely in *Weltenschauung* have done so to any great purpose or profit? And could it be any more certain that, if those questions were now to be more frequently mooted among philosophers, the outcome would be particularly valuable? A marked capacity for abstract thought is compatible with an "attitude to life" entirely ordinary, or even dull. A philosopher's views in this area might be expected to be consistent and reasonably clear; but they might well, while fulfilling those conditions, be absolutely uninteresting. If so, one need not complain if he should keep them to himself.

But second, some philosophers, conscious perhaps of the lack of weight in this first objection, have raised a rather similar point in a more telling form. The view that philosophy is, to repeat an expression employed just now, ideologically neutral is held widely enough for it to be becoming increasingly fashionable to deny it. The fashionable objection is that current philosophical views and procedures are *not* distinct from, unrelated to, matters of the *Weltanschauung* variety; so that for philosophers to disclaim any concern with those matters amounts in fact to their being blind to the implications of their practices. The suggestion is not that questions of a different kind should be admitted within the scope of philosophy, but that those questions necessarily are within its scope already and therefore ought not to be, as they often are, passed over in silence.

It is in any case a rather curious fact that philosophy in general should be made so often a target for public complaint or criticism. There are after all a great many academic subjects in which, as they are at present pursued, the general public neither finds nor could well be expected to find any sort of interest. Yet no one is moved to complain of this state of affairs, or to urge the professors of those subjects to turn their hands to matters that would engage the concern of a wider audience. Why are philosophers not thus allowed to go their own way? No doubt there are many reasons. But one, I think, is this. There is a sense in which philosophy has only rather recently achieved professional status. This has occurred in two ways. First, "where Mill, Huxley, and Leslie Stephen had published their articles in the ordinary reviews, Bradley, Moore, and Russell published theirs in the philosophers' professional organ or in the Proceedings of the philosophers' metropolitan forum. This new professional practice of submitting problems and arguments to the expert criticism of fellow craftsmen led to a growing concern with questions of philosophical technique and a growing passion for ratiocinative rigour. Eloquence will not silence rival experts and edification is not palatable to colleagues. . . . Philosophers had now to be philosophers' philosophers; and in their colloquia there was as little room for party politics as there is in courts of law."[1] Second, it is only quite recently that the subject-matter, or rather the tasks, of philosophy have come to be clearly distinguished from those of other disciplines. In this way too, connected of course with the other, the subject has not long been standing firmly on its own feet in its own territory. For these reasons I believe that philosophy has not yet been accepted as a subject which its practitioners should be left to practice. There lingers a certain sense of the old, kind days of amateurism, the days, as it were, when anyone could join in, could have his own say, and could expect to be listened to. Those who have not moved into, or have moved out of, professional circles have, perhaps; still a sense of a certain deprivation, a vague feeling that the total amateur ought not to be disqualified from engaging in what was, so recently, an amateurish pursuit. (I believe that the position of literary criticism is here very similar.) On the professional side too there is perhaps a certain nostalgia. The old amateurs were occasionally conspicuous public men. Their cogitations were of interest to, and rightly or wrongly were thought to be of importance in, far wider circles than would now be likely to be reached by even the most admirable of contributions to philosophy. Thus, perhaps, it comes about that certain philosophers deplore the present aspect of their own subject, and that, more commonly, certain nonphilosophers discuss philosophy with a plaintive and patronizing impertinence which they would not dream of displaying towards any other subject in which they were admittedly ill qualified. There is not much need to worry about this. The present state of affairs is doubtless temporary and transitional; and in the meantime the complaints that are made are quite certain to be ineffective.

For my own part I am inclined to think that they only need feel strongly hostile to contemporary philosophy who have cause to fear or to dislike a

---

[1]Ryle, *The Revolution in Philosophy*, Introduction, p. 4.

clear intellectual air and a low temperature of argument. It seems to be true that the contemporary philosopher's eye is characteristically cold and his pen, perhaps, apt to be employed as an instrument of deflation. It is largely for this reason that, however narrowly technical, however refined and minute and even pedantic, the pursuits of philosophers may be or may become, any age or society in which those pursuits were wholly neglected would be, in my judgment, seriously the worse for that. In our own case we have, at present, no ground for apprehension.

From G. J. Warnock, *English Philosophy since 1900,* Oxford University Press, London and New York, 1958. © Oxford University Press 1958. Reprinted by permission of Oxford University Press.

QUESTIONS FOR REVIEW AND DISCUSSION

Geoffrey Warnock agrees that "questions of 'belief'—questions of a religious, moral, political or generally 'cosmic' variety [for example, 'What is the meaning of life?']—are seldom if at all directly dealt with in contemporary philosophy." Warnock then asks, "Why is this so?"

1. Is the answer simply that today philosophers deal with what they consider more interesting questions?
2. Is there a different answer to be found, for example, in the earlier section on analytic philosophy?
3. How does Warnock answer his own question?

36

The Inevitability of the Question "What Is the Aim of Life?"

Tolstoy

Count Tolstoy was born in Russia in 1828 and died there in 1910. He was one of the world's great novelists, known especially for his *War and Peace* and *Anna Karenina*. His *Confession* from which the selected reading is taken reveals his deep personal crisis, which led him to a profound search for an answer to the meaning of life.

Reading ────────────────────────────

My Confession

Lev Tolstoy

I was baptized and educated in the Orthodox Christian faith. I was taught it from childhood and through the whole time of my boyhood and youth. But when I, at eighteen years of age, left the second year's course of the university, I no longer believed any of the things I had been taught. . . .

My defection from faith took place in the same manner as it has taken place and still takes place in people of our cultivated class. . . .

I wished with all my heart to be good; but I was young, I had passions, and I was alone, completely alone, when I was trying to find the good. Every time I endeavoured to give utterance to what formed my most intimate wishes, namely, that I wished to be morally good, I met with contempt and ridicule; and the moment I surrendered myself to the abominable passions, I was praised and encouraged.

Ambition, lust of power, selfishness, voluptuousness, pride, anger, revenge,—all that was respected. By abandoning myself to these passions I became like a grown person, and I felt that people were satisfied with me. A good aunt of mine, a pure soul, with whom I was living, kept telling me that there was nothing she wished so much for me as that I should have a liaison with a married woman. . . . I . . . fornicated, and cheated. Lying, stealing, acts of lust of every description, drunkenness, violence, murder—There was not a crime which I did not commit, and for all that I was praised, and my contemporaries have regarded me as a comparatively moral man.

Thus I lived for ten years. . . .

When I came back [from St. Petersburg], I got married. The new conditions of my happy family life completely drew me away from all search for the general meaning of life. All my life during that time was centred in my family, my wife, my children, and, therefore, in cares for the increase of the means of existence. The striving after perfection . . . now gave way simply to the striving after making it as comfortable as possible for me and my family.

Thus another fifteen years passed.

Although I regarded authorship as a waste of time, I continued to write during those fifteen years. I had tasted of the seduction of authorship, of the seduction of enormous monetary remunerations and applauses for my insignificant labour, and so I submitted to it, as being a means for improving my material condition and for stifling in my soul all questions about the meaning of my life and life in general.

In my writings I advocated, what to me was the only truth, that it was necessary to live in such a way as to derive the greatest comfort for oneself and one's family.

Thus I proceeded to live, but five years ago something very strange began to happen with me: I was overcome by minutes at first of perplexity and then of an arrest of life, as though I did not know how to live or what to do, and I lost myself and was dejected. But that passed, and I continued to live as before. Then those minutes of perplexity were repeated oftener and oftener, and always in one and the same form. These arrests of life found their expression in ever the same questions: "Why? Well, and then?"

At first I thought that those were simply aimless, inappropriate questions. It seemed to me that that was all well known and that if I ever wanted to busy myself with their solution, it would not cost me much labour,—that now I had no time to attend to them, but that if I wanted to I should find the proper answers. But the questions began to repeat themselves oftener and oftener, answers were demanded more and more persistently, and, like dots that fall on the same spot, these questions, without any answers, thickened into one black blotch. . . .

My life came to a standstill. . . . The truth was that life was meaningless. It was as though I had just been living and walking along, and had come to an abyss, where I saw clearly that there was nothing ahead but perdition. . . .

. . . I did not know myself what it was I wanted: I was afraid of life, strove to get away from it, and, at the same time, expected something from it.

All that happened with me when I was on every side surrounded by what is considered to be complete happiness. I had a good, loving, and beloved wife, good children, and a large estate, which grew and increased without any labour on my part. I was respected by my neighbours and friends, more than ever before, was praised by strangers, and, without any self-deception, could consider my name famous. With all that, I was not deranged or mentally unsound,—on the contrary, I was in full command of my mental and physical powers, such as I had rarely met with in people of my age: physically I could work in a field, mowing, without falling behind a peasant; mentally I could work from eight to ten hours in succession, without experiencing any consequences from the strain. And while in such condition I arrived at the conclusion that I could not live, and, fearing death, I had to use cunning against myself, in order that I might not take my life. . . .

Long ago has been told the Eastern story about the traveller who in the steppe is overtaken by an infuriated beast. Trying to save himself from the animal, the traveller jumps into a waterless well, but at its bottom he sees a dragon who opens his jaws in order to swallow him. And the unfortunate man does not dare climb out, lest he perish from the infuriated beast, and does not dare jump down to the bottom of the well, lest he be devoured by the dragon, and so clutches the twig of a wild bush growing in a cleft of the well and holds on to it. His hands grow weak and he feels that soon he shall have to surrender to the peril which awaits him at either side; but he still holds on and sees two mice, one white, the other black, in even measure making a circle around the main trunk of the bush to which he is clinging, and nibbling at it on all sides. Now, at any moment, the bush will break and tear off, and he will fall into the dragon's jaws. The traveller sees that and knows that he will inevitably perish; but while he is still clinging, he sees some drops of honey hanging on the leaves of the bush, and so reaches out for them with his tongue and licks the leaves. Just so I hold on to the branch of life, knowing that the dragon of death is waiting inevitably for me, ready to tear me to pieces, and I cannot understand why I have fallen on such suffering. And I try to lick that honey which used to give me pleasure; but now it no longer gives me joy, and the white and the black mouse day and night nibble at the branch to which I am holding on. I clearly see the dragon, and the honey is no longer sweet to me. I see only the inevitable dragon and the mice, and am unable to turn my glance away from them. That is not a fable, but a veritable, indisputable, comprehensible truth.

The former deception of the pleasures of life, which stifled the terror of the dragon, no longer deceives me. No matter how much one should say to me, "You cannot understand the meaning of life, do not think, live!" I am unable to do so, because I have been doing it too long before. Now I cannot help seeing day and night, which run and lead me up to death. I see that alone, because that alone is the truth. Everything else is a lie.

The two drops of honey that have longest turned my eyes away from the cruel truth, the love of family and of authorship, which I have called an art, are no longer sweet to me.

"My family—" I said to myself, "but my family, my wife and children, they are also human beings. They are in precisely the same condition that I am in: they must either live in the lie or see the terrible truth. Why should they live? Why should I love them, why guard, raise, and watch them? Is it for the same despair which is in me, or for dulness of perception? Since I love them, I cannot conceal the truth from them,—every step in cognition leads them up to this truth. And the truth is death."

"Art, poetry?" For a long time, under the influence of the success of human praise, I tried to persuade myself that that was a thing which could be done, even though death should come and destroy everything, my deeds, as well as my memory of them; but soon I came to see that that, too, was a deception. It was clear to me that art was an adornment of life, a decoy of life. But life lost all its attractiveness for me. How, then, could I entrap others? So long as I did not live my own life, and a strange life bore me on its waves; so long as I believed that life had some sense, although I was not able to express it,— the reflections of life of every description in poetry and in the arts afforded me pleasure, and I was delighted to look at life through this little mirror of art; but when I began to look for the meaning of life, when I experienced the necessity of living myself, that little mirror became either useless, superfluous, and ridiculous, or painful to me. I could no longer console myself with what I saw in the mirror, namely, that my situation was stupid and desperate. It was all right for me to rejoice so long as I believed in the depth of my soul that life had some sense. At that time the play of lights—of the comical, the tragical, the touching, the beautiful, the terrible in life—afforded me amusement. But when I knew that life was meaningless and terrible, the play in the little mirror could no longer amuse me. No sweetness of honey could be sweet to me, when I saw the dragon and the mice that were nibbling down my support.

That was not all. If I had simply comprehended that life had no meaning, I might have known that calmly,—I might have known that that was my fate. But I could not be soothed by that. . . . I was like a man who had lost his way in the forest, who was overcome by terror because he had lost his way, who kept tossing about in his desire to come out on the road, knowing that every step got him only more entangled, and who could not help tossing. . . .

"But, perhaps, I overlooked something, or did not understand something right?" I said to myself several times. "It is impossible that this condition of despair should be characteristic of men!" And I tried to find an explanation for these questions in all those branches of knowledge which men had acquired. . . . and I found nothing.

For a long time I could not believe that science had no answer to give to the questions of life. . . .

. . . If you turn to the branch of knowledge which does not busy itself with the solution of the problems of life, but answers only its special, scientific questions, you are delighted at the power of the human mind, but know in advance that there will be no answers there to the questions of life. These sciences directly ignore the question of life. They say: "We have no answers to what you are and why you live, and we do not busy ourselves with that; but if you want to know the laws of light, of chemical combinations, the laws of the development of organisms, if you want to know the laws of the bodies, their forms, and the relation of numbers and quantities, if you want to know the laws of your mind, we shall give you clear, definite, incontrovertible answers to all that." . . .

No matter how strange, how incredibly incomprehensible it now seems to me that I, discussing life, should have been able to overlook all those who surrounded me on all sides, the life of humanity, that I should have been able to err in such a ridiculous manner as to think that my life, and the life of a Solomon and a Schopenhauer, was the real, the normal life, while the life of billions was a circumstance that did not deserve consideration. . . . .

I lived for a long time in this madness, which, not in words, but in deeds, is particularly characteristic of us, the most liberal and learned of men. But, thanks either to my strange, physical love for the real working class, which made me understand it and see that it is not so stupid as we suppose, or to the sincerity of my conviction, which was that I could know nothing and that the best that I could do was to hang myself,—I felt that if I wanted to live and understand the meaning of life, I ought naturally to look for it, not among those who had lost the meaning of life and wanted to kill themselves, but among those billions departed and living men who had been carrying their own lives and ours upon their shoulders. And I looked around at the enormous masses of deceased and living men,—not learned and wealthy, but simple men,—and I saw something quite different. I saw that all these billions of men that lived or had lived, all, with rare exceptions, did not fit into my subdivisions, and that I could not recognize them as not understanding the question, because they themselves put it and answered it with surprising clearness. Nor could I recognize them as Epicureans, because their lives were composed rather of privations and suffering than of enjoyment. Still less could I recognize them as senselessly living out their meaningless lives, because every act of theirs and death itself was explained by them. They regarded it as the greatest evil to kill themselves. It appeared, then, that all humanity was in possession of a knowledge of the meaning of life, which I did not recognize and which I contemned. It turned out that rational knowledge did not give any meaning to life, excluded life, while the meaning which by billions of people, by all humanity, was ascribed to life was based on some despised, false knowledge.

The rational knowledge in the person of the learned and the wise denied the meaning of life, but the enormous masses of men, all humanity, recognized this meaning in an irrational knowledge. This irrational knowledge was faith, the same that I could not help but reject. That was God as one and three, the creation in six days, devils and angels, and all that which I could not accept so long as I had not lost my senses.

My situation was a terrible one. I knew that I should not find anything on the path of rational knowledge but the negation of life, and there, in faith, nothing but the negation of reason, which was still more impossible than the negation of life. From the rational knowledge it followed that life was an evil and men knew it,—it depended on men whether they should cease living, and yet they lived and continued to live, and I myself lived, though I had known long ago that life was meaningless and an evil. From faith it followed that, in order to understand life, I must renounce reason, for which alone a meaning was needed.

There resulted a contradiction, from which there were two ways out: either what I called rational was not so rational as I had thought; or that which to me appeared irrational was not so irrational as I had thought. And I began to verify the train of thoughts of my rational knowledge.

In verifying the train of thoughts of my rational knowledge, I found that it was quite correct. The deduction that life was nothing was inevitable; but I saw a mistake. The mistake was that I had not reasoned in conformity with the question put by me. The question was, "Why should I live?" that is, "What real, indestructible essence will come from my phantasmal, destructible life? What meaning has my finite existence in this infinite world?" And in order to answer this question, I studied life.

The solutions of all possible questions of life apparently could not satisfy me, because my question, no matter how simple it appeared in the beginning, included the necessity of explaining the finite through the infinite, and vice versa.

I asked, "What is the extra-temporal, extra-causal, extra-spatial meaning of life?" But I gave an answer to the question, "What is the temporal, causal, spatial meaning of my life?" The result was that after a long labour of mind I answered, "None."

In my reflections I constantly equated, nor could I do otherwise, the finite with the finite, the infinite with the infinite, and so from that resulted precisely what had to result: force was force, matter was matter, will was will, infinity was infinity, nothing was nothing,—and nothing else could come from it.

There happened something like what at times takes place in mathematics: you think you are solving an equation, when you have only an identity. The reasoning is correct, but you receive as a result the answer: $a = a$, or $x = x$, or $0 = 0$. The same happened with my reflection in respect to the question about the meaning of my life. The answers given by all science to that question are only identities.

Indeed, the strictly scientific knowledge, that knowledge which, as Descartes did, begins with a full doubt in everything, rejects all knowledge which has been taken on trust, and builds everything anew on the laws of reason and experience, cannot give any other answer to the question of life than what I received,—an indefinite answer. . . . Thus the philosophical knowledge does not negate anything, but only answers that the question cannot be solved by it, that for philosophy the solution remains insoluble.

When I saw that, I understood that it was not right for me to look for an answer to my question in rational knowledge, and that the answer given by rational knowledge was only an indication that the answer might be got if the question were differently put, but only when into the discussion of the question should be introduced the question of the relation of the finite to the infinite. I also understood that, no matter how irrational and monstrous the answers might be that faith gave, they had this advantage that they intro-duced into each answer the relation of the finite to the infinite, without which there could be no answer.

No matter how I may put the question, "How must I live?" the answer is, "According to God's law." "What real result will there be from my life?"—"Eternal torment or eternal bliss." "What is the meaning which is not destroyed by death?"—"The union with infinite God, paradise."

Thus, outside the rational knowledge, which had to me appeared as the only one, I was inevitably led to recognize that all living humanity had a cer-tain other irrational knowledge, faith, which made it possible to live.

All the irrationality of faith remained the same for me, but I could not help recognizing that it alone gave to humanity answers to the questions of life, and, in consequence of them, the possibility of living.

The rational knowledge brought me to the recognition that life was meaningless,—my life stopped, and I wanted to destroy myself. When I looked around at people, at all humanity, I saw that people lived and asserted that they knew the meaning of life. I looked back at myself: I lived so long as I knew the meaning of life. As to other people, so even to me, did faith give the meaning of life and the possibility of living.

Looking again at the people of other countries, contemporaries of mine and those passed away, I saw again the same. Where life had been, there faith, ever since humanity had existed, had given the possibility of living, and the chief features of faith were everywhere one and the same.

No matter what answers faith may give, its every answer gives to the finite existence of man the sense of the infinite,—a sense which is not destroyed by suffering, privation, and death. Consequently in faith alone could we find the meaning and possibility of life. What, then, was faith? I understood that faith was not merely an evidence of things not seen, and so forth, not revelation (that is only the description of one of the symptoms of faith), not the relation of man to man (faith has to be defined, and then God, and not first God, and faith through him), not merely an agreement with what a man was told, as faith was generally understood,—that faith was the knowl-edge of the meaning of human life, in consequence of which man did not destroy himself, but lived. Faith is the power of life. If a man lives he believes in something. If he did not believe that he ought to live for some purpose, he would not live. If he does not see and understand the phantasm of the finite, he believes in that finite; if he understands the phantasm of the finite, he must believe in the infinite. Without faith one cannot live.

I was prepared now to accept any faith, so long as it did not demand from me a direct denial of reason, which would have been a lie. . . .

In order that all humanity may be able to live, in order that they may continue living, giving a meaning to life, they, those billions, must have anoth-er, a real knowledge of faith, for not the fact that I, with Solomon and Schopenhauer, did not kill myself convinced me of the existence of faith, but that these billions had lived and had borne us, me and Solomon, on the waves of life.

Then I began to cultivate the acquaintance of the believers from among the poor, the simple and unlettered folk, of pilgrims, monks, dissenters, peasants. The doctrine of these people from among the masses was also the Christian doctrine that the quasi-believers of our circle professed. With the Christian truths were also mixed in very many superstitions, but there was this difference: the superstitions of our circle were quite unnecessary to them, had no connection with their lives, were only a kind of an Epicurean amusement, while the superstitions of the believers from among the labouring classes were to such an extent blended with their life that it would have been impossible to imagine it without these superstitions,—it was a necessary condition of that life. I began to examine closely the lives and beliefs of these people, and the more I examined them, the more did I become convinced that they had the real faith, that their faith was necessary for them, and that it alone gave them a meaning and possibility of life. In contradistinction to what I saw in our circle, where life without faith was possible, and where hardly one in a thousand professed to be a believer, among them there was hardly one in a thousand who was not a believer. In contradistinction to what I saw in our circle, where all life passed in idleness, amusements, and tedium of life, I saw that the whole life of these people was passed in hard work, and that they were satisfied with life. In contradistinction to the people of our circle, who struggled and murmured against fate because of their privations and their suffering, these people accepted diseases and sorrows without any perplexity or opposition, but with the calm and firm conviction that it was all for good. In contradistinction to the fact that the more intelligent we are, the less do we understand the meaning of life and the more do we see a kind of a bad joke in our suffering and death, these people live, suffer, and approach death, and suffer in peace and more often in joy. In contradistinction to the fact that a calm death, a death without terror or despair, is the greatest exception in our circle, a restless, insubmissive, joyless death is one of the greatest exceptions among the masses. And of such people, who are deprived of everything which for Solomon and for me constitutes the only good of life, and who withal experience the greatest happiness, there is an enormous number. I cast a broader glance about me. I examined the life of past and present vast masses of men, and I saw people who in like manner had understood the meaning of life, who had known how to live and die, not two, not three, not ten, but hundreds, thousands, millions. All of them, infinitely diversified as to habits, intellect, culture, situation, all equally and quite contrary to my ignorance knew the meaning of life and of death, worked calmly, bore privations and suffering, lived and died, seeing in that not vanity, but good.

I began to love those people. The more I penetrated into their life, the life of the men now living, and the life of men departed, of whom I had read and heard, the more did I love them, and the easier it became for me to live. Thus I lived for about two years, and within me took place a transformation, which had long been working within me, and the germ of which had always been in me. What happened with me was that the life of our circle,—of the rich and the learned,—not only disgusted me, but even lost all its meaning. All our acts, reflections, sciences, arts,—all that appeared to me in a new light. I saw that all that was mere pampering of the appetites, and that no meaning could be found in it; but the life of all the working masses, of all humanity, which created life, presented itself to me in its real significance. I saw that that was life itself and that the meaning given to this life was truth, and I accepted it.

Lev N. Tolstoy, *My Confession* and *Critique of Dogmatic Theology*, trans. Leo Wiener, Dana Estes, Boston, 1904.

QUESTIONS FOR REVIEW AND DISCUSSION

Tolstoy has produced a candid and detailed description of his life, his thoughts, and his personal crisis of meaning in his celebrated *Confessions*. One question that emerges is why, in your judgment, did he experience a crisis of life's meaning? He read widely in philosophy, studied the insights of scientists, had a deep appreciation for art and poetry, had what he called "a happy family life," and was a highly successful author of such classics as *War and Peace* and *Anna Karenina*, which earned considerable wealth. During his successful career, he said, "I had tasted of the seduction of authorship, of the seduction of enormous monetary remunerations. . . . I submitted to it, as being means for improving my material condition. . . ." How does Tolstoy explain his crisis, and how did he solve it?

37

The Stages on Life's Way

Kierkegaard

Søren Kierkegaard was born in 1813 in Copenhagen. He went to the university there to study theology but was instead captivated by philosophy. He reacted against the dominant mode of philosophy of his day, namely, against Hegel's system of universal knowledge. He was influenced by Friedrich Schelling (1775–1854), a former classmate of Hegel's, who ultimately rejected Hegel's philosophy. Schelling turned from Hegel's universal system to an emphasis on the individual, calling attention to the irrational and darker aspects of man's deepest nature. George Wilhelm Friedrich Hegel (1770–1831) had been professor of philosophy at the University of Berlin, where he formulated a highly technical philosophy attempting to include all of existence in an objective system. Kierkegaard attacked this approach on the grounds that it overlooked the subjective nature of personal life with all its agonizing requirements for making decisions and commitments. Kierkegaard's father left him a considerable fortune, providing the resources for Søren's brilliant literary career, during which he produced over a dozen major works. His father's strict religious convictions coupled with a brooding melancholy strongly affected Kierkegaard. So did Søren's love affair with Regine Olsen. After breaking off their engagement, Kierkegaard left her and spent six months at the University of Berlin, where he wrote his book *EITHER/OR* (1843), which can be read as an attempt to explain his attitude toward her, but it is at the same time a major treatise on the crucial role of decision and choice in human existence. When he died in 1855 at the age of forty-two, he left his remaining possessions to Regine, who by then was happily married to a governor in the Danish West Indies. Kierkegaard's enormous literary output remained almost unnoticed by the world until the Second World War when translations began to appear, creating a powerful impact on contemporary existentialism.

Daily life is the arena where a person's religion is put into practice. Each person has to contend with his human condition. To be alive, to exist, requires that we make countless decisions every day. Philosophers who are especially concerned with the human condition of the existing individual are known as "existentialists." There are theistic as well as atheistic existentialists. Kierkegaard and Sartre represent these two points of view, respectively. Søren Kierkegaard writes from a strong Christian perspective, while Jean-

Paul Sartre tries to show what it means for daily life if one denies the existence of God.

Many of the themes of contemporary existentialism were first expressed in the writings of Kierkegaard. He spent his short life in a brilliant literary career, producing an extraordinary number of books before his death in 1855 at the age of forty-two. Although his books were forgotten soon after his death, they made an enormous impact after being rediscovered by some German scholars in the early decades of the twentieth century.

At the University of Copenhagen Kierkegaard was trained in Hegel's philosophy and was not favorably impressed by it. When he heard Schelling's lectures at Berlin, which were critical of Hegel, Kierkegaard agreed with this attack on Germany's greatest speculative thinker. "If Hegel had written the whole of his *Logic* and then said . . . that it was merely an experiment in thought," wrote Kierkegaard, "then he could certainly have been the greatest thinker who ever lived. As it is, he is merely comic." What made Hegel comic for Kierkegaard was that this great German philosopher had tried to capture all of reality in his system of thought, yet in the process lost the most important element, namely, *existence*. For Kierkegaard, the term "existence" was reserved for the individual human being. To exist, he said, implies being a certain kind of individual, an individual who strives, who considers alternatives, who chooses, who decides, and who, above all, commits himself. Virtually none of these acts were implied in Hegel's philosophy. Kierkegaard's whole career might well be considered as a self-conscious revolt against abstract thought and an attempt on his part to live up to the admonition of one of Hegel's former students, Ludwig Feuerbach: "Do not wish to be a philosopher in contrast to being a man . . . do not think as a thinker . . . think as a living, real being . . . think in Existence."

To "think in Existence" meant for Kierkegaard to recognize that one is faced with personal choices. Men find themselves constantly in an "existential situation." For this reason, their thinking ought to deal with their own personal situation with a view to coming to terms with the problem of alternatives and choices. Hegel's philosophy falsified man's understanding of reality because it shifted attention away from the concrete individual to the concept of universals. It called upon men *to think* instead of *to be*, to think the Absolute Thought instead of being involved in decisions and commitments. Kierkegaard drew the distinction between the *spectator* and the *actor*, arguing that only the actor is involved in existence. To be sure, the spectator can be said to exist, but the term "existence" does not properly belong to inert or inactive things, whether these be spectators or stones.

Kierkegaard illustrated this distinction by comparing two kinds of men in a wagon, one who holds the reins in his hands but is asleep and the other who is fully awake. In the first case, the horse goes along the familiar road without any direction from the sleeping man, whereas in the other case the man is truly a driver. Surely, in one sense it can be said that both men exist, but Kierkegaard insists that existence must refer to a quality in the individual, namely, his conscious participation in an act. Only the conscious driver exists,

Søren Kierkegaard. (*Royal Danish Ministry*)

and so, too, only a person who is engaged in conscious activity of will and choice can be truly said to exist. Thus while both the spectator and the actor exist in a sense, only the actor is involved in existence.

Kierkegaard's criticism of rational knowledge was severe. He revolted against the rational emphasis in Greek wisdom, which, he charged, had permeated subsequent philosophy and Christian theology. His specific argument was that Greek philosophy had been too greatly influenced by a high regard for mathematics. Although he did not want to reject either mathematics or science in their proper uses, he did reject the assumption that the mode of thought characteristic of science could be successfully employed when trying to understand human nature. Mathematics and science have no place for the human individual, only for the general, the universal. Likewise, Platonic philosophy emphasizes the universal, the Form, the True, the Good. Plato's whole assumption was that if one *knew* the Good, he would do it. Kierkegaard thought that such an approach to ethics was a falsification of man's real predicament.

What Kierkegaard wanted to underscore was that even when a person has knowledge, he is still in the predicament of having to make a decision. The grand formulations of philosophical systems are, in the long run, only prolonged detours, which eventually come to nothing unless they lead attention back once again to the individual. To be sure, there are problems that can be solved by mathematics and science as well as by ethics and metaphysics. But over against such universal or general problems stands life, each person's life, making demands on the individual, and at these critical moments, general and abstract thought do not help.

Kierkegaard saw in the biblical story of Abraham the typical condition of man: "God did tempt Abraham and said unto him, Abraham: and he said, here I am. And he said, take now thy son, thine only son, Isaac, whom thou lovest." What kind of knowledge can help Abraham decide whether to obey God, to sacrifice his son? The most poignant moments in life are personal ones, during which the individual becomes aware of himself as a subject. This subjective element is obscured if not denied by rational thought, which considers only man's objective characteristics, those characteristics which *all* men have in common. But subjectivity is what makes up each person's unique existence. For this reason, objectivity cannot give the whole truth about the individual self. This is why rational, mathematical, and scientific thought is incapable of guiding man to genuine existence.

Truth, said Kierkegaard, is subjectivity. By this strange notion he meant for existing, striving, deciding persons there is not available "out there" a prefabricated truth. Anticipating the pragmatic view of William James, who said that "truth is made" by an act of will, Kierkegaard wrote that what is "out there" is "an objective uncertainty"; he argued that "the highest truth attainable for an Existing individual" is simply "an objective uncertainty held fast in the most passionate personal experience. . . ." Whatever may have been his criticism of Plato, he did nevertheless find in Socrates's claim to ignorance a good example of this notion of truth, saying that "the Socratic ignorance which Socrates held fast with the entire passion of his personal experience, was thus an expression of the principle that the eternal truth is related to the Existing individual." This would suggest that the cultivation of the mind is not the only important or decisive thing in life. Of more consequence is the development and maturity of personality.

In describing man's *existential situation*, Kierkegaard distinguished between man's present estate, that is, what he now *is*, and what he *ought to be* or what he is *essentially*. There is, says Kierkegaard, a movement from *essence* to *existence*. The traditional explanation of this movement in theology is made in terms of the doctrine of sin, of the Fall. Kierkegaard translated this doctrine into a profound psychological analysis, in which he isolated man's anxiety over his own finitude as the cause of his estrangement or alienation from his essential being. Sensing his insecurity and finitude, a person tries to "do something" to overcome his finitude, and invariably what he does only aggravates his problem by adding guilt and despair to his anxiety.

Kierkegaard has in mind throughout his analysis the Christian understanding of man. Man's *essential* nature entails his relation to God, the infinite. His *existential* condition is a consequence of his alienation from God. If, then, a person's actions drive him even farther from God, his alienation and despair are compounded. This is why it is not of any help to lose oneself in a crowd. Whatever be the nature of a crowd or collectivity—whether rich or poor or political in makeup or even a congregation in a church—in every case, says Kierkegaard, "a crowd in its very concept is the untruth, by reason of the fact that it renders the individual completely impenitent and irresponsible, or at least weakens his sense of responsibility by reducing it to a fraction." Being in a crowd, in short, unmakes one's nature as an individual by diluting the self. From the point of view of Christian faith, being thus immersed in a crowd appears as an attempt on man's part to derive some meaning for his existence. But this is a wrong attempt, for "to relate oneself to God is a far higher thing than to be related to " any other thing, whether a person, race, or even church. Until man does actualize his essential self in God, says Kierkegaard, his life is full of anxiety. His anxiety is caused by his awareness, however obscure, of a deep alienation of his existential from his essential self. This alienation creates in man a dynamic drive to recover his essential self. In describing this dynamic movement, Kierkegaard speaks of the "stages on life's way."

THE AESTHETIC STAGE

Kierkegaard's analysis of the "three stages" represents the movement of the self from one level of existence to another through an act of will, an act of choice. The first stage in this process, says Kierkegaard, is the *aesthetic stage*. At this level, a person behaves according to his impulses and emotions. Although he is not simply sensual at this stage, he is for the most part governed by his senses. For this reason, the aesthetic person knows nothing of any universal moral standards. He has no specific religious belief. His chief motivation is a desire to enjoy the widest variety of pleasures of the senses. His life has no principle of limitation except his own taste; he resents anything that would limit his vast freedom of choice. At this stage an individual can exist inasmuch as he deliberately chooses to be an aesthetic man. But even though *existence* can be achieved at this level, Kierkegaard injects the element of *quality* into the matter of existence. Later existentialists were to speak of this quality in terms of authenticity. That is, an individual on the aesthetic level is aware, notwithstanding his variety of sense experiences, that his life consists, or *ought* to consist, of more than his emotive and sense experiences.

Kierkegaard distinguishes between man's capacity to be *spirit* on the one hand and *sensuousness* on the other, calling the first the *building* and the second the *cellar*. Man, he says, "prefers to dwell in the cellar." To be able to make this distinction about someone else is one thing, but for each individual to have an awareness of these two possibilities within himself is what triggers the conflict of opposites in the individual. In experience, this conflict produces anxiety and despair when the individual discovers that he is in fact living in the "cellar" but that life at this level cannot possibly produce his *authentic* self (that is, essential self), cannot result in true *existence*. The individual is now face to face with an *either/or*; either he remains on the aesthetic level with its fatal attractions, whose limitations he knows, or he moves to the next stage. This transition, says Kierkegaard, cannot be made by thinking alone but must be achieved by making a decision, or by an act of will, by a commitment.

THE ETHICAL STAGE

The second level is the *ethical stage*. Unlike the aesthetic man, who has no universal standards but only his own taste, the ethical man does recognize and accept rules of conduct that reason formulates. Moral rules give the ethical man's life the elements of form and consistency. Moreover, the ethical man accepts the limitations on his life that moral responsibility imposes. Kierkegaard illustrates the contrast between the aesthetic man and the ethical man in their attitude toward sexual behavior, saying that whereas the former yields to his impulses wherever there is an attraction, the ethical man accepts the obligations of marriage as an expression of reason, the universal reason of man. If Don Juan exemplifies the aesthetic man, it is Socrates who typifies the ethical man or the reign of the universal moral law. The ethical man has the sense of moral self-sufficiency; he takes a firm stand on moral questions and, as Socrates argued, assumes that to know the good is to do the good.

For the most part, the ethical man considers moral evil as being a product either of ignorance or of weakness of will. But the time comes, says Kierkegaard, when the process of choice begins to work in the consciousness of the ethical man. He begins to realize that he is involved in something more profound than an inadequate knowledge of the moral law or insufficient strength of will. He is, in short, doing something more serious than merely making mistakes. The ethical man ultimately comes to realize that he is in fact incapable of fulfilling the moral law, that he deliberately violates that law, and therefore he becomes conscious of his guilt. Guilt, or the sense of sin, says Kierkegaard, is what places before man a new *either/or*. Now he must either remain at the ethical level and try to fulfill the moral law, or he must respond to his new awareness, the awareness of his own finitude and estrangement from God to whom he belongs and from whom he must derive his strength.

Again, man's movement from the ethical to the next stage cannot be achieved by thinking alone but by an act of commitment, by a *leap* of faith.

THE RELIGIOUS STAGE

The difference between faith and reason is particularly striking for Kierkegaard when man arrives at the third level, the *religious stage*. Man's movement from the aesthetic to the ethical level required an act of choice and commitment; it ushered man into the presence of reason inasmuch as the moral law is an expression of the universal reason of man. But the movement from the ethical to the religious level is quite different. The leap of faith does not bring one into the presence of a God who can be philosophically or rationally described as the Absolute and Knowable Truth (and therefore objective) but into the presence of a Subject. The secret of religious consciousness, says Kierkegaard, "is in all eternity impossible because God is subject, and therefore exists only for subjectivity in inwardness."

At the ethical level, it is possible for the existing individual to give his life, as Socrates did, for the moral law that he rationally understands. But when it is a question of man's relation to God, there is available no rational or conceptual or objective knowledge about this relationship. The relationship between God and each individual is a unique and subjective experience. There is no way, prior to the actual relationship, to get any knowledge about it. Any attempt to get such objective knowledge about it is, says Kierkegaard, entirely an *approximation process*. Only an act of faith can assure the existing individual of his personal relation to God. That he must find his self-fulfillment in God becomes clear to him as he discovers the inadequacy of his existence at the aesthetic and ethical levels. Through despair and guilt he is brought to the decisive moment in life when he confronts the final *either/or* of faith.

The existence of God is suggested to man in his awareness of his self-alienation, that subjective awareness of the contrast between his existential and his essential self. That God has disclosed Himself in Christ is a further complication, indeed a *paradox*. To say, as Christian faith does, that God, the infinite, is revealed in Christ, the finite, is an extraordinary affront to human reason, "to the Jews a stumbling block and to the Greeks foolishness." But Kierkegaard wanted to maintain that the only way to cross the span between man and God, that "infinite qualitative distinction between time and eternity," is not through speculative reason, not even Hegel's, but through faith. Again, truth for Kierkegaard was a subjective matter, a consequence of commitment. Without risk, said Kierkegaard, there is no faith. And with faith, the existing individual realizes his true self.

Kierkegaard's existentialism can be summed up in his statement that "every human being must be assumed in essential possession of what essentially belongs to being a man." This being the case, "the task of the subjective thinker is to transform himself into an instrument that clearly and definitely expresses in existence whatever is essentially human." This is Kierkegaard's central point, namely, that each person possesses an essential self, which he *ought* to actualize. This essential self is fixed by the very fact that man must inescapably become related to God. To be sure, man can *exist* at any one of the three stages along life's way. But the experience of despair and guilt creates in man an awareness of qualitative differences in various modes of existence. Some modes of human existence are more authentic than others. But arriving at authentic existence is not a matter of the intellect; it is a matter of faith and commitment, a continuous process of choice by the existing individual in the presence of varieties of *either/or*.

The following reading from *EITHER/OR* was written by Kierkegaard in the form of a letter from "Judge William" to his "young friend," giving some autobiographical references to Kierkegaard's character as a young university student.

Reading _____

The Seriousness of Making Choices
Søren Kierkegaard

My friend, *I think of my early youth*, when without clearly comprehending what it is to make a choice I listened with childish trust to the talk of my elders and the instant of choice was solemn and venerable, although in choosing I was only following the instructions of another person. I think of the occasions in my later life when I stood at the crossways, when my soul was matured in the hour of decision. I think of the many occasions in life less important but by no means indifferent to me, when it was a question of making a choice. For although there is only one situation in which either/or has absolute significance, namely, when truth, righteousness and holiness are lined up on one side, and lust and base propensities and obscure passions and perdition on the other; yet, it is always important to choose rightly, even as between things which one may innocently choose, it is important to test oneself, lest some day one might have to beat a retreat to the point from which one started, and might have reason to thank God if one had to reproach oneself for nothing worse than a waste of time. In common parlance I use these words [either/or] as others use them, and it would indeed be foolish to give up using them. And although my life now has to a certain degree its either/or behind it, yet I know well that it may still encounter many a situation where the either/or will have its full significance. I hope, however, that these words may find me in a worthy state of mind when they check me on my path, and I hope that I may be successful in choosing the right course; at all events, I shall endeavor to make the choice with real earnestness, and with that I venture, at least, to hope that I shall the sooner get out of the wrong path.

And now as for you—this phrase is only too often on your lips, it has almost become a byword with you. What significance has it for you? None at all. You, according to your own expression, regard it as a wink of the eye, a

Kierkegaard house, between town hall and corner house, near Copenhagen. (*Royal Danish Ministry*)

snap of the fingers, a *coup de main*, an abracadabra. At every opportunity you know how to introduce it, nor is it without effect; for it affects you as strong drink affects a neurasthenic, you become completely intoxicated by what you call the higher madness. . . . [You are like] that great thinker and true practical philosopher who said to a man who had insulted him by pulling off his hat and throwing it on the floor, "If you pick it up, you'll get a thrashing; if you don't pick it up, you'll also get a thrashing; now you can choose." You take great delight in "comforting" people when they have recourse to you in critical situations. You listen to their exposition of the case and then say, "Yes, I perceive perfectly that there are two possibilities, one can either do this or that. My sincere opinion and my friendly counsel is as follows: Do it / or don't do it—you will regret both." But he who mocks others mocks himself, and your rejoinder is not a mere nothing but a profound mockery of yourself, a sorry proof how limp your soul is, that your whole philosophy of life is concentrated in one single proposition, "I say merely either/or." In case this really were your serious meaning, there would be nothing one could do with you, one must simply put up with you as you are and deplore the fact that melancholy [literally, heavy-mindedness] or light-mindedness had enfeebled your spirit. Now on the contrary, since one knows very well that such is not the case, one is not tempted to pity you but rather to wish that some day the circumstances of your life may tighten upon you the screws in its rack and compel you to come out with what really dwells in you, may begin the sharper inquisition of the rack which cannot be beguiled by nonsense and witticisms. Life is a masquerade, you explain, and for you this is inexhaustible material for amusement; and so far, no one has succeeded in knowing you; for every revelation you make is always an illusion. Your occupation consists in preserving your hiding-place, and that you succeed in doing, for your mask is the most enigmatical of all. In fact you are nothing . . . an enigmatic figure on whose brow is inscribed Either/or—"For this," you say, "is my motto. . . ."

Now although nothing you say in that style has the slightest effect upon me, nevertheless, for your own sake I will reply to you. Do you not know that there comes a midnight hour when every one has to throw off his mask? Do you believe that life will always let itself be mocked? Do you think you can slip away a little before midnight in order to avoid this? Or are you not terrified by it? I have seen men in real life who so long deceived others that at last their true nature could not reveal itself; I have seen men who played hide and seek so long that at last madness through them obtruded disgustingly upon others their secret thoughts which hitherto they had proudly concealed. Or can you think of anything more frightful than that you thus would have lost the inmost and holiest thing of all in a man, the unifying power of personality? Truly, you should not jest with that which is not only serious but dreadful. In every man there is something which to a certain degree prevents him from becoming perfectly transparent to himself; and this may be the case in so high a degree, he may be so inexplicably woven into relationships of life which extend far beyond himself that he almost cannot reveal himself. But he who cannot reveal himself cannot love, and he who cannot love is the most unhappy man of all.

From *Either/Or* by Søren Kierkegaard, Vol. II, translated by Walter Lowrie with revisions and a Forward by Howard A. Johnson (copyright 1944 © 1955 by Princeton University Press). Reprinted by permission of Princeton University Press.

QUESTIONS FOR REVIEW AND DISCUSSION

1. Kierkegaard distinguishes between a person's *existential* self and his *essential* self. What is the difference between these two selves?
2. Kierkegaard describes life as a journey through three stages requiring choices and decisions along the way. What are these different stages, and why is it necessary to go to each next stage?

38

The Human Condition

Sartre

Born in 1905, Jean-Paul Sartre was educated at the École Normale Supérieure in Paris, exhibiting at an early age his precocious gift for literary expression. He was attracted to philosophy while at the École Normale by Henri Bergson, whose *Essai sur les donnés immédiates de la conscience* left him "bowled over" and with the feeling that "philosophy is absolutely terrific, you can learn the truth through it." He spent the years 1934–1935 at the Institut Français in Berlin, where he studied Husserl's phenomenology. Sartre wrote his *Transcendental Ego* (1936) in Germany while at the Institut, and, as he says, "I wrote it actually under the direct influence of Husserl. . . ." During World War II, Sartre was active in the French Resistance movement and became a German prisoner of war. Afterwards he taught at the lycee at Havre, the lycee Henri IV, and the lycee Condorcet, resigning after this brief teaching career to devote himself exclusively to his writings, which ultimately numbered over thirty volumes, for which he was awarded the Nobel prize and which he refused to accept in October 1965.

While still a student at the elite École Normale Supérieure, he met a fellow student, Simone de Beauvoir, with whom he enjoyed a lifelong companionship. This was no ordinary relationship. Both were brilliant students. Although she was of immense assistance to Sartre in his prolific literary work, Beauvoir herself achieved great fame as a writer. Sartre never published anything before Beauvoir had a chance to read it critically and to approve it. While Sartre was honored by the Nobel Prize Committee, Beauvoir similarly had moved to first place among women of letters. At the time of Sartre's death, she was considered France's most celebrated living writer. Her novel *The Mandarins* won the Prix Goncourt, while her book *The Second Sex,* in which she wrote the often quoted words "one is not born a woman but becomes one," gave her recognition as a well-known feminist. Her literary works gave her money, fame, and independence.

Although Sartre and Simone de Beauvoir did not marry during their fifty-one years together, theirs was a profound relationship of loyalty and love. There were, however, complications along the way. In one of her memoirs, Beauvoir says, "I was vexed with Sartre for having created the situation with Olga." This event became the theme of Beauvoir's first novel, *She Came to Stay,* a couple's intimate secret about the fictional character's relation with another woman, making Beauvoir say about her own situation, "from now on we will be a trio instead of a couple." Sartre had said earlier that Beauvoir was his "privileged" but not his only female companion. Sartre had once

said philosophically that "one can always be free"; Beauvoir asked, "Wha
dom of the women in a harem?" They were a rare couple—she was strikin
and tall, while Sartre was ugly and a full head shorter. Together their fa.... ...
around the world.

Sartre lived simply and with few possessions, finding fulfillment in political
involvement and travel and needing only a small apartment on the left bank in Paris.
In declining health and virtually blind, Sartre died on April 15, 1980, at the age of sev-
enty-four.

Sartre took the more technical writings of the contemporary German philosophers, especially Heidegger, who had probed into the meaning of Being
through the deep recesses of man's anxious and restless soul, and expressed
their findings with great lucidity and popular appeal. What had appeared first
in the heavy language of philosophy now came forth from Sartre's pen in the
open and captivating style of novels and short stories. As a philosopher, Sartre

Sartre in cafe, where he did much of his writing. (*The Bettmann Archive*)

was himself capable of writing about existentialism in the most exacting and complex style, which one finds in his massive major book *Being and Nothingness* (*L'Être et le Néant*, 1943). But his best known work is his lecture *Existentialism Is a Humanism* (*L'Existentialisme est un humanisme*), published in 1946, a work which has become famous because of its brilliance and despite Sartre's later desire to define existentialism in somewhat different terms.

Sartre's version of existentialism is the product of a special mixture of at least three contemporary modes of thought, stemming from Marx, Husserl, and Heidegger. What these three strands of thought had in common for Sartre was their concern about man's active role in forging his own destiny. Marx had expressed his passion for action when he wrote that "hitherto philosophers had merely understood the world; the point, however, is to change it." Husserl also focused his new brand of philosophy, which he called "phenomenology," on the individual, saying that "true philosophy should seek its foundation exclusively in man and, more specifically, in the essence of his concrete worldly existence." And Heidegger, in his great work *Being and Time* (*Sein und Zeit*), which relies somewhat on Kierkegaard and Husserl, wrote that our basic understanding of the large question of Being is achieved best through the existential analysis of the *person*. Heidegger's analysis strongly shaped Sartre's thought, but whereas Heidegger was concerned chiefly with *Being*, and with the *existence* of the *person* only as a means for understanding Being, Sartre became preoccupied almost solely with the existence of the individual. Accordingly, Sartre's classical formulation of the basic principle of existentialism, namely, that *existence precedes essence*, is a reversal not only of Heidegger's intentions, but of traditional metaphysics, which ever since Plato's time has said that essence precedes existence.

EXISTENCE PRECEDES ESSENCE

What does it mean to say that existence precedes essence, and how does this formula bear on our understanding of human nature? Sartre argues that we cannot explain the nature of man in the same way that we describe an article of manufacture. When we consider, for example, a paper knife, we know that it has been made by someone who had in his mind a conception of it, including what it would be used for and how it would be made. Thus even before it is made, the paper knife is already conceived of as having a definite purpose and as being the product of a definite process. If by the *essence* of the paper knife we mean the procedure by which it was made and the purposes for which it was produced, the paper knife's essence can be said to precede its existence. To look on a paper knife is to understand exactly what its useful purpose is. When we think about man's nature, we tend to describe him also as the product of a maker, of a creator, of God. We think of God most of the time, says Sartre, as a "supernal artisan," implying that when God creates, He knows precisely what He is creating. This would mean that in the mind of God the conception of man is comparable to the conception of the paper knife in the mind of the artisan. Each individual, in this view, is the fulfillment or realization of a definite conception, which resides in God's understanding.

Although it is true that some of the philosophers of the eighteenth century, including Diderot, Voltaire, and Kant, were either atheists or else suppressed the idea of God, they nevertheless retained the notion, distinctive of the theist, that man possesses a "human nature," a nature that is found in every man. Each man, they said, is a particular example of the universal conception of Man. Whatever may be the level of development to which various men have attained, whether they be primitive natives, men in the state of nature, or cultured bourgeois, they all have the same fundamental qualities and are therefore all contained in the same definition or conception of Man. In short, they all possess the same essence, and their essence precedes their concrete or historic existence, which they confront in experience.

Sartre turned all this around by taking atheism seriously. He believed that if there is no God, there is no *given* human nature precisely because there is no God to have a conception of it. Human nature cannot be defined in advance because it is not completely thought out in advance. Man as such merely exists and only later becomes his essential self. To say that existence precedes essence means, says Sartre, that man first of all exists, confronts himself, emerges in the world, and defines himself afterwards. At first, man simply is. Whether it follows that man does not have a basic and given nature simply because there is no God who stands in relation to man the way the artisan stands in relation to the knife is questionable. But what Sartre wants particularly to argue is that man is simply that which he makes of himself.

WE MUST CREATE OURSELVES

One's first reaction to this formulation of the first principle of Sartre's existentialism is that it is highly subjective, that each man can presumably set out to make of himself anything he wishes. Sartre's chief point here is that man has a greater dignity than a stone or a table. What gives him dignity is his possession of a subjective life, meaning that man is something which moves itself toward a future and is conscious that it is doing so. Sartre wants to call attention to two different modes of being, which he calls *being-in-itself (l'en-soi)* and *being-for-itself (le pour-soi)*. Applying this distinction to man, one can say that man shares both these two modes of being, the *en-soi* indicating that he *is* (the way a stone is) and the *pour-soi* indicating that he is a *conscious subject* (which therefore differentiates him from a stone). To be a conscious subject is to stand constantly before a future. The most important consequence of placing existence before essence in human nature is not only that man creates himself, but also that the responsibility for each man's existence rests squarely on each man. A stone cannot be responsible. And if man's essential nature were already given and fixed, he could not be responsible for what he is.

What began in Sartre's analysis as an amoral subjectivism now turns out to be an ethics of strict accountability based on individual responsibility. If, that is, man is what he makes of himself, he has no one to blame for what he is except himself. Moreover, when man *chooses* in the process of making himself, he chooses not only for himself but for all men. He is therefore responsible not only for his own individuality, but, says Sartre, he is responsible for all men. This last point seems to contradict the line of reasoning that Sartre has so far been developing, for to say that before one can choose a way of action one must ask "What would happen if everyone else acted so?" is to assume a general human essence, which makes *my* mode of action relevant to *all* men. Sartre does in fact say that even though we create our own values and thereby create ourselves, we nevertheless create at the same time an image of our human nature as we believe it ought to be. When we choose this or that way of acting, we affirm the value of what we have chosen, and nothing can be better for any one of us unless it is better for all. This all sounds very much like Kant's categorical imperative. But Sartre does not wish to invoke any universal law to guide man's choice. He is calling attention to one of the clearest experiences of human beings, namely, that all men must choose, must make decisions and although they have no authoritative guide, they must still choose and at the same time ask whether they would be willing for others to choose the same action. One cannot escape at times the disturbing thought that one would not want others to act as one does. To say that others will not so act is a case of *self-deception.* The act of choice, then, is one that all men must accomplish with a deep sense of *anguish,* for in this act men are responsible not only for themselves but also for each other. Whoever evades his responsibility through *self-deception* will not, says Sartre, be at ease in his conscience.

"CONDEMNED TO BE FREE"

Although Sartre's moral language sounds at times very much like traditional moral discourse, his intention is to carry out the rigorous implications of atheism. Sartre accepts Nietzsche's announcement that "God is dead" and takes seriously Dostoevsky's notion that "if God did not exist, everything would be permitted." In a Godless world, man's psychological condition is one of *abandonment,* a word Sartre takes from Heidegger. "Abandonment" means for Sartre that with the dismissal of God there also disappears every possibility of finding values in some sort of intelligible heaven. Again, there cannot now be any "good" prior to my choice, since there is no infinite or perfect consciousness to think it. Man's sense of abandonment is a curious consequence of the fact that everything is indeed permitted, and as a consequence, man is forlorn, for he cannot find anything on which he can rely either within or outside himself. Man is without any excuse. His existence precedes his essence. Apart from his existence there is nothingness. There is only the present. In his *Nausea,* Sartre writes that the true nature of the present was revealed as what exists, that what is not present does not exist. Things are entirely what they appear to be, and apart from them, there is nothing. To say there is nothing besides the existing individual means for Sartre that there is no God, no objective system of values, no built-in essence, and most important of all, *no determinism*. Man, says Sartre, is free; man is freedom. In a classic phrase, he says that "man is *condemned* to be free." Condemned because he finds himself thrown into the world, yet free because as soon as he is conscious of himself, he is responsible for everything he does. Sartre rejects the notion that human behavior is swept up by a torrent of passion as though such a passion could be regarded as an excuse for certain actions. He rejected the Freudian analysis of human behavior because it appeared to him that it provided an excuse in the form of psychological determinism. Man is responsible even for his passions, because even his feelings are formed by his deeds. Freedom is appalling (Kierkegaard had similarly spoken of the *dizziness* of freedom) precisely because it means that there is nothing forcing me from behind, so to speak, to behave in any given way, nor is there a precise pattern luring me into the future. I am the only thing that exists. We are all free, says Sartre; therefore we must choose, that is, *invent,* because no rule of general morality can show us what we ought to do. There are no guidelines guaranteed to us in this world.

There is an element of despair in human existence, which comes, says Sartre, from the realization that we are limited to what is within the scope of our own wills. We cannot expect more from our existence than the finite probabilities it possesses. Here Sartre believes that he is touching the genuine theme of personal existence by emphasizing man's finitude and his relation to nothingness. "Nothingness," he says, "lies coiled in the heart of being, like a worm." Heidegger located the cause of human anxiety in man's awareness of his finitude when, for example, I confront death—not death in general but *my* death. It is not only man who faces nothingness, says Heidegger, but all Being has this relation to nothingness. Human finitude is therefore not simply a matter of temporary ignorance or some shortcoming or even error. Finitude is the very structure of the human mind, and words such as "guilt," "loneliness," and "despair" describe the consequences of human finitude. The ultimate principle of Being, says Heidegger, is *will*. Sartre concurs by saying that only in action is there any reality. Man is only the sum of his actions and purposes; besides his actual daily life he is nothing. If a person is a coward, he *made* himself one. He is not a coward because of a cowardly heart or lungs or cerebrum, or because of his physiological organism; he is a coward because he made himself into one by his actions.

THE UNIVERSAL HUMAN CONDITION

Although there is no prior essence in all men, no human *nature,* there is nevertheless, says Sartre, a universal human *condition*. He rejects a narrow individual subjectivism as the standard of truth. Rather, to discover oneself in the act of conscious thought is to discover the condition of all men. We are in a world of *intersubjectivity*. This is the kind of world in which an individual must live, choose, and decide. For this reason, no purpose chosen by any individual is ever wholly foreign to another individual. This does not mean that every purpose defines man forever, but only that all men may be striving against the same limitations in the same way. For this reason, Sartre would not agree that it does not matter what we do or how we choose. Man is always obliged to act in a *situation,* that is, in relation to other persons, and consequently, his actions cannot, must not, be capricious, since he must take responsibility for all his actions. Moreover, to say that man must make his essence, invent his values, does not mean that one cannot *judge* human actions. It is still possible to say that one's action was based either on error or self-deception, for any man who hides behind the excuse of his passions or by espousing some doctrine of determinism deceives himself. To invent values, says Sartre, means only that there is no meaning or sense in life prior to acts of will. Life cannot be anything until it is lived, but each individual must make sense of it. The value of life is nothing else but the sense each person fashions into it. To argue that we are the victims of fate, of mysterious forces within us, of some grand passion, of heredity, is to be guilty of bad faith *(mauvaise foi)* or self-deception—of *inauthenticity.* A woman who consents to go out with a particular man knows very well, says Sartre, what the man's cherished intentions are, and she knows that sooner or later she will have to make a decision. She does not want to admit the urgency of the matter, preferring rather to interpret all his actions as discreet and respectful. She is, says Sartre, in self-deception; her actions are inauthentic. All human beings are guilty, on principle, of similar inauthenticity, of bad faith, of playing roles, of trying to disguise their actual personality behind a facade. The conclusion of Sartre's existentialism is, therefore, that if man expresses his genuine humanity in all his behavior, he will never deceive himself, and honesty will then become not his ideal but rather his very being.

Underlying Sartre's popular formulation of existentialism is his technical analysis of existence. In one respect, human nature is no different from any other kind of existing reality. Man is, just the same way anything else *is,* as simply *being there.* Unlike other things, however, man possesses consciousness. For this reason, he is related to the world of things and people in a variety of ways. At one level, man is conscious of "the world," which is everything that is beyond or other than himself and which therefore transcends him. At this level, the world is experienced simply as a solid, massive, undifferentiated, single something that is not yet separated into individual things.

EXISTENCE AS "THE VERY PASTE OF THINGS"

Sartre describes this mode of consciousness in his *Nausea* where the character Roquentin is sitting on a park bench. He looks at all the things before him in the park and all at once he *sees* everything differently, everything as a single thing—"Suddenly existence had unveiled itself." Words had vanished and the points of reference which men use to give meaning to things also vanished. What Roquentin saw was existence as "the very paste of things": "The root [of the tree], the park gates, the bench, the sparse grass, all that had vanished: the diversity of things, their individuality, were only an appearance, a veneer.

This veneer had melted, leaving soft, monstrous masses, all in disorder—naked." Only later, when man reflects, does the world become our familiar one. But, says Sartre, "The world of explanations and reasons is not the world of existence." At the level of Roquentin's experience, the world is the unity of all the objects of consciousness.

EXISTENCE IS "CONTINGENCY" NOT "NECESSITY"

When he views the world as being-in-itself, as simply being there, Sartre says that "the essential point is contingency. I mean that by definition existence is not necessity. To exist is simply to be there." Contingency means that when something exists, it does so by chance and not because it necessarily follows from something else: "Existences appear . . . but you cannot deduce them." The world we experience is "uncreated, without reason for being, without any relation to another being; being-in-itself is gratuitous for all eternity." The meaning anything will have in the world will depend, says Sartre, on choices men make. Even a table will have alternative meanings depending on what a particular person chooses to use it for, to serve dinner or to write a letter. A mountain valley will mean one thing to a farmer and something else to a camper. Here, consciousness shifts a person from simply being there, being-in-itself, to *being-for-itself (le pour-soi)*, where consciousness dramatically differentiates the objects of the world from the conscious self as subject.

THE FUNCTION OF CONSCIOUSNESS

The activity of consciousness is at this point twofold. First, consciousness defines the specific things in the world and invests them with meaning. Second, consciousness transcends, that is, puts a distance between itself and objects and in that way possesses a freedom from those objects. Because the conscious self has this freedom from the things in the world, it is within the power of consciousness to confer different or alternative meanings on things. The activity of consciousness is what is usually called "choice." Man chooses to undertake this project or that project, and the meaning of things in the world will depend to a considerable extent on what project a man chooses. If he chooses to be a farmer, the mountains, the valley, and the impending storm will have special meanings for him, whereas if he chooses to be a camper in that valley, the surroundings and the storm will present different meanings. Man, as man, at first simply *is;* his existence is primary and precedes what he is to become. What he becomes will depend on how his consciousness deals with the world—a world which he views from a distance. From this distance, in this position of freedom from things and persons, man makes a choice regarding how he will relate himself to them. It follows, also, that because man has this freedom from the world, the world does not, cannot, *mechanically and totally* affect man's consciousness and his choices. There is no way for man to alter the fact that he transcends the world, is able to view it, so to speak, from above and must therefore constantly make choices, take sides, undertake projects. In short, man is condemned to be free. By his free choices, man makes himself—not that he creates himself out of nothing, but rather by a series of choices and decisions he converts his existence into the essence of his final self. Man possesses this freedom to create himself within some limitations, such as the conditions of his birth and the circumstances of each particular situation. Nevertheless, Sartre says that any attempt on the part of a person to make excuses for his behavior by attributing his actions to external or underlying causes is self-deception and in bad faith. This strong emphasis on human freedom as worked out in *Being and Nothingness* (1943) was softened by Sartre in the sequel to that book, his *Critique of Dialectical Reason* (1960).

SARTRE VERSUS MARX

Although Sartre believed that Marxism is the philosophy of our time, he was aware of a striking contradiction between his existentialism and Marxist dialectical materialism. Indeed, one reason why Sartre never became a member of the Communist party is, he says, because "I would have had to turn my back on *Being and Nothingness*," in which he had placed such a strong emphasis on human freedom. By contrast, Marxist dialectical materialism emphasized that all the structures and organizations of society and the behavior and thinking of human beings are determined by antecedent events. In this view, freedom of choice is an illusion and man is simply a vehicle through which the forces of history realize themselves. Whereas Sartre had argued that it is man's consciousness that "makes history" and confers meaning on the world, Marxism holds that history is a process which produces the material foundations of social and economic structures, a process which therefore contains within itself the conditions and the reasons for its own development. Rather than conferring meaning on the world, the mind, says the Marxist, discovers this meaning within the historical context as a matter of scientific knowledge.

In his earlier writings, Sartre focused primarily on the individual and his freedom. For this reason, he never would accept Freud's theory of the unconscious, which Sartre saw as an irrational and mechanical causation of human behavior. Later, as in his *Critique of Dialectical Reason*, he focused more specifically on the historical and social context in which man finds himself and which has an effect on man's behavior. He thought that Marx had succeeded more than anyone else in describing how social and economic structures develop and how they bear on human decisions. Sartre accepted increasingly the limitations on human choice—the limitations of birth, status in society, and family background. Earlier, he sought to describe how an individual is capable of deceiving himself by making excuses for his behavior, as if he were not free to have behaved otherwise, a form of self-deception Sartre labeled as "bad faith." He never did depart from this emphasis on the freedom of the individual. But he did adjust his thinking under the influence of Marxism by facing the fact of man's social existence, his relationship with other persons, especially as a member of a group—such as, for example, a labor union. Acknowledging the influence of group structures on human behavior and consciousness, resulting particularly in labor's sense of alienation, Sartre revised his optimistic view of human freedom to some extent. Recalling that he had written earlier (1945) that "no matter what the situation might be, one is always free" (giving as an example that "a worker is always free to join a union or not, as he is free to choose the kind of battle he wants to join, or not"), Sartre says this "all strikes me as absurd today" (1972). And he admits, "There is no question that there is some basic change in [my] concept of freedom." In his lengthy work on Flaubert, he concludes that although Flaubert was free to become uniquely Flaubert, his family background and his status in society meant that "he did not have all that many possibilities of becoming something else . . . he had the possibility of becoming a mediocre doctor . . . and the possibility of being Flaubert." This means, says Sartre, that social conditioning exists every minute of our lives. Nevertheless, he concludes that "I am still faithful to the notion of freedom." It is true, he says, that "you become what you are in the context of what others have made of you"; nevertheless, within these limitations, man is still free and responsible. This is Sartre's way of rec-onciling the fact that historical conditions affect human behavior with his intu-itive certainty that human beings are also capable of shaping history. In doing this, Sartre sought to overcome with his existentialism what he considered the major flaw of Marxist philosophy, namely, its failure to recognize man as a "real person."

Reading _____

The Limits of Atheistic Freedom
Sartre

There are two kinds of existentialists; first, those who are Christian, among whom I would include Jaspers and Gabriel Marcel, both Catholic; and on the other hand the atheistic existentialists among whom I class Heidegger, and then the French existentialists and myself. What they have in common is that they think that existence precedes essence, or, if you prefer, that subjectivity must be the starting point.

Just what does that mean? Let us consider some object that is manufac-tured, for example, a book or a paper-cutter: here is an object which has been made by an artisan whose inspiration came from a concept. He referred to the concept of what a paper-cutter is and likewise to a known method of produc-tion, which is part of the concept, something which is, by and large, a routine.

Thus, the paper-cutter is at once an object produced in a certain way and, on the other hand, one having a specific use; and one cannot postulate a man who produces a paper-cutter but does not know what it is used for. Therefore, let us say that, for the paper-cutter, essence—that is, the ensemble of both the production routines and the properties which enable it to be both produced and defined—precedes existence. Thus, the presence of the paper-cutter or book in front of me is determined. Therefore, we have here a technical view of the world whereby it can be said that production precedes existence.

When we conceive God as the Creator, He is generally thought of as a superior sort of artisan. Whatever doctrine we may be considering, whether one like that of Descartes or that of Leibniz, we always grant that will more or less follows understanding or, at the very least, accompanies it, and that when God creates He knows exactly what He is creating. Thus, the concept of man in the mind of God is comparable to the concept of a paper-cutter in the mind of the manufacturer, and, following certain techniques and a conception, God produces man, just as the artisan, following a definition and a technique, makes a papercutter. Thus, the individual man is the realization of a certain concept in the divine intelligence.

In the eighteenth century, the atheism of the *philosophers* discarded the idea of God, but not so much for the notion that essence precedes existence. To a certain extent, this idea is found everywhere; we find it in Diderot, in Voltaire, and even in Kant. Man has a human nature; this human nature, which is the concept of the human, is found in all men, which means that each man is a particular example of a universal concept, man. In Kant, the result of this universality is that the wild-man, the natural man, as well as the bourgeois, are circumscribed by the same definition and have the same basic qualities. Thus, here too the essence of man precedes the historical existence that we find in nature.

Atheistic existentialism, which I represent, is more coherent. It states that if God does not exist, there is at least one being in whom existence precedes essence, a being who exists before he can be defined by any concept, and that this being is man, or, as Heidegger says, human reality. What is meant here by saying that existence precedes essence? It means that, first of all, man exists, turns up, appears on the scene, and, only afterwards, defines himself. If man, as the existentialist conceives him, is indefinable, it is because at first he is nothing. Only afterward will he be something, and he himself will have made what he will be. Thus, there is no human nature, since there is no God to conceive it. Not only is man what he conceives himself to be, but he is also only what he wills himself to be after his thrust toward existence.

Man is nothing else but what he makes of himself. Such is the first principle of existentialism. It is also what is called subjectivity, the name we are labeled with when charges are brought against us. But what do we mean by this, if not that man has a greater dignity than a stone or table? For we mean that man first exists, that is, that man first of all is the being who hurls himself toward a future and who is conscious of imagining himself as being in the future. Man is at the start a plan which is aware of itself, rather than a patch of moss, a piece of garbage, or a cauliflower; nothing exists prior to this plan;

there is nothing in heaven; man will be what he will have planned to be. Not what he will want to be. Because by the word "will" we generally mean a conscious decision, which is subsequent to what we have already made of ourselves. I may want to belong to a political party, write a book, get married; but all that is only a manifestation of an earlier, more spontaneous choice that is called "will." But if existence really does precede essence, man is responsible for what he is. Thus, existentialism's first move is to make every man aware of what he is and to make the full responsibility of his existence rest on him. And when we say that a man is responsible for himself, we do not only mean that he is responsible for his own individuality, but that he is responsible for all men.

The word subjectivism means, on the one hand, that an individual chooses and makes himself; and, on the other, that it is impossible for man to transcend human subjectivity. The second of these is the essential meaning of existentialism. When we say that man chooses his own self, we mean that every one of us does likewise; but we also mean by that that in making this choice he also chooses all men. In fact, in creating the man that we want to be, there is not a single one of our acts which does not at the same time create an image of man as we think he ought to be. To choose to be this or that is to affirm at the same time the value of what we choose, because we can never choose evil. We always choose the good, and nothing can be good for us without being good for all.

If, on the other hand, existence precedes essence, and if we grant that we exist and fashion our image at one and the same time, the image is valid for everybody and for our whole age. Thus, our responsibility is much greater than we might have supposed, because it involves all mankind. If I am a workingman and choose to join a christian trade-union rather than be a communist, and if by being a member I want to show that the best thing for man is resignation, that the kingdom of man is not of this world, I am not only involving my own case—I want to be resigned for everyone. As a result, my action has involved all humanity. To take a more individual matter, if I want to marry, to have children; even if this marriage depends solely on my own circumstances or passion or wish, I am involving all humanity in monogamy and not merely myself. Therefore, I am responsible for myself and for everyone else. I am creating a certain image of man of my own choosing. In choosing myself, I choose man.

This helps us understand what the actual content is of such rather grandiloquent words as anguish, forlornness, despair. As you will see, it's all quite simple.

First, what is meant by anguish? The existentialists say at once that man is anguish. What that means is this: the man who involves himself and who realizes that he is not only the person he chooses to be, but also a lawmaker who is, at the same time, choosing all mankind as well as himself, can not help escape the feeling of his total and deep responsibility. Of course, there are many people who are not anxious; but we claim that they are hiding their anxiety, that they are fleeing from it. Certainly, many people believe that when they do something, they themselves are the only ones involved, and when someone says to them, "What if everyone acted that way?" they shrug their shoulders and answer, "Everyone doesn't act that way." But really, one should always ask himself, "What would happen if everybody looked at things that way?" There is no escaping this disturbing thought except by a kind of double-dealing. A man who lies and makes excuses for himself by saying "Not everybody does that," is someone with an uneasy conscience, because the act of lying implies that a universal value is conferred upon the lie.

Anguish is evident even when it conceals itself. This is the anguish that Kierkegaard called the anguish of Abraham. You know the story: an angel has ordered Abraham to sacrifice his son; if it really were an angel who has come and said, "You are Abraham, you shall sacrifice your son," everything would be all right. But everyone might first wonder, "Is it really an angel, and am I really Abraham? What proof do I have?"

There was a madwoman who had hallucinations; someone used to speak to her on the telephone and give her orders. Her doctor asked her, "Who is it who talks to you?" She answered, "He says it's God." What proof did she really have that it was God? If an angel comes to me, what proof is there that it's an angel? And if I hear voices, what proof is there that they come from heaven and not from hell, or from the subconscious, or a pathological condition? What proves that they are addressed to me? What proof is there that I have been appointed to impose my choice and my conception of man on humanity? I'll never find any proof or sign to convince me of that. If a voice addresses me, it is always for me to decide that this is the angel's voice; if I consider that such an act is a good one, it is I who will choose to say that it is good rather than bad.

Now, I'm not being singled out as an Abraham, and yet at every moment I'm obliged to perform exemplary acts. For every man, everything happens as if all mankind had its eyes fixed on him and were guiding itself by what he does. And every man ought to say to himself, "Am I really the kind of man who has the right to act in such a way that humanity might guide itself by my actions?" And if he does not say that to himself, he is masking his anguish.

There is no question here of the kind of anguish which would lead to quietism, to inaction. It is a matter of a simple sort of anguish that anybody who has had responsibilities is familiar with. For example, when a military officer takes the responsibility for an attack and sends a certain number of men to death, he chooses to do so, and in the main he alone makes the choice. Doubtless, orders come from above, but they are too broad; he interprets them, and on this interpretation depend the lives of ten or fourteen or twenty men. In making a decision he can not help having a certain anguish. All leaders know this anguish. That doesn't keep them from acting; on the contrary, it is the very condition of their action. For it implies that they envisage a number of possibilities, and when they choose one, they realize that it has value only because it is chosen. We shall see that this kind of anguish, which is the kind that existentialism describes, is explained, in addition, by a direct responsibility to the other men whom it involves. It is not a curtain separating us from action, but is part of action itself.

When we speak of forlornness, a term Heidegger was fond of, we mean only that God does not exist and that we have to face all the consequences of this. The existentialist is strongly opposed to a certain kind of secular ethics which would like to abolish God with the least possible expense. About 1880, some French teachers tried to set up a secular ethics which went something like this: God is a useless and costly hypothesis; we are discarding it; but, meanwhile, in order for there to be an ethics, a society, a civilization, it is essential that certain values be taken seriously and that they be considered as having an *a priori* existence. It must be obligatory, *a priori*, to be honest, not to lie, not to beat your wife, to have children, etc., etc. So we're going to try a little device which will make it possible to show that values exist all the same, inscribed in a heaven of ideas, though otherwise God does not exist. In other words—and this, I believe, is the tendency of everything called reformism in France—nothing will be changed if God does not exist. We shall find ourselves with the same norms of honesty, progress, and humanism, and we shall have made of God an outdated hypothesis which will peacefully die off by itself.

The existentialist, on the contrary, thinks it very distressing that God does not exist, because all possibility of finding values in a heaven of ideas disappears along with Him; there can no longer be an *a priori* Good, since there is no infinite and perfect consciousness to think it. Nowhere is it written that the Good exists, that we must be honest, that we must not lie; because the fact is we are on a plane where there are only men. Dostoievsky said, "If God didn't exist, everything would be permitted." That is the very starting point of existentialism. Indeed, everything is permissible if God does not exist, and as a result man is forlorn, because neither within him nor without does he find anything to cling to. He can't start making excuses for himself.

If existence really does precede essence, there is no explaining things away by reference to a fixed and given human nature. In other words, there is no determinism, man is free, man is freedom. On the other hand, if God does not exist, we find no values or commands to turn to which legitimize our conduct. So, in the bright realm of values, we have no excuse behind us, nor justification before us. We are alone, with no excuses.

That is the idea I shall try to convey when I say that man is condemned to be free. Condemned, because he did not create himself, yet, in other respects is free; because, once thrown into the world, he is responsible for everything he does. The existentialist does not believe in the power of passion. He will never agree that a sweeping passion is a ravaging torrent which fatally leads a man to certain acts and is therefore an excuse. He thinks that man is responsible for his passion.

The existentialist does not think that man is going to help himself by finding in the world some omen by which to orient himself. Because he thinks that man will interpret the omen to suit himself. Therefore, he thinks that man, with no support and no aid, is condemned every moment to invent man. Ponge, in a very fine article, has said, "Man is the future of man." That's exactly it. But if it is taken to mean that this future is recorded in heaven, that God sees it, then it is false, because it would really no longer be a future. If it is taken to mean that, whatever a man may be, there is a future to be forged, a virgin future before him, then this remark is sound. But then we are forlorn. . . .

Actually, things will be as man will have decided they are to be. Does that mean that I should abandon myself to quietism? No. First, I should involve myself; then, act on the old saw, "Nothing ventured, nothing gained." Nor does it mean that I shouldn't belong to a party, but rather that I shall have no illusions and shall do what I can. For example, suppose I ask myself, "Will socialization, as such, ever come about?" I know nothing about it. All I know is that I'm going to do everything in my power to bring it about. Beyond that, I can't count on anything. Quietism is the attitude of people who say, "Let others do what I can't do." The doctrine I am presenting is the very opposite of quietism, since it declares, "There is no reality except in action." Moreover, it goes further, since it adds, "Man is nothing else than his plan; he exists only to the extent that he fulfills himself; he is therefore nothing else than the ensemble of his acts, nothing else than his life."

According to this, we can understand why our doctrine horrifies certain people. Because often the only way they can bear their wretchedness is to think, "Circumstances have been against me. What I've been and done doesn't show my true worth. To be sure, I've had no great love, no great friendship, but that's because I haven't met a man or woman who was worthy. The books I've written haven't been very good because I haven't had the proper leisure. I haven't had children to devote myself to because I didn't find a man with whom I could have spent my life. So there remains within me, unused and quite viable, a host of propensities, inclinations, possibilities, that one wouldn't guess from the mere series of things I've done."

Now, for the existentialist there is really no love other than one which manifests itself in a person's being in love. There is no genius other than one which is expressed in works of art; the genius of Proust is the sum of Proust's works; the genius of Racine is his series of tragedies. Outside of that, there is nothing. Why say that Racine could have written another tragedy, when he didn't write it? A man is involved in life, leaves his impress on it, and outside of that there is nothing. To be sure, this may seem a harsh thought to someone whose life hasn't been a success. But, on the other hand, it prompts people to understand that reality alone is what counts, that dreams, expectations, and hopes warrant no more than to define a man as a disappointed dream, as miscarried hopes, as vain expectations. In other words, to define him negatively and not positively. However, when we say, "You are nothing else than your life," that does not imply that the artist will be judged solely on the basis of his works of art; a thousand other things will contribute toward summing him up. What we mean is that a man is nothing else than a series of undertakings, that he is the sum, the organization, the ensemble of the relationships which make up these undertakings.

When all is said and done, what we are accused of, at bottom, is not our pessimism, but an optimistic toughness. If people throw up to us our works of fiction in which we write about people who are soft, weak, cowardly, and sometimes even downright bad, it's not because these people are soft, weak, cowardly, or bad; because if we were to say, as Zola did, that they are that way because of heredity, the workings of environment, society, because of biological or psychological determinism, people would be reassured. They would say, "Well, that's what we're like, no one can do anything about it." But when the existentialist writes about a coward, he says that this coward is responsible for his cowardice. He's not like that because he has a cowardly heart or lung or brain; he's not like that on account of his physiological make-up; but he's like that because he has made himself a coward by his acts. There's no such thing as a cowardly constitution; there are nervous constitutions; there is poor blood, as the common people say, or there are strong constitutions. But the man whose blood is poor is not a coward on that account, for what makes cowardice is the act of renouncing or yielding. A constitution is not an act; the coward is defined on the basis of the acts he performs. People feel, in a vague sort of way, that this coward we're talking about is guilty of being a coward, and the thought frightens them. What people would like is that a coward or a hero be born that way.

One of the complaints most frequently made about *The Ways of Freedom* can be summed up as follows: "After all, these people are so spineless, how are you going to make heroes out of them?" This objection almost makes me laugh, for it assumes that people are born heroes. That's what people really want to think. If you're born cowardly, you may set your mind perfectly at rest; there's nothing you can do about it; you'll be cowardly all your life, whatever you may do. If you're born a hero, you may set your mind just as much at rest; you'll be a hero all your life; you'll drink like a hero and eat like a hero. What the existentialist says is that the coward makes himself cowardly, that the hero makes himself heroic. There's always a possibility for the coward not to be cowardly any more and for the hero to stop being heroic. What counts is total involvement; some one particular action or set of circumstances is not total involvement.

. . . [Existentialism] defines man in terms of action. . . there is no doctrine more optimistic, since man's destiny is within himself; . . . it tells him that the only hope is in his acting and that action is the only thing that enables a man to live.

From Jean-Paul Sartre, "The Humanism of Existentialism," *The Philosophy of Existentialism*, ed. Wade Baskin, Philosophical Library, New York, 1965. By permission.

QUESTIONS FOR REVIEW AND DISCUSSION

1. What does Sartre mean when he says that *existence* precedes *essence?*
2. Sartre makes the point that "man is condemned to be free." What does he mean by this statement?

3. Why does Sartre say about a person that his or her being a coward is not explained by a "cowardly heart or lung"?
4. In what sense is it the case that, according to Sartre, we create ourselves?
5. As an atheist, did Sartre agree with Dostoevski's statement that "because there is no God, everything is permitted"?
6. What, in the last analysis, is the meaning of life for Sartre?

Glossary

aesthetics The branch of philosophy concerned with the analysis of concepts such as beauty or beautiful as standards for judging works of art.

agnostic One who neither believes nor disbelieves that God exists, since there is no conclusive evidence either way.

analytic An analytic sentence is necessarily true because the predicate is already in the subject, e.g., "all dogs are animals" where the word "dogs" already contains the concept "animal."

a posteriori "After experience" (versus a priori, "before experience.")

appearance How something presents itself to our senses as compared with its true reality. The oar appears bent in the water, but it really is not bent.

a priori "Before" or "independent of experience." Hence, a priori knowledge is what we can know without experiencing it; e.g., "every event has a cause" even though we have not experienced every event.

autonomy Independence from external authority; in Kant, freedom of the will to make its own law or rule of conduct in contrast to heteronomy (being subject to someone else's rules).

becoming The world of becoming is the world where everything in our daily experience, people and things, comes into being and passes away.

being Considered the ultimate reality. For Plato, the realm of the eternal Forms.

Categorical Imperative According to Kant, the absolute moral law understood as a duty by any rational creature, to be compared with hypothetical imperatives, which permit exceptions.

categories Term used by Aristotle and Kant meaning the concepts the human mind brings to knowing, e.g., cause and effect, space and time.

causality The relation of cause and effect, by which one event necessarily follows another.

cause Something that has the power to produce a change, motion, or action in another thing; this change (effect) can be explained in terms of the behavior of the cause.

change The alteration of anything, the rearrangement of something's parts, the coming into being of something that did not exist before, and the decline and dissolution of something.

cognition In the broadest sense, knowledge or the act of knowing.

cognitive meaning A statement has cognitive meaning if *(a)* it asserts something that is true simply because the words used necessarily and always require the statement to be true (as in mathematics) or *(b)* it asserts something that can be judged as true or false by verifying it in experience.

contingent An event that is not necessary; i.e., it may or may not be, depending on other events which also may or may not be.

cosmological argument A "proof" for the existence of God based on the idea that there had to be a first cause for the existence of the universe.

deduction A process of reasoning by which the mind relates the truth of a proposition to another proposition by inferring that the truth of the second proposition is involved in and therefore derived from the first proposition (*see* **Induction**).

determinism The theory that every fact or even the universe is determined or caused by previous facts or events: human behavior and the events of history follow strict laws of causation or necessary connection. Accordingly, in this view, human beings do not possess freedom of the will or the power to originate independently or genuine choices.

dialectic As in dialogue (Socrates), debate over opposites (Hegel), or clash of material forces (Marx) producing dynamic change. Also, a process of reasoning based on the analysis of opposing propositions. Socrates used the dialectic method of teaching by distinguishing between opinion and knowledge. Hegel and Marx developed dialectical conceptions of history in which for Hegel opposing ideas were the key while for Marx history was explained as the conflict of material forces.

dogmatism The act of making a positive assertion without demonstration by either rational argument or experience.

dualism A theory which holds that there are two independent and irreducible substances, for example, mind and body, the intelligible world of ideas and the visible world of things, and the forces of good and evil.

empiricism The theory which says that experience is the source of all knowledge, thereby denying that human beings possess inborn knowledge or that they can derive knowledge through the exercise of reason alone.

epistemology The branch of philosophy which studies the nature, origin, scope, and validity of knowledge.

essence The chief characteristic, quality, or necessary function which makes a thing what it uniquely is.

ethics (1) A set of rules for human behavior; (2) a study of judgments of value, good and evil, right and wrong, desirable and undesirable; and (3) theories of obligation or duty or why we "ought" to behave in certain ways (Greek, *ethicos*; Latin, *moralis*).

existentialism As defined by Sartre, *existence* precedes *essence*; i.e., people have no given identity until they have made specific decisions and have chosen their work and have thereby defined themselves. Existentialism is a mode of philosophy which focuses on the existing individual person; instead of searching for truth in distant universal concepts, it deals with the authentic concerns of concrete existing individuals as they face choices and decisions in daily life.

extension In Descartes, the character of physical things as having dimension in space and time.

finitude   Having definable limits.

form   Plato's notion of eternal and independent reality, e.g., *Man* or *Triangle,* which makes possible particular things like the shape of this piece of pie or this person, Mary.

idealism   The view that mind is the ultimate reality in the world. Idealism is, accordingly, opposed to materialism, which views material things as the basic reality from which mind emerges and to which mind is reducible.

illusion   An erroneous impression (e.g., an optical illusion) or a false belief growing out of a deep wish (Freud).

impression   The same as sensation, or the "sense-data" received by us through our senses (Hume).

indeterminism   The theory that in some cases the will makes decisions or choices independent of prior physiological or psychological causes (free will).

induction   Proceeding from the observation of some particular facts to a generalization (or conclusion) concerning all such facts (*see* **Deduction**).

innate ideas   Certain things we know from birth, without requiring proof from experience.

instrumental   Providing a means for achieving something else (Aristotle) versus *intrinsic* (an act, event, or thing existing for its own sake).

instrumentalism   John Dewey's theory of how thought functions by emphasizing the practical function of thought in determining future consequences; thought is therefore viewed as instrumental in producing consequences.

intrinsic   Referring to an act, event, or thing which exists for its own sake versus *instrumental,* which refers to an act or event as a means for some other end.

logical positivism   The view that statements are meaningful only if they can be verified either directly or indirectly in experience. Logical positivism seeks to analyze all claims to knowledge, all assertions of science and everyday life. Only those assertions have meaning that are verified by empirical facts or are connected logically with such facts and are therefore verifiable.

man   (*As used throughout this book*) a human being, or the human creature, regarded abstractly and without regard to gender; hence, the human race or humanity.

materialism   The view that matter constitutes the basis of all that exists in the universe. Hence combinations of matter and material forces account for every aspect of reality, including the nature of thought, the process of historical and economic events, and the standard of values based on sensuous bodily pleasures and the abundance of things. The notion of the primacy of spirit or mind and rational purpose in nature is rejected.

metaphysics   The branch of philosophy concerned with the question of the ultimate nature of reality. Unlike the sciences, which focus on various aspects of nature, metaphysics goes beyond particular things to enquire about more general questions such as what lies beyond nature, how things come into being, what it means for something to be, and whether there is a realm of being which is not subject to change and which is therefore the basis of certainty in knowledge.

monism   The view that there is only one substance in the universe.

naturalistic fallacy   The mistaken attempt to define a nonnatural object such as *good* in terms of a natural object such as *pleasure* or *self-realization* (G. E. Moore).

noumenal world   The real world as opposed to the world of appearance. The noumenal world, says Kant, cannot be known.

ontology From the Greek *ontos* ("being") and *logos* ("science"); hence, the study of being. Ontological "proof" for God's existence based on the idea of God as the highest Being.

participation The internal relation between different levels of being, e.g., between things in our world and the realm of the Forms in Plato, or the relation between eternal law (God's reason) and natural law (human reason); hence, natural law is man's reason participating in God's reason.

perception The discovery, by the senses, of knowledge about the world; the apprehension of everyday objects, for example, trees, through sense impressions.

phenomenal world The world of appearance versus the world beyond our knowledge (Kant).

pluralism The view that there are more than one (monism) or two (dualism) ultimate and separate substances making up the world.

positivism John Stuart Mill defined positivism as follows: "We [positivists] have no knowledge of anything but Phenomena, and our knowledge of phenomena is relative, not absolute. We know not the essence, not the real mode of production, of any fact, but only its relations to other facts in the way of succession or of similitude. These relations are constant; that is, always the same in the same circumstances."

postulate A practical or moral principle which cannot be proved, such as the existence of God, the freedom of the will, or immortality, which, says Kant, must be believed to make possible our moral duty.

pragmatism According to William James, pragmatism is a method of solving various types of problems, such as "Does God exist?" or "Is man's will free?" by looking at the practical consequences of accepting this or that answer. James says, "The pragmatic method tries to interpret each notion (or theory) by tracing its respective practical consequences. . . . If no practical differences whatever can be traced . . . they mean practically the same thing," and that ends the argument. As a theory of *truth*, James says that an idea is true if it works in daily life.

Prime Mover While every event has a cause, the Prime Mover (in Aristotle—God) is the first cause of everything but does not itself require a cause; otherwise, there would be a constant backward search, an "infinite regress" for the beginning of things.

probable Likely to happen; the middle term in the series (a) definitely, (b) probably, (c) definitely will not; i.e., the choice when there is not enough evidence for (a) or (c).

rationalism The philosophical view that emphasizes the ability of human reason to grasp fundamental truths about the world without the aid of sense impressions.

relativism The view that there is no absolute knowledge, that truth is different for each individual, social group, or historic period and is therefore relative to the circumstances of the knowing subject.

scholasticism The method of learning in the medieval cathedral schools by which a combination of philosophy and theology was taught through emphasizing logical or deductive form, and basing thinking and its conclusions on the sayings or writings of key figures of the past whose tradition was viewed as authoritative.

sense-data The impressions we receive through our senses.

skepticism Some skeptics doubt that any knowledge achieved so far is absolute and therefore continue to seek after more refined and reliable versions of truth; other skeptics doubt whether it is ever possible to attain perfect certainty of knowledge.

solipsism   The theory that the self alone [*solus* ("alone"); *ipse* ("self")] is the source of all knowledge of existence, a view that sometimes leads to the conclusion that the self is the only reality.

Sophists   Itinerant teachers in fifth-century Athens who especially prepared young men for political careers; hence they emphasized rhetoric and the ability to persuade audiences and win debates and were less concerned with pursuing truth.

sovereign   Referring to a person or state that is independent of any other authority or jurisdiction.

substance   A separate and distinct thing; that which underlies phenomena; the essence of a thing which underlies the other qualities of a thing.

syllogism   A form of reasoning: for example, all men are mortal (major premise); Socrates is a man (minor premise); therefore, Socrates is mortal (conclusion).

synthetic   As compared with an analytic sentence (where the subject contains the predicate) a synthetic sentence adds an idea to the subject which the subject does not already contain; e.g., "a dog will help catch foxes," but that is not true of all dogs.

teleology   *Telos* is the Greek word for "purpose"; hence, teleology is the study of purpose in human nature and in the events of history; in ethical theory (teleological ethics) an action is considered good if it is conducive to fulfilling the purposes of human nature.

utilitarianism   In this view, an action is considered good or right if its consequence is the greatest happiness (pleasure) of the greatest number. In that case, the action is *useful* (utilitarian) in producing as much or more good than any alternative behavior.

verification   Demonstrating or proving something to be true either by means of evidence or by formal rules of reasoning.

Additional Suggested Readings

ETHICS

Aristotle, *The Student's Oxford Aristotle*, vol. V: *Ethica Nicomachea*, trans. W. D. Ross, Oxford University Press, New York, 1942.

Augustine, *On Christian Doctrine*, trans. D. W. Robertson, Jr., Macmillan, New York, 1958.

Barnes, Hazel, *An Existentialist Ethics*, Vintage, Random House, New York, 1971. An ethics founded on Sartre's philosophy.

Broad, C. D., *Five Types of Ethical Theory*, Routledge, London, 1951.

Hospers, John, *Human Conduct*, Harcourt, Brace & World, New York, 1972. A comprehensive, but animated, discussion of major moral theories.

Huby, Pamela, *Greek Ethics*, Macmillan, New York, 1967. For those intrigued by Epictetus and Aristotle.

Kaufmann, Walter, *Nietzsche. Philosopher, Psychologist, Antichrist*, Vintage, Random House, New York, 1968. An excellent guide to Nietzsche.

Lerner, Max, ed., *Essential Works of John Stuart Mill*, Bantam, New York, 1961. Includes Mill's *Autobiography* and several important essays.

MacIntyre, Alaisdair, *A Short History of Ethics*, Macmillan, New York, 1966. The title aptly describes the contents.

Nehamas, Alexander, *Nietzsche: Life as Literature*, Harvard University Press, Cambridge, Mass., 1985.

Nell, Onora: *Acting on Principle*, Columbia, New York, 1975. A Kantian ethics done by a contemporary philosopher.

Paton, H. J., *The Categorical Imperative*, University of Chicago Press, Chicago, 1948.

Ross, W. D., *Kant's Ethical Theory*, Oxford University Press, New York, 1953. A straightforward account of Kant.

Walsh, J. J., and H. L. Shapiro, eds., *Aristotle's Ethics*, Wadsworth, Belmont, Calif., 1967. Seven excellent essays on this topic.

Warnock, G. J., *The Object of Morality*, Methuen, London, 1971.

Warnock, Mary, *Ethics since 1900*, Oxford University Press, London, 1960.

Wasserstrom, Richard, ed., *Today's Moral Problems*, Macmillan, New York, 1975. A collection of essays which apply ethical theory to contemporary problems.

POLITICS

Aquinas, Thomas, *On Law, Morality and Politics*, eds. William P. Baumgarth and Richard J. Regan, Hackett, Indianapolis, 1988.

Berlin, Isaiah, *Karl Marx: His Life and Environment*, 3d ed., Oxford University Press, New York, 1963. A useful introduction to Marx.

Bloom, Allan, *The Republic of Plato*, Basic Books, New York, 1968. A lively literal translation with careful notes and a rich interpretative essay.

Commins, S., and R. N. Linscott, eds., *The Political Philosophers*, Random House, New York, 1947.

D'Entrèves, A. P., *Natural Law*, 2d ed., rev., Humanities Press, New York, 1964. A spirited modern defense of natural law theory.

Gorbachev, Mikhail, *Perestroika*, Harper & Row, New York, 1987.

Hart, H. L. A., *The Concept of Law*, Clarendon Press, Oxford, Eng., 1961.

Hayek, Friedrich A., *The Constitution of Liberty*, Gateway Editions, Henry Regnery, Chicago, 1972. A discussion of individualism and liberty by an economist who won the Nobel prize.

Locke, John, *Essays on the Law of Nature*, ed. W. von Leyden, Clarendon Press, Oxford, Eng., 1954.

Marx, Karl, *Early Writings*, McGraw-Hill, New York, 1963. For those interested in reading more Marx.

Warrender, Howard, *The Political Philosophy of Hobbes*, Clarendon Press, Oxford, Eng., 1957.

Yolton, John W., *Locke: An Introduction*, Blackwell, Oxford, Eng., 1985.

KNOWLEDGE

Ayer, A. J., *Language, Truth and Logic*, Dover, New York, 1936.

———, *et al. The Revolution in Philosophy*, Macmillan, London, 1957.

Chisholm, Roderick, *Theory of Knowledge*, 2d ed., Prentice-Hall, Englewood Cliffs, N.J., 1977. A contemporary, clear, and comprehensive discussion.

Cornford, F. M., *Plato's Theory of Knowledge*, Bobbs-Merrill, Indianapolis, 1957. Includes two of Plato's important dialogues (*Theatetus* and *Sophist*) and Conford's helpful comments.

Descartes, René, *Selected Philosophical Writings*, trans. Cottingham, Stoothoof, R., Murdoch, D. ["in clear, readable, modern English"], Cambridge University Press, Cambridge, Eng., 1990.

Flew, Anthony, *Hume's Philosophy of Belief*, Humanities Press, New York, 1966. Exposition and criticism of Hume's views, particularly in the *Enquiry*.

Frankfurth, Harry, *Demons, Dreamers, and Madmen*, Bobbs-Merrill, Indianapolis, 1970. A careful examination of Descartes' theory of knowledge, particularly in the *Meditations*.

James, William, *Pragmatism: A New Name for Some Old Ways of Thinking*, Harvard University Press, Cambridge, Mass., 1976. A good place to start for further reading of James.

Kemp Smith, Norman, *A Commentary to Kant's "Critique of Pure Reason,"* 2d ed., Humanities Press, New York, 1962. Thorough commentary on Kant's first *Critique*. (See also S. Korner.)

Kenny, Anthony, *The Legacy of Wittgenstein*, Blackwell, Oxford, Eng., 1984.

Korner, S., *Kant*, Penguin, Baltimore, 1955. A useful introduction to Kant's difficult philosophy.

Malcolm, Norman, *Ludwig Wittgenstein: A Memoir*, with a biographical sketch by G. H. von Wright, Oxford University Press, London, 1958.

———, *Wittgenstein: Nothing Is Hidden*, Blackwell, Oxford, Eng., 1986.

Mehta, Ved Parkash, *Fly and the Fly-Bottle*, Little, Brown, Boston, 1962. A description of encounters with English philosophers including Russell, Wittgenstein, and Austin.

Russell, Bertrand, *Meaning and Truth*, G. Allen, London, 1951.

———, *My Philosophical Development*, G. Allen, London, 1959.

Ryle, Gilbert, *The Concept of Mind*, Hutchinson, London, 1949.

———, *Dilemmas*, Cambridge University Press, Cambridge, Eng., 1963.

Taylor, A. E., *Plato, The Man and His Work*, Dial, New York, 1936. A standard introduction to Plato.

Wittgenstein, Ludwig, *Philosophical Investigations*, trans. G. E. M. Anscombe, Macmillan, New York, 1953.

———, *On Certainty*, eds. G. E. M. Anscombe and G. H. von Wright, Harper & Row, New York, 1969.

RELIGION AND DESTINY

Auden, W. H., ed., *The Living Thought of Kierkegaard*, Indiana University Press, Bloomington, 1963. A good collection of Kierkegaard's writings.

Beauvoir, Simone de, *Adieux, A Farewell to Sartre*, trans. Patrick O'Brian, Pantheon, New York, 1984.

Cohen-Salal, Annie, *Sartre: A Life*, trans. Anna Cancogni, ed. Norman Macafee, Pantheon, New York, 1987.

Copleston, F. C., *Thomas Aquinas*, Barnes & Noble, New York, 1977. An excellent introduction to the philosophy of Aquinas.

Dean, Sidney, ed., *Basic Writings of Saint Anselm*, Open Court, LaSalle, Ill., 1974. This edition includes Anselm's text, early criticisms, and discussions by later philosophers.

Dostoevski, Feodor, *The Brothers Karamazov*, Critical Editions Series, Norton, New York, 1976. Includes useful discussions of all the topics in our discussion of religion.

Hume, David, *Dialogues concerning Natural Religion: Text and Critical Essays*, ed., Nelson Pike, Bobbs-Merrill, Indianapolis, 1970. This work, by David Hume, is one of the most provocative in the philosophy of religion.

James, Williams, *Human Immortality*, Folcroft, 1977. A clear and careful work on this difficult topic.

Kaufman, Walter, *Critique of Religion and Philosophy*, Harper & Row, New York, 1958. A wide-ranging and influential book.

Kierkegaard, Soren, *Concluding Unscientific Postscript*, trans. David F. Swenson, Princeton University Press, Princeton, N.J., 1944.

———, *Philosophical Fragments*, trans. David F. Swenson, Princeton University Press, Princeton, 1936.

Murdoch, Iris, *Sartre, Romantic Rationalist*, Penguin, London, 1989.

METAPHYSICS, MIND, AND FREEDOM

Aristotle, *The Basic Works of Aristotle*, ed., Richard McKeon, Random House, New York, 1941.

Ayer, A. J., *Freedom and Morality*, Clarendon Press, Oxford, Eng., 1984.

The Empiricists, Doubleday Anchor Books, Garden City, N.Y., 1960. Includes Berkeley's major works along with those of his predecessor, John Locke, against whom many of Berkeley's arguments are directed.

Farber, Austin, *The Freedom of the Will*, A. & C. Black, London, 1958.

Hampshire, Stuart, ed., *Philosophy of Mind*, Harper & Row, New York, 1966.

Laslett, Peter, ed., *The Physical Basis of Mind*, Blackwell, London, 1951.

Lathan, Ronald E., *On the Nature of the Universe*, Penguin, Baltimore, 1951. An excellent prose translation of Lucretius's *De Rerum Natura*.

Lovejoy, Arthur O., *The Great Chain of Being*, Harvard University Press, Cambridge, Mass., 1936. An exciting history of metaphysics.

Malachowski, Alan, ed., *Reading Rorty*, Blackwell, Oxford, Eng., 1990.

Pirsig, Robert: *Zen and the Art of Motorcycle Maintenance*, Bantam, New York, 1976. An engaging novel and yet a serious inquiry into issues raised by seventeenth- and eighteenth-century metaphysicians.

Rorty, Richard, *Consequences of Pragmatism*, University of Minnesota Press, Minneapolis, 1982.

———, *Contingency, Irony and Solidarity*, Cambridge University Press, New York, 1989.

———, *Philosophy and the Mirror of Nature*, Princeton University Press, Princeton, N.J., 1979.

———, ed., *The Linguistic Turn*, University of Chicago Press, Chicago, 1967.

Searle, John R., *Intentionality: An Essay in the Philosophy of Mind*, Cambridge University Press, Cambridge, Eng., 1983.

———, *Minds, Brains and Science*, Harvard University Press, Cambridge, Mass., 1984.

Index